Books by Henri Fesquet available in English

THE DRAMA OF VATICAN II

CATHOLICISM: RELIGION OF TOMORROW?

THE DRAMA
OF VATICAN II

THE DRAMA
OF VATICAN II

THE ECUMENICAL COUNCIL

JUNE, 1962—DECEMBER, 1965

BY HENRI FESQUET

TRANSLATED BY BERNARD MURCHLAND

AMERICAN INTRODUCTION BY MICHAEL NOVAK

RANDOM HOUSE   NEW YORK

1400468

To Mr. Henri Fesquet, the grace and peace of the Lord.

We have always read your regular articles on our Ecumenical Patriarchate and the Vatican Council with great interest.

We appreciate your writing ability; still more, we value your deep knowledge of ecumenical and conciliar questions and the impartiality with which you inform your readers. We see in this an intensely Christian spirit and evidence of the French habit of thought.

We are happy to congratulate you for this precious contribution to the great cause of Christian unity and the progress of interconfessional relations which will enable us to attain "the fullness of the spirit of Christ."

Granting you our Apostolic blessing, we beg the grace and charity of the Lord for you and yours.

Athenagoras
Ecumenical Patriarch of Constantinople

The writing of Henri Fesquet on the Council may at first suggest an aura of discontent. But in reading his work, it seems to me easy to locate behind each sentence a true concern for the Church and to hear a truly Christian heart beating.

What might at first appear sensational is precisely the language of our times and his choice of the angle that could attract general attention to a religious subject—alas, generally held to be scarcely of interest.

Has Henri Fesquet a taste for the indiscreet or are the rest of us merely overly prudent and too timid? The true journalist, like Fesquet, has antennae trained on the signs of the times which sometimes, at least at the start, escape the rest of us. Because there were sometimes, during the course of the Council—and with the best of intentions, one is sure—motions which were to all practical intent maneuverings, one can understand the tendency to be *indiscreet* about them, even if one doesn't necessarily approve of it. About these indiscretions, however, one could say that they are providential.

Helder Câmara
Archbishop of Olinda and Recife
Brazil

. . . The Council has ended.

Its labors will be carried forward in the work of the episcopal synod, the secretariats, and the postconciliar commissions.

But we will not be able to discern the profound meaning, the properly Catholic as much as ecumenical value of what will be begun and accomplished in the years to come unless we constantly refer to the deliberations and resolutions of the Council and relive to some extent its finest hours, hours marked by interventions which, thanks to you, we shall remember.

Thus we will continue to remain in living communion with the many Council Fathers who, having understood what God expected of their Church in the world today, gradually manifested their will to accomplish the reforms whose utter necessity they recognized and to carry out the *aggiornamento* prescribed by John XXIII as the means by which the Catholic Church would recover her youth and her beauty.

Once again, my dear sir, we are indebted to you.

Pastor Marc Boegner
of the Académie Française

I shall begin with certain reservations. Neither I nor others think that Henri Fesquet's articles bear the stamp of Gospel truth (I am sure he agrees with this opinion).

Why? A journalist of his caliber is not content merely to report facts and words. In reporting, he judges. In judging, he commits himself and necessarily puts a good deal of himself into what he writes. Since his reporting was deliberately "selective," it is sometimes difficult to distinguish objective facts from the author's personal opinions. This was undoubtedly the only way he could write, since the best-known journalists of the contemporary press have most often been tendentious.

What is good about Mr. Fesquet's book? He has had the merit of feeling and making felt, from the beginning, the importance of the great events of the Council. He has set an example of a layman passionately involved in the cause of Holy Mother the Church. He has succeeded in making the life of this Church and the ecumenical movement interesting not only to the faithful but to a considerable number of curious or "marginal" sympathetic spirits, who, so to speak, have become part of his school. He has had a great influence in France and elsewhere. I am sure that he himself is aware of the seriousness of his responsibility.

Finally, it cannot be denied that Henri Fesquet's pen is lively and captivating. His style and manner are highly personal. So much so that it is sometimes said in homage to the author's personality: "That sounds like Fesquet."

Joseph Marie Cardinal Martin,
Archbishop of Rouen
President of the French Bishops' Committee for Christian Unity

I know Henri Fesquet's profound intention: to contribute to building the Church of God and thus to constructing the city of man.

Nothing is more difficult, nothing more redoubtable than to interpret facts, intentions, and gestures with a view to forming public opinion. However, I believe in the eminent value of information. It is a means by which the Spirit's work in the Church can be strengthened and communicated. In the order of ecumenism, information has been an instrument for changing the attitude of many.

In this respect, Henri Fesquet is a veritable ambassador of ecumenism in the Church and in the world.

Roger Schutz
Prior of Taizé

TRANSLATOR'S INTRODUCTION

I did not have the opportunity to attend Vatican II. But Henri Fesquet's reportorial powers are such that he creates a sense of presence. This, at any rate, is what I experienced during the months I translated his account of the four sessions. The drama is there. The color and the flavor. But what chiefly impressed me was the clarity with which he delineated the grave and complex issues involved. He takes sides, to be sure. That is only normal. The important thing is that there were sides to take.

There can be no doubt that Vatican II was a historical event of the first importance. Many critical assessments of the Council have been published—both favorable and unfavorable. Some think its achievements were nothing short of miraculous. Others are convinced it scarcely touched the major issues. The truth of the matter is scarcely so extreme. As Hans Küng put it modestly: the Council did more than most expected it to, including most bishops.

I have no intention of entering yet another evaluation. I would, however, like to offer the following reflections. Fesquet attaches great importance to schema 13—the Pastoral Constitution on the Church in the Modern World. In a deep sense this was the crux of the Council. The deliberations over the Church's confrontation with the modern world mirrored Vatican II's failings and aspirations, its inner dynamism and tensions. More than any other topic treated, schema 13 exposed the crisis, and to some extent the bankruptcy, of contemporary religion. Similarly, it pointed to the direction theological thinking must take if religions are to be abolished and religion meaningfully secured. As such, it is a powerful locus of hope. This much has become clear: a religious point of view that is predicated upon the denial or negation of natural values is doomed. The reason for this is not the current wave of secularism. The necessity of affirming natural values is a consequence of the incarnation itself. Modern secularism has called our attention to this necessity. But of itself it has initiated no Christian imperatives.

A unique aspect of Christianity, as has been pointed out, is the fact that revelation took the form of a man. Consequently, nothing inhuman or nonhistorical can be authentically Christian. Anything that diverts our attention and energies from the world in which we live and breathe and have our being, by that same token fails to respect the elementary requirements of an incarnational faith. Is it not ironical that so many noble spirits in the Christian West have so often cast envious eyes upon the life-affirming values of Hellas? Not ironical perhaps in view of the fact that the Church has long lived under the dispensation of alienation. But certainly ironical when we consider that the real demands of Christian faith bear little resemblance to the absurd leaps a Kierkegaard proscribes or the burdensome abstractions of Scholasticism or the refined requirements of mysticism. Absurdity, abstraction, and mysticism may indeed be part of the total enterprise. But by no means the important part. The real issues are far more concrete.

Life is a perpetual problem of how to live. It is always in one sense or another the pursuit, at once painful and glorious, of a Good Life. It is a constant challenge to organize the disparate elements of existence into a harmonious whole. When religion addresses itself to human problems and inspires us to become celebrants of life, it performs most creditably. When the spirit is no longer at ease with its sensual media and can no longer function creatively with the materials of the world, it has become diseased. A good deal of religion, pseudo-religion perhaps we should say, has contributed to this strange malady. Of it we must say: let the dead bury the dead. A new day has perhaps dawned. Vatican II has been described as a work of demolition. I prefer a medical image: it was a surgical operation cutting away the malignancies of hubris and egoism that were killing the Christian soul. Of course, the operation may not be a success. But I for one think the patient stands a good chance.

BERNARD C. MURCHLAND

AN INTRODUCTION

Somehow, the identity of nearly everyone in our civilization is bound up with the fate of the Catholic Church. Almost everyone, in fact, defines himself according to some relation with that church: What else were Protestants protesting, or what else were the enlightened enlightened from? A change in Roman Catholicism, it may readily be observed, affects a change in everyman's image of himself: tamper with Catholicism and you tamper with at least a distant part of him. How else but by some such profound stirring of forgotten memories can we explain the almost unprecedented excitement generated by Pope John XXIII and the four brief years of the Second Vatican Council?

Some of the excitement, surely, arose by contrast with the general lassitude of the immediately preceding era. After the unfathomable, indigestible horrors of the Second World War, men had emerged from a tunnel to find not peace but further, more diffuse, less tangible hostilities: a cold war that threatened to lock East against West for all the foreseeable future. Protestants were not speaking to Catholics. Jews had not yet recovered from tragedies too deep to face. The outlook was not so much black as merely gray, endless, forlorn.

When, in 1959, Pope John first mentioned the prospect of an "Ecumenical Council," there was a ripple of enthusiasm; but caution, pessimism, and indifference were both appropriate and widespread. When the Council finally opened on October 11, 1962, in the presence of a score of Protestant "observers," the ordinary intelligent man manifested, perhaps, a little curiosity; but, after all, the Council was not a pan-Christian affair, merely a gathering of Roman Catholic bishops. The first announced subject for discussion sounded ecclesiastical in the extreme: the liturgy of the Roman Catholic Church.

Gradually, however, the dimensions of what were at stake began to become clear. Pope John made the word *aggiornamento* ("updating") part of the world's vocabulary; his great encyclicals—or, at least, the two of his eleven encyclicals chosen by men to be remembered, *Mater et Magistra* and *Pacem in Terris*—had shown him to be a man eager to address all men of good will. He had shown himself able to distinguish between an abstract ideology like communism and its various, concrete historical developments. He had reversed the century-old stand of his predecessor Pius IX against modern liberties by endorsing religious liberty in a contemporary sense. And at the very first meeting of the Council, Pope John had lent his support to the determination of many bishops that this Council not indulge in condemnations, and that it say nothing at all regarding communism. When Pope John held a friendly audience with Alexei Adzhubei, son-in-law of Premier Nikita Khrushchev, the larger cultural significance of what was afoot in Roman Catholicism took shape in the imagination of the world.

"If the Roman Catholic Church at this late date can renew herself," an agnostic friend of mine at Harvard said in conversation, "there is hope for all of us." Another, in Washington, said: "I know of nothing in my lifetime that has seemed so hopeful."

Thus the drama of Vatican II slowly became a symbol for all of us. At times its human conflicts were intense. As in so many capitals of the world just then, old ideas clashed with new, older men with younger men, career men with men come freshly to the scene. But the scope of the debates was enlarged: as at the United Nations, men from every continent were involved. And in a manner perhaps unique to Roman Catholicism, the mentality of men from societies and theologies conditioned by various centuries—the thirteenth, the sixteenth, the seventeenth, the nineteenth—were involved. Ernesto Cardinal Ruffini spoke for the feudalism of ancient Sicily; Archbishop Michael Conway of Dublin spoke for a paternalistic, scholastically clear, obedience-oriented tradition known to Americans (if in no other way) by obverse reflection in the works of James Joyce; Leo Joseph Cardinal Suenens of Brussels spoke, more nearly perhaps than any other, for the energetic, industrial, democratic nations of the twentieth century.

One world-famous Protestant theologian was to remark, after the second year of debates: "I have heard as wide a diversity of theological opinion in this assembly as I have ever heard at a Protestant gathering." What had happened, then, to the nearly proverbial unity of Catholicism? Nothing except that Catholicism had at last become open to public scrutiny, its debates open to the eyes of the world. "Catholic," the fact became evident, does not mean "universal and the same" but "universal and diverse." No longer on the defensive, no longer shrinking from assaults by Protestant dissent and atheistic denial, Catholic prelates no longer seemed to sense the need to close ranks and to maintain a united front. Even for ordinary Catholics the spectacle was novel, disconcerting, and exciting; when newspapers printed daily stories about their bishops and pope alongside stories of world leaders, teen-age singers, mayors, and corporation lawyers, their own church leadership was "demythologized" before their eyes. Hume did not awaken Kant from his dogmatic slumbers quite so thoroughly.

There are many ways of assessing the achievements of the Council, now that it is completed. But for Catholics who lived through it, no assessment is strongly enough worded that does not include in its description the word "revolutionary." Catholicism in 1966 is not what it was in 1959. No doubt an enormous distance remains to be traversed before Catholicism is genuinely "updated," and before that day, for which many of us long, when the Catholic spirit will take up its share of leadership in intelligence, inquiry, artistic creation, and social and political renewal. For it is obvious that Catholicism is much beholden to the contemporary world, to the contributions of Jews and Protestants, atheists and agnostics, who —often against opposition from Catholics—have secured so many achievements of civilization and science. It is a painful and melancholy duty of Catholics to recognize how seriously in error their Church was in hardening its face against the modern world. On the other hand, a Catholic need spend his time neither in regrets nor in apologies; there is a brotherly future to be built, and far more will be said by his solid deeds than by any number of words.

For more than a hundred years, moreover, there has been an active "underground" of Catholic thinkers and writers, laboring quietly and patiently for the days we have now come to see. Little did they expect, even those working in the still difficult days of 1959, that so many of their dreams would be realized in our lifetime. They were quite prepared to go on steadily for another generation or more. Their faith in the resources of the Catholic people was genuine and unwavering. When they were rejected, as they often were, by the official leaders of this people, they often recalled that so it had always been, and that it was good to follow in the footsteps of a Master who had also been rejected by officialdom. What changed in Roman Catholicism at the Second Vatican Council was not this fundamental law of Christian life, but only the velocity of change. In their own lifetime prophets have been vindicated.

Henri Fesquet will know what I intend by these words, because for years, even in the dark years, he knew many of these prophets and with them waited for the dawn. How else could the mordancy of his wit have grown so sharp, how else could his ears have become so sensitive to the nuances of theological conflict? From the beginning M. Fesquet knew what was at stake in the Council. His friendship with many of the Council's leading theologians and churchmen, particularly from France, gave him an entrée denied to nearly all other journalists. The fact that he was a layman, writing in a world-famous and tersely written journal, freed him from the "discretion" which still bars so many clergymen from saying publicly what they wish to say, as they wish to say it. Fesquet on the Council—he set the mark against which other journalists of the world, in reporting the Council, measured themselves.

MICHAEL NOVAK

Stanford, California
November, 1966

CONTENTS

FIRST SESSION

October–December, 1962

Rome as the Council Approaches

(J U N E 2 8)

John XXIII Desires a Profound Renewal
of the Church's Image

The bronze doors of St. Peter's Basilica. Yesterday it took five people to open its heavy leaves, each of which weighs four tons; its sculptures, sometimes as profane as they are malicious—the work of Philaret—were disappearing under a mixture of dust and verdigris. Today, mounted on ball bearings, the door responds to the slightest touch. Electric brushes and chemical products have gotten the best of the coat of silt five centuries old. This double renovation symbolizes—somewhat ideally, to be sure— the work undertaken by the Second Vatican Ecumenical Council, whose preparation began three years ago.

Although the Council opens in less than four months (October 11), it is difficult to make any predictions. All the members—cardinals, bishops, religious, and priests—of the two preparatory commissions and three secretariats created especially for the Council are in fact bound to secrecy. Nonetheless, the time we have spent in Rome allows us to form some idea of the interplay of forces at work, of the psychology, the hopes, and indeed the fears of the Pope, the cardinals—those in the Curia as well as outside it—and the bishops who have worked on the commissions.

The Council, says Archbishop Thomas D. Roberts (formerly Archbishop of Bombay), is like a ball game which the Pope will umpire. Although we do not know the rules of the game in great detail since the conciliar procedures have not yet been promulgated, we can at least describe the field and talk a little about the ball and the players.

The field, in this case, is the venerable Basilica of St. Peter. These days it is like a theater being redecorated. Paint fumes float around the atrium, whose iron gate has been scoured and repainted; the coffered ceiling has been cleared. The central nave, in the middle of the Basilica, is closed to the faithful. The Council will take up the full length of this nave, which measures over 300 feet. Two lateral platforms separated by a corridor in the middle are presently being constructed. The white wood is still rough, and the sound of sanders is plainly audible. St. Peter's smells more of sawdust than incense. We can imagine these stands furnished with rugs, chairs (red for the cardinals, green for the bishops), desks, and kneeling benches. Three thousand people, including about 2,500 Council Fathers, are to be seated here. Thirty-odd microphones will be at their service.

No Simultaneous Translations   Special seats have been built for the observers. Modern organs to the left of the apse will be added to those which date from the time of Gregory XVI.

To save time, votes will be registered electronically and the Council debates will be recorded. Since the Roman Church is showing signs of modernization in this respect, it is surprising that of the forty-two stenographers from fourteen countries who have been provided for, only one of them is trained in stenotyping.

It is common knowledge that the Council Fathers will use Latin, the official language of the Church. The Vatican has apparently rejected the idea of simultaneous translations, which are deemed essential at all other major international assemblies—notably at the gatherings of the World Council of Churches. The explanation offered for this omission is that the looseness of oral translations could be a source of misunderstanding, and that only Latin can guarantee satisfactory theological exactness. Perhaps. But non-Catholic observers from non-Latin countries will feel rather isolated in spite of the translated résumés that will be distributed to them as the discussions proceed.

Furthermore, these observers will not be permitted to attend all the sessions. There is some fear that the presence of non-Catholics would inhibit the spontaneity of the debates. Protestants have already taken careful note of these restrictive measures, and naturally contrast them with the practice at New Delhi, where journalists and observers were admitted to both plenary and committee sessions. The World Council of Churches wants its meeting to be considered an open house and uses democratic methods. But this cannot be the case at the Vatican Council; the two bodies are scarcely comparable.

An Excess of Discretion   To date the Vatican Council seems more like a fortress with precious few oillets. Moreover, these oillets are covered with colored glass which distorts the natural perspective. The Church is traditionally closemouthed about her affairs; she distrusts public opinion and even more reporters. And she has some good reasons for this. But in the final analysis, is this excess of discretion in the true interests of the Church? What is true in Paris may be less so in Rome since the advent of John XXIII, who created a special press bureau for the Council. The professional consciousness and extreme amiability of the incumbent are not in question; nevertheless, journalists really deserve to be taken more seriously. The press bureau will apparently be well staffed during the Council. The least one can say is that this is a necessity; it is to be hoped that those responsible will be permitted to dispense information which is worthy of the name instead of the kind of abstractions about the life of the Church which can be found in any library. It would also be desirable for Rome to imitate the highly skilled methods used by the press service of the World Council of Churches. Recently John XXIII expressed the desire that all journalists be adequately informed. *Utinam.* . . . Is this not the best and perhaps only way to leash the overactive imagination of certain newsmen?

What about the Pope, the leader of the Council, whom Archbishop Roberts called the umpire of the ball game? John will be eighty-two a few weeks after the assembly opens. His health is apparently excellent, but he is hesitating to undergo an operation his doctors have suggested. We saw him last week at St. Peter's, smiling and relaxed, giving an impression of balance, serenity, and goodness that is characteristic of men who pray a lot. This Italian peasant has a strange face. It is softly contoured, but on closer inspection it is a face of energy and strong will. The whole weight of the Council rests on the shoulders of this octogenarian, who was almost the only one to want it in the beginning. If the Pope were to disappear before October 11, it is said in Rome, the Council would not convene, or at the very least it would be sabotaged.

A Pope of Balance . . .   John XXIII is a complex personality. His manner of governing is disconcerting. When the Italians speak of him, they use the word *furbo*, which means astute, canny, sharp-witted. Like most men who are highly placed and taken up with large-scale planning, he is lonely, often misunderstood and badly advised. He is a man of balance who prefers to pacify rather than affront, to exercise patience rather than cut a knot. Yet John XXIII knows what he wants and can on occasion prove tenacious, and he uses unexpected channels of communication to push ahead.

. . . Who Lives for the Council   Politically, his sympathy for the "opening to the left" is well known, and he himself readily admits to it in private conversations. Equally well known is his opposition to the ideas of Alfredo Cardinal Ottaviani, the redoubtable Secretary of the Holy Office.

This conflict was recently illustrated by a disciplinary rebuke of this prelate which has stirred up a lot of talk. At other times the Pope gives way. He personally removed from the list of nominations for cardinal a personality who would have added to Ottaviani's psychological isolation.

In sum, the Pope lives entirely for the Council. He works on it without interruption, often well into the night. But even in these matters his choices are surprising. For example, he selected Archbishop Pericle Felici, a friend of the late Domenico Cardinal Tardini, as secretary of the Pontifical Antepreparatory Commission of the Council, though Felici's ideas are rather obsolete, while the Pope wants the Council to renew the face of the Church radically and let in fresh air from all quarters, including the non-Catholic faiths.

But make no mistake: John XXIII is very attached to tradition. This is obvious in matters of doctrine. He still seems to oppose the previously disowned worker-priest experiment, just as he does not want to discuss the possibility of a married clergy. Although his humility in anything concerning himself is legendary, he wants a certain decorum to surround his office. Thus, on his election—and this is not widely known—he allowed all of the court protocol to be revived which Pius XII had progressively suppressed. Again, this Pope who dreads doing harm to anyone, this man who has a horror of overhasty action, is leading his Council with drums beating. He insisted that it begin in 1962 and not 1963 as people generally thought it would. He had hoped it would take only one session, but there is abundant material for at least three. The first will last until December 10; the second and third are projected for 1963. This haste can undoubtedly be explained by the fact that John XXIII feels pressed by age and has a presentiment that any putting off of reforms would risk burying them.

(J U N E   2 9)

The Partisans of the Status Quo
Have not Disarmed

A recent incident reveals how hostile certain Roman circles remain to the freedom of speech which the bishops manifested at the time the Council was announced. The Dutch episcopacy (one archbishop, six bishops) had written a collective letter toward the end of 1960 on the "meaning of the Council." It was judged so remarkable that it was translated into several languages. The Italian version has just come out under the auspices of the Salesian Fathers. A few days ago the Salesians were asked to withdraw all unsold copies. Bernard Cardinal Alfrink, Archbishop of Utrecht, in Rome at the moment, has found this rather peculiar. Here is the passage which doubtless gave the most offense:

> The untimely interruption of the First Vatican Council has created the impression that the separate definition of papal infallibility is an isolated dogma. In fact, this personal infallibility is part of the official infallibility of the bishops of the world, which in turn is founded upon the infallible faith of the whole community.

Divinitas, the journal of Lateran University, got ready to publish an article attacking this conception of infallibility. John XXIII opposed this *in extremis,* but he did nothing, it seems, to forestall the withdrawal of the Dutch letter from the market.

A Courageous Book Is Judged Undesirable by Rome Nor did Pope John XXIII defend a book by Father Lombardi, a Jesuit who was often quoted by Pius XII, which met the same fate as the Dutch letter. Father Lombardi was evidently not diplomatic. He said what he thought without circumlocution, but at bottom his observations were not very different from those the Pope himself has made at one time or another. He attacked the Curia with no holds barred; expressing in various blunt ways the hope that in the future careerism would give way to merit and efficiency, that the administration of the Church would be decentralized, that the rules of the Index would be modified, that the Pope would be elected by a larger college, and so forth.

L'Osservatore Romano immediately protested, as could be expected. John XXIII—less predictably, for those who weren't in the know—recommended "to those who write about the Council prudence and a concern for the truth, so that their actions give rise to neither dissension nor disquiet."

Two official documents which appeared in recent months also indicate that the opposition to certain desires for reform has not laid down its arms. The fact that they were signed by the Pope has only increased the uneasiness, as much within as outside the Church, indeed wherever there are people who tend to take their wishes for reality.

An Encylical Unlike Others The first, dated December 9, 1961, is no less than an encyclical, *Aeterna Dei sapientia.* It was written as a eulogy to Pope Leo the Great and deals vigorously with the authority of the seat of Rome. The encyclical explains that Saint Leo long hesitated to ratify canon 28 of the Council of Chalcedon (451), which conceded first place among all the Eastern Churches to the See of Constantinople, in contempt of the rights of more ancient Churches recognized by the Council of Nicaea and which also curtailed the authority of the Apostolic See itself.

There were animated protests on the part of both Protestants and Orthodox. Dr. Visser 'tHooft, Secretary General of the World Council of Churches, publicly regretted the style of this document, which belonged, he said, to an age of monologue one could hope had passed into history. Archbishop Emilianos, Patriarch of Constantinople, thought the text unfortunate, and tending "to rekindle and encourage Roman Catholics to hatred of a sister Church." The same prelate asked the Pope "to recognize all the harm done by this encyclical, to abandon this polemical style, and to admit the synodal authority of the ecumenical councils as did all members of the undivided Church in the early centuries."

Catholic ecumenists, who attach great importance to the climate of friendship John XXIII has created between Rome and Constantinople, were astonished at the content of this encyclical and its tone, which differed rather strikingly from that of other documents John XXIII has signed.

Several Tunes at Once   The second document has stirred even more controversy. This is the apostolic constitution *Veterum sapientiae* dated February 22, 1962, intended to "revitalize" the use of Latin. It especially instructs bishops to forbid those in their charge to write against the use of Latin not only in teaching but also in the liturgy. Professors of theology, philosophy, and Scripture in all Catholic faculties are asked in the decree of application to give their courses in Latin beginning in October, 1963 (see *Acta apostolicae sedis*, May 30).

In Rome the matter has been assessed accurately enough. They say with a smile that it is pointless to take offense at an action prompted by certain persons in the Lateran and elsewhere who are hostile to the spread of vernacular languages in the liturgy and in seminaries. This text, they say, will not go into effect because it cannot, especially in non-Mediterranean countries.

But outside of Italy the reactions have been strong. What is the point of a council, they ask, if it short-circuits on so crucial an issue? The preconciliar commission in charge of studies and seminaries can only interpret this constitution as an insult. In Anglo-Saxon countries the document has caused considerable consternation. In Holland it provoked the laity to write a collective letter of protest to the hierarchy.

Perhaps it is wiser to look upon this pontifical text with a certain skepticism, as the Italians do. In any event, it is undeniable that the clergy's knowledge of Latin is inadequate. In spite of this restrictive measure, the use of the vernacular will continue to spread in the liturgy. As a case in point, the bilingual ritual of Latin America was approved by Rome only a few days ago.

These various examples indicate how careful one must be in interpreting attitudes of the Vatican which to the superficial observer may seem irreconcilable. It is a practice of the Roman Church—and it is more a strength than a weakness—to play several tunes at once. John XXIII is a flexible pope; when he gives in or remains silent on one point, it is most often because he wants to win on another which he considers more important.

(J U N E   3 0)

The Unity of Christians Remains the Pope's Deepest Concern

The documents prepared by the preconciliar commissions, which everyone agrees are of high quality, are collected in 119 brochures with covers bearing the seven colors of the rainbow. In all there are seventy "schemas," all of which have been reviewed by the central commission. At the moment they are undergoing final revision by a subcommission in charge of corrections, a highly important group composed of two Italian cardinals, one Argentine, and one Canadian. These basic documents will be sent to all the bishops of the world in July. The Pope has recently asked them to forward their observations to him (*attentis recum adjunctis*) so that he can consider them before the opening of the Council.

This is a good indication of John's desire to give the Council Fathers every opportunity to express their opinions. For though the schemas were drawn up on the basis of 8,972 *vota* submitted by the bishops in 1960 (the "antepreparatory" period), it is not likely, for practical as well as technical reasons, that they explicitly reflect all opinions. A certain amount of pruning was necessary, and this or that omission could easily displease the bishops. It would be wise for them to speak before rather than after the Council proper begins, when it will be more difficult because of both the number of participants and the inevitable quibbling that the Council's format will provoke.

The best jurists of the Sacred College of Cardinals have been appointed to a special subcommission for the purpose of working out the final details of these rules. They are Francesco Roberti (Italian),

Jaime de Barros Câmara (Brazilian), André Jullien (French), Arcadio Larraona (Spanish), and William Heard (Scottish). The difficulties they have to resolve are rather like those of squaring a circle. On one hand, they must permit each Council Father adequate liberty of expression (otherwise the Council would not be valid, theologically speaking), and on the other, they must keep the interventions within reasonable limits lest the Council go on interminably.

Religious Liberty   Enumerating the titles of the seventy schemas would go beyond the purpose of this report. Briefly, the scope of the questions raised is extremely broad. For example, at the seventh and last meeting of the Central Preparatory Commission, seventeen schemas were examined. One of them was concerned with relations between the church and the state; several others dealt with the role of the laity. Finally, and with this the preparatory work of the Council ended, the Secretariat for Promoting Christian Unity presented five schemas—on Catholic ecumenism, the word of God, prayer for unity, love between the different confessions (particularly the Jews), and, last but not least, religious tolerance.

This thorny subject, so dear to the hearts of Protestants and discussed at length in New Delhi, appears to have brought Augustin Cardinal Bea and Cardinal Ottaviani into polite conflict, the former in the name of the inalienable rights of the human person and the latter in the name of the common good of collectivities.

These debates are evidently ultrasecret, but they have been recorded on tape for the Vatican archives and for posterity. They will not be made public for about fifty years, that is, until after the members of the central commission have died. These are Vatican traditions, and they are very venerable.

Among the schemas are there any concerned directly with the reform of the Curia (requested by a very large number of bishops), a retiring age for bishops and cardinals, the overhauling of the Index, exterior signs of poverty? Who knows? Two points at least seem sure:

1. The patriarchs will henceforward take precedence over the cardinals, a step that will please the united Oriental Churches.
2. A secretariat for the apostolate of the laity will be created at the end of the Council.

It is being said that the question of the diaconate has been put on ice for the time being. The members of the Central Preparatory Commission could not agree on the kind of life (Should deacons be married? Should they take secular jobs?) most suitable to this middleman function, linking laymen and priests, to which many theologians and pastors attach great importance. But the absence (or muted presence) of any of these questions does not mean that the Council will not deal with them directly. In the final analysis, everything depends on the will of the Council Fathers and their skill in making their views prevail. Two or three determined bishops could change the course of the Council significantly. This, moreover, is what Pope John wants, for he called the Council in order to initiate certain fundamental reforms he could not have achieved alone against a reluctant Curia.

It is pertinent here to emphasize that the Council will not go into details. It will be concerned only with defining general directions, and will leave the work of applying them concretely to postconciliar commissions. There is a danger here that certain projects will be buried. In religious as in civil societies, it is not unusual for the work of commissions to get lost in the shuffle.

Will the Powers of Bishops Be Increased? Clearly, nothing is settled. One of the big questions remaining is that of redefining the powers of bishops. It is sure to come up for discussion. But how will it be resolved? It is already being said in Rome that to give bishops more power is practically impossible and even undesirable. In some parts of the world, especially in mission countries where the higher clergy has only recently become indigenous, the bishops lack the experience, so the explanation goes, to justify additional authority. There is also and above all the risk of making bishops "little popes" and thereby diminishing the Vatican's role as supreme arbiter. Perhaps the difficulty can be circumvented by strengthening the powers of national or continental conferences of bishops.

Among the approximately 2,500 bishops who will come to Rome for the Council, there will be about 500 Orientals and fifty Negroes. It is the first time that such a gathering will be so interracial in character.

There are about 300 South American bishops. Their principal preoccupations seem to be the struggle against communism on the one hand and on the other against Protestantism, whose methods of expansion are highly criticized on that continent. The theological competence of North American bishops is notoriously inferior to that of European prelates. The preparatory work for the Council has accentuated the character and value of the German, Austrian, and Dutch episcopacies. France, a country always watched closely by Rome, is known for her theologians.

When the central commission finished its preparatory work,* the Fathers most frequently spoken about and generally agreed to have been most influential were Julius Cardinal Döpfner, Archbishop of Munich; Franziskus Cardinal Koenig, Archbishop of Vienna; Cardinal Alfrink of Utrecht; Archbishop Alfred Bengsch of Berlin; Archbishop Lorenze Jaeger of Paderborn; Cardinal Ottaviani of Rome; Achille Cardinal Liénart, Bishop of Lille; Paul Cardinal Richaud, Archbishop of Bordeaux, and their ilk.

There has been praise, too, of the quiet roles played by Giacomo Cardinal Lercaro, an Italian pioneer of liturgical reform, and particularly Giovanni Battista Cardinal Montini, whose exceptional worth everyone praises. He is undoubtedly awaiting his hour.

The Observers Cardinal Bea merits special mention. Hitherto little known, except in his capacity as confessor to Pius XII, the scholarly Jesuit Scripture authority has occupied a place of first importance since John XXIII entrusted him with the project dearest to his heart: the secretariat for the unity of Christians. Despite his advanced age (he was born in 1881), this prelate has proved his great stature. In a few months he has gained an indisputable influence among non-Catholic Christians, whom he visits regularly, either personally or in the person of his Dutch secretary, Monsignor Jan G. Willebrands, a compatriot and friend of Dr. Visser 'tHooft of the World Council of Churches. Roman circles sometimes take umbrage at the success of this German cardinal and mistrust his bold initiative. But no one dares say so openly, for Cardinal Bea is one of John's favorite prelates, and the secretariat which he heads will very likely become a permanent office in the near future.

Problems relating to observer-delegates from the Orthodox and the Anglican and other Protestant faiths are judged to have been handled in a satisfactory manner. Only the Orthodox Churches behind the iron curtain (in Russia, Rumania, Bulgaria, Czechoslovakia, and Poland) still pose unresolved question marks.

During the Council, Cardinal Bea and his assistants will see to it that the non-Catholic observers are correctly informed, directly or indirectly, on the work and difficulties of the assembly. They will be invited to attend meetings with bishops and theologians. John XXIII has insisted that these special envoys from other confessions be shown

---

* The preconciliar central commission held seven sessions in all. It was composed of 108 members from fifty-five countries. There were sixty-seven cardinals, five patriarchs, twenty-eight archbishops, five bishops, three superiors of religious orders, and twenty-seven advisers.

Vatican I was prepared by thirty-six members, mostly Western, divided into nine commissions. Vatican II will have been prepared by some 800 persons from about sixty countries.

maximum consideration. In fact, the Pope is always mindful, contrary to what some think, of the long-range aim of the Council: better relations with those he no longer calls "separated Christians" but—and the nuance is important—"brothers who do not yet share fully in the unity desired and established by the Lord."

During the summer months, preparations for the Council will mark time. Nonetheless, Pope John has an immense amount of work to do: determine the Council's daily agenda, set up new organs like a general secretariat and a commission of theological advisers to the Pope, and select presidents for the episcopal commissions that will begin to function on October 11 (the Fathers themselves choosing the members).

Toward the Beatification of Pius IX John XXIII wants some large public ceremonies to take place between conciliar work sessions (which are called "general congregations"), such as the canonization of Blessed Eymard, a Frenchman from the region of Grenoble, and of the Italians Francesco Maria de Camporoso and Vincente Pallotini. There will also be several beatifications, among which the most notable will certainly be that of Pius IX, the pope of the *Syllabus*.

A New Era

And so the Council, steering around the reefs, nears the opening date. Unquestionably the preparations have been thought to be hasty and therefore superficial. How successful can the Council be? Opinion is divided. Some expect more from it than it can possibly give. The pessimists call attention to the almost total failure of the recent Roman Synod, though the Pope called it explicitly for the purpose of setting an example in his own diocese. The Synod's stipulations have remained a dead letter because of the lack of energetic men to implement them.*

It is easy to criticize the Pope for being too indulgent. What then can the practical effects of the Council be, even if it does produce some excellent documents?

When speaking of the Council, we must consider its deeper, long-range influence, which is more important. It is wise, at any rate, not to expect immediate spectacular results, as the Pope has specifically pointed out in one of his allocutions.

* There is frequently no sermon or reading from the New Testament in the vernacular at Sunday morning masses in Rome, despite the explicit recommendations of the synod. Militant Catholics in Rome have noted this shortcoming with bitterness. This is further proof that Rome is better suited to command from a distance than on its own territory.

It remains true that this exceptional event in the life of the Church has already provoked widespread ferment among men and ideas. Thanks to the preparatory phase of the Council, the Curia, whose experience is more bureaucratic than pastoral, has come into constant—and practical— contact with all parts of the world. The Vatican has perhaps learned more of the world in the last three years as a result of the preconciliar commissions than in fifty ordinary years. Moreover, the Curia has discovered the existence of ecumenical problems to which it had no previous exposure. In this respect, and whatever happens in the future, a new development has begun; the splendid isolation of the Vatican belongs irrevocably to the past.

OCTOBER, 1962

The Clarity of John's Speech
Impressed the Council Fathers

The clarity—those who felt singled out would perhaps say the severity —of John's opening speech to the Council yesterday very much impressed the Council Fathers.

He complained openly about the "voices of persons who, though burning with zeal, are not endowed with too much sense of discretion or measure. In these modern times they can see nothing but prevarication and ruin. They say that our era, in comparison with past eras, is getting worse, and they behave as though they had learned nothing from history, which is nevertheless the teacher of life," as if formerly, the Pope added, "the Christian idea and life" and "proper religious liberty" had fully triumphed. "We feel we must disagree with those prophets of gloom who are always forecasting disaster, as though the end of the world were at hand."

Although the Council Fathers do not know one another very well, they know whom the Pope was talking about when he spoke of those who lack "broadmindedness, discretion, and balance."

In specifying these faults, to which must be added a total contempt for the modern world, John defined very clearly the integralist tendancy which the Council must contend with.

Twice the Pope took up the subject of "religious liberty"—and not of "tolerance"—which is so important to the Protestant observers and guests who formed a half-circle before him in the first row of the audience. He also mentioned the "interference of civil authority" and "dangerous and self-interested politics" which in former times the princes of the world exercised with regard to the Church.

In another comment, this time a doctrinal one which blends with the concerns of many modern theologians, John declared, "The substance of the ancient doctrine of the deposit of faith is one thing, and the way in which it is presented is another." This formula recalls a distinction made by Pouget between "spirit" and "mentality," ideas popularized by Jean Guitton.

Another statement reveals a quite new attitude in the Church, one that bears the imprint of the Pope's personality: "Nowadays, however, the [Church] prefers to apply the medicine of mercy rather than that of severity," and to refrain from "condemnations."

When the ceremony had ended, one of the Council Fathers said to us, "I hope the moderation and frankness of the Holy Father's words will be an example to us during the Council's sessions so that we will not get lost in a maze of uninteresting details and not be tempted, because of our inability to reform the Church, to tolerate the defects which make it so difficult for men of our times to accept her message."

From Assisi to St. Peter's

An important Catholic journal has written that "The three-quarters of the world who consider the Roman Church a sect are indifferent to the Council."

Among the indifferent, first of all and closest at hand, are the natives of Rome. They have already seen so much of the Council that they have grown quite bored. But above all, in Europe as well as elsewhere, there are the great urban masses who will remember nothing of this pious assembly except the pomp and circumstance.

At the opening of the Council with his fellow ecclesiastics was Bishop José Dammert Bellido of Cajamarca, Peru, a small dot under his white miter in the aula flowing with colors and robes. Not long ago he preached a rousing sermon on the occasion of Social Week in Lima:

> We are a cause of scandal to some and disgust to others because of our lack of moderation in our acts of worship. Quite calmly and innocently, we waste our energies augmenting the outward show, draping silver on statues done in dubious taste. Meanwhile, in our midst are many of God's children who suffer from hunger and sickness. No, our sumptuousness is not really in accord with the miseries of our time.

Some bishops came to Rome in second-class coaches; the majority of them have taken simple quarters in religious communities; but others, and they are not a few—notably from across the Atlantic—have registered at the best hotels in Rome.

John XXIII likes to repeat the complaint made to him by his own brother. "Angelo, you too are now a prisoner of luxury." But there were many in St. Peter's yesterday who remembered that only a week ago the Pope, now seated on his canopied throne, journeyed to Assissi, the home of the *Poverello*. Each has grasped the significance of this unexpected gesture, which was such a radical departure from custom.

Separating himself from the members of his entourage who formed a kind of screen around him, the Holy Father entered into direct contact with the crowd and spoke their colorful dialect. The occasion once again reminded Italian Catholics how much more at ease the Pope is with little people than with the great.

Perhaps more than anything else it is John's desire, and that of a number of bishops, to see the Church do official acts of poverty like Francis of Assisi's and repentance like the recent declaration of the German hierarchy, which constitute the real opportunity of the Council. These gestures hoped for by non-Catholic churches, would not be enough in themselves; but they could in some sense be the breach through which other reforms might pass.

Unknown Factors of Vatican II

Election of Commission Members   The Council at the moment resembles a chess game with the pawns not yet in place. Indeed, the election of members to the ten conciliar commissions will occupy the first four general congregations, that is, plenary work sessions of Vatican II. John XXIII has already named the presidents of the commissions* and reserves the right to select eight members for each one; but the Council Fathers must choose the others—sixteen for each commission, or 160 members in all. Since those with the power to vote number some 2,300, there would have to be not less than 370,000 ballots.

The importance of this preliminary work is evident. By electing 160 men who will constitute two-thirds of the commission members, the bishops will implicitly make known whom they trust for the elaboration of the schemas.

The Council Fathers, barely arrived from the four corners of the

* [These are Alfredo Cardinal Ottaviani (Doctrinal Commission for Faith and Morals), Paolo Cardinal Marella (Commission for Bishops and the Government of Dioceses), Amleto Cardinal Cicognani (Commission for the Oriental Churches), Benedetto Cardinal Aloisi Masella (Commission for the Discipline of the Sacraments), Pietro Cardinal Ciriaci (Commission for the Discipline of the Clergy and the Christian People), Valerio Cardinal Valeri (Commission for Religious), Gregorio Pietro Cardinal Agagianian (Commission for the Missions), Arcadio Cardinal Larraona (Commission for the Sacred Liturgy), Giuseppe Cardinal Pizzardo (Commission for Seminaries, Studies, and Catholic Schools), and Fernando Cardinal Cento (Commission for the Lay Apostolate, the Press, and Entertainment).—Tr.]

earth, don't know one another very well yet. Many of them are not sure whom they should vote for. Because of this the bishops, or more exactly the cardinals, who have had some preconciliar experience are prompted to enlighten the future voters. And quite naturally the lists of "suggestions" that are furtively distributed reflect the interests of those who have drawn them up.

In this very special climate, which is that of an ecclesiastical gathering of some six to seven thousand persons from over 100 countries, tongues will wag if one is patient enough to wait. Most of the Fathers spontaneously barricade themselves behind the "secrecy" of the Council—a secrecy which, to tell the truth, is impossible to describe exactly. But after offering some resistance for the sake of form, they give out bits and pieces of information. Such and such an "expert" (here they are called *periti*) who has the ear of such and such a cardinal goes around recommending a certain number of names. Others from different camps do the same, so that in the final analysis the scrupulous succumb under the weight of *too much* information.

It would be unreasonable to try at present to label the various schools of thought that are emerging and still more to identify their leaders. The physiognomy of so complicated a gathering, where passions are still being held in check—the real battles have not yet begun—will only gradually come clear, after several trial balloons have gone up. The most one can say is that there will be more than two orientations, and that the majority of the Council Fathers have not yet found their way. These undecided prelates will likely rally to the group which has the skill to avoid giving the impression of being "extremist" in either the leftist or the rightist sense; excess might frighten them off. The Council Fathers, it ought not be forgotten, are for the most part men of advanced years and are not inclined to be locked into overly systematic ways of thinking.

Let us note in passing the numerical importance of the Italian Council Fathers—some 400 as against for example only 150 Frenchmen, who nonetheless represent a comparable national population. Also they constitute an unknown factor since many of them have done little in the past to indicate what their true colors might be.

The Seven Schemas Once the preliminary elections are done with, the real work of the Council will begin. The daily agenda has not been determined, but we have learned—not without difficulty—the titles of the seven schemas (out of the seventy drawn up during the preparatory period) which the bishops of the world received in August. We can conclude that these schemas will be brought to the Council Fathers' attention during the first session.

The documents cover about 250 spaciously printed pages. The first four were prepared by the preconciliar commission on theology (president: Cardinal Ottaviani). They are:

1. The Sources of Revelation: Scripture and Tradition. This is a particularly difficult question because of its ecumenical implications. Protestants consider Scripture to be the sole source. The manner in which Vatican II presents the nature of the dependence of the second source on the first will be of the greatest interest, for even within the Roman Church there are several schools.

2. The Moral Order. The dangers of moral subjectivism, for example, and the possible abuses of psychoanalytic techniques will be treated.

3. The Deposit of Faith. This schema will consider pantheism, existentialism, atheism, modernism, liberalism, and so forth. The word *evolutionist* occurs in this schema, and it is more than likely that the Church will take this opportunity to crystallize her position on the thought of Father Pierre Teilhard de Chardin. It is a fact that the Pope said recently before a group of French priests that the monitum of the Holy See was "regrettable." In addition, when Léopold Senghor, President of the Republic of Senegal, came to Rome a few days ago, he told John XXIII that the monitum had created much uneasiness in African and European circles which have benefited from Teilhard's thought. Let us note, in this connection, that if the experts at the Council include Father Gagnebet, who is well known for his "integralist" positions, there is also Father Henri de Lubac, whose book on Teilhard was criticized in *L'Osservatore Romano*.

4. Family and Chastity. This was the theme of John XXIII's discourse at Loretto last week.

5. The Liturgy (eight chapters). This schema is by far the most important. It was prepared with special care by thirteen mixed subcommissions, and was drawn up by the preparatory commission for the liturgy, under the presidency of Gaetano Cardinal Cicognani (and later of Cardinal Larraona). The schema deals especially with the revision of the rites, the mass, and the extended use of vernacular languages. This last point is of great interest to most bishops, who desire more active participation in the liturgy on the part of the faithful. The possibility that the use of Latin will be restricted provokes lively reactions among those who are attached to traditional ways. On the other hand, missionaries and Eastern prelates are decided partisans of the use of local languages.

6. The Means of Distributing Information (six parts). This schema was prepared by the secretariat for the press and entertainment (president: Archbishop Martin J. O'Connor).

7. The Unity of the Church. This document, drawn up by the commission for the Oriental Churches under the presidency of Amleto Cardinal Cicognani, is altogether distinct from that prepared by the secretariat for Christian unity on Catholic ecumenism. The latter, which will be submitted to the Council later, is said to be much more interesting because it was prepared by specialists working under Cardinal Bea.

A Safety Valve   What reception will the Council Fathers give these schemas? In 1869, at the time of Vatican I, the first thing the bishops did when they arrived in Rome was brush aside the reports that had been prepared. "Too obscure," they said. This was scarcely flattering to Father Franzelin, who had made a major contribution to the preparatory work and who was one of the best theologians of the time. His students at the Gregorian University seized on this evaluation gleefully: "We always knew Franzelin was obscure, but it is a dogma now since the bishops have said so."

The atmosphere is very different in 1962. But it must be noted that two-thirds of the Council Fathers live outside of Europe while the proportion on the preparatory commissions was just the opposite. It would be altogether natural for the Council not to find the schemas satisfactory.

Furthermore, the official press bureau informs us with considerable candor that the seventy schemas (2,045 pages) might be considered "the juice produced by straining" the sixteen volumes (10,000 pages) containing the opinions submitted by the bishops during the antepreparatory stage of the Council. The juice? That is a large claim. It is more than likely that the Fathers will not agree entirely with this view and will be surprised, for example, to find nothing on the reorganization of the Curia or the Holy Office.

But John XXIII has seen to it that the Council has a safety valve. He created—and it was an important innovation by comparison with the former Council—a Secretariat for Extraordinary Affairs. It is headed by Amleto Cardinal Cicognani, Secretary of State, and is composed of seven other members: Cardinal Montini, Carlo Confalonieri, and Giuseppe Siri (Italians); Döpfner (German), Leo Suenens (Belgian), and Albert Meyer (American, of German extraction), and also Archbishop Felici (Italian). The Curia is represented by only two cardinals: Cicognani and Confalonieri. With the exception of Cardinal Siri, Archbishop of Genoa, all of the cardinals are reputed to be openminded toward the problems of our times. Moreover, their average age is much less than that of the members of the presidential council. Cardinal Döpfner, who is considered one of the most dynamic prelates at the council, is only forty-nine years old.

It is a good bet that the Secretariat for Extraordinary Affairs will not remain idle and that the Council Fathers will have frequent recourse to it. This is the real unknown factor of Vatican II. By this initiative the Pope has given the lie to pessimists who said that the Council was practically over even before it began. Very flattering for those who worked on the preparatory commissions, of course, but less so for the Council Fathers who want to make maximum use of the Council to bring their views to fruition.

OCTOBER 15

The First Three Surprises of the Council

The prophets went to all their trouble for naught; so far nothing but the unexpected has happened. Vatican II is only five days old and on three different occasions events have shattered the predictions: the vote on the formation of the conciliar commissions has been postponed; Pope John made a resolutely "modern" speech; and Russian observers have suddenly appeared.

Let us begin with the last to occur. According to the calendar distributed by the official press bureau, the Council was to hold its second general congregation this morning, Monday. But it did not take place. In fact it can scarcely be said that the first one met last Saturday. It lasted a mere half-hour. What happened?

The meetings were held to elect the first of the 160 members of the conciliar commissions. Television cameras were standing by to record this historic vote. But after Archbishop Felici, the secretary general of the Council, asked the bishops to begin the proceedings, Cardinal Liénart rose and said in substance, "We are not disposed to accept the list of candidates proposed to us until the Council meets again. We have had too little time to choose our own candidates, since the Council Fathers do not know one another well enough yet. We therefore ask for a further delay in order to get our bearings."

The Marxist *Il Paese* had this to say apropos Cardinal Liénart's intervention Saturday: "The Devil has entered the Council." It hastened to add that this dictum is not its own but Pius IX's.

It is true that Piux IX once said, "In a council, there are three climates: that of the Devil, who tries to set everything topsy-turvy;

that of men, who try to confuse everything; and that of the Holy Spirit, who comes to clarify everything."

Joseph Cardinal Frings, Archbishop of Cologne, then spoke and seconded his colleague. He also remarked that there were no cardinals among the members of the preconciliar commissions, but that there was no reason they should not eventually be elected to the conciliar commissions. That was all. These two declarations were met with a salvo of applause and were unanimously approved, so that there was no need to vote an adjournment.

The Church of France Was the First To Speak Thus the Church of France, in the person of its Cardinal dean, Bishop of Lille, and director of the Mission de France, was the first to speak its mind in Rome. This was a precedent. As soon as the assembly dissolved, the ten cardinals chosen by the Pope to preside in turn over the general congregations met in conference. They are Eugène Tisserant and Liénart (French), Ignace Tappouni (Syrian), Norman Gilroy (Australian), Frings (German), Enrique Pla y Deniel (Spanish), Francis Spellman (American), Ernesto Ruffini (Italian), Antonio Caggiano (Argentine), and Alfrink (Dutch). With this meeting they made it clear that they intend to act collegially from the beginning, and not merely preside individually over the sessions.

For the second time today, Monday, the French bishops met at the Church of St.-Louis-des-Français to agree on their candidates. The other bishops did likewise either by nations or by language groups. Through the instrumentality of their general secretariats, they each agreed to choose three candidates per commission. The next general congregation is set for tomorrow, Tuesday.

The importance of Cardinal Liénart's initiative cannot be over-emphasized, although it met a chilly reception in Roman circles. If the vote had begun as planned last Saturday morning, the bishops, caught unprepared, would have been inclined to vote for the prefabricated lists which were ready for circulation. If that had been the case, the conciliar commissions would have been closely related to the preconciliar commissions—which would not have displeased those who are reluctant to give the Council full liberty.

So much for the first surprise of the Council. The second is already known but it would be well to dwell on it further. The Pope's opening speech to the Council is laden with meaning. In rereading it under more relaxed circumstances, the Fathers have discovered further matter for reflection in a text that was more or less understood when it was delivered in Latin.

Pope John Praises the Research Methods of Modern Thought   The Pope, for example, has given the Church a dynamic image oriented toward the present and the future. "Our duty," he said, "is not only to guard this precious treasure [of the patrimony of faith], as if we were concerned only with antiquity, but to dedicate ourselves with an earnest will and without fear to that work which our era demands of us, pursuing thus the path which the Church has followed for twenty centuries."

No one could illustrate more clearly, in Jean Guitton's words, that "Tradition is the progress of yesterday and progress is the tradition of tomorrow." In other words, one should distinguish between tradition and intellectual laziness.

The Pope further expressed the wish that there be "a step forward toward a doctrinal penetration"; this, he added—and the elucidation has importance—means that doctrine must be "studied and expounded through the methods of research and through the literary forms of modern thought." This is the clearest statement yet made by the Pope on what he means by the *aggiornamento* of the Church. Councils may follow one another and yet bear hardly any resemblance; in 1870, at the time of Pius IX, the word *modern* was used only in an opprobrious progressivist sense.

Finally, in the part of his speech where he spoke of the unity of the human family, John XXIII evoked not only "the unity of prayers and ardent desires with which those Christians separated from this Apostolic See aspire to be united with us" but also "the unity in esteem and respect for the Catholic Church which animates those who follow non-Christian religions." In this sense, the Pope added, "the Second Vatican Ecumenical Council . . . prepares, as it were, and consolidates the path toward that unity of mankind which is required as a necessary foundation in order that the earthly city may be brought to the resemblance of [the] heavenly city. . . ." Ecumenism, as John XXIII sees it, thus goes beyond the limits of Christian confessions to reach the whole of mankind. The Pope explicitly affirmed that the Church's "strength of supernatural unity redounds to the advantage of all humanity. . . ." Concerns of this sort were frequently expressed at the meeting of the World Council of Churches in New Delhi a year ago; they are common currency in many Christian circles. But it is exceptional for a pope to allude to other religions in so positive a fashion.

A Double Paradox   The third but not the smallest surprise of the Council was the unexpected presence of Russian observers. This event is doubly paradoxical. The Patriarch of Moscow, as a matter of fact, had shown his disdain for the Council on several occasions. An article which appeared in the magazine of the Patriarchate was even entitled *"Non Possums."*

On the other hand, while Moscow, against all expectations, has been represented from the time the Council opened, no one represents the Church of Constantinople, whose patriarch had repeatedly praised the ecumenical initiatives of John XXIII.

There is something extraordinary about the fact that the presence of the Church of Moscow today serves as a stimulus to other Orthodox Churches, since her expected absence was a serious block to relations between Rome and Orthodoxy.

Why this sudden change on Moscow's part? Is it only a reflection of the shift at the Kremlin, which has indirectly gained the desired appeasements since Monsignor Willebrands' visit? Is it because the Patriarch Alexei and the Soviet government want to show their independence from Constantinople? Or is it more deeply a gesture of solidarity with a confession which represents an undeniable international spiritual force? Who knows?

OCTOBER 16

The Bishops Question the Schemas Prepared for Vatican II

Vatican II really began today, Tuesday. After three feverish days of interepiscopal contacts, the lists for the 160 members to be elected to the commissions have been put in order.* Gathered in a general congregation in St. Peter's this morning, the Fathers began to vote.

A number of bishops—French, German, and Dutch especially—have questioned the doctrinal schemas prepared for the Council.

Thus the Council is little by little becoming conscious of itself and beginning to flex its youthful muscles. Working out the lists has enabled the bishops, who scarcely knew one another a few days ago, to make international contacts. There are some fifty national or continental episcopal conferences in Rome, and it was at this collective level that liaisons were made.

At the end of these meetings, authorized spokesmen made it clear that the French episcopacy wanted at all costs to avoid the formation

---

* According to the rule presently in force, no Council Father can be a member of more than one commission. However, if the president of the commission (who is designated by the Pope) sees fit, he can seek the advice of any other Father, not a member of the commission.

Ordinarily, the regulations require a two-thirds majority of the votes. In exceptional cases, canon 101 of the Codex is applied. This stipulates that after the invalid ballots have been subtracted, an absolute majority is required or, if this is not attained after two ballots, a relative majority. In case of a tie after the third ballot, the president may cast a vote.

of antagonistic camps. They established numerous contacts with the bishops of other nations, so that the projected lists have had an international flavor from the beginning. As proof of their intention not to go it alone, they decided that their own meetings would be opened to whoever cared to attend, whatever his nationality.

It was learned meanwhile that the Pope had received the ten cardinals of the presidency on Monday. They informed John XXIII of the present spirit of the Council Fathers after the decidedly remarkable intervention of Cardinal Liénart.

France is still effectively holding the limelight and providing leadership in the discussions. By spearheading the effort to prevent rigged elections, the French contributed to creating a climate of freedom and openness that continues to bear fruit.

It is now known that when the Council finishes with the work of the elections, it will question the doctrinal schemas presented for its consideration. The German, Dutch, and French are firmly resolved not to let the schemas come up for discussion right away. The one exception is the schema on the liturgy, which everyone agrees is of high quality. An increasing number of bishops think that Vatican II ought to begin where Vatican I left off, by first considering the important question of episcopal powers. Once they have been satisfied on this point, the Council Fathers could have greater authority for continuing discussions on other matters. Moreover, the doctrinal schemas in their present form have gotten a very bad press. They are described as too scholastic, too juridical, too canonical, too centered on morality, and, perhaps the most serious charge in view of the ecumenical aspirations of the Council, not biblical enough. In this connection, one of the Protestant observers is reported to have said, "What is the point of the immense exegetical work undertaken in the Catholic Church if it comes to this?" The proof of this opinion is that some hope these schemas will be "piously buried." The Latin puts it nicely: *sepelire reverenter.*

The French bishops are not among the least demanding. Monday afternoon they let their unamimous desire be known that these doctrinal schemas be restudied "in light of John XXIII's speech," which means that the efforts of the Fathers ought to be directed, not toward anathematizing the errors of our time or wallowing in abstract considerations, but toward presenting Christian doctrine in a positive manner so that it will be appealing to contemporary man and so that the resultant image of the Church will be more attractive. This is the first time, but certainly not the last, that the Fathers have had recourse to the Pope's speech in an effort to keep the Council forward-looking and centered on the concrete problems that plague the world today.

John XXIII has named five undersecretaries of the Council. Happily, he chose bishops reputed for their liberal tendencies. They are Casimiro Morcillo Gonzáles, Archbishop of Saragossa; John J. Krol, Archbishop of Philadelphia; Jean Villot, Coadjutor Archbishop of Lyon; Wilhelm Kempf, Bishop of Limburg; and Philippe Nabaa, Melkite Archbishop of Beirut.

The Observers Are Asked
To Make Known Their Criticisms

As the Council takes its first steps, the non-Catholic observers and guests are the object of much attention. Last Saturday the Pope received them in special audience and welcomed them with his usual goodness and simplicity: "If you could read my heart," he told them, "you would perhaps understand much more than words can say. . . . Your welcome presence here [moves] our priestly heart, the heart of a bishop. . . ." (It is noteworthy that he did not say, "of a pope.")

Monday evening Cardinal Bea held a special reception for the observers in the Columbus Hotel. He addressed them as "My dear brothers in Christ." This title, he said, "makes us mindful of the incommensurable grace of baptism, which has created bonds that are indestructible, stronger than all our divisions." He asked them "to tell us very frankly . . . everything you dislike, to share with us your positive criticisms, your suggestions, and your wishes." Cardinal Bea regretted the absence of "venerable Orthodox Churches of the East which are not officially represented. This fact," he remarked, "is doubtless painful for both sides, for them and for us."

The representatives from the Orthodox Church behind the Iron Curtain are surrounded with curiosity and reserve. No one in Rome is unaware that despite the Soviet government's gestures of consideration, this church is sorely tried; nor is there any reason to think that the end of her trials are in sight.

OCTOBER 19

The Council's Message
To Be Addressed to the World

Like concentric waves in still water when a rock is thrown in, the excitement caused by the interventions of Cardinals Liénart and Frings is slowly dying down. But there is no telling what will happen next. Surprises like these are and will be the daily bread of Vatican II, which is no prefabricated council.

When a recent visitor asked him what he expected from the Council, John XXIII pointed to a window and said, "A breath of fresh air in the Church." On another occasion he said, "We must come out of our ghetto, and we have more important things to do than cast stones at communism." These and dozens of other quotes are making the rounds in Rome and are gradually creating the climate of this emergent gathering, which is ever the prey of different and indeed contradictory ideas.

As a matter of fact, there is a good deal of improvisation (and this is Italy, not Germany) as the Council gropingly seeks its proper course.

It is hard to tell at this point which way most of the Fathers will lean. Those whose names recur most frequently as likely to influence the Council in a special way are Cardinals Koenig, Archbishop of Vienna; Frings, Archbishop of Cologne; Döpfner, Archbishop of Munich; Alfrink, Archbishop of Utrecht; Paul Emile Léger, Archbishop of Montreal; Montini, Archbishop of Milan; Bea, president of the Secretariat for Promoting Christian Unity; Suenens, Archbishop of Malines-Brussels and Primate of Belgium; and Liénart, Bishop of Lille.

Clearly this is not an exhaustive list, but it does indicate some landmarks for the present and future.

The "List from the Common Market" The results of the voting will probably be known today, Friday. It wasn't possible to process the votes electronically since it would have required too complicated a code. The hand count was a lengthy operation.

The Fathers chose among seven slates of candidates, all of which were more or less international in character. The European list, jokingly called the "list from the Common Market," was the collaboration of the greatest number of countries, perhaps a dozen. There are several other lists—English, African, Asian, Latin American, and so on.

To the Italian list, which proposes five members from this country for each of the ten commissions, the Holy Office has added the names of an additional dozen for the theological commission (Doctrinal Commission for Faith and Morals). They come from different countries, excluding, however, Germany, Austria, the Netherlands, and France (except for one person who has long resided in Rome).

What will come out of this brew of names or the still possible mixture of lists? The mystery still excites speculation. Furthermore, we do not know yet whether the Pope will accept a proposal made by Cardinal Ottaviani that a simple majority vote suffice for election.

A "Message to the World"   There is already a good deal of interest in the "message to the world" which the Council Fathers will be asked to adopt before beginning their labors. This message, in concise and moderate style, is expected to touch upon themes of general interest, such as peace, the brotherhood of men of all races, the struggle against poverty in underdeveloped nations, and the like. It would thus rekindle the hope, often expressed during these past few months, that the Council will transcend specifically religious concerns and take up matters of common interest to all men, whatever creed they profess.

Then on Monday, October 22, the Council Fathers will address themselves to what will probably be the most important item of the first session: the schema on the liturgy. Will discussion of this essentially pastoral and concrete subject hold some surprises for us? It may well be, for liturgical reform has traditionally provoked a good deal of controversy.

We will report further on this in due time since the implications are of immediate concern to the faithful. The ritual of the mass will almost certainly be modified. The celebrant will undoubtedly be authorized to read the epistle and Gospel in the vernacular. African bishops will probably be permitted to base certain rites on animistic religions. Discussion on this schema is expected to last a considerable time since each amendment has to go back to the commissions for redrafting.

The non-Catholic observers and guests, for their part, are gradually acquainting themselves with the atmosphere of the Council, something altogether new to them. Perhaps they will discover from close up an image of the Roman Church very different from the one they discerned from afar.

The number of those who have personal invitations is increasing. Orthodox Bishop Cassien, Rector of the Orthodox Theological Institute of St.-Serge in Paris, has arrived. Day before yesterday the two observers from the Patriarchate of Moscow enlisted the services of an official interpreter, Dr. Nicolas Anfinaguenov, secretary of the Russian Orthodox delegation to the World Council of Churches in Geneva.

The conduct of the Russian observers has been edifying. Shortly after their arrival they asked to be taken to the altar of the Confession of St. Peter to pray before the presumed tomb of the first of the apostles, and they went to meditate at St. Paul's Outside the Walls before the mausoleum of the Apostle to the Gentiles. They were also seen at the Orthodox services celebrated by the Russian Church abroad, thus bearing tangible and unsolicited witness to the truth that religious communion is stronger than political dissension.

The Pope Judges a Single Ballot Sufficient;
Commission Members Declared Elected

The third general congregation of Vatican II opened Saturday morning at nine o'clock and terminated about one o'clock. It was presided over by Cardinal Liénart. At the request of the presidency, the Pope, taking account of the great number of votes (even for candidates who did not have an absolute majority) and eager for the work of the Council to progress more quickly, decided that there should only be one ballot, despite article 39 of the regulations. As a result, all sixteen Fathers for each of the ten commissions were elected. Results have been announced for only seven of them since the count has not yet been completed.

Among the more notable personalities elected to the Doctrinal Commission for Faith and Morals, which is by far the most important, are Archbishop Gabriel Garrone of Toulouse, Cardinals Koenig and Léger, and two Italians, one of whom is Archbishop Ermenegildo Florit of Florence.

In general the lists were found balanced and satisfactory. It was an agreeable surprise to learn that almost all the bishops proposed on the Central European slate—one of the most liberal—were elected.

The Pope has already exercised his right and named eight members of the Commission for the Sacred Liturgy. Among them are Cardinal Jullien, no doubt because of his competence in canon law, and Abbot Jean Prou, O.S.B., of Solesmes, Superior General of the Benedictine Congregation of France. Thus, the twenty-four members of this commission have all been named, and work on the schema on the liturgy can begin Monday morning.

The Message

The message to the world was adopted by a show of hands after a pause of half an hour to permit the Fathers to become more familiar with it. Some twenty bishops spoke from the floor. One of them asked that explicit mention be made of the "Church of silence"; but a Hungarian bishop declared that discretion on this matter would be the best solution, and his view prevailed.

The first version of the message was written by Father Marie D. Chenu, a Dominican. It was extensively revised by the presidency, although the principal ideas were retained. As we have already mentioned, this message is addressed to all men and treats such subjects as peace, racial equality, and social justice. We might note that in the course of the session the five undersecretaries of the Council translated the Latin message, read by Archbishop Felici, secretary of the Council, into five languages—English, French, German, Spanish, and Arabic.

Here are the essential passages of the Council's message:

> Under the guidance of the Holy Spirit, we intend in this meeting to seek the most effective ways of renewing ourselves and of becoming increasingly more faithful witnesses of the Gospel of Christ.
>
> We will strive to propose to modern men the truth of God in its entirety and purity so that they may understand it and accept it freely.
>
> Conscious of our duties as pastors, we wish to meet the demands of those who seek God "and perhaps grope after him and find him, though he is not far from any one of us" (Acts 17:27). . . .
>
> We, therefore, the followers of Christ, are not estranged from earthly concerns and toils. Indeed, the faith, hope, and charity of Christ urge us to serve our brothers in imitation of the example of the divine Master, who "has not come to be served, but to serve" (Matt. 20:28). Neither was the Church born, therefore, to dominate but to serve. ". . . He laid down his life for us; and we likewise ought to lay down our life for the brethren" (I John 3:16). . . .
>
> United here from every nation under heaven, we carry in our hearts the anxieties of all peoples entrusted to us, the anxieties of body and soul, sorrows and desires, and hopes. We turn our mind constantly toward all the anxieties afflicting men today.
>
> Our concern is directed especially to the more humble, the poorer, the weaker, and, in keeping with the example of Christ, we feel compassion for the throngs who suffer hunger, misery, and ignorance. . . . For this reason, in performing our earthly mission, we take into great account all that pertains to the dignity of man and all that contributes toward the real brotherhood of nations. "For the love of Christ impels us" (II Cor. 5:14); in fact, "He who has the goods of this world and sees his brother in need and closes his heart to him, how does the love of God abide in him?" (I John 3:17). . . .

In his broadcast message of September 11, 1962, His Holiness Pope John XXIII stressed two points especially. First of all, he recommended everything that favors peace among peoples.

There is no man who does not detest war and who does not ardently desire peace. This is the greatest wish of the Church, who is the mother of all. Through the voice of the Roman pontiffs, she has never ceased to proclaim not only her love for peace but also her resolve for peace, always ready to give herself wholeheartedly and effectively to every sincere proposal.

She tends with all her strength, furthermore, to unite all peoples and to create among them a mutual esteem of sentiments and of works. Is not this conciliar assembly—admirable for its diversity of races, nations, and tongues—a testimony of a community bound by fraternal love which it bears as a visible sign? We proclaim that all men are brothers, irrespective of the race or nation to which they belong.

Secondly, the Pope urges all to social justice. The doctrine outlined in the encyclical letter *Mater et magistra* clearly shows how the Church is needed by the world today to denounce injustices and shameful inequalities and to restore the true order of goods and things so that, according to the principles of the Gospel, the life of man may become more human. . . .

Tass Quotes Two Extracts from the Council's Message   Two sections of the Vatican Council's message addressed to the world were quoted Sunday by Tass.

The Soviet agency cited without comment the sentence, "There is no man who does not detest war and who does not ardently desire peace," as well as the clause which says that the Council "will take into great account all that pertains to the dignity of man and all that contributes toward the real brotherhood of nations."

OCTOBER 22

Liturgical Renewal Is Vitally Important
for the Catholic Church

Vatican II got down to its real business this morning, Monday, with a discussion on the liturgy. In accordance with the wishes of many bishops, John XXIII thus indicated his will to steer the Council toward concrete, practical, and pastoral problems rather than doctrinal discussions. He made this point explicitly in his opening address: "The salient point of [Vatican II] is not a discussion of one article or another of the Church's fundamental doctrine . . . taught by the Fathers and . . . theologians. For this," he added rather bluntly, "a council was not necessary."

To be worthy of the name, liturgical reform must harmonize cult with modern man's manner of feeling and expression. In industrialized countries a technological civilization has created a new kind of humanity which the Church must reckon with; otherwise, religion runs the risk of remaining on the margin of life.

The spiritual level of a parish bears a direct relation to the quality of its liturgy. This is an infallible measuring rod, and even those who have no faith are aware of it. This is one reason why these problems are of vital interest.

Many liturgical experiments have been attempted in our day, those in Germany and France, for example, as well as in mission countries, where the problem is particularly acute. The Council should take note of these efforts by relaxing some of the restrictions and setting sufficiently broad norms as well as by coordinating the various experiments by defining the basic objectives precisely.

The liturgical commission, constituted last Saturday, includes men of universally recognized competence, like Cardinal Lercaro, Archbishop of Bologna, and Bishops Henri Jenny, Auxiliary of Cambrai, and Guillaume van Bekkum of Ruteng, Indonesia. The schema which the Council Fathers will discuss was prepared with great care, as we noted earlier. Officials of pastoral liturgical centers from many countries worked on it at great length, notably Canon Mortimort of the Catholic faculty of Toulouse.

Protestants have also been impressed by the quality of this document, its Christocentric character, and its numerous scriptural references. The ecumenical implications of the liturgical renewal are obvious. Thanks to it, Catholics will be able to improve their biblical knowledge and spirituality. In the future greater place will be given to noneucharistic services based on the psalms, which are of Jewish inspiration. The mass will no longer be isolated but situated within a cultic context. There is also the question of revising the mass of the catechumens and giving it a more evident pedagogical dimension by making more liberal use of biblical texts. Finally, in certain special circumstances the faithful may be permitted to receive communion under both species. Much discussion is expected on concelebration, or authorizing several priests to say mass together in order to avoid the regrettable dispersion of individualistic piety. Certain passages on this subject are reported to have been cut out of the schema in its present form. The Fathers will have to decide whether or not they want to return to the original version.

The language problem is also a very pressing one. A greater use of vernacular languages is widely desired. The Council should produce a majority consensus on the limits for the use of Latin. This, of course, is a highly delicate issue, but one would surmise that at least the epistle and Gospel will be read in the vernacular.

Missionary bishops are in favor of flexible directives which would permit them to assimilate regional cultures. The boldness of liturgical reform will indicate whether or not Catholicism wants to throw off the iron collar of Western and Latin culture which cripples its dissemination on some continents.

Many liturgists regard it as fundamental that the proposed changes not revert to special historical forms, however privileged these may have once been, but that they introduce new forms compatible with our age. If the liturgy, like sacred art, is not an integral expression of contemporary culture, it cannot be very convincing.

Finally, authenticity demands that liturgical expressions reflect a plurality of mentalities. What is sometimes a serious danger, an exaggerated particularity, would be considerably reduced if the bishops were conscious of their collegial responsibility in the Church.

OCTOBER 23

The Secretariat for Promoting Christian Unity
Added to the Council Commissions

Archbishop Felici, secretary general of the Council, announced during the general congregation of October 22 that the Secretariat for Promoting Christian Unity had been elevated to the rank of a conciliar commission. Consequently, (1) the secretariat itself will present the schemas it has prepared; (2) these schemas will be discussed, corrected, and redrafted according to the same procedures as those of other commissions; and (3) in the case of mixed materials, the secretariat will collaborate with the interested commissions as the regulations provide.

This seemingly anodyne announcement is in fact very important. By making the Secretariat for Promoting Christian Unity a conciliar commission, the Pope has integrated it into the Council and has thus given new weight to a body heretofore considered marginal.

A new step has been officially taken toward Christian unity. The ecumenical objective of the Council has been clarified. It is pertinent to recall that the purpose of the Secretariat for Promoting Christian Unity is to keep the non-Catholic observers and guests informed of what the Council is doing, record their impressions, and pass them on to the Council Fathers.

The secretariat has prepared four very interesting schemas, on Catholic ecumenism, prayer for unity, the word of God, and religious liberty.

The Secretariat for Promoting Christian Unity has retained the same composition from the beginning and has not been subjected to the vicissitudes of elections. The team of specialists who work under Cardinal Bea and Monsignor Willebrands, and who were directly appointed by the Pope in 1960, is thus enabled to work effectively as a cohesive body. Finally, everything points to the possibility that the secretariat will become a permanent office after the Council ends.

The general congregation yesterday, Monday, heard about twenty interventions, some defending and others criticizing the schema on the liturgy. Among the speakers were Cardinals Montini, Archbishop of Milan, and Ruffini, Archbishop of Palermo.

Discussion of the Schema on the Liturgy
Raises the Delicate Question of Episcopal Powers

The Council Fathers continued their general discussion on the liturgy Tuesday morning. On October 22 there were twenty-five speakers from the floor. It is now assumed, given the climate of the first congregations, that most of the important points of this schema will be adopted.

Nonetheless, some matters call for clarification. The most troubling of these is that the text of the schema as it was printed and distributed to the bishops does not correspond exactly with the text adopted by the Central Preparatory Commission. For example, some passages concerning the biblical foundations of the liturgy have been omitted, and an admonition has been inserted to the effect that the schema lays down only general principles for whose application recourse must be had directly to the Holy See. The origin of these modifications is not known, but it is easy enough to recognize the hand of certain Roman conservatives who operate in the shadows. The alterations surprised two German cardinals particularly, who asked in their interventions that the original document be distributed to the Council Fathers so that all would know exactly how much it had been changed.

Many bishops have two principal objectives. First, they want commissions with legislative powers in liturgical matters to be constituted in each country or continent. Second, they would like to see a kind of central commission established in Rome comprised of experts from all over the world who would meet periodically.

But this double reform, which is revolutionary enough since it diminishes appreciably the present powers of the Sacred Congregation of Rites, cannot be effected unless the powers of bishops are defined.

Thus, many Council Fathers continue to think that it would be

fitting to take up fairly quickly two other schemas, the one dealing with
"the relationship between bishops and the Roman Curia" and the other
with "episcopal conferences and the collegiality of the episcopacy."
When and only when these schemas have been adopted will the Council
Fathers feel completely free to propose reforms.

1400468

The Most Ecumenical Council in History

Twelve days after its opening, the Council is in full swing. Meeting in
the fourth general congregation on Monday morning, it began discussion
of the first of the seventy-three schemas prepared by the preconciliar
commissions over a three-year period.

Although brief, this first period has already been rich in events and
instruction. After the solemnity of the opening ceremony, which was
a cause of rejoicing for some but a little disappointing for those who
had hoped the Council would begin with a symbolic gesture of collective penance, the Fathers immediately began to show their spirit of
independence. It was no accident that a French and a German cardinal
revealed the bishops' state of mind; but it is not the most important
factor. It is rather that the suggestion to defer elections met with unanimous approval. Despite their differences, the bishops want the Council
to be theirs and not a docile instrument in the hands of the Roman
Curia. This must have made John XXIII happy, so unlike is he to Pius IX
of Vatican I. Pius IX's formula "I am tradition" has never seemed more
anachronistic.

But this same John XXIII, who has so often in the past chosen to
compromise rather than to upset, found the occasion to reveal his deepest
thoughts the moment the Council opened. After firmly demanding once
more that Vatican II be pastoral and resolutely modern, the Pope in so
many words disavowed the integralist camp, throwing the weight of
his authority on the side of the progressives. This will be of capital
importance in the forthcoming discussions.

The election of commission members has proved, moreover, that
the adversaries of integralism are more numerous than one would have
thought. Of course, the lists naturally represent a wide variety of views,
but the liberal tendency is quite clear. Furthermore, the desire to decentralize has been indicated by a number of spontaneous meetings of
bishops according to area rather than school of thinking. At the moment,
episcopal power has *de facto* increased on the basis of geographical
groupings.

In naming five subsecretaries to the Council—a German, a Frenchman, a Spaniard, an Anglo-Saxon, and an Oriental—when the regulations called for only two, the Pope has further distributed the central power of the Council.

The Fathers have given themselves or received effective working tools. As the message to the world has indicated, they are seriously resolved to undertake a work of renewal. Religious history has markedly accelerated in the Church over the past two weeks. The *aggiornamento* of the Church desired by the Pope seems to be off to a good start. This has not gone unnoticed by the Protestant observers. The era of Catholic isolation is over.

Whatever difficulties lie ahead, Vatican II to all appearances will be the most ecumenical council in history.

Poverty and Simplemindedness of Official Information

Official information about the Council is cripplingly sparse and sometimes amusingly simplistic. This is not only a personal opinion; it is a commonplace that any journalist in Rome who is concerned with serious reporting would subscribe to.

It might be useful to note the conditions under which the reporters work.

Here is a sample of one of the official press releases: "Escorted by acolytes bearing lighted candles, Archbishop Villot, a subsecretary for the Council, carried the missal. . . ." There is a piece of news that is as specific as it is uncompromising.

Here is a better example. At the end of a dry enumeration of the names of sixteen bishops who intervened on October 23 on the schema on the liturgy, we read: "Various opinions were expressed. They indicate different schools of thought, problems, and experiences." That is a commentary well designed to nourish the curiosity of journalists.

Given such substantial food, the journalist has no choice but to chase down the news himself. There is no lack of it in this southern city, where gossip flourishes spontaneously. But how can we separate the wheat from the chaff or assess the rumors correctly? We are constantly being reminded of the Council's "secrecy." But given the fact that it is impossible to keep, does such secrecy serve or harm the cause it was intended to protect? The opinion is almost unanimous, but out of prudence, we will refrain from making a personal judgment.

What did Cardinal Spellman say, for instance, when he intervened on October 22? "I read it in an Italian paper which reported that the Archbishop of New York was in favor of using Latin in the mass," an American journalist told me. This is likely enough to be true. But we have heard conflicting reports. We also were told that Archbishop Dante, Secretary of the Sacred Congregation of Rites, has drawn up twelve objections to the schema on the liturgy. But what are they? No one knows.

OCTOBER 26

Proponents of Latin in the Liturgy
Seem To Be a Minority at the Council

Nothing is less stilted than a conciliar gathering. Rome, of course, would not be Rome without that close familiarity with the sacred which characterizes all Italian churches. When they are among themselves, the bishops soon abandon the air of compunction their flocks know so well. Dispersing after one of the general congregations, the Council Fathers are like college students on vacation. From about 11 o'clock onward, that is, about an hour before the end of the deliberations, which begin at 9 o'clock, the coffee bar does a bustling business. Tired of the series of often boring interventions, the bishops indulge in a cappuccino before slowly making their way back to their seats.

The most solemn moment of the day is naturally the formal religious ceremony that opens each day's session. On Wednesday morning mass was concelebrated by the Melkite Archbishop of Beirut, assisted by two priests and a deacon. Most of the bishops, who are not familiar with the majestic Rite of Antioch and Constantinople used in the Byzantine churches, were surprised that both the Greek and the Arabic languages were used, and they were favorably impressed by the choir of the Pontifical Greek College in Rome. "This makes you want to get on with some changes," said one of the Fathers.

One of the interventions bore on the theme *"Non timeo Petrum sed timeo secretarium Petri"* ("I do not fear Peter but his bureaucrats"). John XXIII, who follows all the deliberations on a private loudspeaker in his apartment, must have smiled when he heard these words. In a speech in June, 1960, he had said, "The government of the Church is one thing; the Council is another. And its structure and organization cannot be confused with those of the curial bureaus." The Curia has not forgotten those words and clings to article 7 of canon law, which dates from 1918: "By the Holy See must be understood, aside from exceptions, the sovereign pontiff, the Roman congregation, the tribunals, officers," and so forth. This is the crux of the matter and one of the central issues at Vatican II.

The problem of Latin is most frequently mentioned in the interventions. The Curia Fathers who speak in defense of Latin are a minority, and their suggestions are largely ignored. Antonio Cardinal Bacci, for example, recalled the expression *vinculum unitatis* (bond of unity); but it is a debatable adage since the use of Latin in fact provokes much dissatisfaction in the Church.

Cardinal Tisserant said that several languages have been and have the right to be used in the Church. He noted the example of Slavic in the ninth century, in the time of Cyril and Methodius. "The ecumenicity of the Church," a Madagascan bishop declared, "does not depend on one language."

In a speech to French journalists, Auxiliary Bishop Jenny of Cambrai, a member of the Commission on the Sacred Liturgy, especially insisted upon the necessity of creating unity in the Churches around the altar and not around the clergy. He deplored the stultification of rites in the Middle Ages and the harm done to the liturgy by an excess of juridical spirit and the "rubricism" consequent upon the Counter-Reformation.

Against Latin in the Liturgy   Given the paucity of information, we cannot be too grateful to Coptic Rite Bishop Isaac Ghattas of Thebes, Egypt, for having printed and distributed some of the theses that the Oriental clergy want defended in the Council. Here are some extracts concerning the liturgy:

> The Oriental tradition would like to see the liturgy translated into the vernacular so it could be understood by the people.

> It is desirable that Sunday evening mass be normally framed in the liturgical office.

> The liturgy has been the guardian of the faith in the Orient. Consequently, the faithful must be given serious formation in this.

> Christians have been fighting for a common date for Easter since antiquity; they still want it. It would be good, then, if all Christendom followed the Oriental date, which has high symbolic value.

A Work of Clarification

About a hundred speakers, some sixty of whom have already been heard, are slated to intervene on this schema. But the work of the Council Fathers is not limited to the plenary sessions and the commissions. Much is accomplished in special sessions during the afternoons. At St.-Louis-des-Français on Wednesday afternoon, the French hierarchy heard Fathers Jean Daniélou and Joseph Lécuyer speak on "The Episcopacy," while Archbishop Neophite Edelby, Auxiliary Bishop to the Melkite Patriarch Maximos IV Saigh, reminded his audience of certain articles in the schema on the unity of the Church which offend the sensibility of the Oriental Church.

The Council, we noted, is not stilted as it begins. This is seen even in the tone of the interventions. Each speaker expresses himself frankly, without worrying about whether he pleases or displeases. That is the purpose of Vatican II. The bishops are keenly aware of this and are taking advantage of it. Too, the Council is contributing to the discovery of the real value of various arguments and persons. If the cause is a poor one and the arguments weak, the assembly soon detects it. The law of collectivities, which is hard on the weak, has full play. Thus, a healthy work of clarification for the Church is being accomplished. Certain fictions are disappearing quickly. The realities of the apostolate take precedence over certain verbal gymnastics.

That is precisely what the Pope hoped for when he put the schema on the liturgy up for discussion first. The Council is going through a trial period before coming to grips with more arduous issues.

The Council and the Atomic Bomb

Will the Council condemn either the production or the use of atomic weapons? It is difficult to say, but there are bishops who desire such a declaration and have so informed the Secretariat for Extraordinary Affairs.

It is worth recalling that this has been strongly urged for some years by Archbishop Roberts, Titular Archbishop of Sygdia (in Georgia, Stalin's country), who relinquished his See of Bombay in 1950 to an Indian, Valerian Cardinal Gracias, who has occupied it since. Archbishop Roberts; Bishop Thunemann of Keimoes, South Africa; Bishop Esser, his coadjutor; Father Yves Congar, O.P., theological adviser to Archbishop Jean Weber, Bishop of Strasbourg; Father Varillon, a Jesuit,

Father G. Michonneau, and dozens of others from different countries have recently signed a document entitled, "A Suggestion for the Council." Part of it reads, "It is urgently necessary to condemn once and for all the weapons of massive destruction, whether atomic, bacteriological, or chemical, as well as testing, producing, and stockpiling them. Such production and stockpiling is immoral, even if these weapons are built and stocked as a deterrent against an eventual aggressor."

For their part, the laity in Rome have circulated an open letter to the Council Fathers, recalling particularly the following quotation from Cardinal Ottaviani, made several years ago. It is extracted from chapter 86, "*Bellum interdicendum omnino,*" in a work called *Political and Ecclesiastical Institutions:* "All war must be prohibited. Those who see clearly that their government is making preparations for the carnage and ruin of the people by means of war can and should overthrow that regime by just means."

The personality of Cardinal Ottaviani, Secretary of the Holy Office, lent singular weight to this double affirmation, one not widely known to the public.

OCTOBER 27

The Quarrel over Latin

When they arrived in Rome, the French bishops had no idea they would have to work so hard. Caught up in the spirit of the Council, they have become aware of the growing demands of their responsibilities in the world today and the perhaps even greater ones in the world of tomorrow. They have also profited by contact with bishops of other countries and have sought instruction from the most qualified theologians. Everyone has confirmed the influence of these latter. Yesterday the Jesuit Father Daniélou spoke to them on the meaning of the episcopacy; today the Dominican Father Yves Congar lectures; and tomorrow Father Henri de Lubac, S.J., will be heard.

The general congregations are getting longer and sometimes more interesting. This was predictable and inevitable in view of the number of participants (over 2,300 on October 26). But the debate is very important in itself. Latin or not Latin continues to be the main issue. It is somewhat odd to observe the suitability of Latin being discussed—rather roughly, it is true—in that language. This creates an additional difficulty. Those familiar with anecdotal ecclesiastical history will recall that at Vatican I two bishops who handled Cicero's language especially maladroitly were dubbed Bishop Contrasense and Bishop Wrongsense.

The Council is not disputing the superiority of Latin for theological or dogmatic expression. It is a good bet that the future code of canon law will be written in Latin, and there are only advantages in this. Latin will remain for a long time the official language of the Church for all her basic documents. The constitution *Veterum sapientiae* urged only this year that seminarians be given more and better courses in Latin. They need it.

But the discussion at the Council bears on an altogether different matter. The question is whether or not Latin must be the language of the liturgy, whether it is normal for the faithful of various nations to follow services in a missal translation or listen to a commentator who intrudes himself between the celebrant and the people in order to understand the priest who is saying mass. Bishops with pastoral experience and concerns are eager to put an end to this confusing situation.

More Catholic than the Pope Would it be normal for a theater to play programs in Latin to audiences who were not familiar with it, on the pretext that it was a more beautiful language? Yet this is the present practice in the Roman Church. When the Pope himself delivers a message, he does not speak Latin. Why should the liturgy be more Catholic than the Pope?

Bishop Alfred Ancel, Auxiliary to Pierre Cardinal Gerlier and the only modern bishop to work regularly with his hands (in suburban Lyon), is reported to have told the general congregation on Friday, "Let the Council Fathers who are not charged with the pastoral ministry recall that a great number of Christians rarely enter a Church in their lives. Is it by speaking Latin that we will reach them?"

There are valid objections, of course. How, for example, could Gregorian chant be replaced? But it might be answered that specialists could be put to work; are composers less talented than church architects? Sometimes the reasons invoked in defense of Latin are less serious. Thus, we read in a document distributed by the Sacred Congregation on Seminaries and Universities, "an attentive reading of a translation cuts down on discreet whispering—which is always indiscreet in church."

"That's a boomerang argument if ever there was one," an old-line Roman declared. "For if the Italians, who are a talkative race, are tempted to talk in church, isn't it precisely because they are not interested in a mass celebrated in Latin in an unintelligible voice by a priest who turns his back on them? And since the proof offered is that a translation in Italian holds their attention, they might just as well recite the mass prayers directly in the vernacular."*

* This quote is from a Benedictine who was a professor in Rome. The general

Prisoner of War Camps Contributed to Liturgical Renewal   The prison camps of World War II are commonly agreed to have been an important influence in shaping the present mentality of laymen. After five years of hearing mass said by one of their comrades at close quarters and in intimate circumstances, Catholics could no longer tolerate the old forms. They felt encouraged to demand more authentic ceremonies in their parishes and to urge that the priest speak their native language. The Council Fathers, among whom there are a number who experienced imprisonment, have made these hopes their own.

OCTOBER 30

Many Bishops Want the Schemas
on Episcopal Powers To Be Discussed Soon

Discipline is not the strong suit at Vatican II. The regulations are taken lightly, even by the Pope. This is a good thing for the Council, which is picking its path, like a caravan, over unknown terrain. The Roman Church, however it looks from the outside, bears little resemblance to an army with conditioned reflexes, and is far from being a monolithic bloc.

There are other relaxations of the regulations besides those already mentioned. Although Latin is required in the general congregations, at least two Oriental Fathers, to our knowledge, have spoken in French— Maximos IV Saigh, the Greek Melkite Patriarch of Antioch, for one. He is very well versed in Latin but wanted to show his refusal to recognize it as the living language of the Church. The same Patriarch, well known for his outspoken attitudes, abstained from participating in the opening session of October 11 ostensibly to indicate his displeasure at not having precedence, contrary to expectations, over the cardinals and his disappointment at not having a train bearer as did the members of the Sacred College (a service that would have considerably aided a man of eighty years in managing his liturgical vestments).

Another relaxation of discipline: article 33 stipulates that the Fathers not speak longer than ten minutes in their interventions. In fact, they often get carried away by their own eloquence. In such cases the assembly shows its disapproval, courteously enough but nonetheless unequivocally, by applauding *the end* of the speech. Applause is also prohibited, but the secretary general can do nothing about it despite repeated calls to order. Clapping is too natural a means of expression in assemblies everywhere.

congregation of October 26 heard interventions by three Benedictine abbots general, those of France, Germany, and England.

Last Saturday one of the Fathers complained that the interventions were too long and too numerous and that it was time to get on with voting on the amendments. His remarks too were greeted with loud applause. It was a spontaneous way of expressing the general weariness.

The Commissions Are 20 Percent Italian

The regulations state in article 6 that each commission must be composed of twenty-four members in addition to the president, eight of them named by the Pope. John XXIII has just decided otherwise. The list of those designated by the Pope which has just been published reveals that he named nine members to each commission. The ninth turns out to be a curial figure whose competence corresponds with that of the conciliar commissions. It is not out of place to spotlight the conservative bent of these men. There is, for example, Archbishop Enrico Dante, Secretary of the Congregation of Rites and named to the Commission for the Sacred Liturgy, who has attracted attention by reason of his many criticisms of the document under discussion. Then there is the renowned Archbishop Pietro Parente, Assessor of the Holy Office, who recently gave vent to his alienation complex during one of the general congregations. "Contrary to popular opinion," he said, "it is we, the members of the Holy Office, who are the real martyrs of the faith, because no one understands us." There were various reactions in the stands.

With the Spanish bishop from Salamanca, the Canadian bishop from Three Rivers, and the American auxiliary bishop from New York who will sit together on the doctrinal commission, the Assessor of the Holy Office should be in good company to defend his conception of orthodoxy. It must be said, however, that the composition of the commissions, now that they are complete, on the whole reflects a concern for a balance of different schools of thought and a geographical distribution in keeping with the spirit of equity and universality. Nonetheless, the Pope named twenty-one Italians out of his ninety, which are added to the twenty elected by the Fathers out of their 160. The Italian representation is doubled: forty-one out of 250 members. And we should add the ten presidents of the commissions, all but one of whom are Italian. Those who think the Italian representation too high (20 percent) might take consolation in the fact that it is less than on the homologous preconciliar commissions, where there were sixty Italians out of 265 members.

The role of the commissions is by no means neglible in an assembly of 2,300 members. The regulations prudently state that a two-thirds majority is necessary in the commissions as well as the plenary sessions.

The commissions have been proportioned in such a way as to make this majority impossible were it a question of ratifying a rash amendment. One Roman prelate expressed the opinion that this composition is a sure means of "closing the door to the unexpected." But to our way of thinking the regulations leave the door half-open because article 39 states, "When the necessary majority cannot be had in the commissions after every effort has been made, then the matter is to be passed on to the general congregation." The authors of the regulations have thus given the Council final control by permitting it to go over the head of the commissions in difficult cases.

The Dangers of Absenteeism

The attendance of the Fathers at the general congregations presents an interesting pattern: 2,365 on October 23; 2,322 on October 26; 2,302 on October 27; 2,277 on October 29. Why the slacking off? For one thing, some bishops have returned home. Also, the auxiliary bishops were informed discreetly but clearly that there was no rule against their leaving. Some have certainly taken advantage of this liberty. Everything indicates that after the four-day respite for the Feasts of All Saints and All Souls, there will be even fewer bishops than at present. And who can say how many will return for the second session?

Given these factors, the Curia and the conservative bishops have a stake in postponing discussion of the important schemas on episcopal powers as long as possible. There is a double advantage in doing so. First, the auxiliary bishops, who are younger and therefore more reform-minded, would be out of the way. Second, the Italians, who are usually more conservative and who live within a day's drive of Rome, could hustle back to cast their votes.

"Chi Va Piano . . ."

To date the schemas on the powers of bishops have not been distributed to the Council Fathers, although those elaborated by the commission on doctrine, presided over by Cardinal Ottaviani, have. These have been severely criticized, and said to bear an amateurish resemblance to extracts from elementary manuals of theology. Are the texts on episcopal powers being deliberately held back, as some think? It is difficult to know. Many bishops, however, have energetically asked that these documents be presented for discussion immediately after the schema on the liturgy.

In any event, when the doctrinal texts come before the Council Fathers, they have every intention of substantially transforming them by whatever means they judge most effective. At last report, it seems the more aggressive bishops have been persuaded that it would not be in their best interests to reject the schemas *en bloc* as they originally intended to do.

However that may be, it is not the central issue. The big battle of the Council, we repeat, will be over increasing the powers of bishops. The Pope, as a good diplomat, would prefer not to precipitate things so as to give the Council time to find its own rhythm, calm its impatience, and perfect its procedural techniques. *Chi va piano va sano*, as the Pope recently said.

At the moment the Council is still feeling its way, and progress is so slow that everyone is bored. Before long the Fathers will have to organize themselves in a more rational manner. They could, for example, limit the interventions to spokesmen for general trends of thought. This would be relatively easy in view of the fact that the Fathers are for the most part already members of national or continental episcopal conferences, and the cohesion of these assemblies, which have met frequently detween the general congregations since the opening of the Council, is increasing day by day.

NOVEMBER, 1962

Liturgical Syncretism Not Incompatible
with Catholicism

The young African Churches have impressed the Council with their vitality and organization. Transcending their ethnic and linguistic differences as well as their former European connections (with France, Great Britain, Belgium, Portugal, and so forth), they have effectively succeeded in grouping their episcopacies about a central secretariat, presided over by Laurean Cardinal Rugambwa, Bishop of Bukoba, Tanzania, the first Negro cardinal in the history of the Church. There are about 250 African bishops, including thirteen Negro archbishops and forty-seven Negro bishops. They are indeed a mixed bag. There is Archbishop Léon Duval of Algiers side by side with Archbishop Owen McCann of Cape Town, Portuguese bishops along with Madagascan. The extraordinary diversity of these religious leaders on the immense continent gives some idea of the problems that can arise. And yet, when an African bishop speaks in one of the general congregations, he speaks in the name of all. This solidarity has made a deep impression on the Council Fathers, and they point to it as an admirable example.

After the interventions of Cardinal Rugambwa and Archbishop Hyacinthe Thiandoum of Dakar, Senegal, Bishop Jean van Cauwelaert of Inongo, Leopoldville Congo, asked the Fathers Wednesday morning not "to stifle the Holy Spirit" by preventing the liturgy from being adapted to local customs. Bishop van Cauwelaert has worked for many years to conform the Roman liturgy with local ceremonies related to births, sickness, funerals, and the like.

The day before, Bishop António Pildáin y Zapiáin of the Canary Islands strongly supported the clauses in the schema recommending the suppression of classes for marriages and funerals; we might recall that Maurice Cardinal Feltin's Archdiocese of Paris anticipated the Council's wishes on this point.

What About Lipstick?   The weakness—to say nothing of the pettiness —of some of the arguments advanced against the use of the vernacular these past few days is exemplified in discussions concerning communion under both species. One bishop said, for example, that it would be awkward to pass the chalice in a congregation with women wearing lipstick.

The Liturgy Behind the Iron Curtain   Bishop Otto Spuelbeck of Meissen, East Germany, gave an argument in favor of using the vernacular which carries considerable weight in view of the number of Christians living in Communist lands. In these countries, where an officially atheistic state appropriates every means of influencing the people—schools, youth movements, the press, radio, and television—the liturgy is the only way the Church can educate the faithful and counteract the neopagan ceremonies of "baptism," "confirmation," and "marriage" honored by the Communist governments.

The latest official communiqué from the Council mentions an expression, extracted from the schema, which will not go unnoticed by Protestants: "The Fathers have on several occasions expressed a desire to develop an awareness of *the priesthood common to all the faithful*" (italics added). The priesthood of the faithful? These words often astonish Catholics, who until recently have scarcely ever heard them. Nonetheless, they form part of the traditional vocabulary of theology; but since the Counter-Reformation this doctrine has not been stressed. The Protestants are happy with this evolution in the presentation of Catholic doctrine.

Enlarging the Common Trunk   Liturgical renewal has ecumenical implications. The common trunk of the liturgies of the diverse Christian confessions could be considerably enlarged. By restoring communion under two species, for example, Catholicism would make a conciliatory gesture toward the Protestant and Orthodox Churches.

Eucharistic communion under two species, which Vatican II will undoubtedly restore in certain circumstances, can only appear revolutionary for those who confuse the Church's long tradition with their short experience. It was the rule in the Catholic Church for the first twelve centuries. Sometimes the faithful drank from the same chalice; sometimes they received bread soaked in the consecrated wine, a practice preserved in most of the Oriental Rites today. Until the end of the fifteenth century, the popes gave communion under the two species on Easter Sunday.

In 1584, Gregory XIII suspended the practice of communion with wine, which had become a symbol of Protestantism. But the practice was retained for the consecration of kings, as for Leopold II and Francis II toward the end of the nineteenth century. In France, Louis XIV was the last to be consecrated under this dispensation. In 1652 the Council of Trent voted by a majority of eight (87 against 79, including the two papal legates) to suspend communion from the chalice permanently in a reaction against Protestantism. In 1912 Pius X authorized communion under both species for those attending a mass of the Oriental Rite. This was incorporated in canon law and is still in effect.

In a conference arranged by the official press bureau, Father Hermann Schmidt, S.J., a professor at the Gregorian University, said there was no reason to put off adopting the rituals of other confessions when their symbolism was better. A case in point might be Protestant marriages in Holland, which are celebrated around a table.

It is interesting to note in this connection that a recent book written by the priests of St.-Séverin favored the idea of a "liturgical syncretism," which the authors opposed to "doctrinal syncretism."

The Latin Rite is the only Catholic rite that does not allow concelebration. Yet in the thirteenth century, the age of Saint Thomas Aquinas, it was prohibited to celebrate two masses separately at the same time in the same church. What would the Angelic Doctor say today before the spectacle of dozens of masses said individually at the same time at such places as Lourdes? Would it not be more in keeping with the community spirit of the eucharistic sacrifice to restore concelebration, which associates all available priests in a single ceremony?

After a four-day intermission, on Monday the Council Fathers will renew their discussion on the liturgy, a topic that is far from being exhausted.

The Italian Representation

We have already reported that since the Pope's recent nominations, 20 percent of the members of conciliar commissions are Italians. This does not correspond with the percentage of Italian bishops at the Council, which is much weaker: 360 out of 2,300, or 15 percent. The divergence is still more striking when we consider, as is logical, that the Italian Catholic population represents only 9 percent of the world total. The

Italian representation at the Council, and *a fortiori* on the commissions, is unduly high, a situation which can only seem abnormal and outmoded in these days when the trend is toward balancing the national representations within the Church.

Roman Wit

In this gay city, where people joke easily and unmaliciously about serious things, two word plays are circulating that are more innocent than they might seem.

The first compares John XXIII's opening speech with Pius IX's speech to Vatican I. The first is said to have been "ultramontane," the second to be "ultramontini." It is rumored that Cardinal Montini himself may have had a hand in Pope John's speech.

The second concerns the quarrel over Latin in the liturgy. In the spring of 1962 the Holy Office published a constitution in praise of Latin. It was entitled, *Veterum sapientiae*. The facetious translation reads, *The Wisdom of the Senile*.

NOVEMBER 2

The Question of the Reform of the Curia
Already Implicitly Raised

The break occasioned by the Feast of All Saints gives us an opportunity to take stock. If we compare the size of the assembly at the Council, the manner in which it has been orchestrated, the quality of the best bishops present in Rome, and the results achieved after three weeks of work, there is a flagrant disproportion. The ponderousness of the sessions and the shallowness of many interventions (which are repeated fastidiously as though the members of the assembly were weak-minded) are disconcerting for the uninitiated observer.

But these impressions are superficial and not entirely accurate. They overlook the complexity of the Roman Church, which has taken root in every part of the world and includes men of all ages, all civilizations, all races, and all mentalities. They overlook as well the fact that the Church finds her *raison d'être* in her fidelity to a message delivered some 2,000 years ago, a message she must defend against the corrosive influence of materialism.

Like any human society today, and perhaps more than many others, the Catholic Church greatly desires a renewal because she suffers from a lack of efficacy. Yet she cannot adapt at the price of changes which might please an elite but would completely baffle the majority of the faithful.

Under these conditions, the Council cannot achieve immediate or spectacular results. Moreover, as in any parliamentary assembly, everyone must get a hearing; thus, the Church must spend a good deal of time seeking her internal balance and collective personality. This is what the Council has been doing, more or less adeptly, for the past twenty days. At the moment two conclusions are clearly discernible from the first eleven sessions:

1. The central government cannot survive in its present state. Immobile in its ivory tower and often ill informed on the vital problems of local churches, the Roman Curia cannot continue to dominate and control everything in its niggling and inflexible fashion without aggravating the discontent of bishops who are most conscious of their responsibilities and without seriously compromising the Church's influence. Young and often old Christians demand, not their independence—for this would be radically contrary to the spirit of Catholicism—but greater autonomy, which would enable them to solve their own problems without constant recourse to Rome.

2. This raises the question of the powers of episcopal conferences. Will they be able to "legislate" in liturgical matters, say, with the approbation of the Holy See, as asked in the first schema drawn up by the preconciliar commission, or only "propose," as it is put in the present document, revised by the Central Preparatory Commission? This is the crux of the matter. And it cannot be resolved until the Council is more mature. We may expect a hard-fought battle, compared with which the early skirmishes we have already reported will fade into insignificance. The dress rehearsals have already taken place, in the preparatory commissions last spring. Since then each party has had time to ready its weapons.

A Document on Psychoanalysis
Circulates Among the Fathers

Presently the Council is getting its breath. The bishops celebrated All Saints, and profited by their leisure time to become more informed on various issues and broaden their contacts with colleagues from other countries. Different mimeographed documents are circulating in the wings; they deal with all sorts of questions. By far the most interesting which we have had the opportunity to inspect is called "The Church and

Psychoanalysis." It was obviously written by someone with an exceptional knowledge of both religious experience and psychology. It is a striking document. Here are some excerpts:

A Challenge to the Church

   The teaching Church's rejection or suspicion of psychoanalysis would contribute to alienating a growing number of influential persons from Christianity. If the Church has lost the working class as a result of her backwardness in social and economic matters, she will lose a part of the white-collar classes as a result of her backwardness in psychological matters. Biblical criticism and evolutionism affect man only exteriorly; but psychoanalysis concerns man in his innermost being, all men and not only, as is often wrongly believed, the unbalanced.

   That is why psychoanalysis presents a transcendental challenge to the Church. We must rethink all of Christian morality in the light of depth psychology. What the Church is presently doing has nothing to do with this gigantic work. Modern man's vitality has torn the old cloth of Christian morality as Christ tore the old cloth of Judaism. Nor will it help to make a few concessions on secondary issues. . . .

The author insists that this work can only be effected by theologians and psychologists who have been psychoanalyzed, although he is aware that this statement will probably provoke

   . . . the mockery and skepticism of many. . . . Only those who have had a mystical experience are qualified to talk about mysticism; the same must be said of depth psychology. It is necessary for priests and religious to submit to psychoanalytic treatment, not for personal problems, but even those who are stable and without evident neurosis.

   To achieve this goal, however, we would have to overcome an obstacle that comes largely from psychoanalysts, namely, the supposed incompatibility between psychoanalysis and the religious man as such. They are afraid to analyze religious experience *ex professo* and directly. This fear stems from the prejudice that to analyze the domain of religion would somehow profane it.

   If we someday achieve true dialogue between psychoanalysts and believing Catholics, it will be highly beneficial for both. . . .

   Some of Freud's remarks can clarify present investigations into the religious myth and eventually lead to a solution of the modernist crisis which rightly continues to worry the Church.

The Fear of Atheism   The document concludes with some original and intelligent remarks on ecumenism and atheism. *Fear* or *faith:* we must choose between these two attitudes. If we choose fear, we will feel beleaguered by enemies from without. Until very recently non-Catholics were considered enemies. Ecumenism has enabled us to discover brothers in the Orthodox and Protestant Churches. But we do not yet dare consider Muslims and Buddhists as brothers, and we still consider atheists as enemies. Will it be possible for us to banish the fear of atheism, which is at bottom the fear of God's absence in our own lives, from our hearts?

"If we choose fear, we will continue to feel beleaguered by enemies from within: conscience, freedom, sanctions, the law, authority. . . . Only faith will enable us to discover friends in everything, even in sin: *felix culpa.*"

Will the Council talk about psychoanalysis? Yes, but in a superficial and almost entirely negative way if the Fathers go by what is in the schema on the "moral order," where the dangers and abuses of this discipline are stressed.

NOVEMBER 3

Observers Are Favorably Impressed

In former times heretics were burned, or at least carefully kept out of circulation; today they are being sought after. In the annals of Vatican II —and indeed of the Roman Church—a recent moment will stand as history-making: when the secretary general, Archbishop Felici, pronounced the first *extra omnes* of the Council on October 13, and followed it with these words, emphasizing each syllable in a loud voice: *"Possunt remanere patres, periti, observatores, et officiales"*; that is, in addition to the Fathers, experts, and approved personnel, the non-Catholic observers invited by the Secretariat for Promoting Christian Unity may remain in St. Peter's. The presence of the thirty-two observers has thus been officially accepted.

At the explicit request of John XXIII and Cardinal Bea, the Council is undertaking what Cardinal Feltin has called "a gigantic examination of conscience" before representatives of other faiths. This constitutes an extraordinary step forward, and it is not difficult to imagine that the Pope's decision must have caused some consternation among the members of the Curia: *horresco!* The *extra omnes* of Vatican II marks the end of a world—the world of the haughty, some would say pharisaical, isolation of the Roman Church.

As if to seal this gesture of reconciliation, some Eastern Fathers prefaced their interventions with the words, *"Carissimi observatores."* One Father even added, *"Clarissimi."*

The observers are in the first seats of a rostrum facing the cardinals, high in the central nave. Here is an ironic detail. The observers, who are not expected to know Latin, have the service of simultaneous interpreters who translate what the Fathers are saying. It is said that this makes some of the bishops jealous, for while they have some familiarity with Latin, most of them are sorely out of practice and miss part of the speeches. This is especially true when the American bishops speak. Scarcely anyone can understand Cardinal Spellman, whose Latin is universally agreed to be unintelligible.

A Vote of Confidence　　Rome doesn't do things by halves. Not only are the observers authorized to participate in the general congregations, but they also receive the same working documents as the bishops. This vote of confidence has very much impressed them. They have received the volume containing the first seven schemas, the only ones that have been circulated so far. The Council regulations ask them not to divulge the contents and to respect the secrecy of the work sessions. However, they may inform their own churches as they see fit.

Truth obliges us to record that the secrecy of the Council is much better observed by the non-Catholics, who are models of discretion, than by the bishops. This is proof of their courtesy and tact, which everyone admires, beginning with the journalists.

The observers have not been reduced to a passive role. Once a week they are invited by the Secretariat for Promoting Christian Unity to a briefing conference, after which they are free to express their observations, criticisms, and suggestions. They have already met with Bishop Hermann Volk of Mainz, one of the best theologians at the Council, who, at their request, spoke on the word of God and the sacraments. Eight days earlier Jesuit Father Schmidt, who helped prepare the schema presently under discussion, had addressed them on the spirit of liturgical renewal.

Oscar Cullmann, a Protestant and a professor at the Universities of Basel and Paris, is one of the better-known observers at the Council. He is a renowned specialist in New Testament studies and, furthermore, no stranger to Rome. For the past fifteen years he has taught exegesis at the Swiss theological faculty here, during the Easter holidays. He has also been in close contact with the Pontifical Biblical Institute, especially when Cardinal Bea lectured there (Cullmann followed his courses). This scholar's views on "the sacraments in the Johannine Church" and on Christ's words "*Tu es Petrus*" have attracted the attention of the whole Christian community.

Hopes and Disappointments The observers complement their official contacts with the secretariat for unity by informal meetings with theologians and bishops. They thus have an opportunity to express their hopes and disappointments. If the schema on the liturgy seems very satisfactory to them, Protestants and Orthodox unanimously criticize the schema on the unity of the Church, prepared by the commission for the Oriental Churches entirely independently of Cardinal Bea's office, as well as the schema on tradition, prepared by the commission on doctrine. "The latter document," one of the observers told us, "seems to take no account at all of the biblical research done by Catholics in the past thirty years. It is a little discouraging. . . . Let us hope that the Council will make itself a duty to redraft these texts." It is no secret that this disappointment is shared by many bishops with special competence in the field. For this reason we may expect a good deal of controversy when the documents come up for discussion.

How have the observers reacted since the opening of the Council? Predictably, the Protestants scarcely appreciated the display of the inaugural ceremonies. The pomp surrounding the papacy reminded them of one of Luther's sayings, "*Regnum papae.*" But they all remarked upon the "striking contrast" between the ceremonial fanfare and the recollected expression on the face of John XXIII, who seemed to accept his role "in all modesty and humility." "If I didn't find the ceremonies too excruciating," one of the French observers told me, "it was solely because of the Pope's personal attitude. He is obliged to conform with the system, but he obviously did so without much enthusiasm." The same person also said his presence in Rome has occasioned a good number of indignant letters from his coreligionists.

A representative of a Near Eastern church declared he was happily surprised by the liberty of the bishops in their interventions. He had no idea that one cardinal could publicly take a position diametrically opposed to another's.

It might be well to note, too, that prayers for the success of the Council have been prescribed almost everywhere in the Protestant world.

Four members of the Community of Taizé have assembled here in Rome, on the second floor of a building on the Via del Plebiscito, for the duration of the Council. Each day, in a little white room bare as a monastery cell which has been converted into an oratory, the monks recite the office and pray, in accordance with their vocation, for Christian unity. In the wavering candlelight they pray indiscriminately for John XXIII, Cardinal Gerlier, Cardinal Ottaviani, Dr. Geoffrey Fisher, Patriarch Athenagoras, and others. For these few minutes at least, the barriers are down and vanities revealed.

Will Vatican II Change Its Work Methods?

"Kindly do not repeat what has already been said and keep your interventions as brief as possible." Thus spoke Archbishop Felici, secretary general of the Council, as today's general congregation opened; they were repeated by Cardinal Liénart, who presided over the session.

Vatican II has not yet found its rhythm. But the interruption for All Saints was propitious for reflection and may hasten the solutions which would permit the Council to advance more rapidly. Local wags have estimated that at its present pace, the Council will be in session for twenty years. Others have gone this one better by declaring that half the bishops will die in the meantime—of boredom rather than old age. Finally, those who are quick to suspect plots even where they probably do not exist wonder whether the present pace is not calculated to tire out the Fathers so they won't be too inclined to argue over amendments.

Whatever the case, John XXIII is not likely to settle things with a show of authority. He thinks the Council must set its own cadence, so that no one will be able to say it was arbitrarily denied absolute freedom of expression.

There are several obvious ways to step up the proceedings. First— and this will necessarily come about, since the example has already been set by the Africans and Japanese—episcopal conferences could appoint a limited number of spokesmen. It may also have been proposed that the Council Fathers express their opinions only in written reports to the competent commissions. Finally, the *periti* (experts) wonder why they are not called on in the general congregations as provided for by the regulations. To let the specialists speak would have several advantages; it would (1) avoid repetitions, (2) permit syntheses properly prepared by trained men, and (3) raise the level of discussion. But however valuable these improvements would be, they would not please everyone, for it is the bishops as such who are sitting in council and not the theologians. Furthermore, it has been stressed over and over again that Vatican II is to be concrete and pastoral in orientation, and therefore the pastors rather than their counselors should speak. Experts were extensively called upon in former councils.

The Eastern Churches Organize The Arabic-speaking Near Eastern Churches have just made a decision considered surprising. The bitterness of the dissension among these churches has given the Fathers the impression that they would be very fragmented. Events have proven them wrong. Following a recent meeting, the patriarchs of six Arabic communities have called for the constitution of a sort of executive committee of twelve bishops (two per church). In order of importance, these communities are the Maronites, the Melkites, the Syrians, the Chaldeans, the Armenians, and the Copts.

That the need for unity took precedence over all other considerations is another proof that Vatican II will, among other results, reinforce geographic solidarity. It is also another indication that the trend is away from the Roman centralization of power.

John XXIII Again Encourages Changes

A mass celebrating the fourth anniversary of Pope John's coronation was sung Sunday by Cardinal Montini, Archbishop of Milan, according to an Ambrosian Rite appropriate to this diocese. It was the first time this mass has been said in St. Peter's. After a brief introduction in Latin in which he stated his intention to speak Italian so as to be better understood, the Pope spoke about Saint Charles Borromeo's role as peacemaker during the violent discussions of the Council of Trent. The Pope also made a discreet but widely noted allusion to the provincial councils that followed Trent. Then he returned to a theme already articulated in his opening speech of October 11 about the legitimacy of changes in the Church: "It is natural for the newness of our times and circumstances to suggest diverse forms and methods of transmitting the same truth, outward, and of giving it new clothing."

The Pope's insistence upon the appropriateness of changing the liturgy and updating the forms of doctrinal expression constitutes precious encouragement for the Council Fathers to overcome the reluctance of a minority who cling to the past.

Reforms in the Mass

The topic of discussion at today's general congregation was the opportuneness of reforms in the mass. This afternoon Bishop William Duschak, Apostolic Vicar of Calapán, the Philippines, held a press conference on "the necessity of instituting, over and above the Roman Rite, an ecumenical mass inspired by the Last Supper which would be said entirely in the vernacular, in a loud voice and facing the people, so that it would be readily understood without explanations or commentaries and acceptable to all Christians of whatever confession. Why," he added, "shouldn't the greatest ecumenical council in history order the study of a new form of the mass adapted to men of our times?"

The boldness of these remarks might be compared with those of the Benedictine Father Marcili, president of the Pontifical Liturgical Institute of St. Anselm in Rome, who also addressed the journalists in an official press conference. He argued for the "elimination of superstructures" and a "disincrustation" of rituals. He specifically proposed that ceremonial vestments for pontifical masses be simplified, and made some humorous allusions to the celebrant's "striptease" act. This expression scandalized certain Roman circles, who, it is true, are easily annoyed and lack a sense of humor. Father Marcili argued against wholesale concessions to the liturgical "new wave," as by translating *Dominus vobiscum* as "Greetings, comrades," or *amen* as "Agreed." But he did suggest that the kiss of peace could be replaced with a handshake. The tone of these conferences gives some idea of the climate of freedom which, to the Council's benefit, presently prevails in Rome.

NOVEMBER 6

Will Vatican II Show That the Church
Is Concerned with the Poor and the Hungry?

Today, Tuesday, the Council Fathers are broaching section 3 of the schema on the sacraments. About 100 speakers are expected to take the floor. This indicates that discussion on the liturgy is far from over. But the subject is not monopolizing the Council's attention. Between sessions work is progressing on other matters that will come up for consideration later. A case in point is exegesis, a controversial subject about which we will have more to say in due time, because it has been a bone of contention in the last several months between those in favor of modern methods and a group of conservatives who have become more aggressive as their following has dwindled.

Against Exterior Signs of Wealth   The questions of poverty, hunger, and exterior signs of wealth, which are so relevant to Catholicism, continue to preoccupy an important number of bishops. This is particularly true of bishops from countries where the workers are alienated from the Church, or where distribution of land is rankly unjust or hunger is endemic. We have already reported the disillusionment of those who had hoped the Council would begin with a concrete gesture in favor of the disinherited. It had been suggested, for example, that a collection of pectoral crosses, many of them of great value, be taken up for the poor. But these projects have not materialized. There is reason perhaps not to regret this, for the Council can later make a thorough examination of the multiple problems of poverty at the level of both theological reflection and practical effectiveness.

Although no schema of this nature was prepared by the preconciliar commissions, the bishops did not come to Rome empty-handed on the subject. Some of them—though with little recognition in rich countries—have undertaken impressive initiatives in this respect. Thus, Archbishop Tulio Botero Salazar of Medellín, Colombia, after a retreat preached at Pentecost by Father Lombardi, converted the episcopal palace he had inherited from his family into a school for workers and peasants and went to live in the suburb of Medellín, where he regularly invites workers to his table. Bishop Ngo Kim Diem of Can Tho, Vietnam, likewise gave up his luxurious residence, which attracted great attention in that land of castes. Bishop Eugenio de Araujo Sales, Apostolic Administrator of Natál, Brazil, interrupted the construction of his cathedral to build homes for workers, and undertook a vigorous campaign in favor of land reform. A Chilean bishop sold the diamond of his pectoral cross to build a professional school.

Another bishop, who wishes to remain anonymous, recently traveled 300 miles to Rome on foot dressed as a beggar to experience total deprivation personally. Archbishop Gregorios Thangalathil of Trivandrum, India, was born into a Communist family and leads a life of extreme poverty, not eating meat during the forty days of Lent. He has transformed his palace into a hostel where anyone can find food and shelter.

Finally, there is the example of Bishop Mercier, who comes from the Sahara, who is indignant that the oil from the desert brings nothing to his people. He spends three months a year in Europe to raise the money he needs for his works.

Applying the Gospel Bishops of this caliber at the Council are not likely to be happy with philosophic statements. They have also discovered that European prelates have similar problems with regard to workers. Men like Cardinals Lercaro and Feltin, Bishop Ancel, and Cardinal Gerlier can readily understand them. Cardinal Gerlier, for example, has said that he will spare no effort to steer Vatican II toward a consideration of these problems. The success of the Council will be gauged to an extent by such a concern, particularly by unbelievers. Patriarch Maximos IV Saigh of Antioch publicly stated his hope that the assembly would get on as soon as possible to what he called the "big packages," the evangelization of workers and the unity of Christians.

Last Sunday, in the apse of St. Peter's Basilica, fifty Little Sisters of Charles de Foucauld made their solemn profession, with Cardinal Tisserant presiding. Some fifty bishops attended this ceremony, so clearly directed to the "Church of the poor" which John XXIII spoke of in his speech of September 11. After the ceremony one religious remarked how odd it was that a Church which has drawn so many practical applications from the *Tu es Petrus* of Saint Matthew's Gospel has not been nearly so creative in interpreting Christ's teaching that Christians will be judged on what they have or have not done to feed the hungry and clothe the naked.

Perhaps Vatican II will heed the Pope's instruction, "You are a council; invent," and give particular evidence of imagination in this domain, which is so crucial for our age. As Father Louis Lebret has put it, "The greatest evil of the century is not the poverty of the have-nots; it is the insensitivity of the haves."

NOVEMBER 7

Vatican II Modifies Its Procedures

The Council is its own critic. Respectful of its liberty, the Pope only proposes; the assembly itself decides. Making use of the powers delegated to it by John XXIII, the presidency decided Tuesday that the moment had come to cut off the Fathers' verbal deluge on chapter 2 of the liturgy schema. Interrupting the succession of interventions, the president accordingly put the following question to the Council: "Are you agreed that this discussion should end?" A favorable vote was to be expressed by standing. Almost all the Fathers, even those who had not spoken although they were duly registered to do so, expressed their agreement.

The new procedure stipulates that those who were registered but had no chance to speak could present their observations in writing to the secretariat, which in turn would pass them on to the competent commission. Finally, and undoubtedly to encourage the Fathers to keep their remarks brief, they have been asked henceforth to present a résumé of their intervention at the time they register to give it.

During the discussion of chapter 3, on the sacraments, it was noted that the ritual ought to encourage a more "enlightened" and "pious" celebration of marriage on the part of the couple, who are themselves the ministers of the sacrament, the priest being merely a witness. The present ceremony, it was said, is too superficial and worldly and tends to conceal the sacred character of marriage as well as its spiritual and social importance.

The updating of the sacraments is one of the principal aims of the schema. This corresponds with a widely expressed desire on the part of pastors to foster ceremonial gatherings and in addition to underline the community value of sacraments which should draw the greatest possible number of the faithful together. This thinking does not go so far as to include penance, which could not be administered collectively under certain circumstances.

NOVEMBER 8

Animated Sessions in the Offing

The procedural reform is bearing fruit. The Council machinery is not yet off to the races, but it is working more smoothly. The twenty-one points of the chapter on the sacraments were reviewed in forty-eight hours, and at the end of yesterday's session the congregation was even ready to begin discussion of chapter 4, on the Divine Office, of which the breviary is the abbreviated form. Unfortunately, this dispatch required six bishops to relinquish their turns to speak.

Also in order to gain time, the presidency has decided that chapters 5, 6, 7, and 8 of the schema on the liturgy (on the liturgical year, vestments and objects of worship, music, and sacred art) will be studied as a whole. At that rate the revision of the schema could be completed within two weeks or less.

Archbishop Felici has just made an important announcement: the second schema to come up for discussion will be "The Sources of Revelation: Scripture and Tradition." Thus, the Council has finally determined its immediate program. The announcement set off lively discussion among the Fathers. Requests to make interventions which are ready for presentation were immediately transmitted to the secretariat. The controversy will be hot, for reasons we have explained. At the least, the schema prepared by the preconciliar commission on doctrine (with Cardinal Ottaviani as president and Father Sebastian Tromp, S.J., as secretary —two theologians who are more feared than fearsome) will be riddled with amendments. At the most, it could be rejected.

There will be uncertainty until the last minute, which will be dissipated only when the interventions reveal the strength of the opposition and its influence over the undecided. There is every indication that there will be a serious confrontation. This is to be expected. Councils have always known critical hours more or less envenomed by passions.

The Sacraments

To return to the present. Currently the Fathers are discussing the sacraments, which is a subject of pressing interest for both the clergy who administer them and the laity who receive them. There is a general desire for simplification and clarification of the rituals. It was suggested, for example, that catechists be allowed to baptize in mission countries. It was also suggested that a formula for the renewal of the baptismal promises be inserted in the confirmation ritual for those over the age of reason to help them understand the obligations of this sacrament. As for godparents, regret was expressed that they do not take their responsibilities more seriously.

Rebaptizing Extreme Unction   There has been a good deal of discussion about the sacrament of extreme unction. It was proposed that the name, which seems to imply imminent death, be changed to "unction of the sick," thus making it less a sacrament of fear and more one of consolation intended not only for the purification of the soul but also for the healing of the body. This sacrament is frequently administered conditionally to those who are unconscious, either because people are ignorant of its true nature or because they are afraid of upsetting the sick. To counter false ideas about the sacrament, a proposal was made to permit unction to be given in less serious cases than those which can be foreseen (as, for example, before a major operation) and that it be repeated in the course of the same sickness. A suggestion was also made that the application of unction be limited to the forehead and hands.

The use of the vernacular and the adaptation of the ritual of each sacrament to the mentality and traditions of different nations was strongly urged, especially by bishops from mission lands.

Funerals   The Fathers spent considerable time discussing ceremonies for the dead. A majority were in favor of making a serious effort to emphasize the riches of this office, which is one of the most beautiful in the liturgy. Again, it was hoped that judicious legislation could make the faithful aware of this.

The vestments for the requiem mass could be violet to diminish the element of sorrow, since this liturgy is entirely centered on hope and resurrection. "*Dies natalis*," the day of birth, the Church sings in speaking of the dead.

The Fathers stressed the fact that a number of nonbelievers attend funerals, so that it is all the more important to draw the maximum instructive value from the ceremonies.

The Breviary in the Vernacular

Five speakers took the floor on chapter 4 before the session ended. Most of them, especially Cardinals Frings and Léger, argued strenuously for the breviary in the vernacular. If this proposal is adopted, the younger clergy will be happy as well as some of their elders, who are grateful for the existing translations but have not so far .been allowed to use them.

NOVEMBER 9

The Importance of the
Interconfessional Dimension of Vatican II

Cardinal Bea Deplores the "Temporary Failure" of
Efforts in Constantinople

In a press conference Thursday, Cardinal Bea said:

Our joy is darkened by the absence of a good number of venerable Churches from the East at the Council. We must recognize, however, that great efforts have been made to overcome the obstacles standing in the way, and although they have not met with success, we must be careful that our mutual relations in Christ not suffer because of this temporary failure. . . .

Is it still possible that one or another of these venerable Orthodox Churches might send official observers to the Council as personal guests of the secretariat? It is very difficult to say. There have been various reports on the many efforts directed toward this end, but so far we have nothing concrete. In any event, we must hope that something can be done, for it would undoubtedly be very important for the two parties as well as for the cause of unity in general.

Cardinal Bea expressed his great appreciation of the calls to prayer for the Council sent out by many non-Catholic communities. He also stated categorically that the secretariat for unity *itself* should argue before the Council for the schemas prepared under its supervision. In this connection, it is believed that the secretariat is drawing up new schemas. The document on the unity of the Church prepared by the Commission for the Oriental Churches, which has already been distributed, will be redrafted and fused with another text which Cardinal Bea's office is working on at the moment.

Evident Solidarity Among the Churches The Pope has recently named three new members to the Secretariat for Promoting Christian Unity. They are Mansourati, Procurator of the Syrian Patriarchate; Bishop Andrew Katkoff, Ordaining Bishop of the Byzantine Rite for Rome; and Archimandrate Teodoro Minisci of the Basilians of Grottaferrata. All three men worked on the preconciliar commission for Oriental Churches, now dissolved.

By making the Secretariat for Promoting Christian Unity a conciliar commission, the Pope integrated it into the Council and increased its prestige enormously. No one can argue now that it is a marginal or secondary office. The fact that Cardinal Bea is not an Italian and that as rector of the Pontifical Biblical Institute he was noted for his liberal exegetical tendencies sometimes causes grumbling in the Curia. The Holy Office is forced to admit that it has lost exclusive control over relations with non-Catholic churches, which previously fell solely within its jurisdiction. That these relations, which were formerly envisaged in a purely negative and defensive way, are now quite different is essentially owing to the influence of the unity secretariat. Everything indicates that it will grow in stature and become one of the most important ministerial departments of the Church of the future.

This revolutionary aspect of Vatican II cannot be overemphasized. If it is true, as is often said, that the Council is "an internal affair of the Roman Church," it is truer still to say that it is surrounded by an interconfessional context. Solidarity among the divers Christian communities has never been so evident as it is today. Nothing that the Roman Church does or fails to do is a matter of indifference to others. This does not mean, of course, that reunion is imminent. Those who forget this or entertain illusions about the difficulties involved harm the cause of fruitful interfaith relations as much as integralists of various beliefs whose fear of compromise leads them to condemn all dialogue.

NOVEMBER 10

Examination of the Schema on the Sources
of Revelation To Begin Immediately

Will priests be allowed to say their breviary in the vernacular (and not Latin as they are presently obliged to do)? Cardinals Léger and Frings hope so and said as much in general congregation. Bishop Louis Guyot of Coutances, France, said before a group of journalists that as a former superior of a seminary for late vocations, he could see advantages in this change for priests who do not have a classical education and for whom Latin is consequently a source of difficulty.

Several Fathers requested that the breviary substitute New Testament passages for some of the Old Testament psalms which are too "imprecatory" and have a vengeful and bloodthirsty tone scarcely in conformity with the Gospel.

Cardinal Bea, for his part, tried to elevate the level of discussion by urging the Council not to lose itself in details and to restrict itself to general themes.

This opinion is shared by a number of participants, who are apprehensive about the seventy schemas waiting in the secretary general's files. It is generally thought that the Pope will be obliged to make some kind of selection because the documents are of uneven importance.

Discussion on the sources of revelation are likely to begin next week in order to give the commission on the Sacred Liturgy time to integrate the many proposed amendments. The amendments alone cover over 150 pages, a cause of some consternation to members of the commission. They hadn't expected such an avalanche of corrections!

How long will it take to complete this thankless task? The Fathers have made it clear that they want voting on the first schema to be terminated by December 8. In fact, the assembly would like to see its work on this subject end before the second session, to which, it is feared, a number of bishops will not return.

NOVEMBER 12

On the Eve of the First Great Battle of Vatican II:
Adoption of the First Doctrinal Schema
Could Seriously Damage Relations with Protestant Churches

Vatican II is about to witness its first great battle. The occasion is the first doctrinal schema, on the sources of revelation. Was it to drain the abscess that Pope John put it on the agenda of this session, when so many other subjects are waiting which are at once more pressing and more in conformity with his pastoral concerns? Perhaps. In any case, sooner or later, the Council will find itself at crossroads and be forced to choose for or against those who want to use scientific methods to study the subject of religion. The two schools are at bitter odds in the Roman Church, and everyone knows what stand the majority of the Curia has taken.

The theologians will have their say on this important matter, although until the opening of the Council, John XXIII himself was evasive enough.

"Are you a theologian?" he recently asked one of the non-Catholic observers.

"No," he answered.

"Thank God," said John. "Neither am I, though I have to pretend I am. You can see for yourself how much harm they have inflicted on the Church with their subtlety, their self-love, their narrowness and stubbornness."

Of course, this remark is not to be taken too literally. John knows better than anyone that theology cannot be neglected in a religion which promotes the value of reason and that only a good theology can deliver us from the evils of a bad one. But he is the kind of pope who is principally interested in spirituality and the needs of the ministry.

So the Council is now confronted with a specifically doctrinal document at the Pope's explicit will. What is the issue here? Briefly, it is a schema characterized by a theology that is narrow, superficial, and retrogressive. It contains two cardinal points.

One or Two Sources?   The first concerns the articulation of tradition and Scripture. The present document considers them as two distinct sources of revelation (*duae fontes*). This distinction is judged awkward and inopportune, for it is of a nature to stir the embers of an ancient quarrel between Protestantism and Catholicism at a time when the work of the best theologians on both sides is making encouraging progress toward abating the dispute.

Moreover, it is asked, why speak of *two sources* today when the Council of Trent, which could hardly be termed progressive, affirmed that the Gospel was the only source (*una fons*) of revelation, which is communicated in a twofold manner through Scripture and tradition (Denzinger 783)? A subtle distinction? Clearly not for those who know the importance of what is at stake and its ecumenical implications. Revelation is more existential than ideal, it was lived before it was written. That is fact and not theory.

If the Council ratifies the schema in its present form, it will deal a severe blow to the interconfessional relations which have been so painfully inaugurated. It would seem to say in effect that tradition has added something to the Gospel, which is denied by some Catholic theologians and is a fundamental reproach of the Protestants.

Modern Catholic Exegesis Ignored   The second point is even more important. The schema questions by omission all the exegetical study which has been carried on in the Roman Church over the past thirty years and which has been followed with great interest, indeed with envy, by the Protestant Churches. To understand the seriousness of the conflict, a brief historical survey might help.

For some time the Holy Office, the Sacred Congregation on Seminaries and Universities and Lateran University have been conducting an extremely violent campaign against the Pontifical Biblical Institute, which is staffed by Jesuits of principally German, French, and Anglo-Saxon origin. Cardinal Bea was the director of this institute until 1949. The tone but certainly not the quality of this polemic, which provoked one of John XXIII's rare losses of temper, reminds one of the era of the *Provincial Letters*. In a seventy-eight-page pamphlet published with Giuseppe Cardinal Pizzardo's blessing, Monsignor Romeo of the congregation of seminaries attacked the members of the institute as "contemners of tradition and the magisterium," "enemies of the Catholic faith," "corrupters of the young clergy," "hypocrites," "termites working in the dark," and so forth. Less than two months ago, Father Sapdafora, a student of Monsignor Romeo's, a professor at the Lateran University, and a member of the preconciliar commission, wrote and distributed a fresh accusation intended for the Council Fathers. He came out strongly against any use of the historical-critical method (literary genres and *Formgeschichte*) in the interpretation of the Bible. Cardinal Ruffini, Archbishop of Palermo, wrote an incredible article for *L'Osservatore Romano* (August 24, 1961), disagreeing with a passage from Pius XII's *Divino afflante spiritu*.

These shady polemics were recently accentuated when the Holy Office asked Fathers Lyonnet and Zerwick, both professors at the Pontifical Biblical Institute, to renounce their chairs of exegesis (although they remain on the institute's staff, one as dean, the other as a professor of philosophy).

Elaborated without consulting any of the exegetes on the biblical commission, the present schema ignores their work. If it were to be sanctioned by the Council, dozens of years of progress in New Testament studies would be canceled out, and Protestant observers, who haven't been at all pleased with this document, would be further disillusioned.

Happily, it seems certain that the bishops will take action. And it is to be expected that the first interventions will be stormy ones.

Keeping the Doors Open   The *aggiornamento* of the Church, proposed by the Pope as the goal of the Council, is incompatible with the tone of this schema which, far from widening the opening of doors newly ajar, threatens to close them again. Furthermore, since the Bible is a natural point of dialogue with the Protestants, and Vatican II is committed to advancing the cause of unity, it seems inconceivable that it would set forth on so antiecumenical a course. Should it do so, the observers would be justified in taking offense for having been invited to witness such a spectacle.

The Fathers will likely take every opportunity to quote from the Pope's opening speech, in which he explicitly urged the Council to be "pastoral in tone," to move forward, and not to condemn "the methods of research of modern thought." By far the majority of bishops desire renewal in accordance with scientific advances; their intentions could scarcely be termed reactionary.

And in fact, they have already taken steps to bar the schema's course. First, they have asked the Secretariat for Extraordinary Affairs to let them vote henceforth on a whole schema at the outset, to see whether it is worthwhile to begin discussing it. The six cardinals on the secretariat have agreed to take this request into consideration and have notified the Pope of it.

Second, substitute texts have been carefully prepared and submitted to bishops of different nationalities so they will not be caught short in case the schema is rejected. However this matter turns out, the Council is slowly maturing. Will it be able to form a united front against those who act "as though they had learned nothing from history, which is nevertheless the teacher of life" (John XXIII's opening speech, October 11) and who would, if they could, issue a new *Syllabus of Errors?*

NOVEMBER 13

Cardinal Feltin Wants Easter To Fall on a Fixed Date; Archbishop Gouyon Proposes That Bishops Renounce the Cappa Magna

In the session of November 12, Cardinal Feltin intervened to stress the advantages of a fixed date for Easter. The present tradition, he said, however venerable it is, is not very appropriate in the de-Christianized world of today, where it is no longer normal for such considerations as the changes in the moon, which nobody is interested in, to cause disturbing irregularities in the calendar. The present system, for example, can inconvenience students and those planning vacations.

Archbishop Ngo Dinh Thuc of Hue, Vietnam, made a speech that must have pleased the Curia. He declared himself in favor of the status quo as far as the liturgy was concerned because it would prevent the collapse of the Latin ritual. He also declared himself hostile to an increase in the powers of episcopal conferences. The Sacred Congregation of Rites, in his opinion, ought to remain the guardian and the guarantee of the uniformity of rituals in both their form (Latin) and their substance.

The interventions which caused the most stir among the Fathers dealt with the simplification of liturgical vestments. Bishop Manuel Larraín Errázuriz of Talca, Chile, said that given the poverty of under-developed countries and the social concern expressed in recent encyclicals, it would be good for the Church to have done with shocking ostentation in churches and liturgical vestments.

Archbishop Gouyon of Rennes, France, made a particularly well-received proposal. Nothing is too good for divine worship, he said. But in our day, when the communications media diffuse liturgical services to the world at large, we must be careful not to offend public taste by an inconsiderate display of wealth. Furthermore, he added, the Church was founded by a man who was born in a stable and died in total deprivation on the cross. The bishops, he went on, might set an example with greater simplicity in clothing, by giving up the *cappa magna*, for instance. The assembly was touched by these simple and direct words and applauded vigorously.

The bishops who had attended the Eucharistic Congress in Amster-dam in 1924 were reminded that the walls of that city were inscribed with various protests against ceremonial pomp, such as "Christ went barefoot." Public opinion has not changed since.

The Council will likely finish discussion on the liturgy today, Tuesday.

NOVEMBER 14

John XXIII Decides To Modify the Canon of the Mass Without Consulting the Council

Discussion on the liturgy ended on Tuesday. There was still considerable discussion about the urgency of adopting vestments "more in conformity with the rules of simplicity, avoiding luxury and displays of vanity, and observing the exigencies of poverty recommended by the Pope." An intervention by Abbot Zillianti of Monte Oliveto, Italy, combined Latin eloquence with strength of conviction. There is a growing consensus in the Church that greater simplicity is demanded in an age which is becoming more and more conscious of the dramatic misery of two-thirds of mankind.

A bombshell fell on the general congregation Tuesday. Cardinal Cicognani, Secretary of State, announced that the Pope has decided to insert the name of Saint Joseph after that of the Virgin Mary in the canon of the mass. "This act," the official announcement said, "is to be a remembrance of Vatican II in honor of the Council's patron." The Sacred Congregation of Rites will see to it that this decision becomes effective throughout the world as of December 8.

This news calls for several comments.

1. This is the first time since the reign of Gregory the Great, who died in 604, that the canon of the mass has been changed. It was thus a major event in the liturgical annals of the Roman Church.

2. This measure is not the work of the Council proper, for no vote was taken. "The Pope," the official bulletin states, "is responding to the wishes of many Fathers." That is a large claim, since the Holy Father received a petition signed by a mere 300 bishops, mostly Canadians, Yugoslavs, and Italians. This is undoubtedly the reason that the announcement met with rather meager applause, most of the assembly—2,209 were present—being disappointed at not having been consulted.

3. The Protestant observers and journalists found the change regrettable. They had not been favorably impressed when the Pope made a pilgrimage to Loretto on the eve of the Council, since the shrine is founded on an obviously superstitious legend: the transference by angels of the house in which the Virgin was supposedly born. Although the Protestants have no intention of interfering in matters which primarily concern the internal piety of the Roman Church, they could not help noting that this maneuver did little to advance the ecumenical aims of the Council.

Massive Approval of the Schema
on the Liturgy

The Council voted for the first time this morning, Wednesday, on two questions which can be summarized as follows:

1. Do you approve of the general principles of the schema on the liturgy?
2. Do you agree that the proposed amendments be sent immediately to the liturgical commission to be integrated into the final draft?

Of the 2,215 ballots (the required two-thirds majority would be 1,476), 2,162 were favorable, 46 negative, and 7 void.

A Decisive Day: Eleven Fathers Oppose
the Doctrinal Schema

The coffee shops did a poor business on Wednesday; few of the Fathers left their seats. Furthermore, when the bishops came down the steps of St. Peter's after the session, they did not have their usual air of distraction or fatigue; they were euphoric, and chatted excitedly. The general congregation had clearly been an exceptional one; some were calling it "historic" and others were saying that the Council really began on Wednesday.

Cardinal Ottaviani had reappeared after an absence of almost two weeks; it was a big day for him, perhaps the greatest battle of his already long and militant career. He came to present the doctrinal schema, written under his supervision, which a slightly malicious wit compared with a thalidomide baby.

The high interest of the session had clearly gripped the Fathers' attention. The Council had given proof of both its firmness and its seriousness. Defense and prosecution briefs were excellent.

"The truth is everywhere and always the same," Cardinal Ottaviani began, "and teaching it is the first duty of the pastor, whose responsibility it is to find the best forms and methods. A clever remark, which dealt a telling blow to the often heard objection that the Council should have a pastoral rather than a doctrinal orientation. Clever too was the preliminary report of Bishop Garofal. Doctrine does not change, he said, although it does develop. He explained on the other hand that a dogmatic constitution promulgated by a council should not have the same tone and content as an encyclical, a homily, or a pastoral letter. And on these grounds he defended the schema against charges that it was too brusque, abstract, and stylistically obscure.

Then the formal interventions began: eleven cardinals, one patriarch, and three archbishops took the floor. Of these fifteen speeches, three defended the schema (two Italians, Cardinal Siri and Ruffini, and one Spaniard, Archbishop Morcillo Gonzáles), one expressed reservations (Fernando Cardinal Quiroga y Palacios, Archbishop of Santiago de Compostela, Spain), and nine attacked it in principle (one Frenchman, two Germans, one Canadian, an Austrian, a Dutchman, a Belgian, an American, and an Indonesian).

"Mihi Non Placet"   Cardinal Liénart opened fire with these unequivocal words: *"Hoc schema mihi non placet."* Joseph Cardinal Ritter declared,

"*Rejiciendum est*" (it must be rejected). Patriarch Maximos IV Saigh of Antioch, speaking in French as is his custom, did not mince words. He said that the text expressed a point of view which is "narrow, negative, and polemical." It seems to derive from "theological quarrels which the Council should avoid." He called it a "condemnatory exposition," whereas the people desire "calm and positive methods of a nature to nourish their Christian life and thus prepare the way for ecumenical dialogue." The text uses "outdated formulas belonging to the Counter-Reformation and antimodernism." He pleaded, "Let us have confidence in scholars and theologians of great renown, and give them a free hand." In conclusion, Maximos summed up, "I propose an outright rejection of this schema."

The Patriarch also asked that the Council get on to its principal objective as soon as possible, which is to resume the discussions of Vatican I by balancing the dogma of papal authority with an examination of the powers of bishops. Immediately after his intervention, an official announcement was made that the schema *De Ecclesia* would be distributed to the Fathers within forty-eight hours.

Cardinal Bea was equally forthright. His double competence in matters exegetical and ecumenical lent special force to his words. It seems clear that this favorite of the Pope is prepared to risk both his position and his purple to block the schemas he considers especially harmful, whether to biblical research or to Christian unity.

As was to be expected, several speakers drew support from Pope John's opening speech. Following the Pope's speech, the theological adviser to an eminent Italian cardinal said, "After such recommendations, the Council will have to redo all the doctrinal schemas prepared by the commissions." A prophetic remark.

A Good Omen   What will the consequences of today's session be? After the interventions at the end of the week, the assembly will likely vote on the acceptability of the schema. In any event, thanks to the initiative of Cardinal Tisserant, who presided over the session on Wednesday, the Council has now expressed its agreement on the general principles of the schema on the liturgy. The results of the voting indicate an impressive concurrence. This near-unanimity is a good omen after the animated debates of the preceding weeks over the use of Latin. It shows the assembly's overwhelming agreement with the pastoral objectives of the Council and the need to renew the liturgy. John XXIII, who has time and again stressed the pastoral responsibilities of the bishops, must have been pleased by this first conciliar vote.

Such unanimity is psychologically important for it may have an influence over the fathers in the heated debates that are to come.

After the Council's Message to the World:
Poverty Is a Life-or-Death Question for the Church

Differences of personality, nationality, or theological school are secondary in the Council. For those who care to look at it from a little remove and with a historian's detachment, Vatican II emerges clearly as a gathering of holy and pastoral-minded men, united in a spirit of faith to seek not their personal gain but a better means of transmitting the evangelical message. This constitutes the exceptional character and dignity of the assembly and commands the respect of all impartial observers.

In their message to the world of October 21, the bishops expressed their interest in and compassion for the suffering, both spiritual and material, of contemporary man. They sincerely meant that. The immense majority of the Fathers at the Council know that priests, laymen, and even unbelievers throughout the world expect from them a renewal of the Church, more vigorous spiritual statements, and more understanding of the needs of twentieth-century man.

Stressing the anguish of those in underdeveloped countries, Pope John exclaimed in a speech a month before the opening of the Council that "the miseries of social life . . . cry for vengeance in the sight of God." Since their arrival at the Vatican, many of the bishops have been working quietly but energetically to see that these questions receive direct consideration.

Cardinal Gerlier of Lyon gave a forceful speech in Rome recently in which he said:

> The Church must adapt herself more sensitively to the situation created by the suffering of so many men and by the illusion . . . that the Church is not deeply concerned with them. The problem takes various forms but at bottom is always the same: the sorrowful situation of such great numbers of men resulting from an unequal distribution of wealth. How can the Church not feel obliged to remedy this situation at both the theoretical and the practical levels?
>
> The efficacy of our conciliar work is related to this problem. If we do not confront it, we are evading the most pressing aspects of evangelical and human reality. The question must be asked. And those in authority must be made aware of it. Whatever else we do will be compromised if this problem is not examined and treated. It is imperative to disengage a Church that does not want to be rich from the appearances of wealth. . . . The Church must appear as

what she is: the mother of the poor. She must orient those who have means to become concerned with those who do not yet have them. As bishops, we must see to it that the problem of evangelizing the poor and the apostolate among the workers are at the center of our conciliar preoccupations. The present Council ought to be the occasion for affirming this.

Patriarch Maximos has declared in a similar vein:

> Poverty is a life-or-death question for the Church. We are faced in some parts of the world, notably in Western Europe, with a serious defection of workers from the Church. It is not so much a question of rich and poor but of workers, who are the living strength of today's world.
>
> We have multiple opportunities to make the Church what the Pope in his speech of last September 11 said it should be: the Church of all, and particularly of the poor.

NOVEMBER 17

The Conciliar Assembly at an Impasse

Vatican II has entered its most critical phase. How could it be otherwise? In a monarchical Church, where the manner of governing has become excessively authoritarian, a council provides a unique occasion for the bishops to make inroads on the central power. Furthermore, the Council has thrown together men who differ in everything but their faith. What is there in common, for example, between a cardinal who has had practically no pastoral experience, whose formation has been almost exclusively juridical, whose only knowledge of religious problems comes from Scholastic treatises, and who is nostalgic for the past and afraid of the evolution of thought and another who has been in contact with men of all faiths, who has acquired experience of the world as it is, who is in touch with recent intellectual developments, and who is accustomed to dialoguing with unbelievers? We could list those who belong to one or the other category. But why bother, since they are on everyone's lips?

The fact is that men of the first category drew up the schema, presently under discussion, on the sources of revelation.

The Tone Hardens   The inevitable has thus happened. Since yesterday, Friday, the tone of the debates has hardened still more, aggressiveness is out in the open, and conflicts between personalities are exaggerated.

Those who habitually close their eyes to the human side of churchmen are a bit shocked by such bitter debate and unrestrained passion. The official press communiqués—which are usually conciliatory, imprecise, and insipid—are beginning to give up trying to dilute reality in empty formulas. They no longer praise the exceptional merits of the preconciliar commissions and the "depth" of the schemas. For the voice of bishops, who are no less successors of the apostles for not being Italian, has given the lie to such praise. One charges that the schema is "outmoded," "pessimistic," "inspires a servile fear of the Scriptures rather than love for them." Another adds that it contains "excessively rigid formulations," that it "lacks the pastoral spirit," that it is "too Scholastic and pedantic," that it risks making "the truth incomprehensible to our separated brethren." A third complains that it says nothing about the salvation of those who are not baptized. A fourth criticizes it for discouraging scientific research in the fields of theology and exegesis.

Toward a Synthesis   In the corridors some bishops talk of the "impasse" the Council has reached and the impossibility of reconciling "irreducible positions." The debates will continue Saturday, and perhaps the Fathers will hear opinions less diametrically opposed than those of, say, the Italians and Germans. But the way it looks now, it is practically certain that the schema will be scrapped, entirely redone, or at the very least substantially transformed. Friday a proposal was made to create a committee to seek a synthesis of the principal propositions by using different official documents which are circulating among the Fathers.

A New Syllabus?   But this presupposes that the Council, after the various schools of thought have had a hearing, will indicate its will by one or more votes on clearly formulated questions. In any event, the assembly is practically obliged to exhaust the problem; otherwise the same difficulties will recur with respect to the next doctrinal schema, entitled "On the Deposit of the Faith," which according to all reports is even less "open" than the present one—so much so that it is being called "a new *Syllabus.*"

It is easy to understand that these conditions have made the Council Fathers very keenly aware of their heavy responsibilities.

Vote To Interrupt Discussion on the Present Schema
Fails To Attain a Majority

On the "day of trickery" which was Tuesday, it seemed as if the evangelical spirit of rectitude, realism, and simplicity momentarily deserted the Council authorities. Perhaps order will be restored soon and the arguments used with suspect cleverness will return like boomerangs against their authors, but the Fathers are not about to forget the maneuvers which they were victims of. Here are the facts.

The majority of bishops have for some days indicated their displeasure with the schema on revelation. This was so clear that the Council president resolved to put it to a vote. Thus, on Tuesday the assembly was asked not, as would have been logical, whether they wanted to reject the schema but—and this was more subtle—whether they wanted to interrupt discussion of it. Cardinal Ruffini took it upon himself to announce that voting in the affirmative would mean the end of the schema; other defenders of the present text were busy trying to influence voters in the benches. Hadn't one of their spokesmen said only a few moments before that to vote against the schema would imply it contained errors, which clearly no one thought or intended?

Furthermore, the way the question was posed was tendentious. Those in favor of interrupting the discussion of this schema and passing on to another were to vote *placet* (yes), and those favoring a continuation of the discussion were to vote *non placet* (no). In other words, "yes" meant refusal and "no" meant acceptance. At this point an air of confusion filled the assembly, and it is not certain that all the Fathers understood in time what was being proposed to them.

The results of the voting were as follows: present, 2,211 Fathers; *placet*, 1,368; *non placet*, 822; the rest invalid.

In spite of everything, this was a numerical victory for those opposed to the schema. But practically speaking, the two-thirds majority of 1,460 had not been attained.* Lacking 92 *placet* voices, the vote therefore had no effect on the agenda of the Council, which continued to discuss the schema.†

---

* Article 39 of the regulations states that a majority of two-thirds is required in the general congregation, unless the Pope decides otherwise.

† Among the 822 Fathers who voted *non placet*, half are probably Italians. Most of these consider foreigners, and notably those the Roman press calls "transalpinists," as near-heretics contaminated with the spirit of the modern world. The other half are Spaniards or Americans (both North and South).

Will the Minority Impose Its Will?   Materially, the operation could not be faulted. The procedure was correct. But on moral grounds, there is room for doubt. It seems likely, in the first place, that had the question been asked differently—that is, *placet* for acceptance of the schema and *non placet* for refusal—there would have been much less confusion and the two-thirds majority would have been easily attained. Second, it is altogether astonishing that a minority of 822 could impose its judgment upon a majority of 1,368.

The official press bureau was undoubtedly aware of this and abstained from publishing the above figures in its bulletin. It reported the affair in these evasive words: "Given the results of the vote, discussion of the present schema will continue." This example is characteristic of the manner in which highly placed authorities think the public ought to be informed. Are the results to be considered part of the Council's secrecy? The Fathers judged differently, in any case, since they talked openly about them. They also deplored the official silence, which they felt was as "embarrassing as it was useless."

A Pyrrhic Victory   How have the tactics of this maneuver been assessed? General opinion holds that it was a question of a stratagem to which the Holy Office is no stranger. It was designed to put off the inevitable defeat of the schema's writers and promoters. But was time really gained? Quite possibly not.

In the first place, further examination of this text will allow numerous speakers to make new criticisms of it and thus bring the Council to discredit it. Also, by not fighting fair, the integralists are becoming more and more unpopular. The formal and temporary advantage they have won is a Pyrrhic victory that could soon turn against their interests. The Secretariat for Extraordinary Affairs will be informed immediately of the situation.

It doesn't seem possible that the assembly will continue to discuss the schema as though nothing has happened. The general will of the Council —which, it is well to remember, began on October 13 with great resistance to prefabricated schemas—cannot be defied indefinitely. It is too late now to make the Fathers dance to the tune of the curial pipers. Moreover, they have not forgotten the energetic words of John XXIII's opening speech, in which he disagreed with those who, "though burning with zeal, are not endowed with too much sense of discretion or measure."

A Catholic Layman at the Council

Regret was often expressed during the preparatory period of the Council that no laymen were represented on the commissions, particularly the commission on the laity.

Nor has any Catholic layman been allowed to attend the general congregations. Justified or not, this state of affairs seems peculiar in an age when laymen are taking on greater responsibilities in the Church.

Now that has been changed. John XXIII has personally authorized Jean Guitton to attend the general congregations of the Council as an observer. Cardinal Tisserant is no longer the only member of the French Academy present in St. Peter's. Mr. Guitton is very much at home on the observers' bench since he has long been interested in ecumenical problems. He has dialogued with Lord Halifax, Cardinal Mercier, and countless Protestants. Among the observers is Mr. Oscar Cullmann, also a professor at the Sorbonne.

Although he doesn't have the title, Mr. Guitton might be considered a sort of expert at the Council. Many bishops will seek his advice. He is particularly qualified to speak for intellectuals. Henceforward it will not be necessary to be "a heretic" or a "schismatic" to have the right to attend Vatican II!

NOVEMBER 22

The Pope Intervenes

The Council Fathers have reacted healthily to Tuesday's deceitful procedures which oblige them to continue discussion of a schema unacceptable to the majority. They have neither given in nor adopted captious attitudes incompatible with their episcopal responsibilities. They have turned confidently to the Pope, the head of the Council and visible leader of the Church, as the final arbiter.

John XXIII—who does not attend the general congregations but follows them over a loudspeaker installed in his private apartment—has responded immediately to their appeal. He has resolved the difficulty with a fairness and prudence all the more appreciated in that these two qualities were so conspicuously absent in the last session.

The Pope's first decision was to stop discussion of the schema. Second, he decided that the contents of the schema are to be modified, and he entrusted this responsibility to a special commission comprising cardinals who are members of the theological commission and the unity secretariat.

This is an important innovation for three reasons.

1. It does not infringe upon the rights of the present theological commission. The latter therefore retains its power to deal with the Fathers' amendments for the second version of the schema. But the actual elaboration of this document will not fall to the theological commission as such, which means that it will not be under the control of Cardinal Ottaviani, who presides over the theological commission and is the author of the contested schema. It is consequently certain that the new text will be appreciably different from the first and will faithfully take into account the observations of these past few days.

2. In giving full conciliar status to the members of the special commission from the secretariat for unity, the Pope has established a collaboration which was impossible during the pre-Council period because of Cardinal Ottaviani. As a result, the ecumenical character of the second version is assured.

3. It is also possible that the special commission will sooner or later have to rework the other doctrinal schemas which, for similar reasons, do not meet with the approval of the assembly.

A New Departure

The atmosphere of the Council is once again serene and joyful. The discussions will be able to begin again on a solid footing after some trying days. But the trials will not have been without value, since they have placed in bold relief the retrogressive and antiecumenical intentions of a clique that is hostile to the *aggiornamento* of the Church called for by the Pope. The issues are now much clearer, and will remain so if the assembly continues to show vigilance and firmness, as there is every sign it will.

Friday the Council will shift discussion to the schema on the communications media (the press, radio, television, and movies). Many might think it will be a noncontroversial subject. But in reality this text can provide a prime occasion to expose the difficulties frequently encountered between the press and the Church in general and the Council in particular. Churchmen generally do not understand the working conditions of journalists or the rules of processing information, and consequently tend to belittle a body that can be of service only in the measure that freedom of expression is respected and the mechanisms of forming opinion are understood.

The Council and the Communications Media

The press, radio, television, and movies entered St. Peter's yesterday, Friday. Not literally, to be sure, for we haven't reached that point yet, but in the form of a schema which treats *ex professo* what conciliar jargon calls "the principal audiovisual means of social communication."

The Council thus honors these media, and in a quite unexpected way. As a matter of fact, there is sometimes a kind of China wall between one of these media—the press—and the Church.

There is great ignorance about the religious press in the first place, because its independence or dependence vis-à-vis the hierarchy is very vaguely defined. To what extent is a Catholic paper in Paris, Rome, or elsewhere official or autonomous? Those directly involved are often at a loss for an answer, and sometimes learn to their chagrin that their freedom is much less than they supposed. This situation explains why it can be impossible in specific cases to determine the degree to which a given article expresses the thinking of the Holy See or diocesan authorities. An anonymous article on Teilhard de Chardin in *L'Osservatore Romano* last summer is a case in point.

The difficulties facing the secular press are of another order. Because they are free from the control of the Church, they are often for that reason looked upon with suspicion. Doors close when they could be opened; silence sets in when dialogue could take place; secrecy is imposed on matters of public notoriety. The right to information is a crucial problem which the schema treats too cursorily, because it involves a whole theology of modern man and society.

Paradoxes Alain remarked in his *Propos* that the Church was the first to lay the foundations of democracy by teaching the catechism to all men. The Church considers it her principal duty to announce "the good news." But she is more reluctant when it is a question of giving public opinion the means to judge for itself the Church's behavior on a given problem. We might at this juncture pay homage to the efforts of Catholic Action groups to alleviate this problem, even though their work has not always been appreciated by the clergy. But there can be no healthy society— Christian or otherwise—unless the people are impartially and abundantly informed. Pius XII himself made this very clear.

The situation here at the Council is an excellent example (and there are many others) of the Church's disregard, despite official declarations, of the public's legitimate curiosity. A supreme paradox was that the day the Council began discussion on this schema, Archbishop René Stourm of Sens, France, had his introductory speech printed and distributed to all the Fathers, the first time this kind of thing had been done since the Council opened; yet the press had access to nothing but a very brief résumé of this text. This is a shame, for much of what he said is of direct interest to the laity and could not in any way have compromised the secrecy of the Council.

"The Middle Ages are finished," he said in substance. "The era of technology has begun. The Church must use modern techniques; otherwise she will cut herself off from the world. It is important that these techniques be baptized and Christianized from within. If Saint Paul were alive today, he would not hesitate to do so."

Besides using the communications media to spread the Gospel message, wouldn't the Church gain by furnishing as complete and objective information about herself as possible? One bishop told me, with creditable candor, "The Church has a mistaken tendency to hide what ought not be hidden. We should be concerned with objective information. But we are not."

Freedom of Expression   As an example, some bishops complained during the seventeenth general congregation (November 12) that official bulletins lacked objectivity, according to a dispatch from the Swiss agency KIPA which appeared in *La Croix*. Others, on the contrary, expressed surprise that certain Roman papers were too well informed on the details of the sessions. The men who run the official press bureau are not to be blamed; but their organization is not properly equipped, nor do they enjoy sufficient liberty of expression (although out of discretion they refuse to complain about this).

Speaking of the virtues of the communcations media, one religious told us:

> It is regrettable that the schema considers these media almost exclusively from the point of view of how they can benefit the Church. It would have been encouraging had the schema insisted in a disinterested fashion on their intrinsic role as extraordinary means of bringing men together and allowing them to share simultaneously in the same joys, the same sorrows, the same artistic, scientific, or religious experiences.

When discussion on this schema has finished, and interventions are not expected to exceed forty, the schemas on Church unity (prepared by the Commission for the Oriental Churches) and the Virgin Mary will be presented.

Vatican II and the Protestants: Oscar Cullmann Hopes "Council Decisions Will Be Inspired by the Bible"

A flutter of cassocks surrounded Oscar Cullmann; the Sorbonne professor, a celebrity in spite of himself, was signing his autograph a few steps away from St. Peter's for a group of young clerics in his customary unruffled and polite manner. It was one of the most picturesque and perhaps most significant scenes we have witnessed since the Council began. An hour earlier today, we jammed into the pressroom to hear the Protestant exegete address the journalists.

Mr. Cullmann gave his impressions of the Council he attends each morning as a guest of the Secretariat for Promoting Christian Unity. He spoke in total openness which, he said, is "a necessary condition" if ecumenical relations are to bear fruit.

After praising the World Council of Churches as a "great reality full of promise which has smoothed the way and whose importance Vatican II must recognize," Mr. Cullmann then pointed out "the immense difficulty of the union of the Churches with Rome, . . . because the Roman conception of unity is very different from ours.

"Even if the proposals for renewal are accepted by the Council," he said, "there will remain an important difference between us and Catholicism."

Mr. Cullmann made these two observations:

> On the one hand, Catholicism has much more varied aspects than Protestantism; [on the other,] this confession can profess entire agreement with most of the positive truths which Protestants, under biblical inspiration, believe and preach.
>
> It is not the positive elements of our faith which separate us; it is rather that there is more in Catholicism (or, from our point of view, there is too much) and conversely there is less in Protestantism (or, from the Catholic point of view, there is too little). I believe that dialogue will make progress when our Catholic brothers cease to regard this "less" in a purely negative fashion, when they consider it not as a deficit, as an arbitrary contraction, but as a concentration inspired by the Holy Spirit.

Professor Cullmann thinks that the Protestant churches also stand in need of renewal: "We have to ask ourselves whether or not, instead of a concentration, there has not been in fact a kind of contraction of the Bible in Protestantism and whether or not we have wrongly let go certain perfectly biblical elements."

A "Miracle"   The speaker stressed the "miracle" which the presence of observers in Rome represents: "I still marvel at the way we are being integrated into the Council, and I am not sure that the laity grasp the significance of our presence here. It is a powerful leap forward."

Mr. Cullmann said with a smile that his interpreter at the Council was a Benedictine who was once his pupil at the Sorbonne, and noted that future historians should point out the "ecumenical influence" of the coffee bar in St. Peter's where the bishops go for refreshments between interventions. Returning to more serious subjects, he remarked that he was particularly pleased with the weekly meetings between the observers and members of the Secretariat for Promoting Christian Unity: "These meetings give us the opportunity to pray in common and to express our criticisms and desires. The fact that so frank and fraternal a discussion is possible, and this on the very periphery of the Council, must be considered as an eminently positive element, and merits special mention by future chroniclers of Vatican II."

In conclusion, Mr. Cullmann expressed the hope that

> . . . the decisions of the Council, which we are as yet ignorant of, will be inspired by the Bible. I say this not only because of my special interest as an exegete but because it is a fact that the dialogue began among exegetes. Today it is being carried on by theologians in general. We hope not only that it will not be interrupted but that it will be further intensified and much facilitated by this Council. We wait with confidence. Whatever the outcome, we shall continue the dialogue.

NOVEMBER 27

The Council Will Broach the Schema *De Ecclesia*
Before the End of the First Session

Despite its shortcomings, the schema on the communications media has the advantage of sharpening the question of the role of the layman, which will be discussed more fully in 1963. Many of those who intervened, including Cardinal Léger of Montreal, insisted on the irreplaceable function of laymen in the evangelization of the world today. The press, radio, and cinema penetrate where the priest never can. The Church must therefore take these modern vehicles of thought, which are in the hands of laymen, very seriously. She will be all the more effective in this area if she concentrates not on moralizing but on real facts and human experiences that speak for themselves.

After this study, which obliged the bishops to reflect upon the missionary role of the Church in an age of transistors, magazines, and television screens, Vatican II entered a new phase yesterday by broaching the subject of Church unity. Elaborated by the Commission for the Oriental Churches alone, this document puts the Council in a false situation once again: because they did not work together, the preconciliar organisms drew up schemas on the same subject but from different points of view. Ecumenism does not thrive on this kind of fragmentation, and it is likely that after a brief discussion, the present text will be reworked by the Secretariat for Promoting Christian Unity, the only body which has played the kind of ecumenical role envisioned by the Pope.

According to the agenda announced two days ago, the assembly will next go on to the schema *De Ecclesia*, one of the most important of Vatican II. For some weeks the bishops have been hoping to get to it as soon as possible. This schema in effect takes up the examination of the nature of the Church where Vatican I left off, after defining papal infallibility. Thus, the central questions of episcopal powers and collegiality will come to the fore, and a detailed examination of them will put authority in the Church in a new perspective.

The end of the first session therefore promises to be a weighty one. Voting on the liturgical schema will continue to December 8, the day the first session will end.

NOVEMBER 28

How Will the Nine Months
of Conciliar Vacation Be Used?

Yesterday, Tuesday, the Council offered new proof of its indisputable cohesion by adopting (2,138 to 15) the substance of the schema on the communications media and by severely criticizing the schema on Church unity. It is becoming more and more evident that the doctrinal schemas will have to be substantially reworked. When? How? And by whom? These are questions everyone is asking as the first session nears its end. It does not seem that the mixed commission newly created by the Pope will be up to the task. There is an idea abroad that a kind of "concentrated council" will take place during the first nine months of 1963.

What are we to understand by "concentrated council"? Bishop Sergio Méndez Arceo of Cuernavaca, Mexico, has suggested the following arrangement:

Each national or continental episcopal conference could send 10 percent of its members to Rome between the two plenary sessions. This assembly of about 250 bishops would constitute a kind of second-level council, and would be representative of the different schools of thought in each conference. It would be empowered to prepare a detailed program for the second session, whose output could thus be much superior to the present session's.

Most of the Fathers are very tired now. They complain of the time lost listening to repetitive interventions. Those who have had anything to say have always spoken in full liberty. The time has now come, it is felt, to stop criticizing and begin building in conformity with the desires of the assembly.

The Slum Bishop

The day on which Pope John gave an allocution praising the *sancta libertas* of the Council, one of the Fathers, who was to say mass and deliver a homily for the journalists, was forced to modify the text he had prepared. The official press bureau had judged the contents of his homily to be out of place and at the last moment had stopped it from being distributed.

Archbishop Helder Camâra, of Recife, Brazil, was the victim of this distasteful incident. One of the most popular prelates in Latin America, he has been nicknamed the "slum bishop" because of his charitable work on behalf of the impoverished of his diocese. In his sermon he protested the pomp of the inaugural mass of the Council, which he said was "difficult to justify in the age of television," and suggested that at the end of the first session it would be more fitting to celebrate a penitential office rather than one of thanksgiving. "It is unpardonable," he added, "that the Council has not yet touched upon any of the major problems of our age." However, the Archbishop expressed pleasure over the Pope's speech, "which, inspired by the Holy Spirit, saved the whole ceremony," as well as over the atmosphere of liberty prevailing in the general congregations which has so highly edified the non-Catholic observers. He revealed that Pope John, at the request of a number of bishops, intended to create a special commission to study the problems of underdeveloped countries, overpopulation, hunger, atomic war, and peace.

If some of his remarks displeased certain Roman circles, they were warmly welcomed by all those who hope for the *aggiornamento* of the Church.

Is the Council a Sickness?

Integralist Italian circles frequently look upon the Council with consternation. They are faced with the brute fact that the Curia's omnipotence is being seriously threatened and that the reformist tendency is gaining new victories each day. The Italian press spares no effort to embarrass the liberals. One paper, for example, has tried to prove that Cardinal Bea—if not the Pope himself—is sympathetic to modernism. Some of the accusations border on the ridiculous. In an article in *Corriere della Sera*, Cardinal Alfrink is called "an activist and an anti-Roman." The writer went so far as to accuse the Archbishop of Utrecht of disrespect because he crossed his legs during a pontifical high mass in St. Peter's.

Some Italian bishops are not far from considering the Council as a "sickness of the Church." One of them is quoted as saying, "We are paying for fifteen minutes of foolishness on the part of the Pope."

While it is not beside the point to note the resistance to the Council revealed in such asides, it would be unrealistic to take them too seriously, for the great majority of the bishops disapprove of them.

DECEMBER, 1962

Last Week of the Session
Promises Heavy Work Load

The Council came within an inch of deciding to end with discussion of the schema on the Virgin Mary. On two previous occasions the question arose of whether to turn to this document right after the one on Church unity. Last Wednesday Cardinal Ottaviani urged this course. His arguments were based upon reasons of logic as well as of piety—logic, because only this short schema (five pages) could be finished before the Fathers disband the end of next week; piety, because the Secretary of the Holy Office appealed to the Marian devotion of the bishops by praising the Virgin of Poland, of Lourdes, and of Fatima.

But this intervention disconcerted the Council's presidency by its impromptu character since Cardinal Ottaviani had not gone through official channels before making his proposal. The presidency consequently resolved not to follow the Cardinal, and to broach the schema *De Ecclesia* this morning, Saturday.

This pleased many of the Fathers, for two important reasons. First, the ecumenical argument stands against the argument based on piety, however worthy it is. Protestants are easily annoyed by anything pertaining to the Marian cult; it would have been regrettable, psychologically speaking, for a council intent on smoothing the path toward unity to end its first session by leaving a bad impression on the Protestant observers.

An Eighty-Page Schema The second reason carries even more weight. By putting off discussion of the schema *De Ecclesia* until 1963, the Council would have to wait nine more months to begin its deliberations on a most important subject. The long interval between the two sessions could not then be used to redraft the text. But if the assembly begins debate immediately, it can put forth enough criticisms between now and December 8 to indicate how the redrafting should be done. Thus, by September, 1963, the difficulties will be largely cleared up.

The schema is eighty pages long and comprises eleven chapters: (1) on the nature of the Church, (2) the members of the Church and the need for them to belong to her to be saved, (3) the episcopacy, (4) residential bishops, (5) states of perfection for religious, (6) the laity, (7) the magisterium of the Church, (8) authority and obedience, (9) church-state relations, (10) the necessity for the Church to preach the Gospel to all people, and (11) ecumenism.

The eleventh chapter will likely be separated from the present schema and grouped with the two schemas on ecumenism, the one which the Fathers finished discussing yesterday and that prepared by the Secretariat for Promoting Christian Unity.

The remaining ten chapters are of great interest. The chapter relative to bishops will be hotly debated since most of the Fathers think that the principle of episcopal collegiality has not been sufficiently determined. The chapter on church-state relations is said to be too theoretical; on the other hand, the chapter on the laity is considered satisfactory. It treats of "the universal priesthood of the laity," "the rights and duties of laymen," "the forms their collaboration can take," and "the autonomy of the terrestrial city."

At the end of Friday's session, the Fathers were in exceptional good humor. The last speaker on the floor provoked them to unabashed laughter, a rare relief in the solemn deliberations. He said, by way of peroration, "As our brother observers can see, we can say anything in this assembly without fear of being punished or imprisoned."

The mixed doctrinal commission is hard at work revising the schema on the sources of revelation. It is divided into five sections, each one comprising two cardinals, bishops, and experts. The debates are proceeding apace, and no one feels at a disadvantage since all schools of thought are equally represented. Those working on this commission, elaborating and refining the conciliar texts, will determine the intellectual life of the Church for generations to come.

DECEMBER 3

The Council Gathers Strength

The Council is gathering its strength to consider the schema *De Ecclesia*. This document, on the nature of the Church and her relationship to the world, pertains to the very essence of the sacerdotal and missionary vocation of bishops. They can be expected to put their best efforts into their interventions, not in a polemical spirit but with a firmness dictated by an awareness of their responsibilities.

Cardinal Ottaviani presented his schema in a somewhat subdued manner. He noted, undoubtedly as a result of his experience with previous sessions, that it would likely encounter many objections.

The assembly is on the point of acquiring a well-defined personality; one detects certain orientations that unite the Fathers in a common cause. For example, there is general agreement on the necessity of exploring the ecclesial vision of the mystical body along the lines of Pius XII's encyclical *Mystici corporis,* considering the Church not as a static reality but rather as dynamic, deploying herself in time and space; the invisible frontiers of the Church must be extended to the maximum by taking account of the universal values of the incarnation and redemption. "The mystery of the Church, in all its fullness, transcends the limits of her canonical developments."

Catholicism has not utilized equally well the means which are rightfully at its disposition. It must recognize that the Orthodox and Protestants have historically better emphasized one or another aspect of our religious heritage (for example, the liturgy and the trinitarian and eschatological mysteries in the case of the Orthodox; biblical spirituality and the value of personal commitment in the case of the Protestants).

Along with her rights, the Church must also remember the duties she must assume toward mankind as a whole; she must define the principle of freedom of conscience, valid *for all* and not just for Catholics or Christians; she must protest against what Bishop Emile Josef Marie de Smedt of Bruges has called "the trilogy of clericalism, legalism, and triumphalism." The phrase can be understood to mean the penchant for presenting the Church in a less than evangelical and unduly optimistic light, for throwing superlatives about out of vanity and prestige-consciousness. As an example, the Bishop of Bruges cited *L'Osservatore Romano* and certain curial documents whose antiquated style scarcely radiates a Christian spirit.

Bishops Are Not Minors   The Council Fathers have insisted and will continue to insist on the collegial aspect of government in the Church. The episcopacy is of divine right, and the bishops have a role to play in the government of the universal Church. The Pope is pope because he is Bishop of Rome and not the other way around. Christ chose his apostles *before* he made Peter their head, as one of the *periti* remarked. In an age when we often talk of an "adult laity," the bishops must stop acting like minors or mere chore boys for the Holy See. In this respect the conciliar assembly will have to treat *ex professo* the powers of episcopal and patriarchal conferences, beginning by distinguishing between the personal power of the pope and that of the Curia or nuncios.

These brief remarks indicate the scope of the problems implied in the schema *De Ecclesia*. The stakes are high, for the very success or failure of the Council is involved.

There are only a few sessions left for the assembly to affirm and assume its destiny *in union with the Pope*. The Council must prepare the schemas itself and make its own will known, without any sense of inferiority which would run contrary to its true nature. Curia officials have often expressed annoyance at the Council's independent attitude, but the Council has much greater reason to be annoyed by the Curia's contempt for it.

DECEMBER 4

Will the Council's Spirit of Reform
Influence the Commissions?

"In this new-wave Council, the bishops are more dangerous than the laity," said an Italian periodical recently. Another stated, "No one is trying to poison John XXIII, but he is opposed by retrograde, fanatical, and obscurantist persons who are afraid of losing their absolute power." A newspaper ran an enormous headline of the kind usually reserved for major disasters: "Ottaviani Defeated." That the Council can provoke such reactions in the secular press is proof that the Catholic Church is turning over a new leaf. Italian circles are in a more or less general state of panic because they confuse orthodoxy with their own narrow conception of it and see infiltrations of neo-Protestantism and progressivism everywhere. But today, by the explicit order of the Pope, the reformists have the upper hand and are in undisputed control of the field.

The World Awaits the Church's Examination of Conscience Bishop Gérard Huyghe of Arras, France, said Monday:

> It sometimes happens that instead of leading souls to Christ, the Church turns them away. The world awaits the Church's examination of conscience. Public opinion eagerly and hopefully waits to discover her true face. We will be judged on the texts we elaborate, texts which will determine the course of Catholicism for centuries

to come. I hope that the Church will dedicate herself totally to
the quest of the Spirit and the Gospel so that she will show herself
to be open, really catholic, missionary, and humble.

These firm but measured remarks were followed, as chance would
have it, by an incredible outburst on the part of Bishop Musto of Aquino,
Italy. In an accusatory tone of voice, he declared that criticism of the
essential principles of the institutional and hierarchical Church ought not
be tolerated within the walls of St. Peter's, and reproached certain
bishops for taking their responsibilities too lightly. He cited a text from
Saint Paul on the duty of opposing false doctors who turn from the
path of sound doctrine, and ended by appealing to the vengeance of
God. The assembly protested these words; several bishops pounded their
desks with their pastoral rings, and others shouted, "Inadmissible!" When
the president of the session stopped this unseemly speech, he was applauded by the Fathers.

So outrageous an intervention defeats the purpose it claims to defend.
It was "painful" and "insulting" to the members of the Council, who are
accustomed to weighing their words, whatever the content of their
interventions.

As the session approaches adjournment, the number one problem remains this: how can the Council's spirit of reform be extended to the commissions in charge of correcting the schemas between December, 1962,
and September, 1963? The presidency and the Secretariat for Extraordinary Affairs are confronted with different alternatives; it is becoming
more and more urgent that a choice be made among them. But the
Pope's illness does not simplify matters.

DECEMBER 5

Two Authorized Opinions
on the Preparation of Vatican II

Cardinal Montini: "Excellent but Uneven Material" Cardinal Montini,
in a weekly letter to his faithful, commented in these terms on the preparation of the documents submitted to the Council Fathers:

There is an immense amount of material which is excellent but
heterogeneous and uneven. It could have been considerably reduced
and better classified had some authority which was not merely extrinsic and disciplinary directed the logical and organic development
of these magnificent volumes and had one central structural idea
polarized the whole. Respect for the principle of liberty and spon-

taneity which gave birth to the Council has eclipsed the central point of Vatican II's program, though it was solemnly and wisely outlined by the Holy Father during the years preceding the Council and especially in his speeches of September 11 and October 11.

Cardinal Suenens: All Schemas Should Be Reworked in Terms of Two Basic Ideas Four days from the end of the first session, there is still a good deal of discussion about what is to be done between now and September 8, 1963, when the Council meets again. Two dangers must be avoided. First, the nine-month interim must not be spent drowsing, or the Council will be faced with the same spineless schemas that were prepared by the preparatory commissions. Second, if serious work is to be undertaken, it must not be in a conservative spirit, for this would not correspond with the spirit of renewal that has been so clearly demanded during the present session.

In a brilliant intervention which was received with loud applause, Cardinal Suenens, Archbishop of Malines-Brussels and a member of the Secretariat for Extraordinary Affairs, proposed Tuesday that all the schemas be revised in terms of two basic ideas: the Church *ad intra*, that is, her nature, constitution, central power, members, bishops, clergy and laity, educative mission, and so forth; and the Church *ad extra*, that is, in relation to the principal problems of the world today: social justice, peace, disarmament, hunger, respect for life, evangelization of the masses, poverty, and so forth.

This plan has the advantage of simplicity, and would give the Council the guideline which it presently lacks. The assembly itself must determine its program and decide to set aside secondary matters which would prolong the sessions uselessly. Reference was made yesterday to Cardinal Montini's pastoral letter, in which he spoke of the "heterogeneous" character of the huge amount of conciliar material and the absence of any real authority sorting out the directive ideas, in conformity with the desire the Pope expressed in his opening speech.

To discard what is superfluous, introduce what has been omitted, and regroup what has been dispersed is a tall order. It seems likely that a permanent commission, truly representative of the majority of the Fathers, will be named to coordinate the work of other commissions. The assembly is expected to support the formation of such a commission in the interests of the Council's future.

Council Themes Reduced to Twenty

The seventy-three schemas elaborated by the preparatory commissions of Vatican II are longer than all the decrees adopted by the twenty previous councils. Aware of the bishops' often expressed desire for a more sharply defined agenda, the presidency has distributed a brochure containing a list of twenty themes; the seventy-three schemas have thus been reduced to a more manageable number.

An introductory note says, "The schemas presented summarily in this brochure will be submitted to the commissions to be reduced to general principles and drafted in a more unified way when the need is felt." This means that the commissions may have to abridge the original schemas appreciably, and that themes treated from different points of view by the various preparatory commissions will be regrouped.

Logic has prevailed. It remains only to know the composition of the central commission which will direct the work of other commissions and see to it that whatever modifications are made in the interim period are in accord with the pastoral, missionary, and ecumenical spirit expressed by the majority of Council Fathers during the session now ending.

Maximos IV Saigh Against "Popolatry"

Besides voting on amendments concerning the liturgy, the general congregation on Wednesday continued discussion of the schema on the Church. The event of the day was an intervention by Cardinal Montini, who has until now maintained a prudent reserve.

In a highly subtle and diplomatic statement, the Archbishop of Milan, while making every effort to remain above the fray, nonetheless agreed with most of the criticisms leveled against the schema, noting especially its inadequate coherence. Cardinal Montini was in favor of having the document reworked. The preliminary work of Vatican I, he said, ought to be taken more into account, for had it not been interrupted by the war, that council would normally have adopted a complete schema on the Church.

Maximos IV Saigh's intervention in French was as usual followed closely. After stating that the schema on the Church was "the master doctrinal text of the Council" and referring to "the infallibility of the universal Church," the speaker deplored the "suffocating legalism" of the text and the "significant omission" of anything about titular bishops from the section on the episcopacy.

Concerning the primacy of Peter, he said, there is "an unhealthy insistence upon this truth in isolation from all others, as if there were only the Pope." Stigmatizing "certain flattering and self-interested exaggerations," Maximos declared, "We are disgusted when we read such intemperate language, bordering on the impious, as this [he cited an Italian publication]: 'The Pope is God on earth. Christ has placed him above the prophets, above Saint John the Baptist, above the angels, on a level with God himself.' "

The speaker concluded by hoping that "the Church will purify herself of such profane slag."

Cardinal Ruffini in the main defended the schema. He proposed that it be left in its present form, although perhaps another, more pastoral in tone, could be added to it. Previously, Cardinal Bea had emphasized the deficiencies of the text and deplored its incoherence and the legalistic spirit in which it was written. Cardinal Suenens ended his intervention by evoking the prophetic figure of Désiré Cardinal Mercier, who had worked so hard for the unity of the churches, an ideal that was now beginning to be realized.

DECEMBER 7

A Coordinating Commission Charged "To Assure the Conformity of the Schemas with the Aims of the Council"

Regulations concerning the work of the Council during the nine-month interim were published on Thursday. They contain important stipulations.

The redrafting of the schemas has been assigned to conciliar commissions and mixed subcommissions whose responsibility it will be to facilitate and accelerate the work of the commissions. However, a new Coordinating Commission will be created to control and direct the enterprise as a whole and "to assure the conformity of the schemas with the aims of the Council." Experts may be consulted.

When the schemas have been redrafted and approved by the Pope, they will be sent to the bishops or the episcopal conferences. When they have been studied by the latter, they are to be returned to the secretariat general of the Council. Then, with due consideration of criticisms made by the bishops, the commissions will proceed with the amendments.

The regulations specify in some detail the spirit and methods to be followed by the commissions:

1. They must concentrate upon the most important principles, leaving secondary matters to be considered later by commissions that will be formed *after* the Council.
2. They must bear in mind that the Council is working for the universal Church and for generations to come. The schemas must therefore avoid irrelevancies and repetitions.
3. Anything bearing on the revision of canon law is to be referred to the competent commission.

The Charter of the Council   The same regulations clarify the aim of the Council by citing long extracts from John XIII's speech of October 11. Here are the principles that may be considered the charter of the Council:

> The salient point of this council is not, therefore, a discussion of one article or another of the Church's fundamental doctrine of the Church which has repeatedly been taught by the Fathers and by ancient and modern theologians. . . .
>
> . . . the Christian, Catholic, and apostolic spirit of the whole world expects a step forward toward a doctrinal penetration and a formation of consciences in faithful and perfect conformity with the authentic doctrine, which, however, should be studied and expounded through the methods of research and through the literary forms of modern thought. The substance of the ancient doctrine of the deposit of faith is one thing, and the way in which it is presented is another. And it is the latter that must be taken into great consideration; this, of course, must be done with patience, everything being measured in the forms and proportions of a magisterium which is predominantly pastoral in character. . . .
>
> . . . the Catholic Church, raising the torch of religious truth by means of this ecumenical council, wishes to show herself to be the loving mother of all, benign, patient, full of mercy and goodness toward all the children separated from her.

Substantial Reforms   The regulations leave no room for equivocation. All of the schemas will be redone in light of the Pope's very explicit instructions, which are in perfect accordance with the wishes expressed by the majority of the Council Fathers during the first session. The experience of the past two months has abundantly shown how the schemas elaborated by the preconciliar commissions depart, both in substance and in form, from the directives given by the Pope. What is needed, then, is not alterations of details but a fundamental revision, especially of the doctrinal schemas.

To make sure that the commissions are faithful to this program, the Pope has created the Coordinating Commission we have already spoken about. It is therefore to be expected that the Council Fathers will have much improved documents in their hands when the second session begins.

It is to be noted that the episcopal conferences are explicitly mentioned in the regulations. This is a *de facto* recognition and an innovation of great importance.

The great majority of the bishops are pleased with these regulations, which take into thorough consideration the experience of the session just ending. Only the minority who were satisfied with the preconciliar documents, in particular those who were directly responsible for them, can feel dissatisfied.

The Church of the Poor

In addition to voting on the amendments to the schema on the liturgy, about which we will have more to say later, the assembly heard twelve interventions on the schema *De Ecclesia* Thursday. Among the more interesting we might note those by Cardinal Lercaro, Archbishop of Bologna, and Melkite Bishop George Hakim of Acre, Israel, which we were able to read in part.

Cardinal Lercaro stated his agreement with the desire previously expressed by Cardinals Montini and Suenens to see the Council confront directly problems of social justice, poverty, overpopulation, peace, and so forth. "Our age," he said, "has a great need to see the evangelical doctrine of poverty developed and implemented. The schema on the Church must therefore clarify the intimate bond that exists between the presence of Christ in the Church and the presence of Christ in the poor."

Bishop Hakim also invoked the theme of the Church of the poor which John XXIII had spoken of in his speech of September 11, a month before the opening of the Council. Then, alluding to the style of the schema, the Bishop of Acre said:

> Let them speak another language to us, the language of our age. We find in this schema a style similar to that of our elementary theology manuals of yesteryear. Let them speak the language of John XXIII and the language of the Gospel to us. Let them show us the Church as a loving mother [*mater amabilis*]. If they presented

papal primacy to us as a service and as the answer to Christ's triple question of love to Peter, such a language would be understood by all Christians.

The Council, Jews, and Freemasons

Bishop Méndez Arceo of Cuernavaca, Mexico, raised the question in the Council of relations with Jews and Freemasons.

Concerning the first, he asked whether "Catholic pastors and faithful show these sons of our common father Abraham a real love, after the example of the Sovereign Pontiff, or whether on the contrary they display a subconscious anti-Semitism."

As for Freemasons, who include "many non-Catholic Christians" in their ranks, the Bishop remarked that they are treated almost exclusively to warnings and recriminations. These Christians could be a powerful force for eliminating any deposit of anti-Christian and anti-Catholic sentiment from Freemasonry if they knew the Catholic Church better.

"The beginnings of Freemasonry were not anti-Christian, and there are certain indications, although weak, that some reconciliation with the Church is possible. Good faith on the part of each and that teacher of life which is history could do much to remedy this deplorable separation. Our merciful mother, the Church, should seek the right path under the guidance of the Holy Spirit."

DECEMBER 8

Closing Ceremonies in Rome:
John XXIII Hopes Vatican II Will End in 1963

The closing ceremony of the first session of Vatican II took place this morning, Saturday, in St. Peter's Basilica. The Pope did not attend the Mass of the Immaculate Conception, which was celebrated by Paolo Cardinal Marella, Prefect of the Sacred Congregation of the Basilica, in the presence of the Council Fathers, members of the diplomatic corps, and delegates from the Protestant confessions.

At the end of the mass, Archbishop Felici, secretary general of the Council, announced that John XXIII would celebrate a requiem mass on December 10 for the bishops who died in Rome during the Council. After a visit from his personal physician, the Pope went to St. Peter's at 11 o'clock. He was greeted by applause as he made his way on foot, and not on the *sedia*, toward the throne installed under Bernini's canopy while the Benedictine choirs sang "*Tu es Petrus.*"

Though his face was drawn from his recent sickness, John XXIII's voice was nonetheless strong and steady as he read a speech in Latin which lasted about fifteen minutes.

"Today's celebration does not bring the work to an end," the Pope said. "Rather, the work that awaits all of us is of the greatest importance, which certainly was not the case during the recesses of previous councils."

Pope John first outlined the three points he intended to consider: the opening of the Council, its continuation, and the fruits expected of it for "spreading faith and holiness and apostolic activity in the Church and in modern society." The first session, the Pope went on, "was like a slow and solemn introduction to the great work of the Council. . . . even [the debates] have a providential place in the triumph of truth, for [they have] shown to all the world the holy liberty that the sons of God enjoy in the Church."

John XXIII continued, ". . . the session which will begin in the month of September of next year . . . will proceed more surely, more steadily, and more rapidly thanks to the experience of these two months of 1962, so that there is hope that the conclusion awaited by all our faithful children may be reached in the glory of the incarnate Son of God in the joy of Christmas in the [fourth] centenary year of the Council of Trent."*

The Church will then have the task of extending the findings of the conciliar assembly into every domain of her life, social questions included, and applying its directives to them with "generous assent and prompt fulfillment" (prayer for the Council).

> This most important phase will see pastors united in a gigantic effort of preaching sound doctrine and applying the laws which they themselves have willed, and for this work the forces of the diocesan and regular clergy, of the congregations of women religious, and the Catholic laity with all its attributes and potential will be called to cooperate, in order that the acts of the Fathers may be seconded by the most joyous and faithful response.

John XXIII characterized these prospects for the future as a "new Pentecost," a "new advance of the kingdom of Christ in the world," a "reaffirmation of the good news of redemption," and a "clarion call of God's kinship, of the brotherhood of men in charity, of the peace promised on earth to men of good will in accordance with God's grace."

* The Council of Trent opened in 1545 and closed in 1563. This is the reason the Holy Father hopes to see Vatican II terminate in 1963.

The Pontiff then wished "Godspeed" to those present, their priests, and their congregations, after recalling the words of Pius IX on the occasion of Vatican I: "Peace, as you know, casts out fear; peace shuts its ears to what is said without real knowledge. May this peace be yours all the days of your life."

The Holy Father then blessed those in attendance and returned to his apartment amid the acclamation of the crowd.

A Council of Dialogue

Nearly 600 Fathers intervened in the general congregations of the first session; over 500 others presented their observations in writing. There were thirty-three votes, twenty-eight of them on amendments to the introduction and first chapter of the schema on the liturgy. Five schemas were discussed: the liturgy, the sources of revelation, the communications media, Christian unity, and *De ecclesia*.

Yet the immediate results of the first session of Vatican II might appear meager. After two months of work, the Council had not finished a single schema. There was much talk but, we might be led to believe, little action.

Yet this first impression is deceptive. Although not apparent, a good deal has been accomplished. Before beginning to build, the Council had to overcome some serious obstacles. And this was gradually done as the Fathers became aware of their nascent strength. The early days were difficult. Directly confronted with a central power accustomed to considering itself untouchable, the bishops might well have hesitated to exercise their dormant sovereignty. But they soon understood that their duty coincided with their rights.

Motivated by their pastoral and missionary concerns, and knowing that they had the Pope's support, they refused to be intimidated. Thus, Scholastic abstractions, intractable rigorism, narrow-mindedness, and unawareness of the outside world had to give way to the meaning of history, that "teacher of life" as Pope John has called it, to progress in religious knowledge, and a desire to enter into contact with "the others." Without this effort to adapt to the real and be present to the world, no *aggiornamento* of the Church—the purpose of the Council—would have been possible. But because of this effort, a new climate came over the assembly, and the non-Catholic observers could see that the Roman Church was becoming a genuine interlocutor.

Vatican II, it is no exaggeration to say, has put an end to the age of the Counter-Reformation and its doctrinal inflexibility. It has brought Catholicism into dialogue with other confessions and with the world at large. This immensely significant achievement was obtained in a few weeks, not without periodic pain, but without serious miscarriage and always with dignity. This was possible because the bishops discovered, beyond secondary differences, common and so to speak contagious aspirations to which no one remained insensitive in the final analysis. The Council eventually manifested a moral unanimity that could not have been hoped for in the beginning.

Everything was done openly. Each said honestly what he thought. Only a council could have brought about such great freedom, which had become rather unusual in a Church where freedom of expression was fraught with personal peril.

Furthermore, Vatican II gave Rome a concrete taste of catholicity. Coming from all over the world, with their different mentalities and their particular needs, the bishops broke the relative isolation of the Curia and proved to themselves that they were in possession of a collegial power. Before the theory of collegiality was elaborated, it was lived in the Council, and not one of its least effects is that it emphasized the role of episcopal conferences, the modern expression of religious cohesion in a nation or on a continent.

The bishops are determined to remain "present" in Rome after the Council in one way or another. They will see to it that the governing body of the Church is truly universal in nature. Everything indicates that a new kind of international government will replace the rusty machinery of a Curia abusively dominated by the Italian element.

Finally, the prestige of the Pope has been enhanced. The bishops are grateful to John XXIII for not imposing his will or interfering with the Council except to nudge it when the need of his authority was clearly felt.

At the end of this session, which was really only a beginning, many hopes were born. What follows will indicate the extent to which they can be fulfilled.

SECOND SESSION

September–December, 1963

Vatican II Prepares
for the Next Session

The Work of the Recess Should Correct Some Shortcomings

Contrary to appearances, the Council has not been interrupted. The nine-month recess separating the end of the first session—December 8, 1962—and the beginning of the second—September 8, 1963—is not an intermission but rather a time of preparation and gestation, in many respects more important than the period which preceded the Council. In his allocution of December 8, John XXIII said, ". . . the work that awaits all of us is of the greatest importance, which certainly was not the case during the recesses of previous councils. . . . Thus, the Council really remains open during the next nine months of suspension of the ecumenical sessions properly so called."

But aside from the schedule of commission meetings, not much of this work is apparent. If conciliar secrecy during the first session became, in Cardinal Feltin's expression, an "open secret," the greatest discretion is being observed presently, for several reasons. First, fewer people are involved. Second, the very nature of the work—fragmentary and scattered—does not easily lend itself to publicity, not to speak of the fact that some modifications are ephemeral since they are subject to later revisions. Finally, silence favors the sometimes delicate negotiations and soothes sensibilities bruised during the trying hours of the first session.

But if the details of what is going on are not known, the climate and general orientations are observable; the spirit and the method are known. The first session set three phenomena in relief: an incompatibility between the doctrinal schemas and the hopes of most of the bishops; the lack of a directive idea about which the subjects under discussion could be grouped; and finally, weaknesses in the regulations which caused the

Council to bog down in repetitions and irrelevant sermonizing. *"Prae-dicatoribus non praedicatur"* (Preachers are not to be preached to), complained one of the presidents, though without much success. Perhaps these three shortcomings are not to be regretted, for they provided the Council with an opportunity to remedy them itself rather than by recourse to unilateral decisions which could have been interpreted as a restriction upon freedom of expression.

The Coordinating Commission In any event, the council now has the spinal column it lacked. Responding to a general desire, the Pope named a Coordinating Commission of cardinals last December and charged it with "determining more clearly the work of the other commissions in the context of the general plan and objectives of the Council." This commission is making satisfactory progress, and its advice seems to be listened to.

The composition of the Commission for the Coordination of the Council's Works reflects the tendencies manifested by the majority of the Council Fathers. Cardinal Cicognani, who as secretary of state is the Pope's right arm, is president. He is energetic and scrupulously careful, and is directly responsible to the Pope. There are five other members of the commission, each in charge of a department: two Italians who are known for their devotion to the Pope, Giovanni Cardinal Urbani, Patriarch of Venice (the apostolate of the laity, the clergy, and the sacraments), and Cardinal Confalonieri of the Curia (seminaries and missions); one Frenchman, Cardinal Liénart (revelation and the deposit of the faith); one German, Cardinal Döpfner, Archbishop of Munich (pastoral action of bishops and religious); and a Belgian, Cardinal Suenens, Archbishop of Malines-Brussels (the Church and world problems, the Blessed Virgin). The three last-named cardinals proved themselves to be both authoritative and liberal during the first session.

Two Theological Conceptions All in all, this commission seems capable of reducing the obstacles that hindered progress in the first session. The schemas, it was said, did not pay enough heed to pastoral and ecumenical needs. Is this because they emphasized doctrine too much? No, and it was sometimes wrongly believed that there was a conflict between the "doctrinal" and "pastoral" viewpoints as though the second were somehow less concerned with orthodoxy.

The real debate is on a higher plane, and involves two theological conceptions both of which were eloquently defended in the assembly. The one emphasizes formulas, the expression of a system; the other emphasizes the mystery of faith which is life, incarnate in the person of Christ. The difficulty consists in trying to maintain the two poles in creative balance without falling into the two opposing errors which philosophers would call "nominalism" and "subjectivism."

Father René Laurentin, an expert at the Council, sees in the following text from Saint Thomas the key to the solution sought: "Faith does not terminate in formulas but in realities." In granting full rights to a theology more centered on the mystery of faith than on textbook formulas which are necessarily imperfect, although necessary to their conception of theology, the Council Fathers would give the Roman Church an image that has been somewhat obscured since the Renaissance and the Counter-Reformation.

Only Seventeen Schemas

The revision of the schema on revelation was done by a mixed commission under the joint direction of Cardinals Ottaviani and Bea. It is reported that the new version abstains from making a rigorous definition of the relation between Scripture and tradition, for the question is still highly controversial. But the present text is said to be worded in such a way that it cannot be interpreted as disowning exegetical research. Pius XII's encyclical *Divino afflante Spiritu*, which Cardinal Bea was partly responsible for, provides a precedent for a more flexible formulation.

Some exegetes are nonetheless still suspect. A collective letter bearing the signatures of nineteen cardinals was sent to the Pope at the end of the first session in order to call his attention to the dangers of certain Catholic publications. Later on five of the cardinals withdrew their names, however, which indicates some irresolution among the opposition as well as a desire not to poison the discussion.

The seventy-odd schemas of the preconciliar period have been reduced to seventeen. This means that the commission has considerably pruned and synthesized the texts by avoiding giving separate treatment to different aspects of the same question. They are said to hold to general themes relevant to the universal Church, leaving the task of treating particular points to special bureaus and to the reform of canon law now in progress. Is there a danger in this that the reforms desired by the majority of the bishops will be buried? To the extent that the Council officially recognizes episcopal conferences, no. This is how the bishops will be given freedom to solve the particular problems of their countries and missions, such as renewing the diaconate.

Finally, Vatican II will have to decide on how much it intends to decentralize. Whatever problem is discussed gets back to the power of bishops, to the question of collegiality that was raised last November in the debate on the liturgy.

A Triptych   The present plan of work is centered on the Church, which is treated either in herself or in her relations with Protestants and unbelievers. All the themes are thus reduced to this triptych.

The commissions will have to take into account the observations made during the first session: the Church is not only a juridical institution, a place where the hierarchy acts; more deeply, she is the mystical body of Christ, the spiritual family of the baptized. The work of the Holy Spirit is not limited to the boundaries of the visible Church. There is, in addition, a "priesthood of the faithful." Other Christians, it goes without saying, are particularly interested in how these complementary conceptions of the Church will be treated. The ecumenical influence of Vatican II will depend partly on how these questions are handled and partly on the attention given to the idea of religious freedom.

The Council Fathers have insisted that the assembly pronounce itself on problems of social and international morality. This large issue will, it is said, form a special schema (number 17) entitled "The Principles and Action of the Church To Promote the Good of Society." Here such themes as respect for the human person, peace and war, nuclear disarmament, aid to underdeveloped countries, overpopulation, and the like will find their place.

Poverty   One subject, however, seems to be missing from the schemas, although it vitally concerned the bishops during the first session: the question of poverty. Cardinal Lercaro had even hoped that "The mystery of Christ in the poor and their evangelization will be central to the doctrinal and legislative work of the Council."

Father René Laurentin thinks that the other objectives of the Council will be attained if this one is.* The psychological importance of exterior signs of poverty in the Church, the anachronism of certain "Seigniorial vestiges" in the episcopacy, and the vanity of honorific titles seem to have been too clear to the Council Fathers for them not to take action in this domain. But just what form it will have is not yet known.

There is finally the problem of modifying the working procedure of the second session. Perhaps there will be fewer plenary sessions (five a week last year) in favor of commission meetings, which could entertain interventions, reserved until now to the general congregations. The Pope has already decided that each new schema will be distributed to the bishops as it appears so that they may make their observations and sug-

* René Laurentin, *Bilan de la première Session*, Paris, Éditions du Seuil, 1963.

gestions known, undoubtedly through their episcopal conferences. The first series of texts is expected to be mailed as early as April. Much precious time will thus be saved when the Council reconvenes in what Pope John hopes will be the last session.

Reform of Church Government:
Paul VI Asks Curia To Relinquish Certain Powers

Will Paul VI be a reforming pope? Those who are wondering now have their answer. The reform of the Curia, as Paul announced it on Saturday, September 21, is certainly one of the most important, necessary, and delicate tasks confronting the contemporary Church. It was no accident that the Pope chose the eve of the Council to speak his mind on this problem.

The last reform of the Curia goes back to 1588. One scarcely knows whether to express surprise or admiration that this body has functioned without a major overhaul for some four centuries of social and political upheavals.

The question of reforming the Curia has come up frequently in the last few years. Pius XII thought about it but did not actually do anything. He opted, as Father Emile Legault has written, to "short-circuit" the Curia by making as many decisions as possible himself. John XXIII was convinced of the necessity of reorganizing the government of the Church, but he first of all sought the support of the episcopacy, and this was one of the reasons he convoked the Council. He died without realizing this goal.

More than other departments, the "Supreme" Sacred Congregation of the Holy Office is in need of radical reform. It has become intolerable to Catholics, not because an office for the protection of doctrinal purity exists but because its methods are contrary to international law (condemnation without appeal, without warning or right of defense; official silence about motives, and so forth). The Index is totally anachronistic; sometimes it even achieves results contrary to its purpose. (Had not the Holy Office interfered, Father Jean Steinmann's *Life of Jesus*, for example, would have had less notoriety and therefore fewer readers.)

"Firm and Open" Obedience   Paul VI's proposals are highly instructive. Each word, carefully thought out, is significant. To a Curia which is afraid of the Council, which bristles under the least criticism and tends to show contempt for some "reforming" bishops, the Pope said: "We

must accept the criticisms that surround us, with humility, with reflection, and even with gratitude. Rome has no need to defend herself by turning a deaf ear to suggestions that come to her from honest voices, especially if these voices are those of friends and of brothers."

He preceded these words with the comment, "The Curia's concern was such as to show at times a certain stupor and apprehension about such an unexpected and sudden conciliar convocation and about the gravity of the problems that it would raise." He recalled that the Council was the will of John XXIII, to whom he applied the scriptural words concerning John the Baptist, and then stressed the fact that

> . . . whatever the origins of the Council's convocation, it is the Pope who proclaimed it, the Vicar of Christ. . . . If ever . . . conformity of minds with what the Pope commands or desires must be rigorously univocal on the part of the Roman Curia, if it must be its law and its pride, this is the moment to give it firm and open profession.

Paul VI further exhorted the Curia never to forget that its behavior should be an example for the Church at large, urging it to spurn ambition and to respect the bishops:

> The Roman Curia . . . is a living organ, faithful and docile, of the head of the Church—an organ engrossed in the serious responsibilities of its function and full of reverence and solicitude toward those prelates whom "the Holy Spirit has placed as bishops to rule the Church of God" (Acts 20:28).
>
> Therefore, let the Roman Curia not be a pretentious and apathetic bureaucracy, as some wrongly judge it, merely legalistic and ritualistic, or a jousting field of hidden ambitions and intractable antagonisms, as others accuse it of being. But let it be a true community of faith and charity, of prayer and action, of the Pope's brothers and sons who do everything, each with respect for the competence of the other and with a sense of collaboration in serving him in his work for the brothers and sons of the universal Church and of the entire world.

Neither "Jealous" Nor "Miserly"   The Pope went on to ask the Curia to relinquish certain prerogatives in favor of the bishops:

> The Roman Curia will not be jealous of the temporal prerogatives of former times, of exterior forms no longer suitable for the expression of high religious meanings. Nor will it be miserly of its faculties which the episcopacy, without damaging general ecclesias-

tical order, can today exercise better by itself and locally. Nor will economic purposes and advantages ever carry weight in organs of the Holy See if that is not required by good ecclesiastical order and by the salvation of souls.

The Pope emphasized that the bishops are already part of the Curia, and added:

We shall say more: should the Ecumenical Council evince a desire of seeing some representatives of the episcopacy, particularly among prelates who direct a diocese, associated in a certain way and for certain questions, in conformity with the Church's doctrine and canon law, with the supreme head of the Church in the study and responsibility of ecclesiastical government, the Curia will surely not oppose it.

This remark alludes to a revolutionary project in which the Pope would associate a certain number of residential bishops with the central government of the Church on a permanent basis. This reform would be of great ecumenical importance since the Protestants, Anglicans, and especially the Orthodox have never approved of the virtually monarchical nature of government in the Roman Church.

Pope Paul indicated the spirit and ways in which the projected reform would be undertaken:

They will certainly be weighed. They will be drawn up according to venerable and reasonable traditions on the one hand, and according to the needs of the times on the other. They certainly will be functional and beneficial, because they will have no other purpose than that of dropping what is ephemeral and superfluous in the forms and in the norms that regulate the Roman Curia, and of putting into effect what is vital and serviceable for its efficient and proper functioning. They will be formulated and propagated by the Curia itself.

Therefore, the Roman Curia will not be afraid of being recruited with a broader supernational vision, or of being educated with a more ecumenical preparation. Did not Saint Bernard say, even in his time, "Why not choose from the whole world those who one day will have to judge the whole world?"?

This weighty speech, which was both subtle and strong, touched on the principal points of curial reform as desired by the residential bishops. It was a capital gain that these things should have been said by the Pope a few days before the opening of the second session.

Vatican II Gets Its Second Wind

The "Novitiate" of the Council   The second session of Vatican II will commence on September 29. It will end on December 4, without having exhausted the agenda of the Council. A third session is thus expected in 1964.

There are two reasons that the beginning of the second session arouses sharp interest. The first session had taken—the word is not too strong— a revolutionary turn. An internal and pacific revolution, to be sure, but a revolution nonetheless if one thinks of the taboos that were overcome and the new direction taken, to the great relief of the progressive wing in the Roman Church. An immense hope was sown in the ranks of Christianity, including the non-Catholic churches. Yet this session was only a preamble, a beginning, a "novitiate," as John XXIII put it. Almost no positive decisions were taken.

A second reason is the death of Pope John. The Council is now in the hands of Paul VI, whose basic thinking is still little known. And since the Pope is the head of the Council, his positions will have a pronounced effect on the direction Vatican II takes.

The Christian world is in a state of expectation. Some are afraid: they think that the second session will fall short of the standards set by the first, and that the bishops will enjoy less freedom of expression. Others are confident that the impetus given by John XXIII will continue to inspire the Fathers.

The first session ended in December, 1962, in a general atmosphere of euphoria. Many bishops said they had not expected the Council to get off to such a good start. They arrived skeptical and constrained; they left confident and relaxed. Why?

The preparation for the Council had misled them. Asked by John XXIII three years earlier to send in their *desiderata*, they had expressed their complaints in total frankness. But with few exceptions, the first schemas prepared by the different preparatory commissions hardly took their opinions into account. The bishops therefore felt uneasy; they had every intention of saying so but were by no means sure of being understood. One of them coined an expression during the first session that has become famous: "I do not fear Peter but his bureaucrats," for which read: the Curia.

But the bishops soon got up their courage. Cardinal Lienart was the first to take the plunge, and the Fathers realized that only the first step was hard. Moreover, they knew they were morally supported by John

XXIII, who, after all, had invited them to come help him reform the Church.

Operation Freedom   Thus, the Council was an "operation freedom," and the outside world soon became aware of this, much to its surprise, since it was used to looking upon the Church as an absolute monarchy. One illusion after another was punctured. Seen at close range, the integralists of the Curia, however highly placed they were, were much less redoubtable than from afar. Their blundering and scheming worked against them in the end. The bishops did not forget John's opening remarks: "In the daily exercise of our pastoral office, we sometimes have to listen, much to our regret, to voices of persons who, though burning with zeal, are not endowed with too much sense of discretion or measure. . . . We feel we must disagree with those prophets of gloom. . . ." Rarely had a pope ever used such language on so solemn an occasion.

That is why the first session was indeed a work of demolition, as it has been called. Except for the schema on the liturgy, which met with the approval of the majority, the doctrinal schemas were denounced, criticized, or rejected one by one. This naturally took time and was attended by some pain. There were days of impatience, of vexation, even of anger. Finally peace was re-established owing to John XXIII's intervention.

At the end of a few weeks, the bishops known as "progressives," who had felt themselves an isolated minority in the Church, saw that the majority of the Council was with them. This was one of the great discoveries of the session: the Church of the bishops, that is, of pastors who exercise their ministry in direct contact with the world, triumphed over the Church of the bureaucrats and legalists. The salt of the Gospel proved a cure for religious sclerosis. The desire to progress and bring the Church up to date conquered. The phrase, moreover, was John-XXIII's: hadn't he proposed *aggiornamento* as the aim of the Council?

What is surprising is that this renewal did not take place behind closed doors. When the *extra omnes* was pronounced at the beginning of each session, the observers invited by the Pope's express will remained. Those who had once been called-heretics and schismatics now became *"carissimi observatores"* or "brothers in baptism." History will one day spell out the exceptional value of the presence of these observers within the walls of St. Peter's. For eight weeks they witnessed the spectacle of the Roman Church examining her conscience. Mountains of prejudice disappeared; rays of sympathy and hope broke through. Reciprocally, the Fathers could not forget that in the seats facing the cardinals were non-Catholic Christians listening to them and judging them. The cause of ecumenism which had been bogged down so long took a prodigious leap forward.

We might make the following assessment of the first session:

1. A considerable psychological "deblocking" has taken place within the Church. Blood has begun to flow once again between the head and the members of the episcopacy. "A breath of fresh air," in John XXIII's words, has entered the Vatican.

2. The bishops have become aware once again of their rights and powers. They feel responsible for the whole Church and not only for their dioceses. Before being formulated in a document, episcopal collegiality was lived.

3. A less important psychological "deblocking" has taken place outside the Church. Non-Catholic Christians and unbelievers have seen that the Roman Church is really interested in the problems of the outside world and that she has something to say about them. The Catholic ghetto is now only a bad memory.

From the purely doctrinal and religious point of view, these important results are to be noted:

1. The chapter of the *Syllabus* (1864 . . . already a century) and anti-modernism has ended. The Roman Church, to the certain knowledge of all, looks with fraternal affection upon a world jealous of its intellectual liberty and proud of its technology.

2. Scientific exegesis has been officially defended against its detractors. The Pontifical Biblical Institute breathed a sigh of relief.

3. The Church is defining herself less juridically and authoritatively and more in terms of spirituality and service; there is less "triumphalism" and more humility.

4. The era of the Counter-Reformation has ended. The basic interests of Protestantism have been taken seriously: emphasis on Scripture, the primacy of conscience and religious liberty, a return to the sources of the primitive Church, the universal priesthood of the faithful, and so forth. Official theology has lost its defensive and polemical character.

At the same time, the bishops have called the Council's attention to the problems of our age: the underdeveloped countries, equal distribution of wealth, overpopulation, peace, and other questions. The progress in a few weeks was greater than in the past several decades. This was possible as a result of John XXIII's pastoral intuitions and the underground work—which was long suspect, but is now approved—of innumerable pioneering "transalpinists." This is the name, shaded with fear and opprobrium, that those in Rome sometimes affix to certain energetic Catholics—whether bishops or theologians—who live outside of Italy.

The importance of the first session is obvious. But at the end of this period of rejuvenation, suspense was still the order of the day. The fruit of so much effort must now be embodied in formal documents. This was one of the last concerns of John XXIII.

The Council on Location

Before closing the first session of the Council, John XXIII published an important directive concerning the interval. His clear and precise objective was to keep the next session free of the wasteful discussions that had mired the first. If the Council was to find its axis, the schemas would have to be entirely reworked, abridged, and synthesized in the direction indicated by the majority of bishops. To this end a bold step was taken: the creation of the Coordinating Commission, whose duty it would be to supervise the work of the conciliar commissions and see to it that the revised texts correspond with the stated aims of the Council. This was an official admission that until then they had not. This move naturally provoked various reactions among the integralists, who had hoped to regain the upper hand by the time the second session opened.

In his directive, John repeated that ". . . the whole world expects a step forward toward a doctrinal penetration and a formation of consciences in faithful and perfect conformity with the authentic doctrine. . . ." He could scarcely have been more precise.

To dissipate any remaining uncertainty, he said in his closing speech, "Rather, the work that awaits all of us is of the greatest importance, which certainly was not the case during the recesses of previous councils. . . . The debates of the first session have shown to all the world the holy liberty that the sons of God enjoy in the Church."

Inspired by the controlling organism (which includes such figures as Cardinals Liénart, Döpfner, and Suenens), the commissions went to work. We know today that their time was not wasted and that they were in the main faithful to the directives of the Pope.

Enter Paul VI   Meanwhile, John XXIII has died. His *Pacem in Terris*, completed so shortly before his death, was addressed to all men of good will, and constitutes a precious example for the next conciliar meetings. Scarcely had Pope John breathed his last than those hostile to the

Council let it be understood that the next pope would be well inspired to adjourn the second session. The official speech *"De eligendo pontifice,"* given in St. Peter's on the eve of the conclave by Monsignor Tondini, said as much: "It will be the new pope's responsibility to judge whether or not the problems and studies [of the council] and especially spiritual dispositions have reached a maturity that would produce the results hoped for by the sanest part of mankind."

But Paul VI had scarcely been nominated when he made it clear that the second session would open in September, only two weeks after the date set by his predecessor. There was now no room for doubt: the former Archbishop of Milan was following in the footsteps of John XXIII. His coronation speech was perfectly clear in this respect. Nonetheless, Paul's personality is very different from that of the deceased Pope. The one was serene, spontaneous, pragmatic; the other is anxious, reserved, methodical. The Council will feel the difference.

To date the bishops have received fourteen of the seventeen schemas which are on the agenda of Vatican II. Seventeen instead of the original seventy! The hatchet commission has done its work well, and it was needed. The first schemas were verbose, "heterogeneous"— the word used by Paul VI—and the more undesirable in that they were not in keeping with the central theme of the Council.

Let us take an example. One of the 1962 documents, entitled "On the Deposit of the Faith," was presented as a kind of *Syllabus* or catalogue of condemned errors in ten sections. The English Jesuit George Tyrrel, the French philosopher Henri Duméry, and Teilhard de Chardin were refuted. There is no equivalent of that schema in the present list. It was scuttled and sent to the archives.

The fourteen schemas now completed run to 550 pages. The Latin text is dense, and it is reported that "even a good Latinist" must have frequent recourse to a dictionary to read it. The central schema *De Ecclesia* consists in two sections totaling ninety pages. It takes up directly where Vatican I left off. There are passages of the highest importance on "episcopal collegiality," which is also treated in another schema on bishops in which the emphasis is on the internationalization of curial departments and on the role of episcopal conferences. The Pope's recent speech on the reform of the Curia will lend extra weight to the bishops' criticisms and suggestions on points essential for the future of the Roman Church and the progress of ecumenism.

The contents of the schemas are theoretically secret, as usual, and only as the sessions progress will we know them in more detail. But it is common knowledge that most of these documents are satisfactory. In particular, attention is called to the radical change in tone, substance, and form from the preceding schemas. The reformists, it would seem, have won the day.

However, two or three schemas appear to be quite unsatisfactory, for example the one on seminary formation and, to some extent, the one on Catholic schools. The theology of the priesthood leaves something to be desired, and this is particularly important because the formation of a ministry more adapted to contemporary needs will depend upon it.

In any event, Vatican II will be the council of the episcopacy and the laity, as Vatican I was the council of the papacy. Developing its ecclesial theory, Rome is in the process of gaining a clearer understanding of the role of the apostolic college, the infallibility of the Church as a whole, and, finally, the rights of the laity. There will apparently be a special schema on the last. The document has been the object of special consideration. In it will be found the first elements of a "theology of the laity," the absence of which has been sorely felt.

Victory for the Ecumenists   The schema on ecumenism is undoubtedly one of the best. It will be a landmark in the history of the Church because of its entirely new emphasis on the positive. The writers took to heart John XXIII's advice to speak of what unites and not of what divides. It is a good method but was never thought of before. Non-Catholics are naturally looking forward to the discussion of this text, which constitutes one of the high points of the Council.

Vatican II is at bottom a council for the union of the Churches. To ignore this or regard it with undue skepticism would be contrary to John XXIII's primary inspiration as well as the legitimate hope of millions of the faithful.

The Council will not be under the direction of a "papal legate" as has been rumored by those hostile to full freedom for the Fathers. Four "moderators" have been named: Gregorio Cardinal Agagianian and Cardinals Suenens, Lercaro, and Döpfner. The last three are widely known for their reformist zeal. They will supervise the debates (interventions must be submitted in writing beforehand). As specified in the Latin text, the presidents, properly speaking, will remain as *tutores legis*.

The agenda is not yet known. We do know, however, that the session will begin with a discussion of the schema on the Church, and this will occupy the Fathers for the first few weeks. The immediate program also provides for voting on the schema on the liturgy; only the preface of this was approved in 1962.

And Poverty?   Schema 17 on the Church and the modern world (which Cardinal Suenens worked on) is now practically completed. It will be distributed to the Fathers upon their arrival in Rome but will perhaps not be examined during this session. This schema will have great repercussions for it treats of conjugal morality, church-state relations, religious liberty, war, and other sensitive subjects.

One question remains: will the theme of poverty, called for insistently notably by bishops of Latin America, France, Belgium, and the underdeveloped countries, find a place on the agenda? When the Council reconvenes, the bishops will undoubtedly do what they can to keep this issue alive. The laity, both Catholic and non-Catholic, would be very puzzled indeed if the Council failed to give the Church, which is still weighed down with medieval pomp and unnecessary wealth, an image more in conformity with evangelical simplicity. If the Vatican and the nuncios in certain countries first set the example of real poverty, the psychological consequences could be considerable.

What will the atmosphere of the second session be like? It will probably be as animated as the first, but for different reasons. In 1962 the reforming bishops claimed most of the attention. This time the conservative bishops will react with equal vigor. They were scarcely listened to during the first session and will make every effort to stem the progressive tide. They are sincerely fearful that the renewal of the Church will take on a demagogic air and that the effort at union of the Churches is merely a pretext to flirt with heresy. It will fall to the reformist bishops to show that these fears have no foundation in fact and that doctrinal orthodoxy is sacred to them as well.

The Integralists on the Alert   The integralists did not disarm during the interval, as is shown by the fact that on May 25 a group of experts (they signed themselves *"Periti qui Romae degunt"*) sent a kind of doctrinal note to the Fathers which attacked willy-nilly the "new theology," certain modern exegetes, Teilhard de Chardin (who was accused of "monism properly speaking"), Bigo for his work on "progressivism," Schlier, *Formgeschichte*, and so forth.

This kind of anonymous pamphlet hardly impresses well-informed bishops, but it indicates the persistence of an attitude. This is not the first time, nor will it be the last, that the integralists have acted in the shadows, spread false rumors, or resorted to the bugbear of schism. John XXIII defined them well when he said they have "learned nothing from history, the mistress of life."

These sidelights on "the great conciliar adventure," as one cardinal has called it, ought not detract from its final meaning. For beyond the discussions, however painful they may be at times, emerges the profile of faith and the Church's fidelity to her founder through the vicissitudes of history. This is what in the final analysis gives the Council its serious-ness and its spirituality. Conformity with the will of Christ preoccupies all the Fathers, whatever their personal tendencies or disagreements over means. A council is not a parliamentary chamber. It is a liturgical act, a celebration of faith. There is only one party: the heirs of the Good News.

SEPTEMBER, 1963

As the Second Session Opens:
Paul VI Asks Forgiveness
for Faults Contributing to the Separation of Churches

The thirty-seventh general congregation of Vatican II—and the first of the second session—was held in St. Peter's this morning, Monday, under the presidency of Cardinal Tisserant. After the mass, the Gospel was solemnly enthroned, a manuscript of incredible beauty dating from the sixteenth century. The presence of this book, which in some sense presides over all the sessions, and the homage given it indicate the primacy which the Roman Church attaches to Scripture.

It was Paul VI's explicit will that the opening ceremonies on Sunday be kept to a minimum. There were no outside processions or special prayers. In this way the Pope wished to emphasize that the second session was simply the continuation of the first; it was the same council, Vatican II.

In fact, the memory of John XXIII dominated the ceremony. Everyone present remembered the heavy features, already marked with the paleness of his illness and yet resolute and optimistic, of him who called himself "a prisoner of luxury."

Today the same cardinals and bishops filed into the seats in St. Peter's. But it was a different pope, and despite Paul's deliberate intention to continue in the line of his predecessor, certain differences are apparent. He has a less sanguine view of today's world, for example. In his address yesterday, he not only drew attention to the empty seats ("Where are our brethren from the nations where the Church is opposed?") but also spoke of other "bitter" subjects, as well as the "crushing sadness of so many other evils" throughout the world.

"Atheism," he said, "is pervading part of the human race. . . . While the light of the science of God and consequently over man's true science of nature is increasing, darkness is spreading over the science of God and consequently over man's true science." The love of Christ "sustains us now because, as we turn our view to the scene of contemporary human life, we ought to be frightened rather than comforted, saddened rather than gladdened. . . ."

But such passages were few enough in a speech that lasted forty-five minutes and made a very strong impression. The allocution, which the Pope himself compared with an encyclical and which he considers to be the "prelude" not only to the second session but to his pontificate as well, has great depth. It is marked by the graceful language and habitually lofty views of a pope who is deeply spiritual, widely read, incisively intelligent.

Some quotations from this forceful speech will help shed light on the present climate in the Church and the Council.

On several occasions Paul VI touched on his conception of the pontifical function. He used such expressions as "the smallest," "the least in merit," "the servant of the servants of God"; he declared that the time had come "to develop the doctrine regarding the episcopate, its function, and its relationship with Peter."

Thus, humility on the one hand and, on the other, a desire to decentralize authority. The Pope also stressed the *absolute* primacy of Christ, "the unique mediator and savior of the world."

Non-Catholic observers appreciated these remarks and found them very much in the spirit of several meetings of the World Council of Churches. "Let no other light be shed on this council than Christ, the light of the world," the Pope said. "Let no other truth attract our interest than the words of the Lord, our only master!"

Necessary Reforms   The Pope was extremely clear about the necessity of reform in the Church. The Church, he said, looks "upon Christ to discern in him her true likeness; if in doing so she were to discover some shadow, some defect, . . . what should be her instinctive, courageous reaction? The answer is clear: her primary duty would be to reform, correct, and conform herself with her divine model."

Then the Pope balanced this statement with another, "that the Catholic Church of today [cannot] be accused of substantial infidelity to the mind of her divine founder."

Concerning the separated brethren and the union of the Churches, Paul VI did not hesitate to speak of "the possibility of multiplicity in the unity of the Church," or of the faults at the origin of the separation of the Churches:

> If we are in any way to blame for that separation, we humbly beg God's forgiveness and ask pardon too of our brethren who feel themselves to have been injured by us. For our part, we willingly forgive the injuries which the Catholic Church has suffered, and forget the grief endured during the long series of dissensions and separations. May the heavenly Father deign to hear our prayers and grant us true brotherly peace.

This passage is considered one of the most important in the whole speech. It will in all probability have profound psychological repercussions among Protestants, who will appreciate the solemn character of this declaration. Added to a similar speech by John XXIII, which was delivered, however, to a much smaller audience, it definitively marks the end of any misconception that the Catholic Church feels no blame for religious disunity.

Homage to Non-Christian Religions Paul VI paid explicit homage to "the treasures of truth and of genuine spirituality" which the separated brethren "seek sincerely to make known and to honor." He expressed himself concisely: ". . . we do not wish to make of our faith an occasion for polemics."

The Pope reaffirmed the intention of the Council to "build a bridge toward the contemporary world." Speaking of the message to the world during the first session, he said it was "a singular and remarkable gesture. . . . It could be said that the prophetic gift of holy Church had suddenly burst into expression." Then the Pope added, "Let the world know this: the Church looks at the world with profound understanding, with sincere admiration, and with the sincere intention not of conquering it but of serving it, not of despising it but of appreciating it, not of condemning it but of strengthening and saving it."

Urging the leaders of nations to work for peace and justice, he told them, "You can make of humanity a single city. God be with you!" The Pope then turned his attention, and this was something truly exceptional, to the non-Christian religions, and affirmed that "the Catholic Church . . . esteems what they contain of truth and goodness and humanity."

The whole of this speech incontestably reflects an openness of spirit that will profoundly influence the Council. With Paul VI, the successor of John XXIII, the Roman Church, after a long period of absenteeism, is now in the first ranks of the ecumenical battle. Thanks to the secretariat for relations with non-Christian religions which will soon be created, Rome will become a unique crossroad in the world. The word *catholic* is regaining its true etymological meaning.

Four Aims of the Council
Outlined by the Pope

Following are some important extracts from Pope Paul's opening speech. Paying homage to the memory of John XXIII, he said:

> Oh, dear and venerated Pope John, may gratitude and praise be rendered to you for having resolved—doubtless under divine inspiration—to convoke this council in order to open to the Church new horizons, and to tap the fresh spring water of the doctrine and grace of Christ our Lord and let it flow over the earth.
>
> . . . As if by divining heavenly counsels and penetrating into the dark and tormented needs of the modern age, you have gathered the broken thread of the First Vatican Council, and by that very fact you have banished the fear wrongly deduced from that council, as if the supreme powers conferred by Christ on the Roman pontiff to govern and vivify the Church were sufficient, without the assistance of ecumenical councils.

Four Objectives

> From what point, dear brethren, do we set out? Bearing in mind that we should pay attention rather to the divine directives than to the practical indications referred to above, what is the road we intend to follow? What is the goal we propose to ourselves? We have a goal which belongs to the realm of earthly history in that it concerns the time and mode of our present life, but we do not lose sight of the supreme and final end which, we know, must be the end of our pilgrimage.
>
> These three very simple and at the same time very important questions have, as we well know, only one answer: that here and at this very hour we should proclaim Christ to ourselves and to the world around us; Christ our beginning, Christ our life and our guide, Christ our hope and our end. . . .
>
> If we place before our minds, venerable brethren, this sovereign conception that Christ is our founder, our head, invisible but real, and that we receive everything from him so as to constitute together with him that "full Christ" whom Saint Augustine speaks about and

who pervades the entire theology of the Church, then we shall be able to understand better the main objectives of this council.

For reasons of brevity and better understanding, we enumerate here those objectives in four points: the knowledge or, if you prefer, the awareness of the Church; its reform; the bringing together of all Christians in unity; and the dialogue of the Church with the contemporary world.

The Church's Awareness

There can be no doubt whatever of the Church's desire, need, and duty to give a more thorough definition of herself. . . .

The First Vatican Council treated of the subject, and many external influences have caused it to receive attention from students, both within the Church and without. Among these influences are the intensification of social life in temporal matters, the development of communications, and the need to judge the various Christian denominations according to the true and univocal conception found in divine revelation. . . .

The time has now come, we believe, when the truth regarding the Church of Christ should be examined, coordinated, and expressed. The expression should not perhaps take the form of a solemn dogmatic definition, but of declarations making known, by means of the Church's magisterium, in a more explicit and authoritative form, what the Church considers herself to be. . . .

For this reason, the principal concern of the session of the Council will be to examine the intimate nature of the Church and to express in human language, as far as is possible, a definition which will best reveal the Church's real, fundamental constitution and manifest its manifold mission of salvation. The theological doctrine has the possibility of magnificent developments which merit the attentive consideration of our separated brethren also, and which we ardently hope may make the path toward common agreement easier.

First among the various questions that this consideration will raise, venerable brothers, is one which affects all of you as bishops of the Church of God. We have no hesitation in saying that we look forward with great expectations and confidence to this discussion, which, taking for granted the dogmatic declarations of the First Vatican Council regarding the Roman pontiff, will go on to develop the doctrine regarding the episcopate, its function, and its relationship with Peter.

For us personally it will provide doctrinal and practical standards by which our apostolic office, endowed though it is by Christ
with the fullness and sufficiency of power, may receive more help
and support, in ways to be determined, from a more effective and
responsible collaboration with our beloved and venerable brothers
in the episcopate.

The Renewal of the Church

. . . another chief subject of the Council's deliberations . . . [is]
the renewal of the Church.

. . . the Council is to be a new spring, a reawakening of the
mighty spiritual and moral energies which at present lie dormant.
The Council is evidence of a determination to bring about a rejuvenation both of the interior forces of the Church and of the
regulations by which her canonical structure and liturgical forms
are governed. The Council is striving, that is, to enhance in the
Church the beauty of perfection and holiness which imitation of
Christ and mystical union with him in the Holy Spirit can alone
confer.

Yes, the Council aims at renewal. Note well, however, that in
saying and desiring this, we do not imply that the Catholic Church
of today can be accused of substantial infidelity to the mind of her
divine founder. Rather it is the deeper realization of her substantial
faithfulness that fills her with gratitude and humility and inspires
her with the courage to correct those imperfections which are proper
to human weakness.

The reform at which the Council aims is therefore not a reversal
of the Church's present way of life or a rupture with what is essential and worthy of veneration in her tradition. It is rather an honoring
of tradition by stripping it of what is unworthy or defective so that
it may be rendered firm and fruitful. . . .

The first requirement of this reform will certainly be a more
diligent study and a more intensive proclamation of the word of
God. Upon this foundation an education of charity will be built
up, for we must give the place of honor to charity and strive to
construct the *Ecclesia caritatis* if we would have a Church capable
of renewing herself and renewing the world around her; there indeed
is a tremendous undertaking.

Charity must be fostered because it is the chief and root of the
other Christian virtues: humility, poverty, religion, the spirit of

sacrifice, fearless truth, love of justice, and every other force by
which the new man acts.

Unity of Christians

The Council has a third object, one which may be called its
spiritual drama. This too was put before us by Pope John XXIII. It
concerns "the other Christians"—those who believe in Christ but
whom we have not the happiness of numbering among ourselves
in the perfect unity of Christ, which only the Catholic Church can
offer them.

This unity, objectively speaking, should be theirs by baptism.
It is something which, virtually at least, they already desire. For
recent movements, at present in full development in bodies of Christians separated from us, show clearly two things. The first is that
the Church of Christ is one alone and therefore must be unique. The
second is that this mystical and visible union cannot be attained
except in identity of faith and by participation in the same sacraments and in the organic harmony of a single ecclesiastical control,
even though this allows for a great variety of verbal expressions,
movements, lawful institutions, and preference with regard to modes
of acting.

There can be no doubt about the attitude of the Council with
regard to the great numbers of the separated brethren and of the
possibility of multiplicity in the unity of the Church. This too is
one of the characteristics of the Council. . . .

It is a council, therefore, of invitation, of expectation, of confidence, looking forward toward a more widespread, more fraternal
participation in its authentic ecumenicity.

We speak now to the representatives of the Christian denominations separated from the Catholic Church, who have nevertheless
been invited to take part as observers in this solemn assembly. We
greet them from our heart. We thank them for their participation.
We transmit through them our message—as father and brother—
to the venerable Christian communities they represent.

Our voice trembles and our heart beats the faster both because
of the inexpressible consolation and reasonable hope that their presence stirs up within us, and because of the deep sadness we feel at
their prolonged separation.

If we are in any way to blame for that separation, we humbly
beg God's forgiveness and ask pardon too of our brethren who feel
themselves to have been injured by us. For our part, we willingly
forgive the injuries which the Catholic Church has suffered, and for-

get the grief endured during the long series of dissensions and separations. May the heavenly Father deign to hear our prayers and grant us true brotherly peace.

We are aware that serious and complicated questions remain to be studied, treated, and resolved. We would wish that this could be done immediately on account of the love of Christ that "urges us on." But we also realize that these problems require many conditions before satisfactory solutions can be reached—conditions which are as yet premature. Hence we are not afraid to await patiently the blessed hour of perfect reconciliation. . . .

Our manner of speaking toward them is friendly, completely sincere and loyal. We lay no snares. We are not motivated by temporal interests. We owe our faith—which we believe to be divine— the most candid and firm attachment.

But at the same time we are convinced that this does not constitute an obstacle to the desired understanding with our separated brethren, precisely because it is the truth of the Lord and therefore the principle of union, not of distinction or separation. At any rate, we do not wish to make of our faith an occasion for polemics.

Second, we look with reverence upon the true religious patrimony we share in common, which has been preserved and in part even well developed among our separated brethren. We are pleased to note the study made by those who seek sincerely to make known and to honor the treasures of truth and of genuine spirituality, in order to improve our relations with them.

We hope that just as they are desirous to know more about our history and our religious life, so also they would wish to make a closer study of our doctrine and its logical derivation from the deposit of divine revelation.

Finally we wish to say that, aware of the enormous difficulties still in the way of the desired union, we humbly put our trust in God. We shall continue to pray. We shall try to give better proof of our efforts of charity. And should historical reality tend to weaken our hopes, we shall try to recall the comforting words of Christ: "Things that are impossible with men are possible with God" (Luke 18:27).

Dialogue with the Contemporary World

Finally, the Council will build a bridge toward the contemporary world. A singular phenomenon: while the Church seeks to revive her interior life in the Spirit of the Lord—thus distinguishing and separating herself from secular society in which she exists—

at the same time she is signalized as the lifegiving ferment and the instrument of the salvation of the world, both revealing and strengthening her missionary vocation, which is to treat mankind, in whatever condition it may be, as the object of her dedicated mission of communicating the teachings of the Gospels.

. . . And as Peter on the day of Pentecost felt the impulse at once to raise his voice and to speak to the people, so you also have unexpectedly determined to treat no longer of your own limited affairs but rather those of the world, no longer to conduct a dialogue among yourselves but rather to open one with the world.

This means, venerable brethren, that the present Council is characterized by love, by the most comprehensive and compelling love, by a love which thinks of others even before it thinks of itself —by the universal love of Christ.

This love sustains us now because, as we turn our view to the scene of contemporary human life, we ought to be frightened rather than comforted, saddened rather than gladdened, anxious for defense and condemnation rather than for trust and friendship.

We ought to be realists, not hiding the savagery that from many areas reaches even into this universal synod. Can we be blind and not notice that many seats in this assembly are vacant? Where are our brethren from the nations where the Church is opposed? In what conditions does religion exist in these territories?

At such a reminder our thoughts are aggrieved because of what we know and even more because of what we cannot know about our sacred hierarchy, our men and women religious, our countless children subjected to fear, to persecutions, to privations, to oppression, because of their loyalty to Christ and to the Church.

How sad we are before such sufferings! How painful it is to see that in certain countries religious liberty, like other fundamental rights of man, is being crushed by principles and methods of political, racial, or antireligious intolerance! It causes us deep sorrow to have to observe that in the world there are still so many acts of injustice against goodness and the free profession of one's religious faith.

But rather than in bitter words, our lament must be expressed as a frank and human exhortation to all who may be responsible for these evils to put aside with a noble heart their unjustified hostility toward the Catholic religion, whose followers ought to be considered neither as enemies nor as disloyal citizens but rather as upright and hard-working members of the civil society to which they belong.

Finally, to the Catholics who are suffering for their faith we send, also on this occasion, our affectionate greetings, and for them we invoke special divine assistance.

Nor does our sorrow end here. The spectacle of the world fills us with crushing sadness because of so many other evils. Atheism is pervading part of the human race and is bringing in its wake the derangement of the intellectual, moral, and social order, the true notion of which the world is losing. While the light of the science of God and consequently over man's true science of nature is increasing, darkness is spreading over the science of God and consequently over man's true science. While progress is perfecting in a wondrous way every kind of instrument that man uses, his heart is declining toward emptiness, sadness, and despair.

We would have a hundred things to say on these complicated and, for many reasons, sad conditions of modern man. But not now. Now, as we were saying, love is filling our heart and the heart of the Church assembled in council.

We look upon our times and upon their varied and contrasting manifestations with immense tenderness and with an immense desire to offer to men of today the message of friendship, of salvation, and of hope which Christ has brought into the world. "For God did not send his Son into the world in order to judge the world, but that the world might be saved through him" (John 3:17).

Let the world know this: the Church looks at the world with profound understanding, with sincere admiration, and with the sincere intention not of conquering it but of serving it, not of despising it but of appreciating it, not of condemning it but of strengthening and saving it.

From the window of the Council, opened wide on the world, the Church looks toward some categories of persons with particular solicitude: she looks toward the poor, the needy, the afflicted, the hungry, the suffering and sorrowing.

Encouragement for Leaders of Nations

She looks toward men of culture and learning, scientists, artists. For these also she has great esteem and a great desire to receive the fruit of their experience, to strengthen their intellectual life, to defend their liberty, to provide a space in which their troubled spirits can expand joyously within the luminous sphere of the divine word and divine grace.

She looks toward the workers, toward the dignity of their person and their labors, toward the legitimacy of their hopes, toward the need—which still afflicts them so greatly—of social improvement and of interior elevation, to the mission which may be recognized as theirs—if it is good, if it is Christian—to create a new world, of free men and brothers. The Church, mother and teacher, is close to them.

She looks to the leaders of nations, and in place of the grave words of warning which the Church must often address to them, she substitutes today a word of encouragement and confidence. Take courage, leaders of nations, today you can give your peoples many good things necessary for their life: bread, education, work, order, the dignity of free and peaceful citizens, provided only you truly know who man is, and only Christian wisdom can show you this in its true light. Working together in justice and love, you can create peace, that greatest good which is so much desired and which the Church has done so much to maintain and promote. You can make of humanity a single city. God be with you!

And then the Catholic Church looks further still, beyond the confines of the Christian horizon. For how can she put limits to her love if she would make her own the love of God . . . ?

She looks, then, beyond her own sphere and sees the other religions which preserve the sense and notion of the one supreme, transcendent God, creator and sustainer, and which worship him with acts of sincere piety and base their moral and social life on their beliefs and religious practices.

It is true that the Catholic Church sees in such religions omissions, insufficiences, and errors which cause her sadness. Yet she cannot exclude them from her thoughts and would have them know that she esteems what they contain of truth and goodness and humanity. . . .

Other vast fields of humanity fall under her gaze: the new generations of youth desirous of living and expressing themselves; the new peoples now coming to self-awareness, independence, and civil organization; the innumerable men and women who feel isolated in a troubled society that has no message for their spirit. To all without exception she proclaims the good news of salvation and hope. To all she offers the light of truth and life and salvation. For God "wishes all men to be saved and to come to the knowledge of the truth" (I Tim. 2:4).

The Pope of the Council

As the second session of the Council opens, the widespread impression is that with Paul VI the Church is in capable, circumspect, but firm hands. He seems determined to go forward without either detour or loss of time. His last speech to the Curia is the best and most recent proof of this. Possessing an even temperament and a deep knowledge of Vatican procedure, having worked there so long, Paul VI has been able to fill in the gap in his background in the three months since his election; he left Pius XII's service—voluntarily, it is said—nine years ago.

Today the Curia knows it is judged and measured by a man of lucid intelligence who has assimilated all the records and knows where he wants to go. Paul VI is imposing by virtue of his will and his zeal. He is aware that the reforms he is undertaking are both imperative and urgent.

The Council regulations, which have just been published, include some innovations. There is a modification regarding clothing, first of all, which is more important than it might appear: the Council Fathers are requested to wear the mozzetta, a cape worn by bishops which is a symbol of their power of jurisdiction in their dioceses. This will emphasize in a visible manner the collegiality of episcopal powers in the Church, to be discussed in the coming session.

Also, the laymen who are allowed to participate in the Council as "auditors"—some dozen in all—will have the right to speak in the same capacity as the experts, provided they are invited to do so by one of the commission presidents or by one of the four moderators. This stipulation indicates the Pope's trust in the laity. It is not his desire that they be reduced, even in the Council, to mere figureheads.

Finally, Paul VI intends to give full liberty of expression to minorities. Any group comprising fifty bishops will have the right to present a "counterschema." The moderators will pass them on to the Coordinating Commission, which will determine what action is to be taken. As of now, such documents can be prepared and appended to schemas already drawn up.

In the case where the majority decides to return a schema for revision or close a discussion, the minority now has the right to designate three speakers who will be allowed to defend their point of view for a period of more than ten minutes by exception to the regulations.

This tactic will provide the "losing" side with some protection for their honor and appease their feelings; it will also reduce the temptation for the "winners" to triumph in an indiscreet fashion. We recognize here the hand of a Pope who has always been able to criticize his own positions.

After John XXIII, Paul VI has become in his turn "the Pope of the Council." It is a difficult responsibility, involving two contradictory duties: to hold the tiller firmly, and to respect in all fairness the liberty and prerogatives of the successors to the apostles who are the bishops. What we know of the present Pope indicates that he will find the right point of balance.

OCTOBER, 1963

The Schema *De Ecclesia*
Favorably Received

After a thorough examination, during which ten Council Fathers intervened, the schema *De ecclesia* was approved at noon today, Tuesday, by an overwhelming majority. Of 2,301 ballots, 2,231 were in favor of this important document and only 43 against; 24 ballots were invalid and 3 recommended amendments.

The secrecy rules of the Council have been much modified. This became apparent on Monday after the first general congregation; it obviously pleased everyone, or almost. . . . The schemas themselves and the discussion in the commissions must be kept secret, but secrecy has been lifted from the debates in the general congregations, which constitute the essential of the Council. "Prudence" and "discretion" have been recommended in dispatching information instead of the Draconian restrictions originally imposed.

This is more realistic, since the former ruling could not be enforced anyway, and it is more in keeping with the spirit of the Council, which, according to Paul VI, wants to be "a window open on the world." The son of a journalist and himself one once (he edited a periodical called *La Fronde*, when he was young), the Pope addressed a group of newsmen today and drew a lesson from the first session. Honest and objective information given out under the responsibility of national conferences of bishops, he said, is more profitable for the Church than weak and vain efforts to hide in one place what is finally revealed in another.

The general congregation lost no time on Monday getting down to a discussion on the schema *De ecclesia*. It fell to Cardinal Ottaviani, president of the theological commission, which elaborated this document, to open fire. He spoke briefly, saying only that the deposit of faith must be safeguarded but that it must be presented to all (*omnibus proponere*). Thus he expressed a double doctrinal and pastoral concern which should not be dissociated. The terrible but intelligent Secretary of the Supreme Sacred Congregation of the Holy Office (who seems to be more subdued these days) seems also to have learned something from the first session: the Council must speak in a manner intelligible to all, Catholics or not.

First Interventions   After Michael Cardinal Browne's introductory speech, Cardinal Frings, Archbishop of Cologne, intervened in the name of sixty-five German and Scandinavian Fathers. He began with the words *"Valde placet,"* "The schema pleases me totally." That the demanding German Cardinal could hand down such a positive judgment, although this does not preclude criticisms of details, indicates that the schema is truly satisfactory. This means it has undergone substantial transformation since last year. The new text was drafted on the basis of a Belgian proposal and was reworked and completed in collaboration with several mixed sub-commissions, notably with members of the Commission for the Lay Apostolate, the Press, and Entertainment.

Cardinal Frings was pleased that the schema avoids an apologetical and juridical style and that it is liberally sprinkled with biblical images of the Church. Scriptural expressions best express the reality of the Church because they are the most suggestive and most concrete. In any case, they are the best received by non-Catholic Christians, which is of the greatest importance in the present situation.

Cardinal Frings also forcefully expressed his gratitude to Paul VI, who in his opening speech "courageously, not for reasons of diplomacy but because it is the truth," recognized the wrongs of the Catholic Church in the drama of disunity and humbly asked pardon for them.

The Archbishop of Hue Desires the Presence of Non-Christian Observers
Among the remarks made in the course of the following interventions, we might note these. Cardinal Siri, Archbishop of Genoa, feared that the expression "the universal priesthood" of the faithful would create confusion. Bishop Carlo Ferrero di Cavallerleone of the Order of Malta, in common with many other Fathers, wanted the schema on the Blessed Virgin, which is now a separate one, to be included in that on the Church; Archbishop Florit of Florence made a similar point about the schema on revelation, an improved version of the 1962 text which, it will be remembered, was roundly criticized. Finally, Archbishop Ngo Dinh Thuc, the too famous prelate of Hue, Vietnam, addressed himself to a number of points which were so unimportant that the moderator had to interrupt

him. He then changed the subject and expressed the desire that non-Christian observers be admitted to the Council. He was probably thinking of Buddhists, because he stressed the numerical immensity of the Asiatic peoples and the inadvisability of ignoring so vast a portion of mankind.

The Contents of the Schema   What exactly are the contents of the schema *De Ecclesia* presently under discussion, a schema that has already prompted the submission of 370 amendments? A series of considerations of great interest and incontestable relevance. Here are some of its principal points.

1. To what extent can infidels hope for salvation, and therefore to what extent are they potentially members of the Church? This touches upon the question of "baptism of desire," which is liberally resolved.
2. The schema proposes admitting "degrees of union with the Church"; the ecumenical consequences of this solution are apparent.
3. The emphasis is on the Church as "the mystical body," which is linked with the visible Church, and on the notion of "the people of God," which predicates the fundamental equality of all Christians and introduces the idea of a universal priesthood shared by all the baptized.
4. The primacy of Peter is naturally reaffirmed, but—and this is new and of capital importance—within the framework of apostolic collegiality. Satisfaction is thus rendered after a delay of almost a century to the bishops of Vatican I, who vainly requested a statement to this effect in 1869–1870.
5. The Church in her totality is said to be "infallible," as well as the body of bishops. Let us recall in this connection that the collective letter of the Dutch bishops for Christmas, 1960 [see the report for June 29, 1962], was condemned by the Holy Office principally because it included a passage about collective infallibility which is to all practical purposes incorporated in the present schema.
6. The *sacramental* character of the episcopacy, "the source of the priesthood," is defined, but the exaggerated notion that the episcopacy is a kind of eighth sacrament is eschewed.
7. The collegial character of episcopal responsibility is proclaimed. The practical consequences of this is to be examined in more detail in a special schema on the episcopacy and the government of dioceses.
8. The schema touches rather indirectly on the question of the diaconate, which is of great importance in Latin America, for example. The attributes of deacons are not fixed, but the possibility of ordaining

married men as deacons is not dismissed. Final judgment in this matter is left to the bishops, which is wise, because conditions change substantially from country to country. (Married deacons would be appropriate in Latin America but less so in India, where Buddhist monks are celibate.

9. The role of laymen in the Church is further clarified. They have a duty to evangelize. They embody moral values in the world; attaining sanctity in their temporal commitments; they have the right to be spiritually nourished by priests and *to make their needs known in a filial way;* they owe obedience to their pastors.

10. All the faithful are called to perfect sanctity (*omnes omnino*) within the context of the life they have chosen (religious, married, and so forth).

Ten Lay Auditors at the Council

The Vatican has published the names of the laymen attending the Council:

Silvio Golzio (Italy), president of the Permanent Committee of International Congresses of the Lay Apostolate.

Mieczyslaw de Habicht (Poland), permanent secretary of the Conference of International Catholic Organizations.

Jean Larnaud (France), secretary general of the Catholic Coordinating Center for UNESCO.

Raimondo Manzini (Italy), president of the International Union of the Catholic Press.

James J. Norris (United States), president of the International Catholic Migration Commission at Geneva.

Henri Rollet (France), president of the International Federation of Catholic Men.

Ramón Sugranyes de Franch (Spain), president of Pax Romana and of the Conference of International Catholic Organizations.

Auguste Vanistendael (Belgium), secretary general of the International Federation of Christian Trade Unions.

Juan Vázquez (Argentina), president of the International Federation of Catholic Youth.

The Archbishop of Winnipeg Proposes an "Apostolic College" To Help the Pope Govern the Church

The Council Fathers voted Tuesday morning in favor of continuing examination of the schema *De Ecclesia* (2,231 for; 43 against). Although this vote has only a very general meaning, it confirms the impression that the attitude of the bishops toward this text is very favorable. "*Argentum probatum*" (steel put to the test), an Italian prelate said.

The exact agenda for the second session is now known. While the voting was in process, Archbishop Felici, secretary general of the Council, said that after the schema on the Church, the assembly would examine in turn those on the Blessed Virgin, the bishops and the government of dioceses, the apostolate of the laity, and finally, ecumenism.

As of now we can safely predict that the schema on the Blessed Virgin will be integrated into *De Ecclesia*. As much has been requested by several Fathers, among them Raul Cardinal Silva Henriquez, Archbishop of Santiago de Chile, who spoke in the name of forty-four Latin American bishops; Archbishop Garrone of Toulouse; and Bishop Méndez Arceo of Cuernavaca, Mexico. The principal advantage would be to emphasize that a study of the Blessed Virgin ought in no case be dissociated from that of the Church, and consequently to avoid excesses and deviations that the Marian cult is not always exempt from. These rightly shock Protestants, and John XXIII, in an allocution to the Diocese of Rome, warned the clergy against the tendency "to cultivate practices and devotions that are particularly excessive in devotion to the Madonna."

Apropos of collegiality, Ukrainian Rite Archbishop Maxim Hermaniuk of Winnipeg proposed that the Council decide to create an "apostolic college" to help the Pope govern the Church. This college would be composed of cardinals, Oriental patriarchs, and bishops delegated by the episcopal conferences.

The "Phenomenon of the Church"

On Tuesday, when the Pope received all the newsmen present in Rome, the audience was brief and, it must be admitted, rather conventional. The disposition of the reception room, which resembles a long corridor, plus the fact that the Pope could enter and leave without passing among the journalists did little to facilitate contact. In his speech he said:

. . . this imposing assembly has some similarity with large human gatherings, [but] in reality it is quite different. One might be
tempted to see in it familiar "fiends": nationalism, conflicting tendencies, parties, as well as historical and geographical differences, as
between East and West.

If we limit our attention to these externals or emphasize them,
we alter or even falsify reality. For all the bishops are striving to
avoid giving any substance to these divisions in order on the contrary to be guided by the divine, objective truth which they profess
and by the fraternal charity which animates them.

Discussion in the Council hall is certainly varied and free. But
while it is undoubtedly influenced by the different backgrounds
of the bishops, it is not for all of that determined by closed minds
or prejudices.

Thus we are very pleased that intelligent persons such as yourselves have this extraordinary occasion to observe the "phenomenon
of the Church" in its human aspects, yes, but also in its characteristic
marks that stir deep reflection: its unity, . . . its universality, . . . its
apostolicity, . . . its spirituality and . . . religious sanctity. . . .

The Curia Again Talked About

After the pontifical audience, the journalists learned from reliable sources
that the sale of one of Father Hans Küng's books has been prohibited
in Catholic bookstores in Rome. This news emphasized the need for
the reform of the Curia announced by the Pope, especially since it is
rumored that this book was to be placed on the Index. Happily, the
rumor proved unfounded, but there's no smoke without fire, and the
hand of the Holy Office was clearly discernible.

We were reminded of the need for reform of the Curia again later
in the afternoon. We had gathered at a coordinating center for information on the Council to attend a press conference by Archbishop Pietro
Palazzini, secretary of the Sacred Congregation of the Council. The
way he spoke, carefully avoiding all specific questions about the future
of the Curia was characteristic of an exclusively juridical and static
mentality. This was not always so. The Roman Curia was founded in the
sixteenth century as "an organ of reform and stimulation."

When will it become so again? That is the question.

"The Church Must Not Seem Like a State Within the State or Against the State," Says Cardinal Gracias

Today the Catholic lay auditors addressed a message to the Council Fathers which read:

> Aware of the historic event which is occasioned by the Holy Father's decision to invite qualified representatives of the laity to attend the Council as observers, these auditors feel obliged to express to the Council the emotion, joy, and profound gratitude of the laity they have the honor to represent and their desire to respond by increased attention to its work and decisions and redoubled prayers for its results.

This message gave rise to a number of comments. It was said, for example, that "It is hardly worthwhile for them to be laymen if they are going to adopt such a platitudinous ecclesiastical tone and such insipid expressions. They sound like the kind of pastoral letters that the laity complain about. Are the laymen at the Council unconsciously developing a clerical complex?" Whatever the case, the Fathers applauded this pious declaration with extreme discretion and none of them took it very seriously.

More Catholic Than the Pope   Let us get on to more serious matters. Two points of great importance were raised in the course of yesterday's discussion on chapter 1 of the schema *De Ecclesia*. Cardinal Gracias, Archbishop of Bombay, declared, "The Church must never appear as a state within the state and still less as a state against the state. There are Christians who are more Catholic than the Pope. The Church is not a power of domination; on the contrary, she exists to serve. We must do everything possible to avoid even the least suspicion of the spirit of domination."

The Cardinal cited Newman, who said that when Catholics are a minority, they ought to make their presence felt not by their numbers but by their quality. "The missionary zeal of the Church," Cardinal Gracias concluded, "must always be translated exclusively into a spirit of service."

The intervention of Cardinal Alfrink, Archbishop of Utrecht, made a strong impression, particularly on the non-Catholic observers. The prelate criticized the schema for saying, "Peter and the apostles," as though Peter were not also an apostle, and proposed the substitution, "Peter and the other apostles." He added, "No one intends to deny or diminish the primacy of Peter, but the pope must be resituated within the apostolic college. The Church has twelve foundations. Peter is the cornerstone."

On the other hand, Bishop Enrico Compagnone of Anagni and Bishop Luigi Carli of Segni, both Italians, feared equivocation if the phrase "Peter and the bishops" were used without making it clear that the powers of the pope are not the same as those of the bishops.

Auxiliary Bishop Ancel of Lyon, together with Cardinal de Barros Câmara, Archbishop of Rio de Janeiro, stressed the spiritual value of the kingdom of God, which is a kingdom "in this world characterized by poverty, humility, and love."

Bishop Jan van Dodewaard of Haarlem, the Netherlands, suggested that the Church's bond with Abraham and the Jews ought to be more clearly pointed out. For in effect, he said, the Church is "the heir of the Jewish people."

Finally, Bishop Ernest J. Primeau of Manchester, New Hampshire, asked that a new way be sought to express the relation between the Church and baptized non-Catholics. He also wanted the schema to go farther and define the nature of the relation between the Church and other Christian communities. This question is of the greatest importance for the cause of ecumenism, and amounts to asking what the ecclesial reality is of non-Catholic communities. The Council would take a great step forward if it recognized the title *church* for Protestant communities. But it remains a highly controversial question for fundamental theological reasons.

At the edge of the Council proper, the question of non-Christian religions continues to preoccupy many prelates. In a press conference, Dr. Eugene Feifel, an expert on Oriental religions, declared that Vatican II "offers the Church a unique opportunity to enter into closer contact with Buddhism, Confucianism, Shintoism, and other religions. We should invite representatives of Asiatic religions to Rome and offer them first-hand information. Our theologians ought to receive as well as give."

Cardinal Bea Becomes Part of the Holy Office

But the most outstanding event of the day was incontestably the announcement that Cardinal Bea has become a member of the Holy Office. *L'Osservatore Romano* reported that the Pope had decided to count two new cardinals among the present members of the Holy Office: Ildebrand Antoniutti and Bea.

Cardinal Bea a member of the Holy Office? This is another revolution to Pope Paul's credit. With the exception of Cardinal Agagianian, who was born in the East but is generally regarded, rightly or wrongly, as a Roman, all the cardinals of the Holy Office are Italians (seven in all). Cardinal Bea is not only a German but is considered in Rome, especially since John XXIII put him in charge of the Secretariat for Promoting Christian Unity, as a leading liberal spokesman, and his prestige is enormous.

Cardinal Bea will thus work regularly with Cardinal Ottaviani, Secretary of the Holy Office. But then they have worked together before—on the mixed conciliar commission for theology which was charged by John XXIII with reworking the schema on revelation. The late Pope named them as copresidents.

This skillful and unexpected move offers two advantages: it will reduce the tension which might exist between these two men, who are so different in thinking and background, and it will help modify Holy Office methods. This is the beginning of reform, the first crack in the much-criticized bastion which is destined in the near future for radical transformation.

The "Sans-Culottes" of Theology

We have further details on the measures taken by the Holy Office against Father Hans Küng's book, which show once again the underhanded methods of that department. Several Catholic bookstores are still selling the book. Out of disobedience? No, because all the bookstores did not receive the same instructions. Some learned of the restrictive measures that we have already reported by telephone; others have just received a letter from the Vicar General of Rome which made no mention of Hans Küng (there seem to be several different letters, moreover, but none of them is available). The problem here is that Küng is a *peritus* at the Council, so it is difficult to attack him openly. Consequently, he was attacked indirectly and no written evidence was left.

In some cases, Archbishop Parente, Assessor of the Holy Office and number-two man after Cardinal Ottaviani, visited bookstores with which he has some special link. He appealed to the Christian sentiments of the dealers and exhorted them not to sell a book that would be "contrary to sound doctrine."

Archbishop Parente is a strange man. He has few friends and sees heresy everywhere. His last public statement is famous: recently, on the occasion of a congress at Assisi, the Assessor of the Holy Office roundly denounced the "Sans-culottes" of theology.

"All the Baptized Are in the Church," Says Cardinal Lercaro

Although the Fathers are speaking in the name of a group of bishops more and more frequently, the coordination of interventions still leaves much to be desired. There is a lot of repetition.

At the end of the first week's work, debating procedure is still far from perfect, as Cardinal Lercaro remarked yesterday. The Archbishop of Bologna called for more preparatory teamwork to avoid wasting time.

Several Fathers laid emphasis Thursday morning on the membership of non-Catholic Christians in the Church.

"All the baptized," said Cardinal Lercaro, "are in the Church (the Code of Oriental Law says so explicitly), whatever schisms or apostasies may have taken place afterwards."

Archbishop Herculanus van der Burgt of Pontianak, Indonesia, took up the same idea, saying that if Catholics are the only ones who participate perfectly in the life of the Church, we should not for that reason deny the real union of Protestants with the Church. Bishop Volk of Mainz addressed himself directly to the non-Catholic observers, calling them *"carissimi observatores."*

According to Cardinal Bea, the schema *De Ecclesia* ought to rely more on arguments drawn from Scripture and tradition before the separations took place; otherwise it will not render the ecumenical service expected of it or respond to John XXIII's wishes.

The Influence of *France, Mission Country?*

The intervention of Archbishop Eugene D'Souza of Nagpur, India, was intended to emphasize the absolutely essential missionary character of the Church. He cited the example of a book published in France entitled *France, Mission Country?* and its "enormous influence" on the renewal of pastoral methods. He regretted, on the one hand, that missionary groups are so restricted and closed, and on the other that the clergy are so badly distributed and that so many priests are involved in teaching secular subjects.

The same missionary concern was evident in the remarks of Bishop Pildáin of the Canary Islands. He also recalled the pastoral experiments in Paris under Cardinal Suhard's initiative. The prelate regretted that the schema scarcely touched the subject of nonpracticing Catholics, especially the working class lost to the Church in the nineteenth century and more generally the poor who are the privileged ones of Christ.

Several times in the course of this general congregation the Fathers emphasized the merits of the expression, "The Church, family of God," notably Archbishop Geraldo de Proença Sigaud of Diamantina, Brazil, and Bishop Simon Hoa Nguyen van Hien of Dalat, Vietnam, who went on at length about the Bible's frequent use of such words as *father, son,* and *brothers.* The same prelate drew a smile from the assembly when he said the bishops should address one another as *"carissimi fratres"* and not *"carissima membra."* By that he meant that the expression "mystical body," which has rightly been restored to a place of honor, was despite its great value less meaningful and less accessible to all than that of *family.*

There were further interventions, by Cardinal Richaud, Archbishop of Bordeaux; Archbishop Martin of Rouen, and others.

Examination of chapter 2 of the schema, dealing with the hierarchical constitution of the Church, was begun today, Friday. It revived interest in the sessions. For it is in fact one of the most burning subjects of the whole Council: the nature and the function of the episcopacy.

OCTOBER 5

"We Will Be Judged on Our Attitude Toward the Poor," Says Cardinal Gerlier

With something of the same vigor shown by Cardinal Lercaro last December 6, Cardinal Gerlier raised the question on Friday of the Church and poverty.

The Archbishop of Lyon referred to Paul's opening speech, which affirmed that "the poor, the needy, the afflicted, the hungry . . . belong to the Church, by the right which the Gospel gives her." He regretted that this aspect was so little emphasized in sermons, in the Council, in the schemas, and in the interventions. In the name of many Western and Eastern bishops and thirteen African prelates, Cardinal Gerlier asked that a theology of poverty be elaborated. "The presence of the poor," he said, "signifies the presence of Christ in our midst. We will be judged on our attitude toward them."

The same concern was expressed by Bishop Charles-Marie Himmer of Tournai, Belgium. "Christ wanted to be identified with the poor," he said, and cited the words of the Gospel: "Whatever you have done to one of these, the least of my brethren, you have done to me."

It was no accident that these two bishops chose to speak of poverty on the Feast of Saint Francis of Assisi. Also Bishop Mercier distributed a declaration through the information center of the White Fathers which read in part: "The Christian world on the whole is rich. The Church is in danger of losing in the future the 'two thirds' of the world that is poor as she lost the working classes in the past. Only the Church is capable of removing the scandalous character and the threat of revolt from the shocking inequality in the human condition."

Opposition to a Married Diaconate

The beginning of the examination of chapter 2, "On the Hierarchical Constitution of the Church, and in particular on the Episcopacy," began yesterday with an outspoken intervention by Cardinal Spellman against a permanent diaconate. In his opinion, to restore the diaconate as the schema proposes would risk diminishing vocations to the priesthood and would thus affect the various religious orders. "Let us not indulge in archaeology," he concluded in rebuttal to the argument that deacons existed in the primitive Church. Similar sentiments were expressed by Cardinal Ruffini, Archbishop of Palermo, and Cardinal Bacci of the Curia. They saw a threat to clerical celibacy in a married diaconate. "Let us not interfere, even remotely, with the law of clerical celibacy," said Cardinal Bacci.

We may now expect opposing interventions on this subject. There will be many of them in the days to come, for a number of bishops are resolutely partisan to restoring the diaconate, married or not.

Among the conservative bishops who spoke Friday, Bishop Filippo Pocci, Auxiliary to the Vicar General of Rome, felt obliged to recall, on behalf of Cardinal Vicar Micara, the teaching of Pius XII's encyclical *Humani generis*. "Grave errors exist today about hell and original sin," he said. "Let us not fear to denounce them, nor let us fear the reactions of the modern world. For we serve the Church by truth."

A different tack was taken by Archbishop Maurice Baudoux of St. Boniface, Canada, and Archbishop Salvatore Baldassarri of Ravenna. Both expressed thanks to the Pope for having insisted on the responsibilities of the Catholic Church in the matter of disunity. "It is necessary to say these things in order that ecumenical dialogue begin in an atmosphere of mutual forgiveness."

Auxiliary Bishop Jenny of Cambrai hoped that the schema would place more emphasis upon the person of Christ, the head and pastor of the Church.

A pertinent intervention was made by Archbishop Antoine Grauls of Kitega, Burundi, in the name of fifty-five African bishops: "Let us never oppose unity and diversity. The Church must assume all values, all cultures. All the Catholic Churches have the same rights and the same dignity. Catholicism is the ability to assume everything."

A closely reasoned debate then got under way on the questions of collegiality, the sacramental character of the episcopacy, and the infallibility of the pope and the Church. These serious problems will occupy the Fathers for several sessions, for they go to the heart of the theme of Vatican II.

Press Service Has Improved

The complaints registered last year were not in vain. The French coverage of the Council is unquestionably the best in Rome at the present time. Each day Father F. B. Haubtmann, director of the general secretariat for religious news which was founded by the French episcopacy, gives a precise, complete, and objective synthesis of the work of the general congregations.

Serious journalists are no longer forced to fish for news, as they were in the first session. This progress would have been impossible without the support of the French bishops. The French press is now able to give accurate reports. This is one of the first fruits of living collegiality.

Cardinal Feltin wrote last January that the secrecy of the Council was an "open secret." Today there is practically no secrecy; furthermore, the press is taken seriously. The day is over, at least in France, when the episcopacy was reluctant to give a good man to press relations.

Here is an example of frankness. Archbishop Stourm of Sens, one of the fifteen members of the international Press Committee, which is directed by Archbishop Martin O'Connor, said last Saturday in a statement to journalists:

> It is remarkable that in so hierarchized an institution as the Roman Catholic Church no new religious order was ever created by the central power. The initiative has always come from the periphery. It was such small and humble persons as Francis, son of an Assisi draper, and Ignatius, a captain in Charles V's army, who created new forms of evangelical life. The Church intervened only afterwards to approve and encourage their efforts.

. . . the Church, because she is confided to men, will always
be in need of reform. She must always be led back to her primitive
purity, to the purity of the evangelical spirit. The Church is presently far too centralized, to the point that the power of bishops is
sometimes reduced. The fault is not only with the Roman Curia,
as is sometimes said. Experience proves that a central power always
has a tendency to centralize more. But it must be admitted that in
many cases the Curia augmented its power only to make up for
deficiencies in the local hierarchy. Wherever the responsibility for
this situation lies, it is clear that it . . . poses serious obstacles to
evangelization today. Bishops must now dispose of more power than
they now have and must feel more responsible with the Pope for
the evangelization of the whole world, as Christ himself willed it in
founding his Church.

OCTOBER 7

Vatican II Examines Relationship
Between Papal Authority and Episcopal Powers

An important week for the Council has begun, a week decisive for the
Catholic Church and for ecumenism. Everyone in Rome is aware of the
importance of the forthcoming discussions. Behind the façade of technical
terminology—science has its own, why not theology?—the physiognomy,
the very style of Catholicism, will be determined for centuries to come.
For the Council, ratified by the Pope, is the supreme power, and
its decisions cannot remain a dead letter without infidelity to the
Church.

In the Church, power comes from the top, not the bottom. To be
in touch with the world is necessary but insufficient. Catholic truths
can and must realize the wishes of the "people of God," but they are
not for that less the expression of God's plan for man. Whence the
solemnity of conciliar assemblies, even though at times tempers erupt
and they look very much like parliamentary gatherings.

At the moment, the Roman Church is in the process of laying the
foundation for what in secular language would be called a constitutional
reform. Everyone now admits that since Vatican I especially (1869–1870),
the Catholic Church has been suffering from a serious imbalance which
has confused and offended many men of good will: hypertrophy of the
papal function and prestige against atrophy of episcopal power and
prestige. John XXIII convoked the Council as a catalyst of the resulting
malaise, to restore order in the "house of the Church" before attempting

to advise others. Two elements of reform will be sifted by theological criticism in the days to come: official recognition of the "sacramentality" of the episcopacy, and definition of the "collegiality" of the bishops. What does this mean?

Definition of the Episcopacy Until now bishops have been looked upon, if one may use the expression, as little more than superpriests, that is, as men who receive the same sacrament of orders as simple clerics with the additional powers of ordaining and confirming. Henceforth the perspective will be reversed, and priests will be looked upon as "sub-bishops." In thinking of the sacrament of orders, we will think first of all of those who are the source and possess the fullness of orders. The bishop will appear above all as a man with the fullness of the priesthood, the father of his priests, rather than a kind of prefect of the pope, from whom he receives his powers. It remains true that in designating a bishop the sovereign pontiff confers on him the right of jurisdiction in a diocese. But this does not mean that the bishop is a delegate of the pope. Bishop Carlos Saboia Bandeira de Mello of Palmas, Brazil, said in a public intervention last Friday, "The priesthood and its powers comes from the bishop." A statement of prime importance.

The updating of the episcopacy toward which the deep current of Vatican II is moving sometimes frightens simple priests, who fear they will be in some sense crushed between the bishops and the laity, whom the Council will consider later. There is another danger: that the bishops might become miniature popes whose authoritarianism could become as offensive on the diocesan level as did formerly that of the pope. Authority in the Church is in a perpetual dialectic with itself, and constant vigilance is necessary to avoid a swing from one extreme to another. Vatican II must correct the definite abuse of centralization, but during this conciliar week, it will be the task of bishops attached to a recent past to provide counterbalance.

Collegiality The debate has already been inaugurated by Archbishop Emile Guerry of Cambrai, who spoke on Friday in the name of all the French bishops. With his customary logic and rigor, he called attention to the practical consequences of the sacramentality of the episcopacy and to its justification, which he drew from the formulas of the liturgy for the consecration of a bishop. One notices in this connection the appearance of a new term at the Council: "episcopalism," by contrast with "papalism." It has even been reported that Archbishop Pietro Sigismondi has privately used the expression "episcopal pharaohism."

The matter of collegiality is a closely related one, as Archbishop

Guerry made clear: "The idea of collegiality is intrinsic in the episcopal order. The two ideas are inseparable."

The term *collegiality* has practically fallen into desuetude in the past fifteen centuries, as Father Yves Congar noted in a brilliant press conference on Friday. The Middle Ages had no conception of it. We have to go back to the age of the early Church Fathers. The concept expressed by *collegiality* is that the Church was founded on the apostles as a group, and that these were succeeded globally and not personally as was Peter. Consequently, each bishop has the right and the duty to share in the governing of the Church, even outside of his diocese. This is an extremely delicate point, for it must be reconciled with the power of universal jurisdiction which Vatican I recognized in the pope. It is not a question of withdrawing that prerogative but of understanding it and establishing its context better. Cardinal Ruffini, whose personality is as arresting as it is aggressive, has taken his stand. He is of the opinion that "it is good and useful to speak of the college of bishops, but we cannot say that this college succeeded the college of the apostles, for the latter did not act collegially except at the Council of Jerusalem. In speaking of the infallibility of the bishops united with the pope, we must note that the pope can exercise infallibility without recourse to the bishops." The Cardinal's intention was clear: (1) to emphasize the monarchical aspect of authority in the Church, (2) to minimize collegiality, and (3) to recognize the value of national or international conferences of bishops but not give them juridical powers of decision.

An Amendment by Archbishop Veuillot   On the contrary, said Coadjutor Archbishop Pierre Veuillot of Paris, "Episcopal collegiality was instituted by Christ himself. Scripture says so. The source of collegiality is apostolic succession. This is not a deduction; it is the will of Christ. We must state this clearly." Archbishop Veuillot judged the point so important that he proposed an amendment to that effect.

This brief survey indicates the complexity and imbrication of the notions of priesthood, episcopacy, collegiality, and infallibility—the infallibility of the pope, the infallibility of bishops acting in council, the infallibility of bishops out of council, the infallibility of the Church as a whole. These various uses of the term will undoubtedly receive some clarification in the days to come. The Protestant observers are keenly interested in these matters.

As this week begins, everyone in Rome thinks the debates will be sharp and hot, since there are obviously contradictory opinions among the bishops. The present content of the schema proves, however, that it is possible to reach agreement on a solution that represents indubitable progress over the status quo.

Twelve Lay Auditors

Mr. Vittorino Veronese, former president of UNESCO and the organizer of the two first World Congresses of the Lay Apostolate, has been named an auditor to the Council. To the eleven auditors must be added the name of Jean Guitton, who has chosen to be an auditor rather than a guest of the secretariat for unity, as he was formerly. Mr. Guitton has just presented his book, *The Church and the Laity*, in Rome. Attending the ceremony were Cardinals Tisserant, Gerlier, Alfrink, and Bea; the Apostolic Nuncio to France, Archbishop Bertoli; and a number of bishops.

Vatican II and Women   Why are there no women at Vatican II? Many are wondering. It is a question the laity are quick to put to bishops and theologians.

The question might seem preposterous, but it is far from that. Superiors general of large religious orders for women would have a natural place at the Council beside their male colleagues. By reason of their education and spirituality, many women religious are highly qualified to contribute to Vatican II's deliberations.

And why not laywomen among the lay auditors recently invited by Paul VI? Bishops are inclined to reason in the following fashion: There is no reason women can't attend the Council, but we must let things mature. They will perhaps be invited to the third session or another Council. In any event, male auditors were invited to be spokesmen for women's organizations as well.

At the present time, woman's position in the Church is doubly paradoxical. On the one hand, it is only too true, as Karl Rahner has said, that Catholicism has become "unduly feminized." By that he meant that preaching and catechetic instruction are marked by a kind of effeminate and sentimental style. That is why unbelievers often say, "Religion is for women and children." On the other hand, clerics have made Catholicism a religion of celibates. The celibacy of the priesthood is the cause of this, and the married woman is not always at ease in a Church where she is basically out of place. The theology of marriage developed in recent years has done something to remedy this situation. But not nearly enough.

A Breach   Moreover, in this day and age when feminism is being promoted, Catholics frequently leave the initiative to Marxists or liberals.

By comparison with Protestants, who ordain women as pastors and admit them to synods, and the Orthodox, who permit priests to marry, the Latin Church is clearly at a disadvantage.

But a breach has been made. It is altogether likely that Vatican II will uphold the law of celibacy presently in force; but the Council is favorable to the idea of a married diaconate. This would not have been possible a few years ago.

This will change the style of Catholicism and theology itself in a singular manner. Women will less and less be regarded as taboo, or suspect.

We need more liberal thinking on this question, something more in conformity with biblical anthropology: "Male and female He created them, and He saw that His creation was good." This would attenuate the misogynic ideologies which have contaminated so many centuries of Christianity. On the other hand, the Church has placed a woman who was both virgin and mother at the summit of humanity. This is the exemplary value of Marian dogmas.

OCTOBER 8

The Idea of Collegiality
Increasingly Accepted by the Fathers

The forty-second general congregation of Vatican II yesterday, under the presidency of Cardinal Lercaro, began with a mass celebrated by Bishop Pierre Théas of Lourdes. It was dominated by interventions by Cardinals Siri, Léger, Koenig, Döpfner, and Alfrink and Patriarch Maximos IV Saigh. In this session, as in the preceding one, the Pope's opening speech played a primary role; the bishops drew on it as justification to go beyond what the schemas propose.

Cardinal Siri's intervention was not so conservative as might have been expected. There is a very discernible evolution among some of the most conservative prelates. This is what John XXIII, who is largely responsible for this change, would have called a "sign of the times." Cardinal Siri emphasized that Peter was the head of the apostolic college and that this college depended on Peter for its existence, rather than the other way around. He said that collegiality is a factor of unity among the bishops and has helped develop the notion. It seems certain now that whatever amendments this schema undergoes, there can be no turning back. The idea of collegiality has made rapid progress at the Council.

Cardinal Léger's "advanced" ideas are well known, and his intervention was progressive in tone. He said, "Collegiality, far from diminishing the doctrine of the pope's primacy, rather brings it out more clearly. The more bishops act collegially, the more apparent is the necessity for a center and a guardian of unity." The idea is appealing; Cardinal Léger wanted to nip in the bud any fear that collegiality might seem to run counter to the powers of Peter in any way.

We enter this college, the Archbishop of Montreal noted further, by episcopal consecration itself and not simply because we have been named a bishop by the pope. (The same opinion was expressed later by Archbishop Florit of Florence.) Then Cardinal Léger returned to a theme dear to him as a result of John XXIII's influence:

> I would make bold to suggest that we regulate the use of insignia, embellishments, and titles in the exercise of our office. The use we make of certain traditional apparatus is an obstacle to the pastoral ministry and evangelical action. Perhaps this kind of ostentation might have seemed necessary in an age when bishops were also temporal princes. But today it no longer corresponds with public mores or with the desires of this assembly.

The Fear of Collegiality Unfounded   What is said about collegiality in the schema, Cardinal Koenig of Vienna asserted, is inadequate. "Paul VI expects us to go farther."

Cardinal Döpfner of Munich answered Cardinal Ruffini's charge of last Friday that a married diaconate would be a threat to clerical celibacy. He saw it instead as a good capable of increasing vocations. "We can ordain a married layman to the diaconate," he said. A few minutes later Bishop Pietro Massa, exiled Bishop of Nanyang, China, expressed a diametrically opposite view.

Cardinal Alfrink of Utrecht also answered Cardinal Ruffini on the matter of the scriptural foundations of collegiality. Joseph Cardinal Lefebvre, Archbishop of Bourges, felt the fear that collegiality would diminish the primacy of Peter was praiseworthy in itself but unfounded. "This fear," he said, "can hinder a serene search for the truth and is a cause of sadness for those who are suspected of infidelity to the Holy See. Do not believe that we are less devoted than others to the primacy of Peter, but we want to discuss the matter in the spirit of Christ." He then quoted Pope Gregory the Great: "My honor is the strength of my brothers in the episcopacy."

The Archbishop of Bourges also thought that Paul VI wanted the Council to explore the question of collegiality further and to draw all of its practical consequences.

"The Pope Is Not Head of the Church," Says Maximos   The intervention of His Beatitude Maximos IV Saigh provoked an incident. It is well

known that the Oriental Patriarch refuses on principle to speak Latin and that he has always expressed himself in French. This time, when he presented his speech in writing as is customary, he was reminded that he must speak in Latin in accordance with the regulations. Maximos refused. He was then asked to translate his text into Latin at least, so it could be read in that language after the French version. He complied with this request, a formality which delayed his intervention from Friday to Monday. He stated:

> It is an error to say that the pope is head of the Church. The Church has only one head: Jesus Christ. The pope is head of the apostolic college. The universal primacy of Peter in no way destroys episcopal power. Let us be mindful that dialogue with the Eastern Churches will be impossible if we speak of this primacy in a defective manner. The power of the popes must always be presented as a service, never as a domination. Paul VI, in his speech, emphasized that Peter received primacy in order to confirm his brothers in the faith. The personal power of the pope cannot be delegated in any way. Properly understood, primacy is altogether indispensable; it is a great grace of Christ which we in no way wish to question. . . .

Bishop John Abasolo y Lecue of Vijayapuram, India, agreed that collegiality could not contradict the infallibility of the pope.

Bishop de Smedt of Bruges turned his attention to some practical considerations. "Collegiality," he said, "is demanded for evident pastoral reasons. It will help the pope better confirm his brothers. Present progress in the communications media makes the practical organization of collegiality easier '*cum et sub Petro*' [with and under Peter]."

He added, not without humor, "Italy has a strong devotion to the Sovereign Pontiff because they see him often. We too would like to see him more often. The internationalization of the central government is not directed against the Italian episcopacy, whose merits are obvious and which has given numerous saints to the Church."

Then Auxiliary Bishop Carmel Zazinovic of Krk, Yugoslavia, asked that a central body be created which would be superior to the Curia.

OCTOBER 9

Ninety-Five Latin American Bishops
in Favor of a Married Diaconate

High mass was celebrated Tuesday morning in Syriac—which resembles Aramaic, the language spoken by Christ—by Cardinal Tappouni, Syrian

Rite Patriarch of Antioch. Most of the bishops obviously do not understand Syriac, and thus found themselves in the same situation as the faithful who do not understand Latin. Explications were furnished in Latin by Bishop Mansourati. "It was an excellent experience," one expert told me after the session, "especially since the bishops are soon to vote on an amendment extending the use of the vernacular in the mass."

Part of the time today was given to the schema on the liturgy, which was studied during the first session. The first five amendments of chapter 2 were voted on; they had been introduced and formulated during the interval by thirteen subcommissions. The ballots indicated this time as they did last year the near-unanimity of the Fathers. The negative votes oscillated between 12 and 31 and the positive between 2,249 and 2,278.

Further interventions were made by those partisan to the restoration of the diaconate as "a stable and permanent state." This is the desire especially of Latin American bishops and many missionaries.

There were two specially solid briefs, one by Cardinal Suenens and the other by Juan Cardinal Landázuri-Ricketts, Archbishop of Lima, who spoke in the name of thirty-seven Peruvian and fifty-eight other Latin American bishops. The Archbishop of Lima specified that there was no question of imposing the diaconate indiscriminately, and that episcopal conferences would judge whether or not this solution was acceptable in a given country. He saw two advantages in the diaconate: it would permit closer contact with the faithful, and it would facilitate the selection of candidates for the priesthood.

The Archbishop was in favor of married deacons because it made the vocation available to those already married and would accommodate Protestant ministers who converted to Catholicism and wanted to continue their ministry.

Cardinal Suenens offered a theological argument. "The diaconate," he said, "is part of Scripture and tradition. Since it constitutes a distinct service in the Church, it is fitting that those who fulfill it receive a special sacramental grace."

He said that the objections made during the past few days were not valid. The diaconate is necessary to compensate for the shortage of priests, especially when Christians are scattered among the pagan masses or buried in cities where the Church must appear once again as "a family on the human scale." He added, "Priestly chastity would then be seen more clearly as a sign of perfect love." He was not of the opinion that the diaconate would diminish the number of vocations to the priesthood, but rather the contrary: "As Christian communities become more fervent because of deacons," he concluded, "there would be more priests."

Archbishop Dino Staffa, Secretary of the Sacred Congregation of

Seminaries and Universities and well known for his integralist views, made some blunt remarks about collegiality and expressed the fear that it ran counter to Vatican I. He said:

> To say that the episcopal college has powers in the universal Church is a very grave matter, both in doctrine and in practice. For in fact, universal jurisdiction was given to one alone, and that is Peter. The pope must retain an authority that is full, total, and superior to all. Bishops are certainly of divine right, but they are created to aid the pope.

Do Not Abandon the Poor to Marxism

Cardinal Gracias, Archbishop of Bombay, expressed satisfaction that the schema did not resemble a manual of bad theology. Then he asked that (1) there be no fear of having recourse to arguments developed after the division of the Churches, (2) the missionary concern be primary in the Church, and (3) the bishops not hesitate to express their solidarity with the persecuted Churches. "When one member suffers," he said, "all should suffer with it."

Benjamin Cardinal de Arriba y Castro, Archbishop of Tarragona, affirmed that "Mankind as a whole is the family of God." "Let us think of the little ones," he said, "of the weak and the poor. Let us not abandon the poor to Marxism. The encyclical *Mater et magistra* demanded a just distribution of goods. It is not enough to proclaim this. The Church must work to abolish poverty. Let us say clearly that we wish to raise the standard of living for the poor."

OCTOBER 10

Two Fathers Defend the Dignity of Priests

The general congregations of this week have been so similar that no detailed analysis of yesterday's meeting is necessary. Collegiality and the permanent diaconate remain the principal themes. The arguments in favor seem to be carrying the day by reason of their quality, if not their quantity; those against seem more like rear-guard combat. They are listened to respectfully but with considerable weariness since they offer nothing new. But isn't a council the place to hear everyone? It should also play a role of leadership. Archbishop Franjo Seper of Zagreb, Yugoslavia, has said this unequivocally: "The Council is gathered to open doors and not to close them or say amen to the status quo."

Some of the Fathers defended the eminent dignity of priests, who could no longer be referred to as the lower clergy and who ought to be treated not with condescension but with paternal love, a quality often enough lacking. Thus, Coadjutor Bishop António Añoveros Ataún of Cadiz called the Council's attention to the fact that it is the priests who are in direct contact with the faithful and nourish them spiritually:

> Priests share in the priesthood of Christ and not only in the priesthood of bishops. It does not seem just to call them "an order of the second degree." The priest is not only the bishop's delegate. It is because of him that the Church takes on democratic meaning. There is also a collegiality of priests. Let us develop this point in the schema.

Archbishop William Conway of Armagh, Ireland, said that by not exalting the priesthood of priests, the authors of the schema were guilty of a "grave deficiency." Coining an aphorism that was widely quoted, he said that "Vatican II must not overlook the priesthood of priests by stressing the value of the episcopacy and the laity as Vatican I rather overlooked the episcopacy by stressing the papacy."

These two interventions will have wide repercussions among the clergy. In fact, they respond to a constant preoccupation of many priests, who complain that their bishops are too removed from their concerns, do not support them enough, and have no cordial relations with them. The great material misery of the French clergy, for example, borders on the scandalous. We can recall very bitter comments by priests that bishops who live in comfort, and in certain countries in luxury, are in no position to speak of the "Church of the poor" while their own priests are their most immediate poor, whom they give no thought to. "Would to God," one of them wrote me recently, "that we received the salary of a simple subway worker or even a day laborer so we would not be forced to live by our wits." This is a serious problem that has not yet been resolved.

The Unknown Bishop   But let us return to the interventions at the Council.

Archbishop Denis Hurley of Durban, South Africa, expressed surprise that the schema gives a mere half-page to priests as against nine for bishops and seven for the laity. "This represents a serious imbalance," he said. The same speaker complained that the bishop remains unknown, that he is too often silent on social and other problems touching the lives

of the laity, that his pastoral letters are read as though they were a telephone book. "Whose fault is this?" he asked. "We do not speak either
enough or at proper times. Therefore, let us not be surprised that we
are left behind."

The restoration of the diaconate continues to bring forth violently
contradictory opinions. Archbishop Seper and Bishop Franjo Franič of
Split, Yugoslavia, are against it. In his country, Bishop Franič said, sixteen
out of twenty-five bishops would be against the diaconate. Bishop Biagio
d'Agostino of Vallo di Lucania, Italy, is also a resolute adversary of the
diaconate.

On the other hand, Cardinal Richaud, Archbishop of Bordeaux, propounded a favorable solution in these terms: "Many young men fear the
priesthood because they see many priests worn out by material burdens.
. . . Deacons could help them considerably." Then he added with a smile,
"Moreover, I have the impression that some priests have a vocation to the
diaconate rather than the priesthood. The diaconate would have the
advantage of bringing out the true nature of the priesthood as such."

On Collegiality

The Archbishop of Bordeaux enumerated some of the tasks that could
be confided to deacons: social questions, Catholic Action leadership, works
of charity, distribution of the eucharist especially in big cities, and so
forth. They could be trained in seminaries for late vocations, but the
study of Latin would not be demanded.

Cardinal Liénart also defended collegiality. In sum he said:

> Peter is part of the Church. Primacy was given him in order
> to confirm his brothers, his brothers and not his servants. Christ
> instituted collegiality as he instituted primacy. There is no opposition
> between the two in the Gospels; consequently, in the Church, author-
> ity ought to be understood in terms of service and not of power.

Seven More Liturgy Amendments

The Fathers also voted on seven more amendments to the schema on the
liturgy, with the usual overwhelming majorities, especially those concerning the reform of the mass "to facilitate more active participation on the
part of the faithful": greater simplicity, suppression of repetitions or superfluous elements, eventual restriction of rituals or texts that have lost their
meaning in the course of time. An appendix gave some examples of what

could be decided later by a postconciliar commission: reducing the number of times the celebrant makes the sign of the cross, kisses the altar, genuflects, and so forth; having texts read facing the people and some passages of the canon read aloud.

Further modifications included a statement on the obligatory character of the homily at mass, permission to use the vernacular in community masses in accordance with the prescriptions of episcopal conferences, a recommendation to use hosts consecrated during the mass attended, and permission to give communion under two species on certain occasions such as ordinations, baptism, and marriages.

"The Promised Land of the Council"

In a lecture given to the African episcopacy, Cardinal Suenens furnished some details on the preparation of schema 13, on the Church in the modern world. Father Congar has called it "the promised land of the Council."

The first draft of the first part (general comments) has been completed. It is now in the hands of the competent mixed commission. The second part will study the human person, culture, social justice, peace and war, the population explosion, and other topics.

Said Cardinal Suenens, "In this age, when a woman has almost landed on the moon, the Church must give her greater responsibility. Let us draw upon the wealth represented by the million nuns in the world."

OCTOBER 11

"Papal Infallibility Is Inconceivable Without or Against the Consent of the Church," Says Archbishop Shehan

The general congregation yesterday, Thursday, terminated with a wise remark by Archbishop Antoine van den Hurk of Medan, Indonesia: "The schema *De Ecclesia* keeps getting back to the primacy of Peter. It has been brought up some thirty times; this is excessive emphasis because it seems to indicate some contempt, whereas no one doubts this fundamental truth."

The interventions were very technical today and are difficult for the uninitiated to follow. They are no less important for all that.

In fact, they shed precious light on the fundamental notions of the sacramentality of the episcopacy, infallibility, and the holding of supreme power in the Church.

Here is a summary of the principal doctrinal points put forth by several Fathers.

1. The sacramental character of the episcopacy is proven *historically* by the fact that several popes—Gregory VII, for example, a monk of Cluny—passed directly from deacon to bishop without having received the priesthood. It is proven *liturgically* by numerous texts from the ritual for the consecration of bishops (Archbishop Joseph Urtasun of Avignon).

2. Collegiality derives from the sacramentality of the episcopacy. Episcopal consecration makes one a member of the college (Cardinal de Barros Câmara, Archbishop of Rio de Janeiro, in the name of 139 bishops of Brazil).

3. The supreme power of the Church as well as infallibility is held by two distinct subjects: the pope and the episcopal college. These are two ends of the chain, and they must never be lost sight of. The infallibility of the episcopacy cannot conflict with that of the pope who guarantees it. It is the same infallibility as that of the whole Church and is the fruit of the assistance promised by the Holy Spirit.

4. The episcopal college enjoys infallibility not only in extraordinary circumstances, such as a council, but also outside of conciliar activity, in an ordinary manner (Archbishop Jaeger of Paderborn).

Consent or Assent? 5. The terms used by Vatican I to define papal infallibility lead to factual confusion, especially among non-Catholics. In order to avoid any equivocation in the future that might hamper the progress of ecumenism, Archbishop Joseph Descuffi of Izmir, Turkey, proposed a modification of the famous formula *"ex sese, non ex consensu Ecclesiae"* by replacing the word *consensu* with *assensu*. The purpose of this change is obviously not to revoke an article of faith, but to avoid giving the impression that the pope does not need the *implicit* consent of the bishops when it is only their *explicit* consent that he does not need. But it should be evident to all that papal infallibility makes no sense if it does not express the infallibility of the whole Church. Archbishop Lawrence J. Shehan of Baltimore agreed with this point of view, and recalled that in his opening speech Paul VI invited the Council to a deeper doctrinal awareness. Infallibility is "never to be understood," he said, "as being against or without the consent of the Church. When the Pope or the Council defines a truth, he or it does so in fidelity to revelation and tradition. Let us state this explicitly." The same prelate proposed that in the matter of the relationship between Scripture and tradition, which was the subject of serious argument during the first session, the "excellent" formulas of the Council of Trent be adhered to.

6. The patriarchal institution, a stumbling block with the Oriental Churches, was defended by Coptic Rite Bishop Isaac Ghattas of Thebes, Egypt, in the name of the Patriarch of Alexandria. "It is providential and

essential," he said. "It is the sign of the unity of the Church in our countries; it was because Catholicism was identified with the Latin Church that ecumenism is so difficult in the Orient."

7. Auxiliary Bishop Eduard Schick of Fulda, Germany, said, "The parish must find its place in the schema. Indeed, the parish is not an administrative entity but a sign of the universal Church. The Church is first of all the local community. The small church is the sign of the universal Church. This is a central theological truth."

Let us note in conclusion that the discussion of the sacramentality of the episcopacy points by contrast to the nonsacramentality of the papacy. There is no papal ordination, as a matter of fact. The papacy is not a sacrament. But the Bishop of Rome, if he is not already a bishop at the time of his election (as was common in the early Church), is ordained as is any bishop by three others to symbolize his entrance into the college. Finally, the pope is not strictly speaking the father of the other bishops. That is why he addresses them as "venerable brothers."

OCTOBER 12

"The Thesis of the Universal Powers of the College Is Neither 'Gallican' Nor 'Anti-Roman,'" Says Bishop Bettazzi

Friday's session began with a gesture of solidarity toward the disaster victims of the Piave valley. The Mexican hierarchy indicated that it intended to send help to these victims as well as those of Cuba and Haiti. Other bishops followed their example.

A liturgical matter was dispatched by an official communiqué, which stated that the lay auditors are authorized to receive communion at the Council mass. They are the only ones to do so since the bishops say mass privately before coming to St. Peter's. We will have to wait for the next Council for the Fathers to receive communion at mass, which will then be concelebrated by all as provided for by an amendment in the schema on the liturgy which has not yet gone into effect.

As discussion on chapter 2 of the schema on the liturgy continues, there is general agreement that Friday's session was one of the more interesting. Despite the regulations, the Fathers applauded the final intervention by Auxiliary Bishop Luigi Bettazzi of Bologna. Consecrated but a few days before, this newest member of the episcopal family has the good fortune of working directly with his diocese's archbishop, Cardinal Lercaro, the most evangelical and social bishop of all Italy. He made a smashing debut at the Council, mixing humor with boldness. Here is the substance of this display of bravura:

Although I am young and Italian, I would speak of collegiality. There is no doubt that it is by his consecration that a bishop enters the episcopal college, which itself is a continuation of the college of apostles, nor that this college enjoys universal jurisdiction over the whole Church. This position is neither Gallican nor anti-Roman. Since the Council of Florence the popes themselves have said this. Many of the most rigorous theologians of renown, like the grand inquisitor Torquemada, agree on it.

This universal jurisdiction is of *divine right,* while the power of a bishop over a given diocese is of *positive right.* If this latter power were of divine right, would someone please explain to me how it is that a bishop cannot go from one diocese to another without feeling that he is committing adultery? Christopoulos, an eighteenth-century theologian, taught that the power of universal jurisdiction is in both Peter and the college. It is impossible to separate these two aspects of the same universal jurisdiction. Here is the heart of our present discussion.

Vatican I did not contradict this position. It simply refused to settle the issue and admitted as much. Scripture, tradition, and the liturgy hold this as certain. The innovators are therefore those who doubt it, and the burden of furnishing proofs of their own theses falls on them!

At the end of this intervention Cardinal Lercaro, who was presiding, was smiling broadly. The majority of the bishops were enthusiastic and showed their feelings by applauding. Most of the prelates of Italy, where the influence of the Curia is most felt, were dismayed and still are.

An Important Intervention by Archbishop Gouyon   That was the surprise of this general congregation. The *pièce de résistance came from Paul* Gouyon, recently named Coadjutor Archbishop of Rennes, who last year asked the Fathers to give up the *cappa magna.* The historical arguments he advanced were based on the usual theological considerations. They prove collegiality and its powers of universal jurisdiction by incontestable facts:

1. In the first centuries of the Church, many bishops, including Ignatius and Polycarp, addressed letters to other churches, and this was accepted as normal.
2. In local councils bishops complied with the majority. They applied the decisions taken even if they had voted against them.
3. The Council of Nicaea said explicitly that it is fitting for all the bishops of a province to be consecrators of a new bishop. Today, it is the

practice without any exception for a bishop to be consecrated by three of his peers. *Even a pope never consecrates alone.*

Therefore, Archbishop Gouyon concluded, nobody can seriously doubt the notion of collegiality. It goes hand in hand with the primacy of Peter. The prelate terminated by recalling that the Pope, in his opening address, addressed the bishops by calling them the successors of the apostles.

New Paths Ukrainian Rite Archbishop Josyf Slipyi of Lvov spoke with deep emotion. After referring to the "miraculous possibility" which was given him to be present at the Council, he said, "In every danger, throughout all the invasions of history, the Ukrainians have remained faithful to Rome. Let us concern ourselves as much as possible here with social questions. Let the poor always have evangelical priority. Let us determine the pastoral adaptations which our times demand."

Archbishop Slipyi affirmed that "The infallibility of the episcopal body comes from Christ and not from the pope," as did Bishop Vittorio Costantini of Sessa Aurunca, Italy. Bishop Helmut Wittler of Osnabruck, Germany, and Auxiliary Bishop José Cirarda Lachiondo of Seville (in the name of sixteen Spanish bishops) stated forcefully that all episcopal powers come from the consecration.

The remaining interventions added little new. We might note a supplementary argument in favor of the diaconate offered by Bishop Manuel Talamás Camandari of Ciudad Juárez, Mexico, who spoke in the name of eight Latin American bishops. The ministry of deacons in areas where there are no priests would enable the Church to reduce the number of civil marriages, aid the dying, teach doctrine with authority, and help form public opinion. He was favorable to the idea of selecting deacons from among the married faithful.

This prospect frightened Bishop Albert de Vito of Lucknow, India, who spoke of the scandal that would be caused by a deacon's bad marriage.

Archbishop Marcel Lefebvre, Superior General of the Congregation of the Holy Spirit, who had previously regretted abandoning the cassock as street wear in France, proved to be one of the most hesitant about the notion of collegiality.

Let us give Archbishop Enrico Nicodemo of Bari the last word. He remarked that the bishops are not only "the teaching Church" but also the Church in search of the truth (*Ecclesia quaerens veritatem*), and consequently the Council should not fear embarking upon new explorations, or blazing "new paths," in Paul VI's words.

In this connection, a *peritus* said to me after the session, "Let us not proclaim as is done too often that the Church is a monarchical structure. The only monarch of the Church is Christ. We still are too inclined to consider the Church from the top down instead of from the bottom up. The point of departure for any study of the Church ought to be the 'people of God,' from whom the faithful choose ministers to serve them. We do not question the insight of Vatican I but the way in which this insight was expressed."

In these conciliar times, it is easy to see, tongues loosen and everybody preaches his own message. The contradictory opinions expressed in St. Peter's stimulate the imagination. "Speak! Invent!" John XXIII urged. The Fathers have taken him at his word.

OCTOBER 14

Begun Under the Sign of Courage, Vatican II Proceeds in a Climate of Openmindedness

"Never did a council begin with such good will," wrote the Bishop of Birmingham, England, at the beginning of Vatican I. We know what followed: the painful controversy about papal infallibility, the excommunication of Doellinger, and in 1871 the schism of the Old Catholics. In a word, what began so well ended rather badly, although the Roman Church was in the long run strengthened by these trials.

Vatican II, on the other hand, began badly enough if we recall the harsh tensions of 1962. But today, after two weeks of work, there is relatively good understanding on some essential points. Only one Father came out against the sacramentality of the episcopacy, and few contest collegiality. Differences center on form rather than substance. As of now we can predict that Vatican II will clarify in a singular manner the powers of bishops. It has taken less than twelve sessions to reach consensus on a subject which a short time before had been considered one of the thorniest.

A Higher Bid?   There was something heroic about Vatican I. Who could have expected that the bishops then would launch a system which would ricochet, and end by limiting their liberty, autonomy, and prestige? This is what was done, with abnegation but not without a struggle. Vatican II is much less dramatic. Now that the iron grip of the Curia has been broken—with the help of two popes—the focus is on favoring the bishops, the agents of the Council. The Fathers who plead their own causes have no difficulty persuading themselves that they are proceeding honorably. Perhaps they are sometimes tempted, for it is only human, to outbid their rivals. After the drawbacks of "papalism," some observers think those of "episcopalism" loom on the horizon. They wonder whether the Fathers slid a little quickly over "the mystery of the Church" (chapter 1 of the schema). They fear that Vatican II will insist too much on the institutional and juridical structures of the Church and not enough on "the people of God" or the pneumatic, prophetic, and eschatological aspects of the Church. These three technical terms refer to the truth that the Spirit breathes on all, that he speaks to all, and that the Church journeys in the expectation of the accomplishment of times to come. Are these fears justified? It is not clear that they are.

For it is clear that the majority of bishops are openminded and willing to investigate. These qualities edify most but disturb those who see favorite taboos overthrown: passive obedience, absolute monarchy, ecclesiastical celibacy (for deacons are clerics and not laymen).

The Council has made it clear that "the teaching Church" is also "taught," a Church in search. It agrees with the saying of Laberthonnière: "If he who teaches is not always alert, always being renewed; if he says, 'That is enough,' then he is dead." The Church is singularly alive at Vatican II. Spanish Archbishop Morcillo Gonzales of Saragossa concluded his intervention honestly with these words: "*Nescio* [I do not know]. My heart is pure, my mind does not see clearly. The Council must decide."

Vatican II also admits of a certain relativity—a *doctrinal* relativity with respect to matters on which there is divided opinion (for example, the power of episcopal jurisdiction over the universal Church, which some see to be of divine right and others only of positive right); a *pastoral* relativity when reforms needed in one place are not desired in another (for example, a married diaconate, mass in the vernacular, communion under two species).

The Council lives daily the experience of a Catholicism whose needs are different, and it is discovering that the only reasonable solution is to permit the bishops of different countries to decide for themselves on the suitability of a given reform. The reign of uniformity, too long confused with the notion of unity, is dead. That of pluralism is beginning. The principle of "subsidiarity" which Rome has so often preached to secular societies is finally being applied to the Church itself. It is a just redress of the balance.

A Thaw in the Italian Episcopacy Furthermore, the Council has already had a happy effect on the mentality of bishops reputed to be the most conservative. Let us take the Italian episcopacy as an example. The dictatorial authority exercised by Cardinal Siri, named by Pius XII as president of the episcopal conference of this country, is beginning to lose its edge. The influence of Cardinal Lercaro increases daily. Italian monolithism had already been shaken in the course of the first session, when it became evident that the Council would reject the schemas on revelation and on the Church which symbolized a total refusal of *aggiornamento*. Today the Italian bishops no longer hesitate to enter into formerly prohibited dialogue with the "transalpinists." Through contact with their French colleagues, they are losing their prejudices, discovering new affinities, and overcoming their inferiority complexes. One has only to look at the window displays of religious bookstores in Rome to realize the prestige enjoyed by the great French, German, and other theologians. The Italian ghetto is shrinking, to the benefit of international collaboration. And what is true in this particular case is true in many others. Before dialoguing with other Christian confessions, the bishops are dialoguing with their peers. This is a first ecumenical step.

Let us recall, finally, that by the express will of the present Pope, the direction of the Council's work and the *de facto* presidency of the sessions are in the hands of four cardinals, three of whom are young, daring, and resolutely reform-minded (Suenens, Lercaro, and Döpfner). These elements combine to create the atmosphere of Vatican II. It began under the sign of courage and freedom; it continues today in a climate that is both healthy and open to all directions.

OCTOBER 15

Positions Harden Between Proponents and Opponents of a Married Diaconate

October 14 will remain a memorable day for the Oriental Churches: the Roman Church accorded the Oriental patriarchs a place of honor which none can dispute them, not even the cardinals, who are the Pope's closest collaborators. Leo XIII had recognized this verbally, in conformity with the promises made in 1439 by the Council of Ferrara-Florence, a synod which marked an ephemeral union between the East and the West.

This lack has now been filled. Who is responsible for this? Once again, the courageous Melkite Rite Patriarch of Antioch, Maximos IV Saigh, who alone refused to bend to custom. Trusting in Paul VI, whose sympathy was known when he was still Archbishop of Milan, Maximos relied on the intermediary of Cardinals Bea and Suenens for a satisfactory solution to be found without further delay.

The patriarchs now sit in seats specially built for them opposite those of the cardinals, and hence at the right and in the front of St. Peter's. They are seven: Patriarchs Stephanos I Sidarouss of Alexandria (Coptic Rite); Maximos IV Saigh (Melkite), and Paul-Pierre Meouchi (Maronite Rite), both of Antioch; Paul II Cheikho of Babylon (Chaldean Rite); Alberto Gori of Jerusalem (Latin Rite); Ignace Pierre XVI Batanian of Cilicia (Armenian Rite); and Cardinal Tappouni of Antioch (Syrian Rite), who sits at the council table of the presidency, of which he is a member.

The ecumenical implications of Paul's new reform are not negligible. The Russian Orthodox observers have already expressed their satisfaction. It is now evident to all that the Latin Church respects the traditions of the East. A great psychological step forward has been taken, and God knows that emotions have played an important part in the quarrels between the East and the West.

Placet Juxta Modum Votes Number 781   On Monday morning the Council Fathers voted on the whole of chapter 2 of the schema on the liturgy. The outcome was unexpected: the required majority of two-thirds was not attained; it fell short by 78 votes. Of the 2,242 ballots cast, 1,417 read *placet*, 36 *non placet*, 8 ballots were void, and 781 read *placet juxta modum* (that is, "yes, with reservations"). The chapter was therefore sent back to the commission, which must draft new amendments on the basis of the modifications requested in writing, according to the regulations, by the 781 Fathers.

Most of the reservations, it seems, have the same message: the text should specify that the bishop of a given diocese is not obliged to comply with a request for liturgical change from a religious order resident in his territory. This is one aspect of the smaller limits Vatican II will place on "exemptions" This term signifies the right of a religious order (which depends directly on Rome) to bypass the jurisdiction of the diocesan bishop. The question will be treated in detail by the Council later on; it will put an end to certain abuses which religious are perfectly well aware of.

The temperature of the Council rose sharply Monday. A series of rather categorical interventions were recorded which prompted rumors that the conservatives had taken the offensive. Answering Archbishop Descuffi, Bishop Carli of Segni, Italy, said he was in favor of retaining the formula of Vatican I on infallibility (*non ex consensu Ecclesiae*). This prelate is of the opinion that "cogovernment" in the Church would compromise papal primacy. The word *college* displeases him.

Applause   Two bishops locked horns over the question of the diaconate. Bishop Jorge Kémérer of Posadas, Argentina, speaking in the name of twenty-five Latin American bishops, vigorously defended a married diaconate: "A man can have an ecclesiastical vocation that does not include celibacy." Then he evoked, with deep emotion, the plight of thousands of faithful who, for want of a priest, are deprived of all spiritual nourishment. Addressing himself directly to his opponents, he said, "Do not take away our hope! The schema opens the door for the diaconate. We do not require you to go through it, but let those who wish to do so enter." These words were greeted with applause from the assembly.

Archbishop Paul Zoungrana of Ouagadougou, Upper Volta, replied with no less vigor, "Let us not open this door! It would have serious consequences for Africa. It would establish a distinction between a higher and lower clergy. It would suppress the sign of sacerdotal chastity, which is the guarantee of conjugal chastity." Nonetheless, the Negro bishop admitted that the Pope could personally and by way of exception authorize an experiment in married deaconship.

Bishop Giuseppe Carraro of Verona was also against a married diaconate. Of the same opinion were Coadjutor Archbishop Segundo Garcia de Sierra y Méndez of Oviedo, Spain; Bishop Petar Ču elfo Mostar, Yugoslavia; and retired Bishop Vincenzo Jacono of Nicastro, Italy. Archbishop Custodio Alvim Pereira of Lourenço Marques, Mozambique, speaking in the name of thirty-eight Portuguese bishops, went farther and rejected the permanent diaconate even for celibates, except as an experiment expressly willed by the Pope. Archbishop Armando Fares of Catanzaro, Italy, aware of the division of minds, proposed to the moderators and the presidency that a special vote be taken on this subject.

A Moderate Intervention by Archbishop Parente   Archbishop Parente, Assessor of the Sacred Congregation of the Holy Office, intervened in moderate terms regarding collegiality. In his opinion, it is indeed of divine right; the pope does not create the jurisdiction of bishops, but he does define it. The schema pleased him in the main, but he had two reservations: first, the primacy of the pope can be exercised either in the college or outside of it; second, he disapproved of the expression "Christ founded the Church on the twelve apostles" because, he said, "Peter is the rock, and there are differences in level between him and the other apostles."

Cardinal Frings, Archbishop of Cologne, was categoric: "All the arguments in favor of [papal] primacy are valid for the college. To deny the one is to deny the other."

Coadjutor Bishop Fortunato da Veiga Coutinho of Belgaum, India, wanted the pope to be considered as "the center of the communion of Churches."

Finally, Bishop Jean Sauvage of Annecy drew on Saint Paul to argue that apostolic succession is a fact and not a theory. "To doubt the power of the apostles," he said, "is to doubt the powers of Peter. They are intimately connected and constitute a fundamental aspect of our faith. But we must not forget that the power of Peter is individual."

There has been one notable departure. Richard Cardinal Cushing, the sportive Archbishop of Boston, has returned to the United States, as he did during the first session. And for the same reason, it appears. He has not been able to persuade the authorities to install a simultaneous translation system in St. Peter's, even though he has generously offered to defray all expenses himself.

And there is a new arrival: a thirteenth lay Catholic auditor has been admitted to the Council. He is Emile Inglessis, who represents the Oriental Catholic communities.

OCTOBER 16

Discussion on Chapter 2 of *De Ecclesia* to End

It was high time to end discussion on chapter 2 of the schema *De Ecclesia*. The interventions had become repetitious, and both the Fathers in the Council and the witnesses on the outside were beginning to get bored. The proposal yesterday by the moderator, Cardinal Suenens, to end the debate was greeted by exceptionally vigorous applause.

We might note, however, that the Pope has instructed the moderators not to hasten cloture on this subject. Paul VI absolutely wanted the opposition to be given the time to say all they wanted to say so that no Father could complain of a lack of freedom. A wise precaution which does honor to the shrewd intelligence and liberal spirit of the Sovereign Pontiff.

Among the nine last interventions on Tuesday was that of Cardinal Siri; it was a clear, precise, and conservative statement on collegiality. He noted that the pope, head of the episcopal college, is also the vicar of Jesus Christ, and in that capacity receives special powers directly from God which dispenses him from the concurrence of the bishops. "The sovereign pontiff," he said, "receives nothing from the college, while the college receives its very existence from the sovereign pontiff."

The same spokesman was against a married diaconate. "I do not wish to close a door," he explained, "but if married deacons are accepted in one place, the whole Church will suffer."

The Church Is for All The remarks by Stefan Cardinal Wyszynski, Primate of Poland, were noteworthy for their irenic and mystical character. He said in substance:

> Rather than presenting the Church in juridical terms as a perfect society, it would be better, at least in countries where she is persecuted, to present her as a mystery, as the mystical body whose spiritual bond with the Trinity remains even where there are no priests. We are not ignoring the public rights of the Church, but we must be realistic. Even where there is no longer any parish or diocese, the Church continues, and it is this intimate presence which saves her. The expression "militant Church" [a reference to the recent intervention by Bishop Franič of Yugoslavia] is not a happy one because it risks being badly understood. It would be better to speak of the sanctifying and vivifying Church.

The Cardinal added, "The Church is for all and not only for Catholics. She is also for those who attack her. The Church is the source of progress and social peace."

A Taboo Subject Auxiliary Bishop Narciso Jubany Arnau of Barcelona intervened in the name of twelve Spanish bishops. He asked the Council not to close the door on a permanent diaconate or even a married one. As on the preceding days, other bishops argued against this position. It is very difficult at the moment to determine where the majority of bishops stand on this question. A specific proposition on this subject will be the subject of a vote on Thursday. The Fathers will have twenty-four hours to reflect on the matter since the text will be distributed the day before, together with other propositions concerning the major themes of chapter 2. This unusual step will clarify the situation and facilitate the work of the commission, whose responsibility it will be to redraft the chapter on the basis of amendments suggested.

It is significant that the question of deacons and their marrying, which occupies only a few lines in the schema, has taken so much of the Council's time and provoked so many opposing and often impassioned interventions. This insistence, which some would call obsessive, might be explained in the following way:

1. The great majority of bishops consider clerical celibacy a religious value which must be safeguarded at all costs, in spite of the many individual conflicts and the many notorious irregular situations in certain countries.
2. As celibates themselves, the Council Fathers find it hard to imagine a

change in ecclesiastical discipline, despite the example set by the canon law of Oriental Churches united with Rome.

3. To admit marriage for deacons would seem to be a weakness in the law of clerical celibacy, an argument those in favor of this solution strove mightily to deny. Whatever the Council's decision on this issue, it remains of the greatest importance that it was aired at Vatican II.

No bishop dares speak publicly in favor of optional celibacy for priests. It will likely be a taboo subject for some time to come. Married Protestant pastors, who do not for that reason consider themselves second-class ministers, are always amazed at the intransigence of the Catholic law. They are not the only ones. We received a letter just today from a French priest who lives in the provinces and whose name we will withhold for reasons of discretion. He writes:

> The real reasons for the critical shortage of priests are (1) the poverty of the priest, which makes him dependent for everything on everyone and causes him the worst problems. Conscientious parents no longer want their children to embark on this painful adventure; (2) celibacy. And at my advanced age I can speak with authority on this subject! It is a great pity that the Council does not confront the question.

Discussion Opens on the Place of the Laity in the Church

But today attention is turned in a quite different direction. In opening discussion Wednesday morning on chapter 3—"On the People of God, and the Laity in Particular"—Vatican II entered a new phase in its development that will have all kinds of repercussions on Christians, Catholic and non-Catholic alike.

The Hour of the Laity   It has become a commonplace to say that the hour of the laity has come in the Church. But it is nothing of the kind that the Council proposes to treat this problem in depth. Although avant-garde theologians have privately worked out a doctrine of the laity and the last four popes have occasionally opened the doors, it remains a fact that a complete and coherent doctrine of the rights and duties of the laity in the Church is officially lacking. The Fathers will spend considerable time on this sensitive subject, whose practical consequences are tremendously important. The "declericalization" of the Church is an urgent task. Each Christian, however humble his rank, must know how he can contribute actively to building the Church. He must know the nature of his relation to the hierarchy and the exact religious value of his so-called profane work, which he alone is capable of fulfilling as a spouse with family responsibilities and an agent of the material and spiritual construction of the world which is the Church's field of action. It is not enough to say that the simplistic and paternalistic vision of the layman merely in his capacity of passive obedience to the clergy is completely outdated. This view must be replaced by another that is solidly thought out. A special schema on the laity will be studied later on by the Council; but for the present the broad principles are stated in chapter 3 of the schema *De Ecclesia*, on which discussion is now beginning.

OCTOBER 17

Archbishop Ammann Proposes
the Suppression of Papal Nuncios

The Council regulations, revised and corrected by Paul VI, are more subtle than they appear. Paragraph 6 of article 57 reads, "The moderator, with the express approbation of the majority of Fathers present, can terminate a discussion that has gone on for some time, but must nonetheless give those Fathers who ask to speak in the name of at least five others the chance to express themselves." This safety valve functioned Wednesday after cloture of the debate on chapter 2, which was decided Tuesday as we noted.

Nine interventions are thus to be added to the discussion on chapter 2. No one regretted this. The Fathers have in fact listened to very forthright statements which would prove definitively (were this still necessary) that Vatican II intends to give a hearing to all opinions, no matter how nonconformist. As often happens in similar cases, the nonconformity expresses ideas that are current in private conversations. The trick is to get them a sort of official recognition by having them introduced at a conciliar assembly.

Thus, in one of the nine interventions, Titular Archbishop Joachim Ammann of the Benedictines of Ste.-Odile, a former missionary and a native of Germany, expressed this opinion on the role of papal nuncios:

> The institution of apostolic nuncios can be considered a venerable tradition and worthy of respect. But many people think that such officials . . . are shadows hiding the visage of the Church and ought to be effaced in accordance with the ideals of John XXIII and Paul VI. Is it required by the most authentic tradition? The institution of

nuncios makes the Church look like a political power in the eyes of the people. The work of nuncios could be carried out by the presidents of episcopal conferences or by patriarchs, who have a better knowledge of the language, the history, and the social, political, and religious life of their respective countries.

This task could also be confided to competent laymen. But no diplomatic measures can compare to the graces of consecration conferred on bishops for the accomplishment of their mission.

These statements provoked various reactions in the ranks of the Fathers and experts, who listened to them very closely. In some countries the nuncios have great influence. Bishop Marcel Lefebvre, Superior General of the Holy Ghost fathers, humorously referred to them in a press conference as the "eye of Moscow."

Archbishop Zoghby Asks that the Primacy of Peter Not Be "Imposed with Bludgeon Blows"

Another no less remarkable intervention followed. Archbishop Elias Zoghby, Vicar of the Greek Melkite Patriarch for Egypt, spoke for the Oriental Churches and, to some extent, for Orthodoxy:

> The schema *De ecclesia* would perhaps be more useful for all if it was equally inspired by the traditions of both the Eastern and the Western Churches, whose ecclesiologies complement each other so well. The two Churches coexisted in peace for the first thousand years of Christian history, each having its own constitution, its own discipline, theology, customs, language, and spirituality. Their separation is an abnormal state.
>
> The Oriental Churches have never denied Roman primacy and have always considered this a principle of Catholicism. But during the centuries of separation, this doctrine has evolved to such an extent in the Roman Church in a unilateral direction that it is scarcely recognizable today by our Orthodox brethren. Formerly, the Roman Church rarely exercised her primacy over the Oriental Churches. This is a fact of great importance, and we must bear it in mind if we wish to initiate any kind of dialogue with Orthodoxy.
>
> The doctrine of primacy as it is expressed in the schema is formulated in such a way as to make it unacceptable to the Orthodox. . . .
>
> Each time the schema speaks of the authority of bishops, it immediately subordinates it to that of the Roman pontiff. This affirmation is repeated too often and in the final analysis becomes tedious; it

leads one to believe that the purpose of papal authority is to firm up that of the bishops. The primacy of Peter is a signal gift made to the Church and must not be reduced to a yoke that is imposed with bludgeon blows. Pontifical authority must not be used to stifle that of bishops but rather to protect and sustain it. We have a great responsibility as conciliar fathers at Vatican II not to exaggerate Vatican I but complete it.

The authors of the schema, obsessed with Roman primacy, seem to have forgotten some essential things.

The interdependence of the head of the college and the college itself is not only in keeping with the truth but necessary for any dialogue with the Orthodox. The pope cannot substitute his power for that of other bishops in their dioceses, as was clearly declared by the German bishops to Bismarck in 1875 in a letter solemnly approved by Pius IX, a letter that might be advantageously inserted in the schema.

The Role of the Laity
Is to Consecrate the World

Discussion on chapter 3, on The People of God and the Laity, began with an intervention by Cardinal Ruffini. It lasted twenty-two minutes, over twice as long as the regulations allow. The Archbishop of Palermo is a brilliant, caustic, and mordant speaker and charms all who hear him even though they may think very differently. He is especially skilled in detecting the weakness of an argument. In this case he criticized certain of the schema's biblical quotations which were either inappropriate or distorted. What is said of the laity struck him as being narrow, inexact, equivocal, and even dangerous (equality of all the people of God, the call of all to sanctity, the frequency of charisms among the laity, sacred function, and so forth). The speaker terminated by begging the Council's pardon for his brusque frankness, saying he felt it his duty to express what he believed to be the truth.

Fernando Cardinal Cento, president of the Commission for the Lay Apostolate, the Press, and Entertainment, was pleased that the schema spoke of a "universal priesthood" of the laity, an expression which, on the other hand, displeased Cardinal Bacci of the Curia, who found it imprecise.

José Cardinal Bueno y Monreal, Archbishop of Seville, expressed satisfaction that the schema showed the role of the laity to be more than purely passive—"to obey, be silent, and give." But he thought the definition put forth still too negative. He asked that the laity be presented as "those who are deputized to work in the world and who live in the world in order to consecrate it."

The Hierarchy Must Dialogue with the Laity and Seek Their Advice

In changing the subject, Vatican II has also changed its tone and climate. It has abandoned to some extent the high abstractions of theological discourse and descended to the more mundane level of lay concerns. The general congregation yesterday, Thursday, was comparatively relaxing for the mind.

The Catholic lay auditors have become the cynosure of all eyes. Bishops begin their interventions with the words, "*Carissimi auditores*"; others seek them out and ask, "Did I speak well? Are you satisfied?" Thus an altogether unexpected exchange has begun in the Council, and from some points of view it is revolutionary. The bishops are becoming more aware that they must echo the aspirations and needs of their flocks. The Church of dialogue is succeeding the Church of monologue. Now that the secrecy of the Council has been lifted, the bishops know that their interventions will be broadcast to the four corners of the world and that the whole Christian people is listening to them and in some sense judging them.

More and more the Council is coming to grips with real issues. Faith and events call and respond to one another, fulfilling the hopes of all on the front lines of the Church who must struggle with the exigencies of existence and, as the Gospel prescribes, endeavor to be the leaven in the dough. At the same time, the language of pastors is being renewed and their thinking enriched.

Here is a brief analysis of the principal interventions on Thursday.

In the name of fifteen Chinese bishops, Bishop Stanislaus Lokuang of Tainan, Formosa, noted that the idea of "the universal priesthood of the faithful" makes sense in a Confucian country where each individual plays a sacerdotal role and all families participate very intimately in the cult of the dead.

Bishop Franz Hengsbach of Essen, after pointing out that laymen helped elaborate the present schema, said, "Today the hierarchy does not seek the opinion of the laity often enough. The laity are also inspired by the Holy Spirit. The Spirit, as Scripture says, touches 'all flesh.' Laymen might be more expert than the bishops. Let us ask their advice as often as possible; it is our duty. The temporal apostolate of the laity not only does not harm the Church but helps her."

"This is the first time," Bishop John J. Wright of Pittsburgh remarked, "that a council has spoken of the laity. This third chapter has great historical and theological importance. We may say without fear of error that the laity have been waiting for this treatment for at least four centuries." He paid homage to the theological studies on the laity done in such countries as France, and added, "It is indispensable to show that the Church is not clerical. Let us emphasize the vocation which the layman holds from God. If the Church is too clerical, the laity will only too easily find their place elsewhere, especially with the Protestants. Christ works through the laity in this world."

Why does the schema not mention the family? Bishop Pietro Fiordelli of Prato, Italy, asked this question. He thought it a grave omission. The advice of Saint Augustine and Saint John Chrysostom was, in effect, "Make your family a church!" Love and the home are not only a representation but a communication of the mystery of Christ.

The Human Caravan   For Archbishop Marcel Dubois of Besançon, "The Council should show itself to be ecumenical by concerning itself with all of mankind. The people of God in the fullest sense of the word is the Catholic Church; but it is also the Jewish people, who listen to Isaias, and all who believe in God and who are sometimes more moral than Christians, as well as all unbelievers of good faith." The French bishop ended by evoking the "whole human caravan" (in French) and Rabindranath Tagore's poem on God.

Auxiliary Bishop Candido Padin of Rio de Janeiro said that the laity must obey the hierarchy, but he insisted on the fact that the bishops too must obey the will of God in listening to their flock. "The good pastor," he said, "is the one who knows each of his sheep. Let us learn how to read the signs from God manifested in the life of the laity. It is indispensable for the hierarchy to dialogue with the laity. This is not to the detriment of authority any more than in the case of a father of a family who dialogues with his children."

Individualism: The Major Heresy of Our Day   Coadjutor Bishop Arthur Elchinger of Strasbourg asked this question, which at first seems surprising:

> Are we all in agreement in recognizing that individualism is everywhere, including in the Church, the major heresy of our times, a truly pastoral heresy which Vatican II must remedy?

Let us stress the dogmatic value of the Church as community. Let us make small communities of Christians in the likeness of those of the Church's early days in order to renew the world. If we do not, some will despair over the Catholic Church and go elsewhere.

Auxiliary Bishop Philip M. Hannon of Washington asked that the bishops create special organisms for soliciting the advice of the laity. "Spiritual advice," he specified. "If the laity are so timid with us, it is because we do not give them the opportunity to express themselves."

Archbishop Ismaele Mario Castellono of Siena regretted that the laity were defined in the schema in a way that was too negative and not biblical enough. Then Archbishop Louis Mathias of Madras and Mylapore focused his intervention on the necessity of forming lay catechists. He would like to see a new pontifical institution created to this end. "If this institution were decreed by Vatican II," he said, "the consequences would be as important as the formation of seminaries was for the Council of Trent."

Bishop William Philbin of Down and Connor, Northern Ireland, wanted the Church to say clearly that she was positively hopeful of human progress and not only that she did not fear it. "May our charity," he said, "be not only individual and only come to the rescue of disasters. Let it be preventive and constructive. Poverty is not a good in itself. Natural goods are from God, and we must see to their equitable distribution. We talk too much of the ideal world and not enough of the real world with its struggles in which the laity must take an active part."

Why Can't Bishops Be Elected by Priests and Laymen? Vatican II loosens tongues. Witness this letter we received from France, which we do not hesitate to print because it touches on crucial matters. Father Léon Reboul, of St.-Sauveur-sur-Tinée, writes:

> If the Church recognized unions and the right to strike, although reluctantly, it was because she had to admit that this was one of man's basic rights against a potential oppressor. Why, then, can't the Church grant this elementary right to the priests as to the laity within her own organization?
>
> Furthermore, why can't bishops be elected by the faithful (priests and laity) for a designated time as they were in the early Church and as superiors of religious orders still are?

Father Reboul asked for the suppression of "the inhuman and totalitarian law of celibacy which is at the root of so much hypocrisy."

Paul VI Receives the Non-Catholic Observers

Thursday afternoon, October 17, Paul VI received the non-Catholic observers in audience and addressed an allocution to them. There are some fifty of these observers, including those who were invited by the secretariat for unity. They represent twenty-two churches or Christian communities, which is to say five more than last year. The newcomers are the Church of South India; the Orthodox Syrian Church of the East, India; the Mar Thoma Syrian Church of Malabar, India; the Armenian Patriarchate of Etchmiadzin; and the Orthodox Church of Georgia.

At the moment, there is little hope in Rome that the Orthodox Churches, other than those of Russia, which went to the Rhodes Conference, will send observers to the Council. At least not immediately. But a common statement issued at the Rhodes gathering said that "The Orthodox Churches desire unity and reconciliation with everyone," particularly the Roman Church, provided it is on "the basis of equality."

Since Rhodes an important event has occurred. As is well known, the Greek Church adamantly refused to participate in the Rhodes meeting. Now, as a result of a change in the administration of the Greek synod which took place on October 1, the Greek hierarchy has added its signature to the Rhodes statement.

There is widespread regret in Roman circles that the Orthodox Churches did not send observers; it could have been the beginning of fruitful dialogue. But there is general satisfaction with the Rhodes statement, even though there is no way of knowing how it will be implemented concretely.

The unity secretariat hopes to receive some specific information soon, although the only present source of information is the Greek newspapers.

According to this source, the Greek Ecumenical Patriarch Athenagoras of Constantinople has recently received a letter from Paul VI in response to greetings sent at the time of his coronation. The letter, it is believed, is more than a mere courtesy note.

Paul VI Tells Observers That He Is in Favor of Developing a "Biblical Theology" Paul VI's reception of the non-Catholic observers was in perfect taste. With his slightly anxious manner, his concern for others, and the humble fervor and affectionate reserve that characterize everything he does, the Pope shook hands with each of his guests. They met in his private library and not in the consistorial chamber as they did last year. Hence the audience progressed in a more intimate atmosphere, "in an altogether familiar and friendly manner," as the Pope said in his address. He spoke in French in response to an address by Professor Kristen Skydsgaard of Copenhagen, a delegate from the Lutheran World Federation, addressing them as "beloved brothers in Jesus Christ": "To draw closer, to meet, to greet and speak to one another, and to get to know one another: what could be simpler, more natural, or more human? . . . But there is more still: to listen to each other, to pray for each other, and, after such long years of separation and such painful polemics, to begin again to love each other."

Because of the serious doctrinal disagreements, Paul VI said, no one could say how long the "great dialogue" would have to go on. He asked his audience not to turn toward the past ("This would mean getting lost in the maze of history and undoubtedly reopening old wounds which have never completely healed") but to look to the present and the future.

Professor Skydsgaard called for "a concrete and historical theology centered on the history of salvation." The Pope "would readily subscribe" to this proposal, and he suggested that a new institution might be created to this end if circumstances warranted it. He continued:

> Like you, . . . we do not expect immediate and miraculous solutions. . . . Merely apparent and improvised reconciliations which would disguise difficulties instead of solving them would hinder rather than help our progress. . . . As for us, . . . we are on the alert, trying to discern and happy to take note of the signs foreshadowing a luminous dawn whenever they appear in the depth of the night. We mean the signs of real progress in the dialogue which has begun. . . .

OCTOBER 19

Cardinal Gracias Asks That Canon Law Protect the Laity Against Abuses of Ecclesiastical Authority

The bishops are too garrulous, the interventions too long, and repetitions too frequent. This is the unanimous opinion. Therefore, the energetic Cardinal Döpfner, who directed the debates on Friday, began the session by begging the Fathers not to talk longer than ten minutes and not to repeat what had already been said.

A little later, Cardinal Gracias of Bombay was courteously interrupted when his time had run out: "*Momenta exhausta sunt*" (literally, "The minutes have been exhausted").

It is a fact that the Fathers are weary of listening to speeches of very uneven interest. One expert joked, "They are having a lesson normally reserved to the laity—that listening to sermons can be real torture." Sixteen sermons in one morning is a lot by any standard, even with coffee breaks in one or another of the two bars set up in St. Peter's.

Two interventions dominated the debates on Friday, those of Archbishop Duval of Algiers and Bishop Michal Klepacz of Lodz, Poland.

The latter spoke in the name of all the Polish bishops who had been received in audience by Paul VI the day before. He talked about church-state relations, which he would like to see treated in the schema. "The state," he said, "plays its own role. It must respect the natural law which holds for all men. In this regard the Church is competent and can intervene."

Then Bishop Klepacz analyzed the two kinds of solution possible in church-state relations, concordat and separation:

> The concordat is more in keeping with tradition and is part of the customary teaching of the Church; but if it has advantages, it also has disadvantages. It limits the freedom of the Church and diminishes the responsibilities of the faithful. It permits the state to mingle in the affairs of the Church and can lead to dissension.
>
> Separation of church and state, if it is worked out well, is a lesser evil. It offers numerous advantages. The Church has greater independence; she and the clergy are closer to the people. Therefore, let us not say anything that might be interpreted as a disavowal of the separation of church and state.

Archbishop Duval remarked that the whole life of the layman must become an apostolate. He said:

> The laity share in the sufferings and labors of mankind. Christians live among unbelievers and members of other religions. They must therefore know how to cooperate with them, as the encyclical *Pacem in terris* asks. Indeed, whatever is right and just works for the glory of God. The mission of the Church is to restore all things in Christ. Love sums up her whole purpose.

Archbishop Duval stressed the virtues of the collective apostolate and the support which the hierarchy ought to give it. All the laity, he concluded, are "witnesses to the glory of Christ. This is especially true in countries where the Church is persecuted."

Bishop Paternus Geise of Bogor spoke for thirty Indonesian prelates. He asked that the schema emphasize that the vocation of the layman is to act in the world through his family, civic, social, professional, and political life. "The world," he said, "must become a prefiguration of the reign of God. The love of God embraces all men."

Bishop Pablo Barrachina Estevan of Orihuela-Alicante, Spain, pointed out that the layman is not merely an instrument of the hierarchy. He has a "specific, essential, and cosmic mission." His apostolate is not one of replacement.

Bishop Joseph Schröffer of Eichstätt, who spoke in the name of sixty-nine German bishops, expressed pleasure that the schema spoke of the "universal priesthood" of the laity. "It was an idea that had been largely forgotten," he noted, "and for this reason the layman was inclined to define himself in relation to the secular world, while in fact he is a religious man charged with the responsibility of bearing witness to Christ in the world."

Bishop Lawrence T. Picachy of Jamshedpur, India, stressed the fact, as did several other speakers, that the laity are called to sanctity in the world. "The duty of apostolate for the layman," he said, "flows from baptism and confirmation. Let us not speak only of the obedience of the laity to the hierarchy. They must collaborate and act as adults."

Cardinal Rugambwa of Bukoba, Tanzania, hoped that the catechism and canon law would teach the rights and duties of the laity (to announce the faith, defend moral values, and bear witness to Christ). The Cardinal regretted that there were no representatives from family, worker, or education movements among the lay auditors at the Council. He urged that this be corrected as soon as possible.

Cardinal Gracias said it was not because of the shortage of priests that the role of the laity was being insisted upon:

> The laity must not replace the clergy. They have their own mission. Let the laity not adopt an evasive philosophy; let them not take refuge in a pious society and thereby forget their duty of struggling in secular life. May they accept all stresses and conflicts courageously. It would perhaps be good if canon law assured the laity of protection against possible abuses of ecclesiastical authority.

OCTOBER 21

After a Romantic Period,
the Real Difficulties Emerge

Is the cause of ecumenism making progress or not? Those who live in the ambiance of the Council ask this question because it is of interest to the whole of Western and Eastern Christianity. It is not an easy one to answer. But let us make some effort to do so.

In the first place, a positive symptom arrests our attention these days: the nature of the Pope's reception of the non-Catholic observers. The word *audience* scarcely describes this encounter since there was very little protocol. One is struck by two facts:

1. After speaking individually to each of his guests, Pope Paul asked them to recite with him, each in his own language, the Pater Noster. This unexpected act is by no means insignificant.
2. The Pope had asked for an advance copy of the speech to be given by the representative of the observers so that he could discuss it seriously and in some detail.

In fact, Paul VI signaled two important passages from Dr. Kristen E. Skydsgaard's address. The first expressed frankly "the ardent hope that . . . a theology nourished by the Bible . . . will shine more and more in the work of the Council." In the second passage, the Lutheran theologian said, "We must seek and find the truth: seek in order to find and find in order to seek again, as Saint Augustine says." Paul VI repeated this word for word in his own speech, and added, "This phrase . . . concerns all of us. A true Christian is a stranger to immobility." The Pope stated further, "Our attitude is without guile. . . . Good faith and charity are the bases we offer to your presence here."

By comparison with a similar reception in 1962, obvious progress has been made. Last year the observers had no opportunity to speak. They had been told protocol prohibited it. Also, Paul VI once again asked pardon for the faults committed by the Catholic Church in the painful history of separation, as he had on September 29. Such things are better said twice, especially to those directly concerned.

Orthodox and Protestants on Dialogue   Paul VI has used the expression "the great dialogue." What exactly does that mean?

The Orthodox observers are extremely sensitive on this point. A perfectly defensible thesis is that discussion about dialogue is nothing but talk as long as the participants are refused equal footing. The Orthodox were deeply offended by the appeal to the Oriental Churches pronounced last August 18 by Pope Paul at the Abbey of Grottaferratta. "We desire," said the Pope, "that the Oriental Churches be grafted anew onto the unique tree of the unique Church of Christ."

One of the most influential personalities in the Orthodox Church retorted, "It is not a question in our opinion of grafting either the Orthodox onto the Catholic tree or the Catholics onto the Orthodox tree, but rather of discovering that we are the same Church, that we must become reconciled to one another in order to resume communion and progress together."

The disagreement could not be more clearly expressed. In addition, many Orthodox were offended because the invitations to the Council extended the patriarchs were not even signed by the Pope. (Here we touch on the crucial problem of the precedence of patriarchs over cardinals.)

Moreover, the absence of most of the Orthodox Churches from the Council is all too obvious. The second session marks no progress in this respect. That there are selfish or political reasons as well as religious ones in no way changes the fact.

The Protestant observers are scarcely less sensitive about the word *dialogue.* But there is a notable difference. They readily accepted the invitation to the Council extended by the secretariat for unity. In their eyes, talk about dialogue can become meaningful only if the Roman Church recognizes that Protestants constitute Churches too and not merely "communities," as Rome customarily calls them; it is the official term, in fact. We know of no official document that uses the word *Church* for the Protestants; neither the Pope nor the schema on ecumenism has uttered it. The closest anyone has come would be Paul VI, speaking on September 29, when he mentioned "the other confessions which claim the name of Christ and bear the title of Church." Does this presage a change of attitude? Hope is slight, because the vocabulary used by the Roman Church expresses a theological fact which is fundamental in her eyes: there is only one church instituted by Christ, and that is the mother Catholic Church. The separated "Churches" can be so called only insofar as the umbilical cord with the Roman Church has not been cut.

Ecumenism, an Equivocal Expression   An official declaration published after the committee of the World Council of Churches met last summer in Rochester contains this passage: "There are serious reasons for hoping that the new atmosphere will make the beginnings of an authentic ecumenical dialogue possible between the Roman Catholic Church and the other Churches." The formula is a cautious one. Still, the observers are very pleased with the weekly exchanges held in Rome on the contents of the schema. Their opinions are solicited and transmitted by Cardinal Bea's secretariat for unity.

Let us consider for a moment the two senses given the word *ecumenism.* As it is used by the Roman Church it means, with or without nuances, the reunion of the separated Churches around a center. By definition this center would have to be Rome. Of course, there is more than one way of understanding such a reunion. The word *return* has disappeared—better late than never—from the Catholic vocabulary. But even according to the most liberal hypothesis, the Roman Church cannot imagine a single church which is not bound to papal primacy in one way or another. The new element is that the Catholic Church now sees herself in a context of historical development, and that the unity hoped for is understood as a regrouping, a recuperation, a movement forward which cannot yet be seen in detail but which necessarily supposes, for all the churches without exception, self-criticism, a deepening of doctrine, and a theological and spiritual ascesis.

For Protestants, on the other hand, the word *ecumenism* evokes an association, a kind of round table of churches none of which can claim to be the formal heir of the Church of the apostles. Is there a possibility of reconciliation between these two positions? We could reply in the affirmative; but that is a wager of faith and not of reason.

How Concerned Are the Protestants? A final point: is the Council's present study of the schema *De ecclesia* making a positive contribution to ecumenism?

Some Protestants say that this schema is purely an internal Catholic affair and that for this reason they are not involved. How could Protestants be interested in, say, whether collegiality is of divine right when in their eyes papal primacy itself is a fiction? They are not touched by matters concerning the government of the Roman Church since they are outside the system. This position, however, is not the only one.

Other Protestant reactions are more inflected. To the extent that Vatican II decentralizes power and considers all authority as a service rather than a power, to the extent that collegiality is defined as a communion rather than a juridical notion, they are interested. Nor can they forget that the present schema is incomparably better than the first draft. They also know that the schema on ecumenism prepared under Cardinal Bea's direction, which will be discussed later, will go much farther than the schema *De ecclesia*. Finally, as Dr. Lukas Visher, an observer from the World Council of Churches, said so well, new ways of expressing the faith exercise a profound influence on the substance of that faith. The relation between the substance and its expression is much closer than that between the body and its clothes. Thus Vatican II, in developing the language of faith, is performing an extremely beneficial work.

It can be said that the romantic period of ecumenism is now over. The euphoria of the first hours, which resulted from the fact that polemical attitudes were abandoned and relations of friendship and respect were substituted for centuries of contempt and calumny, is fading. It is a good sign. What has been lost in enthusiasm has been gained in lucidity. We can now face the real problems.

Both the Pope and the observers agree that the time is not yet ripe. In a "letter to the Churches" written by Charles Westphal, Pierre Bourguet, Etienne Jung, Etienne Meyer, and Edouard Wagner, the presidents of French Protestantism said, "The real differences in questions of faith which set us against Rome remain singularly profound and serious. But it is also true that Vatican II has been extraordinarily stimulating for the Churches. The discovery that the Roman Church is in the process of reform morally obliges the other Churches to renew themselves."

Pastor Georges Richard-Molard, on his return from Rome, wrote in the weekly *Réforme*, "Protestantism, it must be said without equivocation, is in danger of being left behind, or better, of being outstripped by Catholicism if, aware of what is going on in Rome, it does not react healthily and positively."

There is no better proof of the contagiousness of good example.

Regarding the Jews   Exercising a special function assigned to it by Pope John personally, the Secretariat for Promoting Christian Unity will present a declaration for the Council's consideration regarding the Jewish people and their relations with Christianity.

OCTOBER 22

The Archbishop of Conakry
Warns Against Aftereffects of Colonialism

On Monday, Cardinal Ottaviani, Secretary of the Sacred Congregation of the Holy Office, broke the long silence he had held since the opening of Vatican II's second session. His intervention, short and discreet, first protested against three experts who had circulated a text in St. Peter's allegedly recommending that the Fathers vote against a married diaconate.* Such a procedure is in fact prohibited, and was criticized at the beginning of the session when a text against Franco's religious policy was circulated among the Fathers.

* This is a reference to a circular signed by Fathers Rahner, Ratzinger, and Martelet. They strongly favor the diaconate but make no allusion to the question of a married diaconate. Cardinal Ottaviani's understanding of the circular was mistaken. But it should be noted that the weak state of his eyes makes it impossible for him to read a great number of documents submitted to him personally.

Then Cardinal Ottaviani himself spoke against a married diaconate because of the sacramental character of this major order. He proposed a substitute solution: the creation of acolytes who would have the rights now reserved for deacons. There would be no objection, the Cardinal specified, to having ordained acolytes, since it is a minor order and does not require celibacy.

Cardinal Meyer, Archbishop of Chicago, criticized the chapter on the laity for its "lack of realism." The text, he said, did not confront the concrete difficulties which the laity encounter in real life; it makes no mention of the struggle necessary to remain faithful to Christ, a struggle which Scripture and the liturgy frequently refer to.

"The people of God," he went on, "is not only a holy people but a refuge of sinners. The Church is a welcoming mother. And Christ has already told us, 'For I came not to call the just but sinners.' "

Archbishop Raymond Tchidimbo of Conakry, Guinea, presented himself as a pastor and not a theologian. He warned the laity who work in mission countries against the aftereffects of the colonial spirit. There are international organizations of the lay apostolate, specialists, and missionary orders which do not, in his opinion, respect the particular genius of these countries.

"They come with ready-made plans," the Archbishop explained. "They think they have been sent by God to teach everything to local Christians. But the hierarchy is already established in these countries, the bishops know the needs of the apostolate, and it is they who are responsible for it."

The Archbishop humorously cited some examples. To a specialist who offered his services, he answered, *"Ne venias!* Do not come! I am the specialist here." The prelate made reference to some of these movements and said they were not wanted: "We don't need them in our country."

Trust the Laity

Bishop Karol Wojtyla, administrator of Poland's Archdiocese of Cracow, expressed the desire that the schema speak of "the people of God" before discussing the hierarchy, that is, discuss the whole before the part. He was followed by Archbishop Hurley of Durban, South Africa, who declared:

We should not speak so much of "church and state" as of "the Church and human society." The term *state* indicates a political unit.

Human society takes in all men, wherever they may be and whatever their form of government.

Our text should try to show our people how they are to combine in Christian fashion the activities which bring them into contact with the two aspects of their life—Christian and civil. All, even apparently purely civil activities, must bear the stamp of the influence of a Christian conscience. No actions are exclusively of the temporal order.

In the life of the laity, everything depends on Christ, but not everything depends on the hierarchy. The laity must assume their responsibilities without asking directives of the hierarchy. Let us proclaim that the role of the Church is to form the consciences of the faithful, and let us trust the laity.

The Archbishop of Lusaka, Zambia, Adam Kozlowiecki, defined the limits of episcopal powers in new terms: "Bishops understand their teaching and sanctifying mission well enough but not their governing mission. We are not sufficiently aware of the limits of our powers. We also talk a good deal about decentralization in our own dioceses. We speak too administratively of our relations with the laity. Not everything depends on us bishops; many things depend on the laity."

New Contacts Between the French Episcopacy and Laity For the Council to speak of the episcopal obligation to consult the laity is good. But to do it is better. This is what has happened in Rome, with the French episcopacy particularly. Last week leaders of the Young Christian Workers were asked to express their views before the assembly of French bishops. Monday, Rural Catholic Action groups did the same; later on Workers' Catholic Action will have the opportunity.

The bishops praised the magazines *Hello!* and *Rallye Jeunesse,* which have played an important role in the formation of the public. One of these magazines was recently the object of an "unjust" attack on the part of integralists for having published an interview with Father Marc Oraison on the problems of sexual education. The French bishops sided with the episcopal committee which came to the defense of these magazines a few days ago and emphasized their educative value.

The French episcopacy also heard a conference by Father Voillaume, Superior of the Little Brothers of Jesus (founded by Charles de Foucauld). "Our apostolate," the speaker said, "has remained too dated. Let us adapt our methods to the industrial era of our times and to its problems: hunger, overpopulation, nuclear arms, and the like. Let us train men for this important work."

Cardinal Suenens Asks that Women Be Invited to the Council

Tuesday morning's session was especially lively in St. Peter's. The interventions were more vigorous and to the point than usual. There is no doubt that the theme of the laity commands the attention of the bishops and faithful alike. It is as though the laity had incited the hierarchical Church to come out of her cocoon and lead her people.

In this respect, the schema presently being studied is a foretaste of one that is yet to appear, on the role of the Church in the world.

By considering the function of the laity, Vatican II marks the end of a long period during which the Church tried to evade life, to confuse action with Scholastic exercises and reality with juridical fictions or systems.

Speaking after Cardinal Caggiano, Archbishop of Buenos Aires, Cardinal Suenens opened fire with an energetic intervention that was roundly applauded. He took direct aim at Cardinal Ruffini, just as the day before Archbishop Kozlowiecki deliberately addressed the *"carissimi periti"* in answer to Cardinal Ottaviani's attack on them. Cardinal Ruffini argued last week that charisms had become very rare in the Church. (The term comes from Saint Paul and designates the temporary gifts given by the Holy Spirit for the edification of the mystical body of Christ.) The Archbishop of Malines-Brussels retorted authoritatively:

> The Church is the locus of charisms. It is built, as Saint Paul says, not only on the apostles but also on the prophets. We forget this too often. The Holy Spirit is given to all Christians, including the laity. Of course, the latter must be obedient; but the hierarchy must be careful never to snuff out the Spirit. Let us stress the fact that the Church is a charismatic structure. Let us respect the liberty of the children of God.

The Cardinal concluded by asking that the lay auditors at the Council play an active role, that their number be increased, and that women, who constitute 50 percent of humanity, and women religious, some 1,500,000 strong, be represented at Vatican II.

A "Ministry" for the Laity

Bishop Giuseppe Ruotolo of Ugento–S. Maria di Leuca, Italy, made an interesting proposal. "Let the laity," he said, "be given a thorough religious education, and let us found special institutes to this end, especially in Rome. By doing this, Vatican II would take an initiative comparable to the Council of Trent's decision regarding the founding of seminaries."

This prelate further asked that a new sacred congregation be created within the Curia dealing exclusively with lay problems. "Thus," he added, "the bonds between the hierarchy and the faithful would become more intimate."

The Layman's Role

Archbishop Morcillo of Saragossa opined that the proper mission of the layman was to offer the cosmos to God. Consecrated by baptism and confirmation, the layman is the "new man" spoken of in the New Testament who bears the responsibility of renewing all things in Christ.

Bishop Jules Daem of Antwerp remarked that Christ was the only man to have proclaimed himself the light, the way, the truth and life and at the same time the servant of all.

Bishop Vicente Enrique y Tarancón of Solsona, Spain, criticized the schema for not defining the spirituality proper to laymen who must, he said, live the spirit of the beatitudes in their special circumstances— marriage, professional life, civic responsibilities, and the like. The same Bishop recalled the celebrated text of Pius XII affirming that public opinion is an essential dimension in the life of the Church as in any society.

Father Johann Schütte, Superior General of the Society of the Divine Word, urged that the "people of God" not be a "sleeping people" and that the missionary apostolate not be considered a hobby in the Church.

An intervention by Auxiliary Bishop Marius Maziers, Resident Bishop of St.-Etienne, empasized the relationship between temporal work and evangelization. "The Christian faith," he said, "ought not be an excuse for the layman to shirk temporal commitment; rather it should encourage him to increase his commitment."

The Pyramid of the Council Auxiliary Bishop Mark McGrath of Panama took up the same idea, with this addition: "The laity are not only

instruments of the apostolate. The Church is not a clerical pyramid with altar boys at the base."

The Council, with its 2,300 bishops and thirteen laymen, gives a distorted picture of the reality. Bishop McGrath cited Étienne Gilson in asking that the Church favor the development of authentic science in order to offer it to God.

The originality of the intervention by Bishop Jacques Ménager of Meaux, France, was a direct echoing of the opinion of the lay auditors on the schema. They think the definition of the layman is too negative and does not adequately represent their irreplaceable role in the Church.

The Voice of the East Maronite Archbishop Ignace Ziadé of Beirut spoke warmly with the mystical voice of the East. He emphasized what he called the "mysterious" and "pneumatic" side of the Church:

> The sterile legalism of the West must be enriched with Oriental mystery. This is very important for the cause of ecumenism and is, moreover, the only way to overcome the obstacles involved. Before being a visible society, the Church is a sacramental reality centered on the eucharist. The whole apostolate is a parturition of the new creation in search of the Spirit."

Finally, Auxiliary Bishop Alfonso Uribe Jaramillo of Cartagena, Colombia, noted that the whole Church is sacerdotal and that the layman is a priest *ex officio*. He stated, "The two priesthoods, that of the laity and that of the clergy, do not differ 'essentially' but only sacramentally."

This is not the first time that the Council Fathers have said the laity are priests in their own right. It is significant that this quality, today recognized as belonging to the laity, does not contradict the "declericalization" of the Church, although apriori one might believe the opposite. This reversal of perspective is naturally being followed by the Protestants with a good deal of interest.

OCTOBER 2 4

Will Lay Auditors and Observers Speak at the Council?

For a week now, it has been announced that a questionnaire would be circulated the next day bearing on four important questions currently in abeyance: (1) the sacramentality of the episcopacy, (2) collegiality

by divine right, (3) the restoration of a permanent diaconate, married or not, and (4) the inclusion of the schema on the Virgin in that on the Church.

So far nothing has been forthcoming. Why this unexpected delay? The reason is that this procedure is not according to Council regulations. It would nonetheless seem to be a practical means of giving the theological commission specific directives for redrafting the schema. Who has the authority to pass on such questions? The moderators? They tried to do so but came up against the combined objections of the presidency, Archbishop Felici (secretary general of the Council), and some members of the Coordinating Commission.

The Council in fact is suffering from uneasiness at the top. The jurisdictions of its directing organisms are not clearly defined. The Pope and the Secretary of State have had to serve as arbiters, and a solution is expected momentarily.

The Fathers are also complaining increasingly because precious time is lost listening to superfluous interventions. The Council obviously lacks organization. The debates are badly coordinated and unfold in such a disorderly manner that everyone is bored. This problem is difficult to resolve because it is necessary both to respect freedom of expression and not to let the discussion founder. What was the purpose yesterday, for example, of the reflections on euthanasia or the flight of oratory on the hands of Christ?

The most interesting points raised during Wednesday's general congregation can be summarized as follows:

1. The non-Catholic observers constrain themselves to listen to the bishops five days a week. Why not listen to them at least once a week in the conciliar assembly (Patriarch Paul II Cheikho of Babylon)?
2. The laity do not exist simply to believe, pray, obey, and pay. Their spirit of initiative ought to be encouraged. They have had quite enough of being dumb sheep (*oves mutae*). Let them be permitted to speak in St. Peter's (Bishop Primeau of Manchester, New Hampshire).
3. John XXIII and Paul VI have asked the Council to express religious truths in terms understandable by men of our time. The lay auditors do not think this is being done in the discussion of the present schema. The Fathers must therefore improve its wording, and must above all make the schema move in an ascending rather than a descending direction—that is, begin with secular realities and climb to religious truths rather than vice versa (Auxiliary Bishop Rafael González Moralejo of Valencia, Spain).

4. The schema must put more emphasis on the liberty and dignity of the laity and the spiritual character of their mission, and also on the Church of the poor (the same bishop).

5. Let us erase from the schema the qualifier "unfortunate" (*infaustus*) which is applied to the separation of church and state. (Archbishop Shehan of Baltimore, in the name of all the U.S. bishops).

6. Marriage and the graces proper to it, together with baptism and confirmation, constitute one of the theological foundations of the lay apostolate (Auxiliary Bishop José da Silva of Lisbon, in the name of the Portuguese bishops).

7. Charisms are frequent in the Church today, particularly in countries where the liberty of Christians is shackled (Bishop Josip Arneric of Sibenik, Yugoslavia).

8. The laity alone can, if we train an élite among them, overcome the wave of present-day materialism (Coptic Rite Bishop Alexandros Scandar of Assiut, Egypt).

OCTOBER 25

Bishops Close Discussion on the Laity Text

The Council voted Thursday to close discussion of the schema On the People of God, and Especially the Laity. It had entertained seven interventions before doing so. Cardinal Siri's was particularly negative; it even provoked displeasure in the ranks of the Italian hierarchy, who sometimes openly expressed their disagreement. Cardinal Siri made the point that the expression "universal priesthood" was used to please the laity but was injudicious. The term is used in a broadly analogical sense, and account must be taken of the literary genre of Scripture. The speaker insisted twice on the obedience which the laity, whether enjoying charisms or not, owe the hierarchy. But no one in the assembly or elsewhere seems to doubt this point.

Father Aniceto Fernández, Master General of the Dominicans, spoke of the duty to distribute the goods of the earth more equitably. He requested that the Church "multiply economic associations and that a central international commission be organized to this end."

"The Church," said Bishop Pedro Cantero Cuadrado of Huelva, Spain, "is not clerical because the Spirit acts in all the members. It can even be that in matters of faith, the simple faithful might be more expert than theologians. Dialogue with the laity is indispensable to make public opinion operative in the Church."

Laity: A "Pestilential" Expression   Auxiliary Bishop Thomas Muldoon of Sydney, Australia, surprised everyone with an amusing intervention. He had little use for the word *laity*. "The use of this pestilential expression," he said, "is a greater mystery to me than all the supernatural mysteries. Let it be replaced by the term 'people of God.'"

A Declaration Against Racism   Bishop Robert E. Tracy of Baton Rouge spoke in the name of 147 American bishops and drew applause. He asked that the schema include a solemn declaration against racism, "which would have worldwide scope and would be a consolation for all who are deprived of their liberty."

Scriptural Grounds for the Lay Apostolate   Speaking in the name of seventy French bishops and in agreement with the lay auditors, Auxiliary Bishop Ancel of Lyon, criticized the schema for not putting the apostolate of the laity on firm scriptural grounds. He quoted a number of passages to prove that in the Gospel, Christ himself willed this apostolate. The shepherds of the nativity, the good Samaritan, and the good thief all announced Christ. "Let us rely more on Scripture than on theology," he concluded. There is a marked resemblance between this intervention and Paul VI's allocution to the observers in response to Professor Skydsgaard.

Eastern Views   Melkite Rite Bishop Hakim of Acre regretted that the schema was so obviously conceived by bishops and experts from Christian countries. "It seems," he said, "to take no account of the real situation in the world, where two out of three persons do not know Christ. We have become a small flock. Let us then speak with non-Christians in mind."

Reverting to the subject of the diaconate, the Melkite Bishop observed that in the East deacons are chosen from among upright married men, and that this solution is still possible for the West. But, he pointed out, Eastern priests cannot marry after ordination. He also signaled the problem of widowed priests. Finally, he pointed out a "serious omission" in the schema: women.

"It is as though they did not exist," he said, "and yet they are the first batallion [*primum agmen*] of humanity. There is a connection, moreover, between the promotion of woman's role and devotion to Mary."

Whither the Schema on Mary?

At this point cloture on the discussion was voted, and then Cardinal Döpfner announced in the name of the moderators that the Council would be called upon soon to decide whether or not the schema on the Virgin ought to be included in that on the Church. Two cardinals with conflicting views were invited to debate the issue: Rufino Cardinal Santos, Archbishop of Manila, and Cardinal Koenig, Archbishop of Vienna. Judging by the applause, the Fathers seem to favor a single schema, as recommended by Cardinal Koenig. Apart from other considerations, this solution offers ecumenical advantages. The Orthodox and Anglicans and other Protestants have no objection when Mary is presented as the "type of the Church"; it is only when this devotion is isolated that abuses set in.

"The Vocation of a Priest Is Distinct from the Celibate's," Says Archbishop Edelby

Before opening herself to other Christian confessions, the Latin Church owes it to herself to be very attentive to her Oriental branch—the Uniates, who have proven their fidelity to the See of Rome with their blood. Wouldn't the best antidote to Roman legalism and rigidity be a consideration of the special values of the East?

Brilliant in the first session, the contribution of the patriarchical Churches continues to attract attention today. The personalities of Maximos IV Saigh of Antioch and his auxiliaries are particularly impressive. Vatican II already owes them much. For his reason there was a capacity crowd Thursday afternoon when Archbishop Neophite Edelby of the Titular Archdiocese of Edessa spoke at St. Agnes Church on the Piazza Navona. With as much frankness as diplomacy, he spoke of his reactions to the Council as an Oriental:

> The Western Church is still too clerical, both in its ideas and in its behavior. Its basic perspective is different from ours: Christ established Peter as the supreme head, a kind of Roman emperor in a cassock; he then gave him collaborators and finally subjects— the clergy and the faithful. The opposite is true for the Orientals: Christ went first to the faithful, for whom the preaching of the Gospel is a right; next, he gave them the apostles; finally, in order that this college remain coherent, he chose a head for it. In modern

Catholic thought, there is a kind of morbid obsession with papal primacy. One must almost recite a prayer of exorcism. To say that the pope is God on earth is blasphemy. The sovereign pontiff is surrounded with an obsequious respect that is in no way evangelical. Let us return, then, to the Gospel. The rest is worldliness and should not exist. . . .

The schema on the laity is asexual. It does not mention woman, whose role as wife and mother is irreplacable.

Archbishop Edelby then spoke of ecclesiastical celibacy:

The vocation of a deacon or a priest is distinct from the celibate's, which requires a special grace. I am astonished at the attacks heard in the Council against a married diaconate. We have a married diaconate. And yet we think we are the Church. The married diaconate has therefore always existed in the Catholic Church. The Latin Church is the exception to the rule. A married diaconate is no more a threat to priestly vocations than are religious orders. Moreover, 80 percent of our candidates for the priesthood prefer to remain celibate, and their number is increasing. Celibacy is an undeniable source of spiritual fecundity, but it is good that it remains the fruit of a personal choice. Married priests helped save the faith in our countries during periods of persecution because of their family and professional roots in the villages.

Archbishop Roberts Recommends
an "Inquisition of the Inquisition"

A mere stone's throw from the palace of the Holy Office, at 25 Via del Santo Ufficio, Archbishop Roberts, a Jesuit and formerly archbishop of Bombay, recommended what he called an "inquisition of the inquisition" in a press conference. Typically English, diminutive in stature and dressed in simple clerical garb, Archbishop Roberts' way of expressing himself unavoidably reminds one of G. K. Chesterton. Behind thick glasses, his eyes sparkle with roguishness and humor. This old campaigner resigned his see in 1950 for the present native incumbent, Cardinal Gracias. He once published a book on obedience. Practically unobtainable today, it was a model of courage and a democratic spirit.

Archbishop Roberts attaches the greatest importance to the press. In his opinion, journalists inform bishops as well as the faithful of what is going on at the Council. Latin, he thinks, is a big obstacle, and he said he has been struck by the number of bishops who have given up

following the interventions attentively, preferring to make personal contacts in the coffee bars. That is why Archbishop Roberts communicates
his views to the press rather than in the aula. His ideas are simple but
important. He expresses them so wittily and matter-of-factly that he
provokes continual laughter. Yet he is talking of extremely important
matters. The reader can judge for himself:

> If the members of the Holy Office used such methods in England,
> they would immediately be hailed before a court of law. It would be
> good if the inquisition of today conducted itself differently from
> the Inquisition of the Middle Ages. Quite frankly, I personally don't
> see any difference. It is more difficult in the twentieth century to
> kill and imprison; still, reputations are ruined and careers are broken.
> There is no doubt that the inquisition has the right to protect the
> faith, but it has the no less imperious right of respecting the natural
> law, which is made by God and not the Church.
>
> The tendency in the Church is to prevent scandals from becom-
> ing known. In God's eyes it is reparation of scandal that counts. If
> someone's reputation has suffered, reparation must be made at all
> costs. If this involves the resignation of a cardinal or a bishop, then
> it is very important that he resign, for according to the Gospel a
> bishop is above all a man of humility.
>
> Paul VI has said that the Curia must be reformed. That is cor-
> rect; but it depends on the clergy and faithful as well as the Pope
> and bishops. Otherwise, reform will be effected in theory but not
> in practice.

One of the most important and urgent reforms, thinks Archbishop
Roberts, is that of the ecclesiastic courts which handle marriage cases.

"In fact," he said, "one often has to wait years to get any results.
Most of those concerned opt to marry civilly and thus leave the Church."

Archbishop Roberts insisted that public opinion must demand a real
and rapid reform without waiting until canon law is completely revised;
this could take ten years.

> People have written me asking that the Council concern itself
> with the protection of animals. But it is more important to protect
> men and women. . . . In Scandinavia there is an admirable institution:
> the government gives great powers to a high official to deal with
> 'appeals from the humble' who feel they are victims of injustice
> and to conduct investigations. Such an institution would be very
> useful in the Church, for bishops, seminarians, professors of Scrip-
> ture [this was an allusion to certain exegetes who have been the

target of Roman calumny], and finally, for women, who have no voice in the Church and who, surprisingly, have no official capacity at the Council.

Archbishop Roberts regretted that women are not protected by canon law.

"Male religious have a cardinal 'protector.' But whom does he protect? I believe above all that he is on the side of superiors rather than of obscure women religious or humble priests."

Archbishop Roberts noted that he had submitted a written intervention to the Council but preferred , he repeated, to confide in journalists in order to be heard.

OCTOBER 26

The Bishop of Verdun Urges the Church
To Exhibit Exterior Signs of Poverty

Bishop Pierre Boillon of Verdun was the first to speak in the general congregation yesterday, Friday. "The Church," he said, "is a stranger to the poor. Marxism has captured the attention of the poor because it speaks to them of their dignity as men. Why is the Church not heard? Because the exterior signs of wealth deceive the poor."

The Bishop cited the parable of poor Lazarus: "There was a rich man clothed in purple and fine linen." The Fathers understood the allusion perfectly. "Let the Council declare," Bishop Boillon added, "that the poor have a divine right to first place in the Church. Let the Church be poor and appear poor. Vatican II cannot be silent on this question. The rich will not enter the kingdom of heaven."

It was far from the first time the issue of poverty has been raised in the Council. Cardinals Lercaro and Gerlier, Archbishop Gouyon, and others have spoken about it. But repetition is one of the most effective pedagogical techniques; hammering at the same nail will indubitably get results. What must the poor think of the case that has recently been recounted here, to cite but one example, of the Benedictine abbot in Italy who owns three cars: one for his pastoral work, one for official visits, and a third for his personal use? It is likely, at least according to widespread rumor, that Paul VI, the first among the bishops, will soon set an example of poverty that will get a general movement going in the Church. The Vatican, the heart of Catholicism, stands most in need of a reform in this direction.

Religious Liberty

Bishop Méndez Arceo of Cuernavaca spoke in the name of sixty bishops on church-state relations. The policy of separation which exists in many countries, he said, is not a lesser evil, a "hypothesis" that must be tolerated; it is a positive good, and it is mandatory to strike the adjective "unfortunate" from the word "separation" in the schema. In some countries the Church is persecuted and is the object of suspicion; in others she is "too much bound up with the central power." "We anxiously await the schema on religious liberty," the Bishop added, "which has been prepared by the Secretariat for Promoting Christian Unity. Without this text we cannot validly treat the important question of church-state relations."

In the name of all the Polish bishops, Archbishop Antoni Baraniak of Poznan said that in certain countries where bishops cannot exercise their ministry, laymen and even women can replace them, as for example at the Council.

Bishop Michel Darmancier, speaking in the name of the six bishops of Oceania, stressed the ecumenical value of the universal declaration of the rights of man issued by the United Nations which proclaims religious liberty.

Coadjutor Bishop da Veiga Coutinho of Belgaum, India, stated that his country is in desperate need of laymen who can perform sacred functions. A married diaconate, which he favors, would not suffice to carry out the essential work they would be expected to do.

"We should be careful in using the term 'people of God,'" said Bishop Joseph Evangelisti of Meerut, India, who intervened in the name of several bishops from India, Pakistan, China, and Indonesia. "For it can easily give offense to non-Christians, as if we are insinuating that they are the people of the devil. This is false, because Christ died for all men." He proposed that the schema replace this offensive expression with "the Christian people."

On Sanctity

The second part of the session was given over to an examination of chapter 4 of the schema *De Ecclesia*, which is entitled, "On the Vocation to Holiness in the Church."

It was noted that the Sermon on the Mount is addressed to all without exception. In fact, Christ said to everyone, "Be ye perfect as your heavenly Father is perfect." Every Christian is obligated to follow the evangelical counsels.

Bishop Guillaume Schoemaker of Purwokerto, Indonesia, specified that "Sanctity does not consist in exercises but in love."

Bishop Luigi Morstabilini of Veroli-Frosinone, Italy, declared that there is no necessity to do something extraordinary to become a saint; it is enough to live each day as one should.

"More than anyone else," said Bishop Marcello González Martin of Astorga, Spain, "bishops must pursue sanctity."

OCTOBER 29

The Council Gives Homage to John XXIII

The Council paused yesterday, Monday, to render homage to John XXIII, who had succeeded Pius XII six years ago to the day. It was a fundamental gesture of gratitude toward him who in his pontifical solitude decided against his advisers to convoke Vatican II for the purpose of helping him reform the Church. It was also a gesture of reparation—this is the word the bishops most frequently use—to erase the memory of Monsignior Tondini's allocution on the eve of the last conclave [see page 114]. Who could forget the scarcely blunted barbs which that Roman prelate shot at the deceased Pope in his official discourse to the princes of the Church?

With emotion and filial piety, the Fathers listened to the sermon by Cardinal Suenens, which was given in French and not Latin as was expected. He said, "John XXIII was a man who was astonishingly natural and supernatural. Everything he did flowed from a deep spring of spirituality. He was natural with such a supernatural spirit that no one could discern where one left off and the other began. He breathed physical and moral health with full lungs." And the Cardinal quoted Louis Lavelle: "Charity is pure attention to the existence of another."

On this anniversary, an unusual mass was celebrated by Paul VI in St. Peter's: the office was dialogued throughout by the congregation. Everybody participated, which is rare in St. Peter's, where the choir normally intrudes between the celebrant and the congregation. After the ceremony a colleague said to me, "It's just like mass back home."

On the Pope's right was Monsignor Capovilla, former secretary to Pope John, and in the first seats of the Basilica sat members of the

Roncalli family. After the sermon Paul VI flaunted protocol by shaking hands with each of them.

New Commission Elections?

Vatican II got back to work this morning, Tuesday. There is more and more talk in the corridors of the Council about the opportuneness of new elections to the conciliar commissions as a means of overcoming the discouragement of many bishops. There is no doubt that some of them are not representative of the majority of the Fathers; this is especially true of the theological commission, and there is widespread fear that this commission will redraft the schema *De Ecclesia* in a way which could paralyze the Council.

The president of this commission is, of course, Cardinal Ottaviani; his secretary is Father Tromp, a consultor to the Holy Office. Their thinking represents but a feeble minority today. And this is one of the basic causes of Vatican II's present uneasiness.

Petitions from national conferences of bishops have been circulating these past few days which indicate their anxiety about this state of affairs and their desire to see a change. It cannot be said often enough, for it is fundamental, that the Council is directed against the supremacy of the Curia. That is why Paul VI's speech on the reform of the Curia, given before the opening of the second session, remains one of the principal hopes of the bishops. If the Curia, particularly the Holy Office, is radically transformed, Vatican II will have been a success. If not, this would be a setback.

Happily, it seems more and more evident that Paul VI wants a real reform, that he already has a general plan for reform, and that it will be promulgated before the end of the year 1964.

At the moment, the Fathers are looking forward to the schema "On Bishops and the Government of Dioceses," which explicitly treats the relationship between bishops and the Curia. Discussion on it will begin after All Saints'.

Three recent events are presently being talked about in Rome. They reveal the asperity of the rear guard.

First, Father Carolo Balič, a consultor to the Holy Office, president of the International Pontifical Marian Academy, and an expert at Vatican II, has circulated a brochure with his comments on the schema on the Virgin. This is a normal enough procedure. What is less so, and what might mislead some of the Council Fathers, is that it was printed by the

Vatican Polyglot Press, the official printers to the Vatican, which publish the schemas of the Council.

Second, the commission on theology is doing everything it can to block the publication of the schema on religious liberty, prepared by the Secretariat for Promoting Christian Unity and approved several months ago by the Coordinating Commission. This schema is incontestably of the greatest importance from the ecumenical point of view. Cardinal Bea's team drew it up with customary openmindedness. And that is precisely the rub.

Third, it is rumored that Cardinal Antoniutti, Prefect of the Sacred Congregation of Religious, has sent a letter to the superiors general of religious orders with houses in Rome warning them against twelve experts, among them Fathers Yves Congar, Karl Rahner, Hans Küng, and J. Ratzinger.

If this proves to be a fact, it will set in bold relief the distance between some members of the Curia—some but not all—and the Sovereign Pontiff. In fact, the Pope recently said in a private audience (this is no rumor but a fact) that Father Congar is one of the theologians who most contributed to the preparation of Vatican II and whose thought is most respected by the Council Fathers.

In so saying, Paul VI merely echos a truth that is evident to all men of good faith. But if some truths need not be articulated, others do. Especially by the Pope.

OCTOBER 30

Vatican II at a Crucial Stage

"Vatican II ought to play its hand on Wednesday." Such was the opinion of those who see the Council as an indispensable instrument of institutional reform in the Church. This point of view is not the only possible one. Others think the Council will play its hand when it speaks—either well or badly—of ecumenism, religious liberty, mixed marriages, conscientious objection, conjugal spirituality, and so forth.

But it cannot be denied that the issue today, Wednesday, was an important one. The Fathers were asked to answer yes or no to the following question, which is the doctrinal knot of the Council:

> Does it please you that the Council affirm that the body or college of bishops succeeds the college of apostles in its evangelical, sanctifying, and pastoral function? Does it please you that it be said that this college of bishops, united with its head, the sovereign pontiff,

and never without its head—it being well understood that the right of primacy of this head remains safe and entire—enjoys full and sovereign power in the universal Church?*

The question is a weighty one. It demands nothing short of a recognition that the bishops as a college succeed the college of apostles and that there are two subjects of full and sovereign authority in the Church: the Pope and the college. If, as seems likely, Vatican II ratifies this judgment, the Roman Church will have ceased to be—if indeed she ever was—a pure monarchy and will become a collegiality. It follows that the Pope will naturally seek the support of a more or less permanent organism composed of a certain number of *residential* bishops in governing the Church.

The Council was also presented with four other questions:

1. Is the supreme power of the college of divine right (fourth question)?
2. Does episcopal consecration constitute the supreme degree of the sacrament of orders (first question)?
3. Is every legitimately consecrated bishop, in communion with the other bishops and the Roman pontiff, a member of the episcopal body (second question)?
4. Is it opportune to restore the diaconate as a distinct and permanent rank of the ministry to serve local needs (fifth question)?

Silence on a Married Diaconate   The last question prudently avoided the issue of a married diaconate. To raise it would have encouraged a negative response which could be damaging to the interests of the Church. On the request of national episcopal conferences, the Pope can always authorize *ad experimentum* a married diaconate where the need for one is felt.

An absolute majority instead of the normal two-thirds was required in this vote. But it was only a guideline ballot and in no way a judgment on the schema as a whole, which will be taken up later when the hundreds of emendations have been incorporated by the theological commission.

As soon as these questions were put to them, the Fathers' morale rose again after several days of depression. For Vatican II has gotten unstuck. It took more than a week of tergiversations to get this far. But better late than never.

* This was the third of the five questions posed.

A Slim Majority

On Tuesday the Council voted on the suitability of including the schema on the Virgin in the schema *De Ecclesia.* The results were extremely close. Passions and politicking in both camps resulted in an unconvincing majority favoring inclusion. That the Virgin is so controversial a subject in the Church of 1963 is proof that Vatican II must ease into discussion of more serious theological problems with great prudence. Why do so many want a special schema on the Virgin? Is it practical? No one is offended that there is no special schema on Christ or the Trinity, subjects of greater importance.

Vatican II will soon begin discussion on the Marian schema. This will occasion further divisive debate, and no significant results can be expected. The faithful will have little interest in the subtleties of the schools.

Tuesday's session also continued examination of the chapter on holiness. We shall summarize only two points from the interventions. First, several Fathers emphasized the necessity that the bishop be a saint, and regretted that the schema said nothing about this. Second, sanctity is not essentially a moral value or an ascetic effort. It is an ontological value, a gratuitous gift from God, a habitual union with him, the fruit of a mystical union, a work of love. "I seek not virtue," said Theresa of Ávila, "but the Lord of virtue." The thought is similar to Charles Péguy's observation, "Morality is a shield which makes people impermeable to grace."

OCTOBER 31

Several Fathers Again Stress Lay Spirituality

Wednesday's interventions paled considerably by comparison with the voting on episcopal collegiality. Nonetheless, they are important in their own right. Several percussive interventions were heard before the discussion on the schema's chapter 4, on holiness, ended.

Cardinal Léger, Archbishop of Montreal: "Let laymen be allowed in seminaries to teach matters concerning the theology of terrestrial realities."

Cardinal Cento: "Let the Church canonize more laymen."

Cardinal Bea: "The Catholic Church counts many sinning members; otherwise the Reformation would not have taken place."

Bishop Huyghe of Arras: "Canon law wrongly identifies perfection with the three vows of chastity, poverty, and obedience." (Bishop Sebastião Soares de Resenda of Beira, Mozambique, said the same thing.)

"Many Christians work toward perfection by other means. Let us pay more attention to life than to juridical rules."

Bishop René Fourrey of Belley, France: "The need of a spirituality that is specifically lay and not monastic is strongly felt in the Church of today."

Bishop Franič of Split, Yugoslavia: "There are few saints among the bishops [he quoted Virgil: *"Rari nantes in gurgite vasto"*], and many among religious. We bishops lack evangelical poverty: How can we speak of the Church of the poor as long as bishops are rich? Poverty is the foundation of sanctity. Let us renounce the signs of wealth, then. Let us not hesitate to work with our hands as often as possible."

Pharisaism   Archabbot Benedict Reetz of the Beuron Benedictine Congregation said that a monk can sometimes be more full of pride than anyone else, and warned against pharisaism. The right of exemption for religious must be retained at all costs, he said. "Let us look at this from the standpoint more of humility than of legalism."

A Byzantine Mass   Finally, let us note that the conciliar mass was celebrated according to the Byzantine Rite by Archbishop Slipyi, a Ukrainian and a former prisoner in the Siberian prison camps. The Ukranian seminarians in Rome sang the mass brilliantly. When it came time to incense the congregation, everyone noticed that Archbishop Slipyi turned first toward the Oriental patriarchs and only then toward the cardinals.

Voting Acknowledges the Full Powers
of the Episcopal College

The voting on Wednesday recognized the bishops' sovereignty in the Church. On the third question, of whether the college of bishops succeeds the college of the apostles and "enjoys full and sovereign power in the universal Church," the Fathers voted 1,808 yes and 336 no, with 4 void ballots.

On the fourth question, on whether the supreme power of the college is of divine right, 1,717 of 2,138 votes answered yes and 408 no, with 13 void ballots.

On the first question, of whether episcopal consecration constitutes the supreme degree of the sacrament of orders, 2,123 of 2,157 voters said yes and 34 no.

On the second question, of whether every bishop legitimately consecrated in communion with the other bishops and the Roman pontiff (who is their head and the principle of unity), is a member of the body of bishops, 2,049 voted yes and 104 no, with 1 void ballot.

On the fifth question, of whether it is opportune to restore the diaconate as a distinct and permanent state of the ministry to serve local needs, 2,120 voted, with 1,588 saying yes, 525 no, and 7 void ballots.

A New Page in the Roman Church   Unbelievers may be surprised, Protestants may be skeptical, integralists may hide their faces in their hands; the fact is that on October 30 at 11 o'clock in the morning Vatican II affirmed that the college of bishops enjoys full and sovereign authority in the universal Church and that this authority is of divine right.

The schema *de ecclesia*, it is true, has not yet been adopted. Wednesday's decision is not official since the Pope has not ratified it, but it is unthinkable that he will not do so.

"Full and sovereign power"—what does this mean? Since Vatican I the pope has been practically considered as the only holder of universal authority in the Church. The text adopted in 1870 reads, "The fullness of power to shepherd, govern, and administer the entire Church has been transmitted to the pope." Vatican II, without forgetting one iota of the former definitions, now states further that the episcopal body enjoys an analagous power in the universal Church.

Each bishop, therefore, must be interested not only in his own diocese but in all others as well. He has no direct authority over another diocese, of course, but the totality of bishops has authority over the totality of the Church, as does the pope. There are thus two subjects of sovereign authority in the Church: the pope and the college of bishops. However, since the pope is the head of the college, the two cannot logically be in conflict.

Moreover, the power of the college is said to be of divine right. This is a powerful qualification. The expression sounds bad to secular ears. It especially evokes political memories—of the divine right of absolute monarchy. But in this context it has a quite different meaning, a meaning without decadent overtones, which might be formulated in these words: it is Christ's will—and therefore the will of God and not of men—that the episcopal college possess universal authority.

Vatican II has thus explicated a truth that is not of ecclesiastical right but of divine right, and consequently a truth that cannot be changed.

Only 408 Fathers opposed this notion. The small size of the minority surprised many people. This proves once again that these have not understood that Vatican II opened a totally new page in the history of the Church.

The integralists in particular fall behind the Council by about a century. Their efforts and their intimidations have been foiled to a degree one could not have imagined.

Perhaps the beaten minority will now sacrifice their self-interest to the greater good; such humility has not been unknown at crucial moments in the Church's history. For after all, to be a Catholic implies subordinating one's personal judgment to that of the Church.

NOVEMBER, 1963

The Moderators Resume Control of the Council

The success of the voting on Wednesday will have important psychological repercussions now and in the future. Credit for the success must go to the moderators, who, not without difficulty, made the original formula of indicative votes prevail. Their prestige was at stake. If the majority that should have emerged in the voting had vacillated, the impotence of the assembly would have been obvious to all. And that would have been the end of Vatican II on the doctrinal plane.

If the Theological Commission had not received specific instructions, its already difficult work would have become impossible. Without clearly stated directives, how could it have integrated contradictory amendments, and how would the assembly have functioned when it came to a definitive vote on more or less muddled texts? Now the situation is clear. To unequivocal questions the Council gave unequivocal answers, and everyone knows where Vatican II wants to go. It is no longer possible to waver, evade the issue, or turn the clock back. The course has been set. It remains only to follow it.

The authority of the moderators has increased. They will now be able to conduct the daily business of the Council without the loss of time that was becoming more and more intolerable to the Fathers. Vatican II is about to begin again in a new spirit and with new energy. By voting for collegial sovereignty of divine right, the bishops have strengthened their position markedly. The Council, a privileged locus for the exercise of this collegiality, will be the first to feel its effects. A tool has been fashioned; it has only to be put to use.

When the general congregation began on Thursday, one could sense that the atmosphere had changed. Cardinal Döpfner, the moderator for the day, spoke with authority about the order of discussion. Cloture on the last chapter of the schema *De ecclesia* had been decided upon the day before. But in keeping with the regulations, the Fathers could still speak if they did so in the name of five other Council members. Requests on this occasion reached a record number: forty-three Fathers registered! The moderators therefore decided to be stricter: the time for each speaker was reduced from ten to eight minutes, and the new rule would be rigorously enforced. The Fathers were urged to avoid repetition and digressions; they were also asked to submit their interventions in writing whenever possible, since, as Cardinal Döpfner pointed out, they "have the same value" as oral interventions.

"Out of Order"   Nineteen fathers spoke on Thursday. Cardinal de Arriba y Castro, Archbishop of Tarragona, was first in line: he took up arms against the general corruption of morals in our time, the bad influence of the press and radio, the obscenity of stage shows, the growing number of divorces, and so forth. Bishop Isidor Emanuel of Speyer, Germany, wanted the laity and married people to be canonized as well as religious and widows. He was told that he was "out of order." Former Archbishop Juan Gonzales Arbelá of Popayan, Colombia, hoped the Council would say more about parish priests since it is supposed to be pastorally oriented.

Archbishop Joseph Martin of Rouen stressed the ecumenical value of religious vocations: "The whole history of the Orient is dominated by monasticism; the Anglicans restored it to a place of honor at the end of the nineteenth century; and if it is true that Luther rejected the 'vows,' the Protestant Churches are today in the process of rediscovering them." The Archbishop cited the community of Taizé as an outstanding example. This was fitting since the prior of that community and his assistant are among the guests invited to Vatican II by the Secretariat for Promoting Christian Unity.

Speaking for eleven bishops, Auxiliary Bishop Ildefonso Sansierra of San Juan de Cuyo, Argentina, suggested that two paragraphs be added to the schema: one on the poor, who should have evangelical priority as Christ asked, and the other on workers.

Father Giocondò Grotti, Prelate Mullius of Acre and Purús, Brazil, was called to order since the moderator thought he digressed. "We have heard very kind words," he said, "about the separated brethren and about women, who have even been invited to speak in the Council, but nothing about 'fallen' priests."

Archbishop Joseph Gopu of Hyderabad, India, requested that the expression "secular clergy" be replaced by "diocesan clergy."

First Simultaneous Translations

During this session some simultaneous translation equipment was tried out. Some of the Fathers were able to hear an English version of the interventions. It was decided that the hard-pressed interpreters should have an exact and complete copy of the text in advance so as to avoid improvising.

The Council will not meet again until Tuesday, November 5. Many of the ceremonies of All Saints' will commemorate the fourth centenary of the institution of seminaries by the Council of Trent.

NOVEMBER 5

Cardinal Ruffini Urges a Crusading Catholicism

Cardinal Ruffini, Archbishop of Palermo, gave a press conference this afternoon. This prelate doesn't show his seventy-five years. He has regular features, an alert mind, and eyes that peer over his glasses with amused curiosity. He has a sense of humor but is also very aggressive. It is a military aggressiveness, actually, since in his eyes priests are officers and laymen, an extension of the clergy, are second-class soldiers. The Church needs them "to go to the front and conquer the enemy." "What would officers do if they had no soldiers under their command?" he asks.

He also thinks laymen are important "to conquer the key positions of the secular world—in the press, cinema, television, universities, schools, politics, and so forth—to offset communism and devastating materialism."

The Cardinal lamented the immorality of the cinema several times. "Even in Italy," he added, "one feels ashamed when viewing certain films. Shall we remain like the 'silent dogs' Scripture speaks of before these excesses?"

The prelate contrasted license with liberty, which he defined as "the right to do one's duty." He concluded, "Let us pray and study. Laymen frequently have a poor understanding of their faith. We need martyrs and witnesses to the faith who will be of value to the family, society, and economic progress. To love God and fatherland is to serve them. "

This vision of the Church and the world has simplicity, clarity, and a kind of tradition that is still alive in regions where Christianity is established. It corresponds exactly with what in France has been called a crusading Catholicism, dear to movements which have made anticommunism and antimaterialism their chief preoccupations. Identifying Catholicism with an ideology, they end up at the extreme positions we are all familiar with.

It was good that Cardinal Ruffini left the seats in St. Peter's to descend into the arena and preach the "good fight" to journalists. Now we know what to expect. There would have been some questions, but Cardinal Ruffini doesn't seem to like letting laymen interrogate him.

NOVEMBER 6

The Schema on the Bishops
Must Be Completely Rewritten

"People do not put new wine in old wineskins, lest the skins break, the wine run out, and the skins be ruined. But they put new wine into fresh skins, and both are preserved" (Matt. 9:17).

This biblical reflection is perfectly applicable to the present moment. In voting last week to affirm collegiality by divine right, the assembly has put the Church and the Council in a radically new situation—so much so that the schema "On Bishops and the Government of Dioceses" presented on Tuesday seems completely out of date.

This schema treats of (1) the relations between bishops and the Curia, (2) the participation of bishops in the government of the Church, (3) the role of episcopal conferences, and related subjects. It is a capitally important document, without which the dogmatic decisions taken in the past few days could not be put into effect.

An expert at the Council has written that had this schema as it stands been ratified in the time of Pius XII, "It would have been considered a sensational step forward, if not the ecclesial event of the century." That is quite possible; but since the historic vote on October 30, the document has suddenly aged to the point of being useless in its present form. The schema asks that "new faculties" be conceded the bishops to govern their dioceses. It puts the bishops rather in the position of asking the Pope for a little more authority as a *favor* instead of as a *right* given them by the authority of their ministry by divine right. The whole perspective of the schema must therefore be changed. It calls for more than a mere patching job; it must be radically rethought.

Cardinal Liénart Demands a Vote   The day's interventions focused on this central idea. The French did themselves credit. Cardinal Liénart said in substance:

> Now that the doctrine of the episcopacy is clear, let us review this whole schema. The hour has come to respond to the hope ex-

pressed by Paul VI in his speech to the Curia and therefore demand that the bishops be habitually associated with the pope in the government of the Church by virtue of their collegiality of divine right; let us ask the assembly to express their will on this matter by a vote.

The Cardinal then noted the ecumenical value of this kind of reform, which is very much in the direction of Oriental aspirations.

"Every right," said Cardinal Richaud of Bordeaux, "must be based on the divine right of bishops. Let us no longer speak, as the schema does, of 'faculties conceded' but of respect for our rights." (Archbishop Louis de Bazelaire de la Ruppierre of Chambéry spoke in a similar vein.) "As for episcopal conferences, let us clearly state their competence and the fact that they do not require curial approval on numerous matters —the liturgy, seminary curricula, Catholic Action, and the like."

The Reform of the Curia   The question of the Curia itself and its reform was directly dealt with by Bishop Giuseppe Gargitter of Bressanone, Italy, who also agreed that the schema should be reworked:

> The utility of a Curia is evident, but let us insist on the spirit of service and love that should animate it and on the fact that it is an executive organ. A real decentralization of power in the Church is not a concession but a logical consequence of the doctrine of the episcopacy. Let us remember the great principle of subsidiarity. Let us speak openly of the internationalization of the Curia, for in practice [that body] has become the privilege of one nation.

Cardinal Gracias of Bombay spoke of the nuncios or apostolic delegates. He asked that a similar reform be undertaken in respect to them; he said that they should have a detailed knowledge of the political problems, philosophy, and manners and customs of the countries to which they are sent, and that they know how to speak the local language.

Episcopal Conferences and Socialization   Archbishop Garrone of Toulouse spoke vigorously on the question of episcopal conferences:

> The socialization of the world, that is, the multiplication of interdependencies and cross-currents, is a universal phenomenon. All important problems go beyond the borders of a diocese. Now, since there is presently no competent authority to deal with them, either they are not solved or they are solved without the episcopacy. In either case, the bishop is not fulfilling his role. Only episcopal conferences can meet this need. They constitute the necessary condition

for the bishops' fulfilling their pastoral charge. Collegiality is a vital necessity as well as a doctrine, and it is providential that the Council has defined it.

Archbishop François Marty of Rheims, viewing matters in a practical perspective, requested specific rules for action. He emphasized the usefulness of regular meetings of national episcopal conferences, and hoped that these would maintain close rapport with lesser regional assemblies.

Auxiliary Bishop Jubany of Barcelona and Bishop Jean Rupp of Monaco both suggested that canons and cathedral chapters play a more active role in naming bishops and conducting the affairs of the diocese. We might note in passing that the schema says nothing about the nomination of bishops, a matter which is commonly agreed to be in need of reform.

Only one bishop pointed out the possible dangers of episcopal conferences, although he acknowledged the services they could render. James Francis Cardinal McIntyre, Archbishop of Los Angeles, feared that these assemblies would form an obstacle between bishops and the people on the one hand and between bishops and the pope on the other.

Expected Reactions   Bishop Pablo Correa León of Cúcuta, Colombia, speaking in the name of sixty bishops, seriously criticized those responsible for the preparation and presentation of the schema. He deplored that more than half of the members of the competent conciliar commission, presided over by Cardinal Marella, had been neither convoked nor consulted on the schema; he also complained that the present reporter, Bishop Carli, had not been elected according to the explicit stipulations of the rules and that his report had not been submitted to the commission.

At the end of this important general congregation, there was a widespread impression that the assembly, strong in its overwhelming vote in favor of affirming collegiality by divine right, will quickly ask for a radical reworking of the schema on the bishops. But meanwhile the temperature of the Council is certain to rise. The Curia, feeling itself directly threatened, will quite probably react and appeal to all its friends to limit the demanded changes as much as possible. But won't this be a wasted effort? The Council is leaning with all its weight in the opposite direction.

Whatever the case, Vatican II has now come down from the pinnacle of theological speculation to discuss the reform of the Church's institutions in detail. The time has come to translate principles into action.

Paul VI Scolds Lateran University
for Its "Tedious Polemics"

Paul VI is a prudent and deliberate man. Such is his current reputation in many Italian circles. But his prudence does not prevent him from throwing his authority in the balance when he thinks he should do so. His discourse to the Curia on September 21 was a case in point. A few days later, he defended Father Congar in a private audience, thus cutting off the unfavorable comments of those who have long tried to discredit the thought of one of the greatest contemporary Catholic theologians.

Recently Paul VI presided over ceremonies opening the academic year at Lateran University. In a speech given before forty cardinals, the Pope took sides against the polemical acts of certain professors who are known to be more or less directly responsible for violent attacks on the Pontifical Biblical Institute.

Paul VI expressed himself in these words: "It is our wish that the Lateran University express itself in its relations with other Roman institutes in terms of mutual gratitude, fraternal collaboration, loyal emulation, reciprocal respect, and mutual concord—and never in terms of jealous rivalry or tedious polemics, never!" the Pope repeated energetically. And he concluded, "The Pontifical Lateran University will thus have its own mission to fulfill, its particular physiognomy to show forth, and its specific merit to win; and then it will always be favored with our affection and supported with our blessings."

NOVEMBER 7

Many Fathers Hope the Curia
Will Be Simply an Executive Organ

Rejected purely and simply because of its many faults, the schema on the bishops would have impeded discussion on a theme of the first importance and would thus have prevented the bishops from expressing their criticisms and desires publicly before the Council. For this reason, the Fathers agreed that the present schema will serve as a basis of future discussions. The ballots revealed the following results: of 2,100 voters, 1,610 said yes, and 477 no, with 13 ballots invalid.

Before reporting further on Wednesday's interventions, it is important to return to what presently appears to be the number one problem: the theological commission, with Cardinal Ottaviani as president and Father Tromp as secretary. These two persons, in whom practically all power is vested, seem determined to pay no heed to the indicative vote of October 30. "These votes," Cardinal Ottaviani has said in substance, "have no legal value." Cardinal Ruffini expressed a similar opinion yesterday before the conciliar assembly: "The vote of October 30 determines nothing. Only the commission has the right to examine the schema and expand the study of this problem; only then will we know what to do."

Some twenty bishops recently petitioned Paul VI to reorganize the commissions and let the Fathers themselves name the secretaries, until presently named by the Pope. The question now is whether—or rather, when—Paul will do this. More and more of the Fathers are of the opinion that the Council cannot continue unless the commissions reflect the true thinking of the assembly. The voting on October 30 may have been only indicative, but it was eloquent. To try to conceal its significance could in the long run only do harm.

In any case, the interventions of this week are further proof that the Fathers are resolute in their attitude toward curial reform, and it is difficult to see how this can be avoided, especially after the Pope's speech of September 21.

"The Church Was Given to Peter and the Apostles, Not to the Curia"
The intervention of Maximos IV Saigh, pronounced as usual in French, was the event of the day. He said in part:

> Let the Council make it clear that the Curia is the court of the bishops of Rome and in no way the college. . . . The very fact that Roman cardinals are assigned to particular titular churches in Rome shows that they belong more to a particular church, that of Rome, than to the Church of Christ, for the latter is not limited to Rome. The Church should have at her disposal a genuine Sacred College, composed of patriarchs, according to the early Church councils; of cardinals, whose titles would come from the cathedral churches of their dioceses, not from a parish church in Rome; and of bishops elected by episcopal conferences.

> To assist the Holy Father, there should be . . . a permanent synod with members succeeding each other by term. This body would be supreme, even over the curia, with the last word always resting with the sovereign pontiff.

The Patriarch continued:

> All the Roman offices should be subjected to this supreme Sacred College. [Note that he intentionally used the adjective presently

applied to the *Supreme* Congregation of the Holy Office.] These ministries have no right to block all progress in a uniform and sometimes niggling manner.

Moreover, the problems proper to each country should be resolved in those countries. The pope cannot rule the Church with the advice of his familiars alone. The Church was given to Peter and the apostles, not to the Curia. These reforms are urgent. Otherwise we will be courting catastrophe, especially in the East.

He then spoke of the various Churches—African, Chinese, Indian, and the rest—and hoped that they would be able to develop freely and retain their own identity.

The Accusation of Imperialism In other interventions, these points were made:

1. The Curia's role is to execute, not rule; it must become the executive arm of a central organism created by the body of bishops to aid the pope in governing the Church (Cardinals Koenig, Alfrink, and Bea; Archbishop Fernando Gomes dos Santos of Goiania, Brazil, and Bishop Francis Simons of Indore, India).
2. National episcopal conferences could take decisions with a three-fourths majority for serious matters and a two-thirds majority for other questions (Cardinal Koenig).
3. "The Church is often accused of centralization, of curialism, of imperialism. We must answer these accusations with deeds and not words by showing a deep respect for the bishops" (Cardinal Bea, who was loudly applauded).
4. It would be premature to send the schema back before we have clear doctrine concerning the meaning of collegiality; let us wait until this matter is settled (Archbishop Veuillot).
5. Let us clearly affirm the equality of the East and the West in dignity and honor (Coptic Bishop Pierre Dib of Cairo).
6. The primacy of Peter confers a sovereign authority upon him, but sovereign does not mean absolute (Bishop Simons).
7. The cardinals should represent the universal Church. This is not the case. Therefore, let us initiate the necessary reforms or designate another senate.
8. Union between the secular and religious clergy is more important than ever. Let us follow the example of France and create organs of liaison between religious and episcopal conferences, and begin real dialogue between the two clergies (Father Fernández, Master General of the Dominicans).

Finally, an original proposition was made by Archbishop Thomas Cooray of Colombo, Ceylon. Because "the Curia works in the name of . . . the Holy Father," this prelate suggested that all interventions be made in writing so as to be "freer and more objective" while also avoiding scandal. "My intervention," he specified, "will not be popular. I hesitated to make it, but resolved to do so out of love for the common good and respect for the Pope."

NOVEMBER 8

Several Interventions Indicate Disarray
of Bishops Opposed to Collegiality

The reactions during the examination of the schema on the bishops were predictable—sometimes brutal, sometimes subtle, and sometimes moving, as is often the case in life-and-death struggles. They are indicative of the fear and disarray on the part of some before the direction Vatican II seems irrevocably to be taking.

Bishop Méndez Arceo, who spoke on Thursday, put it well. "I have heard some surprising things today," he said. "One would think we were at Vatican I. But this is a mistake, for we are here specifically to complete that council. We are no longer in the era of Constantine, which constrained the liberty of the Church. The Holy Spirit is the source of unity in the Church."

Expressing the fears of many, he added, "The theological commission must work according to the spirit of the Council. I have communicated my thoughts to it in writing. I hope they will be heeded."

Some members of this commission act as if they were above the Council, but the contrary is the case. Its *raison d'être* is to serve the Council, to help it express itself.

Following are some of the more "surprising" interventions of the day.

1. His Beatitude Ignace Pierre XVI Batanian, Patriarch of Cilicia: Our innovations would reduce the Church to a lamentable state. A senate, it has been said, is necessary for the Church. But such a senate exists in the cardinals. Let us not exaggerate the faults of the Curia. The press has done much harm in this respect. The Curia is a very worthwhile institution. Let us avoid scandal. (Light applause.)

2. Archbishop Florit of Florence: The vote of October 30 is of no value. Nothing whatsoever follows from it. The theological commission is the only judge. Let us be prudent and avoid divisions among ourselves.

3. Bishop José Souto Vizoso of Valencia, Spain: Let us thank the Pope for the new faculties he will concede to the bishops.

4. Bishop Michael Browne of Galway, Ireland: Collegiality limits the powers of bishops taken individually. This is a serious disadvantage. It is not our place to talk about collegiality. Everything depends on the sovereign pontiff. The commissions have no right to say what must be done but the pope alone, who has all powers.

5. Bishop Aurelio del Pino Gómez of Lerida, Spain: The Curia is worthy of our admiration. The organ we need is uniquely the Roman Curia. Everything we say against the Curia we say against the pope. It is extremely dangerous to express ourselves on these subjects. Nothing can be said or done without the pope's permission. Some talk incessantly of collegiality; one would think that every bishop wanted to be pope. It is false, erroneous, and against Vatican I to hold that the bishops have all the powers, that the episcopal body possesses full power. Let us not suffocate (*non suffocamus*) papal primacy. Everything comes from the pope; everything must be submitted to the pope. (This speaker was interrupted because he overstepped the time limit. There was a sprinkling of applause, but it was difficult to determine whether it was for the speaker or for the moderator who stopped him.)

6. Bishop Edoardo Mason, Apostolic Vicar of El Obeid, Sudan: The sovereign pontiff speaks through the Curia. The Curia is especially indispensable in these days of extreme nationalism. *Maxime caveamus!* It has been suggested that we renounce the *cappa magna* and the titles of excellency and eminence, and this at a time when we are claiming more powers. Isn't there a contradiction here?

Interesting Suggestions by Archbishop Gouyon Together with these interventions, which we have considerably condensed, there were many others on the usual themes of extending the powers of bishops ("restored" powers rather than "conceded"), on episcopal conferences, the exercise of collegiality, and so forth.

Archbishop Gouyon's suggestions were among the more interesting (it was he who asked the bishops to renounce the *cappa magna* in 1962):

1. Paul VI, in his speech to the Curia, explicitly declared his intention of governing the Church with the aid of residential bishops. Let us vote on this matter.
2. The members of this apostolic council should be designated by episcopal conferences.
3. It is indispensable that this council be above the Roman congregations.
4. The bishops named by the episcopal conferences should meet at least twice a year. They should be assisted by experts and maintain close

contact with their native countries, not hesitating to use the most rapid means of communication such as the telephone.

Bishop Piotr Kalwa of Lublin, Poland, spoke in the name of all the bishops of his country. Like several other speakers, he wanted the schema to speak explicitly of the relations between bishops and the pope and not only of relations between the bishops and the Curia. The Curia, he noted, was instituted only in the sixteenth century. Before that there were direct communications between the bishops and the pope. "Let us therefore respect historical and doctrinal reality," he said. "The vote of October 30 is a clear answer to a clear question. Let us draw the logical conclusions and affirm that there are two forms of supreme power in the universal Church."

All Bishops Are Vicars of Christ   "The Church is not and cannot be an absolute monarchy," said Archbishop António Ferreira Gomes of Oporto, Portugal. The bishop is not the pope's vicar, he stated. Collegiality pertains to the very essence of the Church. The cardinalate no longer corresponds with the needs of the times; the Council Fathers should create something else. Just as civil societies have gone from absolute monarchies to other forms of government, so too, insofar as the analogy is valid, should the Church decentralize her governing power. The bishops whose responsibility it is to govern should be elected. Their mandate could be for three years.

Maronite Archbishop Ziadé of Beirut remarked that the pope is not the only vicar of Christ. "All bishops," he said, "are genuine vicars of Christ. They are vicars neither of the sovereign pontiff nor of the nuncios."

The same speaker then criticized the bishops for their past attitude toward the Curia. "Because of this," he explained, "the Curia has become all powerful. Its permission was requested for every decision. We don't need the Curia to tell us how to wash the sacred linens. *De minimis non curat praetor!*"

A Bout of Fever at Vatican II

Cardinal Frings: "The Holy Office Is a Cause of Scandal in the World"
Cardinal Ottaviani: "To Attack the Holy Office Is To Insult the Pope"
The confrontation in Friday's session was inevitable. In the final analysis, it was a healthy one. Tensions are normal in a living organism. There comes a moment when the newest cells undertake to eliminate the others.

It is not with inpunity that the Holy Office has for so many years caused suffering, either in honor or in reputation, to priests, religious, and bishops whose only desire was to transmit the Gospel to men of their times.

There is no reason to be either unduly alarmed or gladdened by these stresses at Vatican II. Fever is a painful but necessary moment in the course of a sickness. These discussions will scandalize only those who prefer personal peace to the truth and those who are ignorant of the serious conflicts that shook the Church at the time of Vatican I and preceding Councils.

The principal antagonists on Friday were Cardinal Frings, Archbishop of Cologne, and Cardinal Ottaviani, Secretary to the Supreme Sacred Congregation of the Holy Office. The first, a German and a former student at the Pontifical Biblical Institute, was elevated to the purple by Pius XII, and was named to the Council's presidency by John XXIII. He is open to ecumenism, contemporary exegesis, and all currents of modern thought. The second is a Roman who has never lived outside of Italy. His attitudes are well known. Feared for the severity of his judgments, he is a holy and inflexible priest and totally dedicated to the Church. He is very popular among the humble people of Trastevere, where he was born.

Cardinal Frings: "The Holy Office Is a Cause of Scandal in the World"
Cardinal Frings went directly to the point. In a controlled voice he began:

> The vote of October 30 is perfectly clear although only indicative. I am surprised that Cardinal Browne, vice president of the theological commission, could have cast any doubt on this. The commission has nothing further to do than execute and obey the Council's wishes. It has no new truths to invent. The commission is an instrument whose sole reason for being is to carry out the expressed will of the Council.
>
> Moreover, let us not confuse administrative and judicial procedures. This distinction holds for the Holy Office, whose methods are out of harmony with modern times and are a cause of scandal in the world.

At this point the assembly interrupted the speaker with applause. Then the Fathers held their breath to hear what would follow. After thanking the Roman congregations and the Holy Office for the good they have accomplished, the Cardinal went on: "No one ought to be judged and condemned without having been heard, without knowing what he is accused of, and without the opportunity of correcting his views."

In the second part of his speech, Cardinal Frings said that the episcopacy was a charge (*onus*) and an honnor (*honor*), and that it was not normal to be named a bishop merely because one had served for several years on a Roman congregation.

"It is not necessary," he added, "to be a bishop in order to work on a Roman congregation, or even for that matter to be a priest. Many duties could be performed perfectly well by laymen. We have spoken about the laity at some length in the Council; let us give them their rightful place. This is a necessary reform; let us get on with it." (Applause.)

Cardinal Ottaviani: "To Attack the Holy Office Is To Insult the Pope"
Cardinal Ottaviani replied a few moments later, his voice trembling with anger and emotion:

> First of all, I must protest most vigorously against the condemnation of the Holy Office voiced in this Council hall. The criticism stems from pure ignorance—I use this term to avoid a stronger one which would be uncharitable. The Holy Office never acts without the advice of competent consultors and experienced specialists. To attack the Holy Office is to insult the pope, for it should not be forgotten that the prefect of the Holy Office is the pope himself. [Applause.]
>
> Some Fathers have spoken of collegiality of divine right as though it were already defined. This is decidedly not the case. The theological commission alone can decide this. The five points recently submitted for the approval of the Council Fathers were drawn up by the Council moderators. They should have been submitted to the theological commission for careful study. For it and it alone is competent, not the moderators. In this way, very regrettable ambiguities would have been avoided. If the collegiality of the episcopacy is defined, when it is by no means clear that the apostles acted collegially (with the exception of the Council of Jerusalem), the primacy of Peter will be questioned. I am amazed that collegiality is spoken of in the juridical sense of the word since Christ said to Peter, "Feed my sheep," including the apostles.

Cardinal Browne, vice president of the theological commission, flew to Cardinal Ottaviani's support with a statement that the idea of collegiality runs counter to the constitution *Pastor aeternus* of Vatican I. Cardinal Browne concluded pathetically with the words, "Venerable brothers, beware! Beware!"

Archbishop Lefebvre of the Holy Spirit Fathers agreed with Cardinal

Browne and asked that the Council "refrain from speaking about collegiality in any sense except a purely moral one."

Inadmissible Cardinal Ruffini exclaimed with scarcely concealed emotion, "I have listened to a harsh and offensive speech against the Roman Curia in this assembly [he was referring to the intervention of Maximos IV Saigh on Wednesday]. It is inadmissible! Reparation has happily been made by the Patriarch Batanian, my very dear friend and classmate. I thank him publicly in my name and in the name of Cardinal Siri, president of the Italian episcopal conference."

This homage to the Patriarch of the Armenians, whose intervention Thursday provoked mixed reactions, was undoubtedly flattering. One of the members of the assembly said in a loud voice, "Sold!"

In this overheated atmosphere, the firm but dignified speech by Archbishop D'Souza of Bhopal, India, seemed like a salutary return to calm. He began:

> We have heard that the question of collegiality is not yet settled and that our vote of October 30 can therefore be considered invalid and illegitimate. It is sheer mockery to speak in this way, for 80 percent of the Fathers gave a perfectly clear answer to an equally clear question. Furthermore, this response is in total conformity with Paul VI's allocution. I beg you not to reduce the question of collegiality to a juridical matter. What concerns us above all is the good of souls, which is our only reason for existence. . . .
>
> The schema is not pastoral enough. It is not in keeping with the Pope's intention. It proposes additional members in the congregations, but this is not the issue at all. We must go much farther. Otherwise, in a few years, everything will be just as it was before. If 2,200 bishops, gathered together from all over the world for an ecumenical council, find it difficult to resist pressures, what would a few bishops, scattered through the various congregations, be able to do?
>
> And the Curia? It has performed well in the past. But the situation today is totally different from the past. The Curia cannot continue to resolve problems in the old way.

After recalling the verse in the Gospel which says that "the letter kills," Archbishop D'Souza continued:

> Suspicion is cast on some authors without any reasons given; they are not told what is praiseworthy and what is to be corrected

in their work. It falls to the bishops, aided by experts, to judge these authors.

We love the Pope more than ever; we believe in primacy more than ever. Why then this clamor, as if the Church were in danger?

Two cardinals, Lercaro and the African Rugambwa, made interesting practical suggestions: that the formation of an episcopal council to assist the Pope be spoken of outside of the schema, in a separate document, and then presented to the Pope; and that a special commission be designated as soon as possible to prepare this important work. But first of all, a new indicative vote would have to be taken in the assembly.

After this animated session, it seems more evident than ever that the Curia, and more particularly the Holy Office, will not recover from the cleansing operation of Vatican II. The Holy Office must be radically transformed, not only in methods but in name, as was requested by the Fathers. A curious coincidence: in 1542 Paul III instituted the Holy Office to help fight Protestantism; four centuries later, it has devolved on his namesake to undertake the transformation of this anachronistic institution.

NOVEMBER 11

Council to Examine the Schema on Ecumenism
Prepared by the Secretariat for Unity

The Pope received the moderators twice for lengthy audiences over the weekend—Saturday and Sunday afternoon. It is expected that important decisions concerning the machinery of the Council will be announced shortly.

We have also learned that Vatican II will examine the schema on ecumenism after that on the bishops. This text was drawn up by the Secretariat for Promoting Christian Unity; the union of the Churches, we must remember, continues to be a principal goal of the Council, as announced by both John XXIII and Paul VI.

This document comprises four chapters. It treats of the general principles of ecumenism: interior renewal based on a biblical and liturgical movement; a conversion of heart to abnegation, humility, meekness, and forgetfulness of self; a search for an evangelical life, and so forth. It particularly stresses the necessity of knowing non-Catholic communities better, interconfessional meetings, and the suitability of collaboration with all Christians in charitable works and social reform.

The schema emphasizes the importance of the Oriental Churches, their apostolic origin, and the determining role monasticism played in their tradition. It alludes to the diversity of practices and customs in the Church which in no way detracts from unity properly understood. It speaks of the Protestant churches and their "affinities" with the Catholic Church, of what is positive in their faith, and so forth. We have recently been advised that this schema will include a special section on Jews and non-Christians.

There is no doubt that history will consider this text one of the high-water marks of Vatican II. For long centuries, the Roman Church has not spoken positively of the non-Catholic Christian confessions. It is worth noting that this is the first schema to come before the Council that was not prepared by one of the conciliar commissions properly speaking; it was drafted by the Secretariat for Promoting Christian Unity, upon which John XXIII conferred an authority equal to that of the commissions.

World Jewish Congress Comments on Secretariat's Work   "The Jewish people are profoundly moved and happy that the Ecumenical Council in Rome is considering a declaration requesting the Roman Catholic Church to eliminate religious teachings which are capable of inciting contempt, hatred, or persecution of the Jews," said Dr. Nahum Goldmann, president of the World Jewish Congress, in a statement published in London on November 9.

Pope Congratulates Father Rahner

Earlier (October 29) we reported a rumor that Cardinal Antoniutti, Prefect of the Sacred Congregation of Religious, had sent a letter to superiors general of religious orders warning them against twelve experts at the Council, among them Fathers Congar, Rahner, Küng, and Ratzinger. We pointed out that the existence of this letter had not been proven.

This rumor provoked Cardinal Antoniutti to a public denial. He declared that it was untrue and unfounded. Contrary to his wishes, his denial was not published by either the official press service of the Council or *L'Osservatore Romano*, but rather by some Roman papers and different press agencies.

Everyone in conciliar circles was happy with the Cardinal's denial. Does this mean that the rumor we reported was altogether without foundation? Nothing could be less certain. Perhaps it is only a question here of one or several confidential letters sent to a number of recipients.

We are sure, on the other hand, that the Pope recently gave a special audience to the Archbishop of Freiburg im Breisgau, the German publisher Herder, and Father Rahner. Paul VI expressed his gratitude to the last for his theological work and gave him a special blessing. This news was announced in a bulletin from the press service of *L'Osservatore Romano*.

Cardinal Döpfner Reminds the Fathers
That the Moderators Control Vatican II

After the storm, an apparent calm. The fireworks of last Friday are still echoing and the wounds inflicted upon self-esteem are not yet healed. Ecclesiastical bitterness runs deep, as Alphonse Daudet says, but the exception can prove the rule. In any case, there are more important issues. One is the reform of the Curia; another is the abatement of the opposition between the Eastern and the Western Churches.

Cardinal Confalonieri, Secretary of the Sacred Consistorial Congregation, made a conciliatory gesture when he said yesterday that the Curia was not all bad—which is true, of course—but that the Pope ought to be courageous in initiating its reform. "Let us make our desires known to him in a humble manner," he said.

Cardinal Döpfner, who is one of the four moderators, made the following points:

> The vote of October 30 is very important. To hear certain people talk, one could get the impression that the Holy Spirit was absent when the five questions were presented by the moderators and when the Council answered them. They would have us believe that the Prince of Evil sowed bad seed while the father of the family slept. Now, the moderators control the Council. They presented questions whose meaning and wording were based upon the schema itself. It cannot be said, then, that the moderators acted furtively [*furtim*]. This vote was taken to survey the Fathers. It is only indicative, of course, but that indication is perfectly clear, and no one can ignore it.

In this way Cardinal Döpfner answered Cardinal Ottaviani, who had said on Friday that the theological commission, and not the moderators, is the competent authority, and had criticized the latter for not asking the commission to formulate these questions.

The Pope's Role Was Determining   There was some confusion as to how the notorious questions evolved, but the facts now seem clear. Two successive votes were necessary before the moderators, members of the Coordinating Commission, and the cardinal presidents could reach a positive decision.* The first vote ended with 11 against and 9 for. Had the initiative taken by the moderators failed, serious consequences would have resulted, as we have said. Their prestige was at stake as well as their future authority. Such a failure would also have reflected on the Pope, who had personally put the direction of the Council in the moderators' hands. That is why they asked Paul VI to arbitrate the situation. They rephrased the questions so that a majority vote could be reached—the question on collegiality was divided into two, and the issue of married deacons suppressed altogether—and the second vote indicated 11 for and 9 against.

Thus, it is correct to attribute the victory to the moderators. The historians of the Council will undoubtedly consider the day of this secret balloting the most dramatic of Vatican II. Without the Pope's action, it is more than likely that there would have been no outcome of the situation and hence no indicative vote. The value of the latter is contested by a few, but it cannot be denied that the majority of the Fathers made their thinking perfectly clear. The authority of the moderators emerged strengthened from this challenge.

During the second session, as during the first, the Council had the greatest need of the Pope. In both cases, he has supported the deepest trend of the Council. He has placed his influence at the service of the freedom of Vatican II. All, both then and now, are much indebted to him.

Pension Fund for Bishops

Most of Monday's session was given over to a problem that is in itself minor and only moderately interesting to the faithful: what to do when a bishop of a diocese needs help, either because his diocese is too large or because the bishop is old or incapacitated. The schema examines the role of auxiliary and coadjutor bishops as well as the possibility of a retirement age.

A footnote to the schema proposes seventy-five as a retirement age for bishops.

This suggestion, which seems reasonable at first sight, raises many

* [According to Xavier Rynne, these votes were taken at a "summit meeting of the Council authorities" held the evening of October 23 in the Vatican. The point at issue was whether the moderators' powers included the right to call for any conciliar vote; the presidency had protested on this ground against the proposed test vote, which had been announced in the general assembly on October 15 by Cardinal Suenens, the day's moderator. At the "summit meeting," the first vote was 11 to 9 against the moderators; the second was 11 to 9 in their favor. See Xavier Rynne, *The Second Session*, New York, Farrar, Straus & Company, 1964, pp. 164–165.—Tr.]

difficulties. It is in fact contrary to the tradition and radical optimism of Christian anthropology. Some think the solution of coadjutors better. Moreover, if this rule had been in effect earlier, we would not have had John XXIII as Pope.

Should Bishops Be Forced To Retire?   One reason it is difficult for bishops to give up their sees is that no provision is made for decent living conditions for retired prelates. Cardinal Cento proposed that a kind of pension fund be created to remedy this situation. It would be a practical way, he said, of manifesting a collegial spirit.

Arguments for and against a retirement age were presented at length by the speakers. Sixty-two-year-old Archbishop Corrado Mingo of Monreale, Sicily, is in favor of making retirement mandatory at seventy-five. "*Dura lex,*" he said, "*sed necessaria*"—a hard law but necessary. Bishop de Vito of Lucknow, India, thought the whole idea preposterous. "It would be like trying to change the course of the moon," he said.

Coadjutor Bishop Antoine Caillot of Evreux, France, thought the practice of making auxiliary bishops titulars of imaginary dioceses should cease. "This practice provokes amazement," he said. "No one but Benedictines knows where these titular sees are. Many have long since been in ruins."

Passing to chapter 3 of the schema today, Tuesday, the Council began to discuss the question of episcopal conferences and their powers.

Free the African Churches
from an "Inferiority Complex"

Archbishop Hyacinthe Thiandoum of Dakar, a Negro, gave a conference sponsored by the official press bureau of the Council.

> The time has undeniably come to free the African Churches from the inferiority complex that is implicit in the designation "mission lands." We hope that the schema on the missions, by defining the word, will put everyone at ease: first, those who won't use the expression out of fear of displeasing, and the second, those who want to use more general categories. . . .
>
> The examination of the schema on the laity which the Council has just examined has a special interest for us. Everyone knows that religious and priestly vocations are on the increase throughout Africa. But the laity has not followed the same rising line. Yet everyone

agrees that without a native laity, the Church cannot be said to be fully implanted among us.

At the Council's Request, Paul VI Will Soon Specify How He Wants To Use the Bishops in Governing the Church

The Council follows its course imperturbably. The obstacles it encounters fail to stem its progress. Each day the *aggiornamento* of the Church becomes more and more a reality. As time passes, it is increasingly evident that Paul VI, despite his natural discretion, has cast his lot with the reforming progressives against those who fear any change.

In this new week, following last Friday's tempestuous session, there are several interesting items to report:

1. Last Friday evening Paul VI called for Cardinal Frings, who, it will be remembered, had told the Council that the Holy Office was a cause of scandal to the world. The Pope intimated that he approved of the import of his intervention.

2. The same evening the Pope agreed to receive Cardinals Ottaviani, Antoniutti, and Siri, to whom he spoke a quite different language. The Secretary of the Holy Office asked for the Pope's support, but in vain. It is said that he was so upset by this that he is thinking of handing in his resignation. It is likely that the Pope showed displeasure at Cardinal Ottaviani's ungracious attack on the person of Cardinal Frings and implicitly reproached him for his bad behavior.

3. Cardinal Ruffini, who attacked Maximos IV Saigh on Friday, has apologized.

4. On Tuesday morning the theological commission, as we reported, has accepted the schema on religious liberty prepared by the Secretariat for Promoting Christian Unity (18 for, 5 against, and 1 invalid ballot). Before the voting, Cardinal Ottaviani launched into such lengthy explanations that the members of the commission grew impatient and shouted in unison, "Let us vote! Let us vote!" The document is at the printer's and will soon be distributed to the Fathers. It will constitute chapter 5 of the schema on ecumenism. It was not generally expected that the theological commission would act so quickly and positively. There is every reason to believe that the decision can be attributed to the atmosphere which prevails in the Council these days. The opposition is losing ground.

5. Many Fathers have expressed the desire that the Pope inform the

Council of his specific intentions with respect to the concrete exercise of collegiality and the creation in Rome of a permanent episcopal council to help the Sovereign Pontiff govern the Church.

A Document To Be Submitted to the Moderators   That is why a document has been prepared with the assistance of Cardinal Silva Henríquez. It will be read to the Council or submitted in writing to the moderators, who may propose it for a conciliar vote if they judge this opportune, or else transmit it directly to the Pope. Several hundred bishops of Latin America, Canada, Africa, and elsewhere have already signed the text, and it is bound to meet with the approval of the great majority of Fathers.

What does the document say?

The Fathers convey their gratitude to the Pope for the positions he took in his speeches of September 21 and 29:

1. The Pope expressed the hope that the Council would strengthen the doctrine of the episcopacy and the nature of its relation with Peter, and that it would indicate the doctrinal and practical principles according to which the bishops could collaborate more effectively with the Pope.
2. The Pope favored a reform of the Curia so that it would be more in harmony with the needs of our age.
3. Several further points were enumerated: the necessity of decentralizing and of granting the bishops the right to make decisions until now reserved to the central government; the Curia's duty to ask for and heed the advice of the bishops; the serious obligation of the Fathers to help the Holy See bring about the concrete reform of the Curia by adding to it bishops from all countries, imbued with a true ecumenical spirit; the duty of residential bishops to release the most competent men to the central government.

Principles and Methods

Consequently, taking into consideration the desires of many Fathers expressed in the discussions of the schemas on the Church and on the bishops, the Council Fathers respectfully request the Sovereign Pontiff to determine the principles and methods of assistance which will enable him to enlist the greater collaboration of bishops from all over the world.

Just as the Supreme Pastor, according to the Lord's precept, must confirm his brothers, so too his brothers know that the duty is incumbent upon them to offer the Sovereign Pontiff their serious and effective cooperation in supporting the weight of the government of the universal Church.

It is expected, then, that in one form or another the Pope will communicate how he envisages the cooperation of the bishops in the central government of the Church. These indications will encourage the Council in its work. The Pope and the Council will be lending one another a helping hand, so to speak, entering into close cooperation to elaborate the bases of the new collegial government of tomorrow. The Pope's role in this reform will naturally be the preponderant one.

This is the reason the Council is turning to the Sovereign Pontiff to ask for clarifications and give him its advice. But it is also true that the Pope will receive valuable support from the Council to bring about this reform, and he will gladly listen to its suggestions. This collaboration and understanding already prefigure the physiognomy of the hierarchical Church of tomorrow, in which, through the instrumentality of delegates from episcopal conferences, the central authority will be the result of close cooperation between the college and its head, the Sovereign Pontiff.

Discussion Opens on Episcopal Conferences

Tuesday's general congregation began the examination of chapter 3, on episcopal conferences. Five cardinals took the floor. Three of them were in favor of the juridical authority of these conferences, at least in certain important instances which are still to be determined (Cardinals Gracias of Bombay, Ritter of St. Louis, and Landázuri-Ricketts of Lima). Cardinal Meyer of Chicago spoke in the name of 120 American bishops. He did not rule out juridical powers but thought they should be exceptional. Cardinal McIntyre of Los Angeles was categorically opposed to this. He took the opportunity of his intervention to say that "No one should attack the Curia, which is the instrument of the Holy Father."

Bishop Klepacz of Lodz spoke in the name of all the Polish bishops. He was of the opinion that the president of the national episcopal conference and *not the nuncio* should be responsible for church-state relations.

Before voting cloture on the discussion of chapter 2 of the schema, the Council heard varied interventions on the powers of coadjutor and auxiliary bishops. Auxiliary Bishop Jacques Lecordier of Paris made mention of his unusual experience (he lives apart from the residential bishop). Bishop Zak of St. Pölten, Austria, speaks frankly. He declared himself in total agreement with what had been said in the past few days by Cardinals Frings and Döpfner. With respect to Bishop de Vito's intervention of the day before, he said, "Some ridiculous things were said here. We are at a Council and not a circus." (Laughter.)

Cardinal Suenens Vigorously Favors
a Retirement Age

Cardinal Suenens made a vigorous plea for a retirement age of seventy-five:

> Merely exhorting bishops to retire would be like cutting water. Our Council is supposed to be pastoral. Now, the first motor force of every apostolate is the bishop. Present circumstances thrust more and more responsibilities upon the bishop. The accelerated pace of the world demands men who are ready to adapt constantly to evolution. Age creates a hiatus between the bishop and the world. One has only to see what happens in dioceses where old bishops remain at the helm.
>
> Since we require a retirement age for pastors, let us do the same for ourselves, or else people will say, "Physician, heal thyself." In secular society, sixty-five is the normal retirement age. The analogy cannot be pushed too far, but from the psychological point of view, what is true in one society is true in another.

NOVEMBER 14

Episcopal Conferences:
A Danger or a Force for the Good?

A Last Word on "Honors" Napoleon was honored in the Council on Wednesday. With respect to honors, no less. Bishops put great stock in honors, if we consider the five or six interventions the day before which repeated *ad nauseam* that a bishop should not be deprived of the honors due to his rank when he retires.

Coadjutor Archbishop Angel Fernandes of Delhi, India, is not of this mind, and yesterday he cited a saying attributed to Napoleon in support of his view: "Declarations are the toys of adults." "We are always preaching humility," the prelate commented. "Therefore, it is not our role to talk of honors at the Council. Let all hint of careerism be excluded from canon law. The faithful do not understand our distinctions, which are only too human. They remind us of the Gospel, and they are right."

"Let Us Carefully Avoid All Innovations" The assembly heard a bishop who is naïvely hostile to any form of *aggiornamento.* Archbishop Luis Alonso Muñoyerro, Military Vicar in Madrid, was the speaker. His remarks delighted the reform-minded bishops, who bank on such exaggerations to destroy the persuasiveness of conservative positions.

"Episcopal conferences," he said, "constitute an oppression for the bishops. Let there be as few of them as possible, and let them be held at irregular intervals, only by order of the Pope and in the presence of the nuncio. To give them purely moral powers is already too much. It is a dangerous inclination toward democracy. These conferences will contribute to making discipline impossible in the Church.

"Let us carefully avoid all innovations," the prelate added. And to everyone's astonishment, he concluded with this remark: "If it is absolutely necessary to convoke an episcopal conference, the military vicar should be invited."

Bishop Pildáin of the Canary Islands and Bishop Carli of Segni, the reporter for the commission, are also against episcopal conferences, which they think can in no way be justified theologically, but only pastorally. Bishop Carli took the occasion to say what he thought of the indicative vote on October 30. It was "altogether dubious, precipitate, inadequately prepared, too hasty, outside the regulations. The text of the questions was equivocal, incomplete, and obscure."

Cardinal Döpfner, who directed the discussions, and the three other moderators listened to these pleasant words without batting an eyelash. They know full well that they will have no effect on the outcome of the Council, and that by expressing themselves so crudely the opposition gains nothing. On the contrary!

On Juridical Power for Conferences Most of the bishops who have spoken these past few days are opposed to giving episcopal conferences juridical power, even Cardinal Frings, who on this question was in agreement with Cardinal Spellman.

There are presently some fifty episcopal conferences throughout the world. Most of them are of very recent origin. The oldest was established in Belgium in 1845; it was followed two years later by Germany's.

The Archbishop of Cologne, who is president of the German conference, spoke of its excellent results in Catholic Action, educational issues, charitable works, and the like. He said that if juridical power was given the conferences, it should be for exceptional cases, and a majority vote of four-fifths should be required.

Bishop Dammert of Cajamarca, Peru, thinks that episcopal conferences are an extension of a secular tradition, that of the provincial councils, and should be accorded juridical powers.

A False Mentality   The interventions of Auxiliary Bishop Ancel of Lyon and Archbishop Guerry of Cambrai were closely followed, for they introduced new elements which had the merit of getting beyond the present tangle.

Bishop Ancel said the issue ought to be debated from a pastoral rather than a juridical point of view:

> Each bishop in his diocese cannot fulfill his mission if he is not helped by others. A bishop can do nothing alone. The faithful expect that form of collegiality which will particularly bring about a more equitable distribution of the clergy. But we are far from this spirit of collegiality which we talk about so much in theory. This is understandable for historical reasons. We are so accustomed to a regime of absolute monarchy that it is difficult for us to get outside of this false mentality.

The Archbishop of Cambrai took an Oriental viewpoint that is not commonly thought of:

> Each particular Church must stay in communion with the others, with the universal Church, and with the Sovereign Pontiff, who is the sign of unity. All the Churches have the same doctrine, the same Holy Spirit, and are founded on the same Eucharist: this is the real theological basis of episcopal conferences. Let us consider this first before speaking in juridical terms as does the schema.
>
> In the principle of collegiality, it is important to distinguish what is of divine right and what is only of ecclesiastical right. Episcopal conferences depend on the latter and not the former.

Coadjutor Bishop Guy Riobé of Orléans, who is in charge of the French episcopacy's program for aid to Latin America (to date some fifty-five priests have been sent to this continent), said episcopal conferences help overcome a parochial spirit. Today people are thinking more and more in universal terms, and it would be good for each diocese to develop a global outlook and make every sacrifice necessary to this end. In this way the young and poor churches would no longer be placed in a position of begging. There would be normal exchanges among churches considered equal.

Messages from the Jewish Community

"A Great Day in the History of Judaism"   Mr. Zachariah Shuster, European director of the American Jewish Committee, gave a press conference in Rome in which he declared that the project on Judeo-Christian relations which has just been distributed to the Fathers "is certainly one of the great moments in Judaism.

"I believe," he said, "that the Jews of this generation will consider themselves fortunate to have witnessed this historic step on the part of the Church. Now Jews can envisage a new era in which Jews and Christians can begin to understand one another."

He added: "During the elaboration of this document, the Vatican solicited the views of the most competent Christian and Jewish religious leaders. We can say with certainty that there was no group or tendency or direction of Jewish thinkers who did not give their point of view to the authorities in Rome."

Saturday as the Day of the Lord?   In a letter addressed to the Council Fathers through the intermediary of Cardinal Bea, the president of the Association for the Propagation of Judaism proposed that Catholics recognize Saturday as "the day of the Lord."

Dr. Israel Benzeev, the author of this letter, thought such a measure would constitute an essential step in rapprochement between Catholicism and Judaism. Here are his arguments:

> As you know, the Council of Nicaea in 325, under the reign of the Emperor Constantine, decided upon a total separation between Judaism and Christianity as well as a complete abrogation of the ritual practices proscribed in the Law of Moses.
>
> The Council of Lucca in 380 abolished the seventh day of the week as the Sabbath on the pretext that Christians were forbidden to imitate the Jews in this observance, for they are only obliged to sanctify Sunday, the first day of the week, as the day of the Lord.

After recalling that Christ, his disciples, and all Christians until the year 380 observed the Sabbath, Dr. Benzeev said the Gospel contained nothing "opposing the celebration of the Sabbath."

The Right to Information

On Thursday the general congregation voted on the communications schema (press, cinema, radio, television, and so forth), which was discussed on November 23–27, 1962. At that time the assembly approved the schema on condition that it be considerably abbreviated. That condition has been met with, since the present text is only nine pages long instead of the original thirty-nine.

Does this mean that the schema is satisfactory? Hardly, judging by the unfavorable opinion several young French bishops expressed in the last French episcopal conference. The text is so inadequate, said one of them, that "I would have hesitated to present it to my students when I was a chaplain. It is altogether too elementary."

But at least the schema speaks of "the right to information necessary to social life." The Fathers voted separately and without discussion on the schema's two chapters. Those in favor varied between 1,832 and 1,893, those against between 92 and 103, and those in favor but with reservations between 243 and 125.

Dioceses Ought to Correspond
with Modern Needs

Getting back to the subject of episcopal conferences, the assembly heard several interventions. Cardinal Alfrink, Archbishop of Utrecht, said episcopal conferences and collegiality ought to be distinguished since the latter is effected in the conferences only "in a certain way." He answered Bishop Carli's attacks the day before against the vote of October 30 by saying that it had not been improvised; but taking note of the many critical interventions registered for the day, he asked the moderators "to intervene in order to clarify the matter."

"We always forget the Orientals," said Bishop Gérard Coderre of St.-Jean de Québec. He proposed that the schema state explicitly that "in the Oriental Churches, the patriarchical institution corresponds in some degree to episcopal conferences."

Archbishop John Garner of Pretoria, South Africa, said that to abandon any idea of juridical power for episcopal conferences would be "to empty the schema of substance and to waste time in a manner unworthy of a council."

How should the presidents of these conferences be chosen? Bishop Franič of Split, Yugoslavia, who has intervened at the Council on several occasions, asked that they be elected for three to six years only. "This rotation system," he said, "corresponds with the rapid changing in the world, and I would suggest an analogous rotation for pastors, vicars general, and archbishops. I dare not go farther."

Bishop Franič also put forth another interesting idea: that the nuncios are in a better position to deal with civil authorities than the presidents of episcopal conferences because, as strangers, they are more independent.

Further interventions followed, by Dom Reetz, Superior General of the Beuron Benedictines; Archbishop Antonio Santin of Trieste, and Bishop Luis Cabrera Cruz of San Luis Potosí, Mexico. The assembly then voted cloture on chapter 3 and immediately began discussion of the next chapter, on dioceses.

Cardinal Feltin stressed the value of military chaplains and went on to plead for "personal" dioceses—that is, dioceses which are composed of homogeneous groups of faithful independently of the territory in which they live (military personnel, immigrants, and the like).

Commissions to Revise Dioceses Urged Bishop Alexandre Renard then took the floor to elaborate on the criteria which should determine the division of dioceses. The Bishop of Versailles—which is a particularly good example of a dislocated diocese—noted that many dioceses in France trace their origin to Pius VII and are quite naturally anachronistic. He said the schema hardly took any risk by stating that a diocese should be neither "too large nor too small." The ideal diocese, he went on, is one in which the bishop can fulfill his role personally or with auxiliaries, one which does not exceed the bishop's physical and intellectual strength. He urged that a special commission composed of bishops and experts be set up in each country as soon as possible to study this problem.

Bishop Francisco Peralta y Ballabriga of Vitoria, Spain, remarked that two contemporary phenomena ought to be remembered when dioceses are erected: dense urbanization and the apostasy of the masses. He praised the idea of "suburban" bishops and cited the example of Auxiliary Bishop Lecordier of Paris, who resides at St.-Denis.

The silence of the Council Fathers on the government of dioceses surprised the Spanish bishop. He recommended that they give further consideration to an episcopal Curia and comanagement, for if "a diocese is a monarchy, it is not an absolute one." Clergy should be distributed in terms of the realities of life. Many responsibilities could be trusted to laymen; otherwise, there will always be a shortage of priests.

Too Many Italian Dioceses Auxiliary Bishop Franciszek of Opole, Poland, and Bishop Aurelio Sorrentino of Bova, Italy, both complained that there were too many Italian dioceses, relics of the past, which no longer corresponded with the needs of the apostolate. Some have as few as 20,000 faithful and twenty parishes. "Dioceses with depleted resources must be regrouped. The Council offers an excellent opportunity for this reform. Let it not pass. We are confronted with an urgent task, and the faithful know this to be the case. The Church is not the guardian of the past."

Pope Meets with Council Directors

The document given to the moderators, which we analyzed earlier (see the report for November 13), has been signed so far by more than 500 Fathers. Will there be an official vote on it in the near future? Possibly. At any rate, the moderators and the presidential council have been convoked for a meeting this afternoon, Friday, in the Pope's presence. The agenda is secret, but quite likely two questions will come up in the meeting, which is an exceptional one because of Paul VI's participation.

The first question is the problem of how the Pope should intervene in the Council. The collective document referred to earlier shows that his intervention is desired.

The second question is the eventual modification of the conciliar commissions; several of them are hamstrung by presidents, vice-presidents, or secretaries who do not have the confidence of other members of the commissions. The most typical and crucial case in point is the theological commission, which is responsible for drawing up the texts relating to the sovereignty of the episcopal college.

NOVEMBER 16

Paul VI Readies a Motu Proprio
on the Powers of Bishops

Nothing has as yet resulted from Friday's meeting between the Pope and the moderators, Council presidents, and members of the Coordinating Commission. But it is widely rumored that Paul VI is preparing a motu proprio (as a letter with the pontifical signature is called) on the powers of bishops. The essential idea of the document is that over the centuries the Curia has appropriated powers which should normally be exercised by the bishops, and that the time has come to redress the balance. Consequently, the power of the Curia would be diminished.

Paul VI would thus lend the weight of his authority to the desires of the Council. In particular, he would be responding in a concrete way to the collective document signed by several hundred Fathers which we have already analyzed. In it we read: ". . . the Council Fathers respectively request the Sovereign Pontiff to determine the principles and methods of assistance which will enable him to enlist the greater collaboration of bishops from all over the world. [The bishops] know that the duty is incumbent upon them to offer the Sovereign Pontiff their serious and effective cooperation in supporting the weight of the government of the universal Church."

At the same time, the motu proprio would strengthen the vote of October 30 on collegiality of divine right and would perhaps carry a more or less indirect pledge for episcopal conferences, which, while not strictly the expression of collegiality, nonetheless are closely connected with it, and in any case constructively implement the desired decentralization.

The Unity Secretariat Will Submit
the Schema on Ecumenism

The Council finished examination of the chapters pertaining to bishops and the government of dioceses on Friday. Next Monday they will begin the schema on ecumenism. This will be an event of the greatest importance. It is in the fact the first time in history that this subject has been considered by a council. In doing so, Vatican II is fulfilling Pope John's fondest hope. During the short years of his pontificate, the late Pope effected a truly astounding quiet revolution in this respect.

The Roman Church has abandoned her defensive, indeed polemical, and in any case sterile attitude toward other Christian confessions, and has opted instead to enter into the great ecumenical dialogue. Until John XXIII, the position of the Roman Church was roughly this: she was content to state that the Catholic Church was the only true Church and to wait for other churches, which had separated from her over the centuries, to return to her bosom. Meanwhile, the Roman Church was not overly concerned with reforming herself to make her face more in conformity with the Gospel and less forbidding to separated Christians, or with emphasizing the common patrimony of all the confessions. In practice the Holy Office had authority over ecumenical matters, and its activities were principally directed to issuing warnings against the dangers of interconfessional dialogue.

A Sudden Change   With John XXIII, all of that suddenly changed. One of the most important of this Pope's initiatives was the creation of the Secretariat for Promoting Christian Unity, which largely removed responsibility in ecumenical matters from the Holy Office and confided it to specialists. The latter have been in constant touch with other Churches for several years.

The elements of a dialogue are being gathered together. The secretariat for unity, to which John XXIII gave an authority equal to that of a conciliar commission, will present its first schema to the Council.

It will be a great day for the Council and for Christian unity. The Fathers will be confronted with a text which brilliantly exhibits the Roman Church's spirit of openness toward other confessions and lays down the indispensable conditions basic to any ecumenical dialogue.

The schema contains the following chapters. Chapter 1 recalls that ecumenism consists first of all in being attentive to inner renewal so that the Church may appear without stain. The second chapter is concerned with the practice of ecumenism, and indicates how dialogue must be initiated and cooperation undertaken. The third analyzes relations with the Oriental Churches and communities which have arisen since the sixteenth century. Chapter 4 deals with the attitude of Catholics toward non-Christians and particularly the Jews. The fifth chapter treats of religious liberty; this text is fundamental, and will certainly encounter strong opposition. It especially stresses the necessary respect for conscience.

The non-Catholic observers and guests will obviously follow with keen interest the work of the Council in a matter that for once concerns them directly. They will be the center of the Council's attention. Their reactions, registered by the unity secretariat, will give the Fathers precious information. For if there is to be real dialogue among the churches—and there is no doubt that a real desire for it exists—then it is indispensable for the Council to know what non-Catholics think of how it speaks of them.

Several interventions on the chapter on dioceses occupied the general congregation on Friday. They were particularly animated because the subject is vitally important to bishops, who are the pastors and leaders of dioceses. Archbishop Zoghby, Melkite Patriarchical Vicar for Egypt, was not at all satisfied with the fact that six patriarchs have been named to the Sacred Congregation for Oriental Churches, for he said they will be drowned among the thirty other prelates, who are Occidental. Archbishop Zoghby demanded a radical transformation of this curial body, which should be composed, he concluded, of members elected by the Oriental synods.

"Let us have done with individualistic ideas," exclaimed Bishop Stefan László of Eisenstadt, Austria. "The diocese is a member of the body of the Church and not an isolated unit. Each bishop is responsible for the whole Church."

Archbishop Urtasun of Avignon repeated John XXIII's opinion that "The Church is not a museum," and said that she should not hesitate to redistribute dioceses in view of contemporary pastoral rather than merely historical needs. "Let us not wait," he said, "for revolutions or martyrs to transform dioceses. Let us not hesitate to benefit by the results of religious sociology, and let us review the question of the distribution of the clergy."

Archbishop Dominic Athaide of Agra, India, Coptic Bishop Scandar of Assiut, Egypt, and Maronite Bishop Antoine Khoreiche of Saida, Lebanon, all argued in favor of unity of jurisdiction over a given territory in which several rites are found.

After retired Archbishop Antonio Vuccino of Corfu, Greece, was called to order three times for digressing, Bishop Gonzáles Martin of Astorga, Spain, made a widely noted intervention: "The disparity of wealth among the dioceses is scandalous and contrary to the social doctrine of the Church, which constantly preaches a just distribution of goods. It is also contrary to the spirit of collegiality. Let us therefore establish some balance between rich and poor dioceses."

NOVEMBER 18

Affirmation of Religious Liberty Will Serve as a Test at the Ecumenical Début of Vatican II

Will humanity, which is tending toward economical and political unity and has already achieved a large measure of universality in science and technology, be able to achieve religious unity? After centuries of separation, Christianity today evinces signs of convergence or at least of nostalgia for its lost unity. The current of ecumenism has irresistibly caught up almost all of the churches. The Roman Church was among the last to be affected, but today she seems to be making up for lost time and becoming a stimulating force, whereas in the past she was all too often a force of inertia.

In opening discussion on ecumenism, Vatican II touches one of the most sensitive nerves of contemporary religious psychology. Until now the Council has dealt with "professional" themes, to use an expression of Archbishop John Heenan of Westminster. For this reason, the world at large felt little concerned in the Council's deliberations. But now, at least in countries where the various confessions are well represented, the Council's consideration of Christian unity will be followed with the greatest interest.

Everyone is vaguely aware that in treating of ecumenism, Vatican II is handling a delicate key to the future of Christianity. Our century is merciless toward those who have a parochial mentality. And for good reason. In an age of increasing socialization, society, any form of narrowmindedness seems more and more artificial, necessarily including interconfessional quarrels.

Thus, the theme of religious liberty constitutes one of the chapters with star billing. Its examination got under way today with a general exposé by Cardinal Cicognani. Then Archbishop Martin of Rouen reported on the first three chapters of the schema.

The least that can be said is that a serious ambiguity subsists in the Catholic teaching on religious liberty. Curiously enough, lay moralists are more concerned about liberty than many theologians. Religion, which teaches that the act of faith is free, would seem to imply the conclusion that every man has the right, after having selected the creed of his choice, to practice his faith freely. But the "thesis" is still often opposed to the "hypothesis," as if the ideal would be for the state to favor one religion and look upon religious tolerance as a more or less necessary evil.

Vatican II will have to speak clearly, and thousands of Protestants who suffer concretely from a lack of religious liberty in some countries will be listening carefully as it answers these questions:

1. Is the thesis of a Catholic state, wherever several believing families exist, a Christian doctrine, or rather a residue of a politicoreligious amalgam which has nothing to do with the Gospel?
2. Doesn't respect for objective truth lead necessarily to respect for the conscience of those one believes to be in error?
3. Has the state any competence in religious matters?

"The Clerical Unity of Truth" In a press conference given in Rome, Dominican Father Le Guillou stated:

In a world where the light of truth shines in increasingly distinct cultures, it is clear that the religious unity of mankind can result only from a consensus of investigations carried out in all freedom by individuals. The Church must do everything she can to protect the juridical status of this communion among men. She cannot, of course, abandon the objective of bringing about the unity of humanity on the plane of faith; but this attitude specifically implies that we must get well beyond what Paul Ricoeur has called "the clerical unity of truth," a unity that is always more or less necessarily based on constraint. An affirmation of religious liberty by the Catholic Church would undoubtedly be the best proof of her ecumenical orientation as well as of her ecumenical début.

If Vatican II could overcome the contradictions that will be encountered among the Fathers and state unequivocally that freedom is at the very heart of Christianity and break away from her many historical and contemporary compromises, if it could affirm that the lay state properly understood is not contrary to Catholicism but is in fact an essential consequence of it, then it would speak a language understandable by all, whether Catholics or not, and what is more important, it would be in the spirit of the Gospel.

NOVEMBER 19

The Theme of Ecumenism
Provokes Radically Opposed Reactions

The schema on ecumenism is acting like a scouring agent, laying thoughts and hearts bare. Rarely have interventions been more radically opposed than those heard in the Council on Monday as the debates began. Contemporary in age, the Fathers—some of them, at any rate—are scarcely so in mentality. The perceptions of some are not those of others. Some of the Fathers are completely insensitive to the signs of the times. In practice they continue to think as though Catholicism and Christianity had nothing to do with the flow of history, and they see the "separated brethren" principally as suspect and disturbing. But others, because they know non-Catholics, speak with truth and emotion of their good points and the intrinsic value of their faith.

A whole world separates the first from the second. It is difficult to see how they can ever get together. The Council must listen to the opposing positions. We will then see what the majority think, and whether or not John XXIII was right to make ecumenism the principal issue of Vatican II.

No commentary is necessary here; the interventions speak for themselves. Our purpose will be to transcribe the essence of what was said.

Cardinal Cicognani, president of the Commission for the Oriental Churches, presented the schema quickly and referred to the "anxiety" it has sometimes provoked. He recalled the pastoral end of Vatican II. "Let us be under no illusion," he said. "Union will not be achieved immediately, but we must open and not close the doors. May this schema be an effective basis for discussion."

Then Archbishop Martin of Rouen, the reporter, stressed the importance of this schema before God and before history:

> The spirit of the schema is pacific and ironic. The ecumenical question is altogether new, for it responds to a new situation. Divisions among Christians today are a cause of scandal to those who are unbelievers. They paralyze the work of evangelization. This is a fact of daily experience.
>
> The schema, in accordance with the wishes of John XXIII and Paul VI, speaks of the spiritual renewal of the Church, of a conversion of heart, of an evangelical life, and of prayer in common with our separated brethren. It deliberately rejects all spirit of compromise. No one is disposed to subscribe to a superficial and equivocal union. All Christians are children of the light and cannot walk in the darkness. There is only one spirit of quest for and fidelity to Christianity. On the Catholic side, there is no duplicity, no double-dealing, no Machiavellianism.
>
> There is no need to recall at length all that separates us, for we know it well. It is more necessary to seek out a common basis of dialogue, the indispensable path to overcoming our differences.
>
> As regards the Oriental Churches, the schema emphasizes their venerable prerogatives, which go back to the apostles and which were retained and accepted by the Fathers of the Church. It insists on the legitimate diversity of these Churches, not out of opportunism but out of respect for the truth. Concerning the communities born of the Reformation, the schema sets in relief what they have in common with Catholics: the same faith and the same love in Christianity, the same cult of Scripture, the presence of God's ever living word, the sacramental bond of baptism, the same missionary activity, the same Holy Spirit. No one can deny the profoundly amicable and fraternal character of our interconfessional encounters, or that we have always felt the influence of the Spirit in them.

After this preliminary brief on ecumenism, the interventions began.

An Inopportune Subject for Vatican II   Cardinal Ruffini said he admired the manner in which the schema treated Catholic doctrine, but he expressed certain doubts on its "manner of proceeding." He regretted that the word *ecumenism* itself was not more clearly defined; he said that it has one meaning for Catholics and another for Protestants. "Never," he went on, "can the Catholic Church agree to put all communities on the same level. Nothing is dearer to our hearts than unity. But we cannot speak in the same terms of relations with the Oriental Churches, so close to us, and with the communities born of the Reformation, which comprise hundreds of sects which interpret the Gospel differently."

Cardinal de Arriba y Castro, Archbishop of Tarragona, warned the assembly that he was going to speak his mind freely—a wise precaution. He said:

> We magnify the dialogue, we talk of prayer in common; this is all very fine, but let us beware of the dangers and always strictly respect the laws of the Church, such as the Index, which prohibits books favoring heresy. It is inopportune to speak of ecumenism in a council. This will scandalize the faithful of little education, who will be confused and put all churches on the same level.
>
> Proselyting is increasing. Let us ask our separated brethren to renounce all proselyting among Catholics. But the Church's right to preach the Gospel everywhere must be recognized. Let us insist on charity toward our separated brethren but first of all on fidelity to Christ. This schema does not please me. It is very badly done. It is better to avoid such a subject altogether. A secretariat for unity, which works directly under the Pope, is enough.

His Beatitude Stephanos I Sidarouss, Coptic Patriarch of Alexandria, thought that the schema evidenced a "false irenicism." He regretted that the primacy of Peter was not mentioned.

When Cardinal Ritter of St. Louis spoke, the tone of the debates changed radically. "The schema," he said, "responds to the *aggiornamento* urged by John XXIII and Paul VI. It rings the death knell of the Counter-Reformation." However, the prelate regretted that the chapter on religious liberty did not come first, for it is "the essential prologue to all genuine ecumenism," he said. "Religious liberty is not an opportunistic affair; it is a question of theology. The very liberty of the act of faith demands total independence from all civil power. The state has no competence whatsoever in matters religious. It should never meddle in religion, and the Church should never be dependent on any civil authority, even though it be Catholic."

Cardinal Ritter also asked that the word *church* be used when speaking of the Protestant communities since these "are also founded on baptism and Holy Scripture." It was a remark fraught with consequences of the highest importance.

Luther Fought Against the Immorality of Catholic Prelates José Cardinal Quintero, Archbishop of Caracas, urged that the blame for the separation in the sixteenth century not be placed on the Protestants alone but that Catholic responsibility also be recognized. He recalled "the immorality of Catholic prelates at that time," and stressed that "Luther fought against their pagan and dissolute morals. Even since the Reformation, we have failed in charity toward the Protestants. Let us begin, then, with the evangelical attitude of the Publican and not that of the Pharisee. Let the Council issue a statement asking pardon of our separated brethren for the faults we are guilty of and for the indignities we have subjected them to." (Applause.)

His Beatitude Maximos IV Saigh intervened, in French as usual. "This schema," he said, "pleases me immensely. It indicates that we have finally emerged from a period of sterile polemics which have done so much harm to our theology and our spirituality." The Patriarch expressed pleasure that false proselytism is on the wane, and that people are relying rather on the influence of sincere witness and respect for the conscience of others. "As John XXIII and Paul VI have asked, let us not hesitate to recognize our mutual wrongs or to admit that our divisions are the result of sin. I want especially to say how happy I am finally to see the emergence of a true theology and a true ecclesiology in the Latin Church which take the Oriental Churches into account and which lead to the life of the Trinity."

The speakers yesterday agreed on only one point: there should be no mention of the Jews in the schema. To do so, it was said, would seriously compromise the situation of the Christian minorities in Arabic countries. Maximos IV Saigh quoted an Arabic proverb: "He who receives the blows is not in the same position as he who counts them." Furthermore, it is argued, it would offend the separated brethren, who are Christian, to put them on the same level as the Jews. But if the schema must speak of the Jews, then it should also consider the Muslims, Buddhists, and Confucians.

NOVEMBER 20

Schemas on the Jews and Religious Liberty on the Agenda

The general congregation on Tuesday (the seventieth) was dominated by the reports of Cardinal Bea, president of the Secretariat for Promoting Christian Unity, and Bishop de Smedt of Bruges. They defended chapters 4 and 5 of the draft decree on ecumenism, which deal respectively with the attitude of Christians toward the Jews and with religious liberty.

Both questions are highly controversial. Anti-Semitism is indeed not a Christian monopoly. As for religious liberty, it is a burning issue for two reasons: first, Protestant minorities have directly experienced great difficulties living in Catholic countries like Spain; second, relatively recent pontifical statements have attacked freedom of conscience and worship. Jesuit Father Lecler has written in *Études*, "Since the seventeenth century, a whole casuistry has developed about the thesis of absolute tolerance which has allowed the most brutal intolerance to run free."

The memory of such texts as Gregory XVI's *Miravi vos*, written in 1832, remains very much alive: "That each must be granted and guaranteed freedom of conscience, one of the most contagious of errors, is most false and absurd, or rather insane." Pius IX, in the encyclical *Quanta cura* of 1864, spoke of "that erroneous opinion which could not be more fatal to the Catholic Church and the salvation of souls, namely, that freedom of conscience and worship is a right proper to man."

In the *Syllabus*, the same Pius IX condemned the following propositions:

"Every man is free to embrace and profess the religion he deems correct according to the light of reason."

"In our age, it is no longer practical to consider the Catholic religion as the unique religion of the state to the exclusion of all other cults."

"It is false that the civil liberty of all cults and the right of all to manifest openly and publicly all their thoughts and opinions precipitate peoples into the corruption of morals and spirits, and propagate the plague of indifferentism."

Finally, Leo XIII in his encyclical *Libertas proestantissimum* of 1885, called freedom of worship "a liberty totally contrary to the virtue of religion," and stated that "the state cannot treat all religions on an equal basis or indiscriminately accord them the same rights."

Freedom of Religion Is Inherent in the Act of Faith   These quotations, which historic context may explain but not excuse, are necessary to understand Bishop de Smedt's loudly (but not unanimously) applauded exposition yesterday. He spoke of what many call "a kind of Machiavellianism [of the Church] because we seem to them to demand the free exercise of religion when Catholics are in a minority in any nation and at the same time refuse and deny the same religious liberty when Catholics are in the majority."

The Bishop then clarified misunderstandings of the word *liberty*, which he said cannot be confused with "whim." He rejected the errors of "religious indifferentism," "doctrinal relativism," and "dilettantistic pessimism." He next defined religious liberty as "the right of the human person to the free exercise of religion according to the dictates of his conscience," and explained;

Negatively, it is immunity from all external force in his personal relations with God, which the conscience of man vindicates to itself.

Religious liberty implies human autonomy, not from within certainly but from without. . . .

[Catholics] must abstain from all direct and indirect coercion [of any man]. . . . they must respect and esteem the right and duty of non-Catholics to follow the dictate of their own conscience even when, after sincere and sufficient study, it errs in good faith.

What is the reason of faith why non-Catholics can be forced by no one to admit the Catholic doctrine against their conscience? This reason is found in the very nature of the act of faith. For this act . . . is and must be an assent which man freely gives to God.

. . . every man, who follows his conscience in religious matters, has a natural right to true and authentic religious liberty. . . . No person can be the object of coercion or intolerance.

"Fish Out of Water"   Bishop de Smedt continued:

Religious liberty would be fruitless and empty if men were not able to carry out the dictate of their conscience in external acts whether in private life, in social life, or in public life. . . .

Here, however, there arises a most difficult problem. For, if a human person carries out the dictate of his conscience by external acts, there is danger of violating the rights and duties of another or of others. . . .

From this it is evident that the right and duty to manifest externally the dictate of conscience is not unlimited, but can be and at times must be tempered and regulated for the common good.

This ordering of the common good must be done juridically in human society and belongs to public authority. . . . [But] public authority can never act contrary to the order of justice established by God. . . .

Recent Roman pontiffs again and again have bewailed the fact that not a few governments have gone too far in this matter, ignoring and violating religious liberty. [The most recent was] Paul VI, in his allocution to the Fathers of the Second Vatican Ecumenical Council on September 29, 1963.

Bishop de Smedt said that everything in the schema is in accord with traditional thought. To explain the positions taken by nineteenth-century popes (quoted above), recourse must be had, he said, to the laws of "continuity" and "progress." We have gradually learned to distinguish between subjective and objective error. If Gregory XVI used the word "insane" and the *Syllabus* condemned separation of church and state, it was because of the ideology of rationalism then current, according to which the individual conscience was above all laws, and because of the omnipotent state. Similarly, freedom of worship was condemned because of religious indifferentism. Every document, he said, must be interpreted in the "historical and doctrinal context" which gave it birth. Otherwise, it would be like trying to make "fish swim out of water."

Bishop de Smedt concluded:

> The whole world is waiting for this decree. The voice of the Church on religious liberty is being waited for in universities, in national and international organizations, in Christian and non-Christian communities, in the papers, and in public opinion—and it is being waited for with urgent expectancy.

> We hope that it will be possible to complete the discussion and the approbation of this very brief but very important decree before the end of this second session. How fruitful our work would appear to the world if the conciliar Fathers, with the voice of Peter's successor, could announce this liberating doctrine on religious liberty!

Cardinal Bea Deplores Anti-Semitic Thinking Among Catholics Cardinal Bea's speech made an equally deep impression on the assembly. The president of the Secretariat for Promoting Christian Unity recalled that Christ, the apostles, and the Virgin Mary were Jews, and that for Saint Paul Christians were the sons of Israel. He deplored anti-Semitic sermons and attitudes among Catholics. If it is true that some Jews put Christ to Death, the Cardinal said, it is no less true that he asked his Father to forgive them, for they knew not what they did. The disciples of Christ ought to imitate the example of their Master. Moreover, God, according to Saint Paul, did not reject his people, for his election was for all time.

Why raise these matters at the Council? Because, Cardinal Bea answered,

> Some decades ago, anti-Semitism, as it is called, was prevalent in various regions and in a particularly violent and criminal form, especially in Germany under the rule of National Socialism, which . . . committed frightful crimes, extirpating several millions of Jewish people. . . . Moreover, accompanying and assisting this whole activity was a most powerful and effective "propaganda," as it is called,

against the Jews. Now, it would have been almost impossible if some of the claims of that propaganda did not have an unfortunate effect even on faithful Catholics. . . .

For the Jews of our times can hardly be accused of the crimes committed against Christ. . . . Actually, even in the time of Christ, the majority of the chosen people did not cooperate with the leaders of the people in condemning Christ. . . . those among them who cried out to Pilate, "Crucify him," formed a very small part of the chosen people. . . .

If therefore not even all the Jews in Palestine or in Jerusalem could be accused, how much less the Jews dispersed throughout the Roman Empire. And how much less again those who today after nineteen centuries live scattered in the whole world.

The Cardinal then stressed the exclusively religious character of the schema. Answering objections made previously by Council Fathers, he said he realized that the Arab countries could misinterpret the document and see in it, for example, an argument in favor of Zionism. But in fact it is strictly apolitical. For this reason, the secretariat for unity had apprised the Arab states of its intentions.

Other interventions yesterday were by Cardinals Léger, Koenig (he wanted the adjective *ecclesial* added to the expression "Protestant community"), and Rugambwa, the Patriarchs Gori (Jerusalem) and Batanian (Cilicia), Archbishop Charles de Provenchères of Aix-en-Provence, Archbishop John McQuaid of Dublin, Archbishop Garrone of Toulouse, and Coadjutor Bishop Elchinger of Strasbourg.

Archbishop Garrone remarked that "There are great treasures in the non-Catholic Christian communities," and he regretted "that sometimes we are afraid to say this and admire them, while all this belongs to God."

Intellectual Reform in the Church Bishop Elchinger's intervention attracted much notice. He said that the decree on ecumenism was "a special grace and favor" given to our times, for, in the words of Father Congar, it is not only a *text* but an *act* which commits the Catholic Church. Ecumenical involvement must henceforward be considered an obligation which binds the pastors and faithful of the Roman Church in conscience. But, he went on, no sincere ecumenism is possible without an intellectual reform within the Church. "In fact, the methods of research and the customs followed in serving the truth are almost as important as the truth itself."

To this end, he proposed four intellectual conditions necessary to authentic ecumenism:

1. Never fear the truth, and welcome it even when it is uncomfortable. Does God need our pusillanimity to defend his truth? To be afraid of discovering the truth is to lack faith in the Holy Spirit. Thus, for example, we must recognize that at the origin of Christian disunity there were not only errors (sometimes on both sides) but also certain demands of faith which were felt more profoundly by our separated brothers than by us. With respect to Scripture, they have sometimes had more trust in the Spirit and more courage than Catholic theologians. Such remarkable men as Father Reginald Garrigou-Lagrange have been suspect, and other inquirers have been systematically condemned. Who followed Lord Halifax and Cardinal Mercier? Very few.

2. The positions of non-Catholic Christians should not be depreciated apriori and indiscriminately. What is true in them should be honestly admitted.

3. We should not rest lazily on our Catholic truths but should continue to search for the truth, which we will never possess fully. Although our dogmas are defined, we will never finish discovering God and the fullness of his message. Moreover, the questions asked by our separated brothers can stimulate us in this search.

4. Since Saint Paul teaches of the diversity of the gifts of the Spirit, we must not confuse *unity* with *uniformity*, as the Latin Church sometimes does. The sin of man is at the root of our schisms, but so too is a refusal to recognize the diversity of gifts. We must respect the work of God in souls. He acts differently in each of us. To forget this would be to dwarf the richness and the fullness of divine truth.

Ecumenism does not consist in seeking a compromise with respect to dogmas or in renouncing the rules of pastoral prudence. Nor does it consist in asking our separated brethren to become like us in all things.

In conclusion, Bishop Elchinger answered the objection that this conception of ecumenism risks culminating in relativism. To be sure, the Bishop said, in relativism regarding some of our personal ideas, but not at all in relativism regarding revealed truth.

NOVEMBER 21

Schema on Ecumenism Widely Approved

Wednesday's general congregation heard the large majority of interventions praise the schema on ecumenism. It was surprising that there were so few objections, and these were moderate. This favorable situation

makes it possible to hope that the schema will be adopted by a comfortable margin. Dialogue between the Roman Church and her sisters will
be much easier in the future.

Here is a brief summary of the debates.

Cardinal Meyer, Archbishop of Chicago, vigorously supported the
chapters on the Jews and religious liberty. Bishop Angelo Jelmini, Apostolic Administrator of Lugano, Switzerland, was happy that the Church
was showing herself not as a closed society but as one open to the whole
world. He expressed the hope that the schema would speak of Muslims
and even unbelievers as well as of Jews.

Bishop Andrea Sapelak, Apostolic Visitor for Ukranians in Argentina,
regretted that greater attention was not given to the united Oriental
Churches, which are a bridge to Orthodoxy and which have remained
faithful to Rome at the price of their blood.

Archbishop Morcillo González of Saragossa liked the positive character of the schema, and was happy to see that the "injurious words"
of the earlier text on unity presented to the Fathers had completely disappeared. "Let us not be afraid to say," he declared, "that there are
elements of truth outside the Catholic Church."

Archbishop Baudoux of St. Boniface, Canada, said the schema was
"essential" and was glad to see it had come into existence. As a testimony
to ecumenism, he quoted a letter sent to the Canadian hierarchy by the
Anglican synod of that country.

In the name of all the bishops of Great Britain, Archbishop Heenan
of Westminster approved the schema in its entirety, and said he accepted
it "with great joy." He thanked God that the very painful dissensions
with the Anglicans were over, and avowed that the English hierarchy
was determined to do everything in its power to promote ecumenism.

Archbishop Weber of Strasbourg opened the question of mixed
marriages. He hoped the Church would return to the position prior to
1918, when these marriages were considered valid, while since that time
they have been looked upon as not only illicit but invalid. He also asked
that Catholic priests be permitted to distribute communion to the Orthodox and hear their confessions.

Revoking the Decrees Against Freemasonry   Archbishop Méndez Arceo
of Cuernavaca said that the schema pleased him greatly, and then went
on to make some interesting remarks:

1. "Protestant communities should be recognized as 'churches.' "
2. "It is absolutely necessary for us to say here that the liturgical movement and the biblical movement are of the highest importance in order
   to favor unity with non-Catholics."

3. "Let us not forget the sects, such as the Pentecostal movement which have great vitality and a perfectly adapted liturgy."
4. "It is about time to condemn anti-Semitism."
5. "Let us begin the schema with the chapter on religious liberty, which is neither a corollary nor an appendix but an eminently fundamental principle of ecumenism. . . . For unity without liberty is not religious unity.
6. "We should revoke the decrees which the Church has often applied against Freemasonry. . . . There are many anti-Christians among them, true; but there are also many who believe in God and call themselves Christian or who at least do not conspire either against the Church or against the civil society."

Speaking About the Muslims Father Robert Chopard-Lallier, Apostolic Prefect of Parakou, Dahomey, also emphasized the very important role played by the various Christian sects, and asked that ecumenism be thought of in a missionary context. He added, "Let us not wait until Vatican III or Vatican IV to speak about the Muslims."

Retired Coadjutor Bishop André Jacq of Langson and Coabang, Vietnam, thought that contact with the Protestant churches helps Catholics return to their sources. He expressed joy that the schema corresponded with the expectations of the non-Catholic observers present at the Council.

There were two amusing moments during the morning. One was when Cardinal Bacci of the Curia complained to the moderators for having refused him the right to speak on the famous October 30 vote. "I appealed to the Pope," he said. Cardinal Agagianian, the moderator who was directing the discussion that morning, explained what the problem was. It involved a request merely for a modification in the wording of question 3 (*primatus* instead of *primatiale*). "The moderators didn't think this a major issue, so the intervention had to be sacrificed [*immolandus*]." (Laughter.)

The laughter was much louder when Bishop León de Uriarte Benzoa, Apostolic Vicar for San Ramón, Peru, enumerated the different kinds of ecumenism in passionate tones: ecumenism of God, of Christ, of the Virgin, of the apostles, of bishops, of religious, of pastors, of mankind in general. The moderator tried to interrupt this ecumenical litany but in vain. It was said that there has never been such laughter in the aula since the Council began.

Lay Auditors Declare, "We Can Testify That the Council Is Thinking About the World"

The lay Catholic auditors at the Council have just released a statement. They express happiness "in the dynamism of the Council which is questioning a good many superstructures." They note that "the interventions are often very contradictory," and add: "This does not surprise us. History tells us how progress results from the most tumultuous councils."

A reference was made to the impatience of some because of "the apparent slowness of the work," but the statement went on to say that time is necessary for maturation and conciliation. They recall that the laity have a place on the commissions, can intervene, and are often listened to.

"For the first time in history a Council has confronted the question of the laity in all its ramifications," the statement said. "The nature of our participation in the life of the Church will gradually be transformed. This is noticeable throughout the Catholic world."

Concerning the opening to the world, the statement commented: "The Council is surrounded by the world. If the world is not paying much attention to the Council, we can testify that the Council is thinking about the world. It feels responsible for its salvation to the point of pain. It is continually on the alert for signs of the times."

The statement noted, finally, that the lay auditors have procured the services of an assessor to assure closer liaison between themselves and the assembly. This assessor is Bishop Emilio Guano of Livorno, a member of the Commission for the Lay Apostolate and of the mixed commission for schema 13.

NOVEMBER 22

Paul VI Will Modify the Composition and Direction of the Conciliar Commissions

On Thursday, Archibishop Felici informed the Fathers that the Pope had made three decisions concerning the conciliar commissions.

1. The membership of each commission will be raised to thirty, generally an increase of five members per commission. However, the composition of the Commission for the Sacred Liturgy, which has almost completed its work, will remain unchanged. The Commission for the Oriental Churches, which has twenty-seven members, will be increased by three; but the Secretariat for Promoting Christian Unity, which has only eighteen members, will be increased by twelve.

2. In general, four out of five of the new members are to be chosen by a vote in the Council. The fifth will be designated by the Pope. The three new members of the Commission for the Oriental Churches will be named by the Fathers; the Pope had appointed two bishops to it during the recess. Eight members of the Secretariat for Promoting Christian Unity will be elected and four will be chosen by the Pope. The episcopal conferences are to present three candidates for each commission and six for the secretariat for unity. The conferences are urged to reach an agreement among themselves. The lists will be distributed to the Fathers next Tuesday, November 26, and the vote is set for Thursday.

3. Finally—and this is by far the most important measure—when the new members have been added, the commissions themselves will elect a vice president and a secretary to join those already in these positions.

The Pope's purpose seems clear: he hopes to ease the sometimes crushing work load of the commissions. The commission on theology, for example, is faced with the enormous task of inserting the myriad amendments into the schema *De Ecclesia*. Until now, sixteen of the commission members were elected by the Council and nine were chosen by the Pope. Henceforward there will be twenty and ten respectively, which means that exactly two-thirds instead of two-thirds minus one will be elected by the Fathers.

A Concern for Continuity   If the president of each commisison and his secretary—both named by John XXIII—remain unchanged, the new ruling will introduce a clause which is more democratic than before. According to the old system, the vice president was chosen by the president. The present modifications stipulate that a second vice president and secretary are to be elected by the commission members.

The juxtaposition of two vice presidents and two secretaries, one appointed and the other elected, is characteristic of the way the Vatican operates; its changes always occur without bumps and with attention to continuity, so that nobody will be roughly shoved aside. "In Rome," an American theologian said to me recently, "they never subtract; they always add." Thus, without interfering with the Council presidents named by John, Paul VI named four moderators who in practice direct the Council. Again, last year when a new commission was formed to rework the schema on revelation, John XXIII named two copresidents, Cardinals Ottaviani and Bea.

A Half-Measure   In the present instance, it is psychologically difficult to remove Cardinal Ottaviani from the presidency of the theological commission (although many bishops would like to see him go). So the

Pope adopted a half-measure. Like all half-measures, it satisfies no one but gives everyone the impression that he has been at least partially listened to. This is a good example of Paul VI's prudence. He didn't want anyone to feel defeated, short of satisfying entirely the impatience of the many Fathers who desire more radical measures. Would it be wise to accelerate the Church's evolution when *aggiornamento* is bound to change significantly the style and structure of Catholicism in any event? Debatable.

"Yes" Votes Number 1,996 out of 2,082 on the Schema on Ecumenism

On Thursday the Fathers finished their general examination of the schema on ecumenism and voted on the following question: "Do you accept the first three chapters of the schema as a basis of discussion?" The subjects of those chapters, let us recall, are (1) the principles of ecumenism, (2) the practice of ecumenism, and (3) separated Christians. The vote indicated near-unanimity among the Fathers. Of 2,082 ballots, only 86 were *non placet*.

The assembly will vote at some later date on chapters 4 and 5, concerning the Jews and religious liberty.

Only one of the seven interventions on Thursday morning was negative: Archbishop Florit of Florence was sharply opposed to the schema. He thought it was excessive in its praise of the communities born of the Reformation, which, he said, "have very evident faults. Apropos of religious liberty, the Florentine prelate declared, "There is no natural right to spread error. Error is not right but a necessary evil in concrete circumstances; . . . Let us then preserve our unity."

Think of the Atheists   With a touch of humor, Bishop Joseph Höffner of Münster asserted, "Our greatest cross is not primarily the reform of the Curia or a change in the demarcations of dioceses; rather it is militant atheism, which is spreading particularly in the great urban centers among the workers and intellectuals. Let us address a separate chapter to our paganized brethren."

Bishop Endre Hamvas of Csanád, Hungary, spoke from personal experience about the difficulties of dialogue with Calvinists in his own country, and warned against anything that might give the impression of "doctorinal indifferentism." Maronite Archbishop Zaidé of Beirut acknowledged the spiritual riches of non-Catholic churches. "These riches are Christian and therefore belong to all Christians," he said.

With reference to the first chapter, Bishop Volk of Mainz said the Roman Church must be open to everything that is authentically Christian in the Orthodox and Protestant churches. "It is a grave obligation," he remarked. "Let us distinguish clearly between what can be changed in the Catholic Church and what is essential. The episcopal college, for example, is something essential. This has always been recognized by the Orientals, and it has been forgotten by the West."

Bishop Carli of Segni took a contrary tack and said no mention should be made of collegiality, which, he said, is "a litigious notion which has absolutely not been proven." He went on, "Peter is the unique foundation of the Church; he is the head of the Church and not of the college. The apostles are merely auxiliaries of Peter."

Other speakers were Archbishop Nicodemo of Bari, Bishop Talamás Camandari of Ciudad Juárez, and Maronite Bishop Antoine Abed, of Tripoli, Lebanon.

NOVEMBER 23

The Schema on the Liturgy
Represents a Victory for Decentralization

On Friday, Vatican II put its seal of approval on the schema on the liturgy with a vote of 2,158 *placet* votes, 19 *non placet*, and 1 invalid.

To date it is the only schema the Council has finished since it opened in 1962. The intrinsic value and potential influence of this document are universally admitted. It is the fruit not only of intense conciliar and preconciliar work—it was four years in preparation—but also of several decades of convergent efforts.

Countless German, French, and American pioneers (to mention but a few) prepared the way for this breakthrough. They were aware of the growing discrepancy between certain outmoded forms of worship and the needs of the faithful today, and endeavored to remedy the situation both by practical experiments and solid historical and theological research.

It was John XXIII's personal decision that the schema on the liturgy be placed first on the agenda of Vatican II. In his mind it was one of the most important subjects of a Council which he wanted to be primarily pastoral. After the initial controversy about the use of Latin, the agreement of the Fathers grew progressively until it reached the remarkable majority of yesterday's vote.

Vatican II has been strengthened by this vote, which eloquently manifests the agreement of bishops and superiors general of religious orders on how the faithful should pray. The schema also gives great freedom to episcopal conferences to adapt the liturgy to local needs. In this sense, the vote represents an incontestable victory for collegiality and decentralization.

The Asian Religions

Continuing examination of the first chapter of the schema on ecumenism, the Fathers heard several interventions urging the discussion of non-Christian religions. Bishop Vito Chang, former Bishop of Sinyang, China, noted that Confucius made himself an apostle of ecumenism several centuries before Christ. His doctrine was based on the universal love of a God who wishes to save all men and teach us that we are all brothers. "Let us not overlook this," said the missionary prelate. "Let us add chapters on Buddhism and Confucianism. This is absolutely indispensable. The word of God has illumined all men, whatever religion they belong to. All religions which are adapted to different mentalities bear some relationship to the true Church."

Bishops Veiga Coutinho (India) and Pont y Gol (Spain) asked that the secretariat for non-Christian religions, which Paul VI announced he would soon create at the outset of the second session, begin its work.

Neither Return Nor Surrender   In a highly spiritual intervention, Bishop Huyghe of Arras condemned any form of ecumenism which, based on a "return" of the separated brethren, would seem like a surrender. He contrasted the word *return* with the one used by the schema: *approach*.

He then stated the conditions for fruitful ecumenism: "It is indispensable for all Christians, of whatever kind, to be renewed, to pray in common, to collaborate in helping the poor, to reflect together on the theological foundations of the Spiritual life, and to engage in common pastoral action in mission countries."

Violent Attack on the Chapter on Religious Liberty

Father de Broglie-Revel, a Jesuit professor of dogmatic theology at the Gregorian University and formerly of the Institut Catholique of Paris, has distributed a three-page note to the Fathers violently criticizing chapter 5, on religious liberty, of the schema *De ecumenismo*.

The author affirms that the text expounding "man's basic right to religious liberty is unimaginably incoherent." According to him, certain passages "subscribe to the most extreme theses of liberalism without any qualification whatsoever."

The theologian added:

> This incoherence is in fact due to an equivocation, for it attempts an impossible compromise between the principles of liberalism and those of Pius IX. The theological commission's massive approval of this text is a little disconcerting. Far from satisfying our adversaries, this wishywashy text can only inspire them to contempt for the Council and the Church. The Council cannot vote against it without being accused of a retrograde spirit and blind hostility to the rights of liberty.

This outburst proves, if proof be needed, the extent to which theme of religious liberty has stirred up passions.

NOVEMBER 26

Communications Schema Squeaks Through

Monday's session was a dramatic one. First came the final vote on the communications schema. A last-ditch effort was staged on the steps of St. Peter's by those who thought this schema was unworthy of the Council because of its superficiality and cheap moralism. A note was distributed asking the Fathers to vote against so unsatisfactory (*minime convenitur*) a schema, which, if ratified, would hurt the authority of the Council. Twenty-four Fathers had signed this manifesto, including Bishops de Smedt of Bruges, Paul Schmitt of Metz, Maurice Pourchet of St.-Flour, France, Volk of Mainz, and Ramón Bogarin of San Juan de las Misiones, Paraguay; Archbishop Schäufele of Freiburg im Breisagau; and Father Schütte, Superior General of the Divine Word Fathers.

This initiative greatly displeased Cardinal Tisserant, who, from his lofty seat, protested as chief of the Council's presidency, calling the action "unworthy of the assembly." The dry tone of his intervention produced a certain amount of ferment. Some of the Fathers must have been swayed by the lobbying, as the results indicate: 1,598 *placet*, 503 *non placet*, and 11 invalid ballots. The number of negative votes was much higher (by some 400) than the previous voting on individual chapters of the schema. Since the decree obtained the two-thirds majority, it will be promulgated in the public session of December 4, together with the constitution on the liturgy.

On Ecumenism: The Definitions Are Broad

"We Never Possess the Whole Truth" Monday's general congregation continued examining chapter 1 of the schema on ecumenism. Cardinal Léger, Archbishop of Montreal, stressed the necessity of a conception of unity that was not monolithic:

> In our insistence on unity, we have too often lost sight of the advantages of diversity. Charity and truth must not suffer in our discussions. But we must pursue truth in humility as well as in charity. . . . The Church has known many heresies and schisms. The remedy is not necessarily authority, but humble progress in the faith. . . .
>
> When we say that the Catholic Church possesses all truth, we use a misleading formula, and forget that the mystery of Christ transcends our ability to understand it fully. We never possess the whole truth. Saint Paul speaks of the depth of the riches of Christ. This certainly cannot favor doctrinal immobilism. As Paul VI said to the non-Catholic observers, "Seek in order to find, and find in order to seek again."

Cardinal Ritter of St. Louis said that the "division of Christians is a scandal to the whole world. Unity is the common end which all Churches without exception seek in common."

"Pride Is the Root of All Division" Cardinal Bea, in his intervention, answered a number of objections. He emphasized the importance of local "directorates" for ecumenism in order to avoid tactless moves and to accommodate diverse regional situations. "Each episcopal conference should have a secretariat for unity working in cooperation with that of Rome," he said. "We must respect the instructions of the Holy Office, but it falls to the bishops to choose the experts they deem most suitable." And he added, "Nothing is more foreign to the spirit of ecumenism than doctrinal indifferentism."

The Cardinal also said, "We too often forget that this schema is written for Catholics who are presumed to know their doctrine. Therefore, there is no need to repeat incessantly the necessity of the primacy of the pope, while they are most often ignorant of what is good in other confessions."

Bishop Emilio Guano of Livorno hoped that ecumenism would not be the concern of specialists but of everyone. He noted that our age is one of secular unity and that Christians must get in tune.

"Obligatory Latinization," declared Archbishop Joseph Tawil, Melkite Patriarchal Vicar for Syria, "is of ecclesiastical right and not divine right. Let us beware of uniformity; it would spell the end of dialogue with the Orientals."

Archbishop Andrea Pangrazio of Gorizia, Italy, spoke of "the lamentable state of the Church at the time of the Reformation." He remarked that not all dogmas were of equal importance; some were truths of "means" and not of "ends" (such as the hierarchy and the sacraments).

Against Proselytism   Cloture of discussion on chapter 1 was then decided by a standing vote, and the assembly went on to consider chapter 2. This occasioned some energetic interventions. For example, Cardinal Beuno y Monreal, Archbishop of Seville, stated that "Ecumenical dialogue excludes proselytism of any kind on both sides because it is a cause of scandal." Archbishop Nicola Margiotta of Brindisi, Italy, while of the opinion that the Index should be retained, thought that books expounding the doctrine of Protestants should be spared so that Catholics could educate themselves in the tenets of other faiths.

Auxiliary Bishop Stéphane Desmazières of Bordeaux thought that separation came about as a result of "serious faults" committed on both sides. And Bishop Pierre Martin, Apostolic Vicar of New Caledonia, who spoke in the name of sixty bishops, said that the separated brethren expect real dialogue "on an equal footing." "This supposes," he said, "a questioning of our own positions. Why fear to question whatever can be questioned? Let us set the example, since we are asking others to do it."

Then he asked two questions: (1) Does the visible body of the Church truly show forth the spirit of the beatitudes, particularly poverty? (2) Is the visible Church sufficiently aware that we will be finally judged on our attitude toward the hungry, the poor, the destitute? "The poor," he concluded, "constitute two-thirds of humanity. Let us speak of them in the Council because of their importance. This would be of much more value than any abstract principles."

Paul VI to Athenagoras: "Let Us Forget Everything That Is Past"   The weekly *Apostolos Andreas*, the official organ of the Patriarchate of Constantinople, recently published, under the title "The Two Sister Churches," the text of a thank-you letter Paul VI recently addressed to His Beatitude Patriarch Athenagoras. In it we read:

> The charge which the Lord has confided to us as successor to the first of the apostles makes us anxious about anything concerning Christian unity and anything that can contribute to re-establishing perfect concord among men.

Entrusting the past to the mercy of God, let us listen to the counsel of the apostle: "Forgetting everything that is behind, I stretch myself forth to him who is before, to try to seize him as I have been seized by him."

We have been seized by him, by the gift of the same baptism, the same priesthood, the same eucharist, the one sacrifice, the one Lord of the Church.

Religious Liberty Defended by Monsignor Pavan

Monsignor Pietro Pavan, an Italian expert at the Council and one of the principal writers of the encyclicals *Mater et magistra* and *Pacem in terris*, spoke on Monday evening before the French episcopacy. In the present state of affairs, this conference has a special importance. Monsignor Pavan first of all revealed that John XXIII got the idea of writing an encyclical on peace after his message at the time of the Cuban crisis in 1962 because he was impressed with the influence of his proposals. "The Pope," said Monsignor Pavan, "began with facts and not ideas. The key facts are, on the one hand, socialization and, on the other, every man's conviction that he has a right to follow his conscience, especially in professing his religion, whether privately or publicly.

"*Pacem in terris* affirms this right clearly," Monsignor Pavan added. "Only God has the right to judge our conscience. The person himself must decide on religious matters, not external pressures and especially public powers, which have only one responsibility—and that is to create conditions favorable to the expression of the rights of citizens."

These remarks by one of John XXIII's collaborators did not go unnoticed. Ever since the subject of religious liberty came up for discussion, Vatican officials have made every effort to have it dropped or at least postponed for further study. Most of the Fathers, however, would like to see it discussed and at least a preliminary vote taken. Thus they could in a general way sanction an elementary truth that has already been expressed in *Pacem in terris* and expounded in the conciliar assembly of November 19.

A Controversial Document
on Sacerdotal Celibacy

The question of sacerdotal celibacy continues to attract attention. It is being closely studied by the Fathers and experts between the general congregations of the Council.

A text by Paul VI dated May, 1960 (when he was still Archbishop of Milan), is mentioned more and more frequently. Although limited in subject, this text is nonetheless significant; it questions the advisability of clerical celibacy in cases when a priest has been returned to a lay state. The future Paul VI wrote, "The suitability or opportuneness of removing the obligation of celibacy from priests who have been laicized and who find celibacy an intolerable burden should be studied, provided that permanent sanctions are retained so as to discourage others from following suit or causing scandal." The theologians we interviewed envision several possibilities, such as removal from the territory where the priest had exercised his ministry, the obligation of going abroad, etc.

Another important document is circulating among French-speaking bishops. Its author is a well-known religious who has been teaching in Rome for some years. The text, which is moderate in tone and pastoral in character, is entitled, "Should the Latin Church Have Deacons and Even Priests Bearing Witness to Conjugal Chastity as Well as a Celibate Clergy?"

We might note that "conjugal chastity" is a current expression in the clerical vocabulary and was the title of the celebrated modern encyclical on marriage, *Casti connubii.*

After making it very clear there was no question of the value of a celibate clergy or perfect chastity in conformity with the evangelical counsels, the document stated, "We are concerned with adding something which is of apostolic institution and which has in fact never ceased to exist in the Church: the right of bishops, if and only if they judge it opportune, to ordain married laymen who have lived exemplary conjugal and family lives."

Enumerating the reasons in favor of this course, the document continues:

> There are today immense regions in Latin America and Africa where many of the faithful *are deprived of a sacramental life* [italicized in the text] because of a shortage of priests. Yet they have a strict right to the sacraments. Missionaries admit that there are areas where they are constrained, despite the call of the people, to slacken their work of evangelization. . . .
>
> Such an innovation would *ipso facto* purify the Catholic priesthood by eliminating candidates who accept celibacy only because it is a necessary condition of the priesthood.

The Glory of the Priesthood

> Moreover, because of deacons and married priests, bishops would no longer be forced to impose on celibate priests conditions of isola-

tion in which, barring exceptional virtue, they find it very difficult to remain faithful to their vow of perfect chastity. Finally, in dioceses with few priests, the bishop would not be tempted to ordain candidates whose qualifications are not totally satisfactory. For all of these reasons, the glory of the Catholic priesthood, far from being diminished, would in all likelihood shine forth with new splendor.

The author suggested that such an innovation would not unsettle the faithful provided it took place gradually and at first uniquely with the approbation of the Holy See.

A married priest could support himself by exercising a part-time profession. "Nothing," the text reads, "is more in keeping with a tradition going back to the example of Saint Paul, who was totally consecrated to the Lord and yet thought it not unworthy of his vocation to earn his bread by manual labor.

"In Europe and elsewhere Catholic Action has shown that many laymen, without the benefit of a seminary education, are capable of attaining a genuine *apostolic and human maturity* which certainly makes them suited to exercise a properly diaconal or sacerdotal role in the apostolate."

With reference to the solution of the permanent diaconate, which he finds good but inadequate, the author concluded: "They would not be able to break bread, which was essential in the Church of the apostles."

A Document Against Atomic Weapons

A group of technicians from the Atomic Energy Commission in Paris and of economists, under the direction of the National Scientific Research Center, have personally presented the Council Fathers with a document in which we read:

> In no case can a defense of the faith be invoked to justify armaments or war; more generally, no human value or conception of life can legitimize war or probably even nuclear weapons.
>
> Today the absurdity of war is obvious. Our efforts for peace must therefore be more intensive, as *Pacem in terris* indicated.
>
> We do not feel the need for a theology of war but rather the proclamation of the Gospel.

The note contains detailed technical information on the present state of armament in the world and on nuclear war, as well as economic statistics on military expenditures. In 1961, these expenditures were the equal of 80 percent of the total income of underdeveloped countries and could have financed the schooling of at least 250,000,000 children.

Weaponry amounted to forty tons for each inhabitant of the earth.

The French representatives were favorably received by the cardinals and bishops they asked to see. The African episcopacy asked for several hundred copies of their document.

An American Bishop Criticizes Certain Aspects of the Catholic Church in Italy

In keeping with Paul VI's directives, the episcopal conferences have presented, with remarkable agreement, their lists of candidates who are to complete the cociliar commissions. The elections, let us recall, will be held on Thursday. Meanwhile the work of the Council proceeds apace as the synod approaches the close of the second session on December 3 and 4. Only four general congregations remain; there is scarcely sufficient time to complete examination of the schema on ecumenism, which is one of the masterpieces of conciliar labor.

The interest in the schema is substantiated each day by the interventions. Despite the weariness of the Fathers in these final days of the session, the Council is conscious of the momentous import of its deliberations. These hours will long be referred to as the time in history when the Catholic Church began to shed her unjustified superiority complex toward the other Christian churches. She suffers without them as much as they do without her. As proof of the value of ecumenism, the Fathers are becoming aware that a divided Christian community is aberrant.

The assembly heard an intervention by Father Sighardus Kleiner, Abbot General of the Cistercians, who paid gallant homage to the Virgin Mary—courageous because he confessed a monastic spirituality which did not blush to seek emphasis on the Virgin in a context where she had deliberately not been mentioned. "I frankly admit," he said, "that the unity of Christians seems to me impossible without Mary. There can be no fruitful ecumenism without her. But let us speak of her in a biblical fashion."

Humor and Wit Bishop Compagnone of Anagni, Italy, returned to a familiar obsession of some Fathers: that Christ founded the Church on Peter alone. The Bishop cited the famous passage from Matthew (16:18), "You are Peter, and on this rock I will build my Church." The next speaker, Auxiliary Bishop Stephen A. Leven of San Antonio, launched into a flight of oratory such as has rarely been heard on the Council floor.

With humor and mordant wit he lashed out against a certain style of Italian Catholicism:

> Every day it becomes clearer that we need dialogue, not only with Protestants but also among us bishops. For there are some Fathers who speak as if the only text in the Holy Bible were Matthew 16:18. . . .
>
> In every intervention they argue against the collegiality of the bishops. They preach to us and chastise us as if we were against Peter and his successors, or as if we desired to steal away the faith of our flocks and to promote indifferentism. . . .
>
> They speak as if the whole doctrine of the freedom of conscience . . . were offensive to pious ears. They seem to think that the Holy Spirit was given to a select few only. They prefer to blame non-Catholics, whom they have perhaps never seen, than to instruct the children in their parishes. . . .
>
> The prelates who seek a sincere and fruitful dialogue with non-Catholics are not the ones who show disaffection and disloyalty to the Holy Father. It is not our people who miss mass on Sunday, refuse the sacraments, and vote Communist. We love the Holy Father. . . . We have not lost the working classes. We do not cause scandal. . . .
>
> Venerable conciliar brethren, I pray you, let us put an end to the scandal of mutual recrimination. Let us proceed in an orderly way with the examination and study of this providential movement called ecumenism, so that with patience and humility we may achieve that unity for which the Lord prayed at the Last Supper.

This cruel eloquence provoked no less cruel applause.

The Battle Against Misery

Archbishop Zoa of Yaounde took the floor next. "Ecumenism is the condition *sine qua non* of the missions," he said, and then noted the danger of syncretism in his country. Cardinal Gracias of Bombay was the following speaker. He regretted that the schema did not emphasize the battle against misery. "The poor are the images of Christ, the living sacrament of Jesus," he said, echoing Paul VI. He cited impressive statistics drawn from a work by a Jesuit demographer, and made a strong plea that schema 17, "On the Church in the World," be studied at the beginning of the third session.

He then referred to the Eucharistic Congress to be held in Bombay in 1964, which he said would be, "neither a triumph nor an act of propaganda but a manifestation of love for the poor after the example of Christ, who said: 'I have come not to be served but to serve.' "

Cardinal Silva Henriquez, Archbishop of Santiago, Chile, signaled the difficult state of Catholicism in his country, attributing it to the attitude of Catholics toward human misery and the social injustices committed by the rich. "It is indispensable," he said, "to renew our pastoral approach according to the principles of a living Christianity."

Archbishop Conway (Ireland) appealed for better religious instruction for Catholics to prepare them for ecumenical dialogue. Bishop Klepacz (Poland) was of the same opinion. He quoted Gandhi, who was amazed at the religious ignorance of Christians. He also hoped that Catholics would emphasize Scripture as much as the Protestants do. "We need a more biblical theology," he asserted. "Let us study history, and not make an absolute of what is changeable."

Bishop Jean Gay of Basse-Terre, Guadeloupe, made reference to Pastor Hébert Roux, who has asked for "a lucid dialogue full of charity," and regretted that many Catholics and Protestants "retain a latent hostility in their hearts. The kingdom of God cannot be promoted by force or by violating consciences. In the future let us stop forced conversions. Experience proves that a change of religion frequently leads to the ruination of faith."

An Examination of Conscience for Bishops

Bishop Alfonso Sánchez Tinoco of Papantle, Mexico, and Bishop Hengsbach of Essen, Germany, urged that all Christians cooperate in social works. The latter stressed the importance and complexity of mixed marriages, which he said make a reform of canon law necessary. "Millions of families are concerned," he stated.

Finally, Bishop Himmer of Tournai thought the renewal of the Church should be more than internal, that it should be manifested in structures and institutions, in the style of Christian life as well as in our relations with civil power. He said:

> The renewal also concerns the bishops. We share in the sin of all men. If the hierarchy had not been a cause of scandal in the sixteenth century, the schism might not have taken place. Let us examine our own consciences. Hasn't it happened that we take the Gospel out of the hands of the faithful? Do we do enough to make Catholics participate actively in the mass? Are we aware that certain

ceremonies are unintelligible and disgust the faithful? Have we adequately propagated the teachings of *Mater et magistra* and *Pacem in terris?*

NOVEMBER 28

The State Should Not Interfere
in Relations Between Conscience and God

Wednesday's session was routine. Attention turned to the commission elections, which will be held on Thursday. The episcopal conferences have agreed on a common list. It was not surprising that Indonesia, Switzerland, and the religious orders, for different reasons, put forth independent candidates. As president of an unofficial liaison committee for the episcopal conferences, Archbishop Veuillot, Coadjutor of Paris, had the delicate responsibility of coordinating and harmonizing the different lists.

Another subject of curiosity and uneasiness: will the Council terminate this session without taking a decision on the religious liberty chapter? It seems likely that the examination of this sensitive question, which cannot be done in haste, will not be undertaken owing to lack of time. But the moderators can ask the Fathers for an indicative vote on the chapter and to say whether they want to see it included in the schema on ecumenism or inserted in the future schema 17, "On the Church in the World." The latter is not yet finished, but it seems to include a great variety of topics. Psychologically, it would be bad for the Council to recess without saying something concrete about religious liberty. The matter rests with the moderators, and their intentions are not yet known.

There were seventeen interventions on chapters 2 and 3 of the schema on ecumenism. We shall report on the highlights. Bishop Jean Nuer, Coptic Auxiliary of Thebes, urged a common ministry for Catholic and Orthodox priests in such circumstances as marriages, funerals, distribution of communion, and the like. Auxiliary Bishop Frantisek Tomasek of Olomouc, Czechoslovakia, suggested that explicit mention of ecumenism be made in the catechism.

The intervention of Bishop Schmitt of Metz centered on the issue of religious liberty. It should be mentioned in chapter 2, he said, since it is a condition of all ecumenical dialogue. Bishop Schmitt then called attention to the harmful consequences of any state intervention in this matter and the risk of political contamination that necessarily follows from such intervention. "The state," he said, "has no business interfering in the relations between conscience and God. It must recognize public religious liberty."

His Beatitude Maximos IV Saigh was happy to see that the schema mentions the necessity of diversity within unity. He rejected the idea sometimes advanced of combining the Latin and Eastern codes of canon law. This, he said, would considerably harm dialogue with the Orientals.

Bishop Bernardin Collin, of Digne, France, urged a return to the more liberal practices prevailing in the eighteenth century regarding *communicatio in sacris,* or the right of Catholics and Orthodox to receive the sacraments of either church. He strongly deplored a decree of 1949 which declared marriages between Oriental Catholics and Orthodox "invalid." Coptic Bishop Ghattas of Thebes made the same observation, and exclaimed, "Let this clause which is so contrary to a tradition of many centuries be changed!"

Auxiliary Bishop Jenny of Cambrai thought the schema was defective because it made no mention of the validity of the sacraments, apostolic succession, and the eucharist in the Oriental Churches, for "If the Church alone makes the eucharist, the eucharist alone makes the Church," he said, echoing Saint Augustine.

Coadjutor Archbishop Gouyon of Rennes greeted the non-Catholic observers as brothers who profess the same baptism and the same Christ, and then went on to make several interesting remarks. He thought Protestants should be accorded the title *communions* or *ecclesial communities* rather than *communities,* which has heavy sociological overtones. And he regretted that the schema is practically silent on the Anglicans, and suggested three distinct chapters: one on the Orientals, one on the Anglicans, and a third on Protestants.

NOVEMBER 29

A Brief for Intellectual Research

The assembly voted as scheduled on the supplementary commission members yesterday, Thursday.

Also, the first chapter of the schema *De Ecclesia* has been amended; it is now at the printer's and will be distributed shortly. It is hoped the Council will not recess without voting on this text, which would be tangible evidence of the bishops' labors during this second session and proof of the importance of the renewal in ecclesiology achieved by Vatican II.

It is possible that the Fathers will be called upon to approve the chapters on the Jews and religious liberty at the last general congregation on Monday. But there is nothing official as yet.

Thursday the assembly continued examining chapters 2 and 3 of the schema on ecumenism. Nineteen Fathers spoke, including Cardinal Frings, Archbishop of Cologne, who called the ecumenical movement "the evident fruit of the work of the Holy Spirit."

Archbishop Thiandoum of Dakar wished to see ecumenism extended to non-Christian religions, notably Islam, which claims Abraham as a forerunner and has many traditions borrowed from the Old and New Testaments.

Bishop Vicente Reyes of Borongán, Philippines, took exception to the word *vires* in the schema, for it excludes girls, women, and children.

In the Wake of Newman An intervention by Bishop Emile Blanchet, Rector of the Institut Catholique of Paris, was heard with keen attention. Insisting on the value and necessity of intellectual research and the duty to seek truth with an absolutely disinterested love, the Archbishop declared, "When a researcher must be warned of a risk of deviation, let him be treated as a son and not as a suspect, for it takes a great deal of courage to do intellectual work. Let the theologian be a psychologist and the historian a theologian!"

Archbishop Blanchet evoked the memory of Cardinal Newman and struck out against the impression that Catholics must renounce their intellectual convictions. Rather, he said, they should be fulfilled. He quoted John XXIII, who said that the Church is not the exclusive property of Catholics, and addressed the observers in these words: "You are at home here. This is your house. We are servants and not emperors of the truth."

Archabbot Reetz of the Benedictines of Beuron poked fun at what he called an "acrobatic theology" which produces such works as "The Immaculate Conception of Saint Joseph" and "The Assumption of Saint Joseph." He criticized the inadequacies of Scholastic theology, which is hard for Orientals and Protestants to understand, he felt. He scored the deviations of Marian devotions which lead to such pious practices as "the rosary of the tears of the Blessed Virgin." Abbot Reetz added, "Indulgences are difficult for Protestants to understand. And for us as well. Let us make moderate use of them."

In the second part of his speech, Reetz noted the factors favoring union: the liturgy, monasticism, ecclesiastical celibacy (he criticized certain publications for treating this matter uncritically), and the sacrament of penance properly understood.

Bishop Pildáin of the Canary Islands made an original suggestion. "The Council," he said, "talks too much and doesn't get to the heart of the matter, which is the love of the poor that Paul VI spoke of in his opening discourse. Let Vatican II dedicate a whole day to this important subject."

Bishop Garabed Amadouni, Armenian Exarch in France, said there was general ignorance of things pertaining to the Orient. "A good deal of nonsense has been spoken about the Orient," he said. "It is as though the Church were purely Occidental. Let us hope that this state of affairs will change quickly."

Archbishop Anibal Muñoz Duque of Nueva Pamplona, Colombia, complained that there "are Christian practices which attract the faithful with money."

The Treasure of the Poor

Then Bishop Bernardino Piñera Carvallo of Temuco, Chile, made a vibrant appeal for poverty: "Let us abandon our episcopal way of living. Let us shun the exterior trappings of wealth—ostentatious ceremonies, insignia, and honorific titles. Let us live according to evangelical simplicity. Without that, no witness is possible. For we are judged on it. Let us strive with all our strength to be humble. Immediately. Our wealth is the treasure of the poor."

Archbishop Henrique Golland Trinidade of Botucatú, Brazil, spoke in a similar vein: "Let the Church abhor even the appearance of wealth and decide to strip herself of everything for the love of Christ."

NOVEMBER 30

New Commission Members Announced

The names of the forty-three new commission members elected by the Fathers have been announced. The candidates won by votes swinging between 1,738 (the maximum) and 831 (the minimum) on a total of 2,127 ballots cast. They were chosen for the most part from the common list we spoke of Thursday.

Only one Italian was elected: Bishop Luigi Borromeo of Pesaro (1,240 votes). He will serve on the Commission for Religious. Others elected included twenty-two Frenchmen, six Americans, three Spaniards, two Germans, and two Englishmen. Auxiliary Archbishop Helder Câmara of Rio de Janeiro, celebrated for his work with the poor, was elected to the Commission for the Lay Apostolate (1,100 votes).

In addition to Bishop Ancel of Lyons, the theological commission numbers among its new members Father Butler, Superior General of the Benedictines in England; Auxiliary Bishop Joseph Heuschen of Liège, and

Auxiliary Bishop Luis Henríquez Jiménez of Caracas, all of whom are favorable to theological *aggiornamento*.

Vatican II Will Address a Message to the Priests of the World

The text of a message to the Catholic priests of the world has been circulated, and the Fathers will be asked to vote on it Monday. It seems the directors of the Council, with the Pope's support, decided upon this message to appease the concern which has been expressed by the clergy. The schema *De Ecclesia* lumps priests in with deacons and gives them very short shrift. Yet, as Bishop Renard of Versailles has pointed out, they are "in the front lines of the Church."

Many priests have complained that they were not consulted during the preparatory period of the Council. They fear that the increased powers of bishops and the new importance of the laity will work to their disadvantage. There is a certain amount of discouragement among the younger clergy, and the vocation crisis remains critical. Poverty and loneliness are demoralizing factors. By commending the qualities of the clergy and emphasizing the nobility and the difficulties of their ministry, the message hopes to dissipate certain misunderstandings and comfort parish priests and their assistants.

In Praise of Taizé . . . Bishop Lebrun of Autun addressed the assembly Thursday on the Protestant community of Taizé, which is in his diocese:

> The influence of this community, which is near Cluny, is a source of great hope. Bishops, pastors, and the Orthodox have met there for several years with the approval of the Holy Office and the encouragement of popes. At first I was suspicious, but experience has shown the fruitfulness of these encounters in charity and sincerity. Prejudices are giving way to mutual edification. The more I go there, the more confidence I have.

Bishop Charles H. Helmsing of Kansas City–St. Joseph, Missouri, added his voice to many others in asking on Friday that Protestant communities be recognized as churches. "The separated churches," he said, "are part of the people of God. Although they do not have the eucharist, they commemorate the last supper." The same speaker was applauded because he called for an indicative vote on chapters 4 and 5 of the schema, which, let us recall, treat respectively of the Jews and religious liberty.

Bishop Franič of Split, Yugoslavia, urged that the greatest consideration be taken of Oriental theology and the Eastern Fathers. Archbishop Nicodemo of Bari, Italy, recalled that the Orient gave theological formulation to the essentials of our faith.

... And of Karl Barth   Bishop Rupp of Monaco intervened in favor of the Anglicans, who have retained the episcopacy, a point the schema neglects to mention. He praised the Protestants for having a greater awareness of God's transcendence than do many Catholics, and quoted Karl Barth who has written "admirable things" on this subject. The Orientals and Anglicans have produced great saints, he added.

Criticism of Latinism

After Maronite Bishop Dib of Cairo also asked for a deeper study of Oriental patrology, Bishop Zoghby, Melkite Patriarchal Vicar for Egypt, declared:

> The schism with the East has not been without advantage. It has providentially enabled us to preserve traditions which would otherwise have disappeared. Roman centralization constitutes a danger. The present unity is Latin and partial, and will not become total until the Eastern Churches are included. Let us be very careful to avoid anything that might Latinize the Orientals. There must be unity in equality and not in uniformity. The Oriental Churches will give as much as they receive. We cannot overemphasize this.

Abbot Atanasius Hage, Superior General of the Melkite Basilians in Lebanon, asked for a more positive treatment of *communicatio in sacris*.

Finally, Coptic Bishop Scandar of Assiut, Egypt, criticized missionaries for trying to Latinize everything. "In the seminaries," he said, "one would get the impression sometimes that Oriental traditions no longer exist [liturgy, chant, abstinence]. The Orientals are not fond of novelties. They cling to their venerable traditions." The prelate concluded with a flight of mystical oratory in prayer form that won applause from the assembly.

DECEMBER, 1963

Three Protestant Conferences

There can be no real ecumenism without dialogue. Because Vatican II is not properly speaking a council of union between the churches, it does not allow direct dialogue with the non-Catholic observers in St. Peter's. It wouldn't be very profitable anyway, as the time is not yet ripe. For one reason, many bishops lack an ecumenical formation; for another, the ecclesiologists are still too divided. Haste could be fatal to serious ecumenical work. Before dialoguing, one must patiently educate oneself to the other's position. This is the purpose of the weekly meetings organized by the Secretariat for Promoting Christian Unity, as also of the conferences given by some of the observers in Rome.

Last Saturday Professor Oscar Cullmann of the Sorbonne gave a conference that was a conciliar event. He had an enormous audience. Five hundred bishops were present, including Cardinal Tisserant, Dean of the Sacred College and president of the Biblical Commision, Cardinal Gerlier of Lyon, Cardinal Lefebvre of Bourges, and Cardinal Richaud of Bordeaux.

The circumstances preceding this lecture had aroused considerable interest. Despite the request of the secretary of the Sacred Congregation of Seminaries and Universities, the Biblical Institute, the Gregorian University (Jesuits), and the Angelicum (Dominicans) had all declined to invite the Protestant scholar. Thereupon Archbishop Weber of Strasbourg (Mr. Cullmann's birthplace) and his coadjutor, Bishop Elchinger, organized an evening at St.-Louis-des-Français. Monsignor Willebrands of the unity secretariat introduced Professor Cullmann, and emphasized what Catholic theology owed to his work.

Mr. Cullmann began by quoting something Paul VI had told the non-Catholic observers when he received them in audience on October 17: "The developments you wish for in 'a concrete and historical theology centered on the history of salvation' we would readily subscribe to. . . .

should circumstances demand it, the establishment of a new institution for this purpose would not be excluded."

The History of Salvation Is Not a Cemetery The theme of Mr. Cullmann's lecture was "The History of Salvation in the New Testament." He criticized all theology that intends to destroy the history of salvation. To do so, he said, would be to destroy the basis of all ecumenical dialogue. He had particularly in mind the theories of Rudolph Bultmann. The speaker continued:

> The history of salvation is neither a cemetery nor a field of ruins. God's plan unfolds in history. Our faith concerns events. There are mythical elements in the Bible, but they have been demythologized by the authors of the Bible themselves and related to historically ascertainable events. In the Bible the myths are already exteriorized. The history of salvation is characterized both by the continuity of the divine plan and by historical contingency.

Speaking of "the present time in the Bible," Mr. Cullmann said that what Christ added to Judaism was the tension between the "already" and the "not yet." "We are living in the time of the Holy Spirit, the time of the Church," he said. "This is the basis of all ecumenical dialogue. The Church is the anticipation of the kingdom, but it is not yet the kingdom. Between the Catholic Church and the Protestant Churches, which put a different emphasis upon the 'not yet' and the 'already,' dialogue cannot be anything other than fruitful."

To explain the religious importance of events, Professor Cullmann used a striking analogy. "We should place the Bible beside the daily newspaper." Then he stated, "The hand of God can be discerned in our divisions, whatever our responsibility for them is. The diversity of churches is a constant reminder to us to respect the diversity of the gifts of the Spirit. The World Council of Churches of Geneva and Vatican II are signs that the time of schism should not last forever. The history of salvation advances despite our imperfections and our sins."

In conclusion, Professor Cullmann recalled the crisis of gnosticism in the second century, a movement that tried to eliminate the event of salvation. "The history of salvation," he repeated, "is not a cemetery. It liberates us from stasis. It puts us in touch with life."

Neither Nostalgia . . . Dr. Edmund Schlink, an observer delegated by the Evangelical Church of Germany, and Dr. Kristen Skydsgaard, of the Lutheran World Federation, both delivered lectures at the German center.

Dr. Schlink claimed the title of *Church* for the Protestant communi-

ties. He also postulated a principles of "equality" in ecumenism, and refused to consider ecumenism as simply a "return" to the bosom of the
Roman Church, "for which we feel no nostalgia."

. . . Nor Victory   Dr. Skydsgaard expressed pleasure that what as a
student he had taken to be a dogma, the so-called immutability of the
Roman Church, had been set aside by Vatican II. In that respect, "this
Council is an extraordinary event." Where Protestants formerly saw authoritarianism and legalism, the speaker said, they now see openness, a
sense of service, and the spirit of poverty. The Roman Church is in the
the process of self-reform.

Professor Skydsgaard regretted that a historical dimension was missing
from the schema *De ecclesia* and that Roman ecclesiology was not based
on the forgiveness of sins. "This essential depth has not been reached."
He continued, "We look forward to the day when a prophetic word will
break through the limits of institutionalism in the Roman Church." In
conclusion he said, "We all desire unity, but when this unity becomes a
reality, no Church can be counted the victor. Rather they will all have
been conquered in order that Christ may triumph."

Professor Cullmann Praises the Secretariat
for Promoting Christian Unity

During a reception given by the non-Catholic observers for members of
the Secretariat for Promoting Christian Unity, directed by Cardinal Bea
and Monsignor Willebrands, Professor Cullmann said:

> Your Secratariat is the open door of the Catholic Church on the
> non-Roman Churches. In what concerns the Council, you hide abso-
> lutely nothing from us. There is no iron curtain. You permit us to
> see not only the *triumphal* side of your Church, which we are accus-
> tomed to, but also the *difficulties* with which you are confronted.
> And for this we feel particularly close to you. We are also convinced
> that the Spirit acts through the instrumentality of difficulties as he
> acted in the primitive Church despite the many difficulties that beset
> it.
>
> In addition to the tribunal in St. Peter's, future historians will
> note that the Hotel Columbus, where Monsignor Willebrands directs
> our meetings with such great tact, was the site of ecumenical discus-
> sions that represent something truly new.

Cardinal Bea Reassures the Fathers on the Fate
of the Chapters on the Jews and Religious Liberty

In asking Jean Guitton of the Académie Française and Vittorino Veronese, former director general of UNESCO, to speak today in his presence at St. Peter's, Paul VI demonstrated his desire to innovate as well as his interest in the laity. It was a precedent in the annals of the Vatican: the auditors became the speakers and the bishops became the auditors in the conciliar aula.

The philosopher Jean Guitton, who was introduced to the Council in 1962 by John XXIII, speaks on ecumenism, and Mr. Veronese discusses the role of the laity in the Church.

The general congregation on Monday was the seventy-ninth of the Council and the last of the second session. Wednesday's assembly will be a "public session," in the terminology of the regulations, during which the Constitution on the Sacred Liturgy and the Decree on the Instruments of Social Communication will be promulgated, and the Pope will give his closing speech. The bishops will then return to their dioceses after a two-month absence, and the second Council recess will begin. Archbishop Felici, the secretary general, announced Monday that the commissions will meet frequently during the recess, and he asked the bishops to submit their observations on the schemas before the end of January, 1964.

There were two highlights on Monday: the postponement of the Council's message to priests, and Cardinal Bea's energetic intervention.

We reported Saturday that a message to the priests of the world had been distributed to the bishops and that they were to vote on it Monday, taking into account the comments and criticisms made meanwhile. But the vote did not take place; the message was simply postponed. Why? It seems that the text, improvised at the last moment, displeased numerous Fathers, who asked that it be completely reworked. The Council organizers took the consequences. They withdrew it as a bad risk. A satisfactory solution would be to incorporate a special chapter on priests in the schema on the Church, and thus make the message superfluous. The third session will settle the matter.

Cardinal Bea's intervention bore exclusively on the fate of the schema *De ecumenismo*, consideration of which has unfortunately been interrupted by the end of the session without indicative votes having been taken.

To all appearances, the president of the Secratariat for Promoting

Christian Unity intervened to attenuate the bad effect created by the fact that chapters 4 and 5, on the Jews and religious liberty, have not been discussed. "It was uniquely for lack of time and no other reason. No other reason," he repeated in a strong voice. His insistence was clearly intended as an answer to rumors circulating recently that discussion of the first three chapters was deliberately prolonged as a concession to the adversaries of chapters 4 and 5, who have shown their hand since Bishop de Smedt's brilliant and much applauded intervention.

To Put Off is Not To Put Away   "I sincerely believe," Cardinal Bea continued, "that these two chapters are essential, and that they will be studied in due time. Why did the vote the other day bear only on the first three chapters? Because the moderators wanted to stress the importance of these three chapters and leave ample opportunity for the Fathers to speak their minds. This in no way prejudices the other two chapters, which are very difficult but essential." The Cardinal repeated the word *essential*. He then added:

> Everything will be done without haste. These chapters will be seriously treated in the next session. "What is put off is not put away" [*differtur et non aufertur*]. Let us continue to work, and I urge you to send me your observations before January 31, 1964. We will then be able to provide you with better texts. What John XXIII said at the end of the first session, I say to you now: the second session has been very fruitful because of the ecumenical dialogue it began. This dialogue is not merely a written text, a charter; it is a living dialogue in our hearts. Like Saint John resting his head on Christ's breast, we now feel the pulsations of Christ's heart better and have a much clearer understanding that we are realizing his will: *ut unum sint*.

There were twelve speakers before Cardinal Bea. One was Cardinal Ruffini, Archbishop of Palermo, who insisted upon the Church's "infallibility" and "indefectability" even though, he said, "her members are sinners." He also expressed anticipation of that day when all Christians would be reunited around the pope. (Applause.)

Bishop Ernest Arthur Green of Port Elizabeth, South Africa, proposed that the question of the validity of Anglican orders be re-examined by experts. Bishop Tomasek (Czechoslovakia) thought it urgent that a kind of round table be organized—whether at Rome, Alexandria, Istanbul, or Moscow—for the purpose of frank discussion with the Orthodox, without any concern for precedence.

Abbot Butler of the English Benedictines asked that the schema speak of the faults committed in the Roman Church, or that a special declaration be issued concerning the responsibilities of Catholics for disunity.

The mass of the Council was celebrated by Archbishop Ngo Dinh Thuc of Hue for the repose of the souls of his two brothers who were killed tragically in the Vietnam coup.

Cardinal Ottaviani Defends the Holy Office

"Opinions expressed about the Holy Office today are anachronistic because they assume that this Congregation is still the Inquisition," said Cardinal Ottaviani, Secretary of the Holy Office, in an interview with the journal *Orizonti*.

"This Congregation is on the contrary a modern organism which acts prudently to reach true and just decisions." If the Holy Office operates under secrecy, he said, it is in the interests of those being investigated. If they are innocent, their reputation does not suffer. This is particularly true of authors.

During the trial, the person in question is not considered guilty until this is proven, and he may make his position known. Interviewing the interested party would be superfluous since the subject matter of the case is not what the author thinks but what he has written and which could harm souls.

The Cardinal then noted that some twenty consultors examine reports for the chancellery of the Holy Office; then the case is submitted to the judgment of a plenary meeting of the cardinal members of the Holy Office, who in turn submit their decision for papal approval.

Cardinal Ottaviani said that in recent times every effort has been made to avoid condemnations. The author has usually been asked, through his bishop, to withdraw the incriminated book or at least to publish a corrected version.

DECEMBER 4

Jean Guitton: "We Should Not Identify Our Human Mentality and Language with Revelation"

The second session of Vatican II terminated Monday with a salvo of applause for the non-Catholic observers, whom Cardinal Agagianian, the moderator, included in the list of those having a right to the Council's gratitude. The observers doubtless wanted to leave Vatican II with this memory, for many of them did not attend the closing ceremonies yesterday, Tuesday, which commemorated the fourth centenary of the end of the Council of Trent. This reserve is understandable when one thinks of the historical conditions of Trent, which was essentially directed against Protestantism.

Nonetheless, Cardinal Urbani, Patriarch of Venice, handled the situation very tactfully in his speech.

"The presence of our separated Christian brethren at Vatican II," he said, "strikes us as a fulfillment of a burning desire on the part of the Fathers of Trent, as a promise rich in hope and trust, as a comforting sign of a new spiritual climate which cannot but yield good fruit in due time."

Then, referring to the lay auditors, the speaker recalled that at Trent, "Emperors, kings, and princes were represented by delegates chosen largely from among the clergy. Unfortunately, Christianity properly speaking, the people of God, were practically strangers at this Council. We have made progress since then. Many laymen are becoming more and more aware of the responsibility of their proper vocation in the Church's service."

The Testament of Cardinal Mercier, Lord Halifax, and Abbé Couturier
After this speech, Mr. Jean Guitton took his place by the Altar of the Confession where the Pope was seated and, a few feet from him, began to read his allocution in a voice charged with emotion. He said:

> I should like to bear witness as a layman, . . . a personal witness founded on the inner conviction and the experience of a whole lifetime. Forty-three years ago I heard the ecumenical call through a French religious, Father [Fernand] Portal, who was a friend of the future Cardinal Tisserant. At the time of our encounters at Malines, I was a disciple of the venerated [Désiré] Cardinal Mercier and Lord Halifax; then I became the friend of Abbé Couturier. It is the spirit and the testament of these precursors that I should like to communicate. . . .

Unity, according to Mr. Guitton, must avoid two contrary errors: a *minimal ecumenism*, which would work for a kind of new super Church and would be a synthesis of the historical churches; and a *maximal ecumenism*, which would consist in thinking that the Catholic Church should limit herself to waiting for the return and the submission of those churches not in communion with her. The speaker went on:

> We should not identify our human mentality and language with revelation. Woe is me if, in the presence of our brothers desirous

of a new understanding, I confuse for want of competence dogma with its formulation, method with usage, life with a certain kind of life—thus narrowing the path of the unity Christ died for.

Ecumenism demands two complementary sacrifices. As Catholics ask a heroic effort of their separated brethren, so they should set the example by a humble, magnanimous, and sorrowful effort of purification that would rid the Church of the disfigurements which mar her eternal youth. The blood which brings about unity cannot be shed on one side only. . . .

The Catholic Church is charged with the task of proclaiming to the world that she is the unique Church willed by her divine founder, the seamless garment in whom everything must be visibly recapitulated. If we were silent on this, we would deceive our separated brethren and become less than what we are. But to be Catholic also means to proclaim that the realization of unity will not be perfect until the legitimate forms of human and Christian diversity have once more found their place and their liberty in the bosom of the Church.

Mr. Guitton then specified:

We must return to the sources common to us—biblical, evangelical, patristic—to determine whether or not, starting from the same foundation, we might not diminish our differences. Finally, with an effort of imagination, we must strive to express the living identity of the Church in loving inventions, in theological development, in new institutions that would make the Church still more united and one.

After Mr. Guitton's speech, Mr. Veronese took the floor and spoke briefly. He expressed gratitude for the "exceptional privilege" the lay auditors enjoyed, and then stated: "May God's help and the grace of our state [in life] permit us to contribute, with our wives and children, with all men of good will, both within and without the Church, to the realization of a purer personal faith, a greater sense of justice, a more profound unity, and a truer peace." It was a disappointing speech.

Pope Accords Forty "Powers" to Bishops

Paul VI's motu proprio *Pastorale munus* was read to the Fathers on Tuesday. It gives a series of powers and personal privileges to the bishops.

These powers belong "by right" (*ex jure*)—it is an important qualification—to residential bishops "from the moment they take possession of their sees."

The document then enumerates forty "powers," which the bishop may delegate to his coadjutor, auxiliary, or vicar general, and four "privileges."

The powers and privileges are varied. They include the right to grant confessors in special cases the faculty of absolving sins for which absolution is reserved to the bishop or the Holy See, except when serious false accusations against a priest are involved; the right to dispense from the age required for ordination, but not beyond six months; the right to dispense from the impediment barring children of non-Catholics from ordination; the power of dispensing from the impediment against marriage between a Catholic and a non-Christian; the power to validate a marriage that is null because of the impediment against marriage between a Catholic and a non-Christian as stipulated by canon law; the right to admit illegitimate children to seminaries; the privilege for all residential or titular bishops to preach and hear confessions throughout the world if the local ordinary has no explicit objections.

The motu proprio is important in that it represents an initial stage in the increase of the bishops' powers while the Council's adoption of the schemas De Ecclesia and De Episcopis is pending. These documents should guarantee yet further powers. Until now the forty-four cases enumerated in the pontifical document required bishops to go through the Curia. They no longer have to do so. It is a first step, modest but real, toward a realization of the ideals envisaged by the Council, a symptom of the change in relations between the bishops and the Curia. From a practical point of view, the granting of these faculties also represents a saving of time as well as an economic advantage, since the bishops were required to pay a fee each time they had recourse to the Curia's services.

The reshaping of the commissions according to the Pope's instructions is still going on. Thus, the theological commission has elected its second vice president and its second secretary in the persons of Bishop André Charue of Namur and Monsignor Philips, one of the experts. Cardinal Browne was the original vice president and Father S. Tromp was his secretary. It is no secret that their thinking is far to the right. This is not true of the two new officers.

Paul VI Announces a Trip to Palestine in January

This morning, during the closing ceremonies of the second session of the Council, Paul VI announced, that he would go to Palestine in January.

The Last Papal Voyages Abroad   The last two popes to go outside of Italy were Pius VI (1775–1799) and his successor Pius VII (1800–1823). They did so for diplomatic reasons or, as is well known, because they were forced to.

Pius VI went to Vienna in 1782 because he was worried about Joseph II's religious policies. On February 20, 1798, he was taken prisoner by Bonaparte's troops who had conquered Rome. We remember General Haller's terrible answer to the Pontiff when he asked to be left to die in the Holy City: "You can die anywhere." He was deported to Valence and died there.

Pius VII went to Paris in 1804 to consecrate Napoleon in Notre Dame. Diplomatic reasons may have persuaded him to undertake the journey. He could scarcely have liked being considered "a chaplain whom the master calls to say mass," as Ercole Consalvi wrote in his *Memoirs*. Nor could he have been very happy when he discovered, on the eve of the coronation, that the Emperor and Josephine had contracted a civil marriage.

Napoleon reconquered Rome in 1808. In 1812 he took Pius VII to Fontainebleau as a "hostage" (to use Paul Claudel's word). He was given his liberty only in 1814. "Savone . . . Fontainebleau" were his last words on his deathbed in 1823.

Since that time, Pius XII (in 1957) and John XXIII (in 1958) thought about going to Lourdes. But neither did. Since 1870 no pope has gone farther than Castelgandolfo. John XXIII was the first to break with this tradition by journeying elsewhere in Italy, notably to Assisi and Loretto in October, 1962.

Papal Trip To Take Place in January   Paul VI specified that he would go to "the holy places." It is generally thought in Vatican circles that the journey will not be longer than one day, perhaps January 6.

The traditional holy places of Christianity are presently divided between Israel and Jordan. But the Vatican and the Hebrew state will not enter into diplomatic relations. So far it seems the Israeli government has not been notified of the impending trip.

This initiative is likely to be the object of much discussion, particularly in the Near East. Many will be inclined to read political implications into the voyage, relating it to Pius XII's idea of internationalizing the holy places, a project the United Nations approved. Others will wonder whether Paul VI will meet with Athenagoras, the Patriarch of Constantinople, who has expressed interest in Church unity but has not yet accepted an invitation to come to Rome to attend the Council.

It seems likely, as a matter of fact, that the Pope and Athenagoras will meet, especially since they have corresponded in the past.

In any case, the voyage is a "return to the sources" and can only be interpreted as an effort on the part of the Pope to restore an evangelical image to the Church which has been gradually blurred since the age of Constantine. It is also an ecumenical act of the first importance; the Orientals will be watching with keen interest.

Paul VI announced his voyage at the end of his allocution in these words:

The Trip to Palestine

We are so convinced that for the final happy conclusion of this Council prayers and good works are necessary, that after careful deliberation and much prayer we have decided to become a pilgrim ourself in the land of Jesus Our Lord. In fact, if God assists us, we wish to go to Palestine in January to honor personally, in the holy places where Christ was born, lived, died, and ascended to heaven after his resurrection, the first mysteries of our faith: the incarnation and the redemption.

We will see the blessed soil from which Peter set forth and to which not one of his successors has returned. Most humbly and rapidly we shall return there as an expression of prayer, penance, and renewal to offer to Christ his Church, to invite our separated brethren to return to her, one and holy, to implore divine mercy on behalf of peace among men, that peace which shows in these days how weak and unsteady it is, to beseech Christ Our Lord for the salvation of all mankind. May the Holy Mother of God guide our path, may the Apostles Peter and Paul and all the saints assist us kindly from heaven.

And as we shall have all of you present in our heart during our holy journey, so you, venerated brothers, accompany us with your prayers so that the Council may reach its goal for the glory of Christ and the welfare of his Church.

The Pope's words were greeted with applause.

Earlier in the day, the Council Fathers cast decisive votes on the liturgy constitution and the decree on communications. The first was adopted by a vote of 2,147 to 4, and the second by a vote of 1,960 to 164. The relative size of this figure shows that though opposition to the schema had been reduced, it had not altogether disappeared.

It is interesting to note that the formula of promulgation used by Paul VI was different from that provided for by the conciliar regulations. At the last moment the Pope decided to use another formula which would take account of the emerging collegiality in the Church: *"Approbamus una cum patribus,"* that is, "We approve *together* with the Fathers." This modification was received very favorably because it is a further indication that the Pope supports the Council's efforts to begin a regime of collegial government.

Let us return to Paul VI's closing speech. It was distinguished by its discretion, its moderation, and its lack of lyricism. As such it differed noticeably from the pontifical allocution of September 29, which was vigorous and imaginative. It was as though the Pope, thinking of the hesitations of the Council, made a deliberate effort to respect its liberty and offer a vote of confidence that it would find a surer path by means of its own resources. His report was scrupulously honest and stripped of all emphasis in an attempt to supress any undue enthusiasm for a session that left more things unfinished than completed.

The Pope referred to the "laborious" and "complex" character of the conciliar debates. But he rejoiced over the promulgation of the Constitution on the Sacred Liturgy, which, he said, would "simplify our liturgical rites" and "make them more intelligible to the faithful and closer to their language." But he warned that "no attempt should be made to introduce private changes . . . , nor should anyone arrogate to himself the right to interpret arbitrarily the Constitution on the Sacred Liturgy. The decentralization implicit in this document requires strict discipline if it is to be put into effective practice.

Paul VI said little about the decree on communications other than noting that it was "of no little value" and hoping that it would encourage "many forms of activity."

The Pope seemed to refer to the contested vote of October 30 in the following passage: "The Council has confronted many problems. As you all know, it has addressed itself to many questions whose solutions are in part virtually formulated in authoritative decisions which will be published in due time, after the work on the topics to which they belong is completed."

To the commissions which have been somewhat reticent, the Pope recalled that he confidently expected great help from them, and that they should carry out their work by taking into consideration the thinking of the Fathers, particularly as expressed in the general congregations.

The allusion was evident: the commissions are at the service of the Council and not the other way around. Paul VI hoped that the commissions would prepare "proposals profoundly studied, accurately formulated, and suitably condensed and abbreviated so that the discussions, while remaining always free, may be rendered easier and more brief."

With and Under Peter The Pope did not use the word *collegiality*, but it was implied when he said:

> The episcopacy is not an institution independent of, or separated from, or, still less, antagonistic to the supreme pontificate of Peter, but with Peter and under him it strives for the common good and the supreme end of the Church. The coordinated hierarchy will thus be strengthened, not undermined; its inner collaboration will be increased, not lessened, its apostolic effectiveness enhanced, not impeded; its mutual charity stirred up, not stifled. We are sure that on a subject of such importance the Council will have much to say that will bring consolation and light.

Paul VI stressed the fact that the present Council is the continuation of Vatican I, which defined papal infallibility. Then he said:

> As a consequence, the aim of our Council is to clarify the divinely instituted nature and function of the episcopacy not in contrast to, but in confirmation of, the supreme Christ-given prerogatives, conveying all authority necessary for the universal government of the Church, which are acknowledged as belonging to the Roman pontiff. Its aim is to set forth the position of the episcopacy according to the mind of Our Lord and the authentic tradition of the Church, declaring what its powers are and indicating how they should be used, individually and corporately, so as worthily to manifest the eminence of the episcopacy in the Church of God.

The Pope announced that he would call members of the episcopacy to help him, along with the cardinals, in his pontifical magisterium in the work of translating the general decisions taken by the Council "into fitting and specific norms." Thus, the Pope emphasized, "without prejudice to the prerogatives of the Roman pontiff defined by the First Vatican Council," experience will indicate how "the earnest and cordial collaboration of the bishops can more effectively promote the good of the universal Church." This was another reference to the future episcopal council which Paul VI wishes to enlist in the service of Church government.

The Pope spoke of the Protestant observers on two occasions. He thanked them, and said that the Council "has always tried to find means and expressions capable of closing the gap between our separated brethren and ourselves."

He then requested the bishops, upon their return, to address different messages to the clergy, the laity, youth, the intellectuals, and the poor.

Apropos of the schema on the Virgin, Paul VI hoped that the Council would make a "unanimously and loving acknowledgment of the place, privileged above all others, which the Mother of God occupies in the holy Church. . . . After Christ her place in the Church is the most exalted, and also the one closest to us, so that we can honor her with the title *Mater Ecclesiae* to her glory and our benefit."

After the Second Session
of the Council

The end of the second session of Vatican II leaves us with mixed senti-ments. Great hopes were born of the Council, and for Catholics it is a point of faith that these promises will be fulfilled. The Roman Church has rarely appeared so rich in dynamic and gifted men, in new ideas and intelligent dedication. The vitality of contemporary Catholicism reminds us of the "the springtime of the Church," an image John XXIII was fond of. Nor has the Church ever seemed so prophetic.

Yet the Council at this moment could seem somewhat disappointing. Buffeted by internal strife, sometimes muffled and sometimes violent, the leadership of Vatican II—the moderators, the presidents, and the co-ordinating Commission—let the debates drift out of control, and so many discordant pleas were addressed to the Pope that it is difficult to get one's bearings. The Fathers, recessing, leave the impression that they have reached no clear conclusions. The votes concerning collegiality by divine right, and the diaconate, have as yet had no concrete consequences. In fact, they stirred such bitter opposition that the moderators dared not use this method again, though there was ample opportunity: the questions of an episcopal council to help the Pope, the powers of episcopal con-ferences, religious liberty, and the Jewish issue. The incoherent film of interventions, which made it difficult to determine the general thinking of the assembly, continued to unwind, and the last days of the Council were weary ones, unrelieved by any positive accomplishment. Confronted with reforms that called for immediate decision, the Council hesitated, or rather it was intentionally allowed to hesitate, because of bitter internal dissension. The Pope, the supreme and uncontested authority, had none-theless made his own desires clear in his opening discourse. But he seems to have thought it wiser not to interfere more than he did.

Perhaps he thought the time was not yet ripe. A circumspect man, he wants to avoid any abruptness. Internal Catholic unity is something too precious to risk. Moreover, he wants the Council to be responsible to itself and find its own rhythm in "liberty."

But it would be unrealistic and shortsighted to overemphasize this uneasiness and ignore the large view. It is the Council's successes rather than its failures that are amazing and conclusive. In the brief five years since the Church's program of *aggiornamento* got under way, the Council has been running double-time; its present breathlessness shows every sign of being a transitory stage.

In an audience given to the Oriental bishops during the last weeks of this session, Paul VI said, "Do you find that things are not going fast enough? Patience. We could legislate reforms immediately. But it would be to no avail if mentalities and people are not changed. It takes time for that. It is a law of history." This is the heart of the problem. The Council has not finished. If the second recess is as fruitful as the first— and it should be even more so, now that the commissions have been strengthened—Vatican II will have got its third wind in eight months. The as yet uncertain results of the second session will have matured, for meanwhile Paul VI will have perhaps begun a progressive reform of the Curia.

The application of the Constitution on the Sacred Liturgy, the leisurely redrafting of schemas presently in abeyance according to the wishes of the majority, collegiality which has in practice been accepted, the practice of making the cause of the Roman Church one with that of ecumenism—all this may well create a climate favorable to new victories.

✝

THIRD SESSION

September—November, 1964

On the Eve of
the Third Council Session

Vatican II at the Crossroads

The third and next to last session of Vatican II opens on September 14 and will close the end of November to enable the bishops—and perhaps the Pope as well—to attend the Eucharistic Congress, which will be held in Bombay from November 28 to December 6.

What is the state of the Council? What are the results of the first two sessions? What was accomplished during the recess? What is the present mood of the Council Fathers? Has the "opposition" lost or gained ground? We shall attempt, in a summary fashion, to answer these questions.

A remark that is attributed to Pius IX, the pope of Vatican I, holds that "There are three stages in a Council: that of the devil, who seeks to destroy everything; that of men, who try to throw everything into confusion; and finally that of the Holy Spirit, who sets everything in order." Some conservatives think this humorous assessment is equally applicable to Vatican II. They see the first session as a period of intense agitation. Most of the bishops were determined to profit by the liberty given them by John XXIII and not rubber-stamp curial documents. The second session made a confused and, as it turned out, vain attempt to reconstruct what had been destroyed. There is evidence that the third session will be a time of fruition and achievement. Vatican II is in effect at the crossroads. The present session will make decisions that will determine a long future.

Since 1962 In both 1962 and 1963 the Council Fathers were quick to see that the majority of them, that is, those who had pastoral experience and therefore knowledge of the outside world, desired radical changes in the central government of the Church, in the theological and psychological orientations then in favor, and in relationships with Protestants and with the secular world. This immense and urgent enterprise could not be undertaken without serious protest from the partisans of the status quo and painful storms of abuse from integralists who were incapable of overcoming their fear of change and distinguishing the essential, which must be safeguarded, from the accidental, which can be abandoned.

The Council began with what was easiest and in a sense most important: liturgical renewal. This immense reform was concluded within a year. We cannot overestimate the victory represented by the Constitution on the Sacred Liturgy which was solemnly promulgated at the end of the second session. This eighty-page text, which was adopted by a nearly unanimous vote, testifies to the ascendancy of progress over stagnation. It would be an injustice to see in this schema merely a reduction of Latin in favor of the vernacular or an approval of minor reforms. The constitution is truly a return to the sources, and it opens new horizons. It puts an end to four centuries of centralized power by giving episcopal conferences more extensive authority in their own territories. This is an important step toward decentralization, one of the objectives of Vatican II. Moreover, it provided the Pope with an opportunity to carry out a highly significant reform that has gone almost unnoticed by the public: the creation of a postconciliar commission, presided over by Cardinal Lercaro, which is invested with all power necessary to put liturgical reform into practice. The Sacred Congregation of Rites was thereby deprived of its long-standing prerogatives in that domain. This innovation is the first breach in the supremacy of the Curia. And it is painfully resented as such by those affected.

Had the Council achieved only this, it would not have been in vain. Father R. Rouquette wrote in *Études* that the creation of this organ "is of incommensurable historical importance."

Otherwise, it must be admitted, the Council has not reached many concrete decisions. One had best pass over the decree on the communications media in silence; it was pitifully mediocre, although it does express the Church's interest in the press, radio, television, and cinema as apostolic instruments.

The second session struggled spectacularly and sometimes painfully with the problems of the collegiality of the episcopacy, intended as a balance to papal infallibility, defined by Vatican I; the institution of a permanent diaconate; the recognition of religious liberty; and the rehabilitation of the Jews. The awkwardness, delays, and vacillations of the Council's directive bodies, which were on occasion publicly flouted, indicated a certain impotence to an outside world not normally interested in the internal difficulties of the ecclesiastical world. This impotence alternately surprised, deceived, and annoyed the Fathers and was in the end roundly denounced.

Vatican II has been compared with a mountain that brought forth a mouse. But this judgment overlooks the psychological transformation it has effected and thereby neglects an essential factor: the majority of the Fathers approved these reforms. They were simply delayed by the maneuvers or scruplings of certain bishops on the one hand, and by the Pope's prudence and discertion on the other. The latter refused to intervene out of respect for the Council's liberty.

The delay will not have been in vain. In order to be truly effective, reforms—and this is especially true in a closely knit society like the Roman Church—should not be forced and should not crush the minority. Six months lost is not much; it is in fact nothing if it serves to clarify ideas and calm overheated spirits.

The commissions worked overtime during the recess and according to rigorous methods which the Pope personally supervised. The schemas to be presented are clearly superior to earlier ones. The commissions acted on the remarks of the majority with an integrity that is universally recognized. Criticism from the minority has also been less harsh; but it has been taken into consideration in all cases where it was considered valid. Time has helped the commissions get matters into perspective.

During the 1963 debates, for example, there were forty interventions against a married diaconate and thirty for—in other words, a majority of 62 percent. Seemingly, the Council was against a married diaconate. But upon closer inspection this turns out not to be the case. If we distinguish between isolated interventions and those made in the name of groups of bishops, it becomes clear that a mere minority of only 17.4 percent opposed a married diaconate.* For this reason the redrafted schema retains the proposal. In all likelihood, the third session will ratify this proposition, which is close to the hearts of so many missionary bishops.

The same remarks could be made about episcopal collegiality, which has been irreverently referred to as the *pons asinorum* (asses' bridge) of Vatican II. As far as we know, the future schema could scarcely be more positive. It speaks explicitly of the "supreme and full power" of the episcopal college. Such authority is therefore not invested in the pope alone. This was the sense of the famous questions presented to the Fathers on October 30, to which a majority of over 80 percent responded in the affirmative. There is every indication that a like majority will be reached

* See René Laurentin, *Bilan de la deuxième Session*, Paris, Éditions du Seuil, 1964.

in the final vote. And this time there can be no possible misunderstanding. October 30, 1963, was indeed "historical," although chroniclers who used the term then were considered rash.

Thirteen Schemas Still on the Drawing Boards

Thirteen proposed schemas remain on the Council's program. Six will be discussed; seven will simply be presented, theoretically without discussion, though the Fathers can decide otherwise and amendments can perhaps be requested.

The order of presentation of the first six schemas, three of which have been given some examination already, is as follows:

1. The schema on the Church. It has two new chapters, on the Virgin Mary and on eschatology (a total of 220 pages).
2. The schema on the bishops (forty-five pages long).
3. The schema on ecumenism, with appendixes containing a declaration on religious liberty (twenty pages) and another on Jews and non-Christians (thirty-five lines). The Fathers may ask that these appendixes be integrated into the body of the schema (now totaling fifty pages).
4. The schema on revelation, a new and entirely rewritten version of the famous schema on the two sources of revelation, which was rejected during the first session (sixty-four pages).
5. The schema on the lay apostolate (sixty pages).
6. The schema on the Church on the modern world. This is the text called successively schema 17 and schema 13. It includes twenty-five paragraphs divided into four chapters, on man's integral vocation, the Church in the service of the world and mankind, relations of Christians with the world they live in, and the primary functions of Christians in the world (a total of forty-three pages). Five appendixes have been added to this text. Now being written, they relate to the human person, the family, culture, economic and social life, and international order and peace.

The seven other schemas have been reduced to rather short "propositions":

1. On the Oriental Churches.
2. On the missions.
3. On religious.
4. On priests. This proposition is considered very important psychologi-

cally, for the Council was not able to reach agreement last year on a message to the world's priests, and Vatican II has often been criticized for neglecting priests to the advantage of bishops and laymen.

5. On seminaries.
6. On Catholic schools.
7. On marriage. This proposition is concerned notably with mixed marriages.

Improvement of the Schemas   The new schema on ecumenism is much improved. Last year's schema was certainly revolutionary in more ways than one, so much so that specialists considered it upsetting in view of the difference between it and the negative attitude previously held in the Roman Church with respect to Protestant communities.

But the present text goes farther. It no longer speaks of "separated brethren" but of "disunited brethren"; the Oriental confessions are called "Churches" and those issuing from the Reformation are called "ecclesial communities." These changes in vocabulary are highly important in themselves. Too, the text no longer uses the expression "Catholic ecumenism" but speaks of "the Catholic principles of ecumenism." It states that the Roman Church is founded on "the twelve apostles and Peter" (and not on Peter alone). It suggests that non-Roman Christians might be admitted to the Catholic eucharist; interconfessional meetings are recommended *on a basis of equality*; the value of the Oriental Churches is stressed; non-Roman Churches are viewed in the perspective of their intrinsic value and not in relation to the Catholic Church, and so forth.

The encounter between Athenagoras and Paul VI in Jerusalem has had a profound influence on ecumenical events. It is altogether fortunate that the second session did not have time to take a definitive vote on the first schema on ecumenism.

The third session will also finish discussion on the chapters concerning religious liberty and the Jews.

The first has been redrafted. It is as positive in tone as the original but it is more balanced and more thoroughly thought out. The commissions took advantage of the judicious remarks of the Fathers who criticized the text for being too vague.

The chapter on the Jews has been rewritten many times. It is reported that the last version is somewhat weaker than the original because of pressure from Arab countries. Significantly, the word *deicide* has disappeared.

The Star Schema   But the star schema of the third session, the one which will attract the most attention because of its originality and its conformity with *Pacem in terris*, is the draft "On the Church in the Modern World." Father Congar has called it the "promised land" of the Council. It has been reworked some dozen times and is not yet ready for distribution to the Fathers. It treats particularly difficult problems: creation seen in an evolutionary perspective, culture, the rights of the human person, the underdeveloped countries, the family and procreation, the theology of war and peace, international relations, and so forth.

The importance of the schema—together with its appendices—is obvious. It will be debated at length and is certain to undergo numerous amendments. No definite vote is expected on it until the fourth and last session of the Council, in 1965.

The Council must also consider mixed marriages, a problem that Protestants consider as important as religious liberty and one that will serve as a test of the Roman Church's ecumenical good will. If no satisfactory solution is forthcoming, we may expect Vatican II to modify "certain outdated and ineffectual prescriptions" that rightly offend the Protestants.

Will Vatican II have anything further to say on the reform of the Curia, without which its work could be seriously compromised? The future will tell just what Paul VI intends to do in this respect; but there is no apriori reason why the Council Fathers cannot express their wishes publicly, and thus contribute to the inevitable creation of a "senate" which would associate the bishops of the world with the government of the Church in a regular and responsible manner. It is likely that postconciliar commissions will be charged with the details of this much-desired reform within the Roman Church, a reform that would have evident ecumenical repercussions. The question touches on the *exercise* of papal primacy— there is no doubt about the *principle*—and the way it is resolved will determine to an appreciable extent the future of Rome's relations with other Christian churches.

Will the procedures be improved in the third session? Most of the Fathers and the Pope himself want to remedy the sluggishness of the second session and the disadvantages of a many-headed leadership.* Bishop Schmitt of Metz, for example, has regretted "the absence of an uncontested authority." For this reason the Coordinating Commission made some modifications in the Council regulations in July. As a result the powers of the moderators have been strengthened. In the future they will be em-

---

* We might recall the names of the four moderators. They are Cardinals Agagianian of the Curia (Armenian); Lercaro, Archbishop of Bologna (Italian); Döpfner, Archbishop of Munich (German); and Suenens, Archbishop of Malines-Brussels (Belgian).

In addition to the four moderators, named by Paul VI, there are ten Council presidents, named by John XXIII, and the Coordinating Commission.

powered to instruct those bishops intending to intervene on the same subject to appoint one or two spokesmen. Moreover, all the Fathers—including the cardinals, and this is new—will be required to present a written résumé of their interventions at least five days in advance, instead of three. Finally, when those registered to speak have finished, a moderator can let others take the floor if they request it, provided they intervene in the name of seventy bishops, instead of five.

These new stipulations should accelerate discussion and prevent the Council from losing time by listening to isolated opinions. The moderators should now be in firm control of the Council. The original regulations designated them explicitly as delegates of the pope; the amendments give them additional means of asserting their authority.

Aggiornamento Forges Ahead

The strengthening of authority within the Council is an indispensable condition of its success, for the opposition is still very active. The recess proved this on many occasions. Now that Vatican II has reached its crucial phase, the extreme right wing will certainly put up one last fight. But it will not likely amount to more than a face-saving effort.

The Council will undoubtedly make every effort to achieve unanimity, although this cannot be done without generous sacrifices. The history of the Church shows that a beaten minority, rather than persisting in a headstrong position, will rally around the majority in the end. And this is what makes a council different from a parliamentary assembly.

Support for the Council   Paul VI has clearly warned those bishops who have shown less than enthusiastic support of the Council. Speaking during the recess, on April 14, to the plenary assembly of the Italian episcopacy, which was meeting for the first time in history, he said:

> Venerable brethren, we count on your attentive, enthusiastic, and active participation [in the Council]. Your participation should not be timid, uncertain, quibbling, or polemical, but rather frank, noble, prudent, and profitable. . . . Whatever the outcome of the Council, we should consider it in its intentional, spiritual, and supernatural reality as an hour of God, a 'passage of the Lord' in the life of the Church and in the history of the world.

Given the opposition of a large number of Italian bishops to the Council, these words take on great meaning. Isn't it repeated *ad nauseam* by certain parties that Vatican II constitutes a danger for the Church and the sooner it is over the better? But the Pope has vigorously asserted the providential role of the Council and urged full support from everyone.

All things considered, it presently seems that the *aggiornamento* of the Church, which both John XXIII and Paul VI set as the end of the Council, is forging ahead. Of course Vatican II will not magically solve all the problems confronting the Roman Church, which is notoriously behind the times or out of step with the legitimate needs of her century. Will it be able, for example, to say anything that rises above the commonplace or make effective decisions about such issues as nuclear war, aid to under-developed countries, poverty, the choice and formation of the clergy, and the apostolate of the laity? It is still too early to say.

The third session will have its arid moments because it will be punctuated by a good deal of voting. Moreover, many debates by their very nature will not be very original. Public interest is likely to lag. Nonetheless, there seems little doubt that in general the pace will be brisk because there is a widespread desire to get on with things. The Fathers now know one another well enough to obviate long explanations.

Three events of great importance will mark the third session.

The Pope has decided that the session will open with a liturgical concelebration. Assisted by three cardinals (Lecaro, Tisserant, and Larraona) and twenty bishops, Paul VI will concelebrate mass at the Altar of the Confession. This symbolic act, which is the fruit of the Constitution on the Sacred Liturgy promulgated during the last session, will highlight the fact that episcopal collegiality is becoming a reality. What is true today on the spiritual and liturgical level should be true tomorrow on the level of institutions.

Also, fifteen days after the session opens, Paul VI will hold an exceptionally solemn consistory (since all the bishops in Rome will be able to attend) ending with the canonization of twenty-two Negro martyrs of Uganda, victims of the persecutions of 1886. The canonization will take place in St. Peter's on October 18. The ceremony will set in relief the preponderant place which the young missionary churches and particularly black Africa occupy in present-day Catholicism. The twenty-two new saints—beatified by Benedict XV in 1920—will be the first Negroes canonized in modern times.

Africa, which is well represented at Vatican II, is remarkable by reason of the imagination, independent spirit, and activity of its native episcopacy. These show every sign of establishing a unique position for themselves in the Roman Church in keeping with their racial genius, rather than remaining under the long-dominant influence of Europe.

Finally, when the third session ends, many cardinals and bishops will go to Bombay, possibly in the company of the Pope. This event, provided it avoids "triumphalism" and ostentatious display, will be symbolic of the Church's open attitude toward the non-Christian world and her interest in underdeveloped countries. It will be in line with both the encyclical *Ecclesiam suam* and the schema "On the Church in the Modern World." It could give substance to the idea that the Roman Church has come out of her ecclesiastical ghetto to enter into contact with non-Christian peoples.

In the final analysis, what is referred to as the Church of the poor will be the touchstone of the Council's success. The world will judge Catholicism on the tangible evidence of the evangelical spirit it shows forth.

The Council in Chinese The press service of the Council has added a Chinese translation section to the eight already existing: Italian, French, English, German, Spanish, Portuguese, Polish, and Arabic. This is designed to make it easier for Chinese reporters to publish the official bulletins of Vatican II.

SEPTEMBER 12

Vatican II Reconvenes

By plane, train, boat, and perhaps even on foot (one bishop who wishes to remain anonymous walked to Rome in 1963), the Council Fathers are returning to the Eternal City for the third session. Once again they will fall into the familiar patterns of the first two sessions.

The first meeting of the third session will be the eightieth; the first vote will be the hundred twenty-eighth. There were thirty-six general congregations during the first session and thirty-three votes. The second session had forty-three general congregations and ninety-four votes. In all: seventy-nine general congregations and a hundred twenty-seven votes.

An official statistic states that of the 3,070 conciliar Fathers convoked, 2,513 will be present. The remaining 557 have excused themselves for a variety of reasons, principally ill health. In terms of nationality, the bulk of the absent bishops are thus distributed: twenty-four Europeans, two hundred ten from the two Americas, sixty-nine Asians, twenty Africans, and eighteen from Oceania.

There will apparently be the same number of bishops from behind the Iron Curtain in attendance as last year. It is almost certain that Archbishop Josef Beran of Prague will not be present since he failed to obtain a return visa; but it is possible that Bishop Aaron Marton, the only active Rumanian bishop left, will be here. Three Slavic bishops and one from Czechoslovakia are expected to return.

Patriarch Athenagoras I of Istanbul wired the Pope Thursday evening that he had sent two prelates from Holy Cross Greek Orthodox Theological School (Brookline, Massachusetts) to Rome to represent the Ecumenical Patriarchate. They are Archimandrites Panteleimon Rodopoulos and John S. Romanides.

In addition, Archimandrite Andre Scrima will be the personal representative of Athenagoras. These three will attend the Council. It is the first time since the beginning of the Council that the Orthodox, with the exception of churches behind the Iron Curtain, have been represented.

The four moderators met Thursday. On Friday afternoon the Council presidents and the Coordinating Commission conferred on last-minute details. The first general congregation will be held on Tuesday (Monday's assembly is not a working session), and will begin by studying the chapter of *De ecclesia* entitled "The End of Time." There is some humor in the fact that the third session will open by considering the end of the world and will terminate in November with an examination of "The Church in the Modern World" (schema 13).

The two most popular subjects of conversation are concelebration and the presence of women at Vatican II.

Concelebration The concelebrated mass on Monday will be something new for the liturgical assembly. Twenty-four bishops will officiate with the Pope as the rest of the Fathers sing certain parts of the mass. Unfortunately, the twenty-four concelebrants are all Latin bishops since there is presently no provision for interritual concelebration, in which Oriental bishops could take part.

Paul VI's Decision To Invite Women to the Council Surprised Roman Circles "There will be no women at the Council," said spokesmen for ecclesiastical circles in Rome as recently as forty-eight hours ago. They explained that the Pope was not going to follow up this suggestion by Cardinal Suenens, one of the moderators of the Council. It seems these spokesmen mistook their desires for reality. A certain antifeminism, inherited from a Jansenist mentality, is not unknown in Rome.

Then Paul VI announced on Tuesday that there would "be a small but significant and symbolic" feminine representation in St. Peter's as the third session began. Representatives from Catholic women's organizations as well as religious orders would be present. Thus, both religious and laywomen will attend. They will be admitted to the liturgical ceremonies of the Council as well as to the general congregations, where issues of vital interest to them will be discussed.

"These measures were taken," the Pope said, "so that women will know how much the Church honors them in their human dignity and in their Christian and human mission. We hope that women religious will be represented in greater numbers in the life of the Church." He added that the crisis of religious vocations in women's communities must be "squarely faced."

We are not yet sure whether or not women really will be present at the Council. The Italian press, and *L'Osservatore Romano* in particular, has shed no light on the subject. Paul VI's last-minute decision is surely unprecedented. In any case, none of them have yet arrived, so it would be idle to speculate about either the number of women invited or the nature of their participation. At most we might risk a guess that Miss Pilar Bellosillo of Madrid, President of the World Union of Catholic Women's Organizations, will be among the female auditors. Perhaps they will be here by Monday.

SEPTEMBER, 1964

Paul VI Says Vatican II Should Clarify
"the Constitutional Prerogatives of the Episcopacy"

The opening ceremony of the third session of Vatican II, which was held this morning in St. Peter's Basilica, was tangible evidence that the Council has already effected a change in the Roman Church. There was a great difference between the liturgy today and the ceremony which opened the first session. The solitude of the Pope has given way to a chorus of twenty-five prelates—including the Bishop of Rome—celebrating the mass together, with the same voice and the same gestures.

Concelebration is still widely practiced in the Orient, but it has become more and more rare in the Latin Church since the twelfth century. In restoring it to a place of honor, Vatican II has shown forth the unity of the priesthood and ended an overly individualistic style of piety. Since the Pope participated in the ceremony, this new liturgical form illustrates the closer collaboration that will henceforward prevail, thanks to Vatican II, between the sovereign pontiff and the episcopal college of which he is the head.

As psalm 131 was chanted, alternating with *"Tu es Petrus"* sung by the assembly, Paul VI entered the Basilica preceded by the twenty-four concelebrants. In addition to Cardinals Tisserant, Lercaro, and Larraona, the Pope was accompanied by twenty-one other prelates of different countries, including Coadjutor Archbishop Villot of Lyon and two religious —Fathers Benno Gut, Abbot Primate of the Benedictines, and Anastasio Ballestrero, President of the Roman Union of Religious Superiors. Archbishop Yago of Abidjan was also in the entourage.

To make room for the twenty-four Council Fathers, the Altar of the Confession, dominated by Bernini's celebrated spiral columns, had to be completely transformed. The altar was enlarged into a great square, and a red and green podium was built around it to accomodate six concelebrants on each side of the quadrangle.

It was a particularly moving moment when fifty hands were extended over the bread and wine and the words of the consecration were pronounced in unison.

The hosts (three of them) were then divided into twenty-five parts, and each concelebrant gave himself communion. Using a golden spoon, the Pope partook of the consecrated wine. The twenty-four other Fathers then did likewise. The *Credo* and *Pater noster* were recited by the whole conciliar assembly.

After mass was over, Archibishop Felici, secretary general of the Council, recited aloud the canonical profession of faith for the intentions of the new bishops attending the Council for the first time. There are some hundred of them. Then Paul VI, wearing the mozzetta, began his opening allocution.

The "Brother" of All Bishops   The way the Pope referred to himself will not go unnoticed: he said he was not only the "head" of the apostolic college but also the "brother" of all the bishops as "the vicar of Christ" and "the servant of the servants of God."

The Pope noted that Vatican II, without in any way detracting from Vatican I's teaching on the prerogatives of the pope, must "complete" this doctrine and clarify "the constitutional prerogatives of the episcopacy."

Paul VI quoted a formula of Gregory the Great which had been recalled in an intervention during the previous session, "My honor is the strength of my brothers," and told the bishops that they were the "teachers, rulers, and sanctifiers of the Christian people." He also assured them of his "esteem" and "solidarity."

On two occasions the Pope used the word *collegiality* with reference to episcopal authority, and thus definitively legitimatized an expression that had been contested by some Council Fathers.

Finally, speaking of the "restoration of unity" in the Churches, Paul VI greeted the non-Catholic observers and guests and made mention of the Orthodox churches, although no representatives from these have been present at the Council.

At the beginning and end of the ceremony, the Pope was carried on the traditional *sedia gestatoria*, but it was a much simplified version and without the customary flabellums.

The problem of episcopal power constituted the principal theme of Paul VI's allocution. After recalling that Vatican I could not complete the doctrine of the nature and function of the successors to the apostles, the

Pope emphasized that that Council's definition of the "truly unique and supreme powers" of the Pope "has appeared to some as having limited the authority of bishops."

This ecumenical Council is certainly prepared to confirm previous doctrine about the prerogatives of the Roman pontiff; but it will also have as its principal objective the task of clarifying and emphasizing the prerogatives of the episcopacy.

Let it be clear in everyone's mind that this present Council was convoked, freely and spontaneously, by our venerated predecessor of happy memory, John XXIII, and afterwards confirmed by us with the full knowledge that the theme of this sovereign and sacred assembly would be that of the episcopacy. It could not be otherwise, not only by reason of the series of doctrines envisaged but also by reason of the sincere desire to confess the glory, the mission, the merits, and the friendship of our brothers engaged in the work of instructing, sanctifying, and governing the Church of God.

The Unitary Interpretation of the Church

As the successor of Saint Peter and therefore the possessor of full power over the whole Church, we have the duty, despite our unworthiness, of heading the body of the episcopacy. Nevertheless, this in no way deprives you of your rightful authority. We are indeed the first to venerate it. If our apostolic mission obliges us to formulate reservations, clarify terms, prescribe forms, and ordain the modes of exercising episcopal power, you know that this is for the good of the whole Church, for the unity of the Church, which is in greater need of a central guide as her Catholic dimensions spread, as greater dangers confront her, as the needs of the Christian people in different circumstances of history are more urgent, and, we might add, as the means of communication become more rapid.

This centralization, which will certainly always be moderated and compensated for by an ever vigilant distribution of opportune faculties and services which will be useful for local pastors, is not a vain artifice. It is a service, my brothers; it is an interpretation of the unitary and hierarchical spirit of the Church; it is the ornament, the strength, the beauty which Christ promised the Church and accords to her in the passage of time.

Paul VI reaffirmed his concern to defend "the independence, the liberty, and the dignity of the hierarchy in all countries." He asked the bishops to remain near the Apostolic See in close communion, and added: "May this communion, which unites the Catholic hierarchy by vivifying bonds of faith and charity, be deepened and made stronger and more holy by this Council for the glory of Christ, the peace of the Church, and the light of the world."

The Pope then turned his thoughts to members of the clergy and laity, to those who suffer, the poor, and the persecuted, "especially those whose lack of freedom keeps away from the Council." He continued, "O distant churches so near to us! O churches for whom our heart is filled with longing! . . . O churches of our tears which we would like to be able to honor by embracing them in the authentic love of Christ! May our affectionate cry from the center of unity which is the tomb of Peter, apostle and martyr, and this ecumenical Council of fraternity and peace reach you!"

He greeted the auditors and the observers from the non-Catholic Christian churches, and said to the latter:

> Our determination and our hope is one day to remove every obstacle, misunderstanding, and enmity which still prevents us from feeling completely one in Christ and in his Church as "a single heart and a single soul." We will do everything we can to this end. We realize that the re-establishment of unity is a serious matter and we shall consecrate to it the care and time it merits. This is something new, in contrast with the long and sorrowful history which preceded the different separations, and we shall wait patiently until the conditions for resolving our problems positively and in a friendly manner are present.

Disappointment in Protestant Circles
After Recent Declarations by Paul VI

In a recent interview given to the journal *Combat*, Pastor Georges Richard-Molard, director of the press bureau for the Protestant Federation of France, analyzed the attitude of French Protestants toward the Council. He said:

> When that altogether exceptional figure John XXIII was at the helm of the first session, there was reason to believe that the Roman-ocentric conception had suffered a serious blow and that the Roman Catholic Church, discovering in council the deplorable results of its juridical authoritarianism, had again found the secret of gratuitous and humble service to the world.
>
> Today, after the impatience that was evident during the second session, various declarations by Paul VI, and his encyclical *Ecclesiam*

suam in which he vigorously reaffirms that the See of Rome is the center of everything, it is very difficult to hide the disappointment felt in official Protestant circles. The same disappointment is also felt in Istanbul, Moscow, and Geneva. If the reform movement among Catholics is still strong enough to storm certain bastilles, then all hope is not lost; but the evolution will take longer than we thought. The atheistic world, impoverished and everywhere in despair, will not rally to *ex cathedra* statements that are apparently addressed to them; what will impress them rather are authentic gestures of humility and free acts of love.

Observer-Delegates

Five Anglican Observers   Dr. Michael Ramsey, Archbishop of Canterbury and Primate of the Anglican Church, has named the following observers to the third session of the Council: Right Reverend J. R. H. Moorman, Bishop of Ripon, England; Reverend Howard Root, Dean of Emmanuel College at Cambridge University; Reverend Eugene Fairweather, professor at Trinity College, University of Toronto; Reverend Massey H. Shepherd, Jr., professor at the Church Divinity School of the Pacific, Berkeley, California; and Reverend Ernest John, Vicar of the Cathedral Church of the Redemption in New Delhi.

He also named Reverend John Findlow, chaplain to the British Embassy in Athens, as his personal representative to the Secretariat for Promoting Christian Unity.

The Coptic Orthodox Church Also Represented   The information agency of the Middle East has announced that the Coptic Orthodox Patriarch of Alexandria, Kiroloss VI, has named Bishop Amba Samuil and Fathers Marcos Elias and Abdel Messih as delegate observers from his Church to the third session.

SEPTEMBER 15

Paul VI in Profile

As the third session begins, the deeds and gestures of the Pope are a topic of frequent conversation. His recent first encyclical, which lifts a corner of the veil on the orientation of his pontificate; his discreet return from Castelgandolfo Sunday afternoon to an almost deserted St. Peter's Square—no one was notified of his arrival time; his move into his completely renovated apartments, with their modern Swedish furniture and neon lighting; his use of a more modest *sedia gestatoria;* his unprecedented participation in a concelebrated mass; his brief but meaningful speech, which outlined the task before the present session—these are all being discussed in Rome at the present time.

There is general agreement that Paul VI is a born leader. He works privately, ponders his decisions at length, and divulges them at the moment most likely to produce the maximum effect (his trip to the Holy Land and his decision to admit women to the Council* are recent examples). He can be unsettling, owing to such unexpected and sharp statements as his remarks to the Curia before the second session or his unprecedented speech on the pope's independence from the Roman nobility. Or he can charm with bold initiatives or moving flights of oratory.

He is an authoritative pope, to be sure, and lets it be known in unmistakable terms that he is at the summit of the ecclesiastical pyramid, that he is in possession of all powers, and that the pope is indispensable to the stability of the Church (what well-informed Catholic would deny this?); yet he is a timid pope and cuts a rather poor public figure with his cramped and starchy gestures, his frozen smile, his monotonous and almost weary voice. He is an uneasy, even tormented pope who desires and needs to be encouraged. Yet he is a holy priest in constant pursuit of perfection, an apostle eager for spiritual success and impatient to open himself to the world, which he loves and understands with rare insight. Was it not Cardinal Montini who said, "A world which progresses, seeks, and suffers is a world groping its way toward Christ"?

He is an indefatigable pope who perseveres in whatever he undertakes, even though he may defer putting it into effect. Father Bernard Häring, who knows him well, has written, "We should be grateful to Paul VI for his patience in awaiting the opportune moment. He knows that the strength of the Council is in direct proportion to the depth of its conviction."

A Penerating and Restrained Speech   Monday's discourse to the Council Fathers reflects the depth and complexity of Paul VI: humble and firm, penetrating and restrained. He does not want to intrude on the Council's decisions. He dreads nothing more than being accused of interfering with the liberty of the Fathers.

Paul VI is above all a mystic. The whole first part of his speech turned on the Holy Spirit. He called the Council "a moment of profound interior docility, a moment of spiritual intoxication." When he abandons

---

* But the women auditors invited to the Council were not present at the opening ceremony, and their names are not yet known.

the long, balanced sentences of official rhetoric, he has an uncanny ability to coin phrases that go to the heart of the matter. His sensitivity impels him to such utterances as these with respect to the "separated brethren": "O churches that are the nostalgia of our sleepless nights! O churches of our tears!"

Women in St. Peter's

The first woman, if we are not mistaken, has been allowed to receive communion at the central altar in St. Peter's. This event is worthy of note because it runs counter to a custom that is as long standing as it is surprising. Last year Madame Nhu, the sister-in-law of Archbishop Ngo Dinh Thuc of Hue, was not permitted to receive communion during a Council mass. Mrs. Montini, in the company of her husband, the Pope's brother, was also turned aside when she approached the communion rail.

Journalists have sometimes been allowed to attend the mass which precedes each general congregation. But on one condition: that they are not members of the weaker sex. This discrimination has seemed so arbitrary to members of the press present in Rome that they sent a formal protest to Archbishop Felici during the second session. But to no avail.

According to the latest rumors, five laywomen and six religious will attend the Council as auditors.

Will the Third Session Have Time To Study Schema 13 Fully?

The Pope stated that the essential work of Vatican II is to define episcopal powers and thus complete Vatican I, which was interrupted suddenly by the war of 1870. This implies that the episcopacy will be the focus of this session of Vatican II; but there is reason to speculate whether it may not bear for the most part on questions relating to the interior reform of the Church. One wonders, for example, whether the Marian question, which is a new chapter in the schema on the Church, will be deliberated at length. If so, how much time will be left for the examination of the all-important schema on the modern world? Will it be examined briefly at the end of the session, or will it be merely introduced during this session and examined more leisurely and seriously next year?

The Pope said nothing about this problem in his speech, and naturally, those who would like to see schema 13 scuttled are in favor of quick and summary debate. When the time comes, the Fathers will have to decide whether this text, elaborated with such care over the past two years, should be discussed in depth.

Public opinion, Christian and otherwise, would be greatly disappointed if such important questions were to be examined hastily. And it is likely that the majority of the Fathers will be sensitive to public opinion. The Pope, who has not yet said whether he will go to Bombay or not, will also be watching public reaction closely.

With respect to the possibility of the Pope's traveling to Bombay, two hypotheses are currently in favor. One holds that his trip to Jerusalem will remain a unique pilgrimage. The other maintains that it set a precedent for regular journeys of this sort to all parts of the world, both Christian and non-Christian. A certain interpretation of *Ecclesiam suam* would seem to make the second hypothesis the more plausible one.

SEPTEMBER 16

The Question of Secrecy

The eightieth general congregation, the first of the third session, began yesterday morning, Tuesday. There was considerable delay because the Fathers had to be assigned new places in the aula.

After mass, which was celebrated by Bishop Charles Vanuytven, former Apostolic Vicar to the Leopoldville Congo, Cardinal Tisserant recalled that John XXIII intended the Council to be primarily pastoral in its objectives. Then he said that many bishops from all over the world, particularly from Latin America, hoped the Council would be able to finish its work by the end of the third session. "It is nonetheless clear," the Cardinal stated, "that this is a hope and not an order." He then urged the Fathers to be brief, to avoid digressions, and to pool their interventions by means of the episcopal conferences.

Finally, the Dean of the Sacred College reminded the Fathers rather sternly of their obligation to secrecy. He regretted certain "ill-timed" statements and interviews given out during the first two sessions, and repeated that the contents of the schemas are secret until they are finally approved. This is a difficult matter, since the interventions reported on by the press services of episcopal conferences criticize or approve this or that point of a schema, so that something of their content is inevitably revealed. There seem to be only two choices here: either the secrecy should be total, in which case the press services might as well close their doors, or it should be practically nonexistent. The latter is presently the case, and owing to the nature of things it will continue so. Cardinal

Feltin said more than a year ago that the secrecy of the Council was an open secret.

Archbishop Felici Threatens the Experts Archbishop Felici, secretary general of the Council, addressed his remarks to the experts and threatened to withdraw their privileges if they did not respect the secrecy of commission deliberations. He reminded them of the regulation dated December 28, 1963, which requested them "not to instigate currents of opinion," to refuse interviews, and to avoid criticizing the Council under any circumstances.

There was a stir in the assembly when the moderator, Cardinal Agagianian, greeted the women auditors. The bishops stretched their necks in various directions trying to spot the women, who had already been greeted by Pope Paul the day before but who continue to be absent from view in St. Peter's. Why and for how long? No one knows the explanation, and it is the object of much joking in the Council corridors.

Should Vatican II Speak of Hell?

Vatican II began with chapter 7 of the schema on the Church, which treats "The Eschatological Character of the Church's Vocation and Union with Heaven." Predictably, the length of the title drew criticism, principally from Archbishop Justin Darmajuwana of Semarang, Indonesia, and Archbishop Nicodemo of Bari, who spoke in the name of eleven Italian bishops.

In essence, this chapter deals with the "four last things," the destiny of man who is called to become a citizen of heaven and share in the divine life with those who have already completed their earthly pilgrimage. This chapter was explicitly requested by John XXIII, as Cardinal Browne pointed out. It clarifies the supreme vocation of the Christian and of the whole of creation, which was made by God for God, who at the end of time "will draw all things to Him," as Saint Paul says.

This vision measures the gap between a Marxist and a Christian. The first limits his horizon to this world and to life in this world, which he considers self-sufficient and its own justification. The second believes in a beyond, the fulfillment of this present life. But there is a very real danger here that this life and the things of the world will be depreciated, denied a proper and immediate value. An example would be a failure to engage in the battle for greater social justice. A Christian can dedicate himself to such a cause without losing sight of the fact that all these values will be totally perfected beyond death and the end of the world.

The same chapter calls for a correction of abuses in devotions to the saints, and notes that such devotions do not consist in a multiplicity of external gestures of piety. We recognize here an effort to discourage certain immoderate practices which are severely judged by Protestants.

Cardinal Ruffini, Archbishop of Palermo, called attention to imprecisions and errors in the scriptural quotations, and then went on to say that some mention should be made of hell, the lot of those who die in a state of mortal sin, which is an object of dogma. A similar observation was made by Latin Rite Patriarch Gori of Jerusalem. He said in substance that Christ, in his infinite goodness, did not hesitate to speak of hell, but preachers today no longer dare to do so. The impression should not be given that hell is a doctrine of the past. It is a duty of charity to recall its existence to modern man.

The two prelates also regretted that the chapter said too little about purgatory. Archbishop García de Sierra y Méndez of Burgos, Spain, was of the same opinion.

Cardinal Urbani, Patriarch of Venice, thought the chapter as a whole was satisfactory. It is necessary and logical, he said, to discuss the last things in a schema on the Church, and he was pleased that this was done in a "Christocentric" and "ecclesiocentric" fashion.

Bishop José Pont y Gol of Segorbe, Spain, thought the schema did not make it sufficiently clear that the Church is transcendent and also "in this world." The Spanish bishop was afraid of the danger we just mentioned, of giving the impression that Christians pine after eternal life to the detriment of terrestrial values. This is a common Communist criticism of Catholics.

The Holy Spirit Has Been Forgotten   Abbot Christopher Butler, Superior of the English Benedictines, regretted that the chapter mentioned the Holy Spirit only in passing, and then in a "calamitous" manner. Marionite Archbishop Ziadé of Beirut expressed the same idea with much vigor and skill. His was the outstanding intervention of the day. This is a peculiar text, he said, and the Orientals have difficulty recognizing their faith in it. The Father is not spoken of adequately; there is no mention at all of the Son and the Holy Spirit. This constitutes a great obstacle with respect to the Orientals. The Holy Spirit will renew all things at the end of the world, and in a certain way we are already living in an eschatological era, owing to the Resurrection of Christ. Not to speak of the Spirit is to remain at the moral level and fail to rise to a theological perspective. The evangelical life of the beatitudes is the work of the Spirit in us. We say that Christians are witnesses: that is true, but the Spirit is the unique witness who speaks through us.

Ukrainian Archbishop Hermaniuk of Winnipeg was disturbed because the chapter is too ascetic and individual rather than sacramental and communitarian. He emphasized the value of the eucharist, which even in this life is "a sign of the Lord's second coming."

The intervention by Coadjutor Bishop Elchinger of Strasbourg agreed with and extended Archbishop Ziadé's. It was sympathetic to the Oriental outlook, and called for a supplementary paragraph emphasizing the collective, communitarian, cosmic, and ontological aspects of eschatology. All men today, he said, understand Saint Paul, who said that Christ will restore and recapitulate all things unto himself. Let us say this in the schema in a way that respects the mentality and sensitivities of modern man.

Finally, Archbishop Mathias of Madras and Mylapore, speaking in the name of several Indian bishops, stressed the importance of this chapter, which he said demonstrates that all men, whatever their social condition or economic state, could be comforted by an understanding of their divine vocation.

In principle, debate on this chapter has ended since no other speakers have registered. Thus, today the assembly began examination of the chapter on the Virgin, the fruit of long efforts of reconciliation among the partisans of different theological schools.

The World Is in a State of "Implicit Christianity"

There have been two lectures of interest recently. Cardinal Suenens spoke on the reform of seminaries, and Father Edward Schillebeeckx, theological adviser to the Dutch hierarchy, spoke on schema 13.

The Primate of Belgium spoke at the Pan-African Secretariat and insisted on the importance of philosophical and theological reform in the formation of future clerics. He also said it is necessary to give seminarians practical experience in pastoral work, even if this means prolonging their formation by another year. He recommended that a program be adopted, as it is in other professions, by means of which priests could be kept informed all their lives of developments in the theological sciences and pastoral techniques.

An intervention by Archbishop Zoa of Yaounde had pointed out that the contribution of the "third world" was not sufficiently respected within the Church, which is still too Occidental.

Cardinal Alfrink, Archbishop of Utrecht, introduced Father Schillebeeckx of the Dominicans at the Dutch Documentation Center. In passing, he congratulated the Center on its excellent work. The speaker noted:

> World interest in Vatican II will depend on schema 13 [the Church and the modern world]. Christianity is neither a ghetto nor an ideological superstructure. The incarnation teaches us that all of creation can be the vehicle of divine grace. In the economy of salvation, the world is by definition in a state of implicit Christianity. To speak of dialogue between the Church and the world is not to speak of a relationship between the religious and the profane, the natural and the supernatural, but between two complementary expressions; it is to speak of the same life hidden in the mystery of Christ. The Church must recognize that the soil she is tilling in schema 13 is not a sacred but a holy land.

These are highly original remarks when compared with manual theology. Father Schillebeeckx's bold perspective is reminiscent of Teilhard de Chardin, who used the daring phrase "holy matter."

SEPTEMBER 17

Cardinal Suenens: Canonizations Are Too Expensive, Too Long, and Badly Apportioned

Although theoretically terminated, discussion on eschatology continued yesterday morning, Wednesday, as some last-minute speakers took the floor. No one objected since Cardinal Suenens and Bishop Ancel made two courageous statements that were much appreciated by the majority.

The Primate of Belgium spoke about the anomalies of canonizations. He had four complaints against the present system. It is abnormal, he said, that (1) 85 percent of the saints are members of the regular clergy; (2) 90 percent automatically belong to three countries, Italy, France, and Spain; (3) the procedure is so slow (fifty-four to eighty years) that it damages the contemporary appeal of the saint; and (4) the investigations are expensive, which means that many secular clergy and laymen whose connections are less fortunate are barred from the liturgical calendar.

Cardinal Suenens proposed the decentralization of the beatification and canonization process. In his opinion, episcopal conferences could assume responsibility for them. The final decision would be left to the pope.

A council is necessary in order that such unpleasant things be said in Rome itself and publicized by the press services. One agency, perhaps out of delicacy, reported thirteen European countries instead of three. But after checking, we can guarantee the accuracy of the second figure.

Bishop Ancel of Lyon, a former bishop-worker, spoke about how the interests of the religious man ought to bear on terrestrial matters. "Religion," he said, "is not the opium of the people, because it urges Christians to engage more than anyone else in civic and social activities and responsibilities. The eschatological perspective gives the believer greater freedom. Neglect of his social duties would be a serious omission. The world would be different if those responsible for economic and political affairs were aware of the eschatological nature of their vocation."

Bishop d'Agostino (Italy), in a more classical style, agreed with a number of speakers that mention should be made of hell and that purgatory should be treated in more detail. These lacks in the schema are "all the more regrettable," he said, "in that some separated brethren uphold errors in this domain."

Hypersensitivity of the Mariologists

The Council then began discussion on the chapter concerning the Virgin, which has given so much trouble to specialists in Mariology. These are a very thin-skinned lot, and if they do not come out swinging in the discussions, it will be owing to good manners, not lack of passion.

Mariologists are hairsplitters. That is the least that can be said about them. The kind of argument that sets them at odds with one another is like this one: if Mary is the mother of the Church and the Church is the mother of all believers, then Mary must be the grandmother of Christians, as Saint Francis de Sales said. Or again, in the twelfth century Saint Bernard said that Mary is between Christ and the Church; following this, some renowned teachers have concluded that Mary is an "aqueduct," others that she is the "neck" of the Church, and still others that she is "Jacob's ladder." There is a good deal of poetry here and it is not to be scorned, but is Marian theology the place for it? However, it would be unbecoming to treat such images ironically, since the Bible and the litanies are fully of hyperbole and expressions of this sort (tower of ivory, morning star, arch of the alliance, and so forth).

The conciliar debates are chiefly concerned with problems relating to the vocabulary, which encompass the principal differences between the schools. Should Mary be called "mother of Church," "mediatrix," and "coredemptress"? Cardinal Ruffini thinks so; so does Cardinal Wyszynski, Primate of Poland, who recalled that the Polish episcopacy sent a memo to this effect to the Pope. He begged the assembly not to disband before solemnly consecrating the world to Mary.

Archbishop Mingo of Monreale, Sicily, thinks that the expression "Mary, mother of the Church" is a necessary one. He also wants explicit mention of Russia in the act of consecration. (The most dedicated Mariologists, curiously enough, are preoccupied with politics; we might recall the anti-Communist propaganda associated with Fatima.) Bishop Ruotolo of Ugento, Bishop Juan Hervás y Benet of Ciudad Real, Spain, Archbishop Octaviano Marquez Toriz of Puebla, Mexico, and Bishop Eduard Nécsey of Nitra, Czechoslovakia, supported similar views. Bishop Abasolo (India) stressed the exemplary value of the marriage between Joseph and Mary "for family life."

Among those opposed to the chapter in form if not in substance, Archbishop Adrianus Djajasepoetra of Djakarta, Indonesia, who spoke in the name of twenty-four bishops from his country, proposed that the expression "Mary mediatrix" be dropped; he said it is equivocal. Cardinal Bea agreed and said that although some popes have used the expression, there is no good reason to continue doing so. Cardinal Silva Henriquez of Chile, speaking in the name of forty-five bishops, recommended that preachers avoid rhetorical oratory when speaking of Mary. Cardinal Döpfner of Munich, speaking for forty bishops, wondered whether the expression "Mary mediatrix" should be used at all. Cardinal Léger of Canada also warned against "verbal inflation," which must not be confused, he pointed out rather cruelly, with depth of thought. He suggested that firm measures be taken to suppress present abuses in Marian devotion which detract from authentic religion.

Let us report further on Cardinal Bea, whose interventions are always closely followed. The president of the Secretariat for Promoting Christian Unity vigorously urged that the schema note clearly the "Christocentric" character of all Marian devotion and stated that there is an "infinite distance" between God and the Virgin, who is only a creature, however privileged. This is a highly important restriction in view of Protestant reactions to the excesses of popular Catholic piety, still too much encouraged in certain regions.

In concluding, we might note that the schema before the Council is an extremely subtle one. A middle way had been adopted in hope of rallying the majority of the Fathers. It scrupulously avoids mention of any new Marian dogmas, which have been altogether excluded from Vatican II despite the efforts of a few bishops. Any new pronouncement would have a catastrophic effect upon the Reformed churches, though contrary to some opinions they are not totally "anti-Marian," as a recent work on the Virgin by Brother Max Thurian, of the Protestant community at Taizé, proves.

First Votes

The first votes of the third session took place on Wednesday, and concerned the schema on the Church. By a vote of 2,170 to 32 (with two invalid ballots), the assembly first adopted the voting procedure that was proposed by the secretary general of the Council. This procedure calls for fifty different ballots: one for each of the six chapters of the schema, and forty-four for the principal amendments, thirty-nine of which will be on the passage concerning collegiality.

SEPTEMBER 18

Vatican II Begins the Schema on the Pastoral Function of Bishops

Things are moving very quickly at the Council at present. The Fathers have been told that those who want to intervene on the schema on revelation must submit the résumé of their speech before September 25; résumés of speeches on the schema on the laity are due before September 28. For schema 13 and the others now in abeyance, the deadline is October 1 for handing in observations.

Will the Council really end with this session? There seems to be a concerted effort to bring it to a close and thus to satisfy the bishops who have requested this. But it disturbs other Fathers, who want the work to be done well in whatever time is needed, and who want at all costs to avoid giving the impression that Vatican II ended hastily because of boredom after the slow pace of the second session.

We won't know anything definite on this for about two weeks. The bishops who think that schema 13 will be one of the most important of the Council hope there will be one more recess in which to redraft this document in the light of observations and criticisms made by the Fathers. In any case, as Cardinal Koenig told me personally at the French Embassy, the moderators are of this opinion.

For the moment discussion continues in depth, and this morning, Friday, the assembly began examination of the schema "On the Pastoral Function of Bishops."

Is Mary the Daughter or the Mother
of the Church?

Thursday the chapter on the Virgin was still being debated. It is the eighth and final chapter of the schema on the Church. One of the experts made this savory comparison: "The schema on the Church is like a train; the first three cars [for which read, the first three chapters] are first-class coaches and the last five are boxcars."

Let us recall the eight chapters: (1) the mystery of the Church, which has just been voted on by a majority of 2,114 *placet* against 11 *non placet* and 63 *placet juxta modum*, (2) the people of God, which will be voted on today, (3) the episcopacy, (4) the laity, (5) the vocation to sanctity, (6) Religious, (7) eschatology, and (8) the Virgin.

Boxcar or not, the last chapter was drafted with extreme care over a long period of time, and it is generally credited with being a balanced but fragile compromise between the maximalist and minimalist schools.

Father Fernández, the Spanish Master General of the Dominicans, expressed this judgment in his intervention. The contradictory reactions to the chapter would seem to prove him right.

Cardinal Suenens thought the document sins by default. He criticized it for not mentioning the "active" and "actual" role of the Virgin in the work of evangelization. In the name of eighty-two bishops, Bishop Francisco Rendeiro of Faro, Portugal, complained that the chapter lacked superlatives! Bishop Sapelak, Apostolic Visitor for the Ukrainian Rite Catholics of Argentina, desired emphasis on Mary's "patronage" as a means of encouraging the victims of atheism and materialism in their struggles against these evils.

The interventions continued to turn on two themes: the Virgin's titles of "mediatrix" and "mother of the Church." Bishop Ancel, speaking for the second time since the session began, admitted that he had changed his mind since studying Mariology more closely and would not now use the expression "mediatrix."

Luther to the Rescue Archbishop Jozef Gawlina, Apostolic Visitor to Polish immigrants, thought that the cult of the Virgin would not constitute an obstacle to ecumenism—to the contrary; and he quoted Luther's comment on the *Magnificat* that "Mary does not lead to herself but to God."

Bishop Primo Gasbarri of Velletri, Italy, was of the opinion that the last two Marian dogmas, the Immaculate Conception and the Assumption, rather advanced the cause of ecumenism. Archbishop Rafael García y

García de Castro of Granada spoke in the name of eighty bishops and remarked somewhat sharply, "It is not possible not to recognize Mary as the mother of the Church." He was challenged by Bishop Méndez Arceo of Cuernavaca, speaking for forty bishops, who said that the expression is of the order of "literary genres" and dates only from the twelfth century, when it was first used by Béranger of Tours. "It is much more traditional," he said, "to call Mary the 'daughter of the Church.' The Church is our mother." With humorous logic the Mexican Bishop recalled the teaching of Thomas Aquinas to the effect that the angels are part of the Church. But Mary cannot be considered the mother of the angels. The speaker also took up the saying of Saint Francis de Sales we spoke of yesterday: "Mary, the grandmother of believers."

These examples show that the discussion on Mary is of no outstanding importance. It would be better for the Council to get on as quickly as possible to a more fruitful topic, which it is expected to have done today. But this chapter will not have been inserted in vain if it curbs the intemperance of certain Mariologists.

SEPTEMBER 19

Rome Between Madrid and Moscow

Vatican II Is Invited To Vote on a Text Concerning the Sovereign Independence of the Church from Civil Powers   On Friday morning Vatican II began examination of one of its most momentous schemas, that on bishops. It treats of such important themes as the relationship of bishops with the universal Church and the Holy See, dioceses, synods, councils, and episcopal conferences. This copious document, consisting partly of a former text entitled *De cura animarum*, was studied by five subcommissions, which had to take into account several hundred amendments filling eight volumes.

Before this examination began there were several further interventions on chapter 8, concerning the Virgin Mary. Let us recapitulate briefly.

Cardinal Frings, Archbishop of Cologne, saw the text as "the best possible compromise."

Cardinal Alfrink, Archbishop of Utrecht, speaking in the name of 124 bishops from various countries, explicitly requested the suppression of the expression "Mary mediatrix" because it was "equivocal and dangerous" in the light of the fact that Christ is the unique mediator.

Bishop Laureano Castám Lacoma of Siguenza, Spain, announced that he was spokesman for eighty Council Fathers. But when the assembly was over several Spanish bishops told him that they were not in agreement with the extreme proposals he upheld, and complained that he had not sufficiently consulted his colleagues. He said in part: "It is shameful and scandalous to suppress the title 'Mary, mother of the Church.' Let us re-establish it. I urge this insistently, most insistently, extremely insistently. Mary is necessarily the mother of the Church, which is the mystical body of Christ, for if she were only the mother of Christ, who is the head of the Church, she would be the mother of a monster."

These remarks gave the minimalist bishops some cause to rejoice; by making the maximalist position appear ridiculous, its proponents bring it into disrepute. May the Council, as one of our abler contemporary Mariol-ogists has written, help clear away "certain feverish, exalted, superfluous, and self-interested forms of Marian piety."

Two New Paragraphs   A surprise awaited the Council Fathers at Friday's session. They were given two new paragraphs which are to be added to the schema on bishops. The texts are said to be so important that they were kept secret until the last moment to avoid unfavorable reaction from civil powers.

The first paragraph concerns countries behind the Iron Curtain, and the second, countries where a Franco-type regime is in power. They deal with the relationship between the episcopacy and civil powers and with the freedom necessary to nominate bishops. Here is a translation:

[1.] In fulfilling their apostolic office, which is totally directed to the salvation of souls, bishops must enjoy full and perfect liberty and independence vis-à-vis civil powers. It is therefore illicit either directly or indirectly to hinder the exercise of this ecclesiastical office and to obstruct direct communication with the Holy See, other religious authorities, or even with the faithful. But since pastors work for the faithful and for civil progress and prosperity, they must collaborate with public authority in accordance with the nature of their office by exhorting the faithful to obey all just laws and to respect all legitimately established powers.

[2.] Since the apostolic office of the bishops has been created by Our Lord for a spiritual and supernatural end, the Council declares that the right of nominating bishops belongs properly and in an ex-clusive manner to the competent ecclesiastical authority. Therefore, in order to protect the liberty of Holy Mother Church and to promote the welfare of the faithful better and more easily, it is the desire of the Fathers that henceforward the laity have no rights or privileges whatsoever in the election, nomination, presentation, or designation of the episcopal office, and that those who presently have this right renounce it of their own free accord.

The commentator added that it was understood that the state has the right to be informed in advance of the identity of the nominated bishops.

The clarity of this text, which will soon be voted on by the Fathers, is striking. But there is a great distance between theory and fact, and we may suppose that this one will be particularly difficult to put in practice. It does show, however, that the Church clearly intends to have done with systems of nominating bishops which reduce the Church's margin of independence. Bishop Pildáin of the Canary Islands, coincidentally a Spaniard, was the first to comment on this text, which marks such a serious reversal in relationships between the Church and totalitarian regimes. He said:

> I wholly agree with this, and I thank the commission for making it clear that the right of nominating bishops is under the exclusive jurisdiction of the Church and in no way under civil power. I hope in the future there will be no more concessions of this sort. No human society has ever permitted its leaders to be named by another. *A fortiori*, this is true of the Church, which is a perfect society. When the Council votes for this total liberation of the Church and deprives the laity of its privileges in this matter, it will be a glorious day for the Church. When the Council approves this text, it will be as important an event in history as Pius X's decision to end the civil power's right of veto in the election of a pope.
>
> The reaction of the interested public powers remains to be seen.

The Medieval Notion of "Benefices"   The interventions were exceptionally interesting and varied. Coadjutor Archbishop Veuillot of Paris, the reporter for the commission, noted that the sensitive point of the schema is the origin of episcopal power (is it communion with the pope?). Then Cardinal Richaud, Archbishop of Bordeaux, made the following commonsensical remarks:

> Too many questions are being referred to the Commission for the Revision of the Code of Canon Law. The postconciliar commission will not have the same authority as the Council to effect certain reforms. Let us therefore take this matter up in detail. For example, the dismissal or transfer of a pastor raises problems concerning the present state of canon law. . . . Statutes governing pastors

are influenced by the medieval notion of "benefices." We must eliminate all vestiges of this. . . . Some matters can be regulated by episcopal conferences instead of the Holy Office.

Cardinal Browne of the Curia and Bishop Carli of Segni both expressed reservations in principle about the source of episcopal powers,
the sacramentality of the episcopacy, and collegiality. Bishop Rupp of
Monaco, then took the floor to quote Luther—the second time in twenty-
four hours that the founder of Protestantism had been paid respects
at the Council: "Too often councils promote the glory of bishops." The
prelate then applied this to the fact that, in his opinion, there was too
much talk at Vatican II about the supreme power of bishops over the
whole Church. Bishop Rupp further regretted the too-static character of
the schema, which had nothing to say about a matter of major importance:
migratory movements and their consequences for pastoral life.

Direct Contact Between Priest and Faithful Archbishop Fares of Catanzaro, Italy, did not think the schema clarified the principle of episcopal
conferences sufficiently. Archbishop Federico Melendro, expelled Archbishop of Anking, China, proposed that ecumenical councils be convoked on a regular basis, say, every forty years. He was then called to
order for digressing into the subject of the merits of devotion to the
Sacred Heart (there have been several such incidents in the general
congregations).

The Bishop of Monze, Zambia, James Corboy, spoke on the
advantages of the exemption of religious, which he did not think the
schema treated fully enough. Bishop John McEleney of Kingston, Jamaica,
supported this point of view. Bishop Maksimilijan Drzečnik of Maribor,
Yugoslavia, noted that today the parable of the lost sheep has been reversed: ninety-nine out of a hundred are outside the fold. He urged a
theology of adapted evangelization which would take into account the
influence of socialization and industrialization on modern man.

In a similar vein, Bishop Brian Foley of Lancaster, England, declared:
"Nothing is more important for the success of the apostolate than direct
contact between priests and the faithful. Let this be stressed."

Bishop Federico Kaiser of Caraveli, Peru, put his finger on one of
the basic weaknesses of the modern Church and spoke his mind bluntly:

> The division of clergy in the world is scandalously uneven. No
> state anywhere uses its personnel as inefficiently as does the Church.
> Let the bishops collaborate to remedy this evil, and let them show real
> generosity. We must find a solution to this calamitous situation now,

not tomorrow by forming new priests. Let the Council appeal to the Pope for a more equal distribution of clergy. Our collective responsibility is involved.

Finally, Archbishop Robert E. Lucey of San Antonio, Texas, intervened to deplore the negligence of the Church toward her strict duty to teach religion. "The faith is dying," he said, "because of the extreme ignorance of Christians. Neither a Communist nor an enemy of religion said that. Pius XI did."

The next general congregation will be held Monday. Collegiality will be the central issue.

"For Rent"

A joker, cruel perhaps but in any event a cleric who is well aware of what is going on in the religious world of Rome, recently hung a sign on the premises of the Sacred Congregation of Rites which read: "For rent." It was there long enough to become the talk of the Council.

Why this iconoclastic gesture? Because the Pope recently received Cardinal Lercaro, president of the postconciliar commission on the liturgy, in audience. Paul VI confirmed the powers of this commission, many of which had formerly belonged to the Congregation of Rites, traditionally the competent department of the Curia for liturgical matters. Members of the Curia body have been trying to retrieve their prerogatives by something approaching gangland tactics. Now, however, Paul VI has dotted the *i*'s for the benefit of those involved. He doesn't want to have to tell them again.

This typically Roman incident is being bruited abroad by a number of clerics with great relish.

SEPTEMBER 21

Declaration on the Jews
Repudiates Hatred and Persecutions

Vatican II will soon vote on the declaration on the Jews and non-Christians, which was redrafted during the recess just past. This text has set off some violent reactions. Some are indignant because it is less categorical than the former draft; others—particularly bishops residing in Arabic countries—have exerted every imaginable kind of pressure to prevent Vatican II from treating the Jewish question. But the competent commissions have refused to bend before their demands because they consider them inadequately motivated. The protesting bishops are of the opinion that any statement in favor of the Jews will be immediately interpreted in political terms by the Arabs, who will then create additional difficulties for Christians living in these countries.

According to our information, it appears that Cardinal Bea's Secretariat for Promoting Christian Unity is not responsible for all the changes. Some were effected at a higher level—by the Coordinating Commission, which is presided over by Cardinal Cicognani, Vatican Secretary of State.

The new text does not say that "Responsibility for the death of Christ falls upon sinful humanity," or that "The role played by the Jewish authorities in the crucifixion does not exempt all mankind from guilt."

The fact that these passages have been withdrawn in no way means they have been disavowed, of course. Furthermore, that would be impossible, since the catechism of the Council of Trent affirms that all men are in some sense guilty of "deicide."

Another modification is that whereas the previous text condemned the expression "deicide nation," the new text says the Jews should not be called "outcast." It expressly states that "What happened in Christ's passion cannot be blamed upon the Jews of today." The theologians had to balance two truths here: on the one hand, the historical responsibility of certain Jewish authorities in the past cannot be denied; on the other, the Council of Trent has once and for all said that the death of Christ is imputable to all men. Consequently, they decided to make no reference at all to "deicide." The new text states, we might note, that we must not blame modern Jews for the death of Christ as though they could be held responsible for the error of certain of their remote ancestors.

Also, the word *persecutio* has been replaced by the word *vexatio*, which can be translated as *harassment*. This is undoubtedly the most awkward of the changes. Under the pretext of avoiding all political allusions in a purely religious document, the editors of the text act as though we in 1964 can forget that millions of Jews were exterminated by the Nazis. It is indeed difficult to find the word *vexatio* adequate a mere twenty years after the concentration camps, the gas chambers, and the crematory ovens.

However, the new text not only forbids preachers to use language injurious to Jews, as does the old draft, but extends this interdiction to include derogation of any man.

The present text is certainly not final. As of now, at least forty bishops have already registered to speak on it and have asked that it be changed.

In view of the many rumors circulating about this draft and the frequently excessive reactions it has stirred up, we think it wise to present the first and last versions (there have been interim texts) in their entirety. In this way readers will be able to judge on the evidence. The new document, we might note, also includes some mention of the Muslims and a paragraph on racial discrimination.

The Old Text: "On the Relations of Catholics with Non-Christians and Principally the Jews"

(Chapter 4 of the Schema on Ecumenism)

After having treated the principles of Catholic ecumenism, we wish to affirm that these same principles, with due account taken of different conditions, are applicable to dialogue and cooperation with non-Christians who believe in God or who, moved by good will, at least endeavor to observe, according to their conscience, the moral law which is written in the nature of man.

This applies especially to the Jews, however, since they are linked with the Church of Christ in a very special way.

The Church of Christ gratefully recognizes that, according to the mystery of God's saving design, the beginnings of her faith and her election are already found among the patriarchs and prophets. She professes that all who believe in Christ, Abraham's sons according to faith (Gal. 3:7), are included in the same patriarch's call, and likewise that the salvation of the Church was mystically foreshadowed by the chosen people's exodus from the land of bondage. The Church, the new creature in Christ (Eph. 2:15), cannot forget that she is the continuation of that people with whom God, in his ineffable mercy, deigned to establish the Old Covenant.

Moreover, the Church believes that Christ, our peace, embraces with a same love both Jews and Gentiles and has made both one (Eph. 2:14), and that the reconciliation in Christ of all nations is announced by the union of both in one body (Eph. 2:17). Although a large portion of the chosen people remain in the meanwhile far from Christ, it would however be unjust to call them a cursed people, since they remain precious to God because of the fathers and the gifts that were given to them (Rom. 11:28), or a deicide nation, because the Lord by his passion and death has redeeemed the sins of all men who were the cause of his death and passion (Luke 23:34; Acts 3:17; I Cor. 2:8).

Yet the death of Christ was not caused by a whole people then living and much less by those living today. That is why priests must be careful to say nothing in catechetical instruction and in sermons which could engender in the hearts of the listeners hatred or contempt for the Jews. Nor does the Church forget that Christ was born of the flesh of this race, that the Virgin Mary, mother of Christ, and the apostles, the foundation stones and pillars of the Church, were likewise born of the Jewish people.

Since the common patrimony between the Church and the Synagogue is so great, this sacred Synod wishes to foster and recommend that mutual understanding and respect which are the fruit of theological studies and brotherly dialogue. Moreover, just as the Church severely condemns all injustices inflicted on any man, even more does she deplore and condemn with a maternal heart hatred and persecutions against the Jews, whether perpetrated in the past or in our own times.

The New Text: "On the Jews and Non-Christians"

32. *The Common Patrimony of Christians and Jews*   The Church of Christ willingly acknowledges that, according to the mystery of God's saving design, the beginnings of her faith and her election are already found among the patriarchs and prophets. She professes that all who believe in Christ, Abraham's sons according to faith, are included in the same patriarch's call, and likewise that the salvation of the Church was mystically foreshadowed by the chosen people's exodus from the land of bondage. This is why the Church, the new creature in Christ and the people of the New Covenant, cannot forget that she is the continuation of that people with whom God, in his ineffable mercy, deigned to establish the Old Covenant and to whom he willed to confide the revelation contained in the books of the Old Testament.

Nor does the Church forget that Christ was born of the flesh of the Jewish people, that the mother of Christ, the Virgin Mary, and the apostles, the foundation stones and pillars of the Church, were likewise born of the Jewish people.

The Church also has and will ever have before her eyes the words of the apostle Paul about the Jews: ". . . who have the adoption as sons, and the glory and the covenants and the legislation and the worship and the promises; who have the fathers, and from whom is the Christ according to the flesh" (Rom. 9:4-5).

Therefore, since Christians have received such a great patrimony from the Jews, this sacred Synod wishes to foster and recommend that mutual understanding and respect which are the fruit of theological studies and brotherly dialogue. Moreover, just as the Church repudiates all injustices inflicted on any man, so likewise she deplores and condemns hatred and harassment [*vexationem*] of the Jews.

In addition, it is well to remember that the union of the Jewish people with the Church is a part of the Christian hope. Indeed, the

Church, according to the teaching of the apostle Paul (Rom. 11:25), with indestructible faith and great desire, awaits the entrance of this people into the fullness of the people of God established by Christ.

That is why all must be careful, whether in catechetical teaching, in preaching, or in daily conversations, not to present the Jewish people as an outcast nation, or to say or do anything that might alienate the minds of men from the Jews. Let all be careful, too, not to impute to the Jews of today what was perpetrated in the passion of Christ.

33. *All Men Have God as Father*   Our Lord Jesus has abundantly confirmed that God is the Father of all men, as the Old Testament and the Church have stated and reason itself suggests. But we cannot call God the Father of all or pray to him as such if we refuse to behave fraternally toward some men, who are all created in God's image. In fact, the relation of man with God the Father and the relation of man with his brothers are so close that any denial of human brotherhood implies or leads to a denial of God himself, with whom there is no respect of persons (II Par. 19:7; Rom. 2:11; Eph. 6:9; Col. 3:25; I Pet. 1:17), for the first commandment is so closely interwoven with the second that our sins cannot be forgiven if we do not whole-heartedly forgive those who trespass against us. Already in the Old Law it is said: "Have we not all one father? Has not one God created us? Why then does every one of us despise his brother, violating the convenant of our fathers?" (Mal. 2:10)

The same thing is stated with yet greater clarity in the New Testament: "For how can he who does not love his brother, whom he sees, love God, whom he does not see? And this commandment we have received from him; that he who loves God should also love his brother" (I John 4:20–21).

Urged on by this charity toward our brothers, let us carefully consider their doctrines and opinions which, although they differ in many points from ours, nonetheless retain the ray of that truth which enlightens every man born into this world. Thus, let us also and first of all embrace the Muslims, who adore one personal God and who are closer to us in their religious sentiments as well as through many human cultural channels.

34. *Every Form of Discrimination Is To Be Condemned*   The ground is therefore removed from every theory or practice which leads to discrimination between man and man or between nation and nation in the matter of human dignity and the rights which flow from it. It is therefore imperative that all men of good will, and Christians in particular, abstain from any discrimination against men or harass-

ment (*vexationem*) of them because of their race, color, social condition, or religion.

As to Christians, this sacred Synod ardently implores them to "behave honorably among the nations" (I Pet. 2:12), and if possible, and insofar as it depends on them, to keep peace with all men (Rom. 12:18). It enjoins them, moreover, to love not only their neighbor, but even their enemies, if they think they have any, so that they will truly be sons of the Father who is in heaven and who makes the sun rise over everyone (Matt. 5:44–45).

Vexatio and Persecutio: A Comment   We received the following letter from Mr. R. Martin, a professor of Latin at the Sorbonne:

Your correspondent, H. Fesquet, stresses the fact that in the new conciliar schema on the Jews and non-Christians, persecutions against the Israelites are no longer designated by the word *persecutio* but by the word *vexatio*. Mr. Fesquet considers this a particularly "awkward" change, and says that the word "can be translated as *harassment*." Then he writes: "It is indeed difficult to find the word *vexatio* adequate a mere twenty years after the concentration camps, the gas chambers, and the crematory ovens."

I should like to point out that not only is the word *vexatio* adequate but it is altogether the best word to translate the French word *persecution*. It is, in fact, the exact equivalent.

Persecutio, despite appearances, would be much less exact. It comes from the verb *persequi*, to pursue or prosecute. Strictly speaking it signifies a prosecution and especially "a legal prosecution." Only in later Latin did the word take on the modern sense of persecution. In this sense it was uniquely applied to the persecutions of the first Christians in Rome. But it is to be noted that these were the object of "legal prosecution" in the strict sense of the word. So much for the semantic evolution. We might also note that the Latin Christian authors, Tertullian for example, used *persecutio Christianorum* and *vexatio Christianorum* indifferently and attach the same value to the expressions.

In any event, the word *vexatio* in classical Latin has—or can have, depending on the context—a very strong sense and can very well be applied to deportations and even massacres. It is certainly the word Cicero would have used were he talking about persecutions analogous to those of the Nazis against the Jews. It would not have occurred to him to have used *persecutio!* For that matter, consult any Latin dictionary. Persecution is always rendered by the word *vexatio*.

It therefore seems difficult to maintain that, on this particular point, the new conciliar text is weaker than the former. It merely makes a necessary linguistic correction; it replaces a vague term with a precise one.

SEPTEMBER 22

Vatican II Takes a Decisive Step Toward Recognizing Collegiality and Establishing a Married Diaconate

The general congregation on Monday was almost entirely devoted to the presentation of reports on the latest draft of chapter 3 of the schema *De Ecclesia,* concerning the episcopacy and a married diaconate. Vatican II took a decisive step toward accepting the sacramentality of the episcopacy and toward real collegiality, a bone of contention that caused serious altercations during the second session.

By skillful maneuvering the moderators succeeded in having Archbishop Parente, charged with refuting the objections to collegiality, speak last. The conclusions of his report were applauded at length by the assembly. This is the first time during the current session that the Fathers have shown their approval in this way. It was a rare enough spectacle, moreover, to see the Archbishop, who is the Assessor of the Holy Office and who is generally held in low repute by both conservative- and liberal-minded bishops, defend collegiality.

On the other hand, the first report, by Bishop Franič of Split who is a leader of the opposition, was not applauded. This was proof, if indeed proof be needed, that Vatican II will approve collegiality and that the vote of last October 30 was really indicative, despite the efforts of a minority to contest its value. Let us add that Bishop Franič in no way represents the minority opposed to collegiality on the theological commission—a fact that seriously limits the influence of his remarks—for the simple reason that this minority does not exist (according to Cardinal Koenig). Chapter 3 was in fact unanimously approved by that commission.

A brief look at the recent past is in order. The adversaries of collegiality made every possible effort during the recess to make their point of view prevail. The celebrated polemicist Archbishop Staffa, Secretary of the Congregation of Universities and Seminaries, and Monsignor Ugo Lattanzi, professor of theology at the Lateran University, published two studies against collegiality in the journal *Divinitas. L'Osservatore Romano* also published an article last June emphasizing the ecumenical dangers of collegiality. It was signed with a psuedonym.

Another example of the opposition's machinations: pamphlets violently attacking collegiality have been placed in the buses which take the Fathers to their lodgings after the work session each day.

Let us add that a brochure published by the Pontifical Biblical Commission has been distributed to the Council Fathers in the aula. By means of arguments drawn from Scripture, the authors of this document have sought to prove, first, that Christ did not expressly will that the apostolic college survive the apostles, and second, that the power of the "keys" given to the apostles does not necessarily imply the principle of their universal jurisdiction. The pamphlet was not an attack on collegiality; rather, it tried to show the weakness of certain scriptural arguments advanced to support it.

"Obsession with Primacy" The schema itself, now presented for approval by the assembly, also calls for some comments.

While the text comes out clearly in favor of collegiality, it is literally shot through with clauses stressing the primacy of the pope. As early as last year, Father Congar wrote that this constant harping on a truth which nobody contests will in the end become "nauseating." This year there is an even greater insistence on primacy.

Primacy is mentioned seven times in twenty lines on page 7 of the schema, that is, an average of once each three lines and at least once in each sentence. It is thus not surprising that one hears talk of a veritable "obsession with primacy" and "neurosis about primacy." This creates a bad impression, especially among the Orientals and non-Catholic observers. It shows the "fear of the orthodox" and demonstrates the difficulty the hierarchical Church is having extricating herself from eight centuries of theology centered lopsidedly on pontifical monarchy. Only eight centuries, in fact, because until the twelfth century the papacy functioned largely as an arbiter between local Churches. The pope, for example, began to intervene in the nomination of bishops and the erection of dioceses only in the twelfth century. Thus, the hypertrophy of the exercise of pontifical authority, which disturbs the Orientals so, is not coextensive with the tradition of the Church. Too often do we forget this owing to our ignorance of history.

Because it is so contorted—there is no other word—the present schema will certainly not yield positive results on the ecumenical level, at least for the present. This is the opinion of so eminent an authority as Maximos IV Saigh, Greek Catholic Melkite Patriarch, who fears that Vatican II will scarcely be more liberating in the eyes of the Orthodox than was Vatican I.

Whatever the case, the Council is now on the eve of voting on a schema that is truly the heart of Vatican II and the core of ecclesiastical reform in the twentieth century. A historic page is about to be turned. This will become evident in the months and years to come.

The Objections   Let us get back to Monday's session. Here is as faithful a report as possible of the objections presented by Bishop Franič:

1. The question of the sacramentality of the episcopacy is not ripe enough to resolve. It is disputed among theologians, and Vatican II ought not interfere. (Let us recall, though, that in October 30's indicative vote, 98 percent of the Fathers gave an affirmative answer to the question on whether episcopal consecration is the highest degree of the sacrament of orders.)

2. The schema states that the college of bishops equally possesses supreme and full power in the universal Church *ex jure divino* (of divine right). This doctrine is based on the consecration ceremony. There would thus be two subjects enjoying full powers, a proposition that seems impossible and contradictory. Whether we want to admit it or not, this is contrary to the teaching of Vatican I, for it places restrictions on the power of the sovereign pontiff. If the pope has need of the college, his power is not total. The arguments, it is said, are drawn from Scripture. But the interpretation given these texts does not seem to be sufficiently substantial.

3. Tradition is uncertain as regards collegiality. Pius XII, for example, said in his encyclical *Mystici corporis* that the ordinary power of bishops comes immediately from the sovereign pontiff. This means that the bishops do not receive their power *directly* from Christ and their consecration. Tertullian and Saint Thomas Aquinas distinguish between the power of jurisdiction and the power of sanctification. In the schema the two are joined. It is therefore a question of a new doctrine which was still considered quite improbable only a short time ago. It would not be safe to settle so serious a matter quickly. Moreover, the schema says that the power of the episcopal body can only be exercised in communion with the pope. Therefore, in practice the pope's authority is necessary. Under these conditions, what purpose does the college serve?

4. The schema stipulates that married men can receive the diaconate. That is dangerous, for this faculty could in the long run constitute a threat to the priesthood, and clerical celibacy will never be dislocated. Moreover, the schema states that young persons who intend to marry can be ordained deacons without the obligation of chastity. "I am persuaded, as are many," Bishop Franič said, "that it would constitute a serious danger to priestly vocations if the Council approved this proposal."

Archbishop Parente Answers Point by Point Cardinal Koenig, Archbishop of Vienna, took the floor next. He presented a report explaining the reasons for the amendments to paragraphs 18–21 of the chapter dealing with bishops as successors to the apostles and the sacramentality of the episcopacy.

The amendments, he said, paid strict heed to the indicative vote of October 30 on sacramentality. In accordance with the requests of many Fathers, the schema indicates clearly that episcopal consecration confers the three powers of teaching, governing, and sanctifying.

Archbishop Parente then presented his response. He noted at the outset that he was not speaking as "the Assessor of the Holy Office but as the Bishop of Thebes, which is in the desert." He added with a smile, "I hope I will not be a voice crying in the wilderness."

> The problem here [he began] is to put a solid foundation under the constitution on the episcopacy. This in itself would be worth a council. We are responding to the desire of Paul VI, who made it quite clear in his opening speech to the second session that this question should be settled by the Council and that it was the essential end of Vatican II. It would therefore be strange if we vacillated in our duty. . . . [This was a direct answer to Bishop Franič's hesitancies.]
>
> The schema affirms two things. It recalls the teaching of Vatican I concerning the personal power of the pope, and it adds that the college of bishops inherits the powers of the apostolic college. It follows as an exact corollary, then, that the college possesses full and supreme powers, always in perfect communion with the pope. The schema affirms that even outside of a council bishops must be solicitous for the universal Church. The schema also states that bishops, even though dispersed, can define a dogma if there is unanimity among them and agreement with the sovereign pontiff; they therefore share in the charism of infallibility. The episcopal function is always present in a juridical as well as a pastoral manner.

Archbishop Parente then added:

1. It is said that the college is a new idea. But recent studies show that this term can be found almost everywhere in the Church's past.
2. It is objected that the word *college* implies an equality of all the members. This is false, since the pope is the head of the college. To avoid all confusion, the schema also uses the word *body*.
3. The opposition speaks as though the college could be distinguished from the sovereign pontiff; but the contrary is the case since the body and the head cannot be separated.

4. It is objected that if the power of bishops is based upon consecration, there is then no need of further reference to the sovereign pontiff. This is false, because the text explicitly states that communion with the head of the college is required at all times. In order to avoid all equivocation, the schema speaks of the pope twenty times in this chapter.

5. The texts from Pius XII cited by Bishop Franič absolutely do not say that the pope creates the episcopal power, but only that the bishops cannot exercise their power without being in communion with him. We must clearly distinguish between the power itself and its exercise.

6. The references to Saint Thomas are debatable and not so traditional. Moreover, we could cite a quantity of other very recent texts and studies, for example, one by the Italian lay theologian M. Alberigo, and another by a German priest, Father Bertram.

"The text," Archbishop Parente concluded, "can therefore be voted upon. I thank God and pray to the Holy Spirit to enlighten us. It is not a question of opinion but of certainty. It is a question of affirming our faith. Let it never be said that the doctrines of Vatican I and Vatican II are separable, for they are not. The whole ontological structure of the Church rests on sacred orders and the universal priesthood of Christ."

Bestow the Diaconate on Fathers of Families   A fourth report was read by Auxiliary Bishop Henríquez Jiménez of Caracas. It dealt with the amendments added to chapter 3, paragraphs 28 and 29, on priests and deacons.

The reporter recalled that during the second session, 759 Fathers pronounced themselves in favor of the restoration of the diaconate and only eighty-two spoke against it. Moreover, the indicative vote of October 30 was 1,588 for and 525 against. Then he said:

> The schema gives episcopal conferences the power of decision in this matter, as it does for the liturgy; but it is understood that the approbation of the sovereign pontiff is necessary. . . .
>
> Concerning the possibility of married deacons, the schema restricts itself to leaving the door open. It makes no recommendations. If many members of the assembly have envisaged bestowing the diaconate on fathers of families, few are inclined to confer it on young men without at the same time imposing celibacy. . . . In what concerns priests, let me reaffirm that there is no doubt, either theoretically or practically, that we will not give authorization to ordain married men in the Latin Church. . . .
>
> Would the diaconate be a threat to priestly vocations? No, because they are two different vocations.

Neither Archaism Nor Paternalism Toward the end of the general congregation, five Fathers spoke about the pastoral responsibility of bishops.

Cardinal Léger, Archbishop of Montreal, spoke of the necessity of adapting pastoral theology to modern man, and sketched a psychological portrait of such a man:

> Modern man is a technician. He has new ideas about religion. He only accepts what he considers true, genuine. He rejects all forms of paternalism. He wants to protect his personal responsibility.
>
> Our ecclesiastical language is archaic, and this is one reason it is ineffective. It would be opportune to reorganize diocesan curias and revise everything related to our titles, our garb, and our style of life. We must build new and real contacts among bishops, priests, and the faithful. If bishops want to be understood, they must know all the conditions of life of their associates and faithful. Let us not settle matters that are not in our field of competency. Let us be humble.

After Cardinal Confalonieri of the Curia spoke about immigrants, Bishop Compagnone of Anagni, Italy, urged that the privilege of lay "patronage" regarding the nomination of bishops and pastors be suppressed wherever it still exists.

Then Archbishop Angelo Rossi of Ribeirão Preto, Brazil, speaking in the name of 180 bishops, suggested that coadjutors be named to aid old or sick pastors who cannot be asked to resign.

Bishop Rudolf Staverman, Apostolic Vicar for Sukarnapura, Indonesia, proposed that the term *flock* be dropped since it is "archaic vocabulary." He said that priests should be taken seriously and not be considered second-rate assistants. He concluded with this important statement: "Let us seek ways of helping priests in trouble and showing them the Church's goodness. The Church must not seem severe with these priests, who have perhaps fallen because they were not sufficiently encouraged. Let us not be afraid to confront this serious problem. It would be an injustice to priests as a whole to show anxiety about solving this problem or fear that it would open the door to abuses."

Bishop Staverman also spoke of granting priests the right to marry if they have good reasons for doing so. He thus touched on a well-known concern of Paul VI.

Bishops Recognize Collegiality
by Sweeping Majority Votes

There was a noticeable lack of interest in Tuesday's general congregation, falling as it did between the memorable session on Monday and today's assembly, devoted to religious liberty, a burning issue of capital importance for ecumenical dialogue.

Collegiality stirred much passion and left some Fathers uneasy. The minority persists in setting this notion in opposition to the personal authority of the sovereign pontiff as if it diminished the pope's authority. On the contrary, the doctrine of collegiality completes, clarifies, and balances the definitions of Vatican I on the prerogatives of Roman primacy.

Here is further evidence of collective fright: it is reported that some fifteen cardinals have recently asked the Pope to withdraw collegiality from the Council's program. Needless to say, Paul VI paid them no heed. To have done so would have brought him into direct conflict with the Council on the one hand and, on the other, put him in a self-contradictory position, since on several occasions he has explicitly and implicitly expressed his desire to see collegiality defined. As of today, that is a closed issue.

First Votes on Collegiality   During the general congregation on Monday, the Fathers began to vote paragraph by paragraph on the third chapter of the schema on the Church.

The first vote, affirming that the bishops are the successors of the apostles and the pope of Saint Peter, resulted in 2,166 affirmative votes against 53 negative with 1 ballot null. The second, recognizing that the college of apostles received the "perpetual" mission of feeding Christ's flock, was adopted by a vote of 2,012 to 191 with 3 ballots null.

Tuesday morning the important vote on the paragraph which affirms that just as Peter and the apostles formed a college, so too do the pope and the bishops form a college, was approved by 1,918 to 322.

A Peculiar Vote   An odd incident, the cause obscure, took place Tuesday morning in St. Peter's during one of the eight votes between interventions. The last vote concerned this proposition: that the college of bishops has no authority without the pope, whose primacy remains total and who can always freely exercise his supreme power over the universal Church.

When the results of the balloting became known, there was a moment of stunned silence, followed by unrestrained laughter: 2,114 Fathers had voted *placet* and, for some strange reason, 90 had voted *non placet*.

How could so many vote against a proposition whose obvious aim was to reaffirm the doctrine of Vatican I concerning the supreme power and total primacy of the sovereign pontiff? It is not easy to answer this question, for contrary to what some distant observers might think, it is absolutely impossible that any Council Father could doubt for a moment the prerogatives of the pope, which are an article of faith. There are two possible explanations: either these Fathers did not understand the meaning of the proposition, or—and this is more plausible—they were influenced by last-minute appeals from integralists to vote a systematic *no* on all ballots concerning collegiality. Whatever the explanation, it was very peculiar.

In the other seven ballots, the opposition swung between 44 and 328, which is striking proof of the health of Vatican II and the almost total defeat of the minority, who persevered to the end in trying to influence the majority. Hadn't Archbishop Parente spoken the day before of "suspicious goings-on" in the assembly?

The consequences of these votes and their repercussions on the evolution of the Church are exceedingly important. Vatican II has challenged integralism, and it is difficult to see how that camp will ever recover.

The Minority Opposed to Collegiality Seeks an Escape Hatch The approximately 300 bishops opposed to collegiality intend to present a common *modus* (modification), as is their right. This is to be introduced at the last moment during the final vote on chapter 3 of the schema on the Church.

This *modus* will attempt to show that the episcopal college *possesses* full power only when it acts in conjunction with the pope.

Although it is not apparent, there is a serious and intentional equivocation in this formula. The question is precisely this: does the pope *give* the power to bishops, or is it conferred upon them by episcopal consecration? The assembly formally voted on the latter version. In this case the pope intervenes only to permit the exercise of this power.

The victory attained by the majority rests on this subtle but important distinction between episcopal power and the faculty to exercise it. Will it be compromised by the special pleading of this *modus*?

Modern Life Calls for
a Totally New Kind of Bishop

There were some twenty interventions on the theme of Tuesday's general congregation, but with few exceptions they were not distinguished by brilliance, although they bore on pastoral questions that were intrinsically interesting.

"If priests feel neglected by Vatican II they are wrong," declared Bishop Guyot of Contances. "Everything that is said about bishops and the sacramentality of the episcopacy has a corresponding application to priests. I, together with the French episcopacy in whose name I am speaking, would like to see the different passages of the four schemas which treat of priests collected in a single document. If Vatican II offers a firm and coherent doctrine on the priesthood, it will be of great help to priests in difficulty."

Speaking in his own name, Bishop Guyot added, "Priests are not mere executives but collaboraters who should be able to express themselves with confidence. This would necessitate readjusting the structures of dialogue. Bishops and priests should mutually give to and receive from one another." Archbishop Urtasun of Avignon was of the same opinion.

Archbishop Guerry of Cambrai stressed that bishops must stop teaching in a purely cerebral and abstract way and speak of events and the problems of life:

> This is why *Pacem in terris* was so successful. Men of our time, believers or not, have become aware of the Church's presence in their problems. Let us not place artificial barriers between natural life and the supernatural life. And to that end, let us keep in touch with modern life; let us speak of the Gospel, denounce injustice, if need be sacrifice our reputation; let us not be concerned with flattering anyone but speak clearly in order to be understood by everyone. And let us be humble; let us not pretend to know everything, but rather listen to others. Let us change our methods if we wish to avoid speaking in a vacuum.

Let the Bishop Reform His Life   Three other French bishops also intervened. Bishop Sauvage of Annecy said, "Let us modify the structures of evangelization." Bishop Renard of Versailles stated, "The bishop is necessary to priests, but the opposite is also true; the bishop needs the advice of his priests." Auxiliary Bishop Maziers of Lyon asked that the bishop "change his personal life," that he "appear exteriorly as a witness to Christ and consequently live poorly," that he "mingle in the concrete life of his faithful as well as of unbelievers," and that he "constantly reform his life."

The other interventions were characterized by a concern for renewing the current image of bishops and the structures of diocesan government as well as by a dislike of the legal mentality.

A Scandalous Disparity   Thus Bishop Barrachina of Alicante declared:

> Let us find a more mystical and spiritual definition of the diocese. There are still too many categories of parishes and priests, some rich and others poor. This disparity works against priestly vocations and scandalizes the faithful. In the primitive Church, everything was held in common. Let us do the same thing today, insofar as we can; otherwise we have no right to speak of the Church of the poor.

Archbishop D'Souza of Bhopal, India, suggested that laymen be invited to join "diocesan councils" and that they be given real responsibilities. Bishop Herbert Bednorz, Coadjutor of Katowice, Poland, spoke of the dangers of individualism, and invited bishops to take initiatives "without waiting for directions from Rome." Archbishop Miguel Miranda y Gómez of Mexico City said missionary vocations ought to be coordinated with those of the laity. Bishop Juan Iriarte of Reconquista, Argentina, urged bishops to adapt to their age and become aware of the fact that they no longer live in "feudal" times; they must adopt a "new style of life" and incite the laity to dialogue.

Bishop Wilhelm Pluta of Gorzow, Poland, spoke in the name of the bishops of his country and referred to "the drama of abortions, which is a greater tragedy than is atheistic propaganda."

"Let us be simple and humble, as was John XXIII, and learn how to accept criticism," declared Bishop Leónidas Proano Villalba of Riobamba, Ecuador. Bishop Samuele Ruiz García of Chiapas, Mexico, reminded the assembly that episcopal conferences are necessary to draw the bishop out of his isolation.

Archbishop Baraniak of Poznan, in the name of all the bishops of Poland and Lithuania, emphasized the importance of migrations—the third time the subject has come up in eight days—and specified that John XXIII wanted Vatican II to deal explicitly with this question.

The voice of the Orient, always so profitable for the Council, was again heard through Maronite Archbishop Ziadé of Beirut. The schema, he said, is of no worth to the Orient, and he urged that another be drawn up that would be suitable to both the Occident and the Orient. The discrimination between the East and the West is obsolete and un-Christian. The Orient has had to beg unceasingly for the right to exist within the Roman Church, and this must stop. Let the Fathers center their attention on the Holy Spirit and the eucharist. What is the reason for the legalistic mentality found everywhere? A diocese is above all the efficacious sign of the Church. Let us say so.

New Auditors

The Fifteen Women Auditors   The Vatican has just released the names of the women auditors who will be permitted to follow some of the Council sessions.

There are eight religious: Mother Suzanne Guillemin (France), Superior General of the Daughters of Charity; Mother Sabine de Valon (France), Superior General of the Religious of the Sacred Heart; Mother Mary Luke (United States), Mother Marie de la Croix Khouzam (Egypt), Mother Marie-Henriette Ghanem (Lebanon), Sister Mary Juliana of Our Lord Jesus Christ (Germany), Mother Constantina Baldinucci (Italy), and Mother Estrada (Spain).

The seven laywomen are Miss Marie-Louise Monnet (France), named by the Pope himself; Dr. Alda Micelli (Italy), Miss Pilar Bellosillo (Spain), Miss Rosemary Goldie (Australia), Miss Anna Maria Roeloffzen (Netherlands), Marchioness Amalia Lanza (Italy), and Mrs. Iduccia Marenco (Italy).

The last two are war widows. The bulletin announcing their nomination noted that they were chosen to honor the suffering they represent, and that this choice constitutes both a condemnation of war and a symbol of the deepest aspirations of mankind for true Christian peace.

Eight New Laymen   Eight new laymen were named by the Pope as auditors: Baron Léon de Rosen (France), president of the International Union of Catholic Employers' Associations; Professor Luigi Gedda (Italy), president of the International Federation of Catholic Physicians; Mr. Patrick Keegan (England), president of the International Federation of Christian Workers' Movements; Mr. Bartolo Peres (Brazil), president of the International Young Christian Workers; Dr. José Maria Hernández (Philippines), president of the Catholic Action organization in that country; Mr. Eusébe Adjakpley (Togo), African secretary for the International Federation of Catholic Youth (male); Mr. Stephan Roman

(Canada), of the Byzantine Rite; and Mr. John Chen (Hong Kong), president of the Hong Kong Council for the Lay Apostolate.

The Council Opens the Important Debate on Religious Liberty

Six more votes on chapter 3 of the schema on the Church were cast during the general congregation on Wednesday. The results yielded a majority varying between 1,927, and 2,163 votes and a minority ranging from 56 to 307 votes. Thus, the assembly has completed nearly half the voting required for this chapter. The bulk of the session was devoted to the debate on religious liberty, and it did not fall short of expectations. It was worthy of a subject that is as difficult as it is momentous.

The challenge before Vatican II is to make reparation for past errors which the vicissitudes of history only partially excuse. Rome is still for many the country of the Inquisition and the Holy Office, responsible for or at least an accomplice to persecutions or injustices inflicted upon Protestants; more seriously, it is seen as the crucible where the disincarnate doctrine of intolerance was forged, founded on a philosophy which prefers principles to men, abstractions to situations. Happily there have always been laymen, theologians, and bishops in the Roman Church who have protested against such a philosophy, but only with John XXIII did this protest become official.

As a result of the deceased Pope's initiative, Cardinal Bea and his Secretariat for Promoting Christian Unity became the instrument of this doctrinal re-evaluation.

The consequences of this reversal are immense—for liberty is indivisible—and as yet can only be dimly seen. They will be felt both within the Church, where the right of study and pluralism in theologies and viewpoints will be increasingly recognized, and outside of the Church with respect to the Reformed churches, non-Christian religions, and freethinkers.

Considerably later than the secular forces for liberty, Vatican II has come to the defense of the cause of man, irrespective of belief, in the wake of a unique encyclical, *Pacem in terris.*

In a century of political totalitarianisms, it is high time the Church, which claims to be the authentic heir of the evangelical patrimony, solemnly proclaimed her belief in liberty.

The document presented on Wednesday for the approval of the

Fathers was a redraft of one distributed on November 19, 1963. The Secretariat for Promoting Christian Unity went back to work on the text on the basis of 380 observations, filling some 280 pages, which were submitted last year.

The present text seems more balanced than the former. It gives greater consideration not only to the individual but also to the collective aspect of religious liberty, and expresses more clearly the objective demands of divine law which give liberty of conscience its whole meaning.

Bishop de Smedt of Bruges, who was also the reporter of the declaration at the second session, said nonetheless that there were still improvements to be made in the presentation of this document. He enumerated some possible objections to points that were not yet quite clear. "Some will find the expression *religious liberty* unfortunate," he noted. "They would prefer the word *tolerance*." But this is not the mind of the commission, he said, for the issue is the basic liberty founded on the very nature of the human person. Paul VI used the expression *religious liberty* in an allocution in April, 1964. The sincere recognition of religious liberty is a fundamental factor in the notion of internal and external peace. Its ultimate basis is the fact that the human person was created free by God himself. On the simple natural level, man is called to be free. This vocation to liberty obliges us to search for the truth, and in this way the dangers of indifferentism and subjectivism are avoided.

"The limitation of liberty by the state poses very serious problems," the reporter admitted. But the state is an essentially "lay" organization, which is to say that it has no power to pass judgment on the truth of things religious and should under no circumstances make suggestions in this domain.

Bishop de Smedt asked the Fathers to help the commission perfect the document by means of their observations.

Nine cardinals and one bishop took the floor during the session. Their remarks fall into two categories: those in fundamental agreement with the schema and those expressing serious reservations. In other words, there are those who still prefer the theory of "thesis" and "hypothesis," and those who are trying to reach a more solid doctrine of liberty.

Cardinal Ruffini: "This Text Goes Against the Holy See" Let us begin with the negative interventions. Since the subject is so important, we will try to be as literal as possible in reporting them.

Cardinal Ruffini, Archbishop of Palermo, found the title "Religious Liberty" equivocal. He proposed instead "Man's Liberty To Choose His Religion," or "The Free Exercise of Religion." (It is worth recalling that at least three popes since the eighteenth century have called the notion of religious liberty "insane.")

"It is good to emphasize man's freedom because God has willed it," Cardinal Ruffini stated. "The Church rejects violence and has always condemned it," he added, seeming more convinced than convincing. Then he listed his objections:

1. "Let us never separate liberty from truth. The former is defined in relation to the second."
2. "Truth is one, and there is only one religion which in itself and of itself has the right to liberty. On the civil plain, it is quite different. Let us then speak of tolerance as a function of the common good. This distinction is absolutely necessary; otherwise we are on the wrong track and run the risk of scandalizing Catholics."
3. "The schema strays, unwittingly and despite all efforts to the contrary, into indifferentism and agnosticism."
4. "It is said on page 33 that the state is incompetent. But if this is so, how can there be a state religion? This denies the idea of a concordat, especially as concordats were understood in the past, but even today in such countries as Italy, Spain, and the Dominican Republic. This text thus goes against a strong tradition in the Church and against the Holy See itself. That is extremely serious."
5. "The schema says that Catholics must respect the liberty of non-Catholics. Can we imagine that this has not always been the case? This suspicion constitutes an insult."
6. "We must absolutely think of those who suffer because they are deprived of religious liberty, of our persecuted brothers. Let us comfort them."

Cardinal Ottaviani Flies to the Defense of Concordats Cardinal Ottaviani's intervention was a very calm one. He began by saying that everyone agreed with the principle enunciated in the schema, namely, that no one should be forced to practice a religion. He then listed his objections:

1. "The text says, 'Even he who is wrong is worthy of honor.' I don't like this. Error is never worthy of honor."
2. "The schema goes beyond ecumenical perspectives because it is addressed to all men. Now, I notice, as did Cardinal Ruffini, a substantial omission: there is no mention of the liberty of the faithful to observe the true religion. This is a matter not merely of a natural right but of a supernatural right. It is better to obey God than men. Let us speak then of the supernatural basis of religious liberty in

addition to reasons of a philosophical order. A council is a religious assembly and not a philosophical one."

3. "Let us always speak of what concerns liberty of conscience in relation to the divine law."

4. "It is said that the state is not competent. We would therefore have to abolish all concordats, which are however very useful. This doctrine is therefore erroneous."

5. "Different religious groups are said to be free to propagate their own faith. I do not agree. This goes too far. This was not Saint Paul's understanding when he forbade the propagation of false doctrine."

6. "What is said about proselytism could be misunderstood and injure the work of missionaries. Let us therefore be more prudent."

Cardinal Quiroga: "Will the Church Now Contradict Herself?" Cardinal Quiroga, Archbishop of Santiago de Compostela, said he was not asking that the text be suppressed but only that it be perfected.

1. "It was drafted by Cardinal Bea in terms of ecumenism but it lacks a pastoral character for Catholics, and it exposes the faithful to very serious perils. It also creates dangers for Catholic nations."

2. "Its doctrine is obscure on several points. It gives the impression that we want to adapt to modern times without concern for tradition. The transition from the past to the future is too abrupt."

3. "The formulation is too individualistic. Liberalism has often been condemned by the Church. Will the Church now cantradict herself?"

4. "It goes from the internal order to the external. This is incorrect. What is true for an individual is not true for a society."

The Cardinal concluded, "All this is serious enough to justify a total revision of the schema with the aid of new experts."

Cardinal Bueno y Monreal: "Liberty for False Religions Harms the One True Religion" Cardinal Bueno y Monreal, Archbishop of Seville, thought that the text was better than last year's but still "very equivocal." He criticized it chiefly for going on a doctrinal plane to the juridical and political planes and from personal liberty to collective liberty. "Doctrinally speaking, only one religion has the right of propagation," he said. "The others have not. But it is a different question on the political level. Any liberty that harms others must be restricted, the schema says. But liberty for false religions harms the one true religion." And the concluded, "We should adopt a practical point of view and not a doctrinal one."

Cardinal Léger in Total Agreement with the Schema Here is the second category of interventions, those of the Fathers who substantially agree with the declaration. Some of them would even like to see a stronger statement.

Cardinal Léger of Montreal, speaking in the name of the bishops of Canada, said that in proclaiming the right of persons or groups to religious liberty, the text responds to an urgent need. It is timely because:

1. It dissipates doubts about the exact meaning of the Church's doctrine.
2. It corresponds with the expectation of those who suffer persecution for their faith.
3. It fulfills a condition for a dialogue between Christians and non-Christians.

The Cardinal declared, "I laud the prudence of this text, which makes all the necessary distinctions and carefully guards against relativism and indifferentism. The document reminds us that to accept religious liberty in no way dispenses us from propagating the truth. The limits of religious liberty are clearly specified. Therefore, I adhere fully to the spirit and the substance of this text."

The Cardinal did suggest some improvements, however:

1. "Let us describe religious liberty in a way that will express not only the rights of Christians but also those of unbelievers. The present schema is restricted to the first viewpoint."
2. "It is important to formulate the basis of religious liberty in a way that is acceptable to all men of good will and not only Christians. But the schema speaks only of the duty to follow the will of God according to one's conscience (article 26) and of the excellence of the divine vocation of man (article 29).

"This kind of argument," the Cardinal explained, "cannot be accepted by unbelievers. Let us therefore add another basis. We might say, for example, that religious liberty is the highest and most sacred claim of man in the exercise of his reason. Thus would it be clear that no derogation of man himself is intended."

Cardinal Cushing: The Text "Must Remain Intact" Cardinal Cushing, Archbishop of Boston, made a moving intervention that was strongly applauded. He spoke in the name of nearly all the bishops of the United States and addressed himself explicitly to the "dearly beloved" non-Catholic observers:

We are dealing here with a question that is essential for the life of the Church and for civil life. This is the first time that the Church has solemnly expressed her doctrine on this point. All men are waiting to see what we will say. It is a crucial issue for America. Should we amend this text? If it be for the purpose of making it stronger, yes; to weaken it, never! It must remain intact. The Church must declare herself the protagonist of religious liberty in the world.

Throughout her history, the Church has demanded liberty for herself. She has a right to it. Today she demands a similar liberty for all men without exception. The doctrinal principles which form the basis of this right to religious liberty are contained in the encyclical *Pacem in terris*, which has had such great repercussions everywhere.

Cardinal Meyer: "The Schema Will Make Ecumenical Dialogue Possible"

Cardinal Meyer, Archbishop of Chicago, stated:

> The schema is very necessary, and men of our time expect this declaration. Let us demonstrate that what is essential is a free and sincere conscience. The schema will make ecumenical dialogue possible. We must take our stand on this platform of the rights of the human person. Without this declaration, our separated brethren would doubt our sincerity, and with good reason. Without this declaration, whatever else the Council might say would not be accepted by the world.

Cardinal Ritter, Archbishop of St. Louis, thought that "Since it is a matter of natural right, religious liberty is only a particular case of human liberty." Speaking as a practical man, the Cardinal declared: "If the theological bases of this religious liberty are uncertain, then let us not talk of them, and let us restrict ourselves to the fundamental respect for man. This would be shorter and better, and it would win the approval of the whole world."

Cardinal Silva Henríquez: Proselytism Is a "Corruption of Witness"

In the name of fifty Latin American bishops, Cardinal Silva Henríquez, Archbishop of Santiago, Chile, also emphasized the importance of the text for men all over the world:

> Throughout the world, we must dissipate the opinion that Catholics are opportunists and that they apply a double standard depending on whether they are strong or weak. In our pluralistic age, let us demonstrate that the Church is the light of nations. This year the United Nations prepared a document on religious liberty which well expresses contemporary public opinion. . . .

For Latin America, where our people are attached to outmoded ways of thinking, this declaration has a very special interest. Modern man demands that we adapt our methods in terms of the evolution of democratic society. It is important that our sincerity be made perfectly clear. The schema warns against proselytism. [Proselytism] in fact represents a corruption of witness. It has the air of seeking the gain of a human institution without hesitating to intimidate, solid material bait.

An Appeal to the United Nations Finally, the Bishop of Skoplje, Yugoslavia, Bishop Smiljan Cekada, spoke of totalitarianism (Nazism and Communism) and their dogmatic character. He proposed that the Council address an appeal to the United Nations asking the organization to proclaim that the state must respect the law of religious liberty for all and to specify how it might be applied in practice. He also suggested that a special commission be charged with drawing up this appeal.

SEPTEMBER 25

Violent Attacks Against the Religious Liberty Draft

There was a veritable barrage against the declaration on religious liberty in St. Peter's on Thursday. Half of the eighteen Fathers who intervened made every effort to demolish the schema. At first sight this proportion is disconcerting, but it can be explained by considering the background and formation of the prelates in question. They see in the declaration a real collapse of a world based on a tradition which has been well rooted since the days of Gregory XVI and Pius IX, the slayer of liberalism.

But the moment seems undeniably to have come when the Church is finally going to recognize religious liberty for what it is: a highly precious value which follows necessarily from freedom of conscience, which is taught moreover by canon law in the statement that conscience binds even when it is erroneous (*consciencia etiam erronea ligat*). Saint Thomas illustrated this truth forcefully when he said that if a man thought the Christian faith was false, he would have a strict duty not to adhere to it.

The conciliar declaration is concerned above all with affirming that not only the Catholic religion but other Christian and non-Christian religions as well have the right to express themselves. In paragraph 29 we read, "The Catholic Church affirms that religious liberty must be observed not only by Christians and for Christians but by and for all men and all religious groups in human society."

The schema strongly emphasizes the collective aspect of religious liberty and the state's incompetence in matters religious. Thus, on pages 31 and 32 it is written, "The heads of governments are not permitted to impose upon their people the profession or repudiation of any religion as a condition of participating fully or partially in national or civic life."

Violent or insidious attacks on the declaration cannot but make a bad impression on public opinion. But it is important to define their meaning and influence. That twenty bishops out of the more than 2,200 Fathers gathered at the Council feel the need to communicate their narrow and retrograde ideas to the assembly is not very alarming. Freedom of expression in the Council, (especially on such a subject!) is strictly enforced. It is altogether healthy that each can speak in all spontaneity. It is also good that some Fathers forcefully point out that the doctrine defended in this text seems to contradict various texts of Pius IX and even Pius XII, for a council does not meet to repeat what popes have said but to clarify doctrine.

It is at any rate comforting to note that so weak a minority is taking exception to a text that from all appearances will be definitively approved after the improvements mentioned by the reporter have been incorporated.

The opposing interventions can be further divided into two classes: those which are opposed to the schema as such, and those which are in substantial agreement but which call for modifications and complements. Here is the substance of both groups.

"Totally Unacceptable" Cardinal Browne of the Curia: In its present form, the declaration is totally unacceptable. Nor is it necessary for peace. It is too individualistic. It is incorrect to give equal status to a conscience which adheres to the truth and one which adheres to falsehood, even though it is sincere. John XXIII never said this in *Pacem in terris*. He spoke of a correct conscience. The present doctrine is contrary to a statement made by Pius XII in 1946. Cardinal Ritter, who intervened yesterday, is right. Let us not advance theological principles that are not certain.

Archbishop Parente, Assessor of the Holy Office: "Although much improved over last year's version, this declaration is not exempt from serious shortcomings. It does not speak enough about the objective value of truth. What is said about the laicism of the state is not clear enough. A variety of extremely delicate and complex questions of the historical, juridical, social, psychological, and religious orders are treated indiscriminately; they should be handled separately with precision and prudence. It is not necessary or even useful for the Council to enter a jungle of multiple and difficult problems. Side by side with statements that are accepted by all we find others which are highly controversial and which, far from meeting with the consent of all specialists, are likely to stir up different reactions in many countries. Because of this possible disagreement, we must correct the text so that it affirms only what is certain. The declaration could contain principles concerning the dignity of man, freedom of conscience, the right of the Church to spread the Gospel, the right of all to practice religion, and the duty of the state to respect all religions. Afterwards, then another declaration could be added, in the form of an appendix, explaining the mind of the Church on these different principles.

"*A Scandal*" Bishop Abasolo y Lecue (India): Under no circumstances can we maintain that an erroneous conscience has the same rights as any other. In itself conscience can only be followed if it is objectively correct. Only truth has rights. Only the Catholic Church has absolute rights in its internal and external judgment seat. Good faith is not enough. Sincerity and truth are two different things. To accept the declaration as it is would be a scandal. It would amount to proclaiming the right not to reject error and even the right to sow error, which is absurd.

We might note that this speaker paid no heed to the paragraph in the schema which states, "Error must be rejected, the truth preached, and intelligence enlightened. But in the love for truth, we must abstain from all coercion, whether direct or indirect."

"*Must Be Radically Transformed*" Bishop José López Ortiz (Spain): This text must be radically transformed. The political doctrine expressed here takes no account of natural rights. It gives the impression of attacking the Catholic state. There are still, happily, Catholic states. It is too bad there aren't more of them.

"*Opposed to the Doctrine of Leo XIII and Pius XII*" Bishop António de Castro Mayer (Brazil): The doctrine exposed here is altogether opposed to the traditional doctrine of Leo XIII and Pius XII, which holds that error has no rights but that it may be granted rights to avoid a greater evil. It is absurd to say that someone in error is worthy of honor.

Bishop Canestri (Italy), Auxiliary to the Cardinal Vicar of Rome, caused the Fathers a painful moment. It is difficult to understand how a bishop could make such statements in the presence of the Protestant observers, who were expressly invited to St. Peter's by the Pope. He said, "Let us take the example of a priest who converts to Protestantism. Has he the right to religious liberty? Absolutely not, for he cannot be

344 THE DRAMA OF VATICAN II

in good faith and can only be acting for motives of money, ambition, or pride."

The above was reported to us by the head of the French press service, whose coverage is as complete and objective as possible. But his embarrassment was increased by the fact that Pastor Marc Boegner, an observer at the Council, was in the audience that day, an audience that is composed for the most part of members of the French-language press.

The same Bishop added that the declaration seems to justify conscientious objectors and condemn Catholic states. This is not progress and is contrary to article 79 of the *Syllabus* of Pius IX. Likewise, what is said about the neutrality of the state is contrary to the teaching of Leo XIII. What we must do is proclaim the absolute and universal right of the Catholic religion throughout the world.

"The Schema Should Be Redrafted" Archbishop Lefebvre, Superior General of the Holy Ghost Fathers: The schema seems to say that we need new principles because of circumstances. But every right is founded on the right of the Catholic religion. The dictates of conscience are not a criterion for the morality of actions. The schema smacks of relativism and idealism. If we approve it, it would be the end of the veneration which even unbelievers have for the Church, and it would be a scandal.

Auxiliary Bishop Anastasio Granados García of Toledo thought that "The doctrine expounded here is contrary to Catholic tradition, according to which only truth has rights. Is this progress? No. It is impossible to put truth and error on the same plane." The Bishop added that under modern conditions religious liberty must be encouraged and defended insofar as possible and must be recognized by all. But we must proceed with great prudence. The schema should be redrafted and the services of other experts enlisted.

"The Schema Pleases Me Thoroughly" Here now is the second group of interventions. Cardinal Koenig, Archbishop of Vienna: This schema pleases me very much. It is a sincere defense of liberty. But let us also speak of those who have no religious liberty. Let us be clear in demanding religious liberty in countries where the Church is persecuted. This world sins against tolerance, against pluralism, and even against scientific principles. The true scholar does not seek truth with ready-made dogmas. There is nothing more stupid than preventing someone from expressing a sincere conviction from the scientific point of view. This world also sins against its own good, because it deprives itself of useful cooperation. And finally, it sins against the dignity of man. I most strongly urge that we

find a suitable way to state this. Let states recognize the distinction between *ratio gouvernandi* and atheism.

"Let Us Change the Basis of Religious Liberty" Archbishop Cantero of Saragossa: Let us take our point of departure from the fact of a pluralistic society and seek the basis of this fact in human dignity and the role of the state. The old theory of thesis and antithesis is not necessary. Let us distinguish between freedom of conscience and religious freedom. I accept the conclusions of the schema, but we must seek another basis for them.

Archbishop Nicodemo of Bari: This declaration is very timely. It is expected by the whole world. But we are neither a political assembly nor a philosophical assembly; we are a council, for which there can be but one guide—the religious liberty of Christ. Error may have a "putative" right but not a real one.

Father Joseph Buckley, Prior General of the Marist Fathers: Let us be real defenders of religious liberty and thus furnish an answer to historical objections; but let us base religious liberty on the obligation every man has to follow his conscience and not on man's "divine vocation" to God as does the text. We must admit that all men of good faith follow a divine vocation even if they are in error. The evident falseness of this conclusion indicates that the present basis must be rejected.

Bishop Primeau of Manchester, New Hampshire: I am for the schema, but I think that there is a close connection between personal religious liberty and social religious liberty.

Bishop Pieter Nierman of Groningen, in the name of the Dutch bishops and of some Indonesians: I am in favor of the schema, but let us draw some practical consequences from it for the Church herself. In mixed marriages, for example, we should take the conclusions of the schema into account and accord the same rights to both partners. Let us reform canon law on this point. This is of great importance, because it involves our sincerity with respect to what is said here.

"Liberty and Progress Are Connected" Bishop Klepacz, in the name of the bishops of Poland: I agree with the schema. We must affirm that no human power has the right to prevent man from professing his religion in public or private, or to impose another philosophical credo on him by force or trickery. Religious persecution must be considered as a violation of a fundamental right of man. Another principle upon which we base religious liberty is justice, which binds individuals, society, and the state. Propaganda which uses lies, distortion of facts, and trickery violates

justice. Finally, we must say that religious liberty and the progress of mankind are connected.

"Refer to the Bible" Archbishop Dubois of Besançon: The schema pleases me in general, but it is too philosophical and juridical in form. We should introduce a religious basis worthy of the Council by drawing on Scripture, where we read, for example, that God makes his sun shine on all men, that tares must grow with the good grain, that Christ did not resort to violence to defend himself during the passion, and that Christians should be the salt of the earth and the light of the world. Let us also draw inspiration from the Fathers of the Church, particularly Saint Augustine.

This intervention impressed the Protestant observers, who are in the main shocked that this schema is practically devoid of biblical references.

SEPTEMBER 2 6

Cardinal Bea Presents the Report
on the Declaration Concerning the Jews

Examination of the declaration on Jews and non-Christians will begin in St. Peter's Monday. On Friday Cardinal Bea, president of the Secretariat for Promoting Christian Unity, was invited by the moderator, Cardinal Suenens, to present his report on this text. He did so quietly and skillfully.

There was palpable human warmth in the words of this German prelate, who feels jointly responsible with his country for the greatest genocide of all time. The former confidant of John XXIII is among the few cardinals who best communicate the heritage of the deceased Pope. Cardinal Bea said:

> In speaking on the schema of the declaration "Jews and Non-Christians," I can only begin with the fact that this declaration certainly must be counted among the questions which have aroused the greatest public interest. Scarcely any other schema has been so widely talked about. Whatever the reasons for this interest and whatever judgment we may make concerning its value, the very fact of the concern shows clearly that . . . many will judge the Council good or bad by its approval or disapproval of the declaration.
>
> Certainly this is not the only or even the principal reason the declaration is necessary. In the first place it is required by the Church's fidelity in following the example of Christ and the apostles

in their love for this people. Nonetheless, these external reasons must not be overlooked. They make it entirely evident that it is quite impossible to do what some of the Fathers have asked—namely, remove the question completely from the agenda.

. . . the schema now consists of two parts, almost equal in length, one concerning the Jews, the other concerning non-Christians.

With regard to the first part, . . . some new ideas have been added, principally two texts from the epistle to the Romans, on the prerogatives of the chosen people (9:4) and on the Christian hope for the final gathering together of this people with the chosen people of the New Testament, that is, the Church (11:25).

The central point on which major changes were introduced is the question of "deicide," as it is called. It should be noted that the [suppression of the term] has been very fully discussed in the press, but that this occurred without any cooperation or intervention by the Secretariat.

The Cardinal then took up the arguments apropos of the term *deicide*, arguments which he is very convinced of. And let us recall that it was not the Secretariat but the Coordinating Commission which suppressed this passage in the present version.

Is the Accusation of Deicide Valid? Were the Jews a deicide race, the Cardinal asked? The reason a negative answer is desirable is that many who are anti-Semitic use this argument as a pretext. There is no doubt, the Cardinal pointed out, that in the course of history the Jewish people were often called a deicide race. That is why the Jews deplore the deletion of the word.

Cardinal Bea then gave several examples, but did not—undoubtedly out of respect for the Coordinating Commission—take sides.

Certainly the leaders of the Jewish Sanhedrin, even if not democratically chosen by the people, were considered and are to be considered as the lawful authority of the people, in accordance with the mentality of the times and of Sacred Scripture itself.

. . . But the leaders of the people in Jerusalem did not fully understand the divinity of Christ in such a way that they could be formally called deicides. On the cross the Lord prayed to his Father and said, "Father, forgive them, for they know not what they do" (Luke 23:34). . . . Saint Peter also, speaking to the Jewish people about the Lord's crucifixion, said, "I know that you acted through ignorance, as did your leaders" (Acts 3:17). . . . And Saint Paul speaks in a similar fashion in Acts 13:27.

Besides, whatever we may say of the knowledge of the leaders in Jerusalem, the whole Jewish people of that time as such never can be charged with what was done by the leaders in Jerusalem to bring about the death of Christ. . . . And even if we granted [such a charge], which we do not, by what right may those acts be blamed on the Jewish people of today?

No Political Intrusion Will Be Tolerated   Cardinal Bea then said that the declaration was necessary for the cause of ecumenism. He stressed the purely religious character of the text, stating that "we do not treat here any political question whatever." The Church's renewal is so important, he said, that "we must pay the price of accepting the danger that some may misuse this declaration for political purposes." The Cardinal ended his speech vigorously with these words: "In these questions the Church and the Council will tolerate no intrusion of political authority or motives."

Three Important Interventions and a Conference on the Religious Liberty Schema

The assembly had previously heard eleven interventions on religious liberty, after which discussion of the subject was in principle closed. With the exception of Archbishop Hurley of Durban, South Africa, Archbishop Garrone of Toulouse, and Titular Bishop Carlo Colombo of Victoriana, Italy, the speakers said little that was new.

It was noted that Bishop Colombo, a personal friend of the Pope's and one of his favorite theologians, spoke last, as if he had been given the right to sum up the conclusions of the arguments. The debate has at times been perilous, at times sterile, but in the final analysis it has been more constructive than destructive if we weigh the value of the positive arguments against the archaic objections—which are always the same— offered by the conservatives.

Francesco Cardinal Roberti of the Curia asked that the ambiguous expression "freedom of conscience," which he said is likely to be identified with indifferentism, be replaced by "freedom of consciences." The Cardinal then expressed his agreement with the schema as a whole.

The Right To Err   Archbishop Hurley has the rare merit of clarifying problems through historical arguments and recognizing "the right to be wrong." He said:

Certain statements in this schema seem to contradict the magisterium of the nineteenth century and the public rights of the Church. This is because a social and historical evolution has taken place. In classical theory, the ideal was union of church and state. If we adopt this perspective, the schema is unacceptable. But this is not a good way of looking at the problem, because the Church was instituted by God to be concerned with religious life. Consequently, the state has no rights to act in the domain reserved to the Church. If it does so, it takes the place of the Church, and this is regrettable. From this standpoint, the schema is a worthy one. The union of church and state is dangerous but they can come to an agreement with one another for the common good. . . .

We must accept the danger of error. We cannot embrace truth without having some experience of error. We must therefore speak of the right to seek and to err. Liberty is a condition of conquering truth.

Bishop Ubaldo Cibrián Fernández of Corocoro, Bolivia, thought that "The schema is erroneous because it seems to admit that doctrine can evolve. But the truth is immutable." This is a surprising assertion since Christ said that he was not only "the truth" but also "the life." The history of the Church proves, moreover, that doctrine is subject to certain changes as a consequence of the deepening of revealed truths and the fallibility of theologians. Dogma itself develops.

The Danger of Laxity   Exiled Archbishop Melendro of Anking, China, found that there are "many defects" in the schema. "The Catholic Church," he said, "has a right to liberty *ex jure divino*. Other churches do not." Man's dignity does not come from his freedom but from the use he makes of that freedom to adhere to the truth. The state must protect the Church and adhere to the true God. The Archbishop felt that the schema is guilty of laxity, and that the doctrine expounded in it will do much harm. The way it has been reported in the papers is regrettable, he said; the true faith has been called into doubt. The schema should therefore be suppressed, and the Council should restrict itself to a general declaration.

Archbishop Wojtyla of Cracow was of the opinion that the text does not state clearly enough, following Christ, that only "the truth will make us free." He went on, "The human person, contrary to what materialistic and atheistic philosophy holds, is not an economic pawn. It is transcendental."

Archbishop Karl J. Alter of Cincinnati spoke of the criticism leveled against Catholics for not being sincere, since they demand liberty when they are a minority but do not grant it to others when they are a majority. "This causes considerable prejudice and ought to cease altogether after the Council," he said. "The changes effected by democratic regimes have important repercussions on the Church. Countries like Spain which enjoy special privileges should renounce them for the good of the whole Church."

Truth Does Not Depend on the Majority   Father Fernández, Master General of the Dominicans, approved the intentions of the schema but criticized its logic.

> Let us not fall into the error of those who are always inclined to canonize the ideas of the moment. We must not confuse the conclusions of sociology with the truth. Truth does not depend on the majority. I side with Cardinals Browne and Ritter and Archbishop Parente in asking for a much less ponderous declaration that is based on sure principles. . . .
>
> This schema smacks of naturalism. It does not speak of the relationship between man and God. . . . We are wrong to seek a new doctrine in *Pacem in terris,* which is being poorly interpreted.

Bishop Cornelius Lucey of Cork and Ross, Ireland, made this strange statement: "It is difficult to suppose that atheistic Communists are in good faith. Everyone knows they are all in bad faith. However," he added, "if God does not force men, and if he wishes them to be free, how could the state coerce them?"

The Archbishop of Toulouse as Conciliator   Archbishop Garrone made a very interesting intervention in the role of a conciliator:

> It is somewhat difficult to discuss this question as it is presented in the schema, because it is not clearly stated that there is a doctrinal continuity between the past and the future. If we do not show that there is a logical development, our sincerity will be doubted. Doctrine has not changed, but totally different relations between people and the state have come to pass.
>
> In former times the state had absolute power. Everyone thought that there was a necessary connection between the state and religion. *Cuius regio eius religio* was a principle admitted by both Protestants and Catholics. Today the state is pluralistic. This evolution is the consequence of the influence of the Gospel, which promotes the holy

secularization of the state and the increased dignity of the human person.

Archbishop Garrone boldly confronted the thorny question of the *Syllabus*. "It comes essentially to this," he said:

1. The exclusive value of truth in itself.
2. The evil of error in itself.
3. The obligation to seek the truth (this was directed against indifferentism).
4. The right of the Church to preach the truth. It is evident that this right is an evangelical one and is not to be imposed by the state.

"Let us consider, the historical context, which obliges us today to adopt a subjective perspective, and let us take account of the growth of the human person."

Archbishop Garrone called for a supplementary paragraph pointing out that there is no contradiction in the principles of doctrine but that there is a human evolution owing to a deeper understanding of the Gospel. He suggested that "We should ask pardon for the past errors of the Church in this matter."

Dialogue Is Necessary for the Discovery of Truth Bishop Colombo developed a line of thought that made a strong impression on the assembly since everyone in the aula knows that his thinking is close to the Pope's.

First point: method. "This declaration," he began, "is an extremely important one. For those of us from Italy, it is the salient point of the Council. If it does not come to fruition, it will spell the end of dialogue. Let us therefore work with zeal.

"As to its substance, this schema pleases me greatly," the Bishop continued, "but let us restudy and specify more clearly the basis of religious liberty." Though it has been suggested that a general declaration would be sufficient, Bishop Colombo did not agree, feeling that the schema must be based on the doctrine of the Church. "It is fitting, therefore, to furnish all the doctrinal principles necessary. Nobody of good faith should be able to say that there is a compromise between the truth of the Church and pastoral exigences."

Second point: the bases. Bishop Colombo next outlined the bases for the right to religious liberty:

1. "There is a natural right to seek the truth, especially in the religious domain. The first person to state this absolutely clearly was Cardinal Montini, on December 5, 1962, when he spoke of the rights of men to

seek the truth." John XXIII has said the same thing. Whoever opposes this fundamental liberty commits an injustice. Two consequences can be drawn from this:

a. Freedom of study.
b. The common pooling of these studies to find the truth, for "if there is no dialogue among men, they will not find integral truth." There must therefore be social communication. This is a good, not an evil.

2. "The second basis is the right and obligation to follow one's conscience, especially in religious matters."

3. "The third basis is of the supernatural order. There can be no authentic act of faith if it is not free. From this it follows that the state has absolutely no right to interfere in religious matters. Let the state confine itself to the natural order."

"These three bases justify the conclusions of the schema: individual religious liberty and the liberty of religious groups," Bishop Colombo said. "The common good is the only limitation. This holds everywhere and always, whether Catholics are a minority or a majority. Thus we have a solid doctrine."

In conclusion he said, "We have the right to seek truth by using means apt to this end and listening to the magisterium. . . . Revealed truth has a value for every society, even on the natural plane. Religious truth is not given to states, but religious truth can be a great benefit for states."

Monsignor Pavan Speaks on Religious Liberty   Monsignor Pietro Pavan, a professor at the Lateran University, a personal friend of John XXIII's, and the chief coauthor of *Pacem in terris,* delivered a speech on religious liberty at the Dutch Documentation Center that was characterized by the realism, optimism, and insight into "signs of the times" which accounted for the success of *Pacem in terris.*

"I have the misfortune to be optimistic," he said. "Also I am convinced that secular states will be more numerous in the future, for these reasons: (1) monolithism is giving way to pluralism, (2) social mobility (population shifts) is increasing, and (3) the tendency to rationalize all human activity is increasing daily."

It is to be noted that Monsignor Pavan, together with a good many theologians, considers the secular state as the ideal, thus definitively breaking with the theory that defends the Catholic state, a theory that has been defended by more than one Council Father.

A Serious Blow to the Traditional Doctrine of Tolerance

The debates on religious liberty which have just terminated contain rich lessons. In the first place, they show the average doctrinal level of most of the schema's adversaries. It is the level of a textbook theology which systematically ignores contemporary works and has remained imprisoned in the outlook of the nineteenth century, when defenders of liberty were automatically Modernists (in the precise sense of that word) or religiously indifferent.

The deep meaning of the evolution of ideas and morals in the twentieth century escapes these Fathers, as the historical conjuncture of the last century escapes a minority of progressive Fathers. Thus, the latter tend to become indignant without trying to understand the context of the doctrinal hardening that then set in. If Gregory XVI and Pius XI were such extremists, it was because they were responding to the polemical stance of the enemies of religion. This doesn't make them right, but it does explain why they acted as they did and gives them the benefit of attenuating circumstances.

Thesis and Hypothesis We have also learned from the debates that the so-called theory of thesis and hypothesis is obsolete. This theory was first propounded by a Roman journalist in the October 2, 1863, issue of *Civiltà Cattolica*. But its great propagator was Bishop Dupanloup of Orléans, after Pius IX's *Syllabus of Errors* was published in 1864.

What does this theory hold? The thesis consists in the ideal and abstract rule of conduct, and this was the subject of the pontifical directives of the time, which were norms more of thought than of action. The thesis, then, bears little relationship to facts. We might almost say, with no pun intended, that it is an intellectual hypothesis, a vision of the spirit.

The hypothesis, on the other hand, is the rule of conduct that takes circumstances and situations into account. It is therefore real and not theoretical. Translated into terms of the present discussion, a doctrine of intolerance of other religions ("Since they are in error, they have no right to exist") is giving way to a doctrine of tolerance ("Let us support other religions since in the nature of the case we cannot do otherwise. If error has no rights, those in error do. Their existence is a necessary evil; therefore, let us strive to get along with them").

The thesis-hypothesis theory undeniably rendered great service in an age when the *Syllabus* was stirring up such tempests. It was a very useful means of appeasement. But it is no less certain that this doctrine set up a dangerous dichotomy between principles and reality—over-emphasizing the former and devaluating the latter—and led finally to according "favors," with little grace and a highly uncharitable kind of condescension, to persons who otherwise would not have been thought to deserve them in circumstances where the Church was a power.

In sum, this theory is the negation of the real meaning of liberty, a liberty which gives first place to respect for the human person who was created free by God and his "right to error," which Archbishop Hurley proclaimed on Friday.

The conciliar debate clarified this crucial issue for the Catholic Church. Vatican II has delivered a mortal blow to the classical doctrine of tolerance. Historians will record this doctrinal revolution—for it is indeed that—which, in the final analysis, has occurred smoothly enough. The Council in itself had already marked the end of the Constantinian era and the era of intellectual and spiritual tyranny, punctuated in the course of history by the condemnation of John Huss (burned alive in 1415), Galileo's retraction (1633), and other crimes of the Inquisition, and more recently by the unbelievable methods of the Holy Office, which has literally tortured so many consciences. For good reason have so many bishops voiced criticism of those methods. By way of example, we might recall the press conference which Archbishop Roberts, formerly of Bombay, gave in Rome on October 22, 1963, in which he declared that the members of the Holy Office employ methods for which they could be arrested if they were in Great Britain.

Suspicion and Integralism   Two bishops have made astonishing statements in the last few days. One said that a Catholic priest who converted to Protestantism could only do so in bad faith; the other said that an atheistic Communist could not be sincere ("Everyone knows they are all in bad faith," he exclaimed). To these bishops and those like them, it is so evident that Catholicism is the only true religion that to be a Marxist or a Protestant is unthinkable. These remarks horrified many auditors, and they are indicative of an attitude that is still fairly widespread in certain Catholic countries. Such an attitude evinces a scarcely believable narrow-mindedness and total lack of even a rudimentary awareness of the other. This sectarianism is strictly incompatible with the justice and hence necessarily the charity demanded by the Gospel.

It devolved to the Pope's personal theologian, Bishop Colombo, to defend the schema on religious liberty most vigorously and with the greatest depth. He insisted that it be securely founded on doctrine so that its importance could not be taken lightly. Bishop Colombo proclaimed not only the right to liberty and study, which has been scoffed at so often by the Holy Office in the past, but also the necessity of dialogue to find the truth. To consider dialogue as an indispensable source of truth constitutes a significant step forward in Catholic thinking. "If there is no dialogue among men, they will not find integral truth," said Bishop Colombo. One needs no great knowledge of the ecclesiastical mind to perceive the singularity of this position, a position that in a real sense is the mainspring of all ecumenism. We recall, too, the importance Paul VI attached to dialogue in his recent encyclical.

Finally, Vatican II has broached the difficult problem of a proselytism which, as the schema says, employs "improper and dishonest means." This corresponds with a preoccupation of the World Council of Churches regarding the sometimes unfair competition between missionaries of different confessions.

In conclusion, we may say that Vatican II has shaken the conviction widely held by Catholics that doctrine is unchangeable. The whole course of the Council has proven the contrary; everything that is not strictly an article of faith is subject to changes according to the well-known adage, *Ecclesia semper reformanda*. This has surprised some non-Catholic observers, who were convinced that the Church's thinking was monolithic. To be sure, these changes do not amount to a total denial of the past— this would be contrary to the principle of continuity of a society founded upon tradition—but they are not for all that less real and are sometimes very profound.

The traditions of the Church are multiple and discordant. Cardinal Verdier used to remark humorously, "The Church loves traditions too much not to invent new ones." This is what Vatican II is doing, without failing to go back to the sources. For in the final analysis, the Church considers herself the heir of Christ and has no other ambition than always to remain faithful to him.

SEPTEMBER 29

Four Last Interventions
in Favor of the Religious Liberty Declaration

There are many ways to get rid of an enemy: kill him, make him recant, imprison him, silence him by preventing him from saying or writing a word, calumniate him, ignore him and refuse to dialogue with him, make him suspect by condemning him without letting him defend himself. The Roman Church has used all of these means over the centuries and continues to use the last mentioned. Thus we cannot be too grateful for the declaration on religious liberty, which would nip the possibility of such actions in the bud.

After some of the interventions last week, it was a real relief for most of the Fathers to hear four speeches yesterday, Monday, the last to be delivered at Vatican II on this subject. Since discussion was theoretically closed, the bishops were permitted to speak only because they were spokesmen for at least seventy Fathers, a fact that lends singular weight to their pronouncements.

Archbishop Heenan of Westminster spoke in the name of the bishops of England and Wales, Scotland, Ireland, New Zealand, Belgium, and other countries. In realistic English fashion, the Archbishop recalled the religious wars in Great Britain and the innumerable persecutions which victimized both Catholics and Protestants. He noted that in England Anglicanism was the state religion but that this in no way diminished religious liberty for all.

> We approve this schema unreservedly. Let us proclaim a religious liberty that is valid for all countries without exception. People will say that error is a danger. To be sure! Error is an evil, but lack of freedom is an even greater evil. Moreover, who would set limits to religious liberty? The state? Experience proves that whenever this is done, the results are bad. . . .
>
> All religions should be juridically equal. Let us no longer speak of tolerating an evil; let us speak of religious liberty as a good. . . . Let the declaration be based on doctrine; otherwise we will be accused of opportunism. The world must know absolutely that we want religious liberty for all men without exception.

Archbishop Heenan's intervention was loudly applauded. (Let us recall that applause is forbidden, but the moderators seem to have given up enforcing the regulation.)

A Universal Declaration   Bishop Hadrianus Ddungu of Masaka, Uganda, spoke in the name of seventy bishops from Africa and Madagascar, and remarked that in Africa the Muslims and Communists tend to restrict the liberty of Catholics. He asked therefore that the schema not limit itself to speaking of the rights of Catholics but that it be more clearly universal, if possible.

Bishop Wright of Pittsburgh spoke of the dynamic and evolutionary character of the common good. He added this important remark and was thus the first to formulate it so categorically: "We do not conquer errors by force but by the light of Christ and the Gospel. Whatever may have been the case in the past, today religious liberty should be based on doctrine."

The Thesis-Hypothesis Theory Is "Two-Faced" Finally, Archbishop Zoa of Yaounde took the floor in the name of several African bishops who had not yet intervened publicly. "Nothing is more necessary," he said, "than this declaration on religious liberty. The Council is a world fact, and it is normal for it to adopt a universal outlook. Our proclamation ought to concern all mankind."

The Negro Archbishop also expressed clearly what a majority of bishops think in a more or less confused way about the thesis-hypothesis theory. "It is two-faced," he said. "It causes us to be accused of opportunism. . . . We must state doctrinally that no human power can go against the dignity of the human person and that all coercion in the religious domain must be repudiated."

In concluding, the Archbishop asked that those Christians now suffering for their faith not be forgotten.

Thus the debate on religious liberty ended. It remains only to wait for the voting on this chapter, which will take place when the competent commission has incorporated the changes requested by the Fathers.

Near-Unanimity of the Fathers
Indicates That the New Draft on the Jews Is Inferior

Vatican II now moves on to a no less exciting debate on the declaration concerning the Jews, Muslims, and other non-Christians. The constructiveness and concurrence of the interventions on this subject are striking. Almost all defend the Jews and ask that the present text be strengthened. This is a brilliant victory for Cardinal Bea and a severe blow to the Coordinating Commission, which believed the first draft was too strong.

"We Are All Sons of Abraham" Cardinal Liénart opened fire. He had not spoken in a general congregation since November 5 of last year. The Bishop of Lille and dean of the French cardinals is a man for solemn occasions.

"The opportuneness of this declaration on the Jews and non-Christians has been very much disputed, especially in the East. This can be explained by the strong political tensions between the Jews and the Arabs.

But an ecumenical council must put itself on a religious and not a political plane." In this connection, the Cardinal said, the declaration is necessary for two reasons.

1. *To fulfill the ecumenical aim of Vatican II.*

> We wish to unite all Christians. Thus, we cannot forget that the Jewish people is the root [in Latin, *stirps*] of all the Christian churches. All Christians have been grafted onto the olive tree of the Jewish people. By our faith we are all sons of Abraham. [Many Fathers were reminded of the celebrated saying of Pius XII, "Spiritually, we are all Semites."]
>
> We share with the Jewish people the economy of salvation until the coming of Christ. The Son of God chose to be a Jew. Mary and the apostles were likewise Jewish. We should therefore show special reverence to the Jewish people. . . .
>
> I insist that we keep the [old] text of the declaration in its entirety. That is a minimum.

2. *To fulfill the pastoral aim of Vatican II.*

> [The declaration] is a requirement of truth as well as of charity. Peter and Paul never considered the Jews as a lost race. It is they who received the promise, and as Saint Paul says, "God does not repent of his gifts." One day the Jews will return to the faith. Let us therefore avoid anything that could give the impression that we consider this people outcast. . . .
>
> Moreover, let it not be said that they are a deicide nation. Christ was killed by ignorance. The fault of the Jewish people is in not having believed in Christ's divinity. They therefore cannot be deicide. Furthermore, the Council of Trent says explicitly that all men share in the responsibility for Christ's death. Let us therefore strengthen the new text, which does not speak of this.

The Reply of the Orientals Cardinal Tappouni, Patriarch of Antioch, then mounted the platform and spoke in the name of all the Oriental patriarchs (except for the Maronites, who only arrived today), that is, for six patriarchs and their vicars:

> I urgently request that this totally unsuitable declaration be abandoned immediately. It is not that we are against the Jewish religion or for discrimination. Moreover, we are nearly all Semites [in fact, only the Armenians are Indo-Europeans]. We do not want this declaration because it would cause very serious pastoral difficulties.

It is said back home that the Council is pro-Jewish, and this does us much harm.

Cardinal Tappouni was applauded by a few fathers.

Let Us Return to the Original Text Cardinal Frings, Archbishop of Cologne, was very happy that the Council saw fit to speak of the Jews and non-Christians. He asked that the Council speak "more deeply and more at length on the Jewish people."

Cardinal Frings then regretted that the condemnation of the accusation of deicide had disappeared, though it had been included in the first version. He asked for a return to the original text. Similar regrets were expressed in different ways by eight other speakers during the day— Cardinals Ruffini and Lercaro of Italy, Léger of Canada, and Cushing, Meyer, and Ritter of the United States, Coadjutor Archbishop Philip Pocock of Toronto, Canada, and Bishop Nierman of the Netherlands. The arguments advanced were almost always the same: that Christ said the Jews did not know what they were doing, and that the sins of mankind are the real cause of Christ's death.

Cardinal Frings urged further treatment of non-Christians. "We share common elements with them," he said. "They too are enlightened by God, even though they may not be aware of it. Saint John says, 'The Word enlightens every man that comes into this world.' "

Cardinal Ruffini of Palermo intervened again—he has taken the floor far more frequently than anyone else at Vatican II. He declared himself in "total agreement" with all the favorable things he had heard said about the declaration and particularly with Cardinal Bea's words. He then made this statement, which most theologians would contest (it makes one think of docetism, a theory dear to the agnostics of the first century, which held that Christ's body was a mere appearance): "We cannot say that the Jews are deicide, for the good reason that God cannot be killed."

The Archbishop of Palermo nonetheless thought the Jews should admit that they unjustly condemned Christ. He recalled that the chief Rabbi of Italy thanked the Catholics for having saved a large number of Jews during the occupation. "The Jews," he concluded, "should also love Catholics. If we make this demand, it is because the Talmud condemns all who are not Jews, calling them *goyim* and saying that they are 'like beasts.' "

Necessity of a Scriptural Dialogue with the Jews Cardinal Lercaro, Archbishop of Bologna, said that the Council should speak of the Jews not because it is opportune but because of an inspiration coming from the

Christian conscience. In reflecting upon its proper mystery, the Church necessarily encounters the Jewish people. Then the Cardinal said vigorously, "This declaration is the logical consequence of the texts on the Church and on the liturgy. Our point of view is not sociological but ontological. How can we speak of Holy Scripture without speaking of the Jews, of the Christian Easter without thinking of the Jewish Passover?" There is an essential bond between the Jews and Catholics, said the Cardinal, who thought there should be colloquiums—dialogues—with the Jews to enable us to understand the Bible better.

Cardinal Léger of Montreal pointed out that the Gospel did not abolish the Old Testament but fulfilled it. "Our origins are Jewish. The Jewish people should enjoy a special dignity in Christian thinking." Alluding to Nazism, the Cardinal emphasized that all Catholics should denounce the brutalities and outrages which result from false ideologies. "We should not speak of a conversion of the Jews," he added, "but of openness to something new. Let us exhort the Jews to deepen their faith."

Let Us Ask Pardon of the Jews   Cardinal Cushing of Boston intervened in his usual booming voice which made the microphones vibrate so much that part of his speech was unintelligible.

"This declaration should be stronger," he said. "All men are sons of Adam, and we are sons of Abraham. . . . Catholics have not conducted themselves properly toward the Jews. They have often been guilty of indifference, and sometimes of crimes. We must ask them pardon for our faults."

Cardinal Koenig supported those who regretted that the word *persecutions* had disappeared: "The first version, which mentions persecutions, was better and stronger. Let us return to it." (We may recall that the new text no longer says "persecutions of the Jews, whether in the past or in our own times," but speaks only of "harassment," without any specification of time.)

The Cardinal also asked that the phrase "a cursed people" be reinserted into the text so that it can be explicitly condemned. "If there is anti-Semitism among the faithful, it is because of a bad interpretation of Scripture."

Cardinal Meyer, Archbishop of Chicago, also asked for a return to the first text, which was better and more ecumenical, he said. "It is not enough to condemn the 'harassment.' Let us be more explicit and at least speak of the sufferings of the Jews through history, as does the first text."

He quoted Thomas Aquinas' *Summa Theologica* (III, q. 47, art. 5): "No Jew was formally a deicide. Nor were the Jews as a whole, for Scripture says they sinned by ignorance."

Other Non-Christian Religions Cardinal Meyer also regretted that the schema said nothing about the Muslims.

Archbishop Jaeger of Paderborn, Germany, requested a clearer and more explicit text. "I regret that it does not mention the respect due to all religions."

The last speaker, Bishop Daem of Antwerp, denounced anti-Semitism, frequent among Catholics, and added: "Let us explicitly reject homicides, pogroms, extortions, and persecutions." Thus this prelate, like many others, did not understand persecutions by the word *vexationem*. Bishop Daem also wanted the declaration to emphasize that Jews and Catholics share common values, as a matter not of charity but of justice. The conditions of dialogue can be found in Scripture properly understood. "Let us be clearer, more positive," he concluded.

Vatican II and Galileo The year 1964 marks the fourth centenary of Galileo's birth. Many think that if the Church is really serious about her new attitude toward freedom of conscience and thought, Vatican II should request formal reparation for the faults committed by the Inquisition against this great scientist. Isn't this an obligation of justice comparable to what was done in the case of Joan of Arc?

The Schema on the Jews and Non-Christians
Is Also Sharply Criticized

The declaration on Jews and non-Christians has already been the subject of some twenty interventions. To our knowledge only one has been applauded, and that vigorously: Archbishop Shehan's intervention this morning, in which he said that his points had been covered by others, and he would submit his remarks in writing. This shows that the Fathers are tired of listening to so many interventions which repeat themselves with incredible monotony.

We will present a rapid analysis of what was original in today's speeches. We might preface our summary by saying that almost all the Fathers have energetically requested a return to the first version of the declaration. Archbishop Tawil, Melkite Patriarchical Vicar for Damascus, was the only one to ask for the suppression of the declaration, "for pastoral reasons," as he put it.

This near-unanimity indicates the psychological mistake made by the theological commission in presenting a revised version that was weaker than the original. In general the schemas were improved during the recess. The declaration on the Jews is unique in that it was weakened. In rejecting this second version, Vatican II is again displaying its vitality and its insight into what not only the Jews but the whole world expects from the Church.

"Cleansing the Memory of Pius XII"   Moreover, we cannot forget that *The Deputy*, whatever judgment we pass on the play, raised a serious question for the public: did the head of the Church conduct himself responsibly in the face of the atrocities committed by Hitler? The Council here has a unique opportunity to proclaim explicitly the Church's indignation against the crimes of the Nazis. As Archbishop Descuffi of Izmir put it in the last intervention of the day: "This declaration gives us the means of cleansing the memory of Pius XII."

Here is a résumé of the principal points which were brought out in the most interesting interventions today.

Archbishop Seper of Zagreb: The liturgy of Holy Week says, "We share in the dignity of Israel." The blood of Christ was Jewish blood (an allusion to the Nazi ideology). How could the Church not be interested in ancient and recent persecutions against the innocent who suffered such atrocities? Let us return to the first text.

Bishop Yves Plumey of Garona, Cameroun: "This declaration does not go far enough, particularly in what regards the Muslims. Priests living in Muslim countries will suffer because of this." The Muslims are 400 million strong, the speaker pointed out. They reject all fetishes and superstition, and they believe in one God and venerate Mary. Catholics could form a bridge between Muslims and Jews.

Jews and Freemasons   Bishop Méndez Arceo of Cuernavaca, Mexico: The declaration is a religious one and has nothing to do with the Jewish state, which is something else again. A faulty interpretation of Scripture is the basis of anti-Semitism. Let us make some gesture of reparation for historic persecutions. Let us return to the first text, which speaks of deicide.

The second part of the Bishop's intervention was not mentioned by the official press release. Was this because he refuted previous statements by Cardinal Ruffini? In it Bishop Méndez alluded to the Freemasons: "Some, because of an elementary knowledge of history or none at all, attribute the origin of anti-Catholic movements to the Jews. It is said that the Jews were Freemasons. That is possible. But it is no reason we cannot discuss the Jews at the Council in a religious and biblical manner." Then the Bishop expressed his certainty that soon Christians would make their peace with the Freemasons.

Bishop Laurentius Satoshi Nagae of Urawa, Japan: Let us not treat all those who are not Christians as pagans and condemn them. All religions are a preparation for the Gospel. What is said about the Muslims is too brief and may be injurious to other religions not mentioned.

Cicero's Latin Bishop Edmund Nowicki of Gdansk, Poland: Cicero himself used the word *vexatio* in two senses: to mean persecution and lawsuit. Let us therefore add *persecutio* to the word *vexatio* used in the text; otherwise, the text will seem to have lost ground. Furthermore, the present version can be considered false from a linguistic point of view. Since people understand Latin badly, let us avoid classical language and use a common language which all can understand. Cardinal Bea, for example, always uses the word *persecutio* to designate persecutions. Let us imitate him.

In this connection, we have received the following letter from a Dominican father:

The quarrel between Professor Martin and your correspondent, Mr. Fesquet, is not merely a quarrel about words. It is a question of *intention* on the part of the writers of the recent schema on the Jews and non-Christian religions. Mr. Martin's remarks about language are above reproach. Cicero would undoubtedly have used the word *vexatio*. But as Mr. Fesquet says, he is wrong about the intentions of the revised schema's writers. They were not so much interested in embellishing the text with a Ciceronian style as they were in weakening it to avoid possible arguments with Arab bishops and perhaps certain Jewish leaders.

As a matter of fact, both Cardinal Bea and his secretary, Monsignor Willebrands, have denounced the insipid and impoverished character of the latter version by comparison with the previous one. It was a pale reflection and a weak expression of the strong and courageous address which Cardinal Bea gave at the end of the second session of the Council. This speech, which presented the reasons for elaborating a conciliar text on the Jews, was sufficiently strong and precise in its use of language. It was an explicit condemnation of anti-Semitism and the psuedo-theological reasons underlying it, which unfortunately are widespread in Christendom, adding fuel to the fire.

It is therefore surprising that the present text—or for that matter, the original version—contains no explicit condemnation of anti-Semitism, whether doctrinal or racial. This omission can only be understood as an attempt to prevent any political interpretation of a purely doctrinal document. This attempt can scarcely be termed courageous. To avoid a difficulty by blunting the sharp edge of the truth to such an extent does not even meet the elementary courage that has become more and more necessary for the Church in the modern world.

Bishop Elchinger and Archbishop Heenan Recall Tortures and Extermina- tions. Coadjutor Bishop Elchinger of Strasbourg told of a "synagogue of peace" which was erected in his diocese right after the war. In it, he said, Judeo-Christian dialogue is going on at different levels. Sketching a portrait of the Jews, Bishop Elchinger noted their profound knowledge of the Old Testament, which is "contemporary history" for them. He also emphasized their "instinct for the absolute," their "theocratic conception of obedience," their highly "developed family sense," and their "refined understanding of monotheism."

"The present declaration," he went on, "is of decisive importance. It can open or close the door for a long time to come." Also, we must radiate the evangelical spirit which caused the Jews to admire Pope John so much. The Bishop then said:

> The Jews expect an act of justice. They have been the victims of grave injustices in the past: torture, forced baptisms, various humiliations. And they suffer injustices today. For example, doctrinal errors are preached in their regard, and some catechetical books do them less than justice. Let us be honest enough to recognize and repudiate these. Let us be magnanimous enough to ask pardon in the name of all guilty Christians. It is in the spirit of the Gospel to proclaim our faults without expecting the Jews to do the same."

The Bishop concluded by quoting a passage from Paul VI's speech in Jerusalem: "Blessed are we if we choose to be the oppressed rather than the oppressors."

Archbishop Heenan of Westminster: I reluctantly accept this second text which is inferior to and less friendly than the original. The secretariat for unity is certainly not responsible. What expert is responsible for this text? He clearly is very ignorant of the subject. In Germany six million Jews were exterminated. Because some Christians cooperated in this nefarious enterprise, the Christian people as a whole cannot be accounted guilty. Likewise for the condemnation of Christ. In keeping with the prayer of the Council, let us not be "disturbers of justice."

Archbishop Joseph Parecattil of Ernakulam, India: Let us present Christianity as the fulfillment of everything members of other faiths find in their religion. Let us specify that missionaries must be disinterested and not succumb to proselytism. Furthermore, the Church needs the values of other religions to become truly Catholic. Let us learn how to recognize the action of the Spirit in the whole world.

Bishop Donal Lamont of Umtali, Rhodesia, observed: "It would be insulting to suggest that anti-Semitism exists among Catholics." (*Sic*.)

Archbishop Descuffi thought that "in some respects" the Muslims are closer to Christians than the Jews. "Let us enter into serious dialogue with them," he concluded.

"Jewish-Masonic Activity at the Council"   The bishops have received a brochure entitled "Jewish-Masonic Activity at the Council." It will delight extreme right-wing Catholics who think the Church is slipping into the hands of a Jewish-Masonic fifth column. An introduction states that the pamphlet was written "by a group of priests and religious of one diocese, two of whom are participating in the Council."

"Our hearts are saddened," reads the text, "because of certain rash deeds which we consider to be the result of some Council Fathers' having lost their faith. They are spreading false doctrine. They are converted Jews who are making yet one more effort to destroy God's work."

Here are some further passages, which make their authors look ridiculous to any sensible person:

> Elated by its temporary triumphs, international Judaism has launched a new attack against the Catholic Church by trying to rehabilitate the Jewish people in the eyes of mankind, an attempt which contradicts the traditional teachings of the Church. . . .

> Jews who have reached a high place in the Church's hierarchy fraudulently convinced John XXIII to create a Secretariat for Promoting Christian Unity. This served them as a platform from which to spread propaganda in favor of the Jews, who will always be anti-Christian.

> These Jews were Cardinal Bea, Monsignor [John] Oesterreicher, and Father [Gregory] Baum. . . . They were later joined by Bishop Karl Kempf, Auxiliary of Würzburg, and Bishop Méndez Arceo. With the exception of a few Council Fathers who might have been influenced by powers outside of the Church, all who support the pro-Jewish theses were deceived by the above-mentioned, who have until now succeeded in concealing their true faces. . . .

SEPTEMBER 30

The Restoration of a Permanent Diaconate:

38 Percent of the Fathers Want a Married Diaconate

Discussion on the Jews was interrupted for a few hours on Tuesday to vote on the suitability of a married diaconate and other questions. On

Monday 1,903 fathers (against 242) had voted in favor of "restoring the diaconate as a permanent order." This means that henceforth the diaconate will not be a mere step to the priesthood but a terminal order. Let us recall that deacons have all the powers of a priest except those of celebrating mass and hearing confessions. They can distribute communion, administer the other sacraments, preach, preside over devotions in church, and so forth.

This decision will have profound repercussions in countries where churches have had to be closed because of the shortage of clergy, as well as in areas where priests need the assistance of non-lay auxiliaries.

Here is another immediately perceptible consequence of the Council's deliberations, and it too is an important one: from now on, episcopal conferences (and not the pope) will decide whether it is opportune to institute the diaconate. The pope's approval will of course remain necessary. This was yesterday's first ballot. It is worth noting that the two-thirds majority was barely attained, with 1,523 in favor and 702 against.

Moreover, the Council decided—and this is more revolutionary— that the diaconate can be conferred "on men of mature age, even if they are married." Of 2,229 voters, 1,598 were in favor and 629 against, with 2 invalid ballots. Hence, the prelates who want to confer the diaconate on fathers of families, who hold a job and are firmly rooted in their community, carried the day.

In view of the Council's decision, the question is now settled. In the future women will be able to support their deacon husbands in the apostolate. The laywoman is no longer forbidden to cross the sanctuary line.

The Council attempted to go farther in putting this question to the Fathers: can the supreme ecclesiastical authority decide to confer the diaconate on young men without obliging them to celibacy? Thus, the theological commission did not want to rule this possibility out apriori, although there was little chance that it would be accepted. Of 2,211 voting, 839 were in favor and 1,364 were against, with 8 null ballots.

These results merit some consideration. Father Haubtmann, director of the French National Secretariat of religious news, analyzed the vote in this fashion: "Last year there was some indication that the Church was moving toward a married priesthood [this is a reference to a controversial article that appeared in *Paris-Match*]. In voting against this question, the Fathers have indicated that they want the ecclesiastical law of celibacy to remain as it is."

Yet we would remark that there were nonetheless 839 Fathers in the aula—one out of every three—who are favorable to the idea of a young deacon's marrying. Given what we know of the mentality of the average bishop, this seems a striking percentage. Indeed, one religious told us: "Vatican III will accomplish what Vatican II was not mature enough to do. That is, it will authorize a married diaconate and will perhaps even restore the tradition that has been uninterrupted in the East, of permitting married persons to enter the priesthood."

Four Chapters of the Schema on the Church Adopted Four chapters of the schema on the Church were adopted today by the Council, including chapter 3 on collegiality, sections of which have already been the object of thirty-nine ballots. This chapter was divided in two. The results were as follows: for the first part, 1,624 votes in favor, 42 against, and 572 *placet juxta modum* (yes with reservations); for the second part, 1,704 votes for, 53 against, and 481 *placet juxta modum.*

Chapter 4 was adopted with a vote of 2,152 against 8, with 76 *juxta modi.* Chapter 5 drew 1,856 votes for and 17 against, with 302 *juxta modum.* Chapter 6, on religious, was adopted by a vote of 1,736 against 12, with 438 *juxta modi.*

Vatican II and the Non-Catholic Observers

The Council deliberations take place, as is well known, in the presence of observers or guests from non-Roman Christian churches.

It is therefore in order to question these observers periodically in order to sound their thinking on the Council and to learn what they hope for and complain about. To this end I have interviewed three of them.

The first, a French Protestant pastor, is not an observer in the strict sense of the word; he has followed the three sessions as a journalist. This is Pastor Georges Richard-Molard, assistant director of the weekly *Réforme* and director of the press service for the Protestant Federation of France. I shall record some of his impressions, which, as will be seen, reflect his double mission as pastor and journalist.

Then I shall record interviews with Mr. Oscar Cullmann, professor at the Sorbonne, and Dr. Nikos Nissiotis, an Orthodox theologian and an observer at the World Council of Churches.

Pastor Georges Richard-Molard: *"The Process of Renewal in the Roman Church Is Practically Irreversible"*

Whatever we may think of the press, we have to agree on the important role journalists play. The Council, which gives them special consideration, is well aware of this. It is in fact because of their reports that their public, which constitutes so to speak a macrocosm of their own differences, can understand what is going on at the Council and find arguments to criticize its deliberations.

Actually, every journalist is one with his spiritual family, with its spirit, its attitudes, its language, and its history. Most don't consider this a limitation but an almost biological solidarity, because much of what one is he owes to this family.

Thus one, as a pastor of the Reformed Church in France, has followed an intellectual and spiritual course which, far from alienating him from his people, brings him closer to them. Could he possibly forget the history of his family? He would perhaps need only to walk beneath the walls of certain Roman palaces to be reminded of the unlikely historical calvary of his "poor little Church," as well as of the Churches of Italy, Spain, and elsewhere. And if he wanted to erase this nauseous past from his memory, he might be prevented from doing so by certain religious—who are very rare, it's true—who seem to have stepped out of a medieval fresco. And if he were tempted to water down some of the major proclamations of the Reformation which are the foundation of his spiritual family, he would, unintelligently and deafly, not be seeing or understanding that for more than two years—and undoubtedly longer—many Catholic believers, lay and cleric alike, have been sounding the depths of Scripture, studying, praying, and suffering, to come now by these and other paths to the same proclamations.

However—why must there always be a "however" at the heart of the greatest affections?—in proportion to his love for his spiritual family, which sometimes sustains his purity in solitude, he can't stand for that family to refuse to see or hear the gestures and prayers of the Catholic family. He would wish that these two families born of the same Father, who alone knows whether or not we are destined to remain separate, could at least unite in their sense of guilt for the increasing agnosticism of men today. He would wish that instead of saying "Lord, Lord!" and invoking his powers, privileges, and royalty, they could both finally accept to share in his death. Not intellectually or even piously but in concrete acts, where each family would lose itself to find itself: lose historically outmoded traditions, human privileges, ineffectual rituals, and closed doctrinal systems in order to offer itself, stripped, in the service of mankind.

But perhaps these thoughts would not be accepted by those of my faith. They might counter, what could be more stripped than our Protestant parishes, their organization, their liturgy, their faith? Isn't our doctrine that of the Gospel? Compared with this simplicity, what do we see in Rome? A church more weighted down than ever with the barnacles of history; a pope asserting his primacy *ad nauseam*, inviting the "separated brethren" to return; a council wondering whether or not Mary is a mediatrix; unintelligible ceremonies with or without relics; antievangelical devotions supported and propagated by the clergy; an increasingly unwieldy and irredeemable tradition.

Such convictions constitute an immense difficulty for a journalist and a pastor. He is one with his people; he also thinks what they think and obviously sees things as they do. But privileged by his position, he goes beyond the first level of this kind of diorama and is aware of seeing farther than they do. Not only is it given to him, as a result of his experience, to discern the remarkable energy stimulating Catholic reform, but he is also convinced, despite surface appearances, that the process of renewal is real, almost irreversible, and fraught with considerable consequences for the future.

Owing to the disagreeable climate created by the interpretation of a speech delivered in Bethlehem, by an unfortunate event that occurred in the Netherlands, and by a manner of acting and talking that some find difficult to justify, this pastor was advised, before returning to Rome, to be tough.

Of course, he intends to be, on the condition that firmness can help Catholic renewal even a little. But not if such firmness would have no other end than to reassure a certain brand of Protestantism and to confirm it. The controversy in the Council stems in large part from the fact that a small percentage of the Catholic hierarchy confuses truth with "Catholic" truth. It is all the more necessary that Protestantism not fall into the same confusion; otherwise all hope of renewal is dead on both sides.

That is why this pastor will strive to enlighten his people, progressively and without unnecessary shock, on the development of Catholic ecclesiology, ethics, and outlook. Beginning with the dark picture Protestants have long had of the Roman Church, he will touch it with highlights little by little, not only because he knows he can do it, but so that Protestantism, called to intercede for the mission of the whole universal Church, will also receive its part of the light.

Oscar Cullmann: *The Texts Elaborated by Vatican II "Will Not Be an Obstacle to Future Discussion as Were the Dogmatic Decisions of Previous Councils"* Professor Oscar Cullmann, a Protestant exegete who teaches at the Universities of Paris and Basel, follows Vatican II as a guest of the Secretariat for Promoting Christian Unity. He was good enough to share some of his impressions of the third session:

It is undeniable that a certain indifference on the one hand and disappointment on the other were apparent at the beginning of this session, both inside and outside St. Peter's. Are the indifference and disappointment justified? Certainly not indifference, for the reason that this third session is the most important of the three because it is the most decisive. Moreover, the extremely fast pace of the debates, the many votes, the waiting for the results, the introduction of new topics after only two or three days' discussion do not leave enough time for either the Fathers of the Council or the observers to get bored.

At first sight, it is more difficult to answer whether the disappointment is justified. I would say that while regretting in principle certain compromises, I do not share the pessimism of some of my coreligionists or of some Catholics. For one thing, I never entertained false hopes about the Council. In my first statements, at the beginning of and during the first session, I warned against expectations that were contrary to the aim of the Council itself. For another thing, that real aim seems to me now to be well on the way to fulfillment.

I have always said that real union of the Churches is impossible at the present time because their very conception of unity is different, and is rooted in our faiths as Protestants and Catholics respectively. To ask the pope to accept our conception and give up primacy would be tantamount to asking him to become a Protestant. Likewise, to ask Protestants to submit to the Roman conception of primacy would be to ask them to cease being Protestants. Our real ecumenical task, on the contrary, is to come closer together and continue the dialogue on unity and primacy, without obliging the pope to abandon his claim to primacy which is guaranteed by the Roman conception of apostolic succession and without obliging Protestants to recognize it.

That is why Paul VI's very clear statements about primacy in his encyclical and in his opening speech for this session (as for that matter in the one for the second session) do not seem to me to justify the disappointment some Protestants feel.

Clarity must be the basis of dialogue. It is only the statement in the encyclical, to the effect that this conception of primacy and apostolic succession would be the only condition, that is unacceptable to us.

The present Pope is currently being contrasted with his predecessor, John XXIII. But while John XXIII insisted on the primacy as much as Paul VI has, which is understandable psychologically, and never spoke differently of the primacy when he had occasion to mention it or thought of Christian unity outside of this Roman conception, his warm personality was different from that of his successor. It seems to me false and unjust to blame Paul VI, as has become popular, for destroying by diplomacy the work begun by John XXIII. John XXIII was necessary to convoke this Council in a moment of prophetic inspiration. But how would he have resolved the great difficulties that could not be foreseen at the beginning and which certainly he foresaw least of all? I don't in the least deny the dangers and harmful influence of too much diplomacy. The same problem exists outside the Roman Church, in our own ecclesiastical organizations, where often diplomatic considerations stifle the prophetic word. It also seems to me unjust to deny that Paul VI has any appeasing inclinations, though his natural reserve often does block him from showing them.

In any case, the new Pope does not seem to me to be responsible for the undeniable slacking off of interest, indeed the disappearance of the earlier conciliar enthusiasm. In all reform movements, enthusiasm is ephemeral. What is essential is that the will to reform persist and become the basis of a work in depth. Whatever people say, from this point of view there is no reason to feel disappointed as the third session begins.

Without making predictions about what will take place in the weeks to come, we can say, after the voting of these two first weeks, that the majority of the Council Fathers who are asking for reforms have consolidated. Many things that were considered revolutionary during the first session are now accepted as natural.

Since the second session, the role of the observers has taken on an importance that we would not dared have hoped for at the beginning of the Council. The commissions in charge of redrafting the texts take account of our weekly discussions organized by the secretariat for unity.

To answer whether or not the pessimism and disappointment I spoke of are justified, the real aim of this Council must not be lost from sight: to increase the power of the bishops. And, secondly, adapting the doctrine and life of the Church to the needs of our times in a pastoral and ecumenical way.

There is much to be said about the collegiality of bishops. From a Protestant point of view, it raises theological problems that I cannot go into here. But be that as it may, the institution of a worldwide council of bishops which the pope may consult, together with episcopal conferences, will diminish the influence of the Roman Curia. The other texts under study during this session—religious liberty, ecumenism, revelation, the modern world—clearly do not yet show that adaptation to the needs of our time, but they may serve as the basis for future reforms. For in the final analysis, they are inspired by a desire for reform.

The disappointment is justified in the sense that the final texts will for the most part be a result of compromise. They too often juxtapose the two conflicting points of view without establishing a real internal link between them. Thus, every affirmation of the power of bishops is accompanied almost wearisomely by a statement stressing the power of the pope. The difficulty here stems from the fact that the present Council is bound by dogmatic decisions to Vatican I, whose spirit was contrary to that of Vatican II, whatever anyone might say.

To find a solution to the problem of collegiality it would have been necessary, had the Council not been obliged to make the dogma of 1870 a starting point, to take up again the problem of papal power as well as the exegesis of Matthew 16, instead of considering it already settled. But we recognize that it would be difficult for a Catholic council to proceed otherwise.

As for the text on the Virgin Mary, we hoped with many Council Fathers that the word *mediatrix* would be suppressed. However, it represents a happy effort to have done with excessive Marian devotion, although even here previous Marian dogmas make it difficult to go beyond a certain point. The juxtaposition of conflicting theses also characterizes the schema on revelation, discussion of which is to begin soon.

But all of these documents are motivated by a desire for renewal. They can serve as a basis for postconciliar reforms.

That is why, even with respect to these compromise texts, I do not share the pessimism of those who proclaim, "Nothing will come of the Council!" All the documents are formulated in such a way as not to close doors; they will not be an obstacle to future discussion among Catholics or to dialogue with non-Catholics, as were the dogmatic decisions of previous councils. On the contrary, they will be a point of departure and a stimulus for future reforms if the desire for renewal remains alive in the Catholic Church. And since there is an ecumenical solidarity, I would add: if this desire also remains alive in the non-Catholic Christian Churches, which stand just as much in need of continuing renewal.

Professor Nissiotis: *Vatican II "Is an Example of the First Order for Us"*
We asked Professor Nikos Nissiotis, a Greek Orthodox observer at the Council delegated by the World Council of Churches, for his impressions of the beginning of the third session. Mr. Nissiotis, a layman as are most

of the Orthodox theologians, is associate director of the World Council's Ecumenical Institute in Bossey, near Geneva.

Making it clear that he spoke in his own name and not officially, he told me:

> I think that at this third session the principal aim of the Council and the attendant difficulties have become very clear. I mean that it is now seen as an effort to complete Vatican I with the doctrine of the collegiality of bishops. From my point of view, this is the chief problem of the Roman Church. What has taken place in fact is an attempt to raise the bishops to the dignity of the Bishop of Rome in order that they may share in the exercise of authority in the Church.
>
> My first reaction as an Orthodox is positive. I am also aware of the enthusiasm of the majority of the Fathers for the course the Council has taken. Now let me state frankly some criticisms.
>
> First, I don't think it is a matter of completing but of correcting Vatican I. That is what the Orthodox expect Vatican II to do. To be sure, we can agree that the college already constitutes a correction. At the moment, it is difficult to make a definite estimate of the Council's achievement, but I fear that collegiality is conceived on the basis of papal primacy, which for the conservatives must be preserved and I would even say strengthened by collegiality. The question for an Orthodox is this: we feel that something extremely important is lacking alongside the hierarchy. Call it if you will the fullness of the people of God, of the whole Church, whose conscience in our view is the supreme authority with the hierarchy as its spokesman;
>
> Second, in the schema on bishops, the episcopacy is constantly referred to as a sacrament. This seems to us somewhat limited in that the whole priesthood is not included. Thus we have the impression that the Council is too hierarchized and concerned only with the higher levels of administration in the Church.
>
> My basic criticism is that the schema *De Ecclesia*, as well as the discussion it has provoked, betrays a weakness with respect to the place of the Holy Spirit in conciliar theology. It seems to me that the Spirit as the Paraclete completes the work of Christ, who founded the Church on Pentecost. Afterwards in the local communities bishops, presbyters, and deacons were chosen to manifest on the one hand the apostolicity of the Church, which is one and indivisible, and on the other the fullness of the truth of each local church gathered about the eucharistic table and presided over by the bishop.
>
> In the third session, we see the Virgin exalted in a manner which for us, who are outside the Roman Church, seems to fill the void

between Christ and his people. This seems to be the reason behind the title *mediatrix*.

As Orthodox, for whom the Virgin occupies a central and unique place in the Church, in union with the people praying through her intercession, the dogmatizing of Mariology fills us with anxiety. It is not that we wish to deny the importance of the Virgin for piety and spirituality, but we hold that the true locus of Mary's glory is in humility, suffering, and complete devotion.

Finally, for ecumenical reasons, I think this subject ought to be treated with great care and in a truly pastoral spirit.

In conclusion, I would say that the fact of the Council is very important for all the churches. It is a school for all, Catholics as well as non-Catholics, because even criticism of certain aspects of it are made in a positive spirit for the purpose of contributing to its success. Moreover, the Spirit urges us to make even stronger criticisms of ourselves, the Orthodox. The Roman Church is today publicly engaged in an open discussion. This is an example of the first order for us.

We also have our problems and we should undertake a similar self-criticism, as indeed should the Reformed churches. The World Council of Churches, which represents the model of an open ecumenism without any ecclesiological conditions, follows the proceedings here in Rome with great interest, and strives to be always cooperative and to exhibit the greatest possible solidarity.

OCTOBER, 1964

After Two Years of Reflection,

Vatican II Re-examines the Schema on Revelation

The Council has abruptly changed direction. Having finished discussion on religious liberty and the Jews, it now takes up the draft on revelation. This is very different kind of schema. After the Church *ad extra*, here is the Church *ad intra*. The source of faith itself is involved. Although less spectacular and far more subtle, this is nonetheless a discussion of capital importance. A Protestant pastor told me, "This is the most interesting part of the whole Council for me." Why?

Because the Church is examining the very basis of revelation: the Bible and its relationship with postbiblical tradition. This is a major area of friction between the Reformed churches and Catholicism. Is Holy Scripture the unique and self-sufficient source of revelation? (This is what the Protestants think.) Or does tradition add something substantial to the Bible? Is tradition distinct from Scripture? Are there two sources of revelation, as the first schema indicated? (This, with many further ramifications, is the Catholic position.)

Upon closer inspection—and the Council has noted this—the matter is more complex still. Even for Protestants, Scripture forms part of tradition. We cannot ignore the evidence that the Bible itself is a written tradition. In Montreal, during a conference on Faith and Constitution, a text using the expression *sola traditio* was almost adopted. An intervention *in extremis* by Brother Max Thurian of the Taizé community was necessary to bar this revolutionary term, which could have caused considerable confusion. For Protestants have long used the expression *sola Scriptura*. In any event, the present conciliar schema is of obvious ecumenical interest.

During the first session, Vatican II rejected the first version of this schema, which was entitled "On the Sources of Revelation," by a vote of

1,368 to 822. It fell short of the two-thirds majority by less than 100 votes. John XXIII's personal initiative was required to send the schema back for revision. The Pope then decided to create a special commission, with Cardinals Ottaviani and Bea as copresidents, in addition to some members from the unity secretariat. That day marked the end of the Counter-Reformation. The new commission was not under the exclusive control of Cardinal Ottaviani, the author of the first schema, and the two conflicting tendencies in the Church would thenceforth work together toward a new version.

A Marriage of Convenience The present schema is the child of that marriage of convenience. It encountered serious difficulties. But the result proves that the union was not all bad. The present text is considered to have attained the optimum perfection possible, given the differences of doctrine: it carefully refrains from stating any partisan theological opinion, and speaks only of what is incontestable. Thus, the document does not mention two sources; nor does it say there is only one. Nonetheless, the previous impasse has been overcome. The serious defects of the first schema have almost entirely disappeared. The perspective has completely changed.

The two reports presented in the Council on Wednesday, by Bishop Franič, spokesman for the minority on the commission (seven out of twenty-four members), and Archbishop Florit, spokesman for the majority (seventeen members), will clarify what we have said.

Bishop Franič, representing the school that had been much in evidence during the first session, declared:

> The present schema does not sufficiently respect the original aspect of tradition insofar as it is distinct from Scripture. Let us accentuate this tradition more strongly. This will be an ecumenical advantage in relation to the Orthodox, who hold tradition in very high honor.
>
> Moreover, Vatican I would seem to attribute something to tradition that is not found in Scripture, as do likewise the encyclicals *Mortalium animos* of Pius XI and *Humani generis* of Pius XII. The latter speaks explicitly of "two distinct sources" of revelation. John XXIII, in his first encyclical, seems to move in the same direction, and so does Paul VI himself. Certain provincial councils also used the expression "two sources," as have many catechisms.

It is clear that the arguments in Bishop Franič's report derive more from authority than from theological reflection properly speaking.

Archbishop Florit's report, on the other hand, offered well-reasoned arguments. Without entering into their subtleties, we will indicate some of the salient points.

1. Faith cannot be reduced, as has been largely taught since the Counter-Reformation, to pure adherence by the intelligence. It demands the adherence of the whole person. The present schema brings that out. Faith, the object of revelation, is man's total response to God, as the Bible clearly shows. It demands meditation and an involvement of the interior life, which concern the whole Christian people.

2. All revelation is incarnate in a man. This man is Christ, who is a person and not an abstract principle. The totality of revelation is found in Christ. No previous council has so clearly explicated this existential aspect of faith.

3. Scripture is the norm of tradition. This does not mean that tradition is of no interest—on the contrary. But it does mean that there is nothing in tradition that is not found at least implicitly in Scripture.

If, leaving aside the reports of the day, we inquire into the heart of the problem implied in the schema, we can say that there are two conceptions of theology: one stresses the pronouncements of faith, formulas, norms, and the necessity of clear ideas which satisfy the intelligence; the other emphasizes the mysterious sense of revealed realities, the fact that they transcend all formulation, that they are given to enlighten our lives rather than comfort our intellect.

The second conception of theology, which has been restored to a place of honor by the Council, is deeply scriptural. It constitutes a return to the sources; it remains close to the spirit of the Bible. This, of course, pleases the Protestants, whose distaste for dogma is well known. The right balance between the two points of view, that of the Protestants and that of integralist Catholics, is difficult to establish. A thought inspired by Saint Thomas may give the key to the difficulty: faith is not limited to pronouncements, even though these are useful in their place; rather, faith consists in the realities which they express without exhausting.

In any event, Vatican II has taken an important step in the official theology of the Church. The complexes of the Counter-Reformation have been shed in favor of an approach in depth which will make the faith more appealing to the contemporary mind. In a certain sense it can be said that the influence of Newman and Maurice Blondel is present in the Council. Life has emerged the victor over the system, and more heed is being paid to Christ's saying, "I am the way, the truth, and the life." In the last three or four centuries of Catholicism, there has been too great a tendency to neglect the first and third terms of this statement, which reveal the fundamental link between truth and act.

On the Outskirts of the Council

Sometimes the most interesting ecumenical events take place on the outskirts of Vatican II.

Paul VI Addresses the Observers   Thus, the reception of the non-Catholic observers by Paul VI on September 29 was the occasion of a discourse by the "Bishop of Rome, successor of the Apostle Peter." This was the expression the Pope used when he responded to an allocution by Archimandrite Panteleimon Rodopoulos, a representative of the Patriarchate of Constantinople (Istanbul). The Pope said in part:

> Any abyss of distrust and skepticism has been largely overcome. Your presence here is the sign and the means of a spiritual rapprochement that we have never known before. A new method has come into effect; a friendship has been created; a hope has been lighted. . . .
>
> You will note that the Council has had nothing but words of respect and joy because of your presence. . . . Even more, words of honor, charity, and hope for you. This is no small matter if we consider our past disputes. . . .
>
> The Church is in no hurry; she leaves the task of concluding the dialogue we have begun to God's providence in a manner and at a time pleasing to him. . . .
>
> Although she is committed to defend certain doctrinal positions, the Catholic Church is disposed to study how difficulties can be removed, misunderstandings dissipated, and the authentic treasures of truth and spirituality which you possess be respected; how to enlarge and adapt certain canonical forms in view of facilitating a return to unity of the large and by now centuries-old Christian communities still separated from us.

When he had finished, the Pope and his guests recited the Our Father together.

A Speech by the Representative of Athenagoras I   The personal representative of His Beatitude Athenagoras I, Ecumenical Patriarch of Constantinople, also delivered a speech of the first importance. Archimandrite Andre Scrima (of Rumanian origin) addressed the Pan-African Secretariat, and by reason of his position what he said is destined to have a great influence.

Before a large audience of prelates and experts, the speaker sketched a historical fresco of relations between the churches of the East and the

West. I would like to be able to quote the whole of this closely reasoned, sensitive and profound lecture, so illuminated with the philosophical and theological *Weltanschauung* which the Orthodox have mastered.

He said that the ecclesiology of the first millennium, that is, before the separation, was centered on the Holy Spirit. It was sacramental and conciliar. The existence of patriarchates corresponded with the modern desire for episcopal conferences. Then came the split in the eleventh century and the ensuing tendency for the Latin Church to extend to the Orthodox the structures and ways of acting that developed about the See of Rome.

Archimandrite Scrima alluded to the different phases of estrangement. "I am painfully surprised," he said, "that the Roman Catholic Church has acted as though she did not belong to the same Church as we. . . . Vatican I might be considered the climax of this development," declared the speaker. Then he added the following highly intelligent explanation:

> The Orthodox could never understand the justification of Vatican I. The West was in the agony of the death of God [Nietzsche]; in the East, Dostoevsky was saying that if God did not exist, everything was permitted to man, while in Paris Renan was inquiring into the meaning of the relativity of history. In this tormented atmosphere Vatican I had to take a rigorous stand. Between Vatican I and Vatican II we lived through the most bitter period between our two Churches. There was a tragic impression in the air of impotency and discouragement.

Archimandrite Scrima then spoke of the present Council, which he described as "a sign of hope."

Cardinal Bea's Allocution to the Orthodox   The Secretariat for Promoting Christian Unity has distributed the text of Cardinal Bea's address at Patras, Greece, on the occasion of the restoration of the relic of Saint Andrew to the Orthodox. This speech gave new and vigorous expression to the bonds which unite the Orthodox and Catholics. It was pronounced in the presence of twenty-five Orthodox metropolitans, although Patriarch Chrysostomos, Archbishop of Athens, was absent. It is worth pointing out that Patriarch Chrysostomos is over ninety years old, and that his well-known anti-Romanism has but a minimal influence on the more dynamic elements of the Greek Church. Said Cardinal Bea:

> For centuries we have lived like strangers to one another, even though a common baptism has made us sons of God in Christ, brothers of one another. For centuries we were often, too often unfortunately, in conflict with one another, even though by the gift of the same

priesthood we celebrated the same eucharist, partook of the same bread of life, and shared the body of the same Lord, who came to give his life in order to gather together the dispersed children of God.

OCTOBER 2

The Schema on Revelation
Meets with Widespread Approval

The first skirmishes on the schema *De Revelatione* were perfectly tactful. But beneath the moderate tones, the initiate could easily detect the two schools of thought we spoke about yesterday. It is a wonder that the balance struck in the schema did not give greater ground for controversy. This is a sure sign that the turnabout begun by the hierarchical Church is now, if not accepted, at least recognized by all, whether they like it or not, and rearguard fighting will no longer be tolerated.

As always, Cardinal Ruffini was first to the attack. "I am astonished," he said on Wednesday, "that this schema on revelation makes no mention of the fact that tradition is not only explicative but also 'constitutive.' The magisterium has taught this everywhere and for a long time." Revelation has an essentially intellectual character, he said, and he requested that relevant passages from the Council of Trent and Vatican I be quoted in their entirety in the schema. Archbishop Joseph Attipetty of Verapoly, India, was of a similar opinion; he saw serious dangers in this omission.

Cardinal Döpfner, speaking in the name of the German and Scandinavian bishops, was happy about what the schema said on the relationship between Scripture and tradition. He requested that the text go no farther. He was also pleased because the document encouraged the development of study and did not present the faith in a purely cerebral manner. The points raised by the minority, he said, surely were not without value, but he did not agree with their interpretation. "Let us not repeat Vatican I," he said; "let us expound on it."

The Deficiencies of the Magisterium Cardinal Meyer, Archbishop of Chicago, found that the schema still puts too much and too onesided an emphasis on the place of the magisterium in tradition. "It is only a guarantee," he said. "Let us avoid describing the faith in terms that are too intellectual. The teaching of morality has been too casuistic and not centered enough on God." Despite the inerrancy of the Church, the magisterium can be deficient, he said. "Let us recognize such deficiencies."

Cardinal Léger's intervention dominated Thursday's general congregation. The Archbishop of Montreal also denounced the shortcomings of the magisterium. "An examination of conscience in this respect would not be out of order," he stated. "Let us be very clear about the transcendence of the revealed deposit; revelation alone is the word of God, and not the magisterium. The magisterium is not constitutive. We sometimes emphasize the infallibility of the magisterium imprudently. Although infallible, the interpretation of the word of God remains perfectible."

The schema's use of the expression "intimate experience" to describe man's grasp of revelation disturbed some, Archbishop Ferrero of Reggio di Calabria, for one. He thought it smacked of modernism. Bishop Guano of Livorno answered that the expression had a totally different meaning in this context.

Bishop Compagnone of Anagni and Archbishop Fares of Catanzaro expressed pleasure that the schema clearly stated, "Revelation is Christ, the living Word of God." Archbishop Zoungrana of Ouagadougou, Upper Volta, noted that this personalization of revelation was very important to the modern mind.

The twenty-odd bishops who spoke were generally satisfied with the schema and proposed only minor corrections.

The audience found these debates rather dull. This was the first time that there was no voting, and the aula was largely deserted in favor of the coffee bars in St. Peter's.

OCTOBER 3

The Schema on Revelation
Recommends Exegetical Studies

There was an interesting conciliar session on Friday morning. Further technical clarifications were made on the difficult problem of the relationship between Scripture and tradition. This question, we repeat, is at the heart of our differences with Protestantism.

Let us take a salient example: did Pius XII have the right to define the dogma of the assumption when apparently nothing in Scripture authorized it? Protestants obviously answer this question in the negative since they recognize only one norm—the Bible.

Not all Catholics are comfortable with this dogma. But while agreeing that its promulgation was undoubtedly inopportune (which is a quite different matter), they argue in this fashion: the Pope had the right to act as he did—not without consulting the bishops of the world, moreover—for he was justified by the living tradition of the Church, which has always believed in the Virgin's physical ascension into heaven at the time of her death. Also, it cannot be stated unequivocally that there is no scriptural basis for this dogma. The Pope claimed that the formulation of this definition was based on Scripture.

Tradition and Scripture   This is the nub of the problem: is there more in tradition than in Scripture? Opinions differ, even among Catholic theologians. Some have no doubt that tradition contains truths which cannot be found in the Bible. Others maintain that there is nothing in tradition which is not contained implicitly in Scripture. The differences of opinion arise over the interpretation of the word *implicitly*.

The Council of Trent did not settle this question. For reasons that are historically difficult to clarify, that Council refused to use the prepared formula, "Revelation is found partly in Scripture, partly in tradition." The two adverbs were replaced at the last moment by the conjunction *and*, which made different interpretations possible.

Should Vatican II be more explicit? Archbishop Baldassarri of Ravenna thinks so. He asked, with good reason, "What is the good of a council if it merely repeats previous ones? The question is important enough for us to feel compelled to resolve it." The prelate proffered his solution by stating that all dogmas are found in Scripture at least "*fundamentaliter*." Thus, this bishop supported the formula *sola Scriptura*, which, he pointed out, was the common doctrine before the Reformation.

At Loggerheads   Father Luciano Rubio, Prior General of the Order of Saint Augustine, was of a quite different opinion. He drew support for his argument from Saint Augustine's writings, which he obviously knows by heart: "There are truths in tradition which cannot be demonstrated from Scripture alone."

Abbot Butler, President of the Benedictine Confederation of England, referred to Cardinal Newman, the defender of a dynamic rather than a static exegesis, and stated, "Tradition and Scripture are each sufficient unto themselves." This was the position of Thomas Aquinas and might be summarized in these words: "Everything is in Scripture, everything is in tradition." We are thus at the opposite pole from the *partim-partim* position.

The Fathers are at loggerheads. In fact, Vatican II cannot possibly agree on this point. That is why it seems wise for the schema to leave the question open.

Let us note the intervention by Archbishop Marty of Reims, who showed how historical events are not without influence on dogmatic truths. "The Holy Spirit," he said, "uses events to clarify truth. This gives a theological basis to schema 13 [on the modern world] which speaks of the 'signs of the times,' after the example of John XXIII in *Pacem in terris*."

Two other important aspects of the schema on revelation were brought out Friday.

1. The text strongly recommends the reading and meditation of Scripture. The document expresses the desire that translations of the Bible be made in collaboration with the separated brethren.

2. The schema gives firm support to exegetical studies. This is one of the interesting additions in the present text as compared with the first version. It thus takes up the message of Pius XII's *Divino afflante Spiritu,* which has often been the cause of much controversy. This is not the place to recall the innumerable instances of interference and suspicion visited on some Catholic exegetes whose only crime was to make their findings known. Vatican II is restoring them to honor, thus giving an example of religious liberty within the Church itself. Paul VI's approach is liberal on this question as on so many others. Fathers Lyonnet and Zerwick of the Pontifical Biblical Institute were recently authorized to go back to their teaching.

Cardinal Ruffini, who is indefatigable, took the floor on chapter 3 to warn against the expression "literary genres" as applied to the Bible. This permits the exegetes, he said, "to invent novelties and make the Bible say what they want it to." He added elsewhere, "Let us specify clearly that exegetes must have as norms the magisterium, the Church Fathers, and the *sensus Ecclesiae*."

The Errors of the Bible   Cardinal Ruffini also objected to the word *maturatio* as applied to revelation. It is, he said, "a harmful word."

In the name of all the German bishops, Cardinal Koenig retorted: "Knowledge of the Orient, archeological discoveries, and the like help the Church to understand and interpret the revealed deposit better. Let us not forget, furthermore, that the authors of the sacred books made various mistakes. Let us state this clearly so we will not be tempted to present things that are false as articles of faith." The Cardinal then gave some examples of typical errors in the Bible: incorrect attributions and quotations, erroneous dates, geographical and scientific errors, and so forth.

For the First Time, a Council Admits the Evolution of Dogma   Father Schillebeeckx, theological adviser to the Dutch episcopacy and a member of the commission for revising schema 13, made the following comment on the schema on revelation:

> Some will think that certain parts of this text are very Protestant. But they will be wrong, because the schema deals with opinions which were taught by the Roman Church in the past but which have not been stressed since the Counter-Reformation out of fear of Protestantism.
>
> For the first time a council is acknowledging that dogma can evolve and that our knowledge of revelation increases with the passage of history. Revelation is above all a living reality, a history of salvation, and not merely a communication of concepts.

The Embattled Minority Makes an Issue
Over the Vote on Collegiality

Not a day goes by but what the embattled minority tries to arrest the progress of the Council. These prelates feel strong because they are for the most part Italians who are geographically close to the Curia and therefore to the Pope.

Last year the partisans of the status quo fought hard enough to succeed—at least temporarily—in casting suspicion on the indicative votes of October 30 and preventing this new method of getting the Council moving from being used again.

A Trial? This year the same minority group, weak in numbers but admirably well situated to play at intimidating even the Pope, have not resigned themselves to accept the positive vote on collegiality. They have found a means of defense. "It is contrary to the regulations of the Council," they have announced, "to vote twice on the same chapter in order to divide the difficulty" (collegiality on the one hand, and the diaconate on the other). Yet this procedure was accepted by a standing vote in the assembly. It was thus not irregular, and in fact enabled the assembly to reduce the *placet juxta modum* votes to less than one-third. The question is therefore juridically settled. But the opposition does not see it that way. They chose as spokesman Bishop Carli of Segni. Father Wenger, editor-in-chief of *La Croix*, wrote of him last summer that he used "specious arguments in favor of the primacy and against collegiality."

This Bishop, who belongs to the Lateran School, decided to take action against the Council directors, who in his eyes are "guilty of having broken the regulations." (The regulation in question—chapter 9, article 37, section 2—says only this: "For each amended schema, whether in whole or in part, the formula for voting is: *placet, non placet, placet juxta modum*.")

Emotions ran high in St. Peter's on Friday when this new maneuver on the part of the integralists became known. Next Wednesday the moderators, the presidents of the Council, and the Coordinating Commission will meet to examine the situation. It doesn't seem too serious, however, because Bishop Carli doesn't have sufficient stature to bring it off.

The majority of bishops have total confidence in the Pope and the directors of the Council. They are not likely to be impressed; such tactics have been employed before and likely will be again.

OCTOBER 5

Will Paul VI Suppress the Index, That "Cemetery of Catholic Intellectual Life"?

The time is gone when one needed courage to attack the Index. But this takes nothing away from the interest of a small book by Hans Kühner entitled *Index Romanus*. It was translated and published recently in France by the Catholic house of Spès, and is a violent attack against the catalogue of prohibited books. The work is timely at this period in the Council. It begins with a humorous reflection by Georges-Christophe Lichtenberg: "The one book in the world that most deserves to be prohibited is the catalogue of prohibited books."

A Catholic who reads a book on the Index without permission from his bishop still commits a mortal sin, at least in theory.

The Index is a tome of some 300 pages that was begun in 1557 under Paul IV. The most recent edition was put out in 1948. But it has been brought up to date (pardon the expression), since all the works of Jean-Paul Sartre were condemned later that year; in 1952, those of André Gide; in 1954, Nikos Kazantzakis' *The Last Temptation of Christ*, which every educated Catholic has read; in 1956 Simone de Beauvoir's *The Second Sex* and *The Mandarins*; in 1961, *The Life of Christ* by Father Jean Steinmann.

The Index condemns the complete works of ninety-three authors of the seventeenth century, fifty-two authors of the eighteenth century, nineteen authors of the nineteenth century, and sixteen authors of the twentieth century. Albertus Magnus, who was canonized by the Church, was put on it, as were Maeterlinck, Pascal's *Pensées*, Spinoza's *Treatises*,

Alexandre Dumas, father and son—and the nineteenth-century *Grand Dictionnaire universel Larousse.*

The Index is nourished largely by denunciations, which are sometimes anonymous and are encouraged by canon law. Several works which have received the imprimatur are on the Index. Frequently a priest will learn through the newspapers that his book was put on the Index. I personally announced this news to Father Steinmann.

Toward the end of 1960, thirty bishops and ten Catholic universities appealed to John XXIII, who formed a special commission for the revision of the Index, Hans Kühner informs us. "The Index," he writes, "is laughable. It is a fossil. It is forever discredited." He quotes Jean Baptiste Sherer, who wrote in 1957, "It is the cemetery of Catholic intellectual life."

The author concludes by saying that "All of Christianity confidently expects Paul VI to put an end to the permanent crusade the Index wages against the mind and against man."

OCTOBER 6

Revelation: "History" or "Message"?

"The schema on ecumenism is a star preceding the dawn," declared Cardinal Martin of Rouen yesterday as he gave the report on chapter 1 of this document. The first four ballots on this schema once again exhibited the cohesion and health of Vatican II, since of over 2,100 voters the number of *non placet* ballots swung between 16 and 57.

Monday's assembly then continued the debate on the schema *De Revelatione*, chapters 3–6.

Fifteen speakers took the floor. Almost all praised the schema. The most critical remarks were as follows.

Bishop Gasbarri, Apostolic Administrator of Grosseto, Italy, focused on the historical value of the Gospels and requested that the schema not give the impression of siding with "recent and not too solid" exegetical schools. "Let us be careful," he added, "not to disturb the faithful. Let us not purely and simply reduce the sacred books to ordinary historical works." He reminded the Fathers of the desire expressed before the Council opened by the congregation of seminaries, "which requested us to react against certain innovations."

Archbishop Morcillo of Madrid, felt that Revelation was treated in too "subjective" a manner.

Bishop William Philbin of Down and Connor, Ireland, also regretted that the historical character of the Gospels was not sufficiently stressed.

To speak of revelation as a "message," he thought, is "dangerous and equivocal." He added, "Let us not follow imprudent schools with our eyes closed. Let us be on our guard against false interpretations of the sacred texts.

Auxiliary Bishop Heuschen of Liège disagreed with this opinion; he found the word *message* (in Latin, *praeconium*) perfectly adequate since, he said, the Gospels are narrated to nourish the life of the Church. "Why oppose history and message?" he asked. And he added, "The magisterium should not limit itself to disciplining the work of exegetes; it should also encourage them."

The same speaker defended the German method of *Formgeschichte*. "Just because this method has been abused does not mean that it is wrong. Let us understand this clearly."

Cardinal Meyer of Chicago warned against too material an interpretation of revelation, which is, he said, "an interpersonal colloquy from God to man." He added that "If we understand the inerrancy of Scripture correctly, there is no difficulty in admitting errors in the Bible."

Cardinal Bea was pleased with the contents of the schema as well as its triple biblical, positive, and pastoral character. He hoped that it would be more explicit about the values contained in the Old Testament (the psalms, the decalogue, and so forth).

"Sorores Carissimae" Archbishop Weber of Strasbourg addressed the women auditors as *"sorores carissimae."* He went on to say that an exegete must know the nonsacred texts of Egypt, Syria, Babylonia, and so on in order to understand Scripture better. "The sacred books form a whole," he said. "Let us never lose sight of the context."

Archbishop Edelby, Patriarchical Consultor to Maximos IV Saigh, the Melkite Patriarch of Antioch, made the most distinguished intervention.

"The Latin Church," he said, "is having trouble getting out of the post-Tridentine period." The West has a tendency to oppose tradition and Scripture. This is a nominalist mentality. The East does not have this problem. Scripture is considered the mission of the Spirit. It is pneumatic, prophetic, and liturgical; it testifies to the Spirit's entrance into history. The speaker drew a parallel between "the liturgy of the word" and the "eucharistic liturgy." Theologians, he regretted to say, "have tried to confine truths to formulas. This is a mistake. What is said by the Spirit transcends all formulation."

Auxiliary Bishop Schick of Fulda, Germany, was glad that the schema puts an end to the charge that the Catholic Church discourages Bible reading.

Archbishop Joseph Cordeiro of Karachi, Pakistan, alluded to the Protestant exegete Rudolf Bultmann and his thesis of "the creative community of myths." "Let us not take Bultmann seriously," he said. "He is very out of date."

Bishop Manuel del Rosario of the Philippines defended the Apocalypse.

OCTOBER 7

For the First Time in History,
a Council Treats of the Laity

For the first time in the history of the Church, the theme of the laity has been made the subject of conciliar deliberations. On Tuesday morning Vatican II heard the first report on the schema entitled "On the Apostolate of the Laity," presented by Cardinal Cento. "This text," he said, "constitutes the best answer to the criticism that the Church is the hierarchy. It corresponds perfectly with the dual pastoral and ecumenical aim of the Council." Then the Cardinal added in typically Italian fashion, "Its importance is not great or even very great; it is supreme for the life of the Church. All laymen share in the priesthood of Christ to some degree."

The Latin Church, it is only too clear, has been clerical for many centuries, and Protestants have had royal sport criticizing this. The essential role of the laity was to put up funds. The clergy took charge of everything else. Catholics had to wait for a Pius XI to hear a special apostolate of the laity spoken of. Even today numerous pastors give Catholic Action movements grudging support at best, and try to restrict them as much as possible. Because of her authoritarianism, the Roman Church helped create a race of laymen whose principal virtue was passive obedience. Happily, this race is dying out.

Sometime soon, it is said, the voice of a layman will again be heard in St. Peter's. The Pope has made this decision. It will be remembered that last year he authorized speeches (which were, it is true, academic) by two laymen, Jean Guitton and Vittorino Veronese, who addressed the Council just before the second session closed.

This time the layman will be a representative of the Catholic Action movements. In addition, a number of Fathers would like the discussion of schema 13 to be preceded each morning by technical comments from well-known lay experts. This would be a good way, say the bishops, of proving to the laity that the hierarchy needs to learn from them everything the bishops may not know about the pressing secular questions of our time: demography, underdeveloped countries, social and economic life, the family, culture, and so forth.

For some years now the laity have heard many flattering words spoken about them, but they have been asked to do very little that was positive. Pastoral letters on the role of the laity are beyond count. But it is a long way from words to actions. Where are the days when a Louis IX locked horns with the clergy, thus proving that one could be both a saint and anticlerical in the precise meaning of those two words? "The clericalization of the Church was the great lever of the de-Christianization of the people," wrote Michel Carrouges.

Historians will undoubtedly consider Vatican II as the link between two eras: the one when the laity were more or less used as "fuel for the ecclesiastical locomotive," as the saying goes, and the one when the laity were recognized as mature, the requisite for an authentic presence of the Church in the modern world. This presence is deeply desired, but as yet means have not been found of assuring it other than by such suspect secular institutes as Opus Dei.

Final Interventions on the Revelation Schema

The general congregation on Tuesday finished examining the schema on revelation. At least two Fathers, Bishop Costantino Caminada of Ferentino, Italy, and Bishop Cekada of Skoplje, Yugoslavia, denounced "the total biblical ignorance of many Catholics." The first noted that reading Scripture "is difficult, especially for uneducated people," who need commentaries. The second speaker remarked that Protestants were far superior to Catholics in this respect. He proposed that Rome create a body analogous to the British and Foreign Bible Society (Protestant), which has the distribution of 1,800 translations of the Bible to its credit.

The intervention of Bishop Carli, the great adversary of collegiality and of ecumenism as it is presently understood, deserves special mention. It was in fact the only really negative intervention during the whole debate over *De Revelatione*.

"The schema," he said, "does not take sufficient account of the errors that are multiplying rapidly, such as *Formgeschichte*. Why was the passage suppressed from the first version which spoke of 'dissipating the errors of our time'?" Bishop Carli also found it regrettable that the text says nothing about the historical veracity of the Gospels concerning Christ's infancy and the post-resurrection. Tradition is as immutable as Scripture. This is not stated, and it is a serious defect. Tradition is not sufficiently respected in the whole of chapter 3, he asserted.

Bishop Carli stated that it is said the Council does not want to resolve the difficult question of the relationship between Scripture and tradition, but that this has been done, and badly. "For false diplomatic and ecumenical reasons we have not dared say that tradition is more ample than Scripture. Yet the Orientals are very attached to tradition."

Bishop Barrachina of Alicante, Spain, noted that during the first centuries Bible-reading was the principal form of catechesis. "Because of present ignorance, the sacramental life is not bearing fruit."

Bishop Volk of Mainz regretted that theology was not more in the service of the Bible which is totally centered on the spiritual life. Bishop Boillon of Verdun was of the same opinion. He said:

> Scripture should be the soul of theology, but unfortunately, that is not the case in our modern manuals, which are too abstract and too cut off from life. Scripture seems more like an ornamentation than a source. Recourse is had to Scripture to prove a thesis, but the opposite should be the case: begin with Scripture to establish a thesis. . . .
>
> The magisterium is an essential factor in the Church, but it is always perfectible, as is the Church herself. The Church should always be spoken of in a dynamic fashion.

Truth Is Not To Be Confused with Dogmatic Formulas   Abbot Butler of the English Benedictines made three pertinent remarks: (1) Catholic truth should not be confused with formulas, even dogmatic ones, because they are not exhaustive. (2) Exegetes should be given great freedom; it is impossible to seek truth without falling into error from time to time. (3) Scientific truth should never be a cause for fear; it cannot, by definition, go against the true faith.

Catholics May Participate in Liturgical Prayers with other Christians

By a vote of 1,926 against 30, with 209 *placet juxta modum* votes, the Council adopted the first chapter of the schema on ecumenism Tuesday.

Then the Fathers voted on the four parts of the second chapter.

By a vote of 2,120 against 46, they admitted that unity is a problem for the whole Church, which ought to reform herself if necessary to achieve this unity.

By a vote of 2,076 against 92, they affirmed that Catholics must undergo a "conversion of heart" so that the suspicions and misunderstandings that impede the ecumenical movement may disappear.

By a vote of 1,872 against 292, they approved the possibility of Catholics' participating with other Christians in the same cult. Application of this measure was reserved to episcopal authority.

Finally, by a vote of 2,099 to 62, they requested that Catholic education be revised if necessary to conform with the principles of unity, and invited Catholics to collaborate with Protestants in all domains of practical life "to give a common Christian witness to the world."

OCTOBER 8

Rome's Responsibility in the Schism with the East

The ninety-sixth general congregation included some interesting interventions, both on ecumenism and on the laity. Suggestions by Cardinal Ritter, Archbishop of St. Louis, and Archbishop Duval of Algiers were widely commented upon.

Archbishop Hermaniuk of Winnipeg delivered the report on the first part of chapter 3 of the schema on ecumenism, concerning the Oriental Churches. It was a real revelation for many Fathers. "The Roman Church," Archimandrite Scrima told me, "discovered today just how she repudiated the Oriental Church and how unsubstantial the schism is."

Here are the historical facts as reported by Archbishop Hermaniuk:

> It is necessary to know the causes of the separation between the East and the West in order to be sincere and to make reparation for the wrongs of the Latin Church. In the time of Patriarch Michael Carularius of Constantinople, Cardinal Humbert [originally of Lorraine], the pontifical legate, attributed every manner of heresy to the Oriental Church in order to condemn her. But that was false, since the Patriarch of Constantinople held the same faith as the Roman Church. These unhappy events, let us note, took place in 1054 during a pontifical interregnum, since the Pope had been dead for three months.

Cardinal Humbert proved his total ignorance of the Oriental faith by accusing that Church of having suppressed the term *filioque* from the Credo. This accusation was entirely without foundation, for the good reason that the expression never figured in Oriental terminology. Thus, the schism with the East took place in an atmosphere of calumny. Few Latin bishops have ever understood this clearly.

Intercommunion Permitted with the Orthodox The assembly voted 2,119 to 39 yesterday for a relaxation of the rules concerning *communication in sacris*. This expression refers to the possibility that Orthodox and Catholics may receive the eucharist and go to confession in either Church.

Laymen Are Not Assistants to the Clergy

After reports of the voting on ecumenism, the assembly began examination of the schema on the laity. Bishop Hengsbach of Essen, Germany, gave an account of the genesis of the present texts, which had been amended, after some ninety-nine interventions, by five subcommissions.

Bishop Hengsbach's report described some highly technical interventions whose sole purpose was to improve a schema Cardinal Ritter still considered "insufficiently pastoral," "confused," "too clerical," "legalistic," and marked with "an unbecoming favoritism." The American prelate thought that the specific role of the laity is not clearly brought out. "The schema speaks as if the laity were simple assistants to the clergy," he said, and added that too much emphasis is put on Catholic Action, to the detriment of other possible forms of the apostolate. Also, the laity should have a proper spirituality which is not a mere carbon copy of clerical spirituality.

Cardinal Browne of the Curia was surprised that the schema did not speak explicitly of the obedience which the laity owe their pastors.

In the name of fifteen Canadian bishops, Bishop Remi de Roo of Victoria, British Columbia, said, "Creation has a Christian value, and Christ is not added to this creation but represents its summit. The laity have the duty of completing creation and therefore of engaging in temporal activities. Let us not confuse the apostolate of the laity with the apostolate of the hierarchy. Let us adopt a more biblical theology."

Bishop Paul Charbonneau of Hull, Quebec, declared that it is false to say the laity must second the clergy; their task is quite different. He complained that the schema lacks a biblical spirit, and said the laity must become incarnate in the world, according to the image of Christ. Otherwise, the redemption will not be accomplished. The Church should not be presented as a society outside of the world. Without the laity the Church cannot be the leaven of the world as the Gospel demands. Cooperation between priests and laity ought to work both ways. "Let us respect the laity," Bishop Charbonneau concluded, "and avoid clericalism at all costs." Coadjutor Archbishop Fernandes of Delhi said, "The obligation of justice comes before that of charity. Where Catholics are a minority, it is essential that they collaborate with nonconfessional groups."

Archbishop Duval of Algiers spoke in the name of all the bishops of North Africa, and said: "The apostolate is above all a dialogue with all men. The solidarity among all men is a fact of capital importance and well founded theologically." Indeed, the Church transcends her limits; the unbaptized are not deprived of grace. The natural and the supernatural should not be unduly separated. "In my own diocese," the Archbishop said, "I consult non-Christians as well as Christians, and they have made many constructive suggestions."

A Document Against Collegiality

With a perseverance that is worthier of admiration than imitation, the integralists continue their maneuvers against collegiality. Members of the theological commission received copies of a document requesting Paul VI to have Vatican II's decision concerning collegiality annulled. The document was signed by Cardinal Ruffini of Palermo and another Italian cardinal.

The way this document was circulated is even more extraordinary than the fact that it exists: it was distributed in the building where the theological commission conducts its official business.

Hans Küng Denounces "Hypocrisy" in the Church

In 1963, during the second session, an angel passed—in the figurative sense, at least—when Archbishop Roberts, formerly of Bombay, proposed that the Inquisition be inquisitioned.*

The same angel visited us again on Wednesday at the Dutch Documentation Center, where Professor Hans Küng, director of the Ecumenical Institute at the University of Tübingen, Germany, put hypocrisy in the Roman Church on trial.

Professor Küng is well known for his courageous books on the Council† and for his pronouncements in Rome, which have been so outspoken that one Italian journal, in a significant lapse, referred to him as a Protestant speaker. But Professor Küng is a theologian and Catholic to the marrow of his bones. His understanding of the Church is, however, demanding. In this conciliar time, his propospals have great importance and

* See pages 191–193.
† See the reports for October 2 and 3, 1963.

exert considerable influence. By way of proof one needed only to observe the reactions of his audience, which included several bishops on Wednesday, and listen to the vigorous applause that followed his talk.

Father Küng's subject was not an entirely original one. Some two years before the Council opened, a French Catholic gave a talk entitled "Contempt for the Truth," in which he upbraided Catholicism for being "a school of hypocrisy, a school of class distinction, of monopoly and contempt." He recalled Leo XIII's words, "God has no need of our lies," —and he added, "Under the pretext of avoiding scandal, supposedly in order to defend the cause of the Church, how many lies have been uttered by those who teach the decalogue!"

Hans Küng developed a similar theme in Rome before the conciliar Fathers. This is to his credit. He did so without subterfuge, with the bold tranquility of those who know that they will not be contradicted because the very stones would cry out what the clergy want hidden.

Here is a condensation of his talk, whose applications seem obvious:

> Contemporary architecture, painting, the theater, cinema, and literature refuse everything that is not sincere, honest, and genuine. Even modern philosophy encourages us to absolute veracity.
>
> And the Church? Does she give the same impression? Of course, since John XXIII and Vatican II, immense progress has been made. But it is a pity that veracity is not one of the four cardinal virtues. Isn't prudence the cardinal virtue most emphasized?
>
> Why all the fuss over the sixth commandment, about whether or not impurity is a mortal sin, when false witness, condemned by the eighth commandment, is considered a venial sin? The Church frequently recognizes her errors too late—Galileo, the interpretation of Genesis, and so forth.
>
> And yet the truth of the Gospel demands the truthfulness of the Church. The demands of the Gospel and of the modern world call to each other. The world expects absolute and concrete sincerity of the Church. The world expects the Church not so much to pronounce these truths as to engage in the truth without compromise.

Some Examples   Here are some specific examples:

1. "Rather than the Council pronounce on evangelical simplicity, the world expects it to abolish feudal titles, vestments, and customs which appear more and more ridiculous."
2. "Rather than the Council pronounce on poverty, the world expects it to reduce the pomp and extravagance of liturgical ceremonies."
3. "Rather than the Church exhort the secular press to accurate reporting,

the world expects her to renounce triumphalism and onesided statistics, and stop camouflaging her own failures."

4. "Rather than she demand liberty for herself, the world expects the Church to accord more liberty to ecclesiastical scholars and theologians of various schools and to reject the Index and the methods of the Inquisition."

5. "Rather than the Council demand freedom for Catholic schools, the world expects it to reform the legislation on mixed marriages."

6. "Rather than it offer beautiful and profound words about conjugal love, the world expects the Council to pronounce on the problem of birth control."

7. "Rather than Vatican II assert that Catholicism transcends all civilizations, the world expects it to abolish the last vestiges of Latinism in mission countries."

Professor Küng concluded with these words: "The weakness of the Roman Church consists in ambiguity, hypocrisy, and lack of sincerity and authenticity. The strength, the youth, and the future of the Church consist in her veracity and her fidelity to the Gospel message."

OCTOBER 9

Will Schema 13 Get the Attention
Its Importance Requires?

For the first time since the third session began, the Council Fathers are somewhat uneasy. The high-level meeting of the moderators, presidents, secretaries, and undersecretaries of Vatican II which was held Wednesday evening profoundly disappointed those who know the results. Or rather the absence of results. In effect, the high command of the Council could not agree on whether or not there should be a fourth session. They were almost equally divided on prolonging the Council.

Furthermore, the Curia is applying pressure to get discussion of schema 13 over with as soon as possible. This schema is not ripe, they say. What is the point, therefore, in losing time over it? Let us have done with it so the bishops can resume control of their dioceses and the Pope can regain his freedom so as to restore order in the Church after more than three years of dangerous ferment.

It is true that schema 13 is not yet adequate, even after seven drafts. But this has been the case with all the other schemas as well; they had to be more or less taken apart after the Fathers had made their criticisms. It would seem that the only way to bring this schema to maturity is to have it discussed in the assembly. Then during the next recess it could be redrafted.

More than 110 Fathers have already registered to intervene on this schema, which indicates the great interest it has aroused. This is precisely what bothers the conservatives. That the Council should speak, with the supreme authority which it has by right, on such burning questions as contraception, conscientious objection, disarmament, hunger, and culture seems literally to madden the adversaries of *aggiornamento* in the Church.

Vatican II spent three years talking about purely ecclesiastical problems. Will it be so ungracious as to spend a mere two weeks discussing the real problems of the modern world? The laity, who are assured that their opinion is of great importance, would find it difficult to forgive the bishops for such unjustifiable haste. The heritage of John XXIII, which Paul VI more than anyone wants to take up, urges the Council to follow in the spirit of *Mater et magistra* and *Pacem in terris*, which unhesitantly treated in depth matters that preoccupy millions of men today.

The Pope and the moderators met on Thursday evening, as they do every week. From what we can gather, they discussed these problems. We won't know for some days the conclusions they reached. But we do know that the immense majority of French, Belgian, Dutch, German, and English bishops want a fourth session.

Youth Today Are "More Capable of Idealism Than Ever"

Discussion of the laity in Thursday's general congregation. Eighteen Fathers spoke. Here are some of the more interesting remarks made.

Archbishop D'Souza (India), a member of the Congregation of Missionaries of Saint Francis de Sales at Annecy, provoked loud applause:

> We must absolutely consider the laity as adults. It is said that nothing must be done without the bishop. To be sure! But what abuses this expression serves when it merely means: nothing "against" or "outside" of the bishop. The people of God is not a totalitarian race. Let us never forget the liberty of the sons of God. . . . Catholic Action is merely one form of the apostolate among others.
>
> The aim of this Council is to renew and reform the Church. The first challenge is to liberate the Church from clericalism. Are we ready to do this? . . . Let us treat the laity as brothers, for in God's eyes they are equal to the bishops. Let us give them real freedom in their temporal decisions.

Laymen as Nuncios? Archbishop D'Souza continued vigorously:

> Why not have laymen in the sacred congregations at Rome or in
> the episcopal curias? Why not laymen as nuncios? Everything we
> de here will be in vain if we do not proceed with the radical re-
> organization of the Church. . . . Of course laymen can make mistakes
> and commit indiscretions; they will perhaps cause us some suffering.
> But isn't it a law of life that we only grow through crises?
>
> Prudence is a cardinal virtue. But if we exaggerate it, we will
> fall into immobilism. If we push forward, the Church will experience
> a new spring. Otherwise we are doing nothing very serious here.

This forthright language obviously pleased the Fathers.

Bishop de Smedt (Belgium) said, "Let us proceed by way of dialogue
and not as schoolmasters. Modern man no longer expects to be treated
like a child. This is particularly true of young people, who have proven
themselves capable of taking an active part in politics and even setting
off revolutions. Let us not repress our youth; let us help them."

Auxiliary Bishop Bettazzi of Bologna also expressed admiration for
youth. "Two-thirds of the world consists in people younger than we.
It is unfortunate that this schema doesn't say a word about those who
will be the leaders of the world of tomorrow."

Archbishop Conway of Armagh, Ireland, continued the same line of
thought and requested that responsibilities be given to today's youth, who
he said "are more capable of idealism than ever."

Maronite Archbishop Ziadé of Beirut said, "Let us be careful not
to give substance to the charge of neoclericalism."

Bishop Stefan Barela of Czestochowa, Poland, asked that the schema
say something about atheism.

Auxiliary Bishop Leven of San Antonio said, "This schema lacks
punch," and then made the Fathers laugh when he remarked, "We sometimes get the impression that the only laymen the bishop has occasion to
dialogue with are his doctor and his housekeeper."

Bishop Gerhardt de Vet of Breda, the Netherlands, affirmed the
"autonomy" of the temporal world.

Bishop de Vito of Lucknow, India, boldly declared, "All laymen participate truly in the triple function of bishops: sanctifying, teaching, and
governing."

Bishop van Lierde, Vicar General of Vatican City, said, "Let us not
give the impression that the Church wants to control the temporal order.
The problem is rather to infuse it with a Christian spirit."

Coadjutor Archbishop Veuillot of Paris emphasized the obedience the laity owe the bishop: "Bishops must listen to laymen, but the latter are subject to bishops."

Votes and Amendments

The third chapter of the schema on ecumenism was approved on Thursday by a vote of 1,843 to 24, with 296 *juxta modum* votes.

Chapter 3 of the schema *De ecclesia*, which was recently adopted by the Council, will be redrafted in keeping with 4,800 amendments: 3,600 on collegiality and 1,200 on the diaconate. These figures show the effort which the Fathers are putting into the basic texts for the renewal of the Church. The commissions have a good deal of work ahead of them.

OCTOBER 10

The Universal Church in Conclave

Yesterday was the ninety-eighth general congregation since the beginning of Vatican II; hence this type of assembly is not hard to describe. One is struck first by its disjointed character. With the same sincerity but unequal talents the Fathers contradict one another, though not intentionally; the text of interventions is submitted five days in advance, so the bishops have no way of knowing what others are going to say. Theoretically, then, the speeches should be a series of monologues, but in practice they often do seem to be related by a kind of pre-established disharmony.

What could there be in common between a young African bishop, a native of a newly liberated country, and a venerable prelate from a quasi-medieval Christian country like Spain or Portugal; between a bishop who has been expelled from China and has good reasons to hate communism, and a brilliant prelate from Holland or Denmark or Germany who is in contact with the Protestant Churches, which have strongly influenced the Catholics in his country; between a Frenchman from the Vendée and one from Alsace; between a Latin American promoter of agrarian reform in an underdeveloped country and a Polish bishop who is struggling for clerical liberty; between a missionary bishop with few priests and a prelate whose diocese is exceptionally rich in vocations?

The only common denominator, though a vital one, of these men from all races and all social backgrounds—sons of African kings, of workers, of aristocrats, of captains of industry, of farmers—is their unconditional attachment to the Roman Church and the Pope.

The value of the interventions is extremely varied. Some speakers sound like a third-year catechism teacher rattling off basic truths. Others, forgetting that they are speaking to preachers, launch into pious homilies. The audience smiles more or less indulgently. A rare Father will try to break the terrible monotony (there are more than twenty inteventions each session) with a flash of humor. Some read their breviary to pass the time, others novels. The latest example in this category we have heard of concerns a French-speaking bishop who thumbed through Michel de Saint-Pierre's *The New Priests*, scowling all the while. When the clock strikes 11, many Fathers repair to one of the coffee bars for a nonalcoholic drink. There are two such bars, one on the right and one on the left, and it is said jokingly that the bishops make their choice according to their political sympathies.

Some interventions have no other purpose than to criticize a given word used in a schema on page *x* at line *y*. Others reach the rarest theological heights. Still others, carried away by their own oratory, go beyond the limited time without adding anything essential. The moderators then call the speaker to order, usually courteously but sometimes sternly if the orator keeps going all the while he is saying that he is concluding. Some speeches are profound, other laughable, and others completely beside the point. Some are mild-mannered, others bitter or deliberately polemical. Some are delivered with marmoreal calm, others in such a hysterical voice that the microphones vibrate and no one can understand. Some Fathers deliver their speeches in carefully polished Ciceronian Latin; others, whose eyesight is poor, can scarcely decipher a text obviously prepared by an expert. Some pronounce Latin so badly they are very hard to follow.

Some are as clear as spring water; others wander, or are deliberately vague in their criticisms or praises. The most frequently used expressions are "We must emphasize . . . ," "Let us stress that. . . ." Superlatives are used liberally; sobriety is not particularly an episcopal quality.

A Good-Natured and Happy Atmosphere Sometimes, when something important is expected, one can hear a pin drop. But generally the intervention is given to the accompaniment of a buzz of whisperings and squeaking seats.

With very few exceptions, everyone looks at his watch as 12:30 approaches, the time when the session ends. As the Fathers begin to descend the immense steps of St. Peter's, their robes blazing in the sun, one is inevitably reminded of a group of students coming from a lecture that has lasted too long.

Upon close inspection, and leaving aside the liturgical ceremonies that begin each session, nothing could be less solemn than a conciliar session. The word *collegiality* contains the word *college*. Its meaning immediately implies a fraternal, happy, and good-natured atmosphere. The bishops gather in small groups on the pavement to talk about the most interesting interventions of the morning.

Friday morning, for example, the Fathers excitedly discussed a virulent speech by Bishop Alexander Carter of Sault Sainte Marie, Ontario. A résumé follows.

The Royal Liberty of the Laity

The document on the laity was conceived in sin, the sin of clericalism. Clericalism is the original sin of this schema. Laymen were invited too late by the commissions to help the bishops draft this text. Moreover, it was a mistake to have abbreviated the first version of the schema and yet retain all of its ideas. The result is an evisceration [*evisceratio*].

The laymen are not happy with the text, and they are right. We are not dialoguing with them. The clergy are talking to the clergy. Let us redraft this schema in its entirety with the real collaboration of the laity.

Nor was Cardinal Suenens happy. He wondered why the term "Catholic Action" was reserved to groups explicity authorized by the hierarchy. "All groups of laymen," affirmed the Archbishop of Malines-Brussels, "should be considered Catholic Action movements. Let us give a catholic (which is to say, universal) definition of Catholic Action." The Cardinal added, "In the beginning it was practical for the hierarchy to organize the apostolate of the laity. But now that the latter have awakened from their sleep, times have changed."

Archbishop Kozlowiecki of Lusaka, Northern Rhodesia, thought the definition of the apostolate given in the schema was too narrow: "Whatever Christian activity the laity engage in is apostolic. Let us respect the royal liberty of the laity. Clericalism is the number one enemy of the Church."

This idea recurred like a lietmotif in many interventions. It is a sign of the times, and only an ill will could suppose that a spirit of demagogy lies behind these repeated statements. The truth is that most of the bishops are still aware of the harmful effects of the many centuries when the hierarchy held the laity in subjection, silent and passive. They really want this situation to change. And at least they say as much with energy and sincerity.

The Priesthood of the Faithful In the name of thirty Latin American bishops, Bishop Marco McGrath of Santiago-Veraguas, Panama, said: "The foundation of every lay apostolate is the common priesthood of the faithful by virtue of the sacraments of baptism and confirmation which they have received."

Archbishop Seper of Zagreb rightly remarked that there is as yet no serious theology of confirmation, the sacrament of adults in the faith. The same speaker thought it highly important for laymen to meet once a week at church for formation, and urged Vatican II to make this obligatory, on the same level with Sunday mass.

Bishop Soares de Resende of Beira, Mozambique, was of the opinion that the clergy ought to be formed to a better understanding of Catholic Action. He then raised his voice unexpectedly to say, "Let us create in Rome itself an international university for Catholic Action." He thought this would be the most important result of the whole Council.

The Italian Bishop Ruotolo is an authoritarian prelate. He said that all Catholics without exception should be obliged to join a Catholic organization. Nor was that all: he thought further that all laymen should make a spiritual retreat at least once a year. And to head off any objection, he specified that these spiritual exercises should be "free."

On the whole the Fathers, who accepted the schema as a "basis of discussion" by a standing vote, agree on its doctrinal weakness, its clerical character, and its lack of precision. The criticisms are such that the commission will likely have to redo the present schema. A great many amendments are expected.

Miss Marie-Louise Monnet Calls on the Council Fathers Miss Marie-Louise Monnet, an auditor at the Council, recently gave a lecture for the benefit of the Council Fathers at the Pan-African Secretariat. She said:

"If the world is so harsh, couldn't it be because it is in the exclusive control of men? God does not will this state of affairs."

In a suppliant voice, she went on: "Gentlemen, put your most apostolic and most human priests in diocesan ecclesiastical courts which deal with marriage cases. I have seen miracles happen with respect to such problems, but I have also seen tragedies. Perhaps the Council could discuss this matter.

"Woman is equal to man in dignity. She should be free to pursue her vocation. Could you, gentlemen, stress this point in your interventions? If schema 13, which few people will read, is to have a universal influence, it will be necessary for everyone—bishops, priests, and laymen—to make a gigantic effort. Gentlemen, invite the women of your dioceses to organize."

At this point a bishop rose to say that laymen should be allowed to speak in the conciliar aula on this schema. Bishop Ancel expressed the hope that many African bishops will intervene on schema 13, which is "much too Occidental" in his opinion.

In a preliminary exposition, the Auxiliary Bishop of Lyon, who is also the Superior of the Prado and has worked on the economic and social life section of schema 13, easily refuted the objection leveled against the schema by conservatives that it treats of a domain that is not the Church's concern.

OCTOBER 12

Schema 13 Reviews the Great Problems of the Contemporary World

For the majority of Christians, or at any rate for those who are more or less interested in Vatican II, the Council will begin when it takes up the problems of the secular world, that is, with the examination of schema 13, "The Church in the Modern World." Most men of our times are in fact little interested in the liturgy, collegiality, or even religious liberty, for this last problem has been positively resolved in all countries which were influenced by the French Revolution.

In the corridors of Vatican II, everyone is talking about schema 13; some are for it, others are against it, but none are indifferent. This "promised land" of Vatican II, as Father Congar put it, is now in sight. It is only a matter of days. Will this schema furnish proof that the Church is capable of transcending her internal problems to confront the problems of all mankind directly?

Theologically speaking, the Church was not founded for herself but for the world. This world, which looks at the Church and sometimes judges her severely, has aspirations with innumerable religious implications. The Church's role is less to view the world with paternal condescension, either to pity it or to criticize it, than to listen to it with patience and humility in order to understand it and help it fulfill itself. The world, which Genesis says was created by God, is a "holy land." Chrisianity's mission in it should be as educator and prophet rather than judge. If it is true, as Isaiah prophesied, that the world has germinated its savior in Christ, it falls to the Church, the continuation of Christ, to assume responsibility for this world, less to moralize over it than to spiritualize it interiorly in liberty. The world can give the Church almost as much as it receives. The implicit Christianity of the one corresponds with the explicit Christianity of the other. It sometimes happens that the implicit is more evangelical than the explicit.

This is the ideal that schema 13 expresses, more or less well. The schema, with its five appendixes, is the labor of Fathers Chenu, Congar, Lebret, and Haubtmann (France), Rahner (Germany), de Rietmatten (Switzerland), Dingemans (Belgium), Schillebeeckx (Netherlands), and others. Cardinal Suenens was one of the first to praise it. The Pope, who it is said will create a special secretariat for atheism in the near future, confided the production of the schema to Bishop Guano of Livorno, president of a special subcommission composed equally of members of the commission on theology and members of the commission for the lay apostolate.

The evolution of this schema has been extremely complex. Innumerable obstacles had to be overcome, not the least of which was the objection that a religious assembly has no business occupying itself with secular matters. This ecclesiastic ghetto mentality has prevailed so long in the Church that it has become almost second nature.

We shall present an analysis of schema 13 and its appendixes, accompanied by extracts that seem to us most characteristic. Since it is destined for the world, it is fitting that this important document be known to all in advance. The information will help us understand the interventions.

After stating that "The joys and hopes, the griefs and the anxieties of the men of this age, especially those who are poor," are those of Vatican II, and that the Church rejoices in the progress of science and technology, the schema goes on to say that the Council recognizes the work of the Spirit in different events which concern the whole human race. The text is addressed to all men of good will, whether Christians or not. "All Christians must cooperate with all men in a spirit of fraternity, poverty, and service. They must confront the urgent challenges of our time with vigilence and promptitude."

CHAPTER I. THE INTEGRAL VOCATION OF MAN

[By becoming incarnate and living a life of labor and humility, the Son of God] not only sanctified human nature but also ennobled all of creation. The Council notes with keen sadness the short-sightedness of those who reduce human life to its terrestrial dimensions. Christ severely reprimanded those who had an immoderate love of the goods of this world and accused them of idolatry of the god of money.

Humanity gives constant proof that its happiness has been ruined by injustice, falsehood, and violence. . . . Man needs the gifts of God, not only to attain eternal beatitude but also to build up the terrestrial city in justice and charity. . . . A humanity which would seek God without building a more human world would defeat its search. The construction of a more fraternal city constitutes a spiritual necessity.

By liberating a mass of men from the oppression of basic material needs, we enable the human spirit to achieve higher values. . . . Let no one who has been called to the things of God show scorn for the terrestrial tasks of humanity or dispense himself from remedying the misery of his brothers. Let all be mindful that man needs spiritual food as well as material food.

CHAPTER 2. THE CHURCH IN THE SERVICE OF GOD
AND MANKIND

The Church, which is in this world but not of it, is bound by multiple and mutual relations to the world, that is to say, to all men. These mutual relations are fruitful for the Church herself and for the world, despite the divergences and the sometimes inevitable difficulties.

The Church herself uses these temporal things insofar as her proper mission requires them. However, she places no hope in the privileges offered by civil authority. Moreover, she willingly renounces certain rights which were legitimately acquired if they call into doubt the purity of her witness. . . .

The Church especially cherishes the ideal of promoting, with the aid of all men of good will, true freedom of the spirit to the exclusion of every form of coercion which wounds human dignity. Indeed, the Gospel calls for the free response of man, and in no way asks for a purely exterior assent; on the contrary, it requires a sincere interior conversion.

The schema recalls the teaching of the Church concerning the distinction between temporal and spiritual powers: "Pastors must never interfere in the proper domain of civil power, even if they must sometimes judge temporal things from the point of view of faith and morals."

After clearly stating that churchmen must never be distracted by "the lust for power," the schema asks God that they "become increasingly less involved in temporal affairs."

The Ignorance and Sins of Churchmen

The Church listens with simplicity to those who criticize her because of the faults of her members and their lack of evangelical spirit.

For she knows that the Spirit dwells within her, and through her instrumentality spreads his gifts throughout the world. But she also knows she is composed of men whose ignorance and sins can impede the work of the Spirit, and that she must constantly reform herself until the end of time. . . .

The grace of Christ has given birth in innumerable Christians to a continuous tradition of humble devotion to the poor, the abandoned, and the despised. And this tradition is an inspiring example today to all those institutions which nations have developed for the protection of human dignity.

The next chapter, 3, contains a "solemn warning" to all the faithful to accept the concrete conditions which charity and justice dictate today.

CHAPTER 3. CHRISTIAN ACTIVITY IN THE
CONTEMPORARY WORLD

The disciples of Christ must acquire better information about the spiritual, moral, corporal, and material needs of all men, without distinction of race, nation, or social class.

This information, joined with a profound concern to be all things to all men, will extend the concern of the disciples of Christ beyond family, local, or national circles, and will inspire them to conceive of their vocation and their activity in terms of the world and the universal Church.

Desirous of reflection and action, the Christian will always be disposed to participate in collective organizations, particularly if the Church calls him.

The Christian cannot remain indifferent to the progress of the natural and human sciences. Let each contribute to them directly or indirectly. This true spirit of faith will eliminate all fear of an insoluble conflict between faith and true science.

Let the young Christian generation bring its enthusiastic cooperation, rooted in fidelity to the Gospel, to humanity, so concerned with greater justice. . . .

The Desire for Wealth and the Service of the Poor

The evangelization of the poor, which is a visible sign of the coming of God's kingdom, begins when the poor are truly loved in themselves for God and are elevated in such a way that they grow in dignity as human persons. The disinherited will not be transformed by a mere exterior exchange of material goods; they themselves must be transformed in order to live a true divine and human life.

But how can this be done if they do not hear the Good News by way of teaching and example that are capable of convincing them?

Let Christians identify with all their brothers, leaving aside their own ambitions and interests in order to let the Lord's call to all men of good will shine through their activity and example. Let them suffer with those who suffer, weep with those who weep, and be poor with those who are poor. In a word, let them be all things to all men in order to win them for Christ.

May the desire for wealth not turn us away from the accomplishment of our sacred duties, or lead us to be guilty of injustice, or impede us from consecrating our energies to the service of our brothers. Let Christians not despise their flesh, and let them not remain in possession of plenty when they know that so many men live in poverty and misery.

Chapter 3 ends with an invitation to dialogue "in a spirit of humility and disinterest."

CHAPTER 4. THE PRINCIPAL DUTIES INCUMBENT UPON CHRISTIANS TODAY

No discrimination, whether of race, sex, or social class, can be allowed, nor should this be suppressed only or principally by just laws. The social and economic order ought to favor the cessation of slavery and promote a genuine moral, intellectual, and cultural evolution as well as security in work and leisure.

The schema speaks of the equal dignity of men and women in family life as well as in social and civil life, and of the rights of laborers.

Concentration Camps, Torture, Slave Trade of Women, and Abortion
Denouncing the oppression of "collective domination," the schema says:

In our century horrible crimes have been and are still being committed: there are concentration camps where men, without due process of law, are deprived not only of freedom but also of almost every human right; deportations, physical and psychological torture; the infamous sale of women for the pleasure of corrupt men; and many crimes against the right to live of those who are not yet born.

One section is given over to the family and marriage, the nature of conjugal love, the indissolubility of marriage, and similar subjects.

Marriage Is Not Merely an Instrument of Procreation
Marriage is not merely an instrument of procreation. Its indissoluble nature and the rights of the children require that parents truly

love one another . . . , that they cooperate generously in the love of the Creator who through them increases and enriches his family.

With regard to the number of children, Christian spouses know that they are not subject to blind instinct, but that truly they glorify God and perfect themselves in Christ when they try to fulfill their function of procreating with a full and conscious sense of responsibility in conformity with God's grace and the norm of true love. They must rely on prayer and hard work to form a prudent judgment in this matter, not once and for all but for each particular occasion, seeking in economic and pedagogic conditions the salvation of the soul and the body, and also the good of the family and the Church as well as the needs of society.

Turning to married couples, the Council is aware that they are confronted with many serious economic, social, psychological, and civil difficulties; as long as these last, the intimate strength of conjugal love has difficulty surviving except between those who are already endowed with great personal gifts. The Council especially recognizes the great difficulty of balancing the necessity of limiting the family, at least for a while, and the expressions of love and tenderness without which the couple often become strangers to one another; thereby fidelity is endangered as well as the good of the children, with regard either to the education of those already born or to the conservation of a living and open spirit for the later procreation of children when conditions are more favorable.

The Church is aware of all this, and exhorts couples not to lose heart when priests do not resolve conflicts between the law of God and concrete difficulties. Frequently the difficulties stem from serious social defects or from human weakness and malice. Moreover, when the Church recommends chastity, she simultaneously defines the family, true love, and the happiness of the couple in marriage. For this reason she exhorts all specialists in the anthropological, psychological, medical, and sociological sciences, as well as husbands and wives themselves, to collaborate with theologians in a deeper exploration of the complex order of nature. In this way practical solutions to many difficulties are already appearing in part and may be hoped for, again in part; but this hope will never eliminate the imitation of the crucified Christ.

Another section of the chapter concerns "the genuine promotion of culture." It notes not only the Church's contribution to culture but also the fact that "The Church is not bound to any culture, and recognizes the values that are to be found in every culture."

The schema exhorts missionaries and theologians to learn to translate revelation into forms current in the surroundings in which they work, and to "be aware of the limitations of their own culture."

The Suppression of Nuclear Arms   The third section of chapter 4 treats of economic and social life. Three facts are noted: (1) The growth of socialization, (2) the universal character of economic and social problems, and (3) their legitimate diversity. "Much good can come from this new state of things," the schema affirms.

A number of principles are enumerated, among them:

1. An increasing number of persons should participate actively in human enterprises so that a small élite (experts, organizations, particularly strong nations) cannot turn the social organism to their own advantage to the detriment of others.
2. Progress should benefit all men without exception; economic evolution should never be left to itself as though the lure of profit, ambition, or power or interminably expanding production were its true end.

The schema includes this interesting point: "Systems of appropriation, production, and distribution can vary greatly. The Church is not bound to any particular economic system."

Eliminating Social Injustices   "Every effort should be made, without injuring the rights of anyone and taking into account the proper character of each race, to diminish and eventually eliminate social injustices."

The schema also emphasizes the necessity of "truly and efficaciously" organizing laborers in a common work. "Let workers participate through their freely elected representatives in the economic and social decisions upon which their lot and that of their children depends so much."

A fourth section treats of "the solidarity of families and races." It is noted that Christian countries are the richest, and that this might create a "scandal." The principle of subsidiarity within mankind, which constitutes one family, is invoked to encourage richer nations to help those that are less favored. "There is no doubt that a grave obligation in justice and charity binds those nations which are materially prosperous and technically advanced."

The distribution of wealth is the only possible solution to the problems posed by a rising demography. "In what concerns the number of children, the final judgment rests with the parents," we read in the schema, which thus condemns any birth control programs imposed by the state. It adds, however, that parents must bear in mind the common good, not only of their families but of their country as well.

The last section concerns "fostering peace."

[The Council,] responding to the supplicating appeals addressed to it from all sides, adjures, before God, all men and all races and especially their leaders to make every effort to stabilize the peace by recalling their very serious responsibilities, by uniting their powers, and by taking the complex situation into account. There can be no true peace if war is avoided out of fear based on a balance of power rather than out of a genuine spirit of cooperation and concord. That is why anything which divides rather than unites, and especially all words, doctrines, or actions which spread hatred, contempt, vengeance or unfounded suspicions against nations, must be held contrary to peace. The same is true of too great an esteem for one's own country or the desire to acquire too much power. That is why all, and especially those who influence public opinion, must discuss the issue of peace and promote mutual respect among nations.

Even though it is licit to take up arms against an unjust aggressor after every other effort has been made, this use of arms, especially nuclear weapons, whose consequences are greater than can be foreseen and hence cannot be reasonably controlled by man, must be accounted unjust and therefore criminal before God and man. For this reason, every honest effort must be made by all nations not only solemnly to ban nuclear war as an inhuman crime but also to suppress nuclear arms or similar destructive forces altogether.

The Council disapproves of the headlong armaments race because this harms and hinders true peace, concord, and trust among nations, endangers the lives of a great portion of mankind, and wastes the material goods necessary for higher ends.

The Appendixes of Schema 13

The schema proper has five appendixes, which alone form a booklet of fifty-five pages, twenty more than the schema itself. The appendixes take up in detail what the schema proposes in general. In the manner of *Pacem in terris*, each appendix begins with a paragraph discussing the "signs of the times."

Appendix 1. Man in Society   This appendix contains fourteen articles in four chapters, which are on (1) man as a person, (2) man in society, (3) man's relations with society and public powers, and (4) the church in human society.

The idea of progress is repeated frequently in this text. The common good is viewed not in a static manner but always as something to perfect. Likewise, the social order is not considered as fixed once and for all.

The appendix develops what was said in the schema about the equal dignity of the sexes, which does not imply "an equality of responsibility."

On the subject of youth, we read:

> The Church expects much from young people. Modern civilization's solicitude for youth is a sign of progress in human awareness. We must be careful at all times to see that young people are treated as real persons. Let parents see to it that children and adolescents are not treated as objects of delectation or utility; rather let them be educated to a sense of personal and collective responsibility.

Appendix 2. Marriage and the Family   This appendix is in large part the work of Father Häring, who is a specialist in problems relating to birth control. The topics discussed include the renewal of a sense of family, love, fidelity, the conscience and love, preparation for marriage, the conjugal vocation, the sanctifying value of marriage, charity in the family, and fecundity.

It is noted that conjugal chastity stems from the nature and strength of love, and that since marriage is not a mere instrument of procreation, a lack of fecundity in no way affects the indissolubility of the union.

On the difficulties that spouses face regarding number of children, the schema says, "The ultimate decision and practical application of general principles rest with the couple themselves. Let them act, however, according to a conscience that has been formed in conformity with the doctrine of the Church."

This is the first time an official ecclesiastical document has stated clearly that the couple themselves must be the final judges of how to apply the principles of family doctrine in their particular circumstances.

The problems of housing are treated: "Whenever large industrial complexes attract great numbers of workers to the cities, suitable housing should be provided for them and their families. City planning should be adapted to these family necessities and not the contrary."

Appendix 3. The Progress of Culture Is To Be Promoted   This appendix deals in turn with (1) the conditions of culture in the modern world, (2) culture and the person, (3) culture and the community, (4) culture and the glory of God, (5) the Church and culture, (6) the Church and the diversity of cultures, (7) what the Church can contribute to culture, (8) what culture can contribute to the Church, and (9) the Church's concern for culture.

Appendix 4. Economic and Social Life   This appendix is particularly important and extremely clear. It is organized as follows:

A. The growth of the human race.
  1. Causes of uneasiness and anxiety.
  2. The Church scrutinizes the signs.
B. The nature and end of the Church's social doctrine.
C. General principles and orientation for our times.
  1. Conditions for a harmonious and humanizing economic growth.
  2. The participation of all citizens.
  3. The communal purpose of goods and the acquisition of property.
  4. Services and obligations of payment by society.
  5. The common good as distinct from the status quo.
  6. The dignity of work and the lightening of labor.
  7. Systems of producing goods.
  8. Public power.
  9. Relationships between different groups.
  10. The right to private property and its abuses.
  11. Relationships with underdeveloped areas.
D. Conclusion: the necessary conversions.

The right to private property is discussed only in tenth place, much later than the communal purpose of goods (in third place). This order is indicative of the thinking that has inspired the document. Immediately after defining the right to private property, the appendix comments vigorously on its abuses:

> Legitimate in itself, private property nonetheless remains subordinate to the communal purpose of goods and therefore implies a social function which is intrinsic. Where this communal purpose is neglected, denied, or forgotten, private property becomes the occasion of much temptation, greed, and serious disturbances.
>
> Among these abuses, very common today, it is necessary to condemn the high price of property which is caused by the phenomenon of urbanization. These speculations are scandalous.

The same appendix proclaims "the absolute necessity" of land reform in countries where land is unjustly distributed.

Appendix 5. The Community of Peoples and Peace   Here is the outline of the final appendix:

A. The building of peace.
  1. The universal brotherhood of peoples.
  2. The foundation and purpose of the international community.

3. Rights of the human person in the international community.
4. Rights of the political community in the international community.
5. Duties of political communities in the international community.
6. Love of country.
7. Cooperation between prosperous and underdeveloped nations (the idea of development referring not only to economics but to cultural, moral, and social factors); the grave responsibility of advanced nations; the coordination of international bodies.
8. International cooperation on population problems.

B. The conservation of peace.
1. The essential conditions of peace.
2. Means of strengthening peace: opposition to the balance of power; international organizations; methods of conciliation; opposition to the use and production of nuclear weapons; the proscription of war as a solution to conflicts; censure of the arms race; condemnation of immoral acts, the death of the innocent, torture; conscientious objection; humane rules of warfare; the duty to study this problem.

C. The mission of the Church and the Christian.
1. The mission of the Church vis-à-vis the international community.
2. The active presence of the Church in the international community.
3. The role of Christians in international organizations.

Regarding conscientious objection, the schema says this: "In the present circumstances it seems fitting that the law take into consideration those who, either for reasons of religious conviction or out of respect for human life, refuse in conscience to bear arms in time of war."

It is to be noted that the schema speaks of the refusal to bear arms *in time of war* and not during peacetime. There is more here than a nuance.

Commotion Over the Declarations on the Jews and Religious Liberty

The Council Fathers were up in arms after they learned the following facts.

Cardinal Bea received two letters signed by Archbishop Felici, secretary general of the Council, advising him that the two solutions below were envisaged "by superior authority":

1. The declaration on the Jews should be re-examined by a commission composed in part of three members named by Cardinal Bea and three members named by Cardinal Ottaviani. Moreover, this declara-

tion would be incorporated into the schema *de ecclesia*, but in a shorter version.

2. The declaration on religious liberty (which has just been redrafted in the light of the observations made by the Fathers) would be reviewed for a last time by a commission including Cardinal Browne, Archbishop Marcel Lefebvre, and Father Aniceto Fernández, all well known for their conservative tendencies. A fourth name has been added (and here we may detect the diplomatic hand of Paul VI), in the person of Bishop Carlo Colombo, the Pope's former personal theologian.

If this news is confirmed, it will tend to show that authoritarian decisions are being forced upon the Council.

Sixteen cardinals, including Liénart (Lille), Richaud (Bordeaux), Joseph Lefebvre (Bourges), Döpfner (Munich), Koenig (Vienna), Alfrink (Utrecht), and Léger (Montreal), immediately sent a letter to the Pope which began with the words "*cum magno dolore*," in which they express their astonishment at the procedure used.

Protest Against the Declaration on the Jews   The Arabic commission in Palestine is to send a delegation to the Vatican to protest against the introduction of a declaration on the Jews, according to an announcement released in the Lebanese press. The bulletin notes "the efforts made in the Council to absolve the Jews," and adds: "These maneuvers conceal imperialistic and Zionist attempts to make the Church take a position in the Palestinian conflict that is favorable to international Judaism."

OCTOBER 13

Will Paul VI Appease the Concern Aroused
by the Offensive Against the Declarations
on the Jews and on Religious Liberty?

The excitement produced by what Rome has been calling the Bea-Felici affair for the past forty-eight hours has not died down. The letter from sixteen cardinals sent posthaste to Paul VI shows the heat of the counter-action by those who are determined not to let the declarations on religious liberty and the Jews be boycotted.

Everyone understand and approves Paul VI's desire, as supreme arbiter of the Church, to obtain the near-unanimity of the Fathers on these two declarations, which are decisive for Rome's relationship with other confessions; the Roman Church wants to be the church of all bishops of good will, and everything must be done to assure the cooperation of all in the conciliar labor. But there is an abyss between this concern and the tenacious efforts of certain conservatives to undermine the two declarations and call them into question again at the last moment, using totally unexpected means. The sixteen cardinals wrote to the Pope with firmness and confidence. Paul VI's personal opinion is expected to be known any day now. Archbishop Felici acted, it is said, with the more or less implicit approval of Cardinal Cicognani, Secretary of State.

Inserting the declaration on the Jews into the schema on the Church is perhaps not a bad idea in itself, but it could serve as a pretext to shorten and weaken a text which was long in preparation and which was morally approved by the conciliar assembly. Will the Arab countries, which have increased their political pressure on the Vatican, carry the day, at least partially, over the will of the majority of the Fathers?

Moreover, staffing the four-man commission to amend the religious liberty text with three bishops who are resolutely hostile to the declaration would be tantamount to emasculating the document, which was prepared by a competent commission with scrupulous attention to the interventions of the Fathers. Is Paul VI afraid that a significant minority will be opposed to the text in its present form? This is possible, and it would show that the declaration's enemies have been able to take advantage of the Pope's fear to propose a solution.

In any case, it was rumored this morning, Tuesday, that Cardinal Bea had forced Archbishop Felici to admit that it was not the Pope who had named Cardinal Browne, Archbishop Lefebvre of the Holy Spirit Fathers, Father Fernández, and Bishop Colombo. If this is confirmed it will give substance to those behind the scenes who are saying this morning, "There is only one unforgivable sin in Rome: to misrepresent the Pope's thinking."

As for the declaration of the Jews, it seems that it will be part of the schema on the Church, although in a different form from the present text. Everyone—or almost everyone—hopes that the new text will conform with the one presented by Cardinal Bea last year.

On the Laity

An Intervention by Mr. Patrick Keegan This morning a layman spoke in the aula, and in English, for the first time during a working session of the Council. He was Patrick Keegan, an Englishman, president of the International Federation of Christian Workers' Movements, a former Young Christian Worker, and recently head of the international Independent Catholic Youth. He represents the opinion of the workers to the Council; in him the voice of the working class is receiving an official hearing. This symbolic gesture, which was expressly desired by the Pope, will help somewhat to narrow the gap that still separates Catholicism from the working class. It is interesting that Mr. Keegan should be neither an intellectual nor a theologian but a man of action and a militant with a reputation for speaking his mind.

Among his remarks were these:

He sincerely hoped that the schema on the laity will mark the beginning of a new era. The very existence of this document proves that today the lay apostolate is neither a luxury nor a temporary arrangement.

The debate on the Church and the world is awaited with special impatience. Everyone knows how great are the needs, both spiritual and material, of the contemporary world.

The development of organized groups should be strongly encouraged. If the laity's work is to be effective, however, they need the help of priests. The lay apostolate requires constant and regular dialogue between the hierarchy and the laity. The "familiar dialogue" Pope Paul VI has frequently mentioned must become a reality among laymen. There is a distinction between the hierarchy and the laity, but there should be no distance.

Among the speakers during yesterday's discussion of the laity were the following.

Cardinal Liénart, Bishop of Lille: The apostolate of the laity is not only the business of clerics. Laymen should be the leaven which Christianizes the world from within. Their role is not only to aid the clergy but to complete their work. Let us emphasize the formation of youth, who are at an age of dedication; they must be given real responsibilities.

Bishop Renard of Versailles referred to Descartes, saying that *The Discourse on Method* has done us much harm. Conversion is not a purely cerebral phenomenon; it is a mystery. Let us not consider everything with reason alone as did Descartes. The Bible does not do so; it speaks of the "heart" of man, which is infinitely richer than his reason. The apostolate is heart speaking to heart (*cor ad cor loquitur*).

Bishop André Fougerat of Grenoble asked that the importance of international Catholic organizations, solemnly proclaimed by Pius XII, John XXIII, and Paul VI, be much more strongly emphasized.

Archbishop Heenan of Westminster made a humorous intervention: "In French and English the word *cleric* is a synonym of *scholar*. In Italian *layman* is *idiota*. Yet it often happens that laymen are more scholarly than clerics. Let us permit laymen to become theologians."

Bishop Larraín of Talca, Chile, president of the Latin American bishops' council, said that some Christian institutions are barriers and constitute ghettos. "Let us learn to listen to God in the 'signs of the times,' as did John XXIII," he said further. "It is because we forget this that modern errors are rampant. They signify our absence and are a criticism of our faults."

Bishop Stjepan Bäuerlein of Srÿem, Yugoslavia, declared, "The true instrument of the apostolate is public opinion. Without it we are voices crying in the wilderness." He recalled the celebrated line of Gregory the Great: "It is better to risk causing scandal than to be silent about the truth."

Let Us Fill Stomachs Bishop Luigi Civardi, ecclesiastical adviser to Catholic Action in Italy, remarked, "Many workers belong to unions that have Marxist tendencies. This is not for ideological reasons but for purely economic reasons. Let us do more than form brains; let us fill stomachs."

A Microphone Cut Off The general congregation yesterday was enlivened by an altogether astonishing intervention by Bishop del Piño Gómez of Lerida, Spain, who said in part:

> Let us no longer use the terms *clericalism* or *liberty*. They are quite inappropriate. All of us—bishops, priests, and laymen—are subjects of the pope. . . . Religious liberty is inadmissible. It cannot exist. It has been spoken of here in inexplicable terms. Christ said that those who did not have the faith would be condemned. Hell awaits unbelievers. . . .
> The right to private property is a way of glorifying God.

As Bishop del Piño Gómez persisted in speaking beside the point, the moderator, after two ineffectual warnings, cut his microphone off. To our knowledge this is the first time that has happened at Vatican II.

Monsignor Romeo and Vatican II

"A sinister comedy of three thousand good-for-nothings, with gold crosses on their chests, who don't even believe in the Trinity or the Virgin, at least some of them don't!" This rather peculiar definition of the Council was formulated by Monsignor Romeo of the Sacred Congregation for Seminaries and Universities. He is especially well known for his pamphlets attacking members of the Pontifical Biblical Institute, recently rehabilitated by Paul VI. Readers will recall that he was at the center of a good deal of controversy during the first session.

The exaggeration apart, this way of looking at things is not so uncommon in certain Roman circles, where people seriously think that John XXIII's "moment of folly"—as is sometimes said—in which he convoked the Council has cost the Church much. Of course, it is true that the Council has laid to rest a number of so-called traditional positions and that the Roman integralists know that they have lost the ball game. Some, like Monsignor Romeo, are bad losers. Others, fortunately more numerous, are making an effort to adapt. One of the greatest merits of the Council is to have brought about a mental evolution in those who are not inclined to change their minds. This is true of Cardinal Ottaviani, Archbishop Parente, and many others.

Paul VI knows the Roman mind well. That is why he got the jump on them and declared last April 14, "Whatever the outcome of the Council, we should look upon it as an 'hour of God' in the life of the Church and the history of the world."

The Schema of Propositions on Priests
Judged Inadequate by Many Fathers

"The priests are the forgotten ones of the Council. They are telescoped between the bishops, whose powers are increased, and the laymen, who are trying out their new strength." This is the impression that prevailed last year during the second session. Today Vatican II is trying to dissipate it. On Tuesday pastors attended the general congregation (the hundredth of the Council) for the first time. This session took up the schema of propositions entitled "On the Priestly Life and Ministry."

It would be vain to try to conceal the real malaise noticeable almost everywhere today among the secular clergy. The grounds are multiple. The number of priests continues to decrease while the number of bishops is increasing, as Bishop Théas noted. Priests are distributed in the most unintelligent and unjust way, with respect both to geography and to sacerdotal responsibilities. Many of them live in utterly inhuman solitude. In many countries, there is a very unfortunate gap between the higher clergy (usually urban) and the lower clergy (generally rural). Cordial contacts that would promote a real dialogue between bishops and priests are extremely rare. And the formation received in most seminaries is so artificial and so cut off from life that the young priest must make a considerable effort to adapt to his ministry. Not everyone can make such an effort.

A study recently conducted among the Belgian clergy concluded that after coming out of the seminary, priests felt incapable of relating to God, to their bishops, their pastors, the faithful, and women.

The theology of the priesthood is far from adequate. As Father Haubtmann remarked, the theology of the episcopacy was a necessary prerequisite to a theology of the priesthood. Now that the former has been established, will the latter be broached?

It is time to distinguish between the priestly functions properly speaking and the very being of the priest, and define clearly how the cleric can be part of life; to find what Father Paul Barreau calls "means of communication" with the people he must evangelize; and to put an end to a chronic awareness of impotence that even the most generous priests experience. How deep is the need for an education and a professional life that would root them in society? The Theological Committee of Lyon has cited the unusual but meaningful cases of priests who have asked to be laicized "in order to serve mankind better."

The Council will likely have little to say about these serious problems. In any case it will not dare confront the serious question of ecclesiastical celibacy, despite the evolution that has taken place in minds and hearts.

An Unbalanced Text   Cardinal Meyer of Chicago had the courage to say that the schema was very inadequate and to deplore the fact that the Council did not give so much attention to priests as to bishops. "The text speaks in terms of obligations without a word of comfort and encouragement. This does not serve the good of the Church. . . . This schema is unbalanced. I request a radically improved one which would respond to the expectation of priests."

This intervention was vigorously applauded.

Archbishop Julio Rosales of Cebu, the Philippines, spoke next and made the Fathers smile when he sang the praises of the schema, which in his eyes is absolutely perfect. True, this bishop is a member of the responsible commission, which explains but does not justify such thorough satisfaction.

Archbishop Evangelisti of Meerut, India, was surprised that the schema said nothing about the missionary spirit, "the number one problem of the Church," he said.

Canons and Tourism   Bishop Añoveros Ataún of Cádiz, Spain, regretted the abbreviated character of the text. He had an ironic word to say about canons: that they no longer offer anything but "touristic interest" (*sic*).

Maronite Archbishop François Ayoub of Alep, Syria, called for closer union between priests and bishops.

Auxiliary Bishop Joseph Hiltl of Regensburg was thoughtful enough to greet the pastors in the aula, and then preoccupied himself with the proper salary for housekeepers. "It is a question of social justice," he said.

Auxiliary Bishop Jacobus Komba of Peramiho, Tanzania, said that before speaking of the spirit of poverty for the clergy, the Council would be well inspired to begin with the question of poverty and the bishops. He added with touching frankness, "I am sometimes the cross of my priests. This happens to other bishops, too."

Loneliness and Nervous Breakdown Archbishop Leonardo Rodríguez Ballón of Arequipa, Peru, spoke about the dangers of loneliness for priests.

Archbishop Giovanni Perris of Naxos, Greece, was disappointed that the schema was silent about the painful situation of rural priests, addressing himself especially to a French country priest (from Maine-et-Loire) who was in the aula.

Auxiliary Bishop John A. Donovan of Detroit spoke of the cases of nervous breakdown among priests, and urged that modern psychiatric techniques be used to cure them. "These priests need hospitals rather than prisons," he said, undoubtedly making an allusion to monasteries where priests are frequently sent for a rest.

Auxiliary Bishop Franjo Kuharic of Zagreb attacked "benefices" as "residues of a feudal scandal" and declared the schema inadequate.

At the beginning of the session three bishops intervened on the schema on the laity. Archbishop Guerry of Cambrai distinguished two separate but related aspects of the apostolate, "evangelization properly speaking and the spiritualization of the temporal," and emphasized the "autonomy" of the city. The other two speakers were Auxiliary Bishop Santo Quadri of Pinerolo, Italy, and Archbishop Zoghbi, Melkite Patriarchal Vicar for Egypt.

OCTOBER 15

The Priesthood Is the Number One Problem
of the Council, Say Several Fathers

There was an important session on Wednesday in St. Peter's: Vatican II again strongly displayed its spirit of independence. This corroborates the trust John XXIII placed in the bishops' sense of freedom. In the day's nineteen interventions, the Fathers made it absolutely clear that the Council was not about to let a subject as important as that raised in the schema of propositions on priests be conjured away. The contents of this schema, we might recall, are extremely brief. With almost total accord, a fact that greatly impressed the observers, the Fathers interrupted Archbishop Gomes dos Santos of Goiania, Brazil, who intervened in the name of 112 bishops (he was the first of the morning not to speak in his own name), with loud applause. He said with great urgency, "We demand that the present schema not be submitted for the Council's approval and that a new text be proposed at the fourth session."

This killed two birds with one stone. For the Fathers' applause expressed agreement not only with the redrafting of the schema but also with the convocation of a fourth session, a possibility that certain parties have bent every effort to play down recently. The bishops are tired, so it is said, and those from Latin America are particularly anxious to return to their dioceses for good.

With energy and clarity, Archbishop Gomes dos Santos explained himself to his colleagues:

> It would be a great disappointment if this schema, even in amended form, were voted on. It would be incomprehensible and inconceivable that we could speak so briefly and so badly about priests. This text is paternalistic, untheological, and not pastoral enough. It gives much advice to priests, while we did not dare do as much for ourselves. . . . Let us not sacrifice a subject of such importance for reasons of haste.

Archbishop Gomes' peroration was once again applauded. This is the first time an intervention has been applauded twice.

Bishop Demetro Mansilla Reoyo of Ciudad Rodrigo, Spain, also thought that the priesthood ought to be the number one problem for the Council. Bishop Proano Villalba of Riobamba, Ecuador, regretted that the schema was so inadequate. He also called for the abolition of honorific ecclesiastical titles for priests.

A Counterweight to Arbitrary Action by Bishops Bishop Victor Garaygordobil Berrizbeitia of Los Rios, Equador, made this important statement:

> Since bishops are being accorded more and more powers, it is fitting to augment the authority of the clergy in order not to upset the equilibrium of the whole. How can this be done? By speaking explicitly of the rights of priests in relation to the bishops, personal

rights and collective rights. The presbyterium [the sacerdotal body] is the necessary counterweight to abitrary action on the part of bishops. For we are not infallible, and we have also been conceived in sin.

Bishop Cekada of Skoplje, Yugoslavia, feared that the Council was going too far.

Bishop González Martín of Astorga, Spain, said it was scandalous that "In our country each year, we must refuse from one to two thousand young men with sacerdotal vocations for lack of space and money." This singular avowal stupefied the bishops of Latin America, where there is a tragic shortage of priests.

Three different bishops demanded decent remuneration for priests, and deplored the fact that there were rich and poor priests.

Today, Thursday, Cardinal Alfrink of Utrecht said the following about celibacy during his intervention, the first of the day on the schema on priests: "Let us clarify this issue further, for it is a critical point. Ecclesiastical celibacy is even more necessary in the modern world. Priests should not find it a burden but a source of strength."

One of the more interesting events on Wednesday occurred when Archbishop Felici declared that voting on the schema could not begin on Thursday as originally planned. The reason given was that many Fathers had requested to intervene. This change of plans is equivalent to annulling the decision taken in principle at the beginning of the session to discuss the schema of the proposition very briefly in order to gain time.

The intention of the Fathers to accord priests the importance they merit ruled out other considerations. This news will be warmly received by the clergy throughout the world, who have feared they were being treated as the poor relatives of Vatican II.

OCTOBER 16

The Letter to Paul VI

After a meeting of several cardinals held in Rome on October 11 near the Piazza Navona, a letter was sent to the Pope, as we reported. It was signed by seventeen Fathers: Cardinals Frings, Alfrink, Döpfner, Koenig, Meyer, Ritter, Léger, Lefebvre, Richaud, Liénart, Silva Henríquez, Landázuri-Ricketts, Quintero, Suenens, and Rugambwa. The sixteenth signer seems to be Cardinal Lercaro, Archbishop of Bologna. The name of the seventeenth is unknown. We have also learned that Cardinal Bea sent a personal letter to the Pope. Cardinal Tisserant told several people that he was familiar with the two letters Archbishop Felici sent to Cardinal Bea.

It will be noted that this letter, which follows in its entirety, speaks only of the declaration on religious liberty, which is endangered by the measures Archbishop Felici announced in a letter which Cardinal Bea received on Friday, October 9.

One is struck by the great uneasiness expressed in the letter to the Pope and also by its firmness. The authors did not hesitate to deplore "any apparent violation of the Council regulations." The text of the letter is as follows:

> Most Holy Father:
>
> Not without great sadness have we learned that the declaration on religious liberty, although it meets with the deep approval of the majority of the Fathers, is to be remitted to a certain mixed commission. We are told that four members have already been named to this commission, and that three of them seem at odds with the orientation of the Council in this matter. This news is a source of extreme concern and the greatest uneasiness for us. Innumerable men throughout the world know full well that this declaration has already been prepared, and they know too its general contents.
>
> In a matter of such gravity, any apparent violation of the Council's regulations and its liberty would severely prejudice the whole Church before universal public opinion.
>
> Urged on by this concern, we beseech Your Holiness that the above-mentioned declaration be remitted to the normal procedure of the Council and treated according to the prescribed rules to avoid great evils for the whole people of God.
>
> However, if Your Holiness believes a mixed commission is necessary, such a commission, in our humble opinion, should be formed from the conciliar commissions as provided for in article 58, paragraph 2, of the regulations.*

It has been confirmed that not only will the whole of this declaration not be watered down but that on the contrary, in accordance with

---

* Article 58 reads as follows:

Paragraph 1. "When discussion of a schema or part of a schema has been completed, the president [of the general congregation] is to order the proposed amendments to be transmitted to the competent commission."

Paragraph 2. "If the amendments concern two or more commissions, the president is to decide which commissions the amendments are to be sent to so that the latter may examine them together and make only a single report on them."

Paragraph 3. "The secretary general is to transmit the amendments which he has collected to the commission or commissions designated by the president."

the desire expressed by the majority of the Fathers, the definitive version prepared by the competent commission will resemble the first version presented during the second session by Cardinal Bea.

Maximos IV Saigh Refuses To Be Considered as a Simple Subject by the Roman Congregations

Vatican II continues at an accelerated rhythm. Every three days the subject of discussion is changed, so that the Fathers—at least those who are working hard on the schemas—are harassed. They would like to have only four general congregations a week instead of five so they could catch their breath.

Since it now seems that a fourth session is inevitable, there is no good reason, they think, to carry on the work of the plenary sessions at such a fast pace. In particular, the bishops who are interested in schema 13 would like time to study it in more detail (it is ninety pages long in all) and prepare their interventions.

On Thursday the Council took up the schema of the proposition on the Oriental Churches. This document introduces three spectacular decisions which will have great repercussions on relations between Orthodoxy and Catholicism.

1. Contrary to Pius XII's motu proprio in 1949, which caused "such great evils," in the words of Coptic Patriarch Sidarouss of Alexandria, the schema declares that mixed marriages will be *valid* which are contracted between a Catholic and a member of the Orthodox Church and celebrated before a minister of the Orthodox Church. Legally, these marriages will remain *illicit*, but their validity will once again be recognized, as it always was in the Church until the time of Pius XII.

2. The promise to raise children in the Catholic faith will be required only of the Catholic party and not of the Orthodox spouse.

3. Orthodox will be permitted to receive communion, absolution, and extreme unction in the Catholic Church. Inversely, Catholics will be allowed to receive the same sacraments from an Orthodox minister in case of necessity.

The bishops will be charged with effecting these principles in practice.

His Beatitude Maximos IV Saigh, Melkite Patriarch of Antioch, made an intervention with his customary vigor. This elderly prelate can afford total frankness by reason of his uncontested prestige and his exceptional spiritual qualities. He is certainly one of three or four most authoritative Council fathers. His intervention is among those very rare ones that

deserve to be quoted almost in toto. Free expression, rigorous reasoning, and deep charity characterize it. What makes Maximos IV's remarks
even more important is the fact that he refuses to dissociate himself from
Orthodoxy, as will be seen:

> This schema certainly represents progress, but its central and
> ecumenical vision is altogether wrong. It is said, for example, that
> the Catholic Church respects the Oriental Church. It thus seems to
> insinuate that there are two churches. Are we then not the Church?
> Is the Latin Church the only one?
>
> What is said of patriarchs makes a mockery of history. This
> is totally inadmissible, for after the papacy it is the most venerable
> institution. Patriarchs are spoken of mincingly, and then only on a
> canonical level.
>
> *It is false to consider the patriarchate as an institution peculiar
> to Orthodoxy.* It is an institution common to the universal Church.
> The pope is the patriarch of the West, as the *Pontifical Roman
> Yearbook* notes. St. John Lateran Church was once called the
> principal patriarchate. The patriarchate in no way compromises papal
> primacy, quite the contrary.
>
> As Bishop of Rome, the pope is equal to the other bishops. In
> the West the patriarchate has been confused with honorific titles.
> There are patriarchs of Venice, Lisbon, Madrid [and elsewhere],
> which means nothing. Let us bear the Oriental patriarchs in mind.
> This is an indispensable condition for dialogue.
>
> *The patriarchate is not an anonymous institution.* The sees are
> determined by precise historical reasons. We cannot speak of Or-
> thodoxy without citing the great patriarchal sees and especially that
> of Constantinople. The writers of the schema seem ignorant of the
> meeting between Paul VI and Athenagoras.

At this point, Maximos IV was loudly applauded. He continued:

> Doesn't this historical meeting mean anything to the writers?
> The titularies of the historical patriarchates have always been inti-
> mately associated with a concern for the universal Church. In former
> times the pope sent his profession of faith to the four great patri-
> archs before his elevation.
>
> The patriarchal college has inalienable rights. Formerly the patri-
> arch of the West commemorated the patriarchs of the East in the
> mass. If we re-established these traditions, we would be taking a
> serious step toward unity. This schema should constitute a blueprint
> of the charter of union.
>
> *It is not enough to heap honors upon us and then treat us as*

subalterns and simple subjects of the Roman congregations. This situation must change.

An ultimate instance is the patriarch and his synod. This could be a valuable example and be followed with regard to other religious groups.

The speaker was apparently thinking of the Anglican Church.

His Beatitude concluded, "When we speak of the Orient, let us not only think of the churches in communion with Rome. Let us make room for those which are absent, not only for those which have been assimilated. I speak not for us, but for those absent."

Outside of the aula, the Patriarch declared, "The Latinization of the Orient is still openly preached today despite repeated warnings by the popes. In view of this it seems ironic to claim as the schema does that the Catholic Church has always had great respect for the institutions of the Orient!"

OCTOBER 17

"The Oriental Catholic Churches Are Not Appendixes of the Latin Church"

Vatican II is taking the bit in its teeth. It is as though the crisis overcome during the past week has given the Fathers an increase of freedom. Never was applause so frequent in the aula; rarely have the bishops expressed themselves with such vigor. The tone was set by Maximos IV Saigh, whose intervention we reported on yesterday.

These two days of the Council will go down in history as the time when the Latin Church fully understood—better late than never—all that she lost in rejecting the Orientals as schismatics.

Among the ten interventions we will report on the most original.

Archbishop Slipyi of Lvov, Ukraine, a compatriot of Nikita Khrushchev's, spoke out against the Latinization of the Oriental Churches. "This attitude," he said, "was catastrophic. It was a disaster for the Latin Church to lose the riches of the Oriental liturgy. Let the Council learn from the respect Paul VI displayed toward Athenagoras on the occasion of his visit to Jerusalem. Have pity on us," he concluded humorously, "because we are Orientals!"

Coptic Bishop Ghattas of Thebes, Egypt, made this savory and theologically irrefutable remark: "The Latin Church is one church in the universal Church. Moreover, all churches without exception are particular churches. The Catholic Church is the communion of all these churches."

Archbishop de Provenchères of Aix-en-Provence went this one better: "Who has recalled the most basic theological perspectives at Vatican II? The Orientals. Who has shown that collegiality is not merely juridical but also sacral and mystical? The Orientals. We owe them much. May the Orientals in communion with Rome remain faithful to their vocation as a bridge between Catholicism and Orthodoxy."

Archbishop Zoghby drew a historical portrait:

> When the Crusades were launched by the Roman pontiffs, Latin patriarchs were placed on the Oriental sees in place of the legitimate pastors; but they were mere puppets of the papacy. In the following centuries and until this very day, Latin missionaries, scarcely more enlightened, have instituted Latin churches in the Orient which have given rise to rivalries unfavorable to the Oriental Churches.
>
> The present schema has been conceived as though the Oriental Catholic Churches were appendixes of the Latin Church; this in all logic cannot be admitted. Let us rework the text in its entirety in order to eliminate this false perspective.
>
> Even after the schism, the churches of the East and West retained their communion in the faith. The conflict was between particular and local churches, and between the Oriental patriarchs and the Roman pontiffs who wanted to extend their patriarchical power to the East. The Orthodox have never considered themselves separated from the Church, for they have never considered themselves as being other than the true Church. They constituted the most important part of Christianity; they defined the truths of the faith in their own councils; they gave the Church her best theologians and almost all the Fathers of the ecumenical councils.

Archbishop Zoghby concluded:

> Let us be wise; but still more, let us be good and tolerant. Let us not judge the quarrels and divisions of past times with the mentality of our ancestors but with our own. We live, thanks be to God, in a century of openness and liberty, including religious liberty. We can have within the same Church and the same Council Fathers who have the right to think and express themselves differently from others. Such liberty was unknown in former times.

Bishop Basilio Cristea, delegate of the Congregation for the Oriental Church to Rumanians in exile, drew attention to the persecutions suffered by the Rumanians and Ukrainians after 1945. Six bishops are in prison and five have died, he pointed out.

A Skeleton   Bishop Joseph Stangl of Würzburg regretted that the present schema has been reduced to a veritable "skeleton."

Latin Patriarch Gori of Jerusalem intervened primarily to defend the right of Orientals who entered the Roman Church to choose their rite.

The day before, Cardinal Koenig of Vienna had expressed satisfaction with the treatment of *communicatio in sacris*, but had called for dialogue with the Orientals on the subject so that the measure would not be unilateral.

Friday, Archbishop Felici, secretary general of Vatican II, made the following announcement, which was repeated in all the official vernacular languages of the Council:

> Since many Fathers have asked the moderators for the schemas which have been reduced to propositions to be returned to the commissions after discussion, the Coordinating Commission has decided that after brief discussion in the general congregation, the assembly will vote to determine whether or not these schemas should be submitted immediately to a vote. If an absolute majority (that is, 51 percent) respond affirmatively, we will vote at that time. Otherwise, the schemas will be returned for rapid amendment.

This decision amounts in practice to giving the proposition schemas the same importances as the regular schemas; that is to say, it cancels out earlier official decisions which tended to brush aside the themes treated in these propositions. This is a significant victory for the partisans of *aggiornamento* and for those who have always thought that a fourth session was inevitable.

OCTOBER 18

The Catholic Church Goes To Meet the World

Paul VI will go to Bombay. This announcement surprised most of the faithful gathered at St. Peter's but was expected by those in the know. It was learned on September 5, in fact, that a special envoy of the Secretariat of State, Monsignor Marcinkus, had gone to Bombay to make preparations for the Pope's voyage.

Since Saturday it has been known that a special plane was being readied under the cloak of great secrecy. Furthermore, those who know Paul VI realize that he chose the name of the Apostle to the Gentiles because he intended to give his pontificate a missionary character and burst the corset that has bound popes to Italian and Western locales.

After Jerusalem—an unprecedented pilgrimage—the Pope wants to make longer trips, beginning with countries that are most distant and most foreign to Christianity. In India there are some 6,000,000 Catholics in a population of 460,000,000. In Bombay the proportion is 200,000 Catholics in a population of 4,000,000.

Paul VI made it clear that he intends to visit only one city and not go to New Delhi as the President of India has urged him to do. Moreover, he has declared that his trip, which will take place early in December, will be "brief," "humble," and "very simple." Paul VI is accustomed to weighing his words well. He seemed to mean by the above that his visit would avoid a triumphal character as much as possible. It is predictable that he will be escorted by a minimum of ecclesiastical dignitaries from the Curia or by laymen.

What will the Pope wear to Bombay? He hasn't said anything about this, but the Pope once said that it is more fitting for the successor of Peter to be clothed in "the mantle of a pilgrim and a sinner" than in royal robes. It is therefore quite possible that Paul VI will be more modestly dressed in Bombay than he was in Jerusalem.

The Pope is not unaware that he is going to a country where millions of people are dying of hunger, and that in Bombay itself 600,000 people sleep in the open because of the housing shortage.

For three years now there has been much talk about "the Church of the poor," most of it irrelevant and sentimental. If this idea is to have any substance, the first thing that must be done is to abolish from the Roman Church all ostentation that is not *directly* connected with the liturgy.

Mr. Bourguiba and the "Crusaders" of Carthage   The international Eucharistic Congress of Bombay will be hard put, if one is to believe those closely associated with organizing it, to avoid falling into the trap of triumphalism. It is a difficult problem to resolve, it is true. It will require infinite tact and a resolute will to banish all unnecessary pomp to avoid giving the Indians the impression that Christians are flaunting their opulence before people living in incredible poverty.

It would be disastrous for Christianity if the congress in Bombay had consequences similar to those of the congress in Carthage in 1930. At that time, Tunisia's President Habib Bourguiba put it in words that were a slap in the face of Christians: "The Eucharistic Congress in Carthage was in part the origin of my struggle for the independence of my country. I saw Europeans there disguised as 'crusaders,' parading with great pomp through the streets of our Muslim city."

We might point out that they were obviously peaceful "crusaders," wearing the white uniform with a cross of the "Eucharistic Crusade" and therefore of a purely spiritual nature. But the effect it produced was no less deplorable.

Will the organizers of the congress in Bombay be better advised? What we know of preparations for this occasion is not totally reassuring. But we must take into consideration the mentality of the missionaries in this country. The chapel of the major seminary in Bombay, for example, which was constructed with American money sent by the Cardinal Archbishop of Boston, is covered with imported marble. Many Christians consider such a church, if not an insult to the poor, at least a distortion of the Christian religion.

In this difficult context, the presence of Paul VI can help matters greatly. In the final analysis, it will depend on how well his instructions are carried out.

One prelate has said this: "You would have to be utterly insensitive to honor the eucharistic bread showily in a country where the people suffer from endemic hunger."

Let us recall, finally, what Paul VI said in a speech of June 23, 1964: "The Eucharistic Congress in Bombay is an extraordinary event in itself. It will bring to the whole Church, and especially to the Asiatic world, the eternal message of the mysterious sacramental presence of Christ and will reveal something of his vivifying power for humanity."

If the congress in Bombay is successful, it could be the crown of schema 13, which will be discussed in the Council this week. It will be a sign that the Roman Church is going forth to meet the world, however indifferent or distant it be.

OCTOBER 19

Africa Is "a Land of the Gospel"
and "a New Country for Christ"

Here are some characteristic passages from a speech pronounced by Paul VI during the canonization ceremony of the martyrs of Uganda:

> These martyrs of Africa inaugurate a new era. We want to think that it will be one not of persecutions or religious wars but of a regeneration of human society with a Christian orientation. Africa, watered with the blood of these martyrs, the first of the new era (and please God may they be the last!), is reborn free and redeemed. . . .
>
> The tragedy which took their lives is so extraordinary that we find in it ample lessons for founding a new spiritual tradition, and enough elements for illustrating and promoting the passage of a civili-

zation, which assuredly contains high human values although it is not proof against weakness and is in some sense a prisoner of itself, to a level where it is open to the highest expressions of the spirit and superior forms of social life. . . .

Christianity finds in Africa a particular destiny, and we do not hesitate to consider it as a secret of God, as a special vocation of this land, as a historical promise. Africa is a land of the Gospel. Africa is a new country for Christ.

At these words, applause broke out in St. Peter's.

Evangelization and Colonialism

This phenomenon makes it possible to draw a comparison between Christian evangelization and colonialism, so much talked about today. In both cases it has been a question of importing civilization into lands with ancient cultures, certainly respectable from many points of view, but rudimentary and frozen in immobility. These importations have introduced factors of development and established relationships which have transformed the society. But while evangelization introduces with the Christian religion a principle that tends to liberate and develop innate energies, native virtues, and latent capacities of the indigenous population, in other words a principle that tends to liberate this population and lead it to autonomy and maturity, to make it able to express itself in an increasingly perfect and broader way in cultural and artistic forms, colonization, on the other hand, if it is guided uniquely by norms of the practical and materialistic order, pursues other ends which are not always in conformity with the honor and the interests of the native population. Christianity educates, liberates, ennobles, and humanizes; it bestows riches of the interior and spiritual life, and promotes better organization on the communitarian level. Christianity constitutes the true vocation of humanity.

Then the Pope launched an urgent appeal to dioceses and religious communities in Europe and America to send many priests to Africa, which is in such need of them.

The entire world seems to be awakening and seeking the path of its future. Here are new peoples, until now inert and passive, convinced as they were that they did not need seek elsewhere for other forms of life than the one they had inherited from the slow labor of centuries, animated and on the march, capable henceforward thanks to the progress of technology, of new ideals and enterprises.

The Pope's Obligation To Draw Near Peoples

Seeing this awakening of peoples, we feel the conviction grow in us that it is our duty, an obligation of love, to come closer to them in more fraternal dialogue, to show them the esteem and affection we have for them, to demonstrate that the Catholic Church understands their legitimate aspiration, to help their free and just development by the peaceful paths of human fraternity, and thus to make it possible for them, if they so desire, to come to a better knowledge of Christ, who is the true salvation of all men and who in a unique and marvelous way can assume all their profound aspirations. The force of this conviction is so great that it seems to us we should not refuse the opportunity now before us, and still less the pressing invitation addressed to us to meet a great people in whom we like to see the symbol of an entire continent in order to bring them our sincere message of Christian faith. We thus inform you, brethren, that we have decided to attend the coming International Eucharistic Congress in Bombay. [Applause.]

At the Gates of Asia

This is the second time we have had occasion in this basilica to announce voyages which we have decided to take and which until now have been entirely foreign to the normal manner of exercising the pontifical apostolic ministry. But we think that, in the light of the first journey to the Holy Land, this second, which will take us to the gates of the immense continent of Asia, of the new modern world, is not foreign to the character or even the mandate of our apostolic ministry itself. For we hear these words of Christ, who is ever present, echoing urgently in our heart: "Go forth and teach all nations." Truly it is not the desire for novelty or traveling that prompts us to this decision; it is our apostolic zeal to shout the evangelical Good News to the immense human horizons which our age opens before our steps, and this with the sole aim of offering to Christ the most generous, most burning, most humble testimony of faith and love.

Response to the Missionary Call of the Council It will be noted in the following passage that the Pope declared that this trip is a first response to the missionary call of the Church, meaning that he intends eventually to go to other continents:

The Pope has become a missionary, you will say. Yes, in taking to the road, the Pope becomes a missionary, which means a witness, a pastor, an apostle. We are happy to repeat it on this day which commemorates the world missions. Although our journey will be brief, very simple, and limited to a single city, where solemn homage will be rendered to Christ present in the eucharist, it is intended to be a testimony of gratitude to all missionaries of yesterday and today, who have dedicated their lives to the cause of the Gospel, and especially to those who, following in the footsteps of Saint Francis Xavier, have established the Church with such devotion and such fruit in Asia and particularly in India. Our journey is also intended to be a symbolic participation in as well as an exhortation and an encouragement to the whole work of the Holy Catholic Church. It is intended to be a first and prompt response to the missionary call which the ecumenical Council presently in session has made to the Church.

OCTOBER 20

The Council Begins the Examination of Schema 13

Vatican II began examination of schema 13 this morning, Tuesday. The efforts of some conservatives to block this text were thus foiled, although they came close to succeeding, according to the judicious expert Father René Laurentin.

Simple truth obliges us to recognize that since the beginning of the Council it has always been the minority who attack, while the majority must defend its rights.

Schema 13 was defended Monday afternoon with much gusto by Father Jean Daniélou, S.J., editor of *Études,* in a press conference for a large audience. His talk constitutes an excellent introduction to the great debate which opened this morning and for which 120 Fathers have already registered their interventions. Here are the principal ideas expressed by Father Daniélou.

He recalled that Cardinal Suenens was the inspiring force behind the schema. The Cardinal had said in 1963 that it would be unthinkable for Vatican II to terminate without analyzing the fundamental problems which agonize men today.

It is the first time in the history of the world that a council has concerned itself with such questions, whose religious implications are nonetheless obvious.

One of the essential aims of this schema is to make Christians understand that they have a serious obligation to work to build a human order. "To go into the world is not to leave the sanctuary, for God is equally present there. Christians have a duty to say *yes* to creation, which is the work of God, and to say *yes* to the building of the terrestrial city, which is also willed by God."

Schema 13 is not to be considered from either a missionary or an apologetical standpoint, nor even from the standpoint of the Christian influence on the world, which is the subject of the schema on the laity. It is intended to present the broad principles of a theory of human values, to recognize the ground of the natural law.

Schema 13 puts mortal sin in its true light. It is not found, as our manuals long pretended, in such moral shortcomings as white lies or gluttony. It is located primarily in habitual violations of social justice. No one stigmatized the abuses of private property with such vehemence as did Isaias. He did so not in the name of class struggle but in the name of God.

It would be tragic to channel schema 13 away from its concrete objectives and replace them with theologico-philosophical abstractions.

It is desirable for the Church to make a fresh study of means of contraception which, whatever they are, modify nature. Let it be clearly stated that this question remains open so that specialists, scientists as well as moralists, can contribute the results of their research.

The Church's respect for conscientious objection stems from her respect for freedom of conscience rather than from the moral precepts of the beatitudes. Protest pertains to the very essence of human nature.

The Church must scrutinize the signs of the times through which God speaks to us. That is why each appendix begins with an analysis of such signs, following the example of John XXIII's *Pacem in terris*.

It would be absurd if schema 13 were a purely Western text. Each country should examine those signs which concern it especially.

The "Necessary Reform"
of the Church's Central Government

The general congregation on Monday completed discussion of the schema on the Oriental Churches.

Fourteen fathers took the floor on that day. The two interventions which were most applauded were those of Cardinal Lercaro, Bishop of Bologna, and Abbot Johann Hoeck, President of the Bavarian Benedictines.

Cardinal Lercaro, whose thinking is close to the Pope's, declared, "It is necessary to reform the bodies of the Church's government." The Cardinal referred to his intervention of November 8, 1963, in which he had judged that the Council had "not only the right but the duty" to consider how the bishops could help the Pope govern the Church. He had suggested then that the moderators confide the examination of this serious question to a special commission comprising elected members and members named by the Pope. This commission could draft a precise text which would then be submitted for the Pope's approval.

Father Hoeck commanded an impressive silence as he made the following declaration, which mainly concerned the restoration of patriarchates. This intervention is considered to be of capital importance for future relations between Rome and Constantinople.

The Total Autonomy of Patriarchs

The essential question of this schema is the patriarchal structure. This was the structure of the Church during the first thousand years. . . . The schism was provoked by false documents. It was said then that Constantine had bequeathed the universal empire to the pope, a fact that caused much harm to the cause of unity between the East and West.

Presently, the patriarchates are mere shadows of what they once were. There has been a consequent contempt for patriarchates which has influenced Catholicism. . . . The patriarchal institution is the true hinge of the whole Orient.

Our separated brethren judge us on this patriarchal institution. In their eyes, it is the essential test. They are secretly asking themselves what would happen to them if they returned to Rome. Would they be subject to cardinals? To the Curia? This would be quite impossible and contrary to their tradition.

No one thinks of touching papal primacy. But the dogma of primacy is one thing and the manner in which it is presently exercised is another, indeed something quite different [*toto coelo differet*].

For a thousand years the Oriental Church freely elected her patriarchs and bishops; she erected her own dioceses; she had control over her liturgy, canon law . . . and so forth. The autonomy of the patriarchs was total within the universal Church. Recourse was had to the pope only in serious matters, and that not more than twenty times in a thousand years!

Let us stress this patriarchal structure in the schema. Otherwise we will be guilty of an unforgivable sin. Likewise, let us consequently revise the schemas *De Ecclesia* and *De Episcopis*. . . .

The Orientals who are on the competent commission are too Latinized. Therefore, they should not be working on this revision. . . .

Why not create new patriarchates in the Latin Church?

Seven Votes on the Schema
on the Oriental Churches

The schema on the Oriental Churches will be the object of seven votes, corresponding with the introduction and the six propositions of this document. On October 20, the Fathers decided 1,911 to 265 to vote on the whole schema the next day. On October 19 they rejected a similar method for the schema on priests.

OCTOBER 21

Eight Cardinals Intervene on Schema 13

It was a great debate. This was the unanimous opinion of the Fathers as they emerged from St. Peter's Basilica on Tuesday. Discussion of schema 13 has in fact been inaugurated under the best auspices. A new phase of Vatican II has begun. The Council members feel profoundly involved in the contents of this document. They listened attentively as Cardinal Cento, president of the Commission for the Lay Apostolate, and Bishop Guano, president of the plenary subcommission, traced the history of the schema and described the fundamental reasons which prompted Vatican II to take up this subject, as well as the objectives it aims to achieve.

Then eight cardinals—a Frenchman, two Americans, two Italians, a German, a Canadian, and a Chilean—took the floor. Most of these interventions made a deep impression. It now seems clear that Vatican II will devote the necessary care and patience to this schema. The next recess will enable the commissions to perfect the text, which has been generally judged defective although suitable as a basis for discussion.

One of the major faults of the schema—I speak of the schema itself and not of the five appendixes, which were much better drafted—is its presentation. The style is ecclesiastical, in the worst sense of that word—heavy and redundant. It inappropriately sounds like a homily, as Cardinal Liénart pointed out. This is the more regrettable in that schema 13 is addressed to the laity and even to unbelievers. It is to be hoped that laymen will be among the writers of the new version so that a readable style will be guaranteed.

Addressed to Nonbelievers The first report was presented by Cardinal Cento, who spoke for himself and for Cardinal Ottaviani, president of the theological commission, members of which collaborated on this schema with members of the lay apostolate commission. Cardinal Cento said in part:

> The Church, our mother, knows that she can show her message to the world, to a world afflicted with so much suffering and so many difficulties, a world which lives in terror of an apocalyptic conflagration. . . .
>
> Despite the considerable work expended on this schema, a certain doubt bothers us. Is this schema adequate? Has it interpreted the world's expectations properly? Have we kept a proper balance between the immense and very difficult questions we touched upon?
>
> Do not be surprised at the shortcomings of this text. Think of the difficulties we encountered. We will be happly to improve this text in the light of the wise remarks you make. For we must address this document to the whole world, to Christians and non-Christians, to believers and nonbelievers.

A Change of Style   Bishop Guano, president of the plenary subcommission, presented the second report:

> In the world today men are worrying about their food, about peace, and about harmony among peoples. Many of them think that the Church is indifferent to their problems, and they sometimes even think that they are our enemies. Others are aware of our solicitude and wait for us to say something of interest to them. They want to know if they can count on the Church to help them resolve their problems.
>
> The originality of the schema is this: it is concerned not with proclaiming what the Church thinks of divine revelation but with establishing closer dialogue with all men, taking into account their concrete circumstances of life and their outlooks. . . .
>
> It is important to emphasize that the Church speaks of the problems of the world from her own point of view and to the extent that they are related to her mission. As for the style of this schema, it should be adapted as much as possible to contemporary ways of talking and thinking without for all that diluting the fullness of the evangelical message. . . .
>
> It is not easy to keep a correct balance between the great evangelical principles and a precise description of the modern world. It is very difficult to grasp what characterizes our times. Many people expect too much from this schema, as though we were about to give an immediate answer to all their problems. Certainly we shall indicate lines

of investigation, but we shall do so with honesty and humility, recognizing our limitations.

Bishop Guano noted that several laymen had worked with the Fathers and experts in the plenary subcommission and on the other commissions that contributed to this schema.

The Value of the Appendixes   Bishop Guano finally made some important remarks on the appendixes, whose value has recently been contested:

> The mixed plenary commission recalled last October 13 what had been decided during the month of June, 1964, namely:
>
> The appendixes were elaborated by order of the mixed plenary commission, and this same commission requested that each of these appendixes be drawn up by subcommissions.
>
> The appendixes remain the responsibility of each of these competent subcommissions.
>
> They are not proposed for discussion or deliberation in the Council; rather, they are offered to the Fathers as aids to their work in order to serve the study of the schema proper.
>
> The mixed plenary commission proposes, and has so intended for some time, to study the appendixes when time permits.
>
> Consequently we ask you to submit your observations on the appendixes immediately.

The Cardinals Take the Podium   The eight interventions then followed. We shall excerpt the most important passages.

Cardinal Liénart, Archbishop of Lille, made several observations:

> The style of this schema must be modified. It is too exhortatory. The world expects more than a homily. It expects the Church to say how she can help it in its anguish; it expects a clear presentation of our Christian principles, and it is in terms of what we say to it that men will judge: either the Church can help us or we can forget the Church. . . .
>
> It is important to make a clearer distinction between the natural and supernatural orders. To be sure, there is a real unity between the two, for grace does not destroy nature but perfects it. But the schema goes from one to the other without warning. . . .
>
> We must first of all consider those natural values in which all men, Christian or not, believe, and then clarify this order in the light of the faith which teaches us that man is of intrinsic worth.

Cardinal Spellman, Archbishop of New York, declared, "These questions are difficult, and it must be admitted that the Church lacks the vocabulary to speak about them. Therefore, let us recommend that each form his conscience and follow it."

Then the Cardinal made this qualification: "It is indispensable to stress heavily obedience in the Church and to the Church at great length, as did Paul VI in his encyclical. A filial rather than a legal obedience, it goes hand in hand with liberty. Obedience to the Church is necessary if dialogue is to be efficacious."

Human Nature and Evolution Cardinal Ruffini, Archbishop of Palermo, congratulated the authors of the schema but regretted the many repetitions which unduly burden the text. He said:

> The dignity of man is mentioned seven times with no reference to redemption. The word *vocation* recurs frequently but is never defined, and it is used in different senses. The struggle against injustice is mentioned five times in one page. . . . It is more a sermon that a conciliar constitution. . . .
>
> Some things are badly phrased, or at least I don't understand them. For example, on page 10, line 4, it is said that human nature appeared after a long evolution. I don't like this. To say that human nature was prepared by an evolution is contrary to the doctrine of the Church.
>
> On page 15, line 25, it is said that the faithful must enlighten their conscience with the help of intelligence and prudence. This smacks of situation ethics. It seems in fact to be saying that conscience should be the norm rather than the principles of the Church.

Cardinal Ruffini was then called to order by Cardinal Döpfner, the moderator, who reproached him for discussing details rather than the general import of the schema, as had been requested. Cardinal Ruffini answered that he had prepared his intervention before he knew this, and continued. His conclusion was categorical: "I dare to propose that this schema be redone in its entirety, and there is only one way of doing this: review all of the encyclicals of John XXIII and Paul VI."

This intervention is indicative of the minority thinking in the Council. It wants Vatican II to limit itself to repeating what the popes have said, and rejects the innovations contained in the schema. We can legitimately ask: why convoke a Council if it adds nothing new.

Cardinal Lercaro: Let the Church Reform Herself Cardinal Lercaro, Archbishop of Bologna, made a very different kind of intervention:

> Let us discuss this schema, without delay but without haste. We could use its faults as a pretext for tabling the schema. This would be

a mistake. This text is in the spirit of Paul VI's message, and is adequate as a basis of discussion. Experience has shown that only discussion improves the schemas.

This discussion should go on for some time. More than in the case of other schemas, it is indispensable that many Fathers from different continents intervene so that this text will lose its excessively Western quality. . . . It is impossible to elaborate a satisfactory document during this session. A fourth session is absolutely required for this.

The Cardinal then added this highly interesting remark: "It is excellent that this schema is looked forward to. But too much is expected of it. Miracles are expected, and this illusion should be dispelled."

Cardinal Lercaro's conclusion was vigorously applauded:

The best way the Church can respond to the expectations of men is to reform herself. This is the heart of the matter; the rest will follow. We have already initiated this reform, but perhaps our efforts have been too timid. Let us first of all have a spirit of simplicity and evangelical poverty. Let us infuse the present schema with this spirit, and all the others as well. Only in this way will we respond to the world's hopes.

Cardinal Léger: Let Laymen Speak in the Aula Cardinal Léger, Archbishop of Montreal, agreed that the present text is a good basis for discussion. He made his a suggestion offered last year by Father Congar that lay experts, men and women, give technical expositions in the aula on the great problems confronting the modern world. "It would be very fitting," he said.

He also expressed this desire: "Let us state more clearly the relationships between terrestrial and eternal vocations. Let us affirm more strongly the exigencies of the evangelical law in profane life. The *aggiornamento* of the Church should have as its end the conversion of Christians to greater fidelity to Christ."

Cardinal Döpfner: Let Us Speak About Atheism In the name of eighty-three German and Scandinavian bishops, Cardinal Döpfner, Archbishop of Munich, said in particular:

Let us speak more clearly here of atheism and dialectical materialism. It is not surprising that this is not done because these are difficult subjects which require us to seek the proper doctrinal expressions. . . .

It is feared that public opinion will spread inexact and immature reports to the world. But on the one hand, I do not doubt the prudence of the Fathers, and on the other, it is impossible not to talk of these questions and not to give at least general norms. This is precisely what is expected of the Council, and it is our duty to do it. . . .

With Cardinal Lercaro, I think that this will take time, and that we should accept the schema as a basis of discussion.

Cardinal Meyer: Intimacy Between the Church and the World   Cardinal Meyer, Archbishop of Chicago, thought it "evident" that discussion of the schema should be especially searching. He called for a better theology of the relationship between the Church and the world, "a biblical theology of quality." He continued:

> We are excessively fearful of terrestrial values. Too many Christians are like travelers who are afraid to stop and enjoy the scenery.
>
> Nowhere does the schema say that the world is not only a means but an object of redemption. The entire cosmos, and not only man, ought to be glorified. All of creation, as Saint Paul says, groans in expectation of Christ's return. . . . It is not a matter of delivering the soul from the body but rather of saving the soul from the body of sin. The parousia is the day of transformation for the cosmos. Let us speak of the human order in terms of the transfiguration which awaits it. In this light we can assess all our present efforts, whether economic, social, political. . . .
>
> Only an exact biblical theology can communicate the *intimacy* that exists between the Church and the world.

Cardinal Silva Henríquez: Let Us Develop a Christian Anthropology   The final speaker was Cardinal Silva Henríquez, Archbishop of Santiago, Chile. He also asked that the present text be used as a basis of discussion. Then he made a series of interesting remarks:

> We must speak of man because the Church exists for men and inversely. . . .
>
> The Church must love the world as Christ loved it. . . .
>
> Eschatalogy is not an escape but a transfiguration. . . .
>
> Let the Council propose a Christian cosmology and anthropology. . . .
>
> Let us inaugurate a dialogue with modern humanism. Contemporary atheism draws its strength from an affirmation of temporal values. The Church must also affirm these. Only on this condition can a consequent and efficacious collaboration be brought about with all men of good will. . . .

Revelation manifests not only God but man in his fullness as well. Christ is truly the new Adam and king of the world. . . .

Let us create a cosmic liturgy really to sing the glory of God.

Schema 13 in the Crossfire of Criticism

The importance of schema 13 is such that it threatens to overshadow the previous work of the Council. But this would be unjust, as Father de Lubac, one of the better-known French experts at Vatican II, has pointed out. The liturgical reform concerns the religious life of all the faithful; the schema on the Church stresses the notion of the people of God; that on revelation restores Scripture to a place of first honor, thus showing all men that the Church is returning to her sources, and so forth.

Moreover, it would not be true to think that the Church waited for schema 13 to deal with the problems of the world. The great encyclicals from Leo XIII to John XXIII (especially his popular *Pacem in terris*) are proof enough. Add to this the Catholic Action movements founded under Pius XI, whose essential goal was to evangelize different strata of society by giving spiritual inspiration to all who struggle for greater justice and fraternity.

Yet for millions of men the adoption of schema 13 might remain one of the most crucial moments in the life of the Church. It is the first time that a council, to quote Bishop Guano, has thrown open the ecclesiastical "citadel."

Another factor, determining in our eyes, gives schema 13 enormous value: it implicitly elaborates a theology of human progress. Thus it counteracts the prejudice, which has led many men today to lose their faith, that the Church is synonymous with social and intellectual immobilism. It is a strange but palpable scandal that the Church could have lost the Pauline and Johannine vision of a world on the march toward God. A council which for the first time in the history of the contemporary Church is not afraid of evolution could adopt the celebrated expression of Henri Bergson: "The universe is a machine for making gods," adding perhaps the qualifier "Christian" to "universe."

A brief résumé follows of the interventions during Wednesday's general congregation.

Said Cardinal Landázuri-Ricketts, Archbishop of Lima:

Formerly the word *spiritual* was synonymous with an escape from the temporal. Today we are trying to include the spiritual within the temporal. . . . Schema 13 responds not only to a need but to a necessity. Nonetheless, it has a serious weakness: it speaks very inadequately of the hunger that plagues one-third of mankind while another third lives in abundance. We cannot remain silent on this flagrant injustice. No peace will be possible as long as one man is hungry.

Integrate the Appendixes   Cardinal Suenens, Archbishop of Malines-Brussels, declared:

> The Church cannot speak of the problems of the world by putting herself on the same wavelength as the world. Let us distinguish carefully between civilization and evangelization, and recall Pius XI's words [to Bishop Roland Gosselin, former Bishop of Versailles]: "The Church civilizes by evangelizing and does not evangelize by civilizing." . . .
>
> The schema does not say enough about militant antheism in all of its forms. This phenomenon should be studied, and we should determine what kind of God the atheists refuse. Have we for our part given an exact idea of divinity? . . .
>
> The appendixes are excellent. They should be integrated into the schema itself.

Cardinal Bea stated, "This schema is not sufficiently in the spirit of the Bible, which says, 'Everything is for you; you are for Christ and Christ is for God' [Saint Paul]."

Maronite Patriarch Meouchi of Antioch said that the Church has an eschatological vision. "She is not on earth to rule the world. She is not of this world but in this world." Her responsibility is "to recapitulate all in Christ," as Saint Paul says. The schema lacks a historical and communitarian sense. It is too individualistic.

Bishop Alphonse Mathias of Chikmagalur, India, warned that "The notion of providence is not an invitation to laziness, nor is it a remedy for all our problems. . . . Let us emphasize the natural law and the human virtues."

Bishop Giuseppe Vairo of Gravina, Italy, stated, "This schema is too indulgent toward the modern mentality. It forgets Christian thought. The world does not see things as the Church does. It forgets divine transcendence and remains at the level of pure immanentism. It does not believe in absolute truth; it lacks an adequate metaphysics. John XXIII did not hesitate to speak the truth, notably in his first encyclical."

Archibishop Morcillo González of Madrid declared, "I doubt that this schema will be accepted by those to whom it is addressed. Its Latin language is lamentable. We should not speak the same language to both

Christians and non-Christians. . . . The schema contains nothing about labor, migrations, sexuality, peace, or hunger, or it speaks badly about them. The encyclical *Ecclesiam suam* was much better."

The intervention of Archbishop Conway of Armagh, Ireland, was an example of how intelligent opposition can be constructive:

> This schema is much too timid with respect to the world. It is altogether surprising that it says nothing about the Church of silence. . . . Real dialogue supposes honesty and the whole truth. . . . The schema says nothing about sexual excesses or prostitution. The Marxists set an example for us when they criticize the sexual license of our civilization. . . . Our Lord, who was meek and humble of heart, was outspoken. . . . Moreover, the schema seems to make the individual conscience the norm of morality. This is excessive and false. . . . Let us send this schema back to the commission. [Scattered applause.]

Coadjutor Bishop Elchinger of Strasbourg said:

> The Church does not seem to be deeply enough inspired by this primordial concern: that man be truly alive. It would seem that for some sadness is a Christian virtue; the Church is criticized for mistrusting joy. But life is the first obligation of man and *a fortiori* for the Christian. Let us avoid, however, the double danger of naturalism and a caricatural supernaturalism. . . .
>
> Some sacrifice human life for gain. In this case life is nothing more than a means. But it is an absolute. Many Christians are victims of the contagion of economic and biological idolatry. The Church must safeguard the transcendent character of life and work for its fulfillment. A pastor should be a defender and servant of life. These problems should be treated not with Scholastic reasoning but with the inspiration of the prophet.

When Bishops were Princes   Archbishop Zoghby, Melkite Patriarchal Vicar of Antioch, had his troubles with the moderator, Cardinal Döpfner, who interrupted him twice for digressing. But this prelate had some sensible things to say: "Formerly the bishops were cut off from the poor. They were princes." (This idea was more vigorously expressed by Father Häring in a recent conference in Rome: "To honor a bishop as a prince of this world is to dishonor him.")

"It is better," continued Archbishop Zoghby, "to be a good pastor than a good administrator. This schema satisfies nobody. It is already out of date. What will it be in ten years?"

Ukrainian Rite Archbishop Hermaniuk of Winnipeg had this criticism: "The schema says nothing about one of the two great ideologies which divides our world: Marxist materialism. This is a serious shortcoming." Transcendence properly understood favors human progress; only in this way can we fight communism. Let us honor the contemporary martyrs of the Church. In the name of freedom of conscience, let us condemn every form of persecution.

Archbishop Wojtyla of Cracow spoke in the name of all the Polish bishops: "It is not the Church's place to teach unbelievers. She must seek in common with the world." If the schema said this, we could avoid the ecclesiastical tone of this text and stop lamenting over the world. Let us avoid any spirit of monopolizing and moralizing. One of the major faults of this schema is that the Church appears authoritarian in it.

OCTOBER 23

Several Experts Are Both Attacked and Defended by Council Fathers

Schema 13 has visibly changed the atmosphere at Vatican II. Faces are animated. Some are gay; others are determined to do battle. Thus, an intervention by the Archbishop of Westminster, in everyone's opinion, bordered on a settling of old accounts by singling out the German Redemptorist Father Bernard Häring, who is a specialist in birth control problems and secretary of the central mixed subcommission for schema 13. Father Häring enjoys the confidence of the Pope since he was chosen to preach the Lenten retreat at the Vatican. But he has taken a position on the pill contrary to the English episcopacy's, and has never been forgiven for this.

Another Father praised Teilhard de Chardin; a third launched out against the Devil; a fourth deplored the Crusades.

In a word, the Council is lively. Everyone speaks with a spontaneity that has been rarely attained here. It is as though discussion of questions relating to the world has given a new *élan* and a youthful spirit to the assembly.

Here are some of the more notable interventions.

Pill and Panacea Archbishop Heenan of Westminster declared, "The schema is totally unworthy of a council. Better say nothing than utter such banal and empty phrases. This pitiful attempt will make us the laughing stock of the world. Even with the appendixes, it remains inadequate and ambiguous. Without the appendixes, it would be injurious."

Then Archbishop Heenan paraphrased Virgil: "*Timeo peritos annexa ferentes!*"

The experts I have in mind are few in number but they have international reputations. Who are the real experts? Those involved in these problems, that is, married people, economists, doctors, biochemists. . . . There is no point in questioning others, for they don't know anything. They have the simplicity of a dove but not the wisdom of a serpent. Thus they pretend to settle everything with the pill. To make a panacea of the pill is a monumental joke!

What will we say later to married couples? If they ask for bread, shall we give them stones? Let this schema be entrusted to a new commission comprised of laymen and priests who have remained in the ministry and are not from universities. . . .

In three or four years these questions will be discussed again. By then many of us here will be dead. But it will profit the Council if they help with their prayers from heaven. It would be scandalous to proceed too quickly. [Loud applause.]

Archbishop Maurice Roy of Quebec said, "Let us not hesitate to adopt a common language. Let us suppress such expressions as 'sacrosanct synod.' Let us be close to the people. The totality of the Christian people should be addressing the world through this schema in friendly tones."

Bishop Soares de Resende of Beira, Mozambique, spoke about poverty in simple and strong terms: "Poverty is the essential point. The world will recognize the Church if she is not only the Church of the poor but poor herself. Let us once and for all abandon gold, precious stones, the *cappa magna*, the *mantelletta*, red and purple."

"The Very Illustrious Father Teilhard de Chardin" Archbishop Hurley of Durban, South Africa, praised the eschatological vision of "the very illustrious and well-known Father Teilhard de Chardin, a son of the Church," and compared it with that of Saint Paul. "Let us employ good experts," he added. "There are still some left. And let us work them day and night."

Archbishop Endre Hamvas of Csanad spoke in the name of ten Hungarian bishops: "The Church is bound to no system or regime, neither to the East nor to the West. She should be a factor of unity between the two."

Bishop Charue of Namur asked:

Let us speak a language that would be understandable in the newspapers. . . . The Gospel does not despise the body, which is promised for resurrection. Let us elaborate a theology of terrestrial values. . . .

The Church must become the conscience of the modern world.

... The appendixes should be published in the name of the Council.
... The commission has some excellent experts. Let us keep them.

The Bishop of Namur was vigorously applauded. The honor of the experts had been vindicated.

Understanding the World   Archbishop Duval of Algiers said, "If we want the world to understand us, let us begin by understanding the world. Let us posit the bases of an ethics of scientific research."

Archbishop George Beck of Liverpool said, "The appendixes should be included in the schema."

Italian Bishop Raffaele Barbieri declared:

> Atheists are more deicidal than the Jews because they kill God intentionally. They are worse than the Devil for the Devil has never denied the existence of God. Atheism is a river of ink that spreads darkness, tarnishes the wellsprings, and would even put out the stars! Atheists are leading us toward universal destruction! It would be a monstrous crime not to discuss this subject. Formerly we did not hesitate to defend the Holy Sepulcher with arms. Today let us avenge God's name.

The Bishop then went on to talk about interplanetary rockets, the atomic bomb, and other subjects. The moderator interrupted this flow of eloquence twice, and then, since the Bishop persisted, finally cut the microphone.

A Bulletin from the Council's Episcopal Committee for the Press

An unexpected event that could have serious consequences took place Thursday afternoon. The official press bureau of the Council released the following text under the title "A Bulletin from the Council's Episcopal Committee for the Press":

> During its last meeting, on October 21, the Council's Committee for the Press, attentively examined different articles published in the press of several countries concerning the activities of persons and bodies at the Council.
>
> The committee noted with great sorrow that, on the basis of deplorable and partial indiscretions, certain papers indulged in a series of deductions that had no foundation concerning nonexistent maneuvers that interfere with the regular work of the Council.

The committee condemns this method of reporting; it is contrary to the truth and unjust toward persons and bodies connected with the Council.

The committee further thinks it must deplore the repeated publication of the entire texts of schemas before they are discussed in the conciliar aula. In this regard it recalls the provisions set by Paul VI at the beginning of the second session, which are still in effect and which reaffirm "the bond of secrecy both for the contents of the schemas and for the work of the commissions." These provisions also recommend prudence and moderation for all, everywhere and always, in what concerns the proceedings in the conciliar aula.

The committee reminds all that the obligation to both secrecy and moderation is binding upon journalists as a matter of professional loyalty and solidarity with their colleagues. All are obliged to observe this regulation of the Council as an important moral duty.

The committee is grateful for the way in which many journalists work in the service of the truth and the Church; it wishes to thank them and encourage them. The Committee has renewed confidence in their work.

The episcopal committee was organized before the second session in 1962, at Paul VI's request. It is presided over by Titular Archbishop Martin O'Connor, from the United States. His secretary is Monsignor Fausto Vallainc, who is in charge of the Council's press bureau. The committee is composed of fourteen archbishops and bishops from various countries, and is directly dependent upon Archbishop Felici, secretary general of the Council.

One of the sentences in the bulletin set off a lively controversy: "nonexistent maneuvers that interfere with the regular work of the Council." This phrase seems to contradict the import of the letter which seventeen cardinals sent to the Pope.

It seems as though the authors of the bulletin are trying to settle the uneasiness which this letter stirred up in public opinion.

The point of this letter, it will be recalled, was to express the "extreme concern and the greatest uneasiness" of the signatories with respect to the creation of a special commission to review the declaration on religious liberty. Three of the commission's four designated members "seem [to the cardinals] at odds with the orientation of the Council."

The cardinals went so far as to mention the "severe prejudice" of what was an "apparent violation of the Council's regulations and its liberty," and respectfully but firmly requested the Pope to take action against such machinations.

What is most surprising is that most of the bishops on the committee are in an excellent position to know that it is contrary to the truth to affirm the nonexistence of maneuvers at the Council.

Moreover, that fourteen bishops could confirm a bulletin on a serious matter that contradicts the opinion of seventeen cardinals struck us as so unlikely that we went to the source and interviewed one of the bishops on the committee. He told us:

> I don't know yet how the bulletin was worded. We did meet on Tuesday evening, and we entrusted Archbishop O'Connor and Monsignor Vallainc with drawing up a statement in our name recalling the secrecy of the schemas. But there was no question of mentioning maneuvers. That phrase certainly does not reflect my thinking, and I am sure it does not reflect the thinking of many of my colleagues on the committee. I for one am very disappointed, and we may expect lively reactions when the communiqué is distributed to all the members of the committee. This will be a lesson to us for the future. It is in fact altogether false to speak of "nonexistent maneuvers" during this session, especially after the letter from the seventeen cardinals to the Pope.

An interesting affair. It is indicative of the great tensions at Vatican II.

A Certain Conception of the Sexual Act
Is at Least Disputable, Say 155 Catholic Laymen

A hundred and fifty-five Catholic laymen—doctors, psychiatrists, psychologists, gynecologists, psychotherapists, sociologists, professors, judges, magistrates, biochemists, editors, journalists, lawyers, engineers, and more, from eleven countries—Belgium, the Netherlands, France, Germany, Austria, England, Italy, the United States, Canada, Bolivia, and the Leopoldville Congo—have sent the Pope and the Council Fathers an "address" requesting the Roman Church to revise her position on birth control.

It is a strongly worded text, as the following extracts indicate.

> Within the framework of present directives, millions of Christian couples of good will encounter great difficulties when they try to reconcile the different objectives of marriage: procreation, education, conjugal love. The result in innumerable cases is that conflicts arise, consciences are deformed, the couple leave the Church, or the marriage breaks up. Another result is a pastoral theology that considers itself forced to make a painful distinction between the formal directives and their application.

The Church's teaching should be subjected to a thorough examination and confronted with the basic postulates of contemporary thinking.

It is difficult to conceive the natural law otherwise than as oriented toward the fulfillment of human nature and as a protection for the person and human life. Man's intervention in nature can raise difficult problems; but their resolution should be guided by the norm of the good of individual man and humanity.

It is extremely difficult to think that respect for the biological order in one of its relative aspects is the supreme norm.

We are now aware of the continuous and dynamic character of spermatogenesis, which is a permanent process of creation and resorption of millions of spermatozoa.

Even on the physiological level, the connection between sexual intercourse and procreation is much less rigorous than was long thought. Given the fact that most acts of sexual intercourse are recognized today to be infertile, it is no longer possible to view fecundity as the direct object or the immediate meaning of each particular act. What is known and experienced as impossible cannot be considered an end.

In the present view, regulation of fecundity is admissible only at the price of a contradiction between the effective and intentional content of an act and its exterior form.

The human values at stake here lead us to believe that there can be limits to conjugal continence, as Saint Paul recognized. The couple must be responsible for determining these limits even when there is no question of birth control.

Certain conceptions, especially a certain vision of the natural order and man's right to his body as well as the meaning of the sexual act, are at least disputable today.

Given the complexity of this matter and its vital importance for millions of people, we are inclined to believe that the spiritual task to be accomplished calls for a time of maturation. This would be necessary not only to reflect upon the Church's teaching but also to form consciences.

We respectfully present these considerations with the conviction that the quest for truth for the spiritual good of mankind is every man's first duty.

Official Announcement of a Fourth Session

Archbishop Felici confirmed yesterday that the closing of the third session will be November 21. On that day the Pope will concelebrate mass with twenty-four bishops from the dioceses in which the principal Marian shrines are located. Also, the first official announcement of a fourth session was made. The secretary general of the Council said the date would be determined in due time by Paul VI.

Archbishop Felici drew applause with a remark about the experts, who were given rough treatment the day before by the Archbishop of Westminster. "Many experts," he said, "have greatly helped the Council by their knowledge and activity."

Archbishop Felici then called upon Bishop Guano, president of the central subcommission of schema 13. But he was not present. Rumor had it that he had just come from seeing the Pope when he arrived some minutes later. Consequently, Guano's words were listened to with much greater attention.

"Schema 13," he said, "cannot be completed until the fourth session. The commission will pay the strictest heed to observations expressed in the aula. Only one Father, to my knowledge, sent the schema to hell outright. Laymen and experts were in agreement as to the preparation of this schema. However, the Fathers and not the experts had the last word." This was in answer to attacks that had been made upon the experts.

Bishop Guano then recalled "the extreme delicacy" of the birth control problem. The Pope will reserve judgment on this matter until a group of specialists—doctors, gynecologists, sociologists, psychologists, and others—have completed their work. "That is why the schema is deliberately vague on this matter."

Finally, the Bishop made this important statement, which was taken as a reflection of the Pope's thinking: "Let the Council be careful not to terminate this session without saying something about such serious problems as peace, hunger, poverty, and atheism in all its forms."

Schema 13: General Interventions End and Specific Examination Begins

Here are excerpts from the seven last interventions on schema 13 as a whole.

Too Occidental Archbishop Tchidimbo of Conakry had these criticisms to make: "This schema is mediocre. It seems intended uniquely for America and Europe. It doesn't touch on the problems of Africa: underdevelopment, colonialism, all forms of discrimination, and the conditions of progress." The Archbishop also felt that the schema is too individualistic. It doesn't say enough about the kind of socialization Cardinal Suhard spoke about in his pastoral letters. The poor have an "evangelical right." Let us present the Church as the great defender of freedom, and "Let us speak about apartheid, the cancer of our times." Let Africans form part of the next commission.

Abortion and Highway Regulations Bishop Franz von Streng of Basel and Lugano mingled two very unlike subjects. "The schema doesn't say enough about abortion," he said. "Let us solemnly insist that life in all of its forms cannot be interrupted even if the civil laws so permit. This is one of the most terrible evils of our time." Then the Bishop asked, "Let us also say something about the training of automobile drivers. Respect for traffic rules is not only of the penal order. It is an obligation of conscience, since violation of them endangers the lives of others."

Archabbot Reetz, Superior General of the Benedictines of Beuron, Germany, provoked laughter when he declared:

> I fear to address the Council, for obviously those who have spent their lives in religious houses know nothing about the world. Yet Saint Gregory the Great sent Saint Augustine to convert England, and he became Bishop of Canterbury. Saint Benedict, who obviously knew nothing of the world, is to be proclaimed the Father of Europe by Paul VI. . . .
>
> I have the simplicity of a dove but not the wisdom of a serpent. The experts who prepared the schema, and especially the five appendixes, are highly qualified. Still, others can be added. . . .
>
> Let us believe not only in the devil but in devils.

Teilhard's Popularity with Young People For the second time in two days, Teilhard de Chardin was favorably mentioned in the Council. But Father Reetz, though noting that this Jesuit "is known throughout the world and enjoys a considerable audience among young people," thought his vision of the world does not give enough place to the redemption and that his doctrine smacks of Origenism.

Exiled Archbishop Paul Yu Pin of Nanking, now rector of Fu Jen Catholic University in Taipei, Formosa, spoke in the name of seventy fathers: "Let us make a statement on atheistic communism. The Catholic and Communist ideologies cannot coexist. . . . Catholic communism is a serious error." (Scattered applause.)

Auxiliary Bishop González Moralejo of Valencia, Spain, urged:

> Let us dissipate the error committed by most men and even by Christians who see the Church only as a power and little understand her profound mystery. . . .
>
> This schema should be drafted in such a way that it can be read by millions of men. Let us call upon expert laymen. The appendixes should be rewritten and translated into all languages, and they should be published officially.

Archbishop Guillermo Bolatti of Rosario, Argentina, echoed Archbishop Yu Pin: "Communism, which holds a third of humanity under its yoke, constitutes one of the most obvious signs of our time. If we do not speak about it, how will history judge us?"

Archbishop Darmajuwana of Semarang, Indonesia, was the last speaker on the schema in general: "This schema is too superficial. Let us show the profound unity of all creation which tends towards salvation. . . . Let us respect the proper laws of terrestrial activities."

The Historic Meaning of Man   The first seven Fathers to intervene on the introduction and chapter 1 of the schema were the following:

Archbishop Gouyon of Rennes:

> The vision of the world proposed here lacks amplitude. We must clarify the theological foundations of technological progress, the means of communicating thought, the triumphs of medicine. . . . All of this represents the fulfillment of the command given by God in Genesis: "Fill the earth and subdue it." . . .
>
> The style of the schema is too weak. After the example of the prophets and Christ, the Church should not hestitate to use strong and harsh language. Let us not fear to use a prophetic voice.

Bishop Schmitt of Metz:

> The Holy Spirit, who is a missionary, has not always been listened to. . . . We are experiencing today an exceptional *élan*. Let this appear in the introduction to the schema. Our present world, which has been taking shape for four centuries, is a planetary world and not merely a European world. It is dynamic as well as traditional; it is highly socialized; it forms a unity. The world claims its proper autonomy in such a way that mankind today does not experience the need of God as its point of reference. . . .
>
> Let the Church reveal to this world the historic significance of

man. . . . This is the first time a council has gathered in an atheistic world. The elaboration of a Christian anthropology would be most practical. . . .

The tone of the Church's presence in the world should no longer be authoritarian as in the Middle Ages. The autonomy which the world claims is legitimate; it is not necessarily the result of a Promethean pride. Let us find other ways. For the presence of authority, let us substitute the presence of interiorized friendship. A dynamic solidarity exists between the Church and the world.

Bishop Felix Romero Menjibar of Jaén, Spain: "The Church continues the incarnation. This is the basis of dialogue between the Church and the world. . . . Let us stress the autonomy of the world."

Bishop de Vet of Breda, the Netherlands: "The process of secularization is normal. Let us study the development of peoples in the light of God's will." The schema shows the Church as a foreigner to the world, as though she were above everything or were identified with the hierarchy. "Let us propose a new version, because the present one is not likely to arouse the least enthusiasm."

Archbishop Luis del Rosario of Zamboanga, the Philippines: Chapter 1 can be read in its entirety without revealing any idea of what it wants to say. "The schema is an unhappy compromise between two themes: man considered as a pilgrim on earth, and therefore obligated to escape from terrestrial concerns as much as possible; and man considered as responsible for the perfection of all of creation and for giving it value."

Bishop Joseph Schoiswohl of Graz-Seckau, Austria: "Let us remind man of the central idea that he is immortal. Thus we will fight effectively against the despair that is one of the characteristics of our world. Hope leads to faith. Man is uneasy as long as his heart does not rest in God."

Archbishop García de Sierra of Burgos, Spain: "We need a healthy anthropology. This should become the backbone of the whole schema. Man was created in the image of God; God remains the conductor of history; evolution is not blind. . . . True humanism cannot be atheistic, for atheism truncates reality. To forget God is to cut off a source of light."

Cardinal Bea to the Non-Catholic Observers: "Your Contribution Was Determining in the Vote on Ecumenism"

At a recent reception for the non-Catholic observers, Cardinal Bea pronounced the following allocution:

The fact that the final vote on the first three chapters of the schema on ecumenism was almost unanimous is a cause for deep joy and great expectation. The schema was adopted with a majority of 98 percent. We would not have dared hope for such results two years ago. This unanimity shows that the Roman Catholic Church, through her highest and most qualified representatives, is seriously committed to the cause of Christian unity.

This vote is at the same time a testimony to the contribution made by the non-Catholic observers to the Council. Their presence in the assembly and their participation in the Council's work by prayer and study made the Council Fathers aware of the problem of disunity in a striking manner. The numerous daily contacts between them and the Fathers have made us realize that there is already a unity in Christ, in the work of the Spirit, in our common faith in and love for Christ. Yet these same contacts have also given us a more painful consciousness of the wound of disunity that still exists."

Vatican II and the Congress in Bombay Will Contribute to the Development of the Idea of Poverty in the Church

Let us underline the conditions Paul VI has set for his Bombay trip: (1) it will have a Gandhi-like simplicity; (2) he will meet the president of India not as a head of state but as a "pilgrim"; (3) he wishes to mingle with the poor masses, whatever religion they belong to.

These three provisos will undoubtedly help subdue the triumphal character of the international Eucharistic Congress. Since the example of humility and simplicity comes from no less a personage than the Pope, it would seem that the ceremonies of the congress will not be such as to offend the millions of Indians who live in hunger and without shelter.

Aware of the dangers of ostentatious display, the Catholic bishops of India have drafted a collective letter, which reads in part: "Natives of the city of Bombay and visitors from India or abroad, remember that during the time of the congress millions will judge Christianity in terms of how Christians behave. Faithful to the religious patrimony of our race, they consider all forms of ostentation and extravagance as incompatible with a true religious spirit."

One of the organizers of the Congress said that Bombay would be a "triumphal failure" if Catholics participating in it do not give concrete proof of authentic charity, such as visits to hospitals, orphanages, prisons, and so forth. We already know that a special afternoon will be reserved for a rally of poor children from the city, and that the last day of the fraternal meetings will be celebrated in some forty centers to which men and women of all religions and social classes will be invited.

Some dozen specialists of the United Nations Food and Agriculture Organization will lecture during the congress on demography, hunger, and underdevelopment problems in India.

Some 30,000 foreigners are expected; they will be lodged partly in private homes, partly in hotels, and partly aboard steamboats.

The congress in Bombay could have the happy effect of rapidly clarifying the question of poverty in the Church which the Council is wrestling with. Once Paul VI has stripped himself of all outward pomp before the poor of the city, how can the "Constantinian" habits of the Vatican survive? Paul VI cannot return to Rome as he left, and the faithful of his diocese should understand that they can hardly continue to treat the Bishop of Rome like a Renaissance king. (In Rome a complete cardinal's regalia costs 1,300,000 lire plus an additional 350,000 lire for the garb of his retinue.)

At Vatican II the problem of the "Church of the poor" continues to be studied in different workshops by Cardinal Lercaro of Bologna, Archbishop Helder Câmara of Recife, Father Paul Gauthier of Nazareth, Sister Mary Theresa of Bethlehem, and others. The results of their labors will soon be known.

A Spirit of Simony   Speaking recently to this group, Father Häring said:

> The hierarchy, which is sent to preach the Gospel, should use the *feeble* means which led Christ to the resurrection. Poverty is a condition of dialogue. Using the most sacred things to exalt a human culture evidences a spirit of simony. The Church is the servant of all cultures and not the protector of the Latin culture, which is considered her indispensable property.
>
> Poverty is not a beautiful ideal for special vocations. It is a strict moral obligation for bishops. Since bishops have received the fullness of the priesthood, they have the privilege of total poverty. This is an obligation for the bishops; otherwise, the Council will be a failure.
>
> Collegiality itself is linked with the spirit of poverty; it helps free bishops from the temptation to dominate.

Archbishop Trinidade Golland of Botucatú, Brazil, said during one of these meetings, "We are so cut off from the poor that when I try to be poor and go among poor people, I remain a stranger to them, like someone visiting from another world. There should be a commission where everyone would be free to say what he expects of us, for we do not know what people really think of us."

Manual Labor for Priests Archbishop Motta of Vitória, Brazil, had this to say: "If we do not train priests specially to live and work with laborers and the poor, we bishops will never be able to understand the poor any more than they understand us, for we are on the periphery of their lives. I would like to intervene on the subject of manual labor for priests in the conciliar aula."

Thus, ten years after the death of Father Henri Perrin and ten years after the crisis of 1954—necessary, perhaps, but painful—the idea of priests working is coming to the fore once again. The number of bishops in favor of this idea is increasing daily.

The problem lies in avoiding former errors by giving these priests an exceptionally solid intellectual and spiritual formation. Only extremely robust and balanced men should be accepted for such a difficult apostolate.

OCTOBER 25

Aftermath of the Episcopal Committee's Bulletin

There was a stormy press conference Saturday at noon at the headquarters of the official press bureau of the Council. Present were two of the journalists who were directly affected by the bulletin: a Frenchman [Henri Fesquet] and the Chilean Dr. Antonio Cruzat, press director for the Latin American hierarchy, who has been forced to resign as a result of pressures from the Curia, owing to his published report—the first—on the letter from the seventeen cardinals. They explained themselves in the presence of Archbishop Martin O'Connor and Monsignor Vallainc. Some strong words were exchanged. The audience left no doubt as to which side it was on. There was a good deal of muttering when Monsignor Vallainc said, "I don't know about the letter from seventeen cardinals"—obviously a Roman way of saying that he hadn't heard of it through official channels.

At the end of the conference, it was a proven fact that at least some members of the Episcopal Committee were in disagreement with the document which was released in their name. The two journalists were later congratulated by Bishop Wright of Pittsburgh and a member of the theological commission presided over by Cardinal Ottaviani. We hadn't expected this.

Bishop Wright, who spoke on schema 13, made this public statement: "Service to the truth is one with the service to the Church."

Aggiornamento Progresses

Monday's general congregation on schema 13 was distinctly one of the most interesting of the whole Council. Such burning issues as Marxism, atheism, the ontological meaning of the incarnation and resurrection, sin, how the Church should be present in the world, the relationship between science and faith, and poverty were commented upon in turn.

Schema 13 furnishes Vatican II with the opportunity to speak truths that have too long been hidden under a bushel. For the third time within a few days, Teilhard de Chardin was praised. We now understand better why the conservative bishops were so anxious to scuttle this schema: it gives the *aggiornamento* of the Church her real meaning.

The Church is feeling her way toward a theology of evolution and redemption that is scattering the residues of Jansenism, a false duality between the natural and the supernatural and an unjustified contempt for terrestrial values. The next generation will discover in schema 13 a theology of relationships between the Church and the world that the present generation was never taught. This rejuvenation and relevance are due to John XXIII, who patiently but firmly wrested the Church progressively from the control of legalists and politicians, and placed her in the hands of pastors who have a feeling for progress and truly love their times. We are witnessing today what John XXIII called the "springtime of the Church," whose implications have not yet been fully grasped. Vatican II is less a terminal point than a point of departure whose consequences will unfold little by little in the years to come.

There were eighteen interventions on Monday, and here are some of the more notable passages.

Harmonize the Profane and Religious   Cardinal Léger:

> Schema 13 gives the impression that the only temptation of Christians is to neglect the temporal. There are other dangers, such as neglecting spirituality. The world today has no taste for silence and prayer. . . . The crucial problem is to harmonize the profane and the religious. . . . The schema is silent on the problem of evil and suffering, which is an essential obstacle. We should say that suffering draws its value from the fact that it is a participation in the redemptive work of Christ.

Abbot Jean Prou, Superior General of the Benedictine Congregation in France, put his finger on a capital difficulty: "What is the relationship between dedication to the world and the incarnation? Some think that the incarnation transformed the world *intrinsically*, a conception which the schema seems to favor and which is in conflict with faith. To be sure, Christ is the alpha and omega, but I think that this transformation was *extrinsic*. Only man, and not all of creation, can be raised up to God."

This position is directly opposed to the vision of the world entertained by Teilhard de Chardin and Father de Lubac.

Understanding Marxist Humanism   Auxiliary Bishop José Guerra Campos of Madrid:

> It is regrettable that the schema doesn't mention Marxist atheism. Marxist materialism is subtle. It proposes a humanism whose end is a profound correspondence between man's conscience and the world. At the present time, man is still alienated, principally by religion. To deny transcendence is thus a virtue and not a fault for the Marxist. It is important to judge Marxist eschatology from within: man must do for himself what others expect from religion; one day the tension between the objective and subjective orders will disappear. This explains why Marxists deny the subjective aspirations of man.

Bishop Guerra concluded, "Let us not indulge in cheap apologetics. If we wish to dialogue, let us begin by understanding Marxism. Marxist blindness might have had its origin in inadequate religious instruction. Let us at all costs avoid presenting the Christian religion as an ideology, because it is a reality."

Respecting the Spirit   Archbishop Josip Pogačnik of Ljubljana, Yugoslavia, made these practical remarks:

> It is not enough to have a social doctrine. We must put it in practice. Pastoral letters and pontifical documents do not guarantee action. *Mater et magistra* was much more seriously studied by the Communists than by some bishops. . . .
> Vatican II must ask itself before the world why the Church has not understood the signs of the times. Many founders of religious orders, for example, were not understood by the Church; they were rather suspect. How can we avoid this? By a renewed theology of the Holy Spirit, who is present both in the world and in the Church. We must believe in the charisms of the people of God. . . . Let us proceed with charity and broadmindedness. . . . The crisis of authority has engendered a servile obedience. Let Vatican II say some-

thing about the duty of bishops to respect the Spirit wherever it manifests itself.

Loving the World Bishop de Roo of Victoria, British Columbia: "Let us avoid the danger of a dichotomy between the natural order and a supernatural vocation. The mystery of Easter, which is at once death and resurrection, enables us to understand that all of man's activity is secured: this is the key to everything. . . . Christ neither condemned nor despised the world. He loved it and lived in communion with the men of his time. Let us imitate him."

A Theology of Work Auxiliary Bishop Santo Quadri of Pinerolo, Italy, is a young bishop. He addressed himself to the experts (he was one himself during the second session): "Let us insert a special paragraph in the schema on work. It is through work that we transform things and discover their nature. To work is already to participate in the universal priesthood of Christ. . . . The chief problem is to determine the nature of the relationships between man's action and the parousia. It is an extremely difficult problem."

The Need for Prophets Maronite Archbishop Ziadé of Beirut: "Let us draw up a more theological schema. The sign of the times *par excellence* is the resurrection, which is ordered toward the parousia. The resurrection embraces all the other signs of the times. We have great need of prophets who know how to read these signs."

Auxiliary bishop Ancel of Lyon: "One of the serious weaknesses of the schema is its failure to show how the Church's interests in temporal affairs proceeds from her overall mission, which is evangelization."

On Mortal Sin Bishop Louis Morrow of Krishnagar, India, made a very important intervention: "How can men and women today understand that God is good if we continue to teach them that those who eat meat on Friday will go to hell? An infinitely regrettable contempt for the authority of the Church is the result. Let us not speak falsely or irrelevantly about mortal sin. Let us continue our *aggiornamento* by simplifying our legislation."

Auxiliary Bishop Anthony Hacault of St. Boniface, Manitoba: "The Church should not be afraid of her human condition. Nothing that is human was foreign to Christ. . . . The Church ought not appear as an authority exterior to the world. Let her espouse the joys and anxieties of the world. The faith and the presence of God in the world is the basis of all dialogue."

The Church Does Not Need Privileges   Archbishop Marty of Reíms, also took up this theme:

> Let us seek a new mode for the Church's presence in the world. Our present mode is too sullied by the past. Formerly, this presence was institutional. Today, when the world is organized without or against the Church, the only possible mode of presence is that of the leaven in the yeast.
>
> Let us avoid saying that the laity are the bridge between the Church and the world. It insinuates on the one hand that the Church is a stranger to the world, which is false, since even priests are in the world, and on the other that the laity are outside the Church, which is equally false. We cannot promote the laity enough.

Bishop Čule of Mostar, Yugoslavia: "Let the Church reject all clericalism, all Caesaro-papism, all spirit of domination." No political party should act in the name of the Church, he said. The Church has no need of privileges, nor does she want them, as Lacordaire once said.

"Without the Church there is no possible liberty of conscience or autonomy of the human person, for the basis of this autonomy is the transcendence of God. Faith implies a radical negative of all tyranny. . . . Christ is man's real physician."

The Divorce Between Faith and Science   Bishop Otto Spülbeck of Meissen, Germany:

> Men of science bitterly regret not being able to dialogue with the Church and not being able to become theologians. Yet they hope for much from the Church. A striking proof is the extraordinary influence of Teilhard de Chardin, who could talk to scientists in a language they understood. That is why official atheists see in Teilhard de Chardin their number-one enemy. . . . It was our fault that Galileo was condemned. . . . Our catechisms do not use a language that is comprehensible to men of science.
>
> We should integrate appendix 3, on culture, into the schema itself.

Seven Million Italian Communists Rejoice in the Church's Wealth   Archbishop Golland of Botucatú, Brazil:

> Let the Church come down from her thrones and palaces and rid herself of ornamentation. The secretary general of the Council sometimes addresses us as "very adorned Fathers" [*ornitissimi patres*].

The people also address us that way, but in a different sense, because they see us each day, here in Rome and elsewhere, clothed from head to foot in our luxurious garments. We seem rich while they are poor. . . .

The Communists, who seem to be ignoring the Council, are seven million strong here in Italy. They see the immense distance between the Church and the people. They rejoice in this. We ought to wear black soutanes at our general congregations. Archbishop Bartholomé of Braqua recommended this at the Council of Trent and recalled to the Fathers the decree of the Fourth Council of Carthage: "Let bishops wear ordinary clothes and eat humble food."

Bishop Fourrey of Belley, France: "Let us show our poverty of spirit in actions. Let our collective institutions be poor, beginning with religious orders. . . . Let us condemn the modern forms of usury. Trusts are perhaps useful, but they profit at the expense of the poor, and this is a very serious sin. Let rich nations help poor nations."

OCTOBER 28

Morality, Tourism, and the Index

The conciliar session on Tuesday was dominated by four speakers: Patriarch Maximos IV Saigh, who was equal to himself—remarkable for his wit and bite; Archbishop Garner of Pretoria, South Africa, who was one of the most amusing to date; Bishop Méndez Arceo of Cuernavaca, Mexico, on mortal sin; and Bishop Huyghe of Arras, on the necessity for freedom within the Church.

It might also be noted that two bishops attacked the Index. But so much water has flowed under the bridges of the Tiber since last year that no one is surprised by such boldness.

Maximos IV Saigh: "Let Us Radically Transform Our Way of Teaching Morality" Here is a substantial part of Maximos IV's speech:

The Church should be interested in all the vital problems of her children. She should look upon them not as servants but as friends. The principal matter is to form the faithful according to Christ's law of love, and to inculcate in them a sense of responsibility. . . . The Middle Ages, that period of humanity's infancy, is finished. We have now entered the age of maturity. Let us impose no law without giving a good reason for it.

Let us radically transform our way of teaching morality. It is presently too legalistic. We no longer have to deal with a closed and absolutist society. We are still too influenced by a juridic perspective. . . . Christ should be the center of all morality. Roman legalism has even contaminated us in the East.

Take the catechism, for example. We oblige the faithful to abstain from meat on Friday and go to mass on Sunday under pain of mortal sin. This is not reasonable; no one believes us. Unbelievers pity us. Even the sacrament of penance should be revised. . . .

A revision is obligatory. The purpose of the commandments is to guarantee human joy. Let us proceed by way of love rather than authority. A mother is not inclined to use the stick very often on her children. Modern man rebels against every form of coercion. . . .

John XXIII wisely said, "We have not yet discovered the real demands of charity." . . .

I suggest a commission of theologians to revise our teaching of morality and positive laws. This would be real *aggiornamento*.

Maximos IV was applauded at length.

No Aggiornamento *Without Tourism*   Archbishop Garner provoked unrestrained laughter. Amazingly enough, he spoke in the name of eighty-four bishops from Europe, Asia, and Latin America.

Tourism is a consequence of the incarnation. It is a sign of the times. It is extremely annoying that schema 13 does not mention it. Last year there were 600,000,000 tourists in the world, without counting athletes and weekend vacationers. There can be no *aggiornamento* without tourism! John XXIII referred to tourism to emphasize its influence on the exchange of ideas and the modification of mentalities. Tourism is an instrument of dialogue.

Center Attention on Paschal Joy   Bishop Arceo Méndez, who has already spoken twice about Freemasonery at Vatican II, made a brilliant intervention on the moral law that was inspired by an open letter from a French mother:

I entirely agree with His Beatitude Maximos IV. One of the principal signs of contemporary times is the growth of a sense of responsibility and liberty. The Church must defend not only religious liberty but liberty as such, wherever it is found. We must preach the spirit of liberty and love. This spirit of liberty is difficult to reconcile with the multiplication of precepts in the Church. We too often talk of mortal sin with respect to these positive laws. In this, schema 13 is good; facts are more important than words. If it is wrong for the state to multiply laws, imprisonments, and the like, for much greater reason it is wrong for the Church to multiply sanctions.

But what do we teach seminarians? In current manuals of morality, the Church imposes 200 positive laws (including the wearing of sacred vestments) under pain of mortal sin. We have only to remind ourselves of what was recently taught about the eucharistic fast. A single drop of water before communion threatened Catholics with hell; but a slight infraction of divine law was regarded as a venial sin.

Likewise, we are forbidden to eat meat, even bad meat, on Friday; but a banquet prepared with the finest of fish opens the gates of heaven.

Many of our positions are no longer relevant. Let us revise them and emphasize evangelical law, because the impression is given that this is of less importance than positive laws.

How ugly it is to think we have to rant about mortal sin to fill our Churches! . . . Let us center our attention on the essential, which is paschal joy. . . .

The manuals say that embroidering on Sunday is not a sin, although knitting is considered a sin if it is continued over several hours. We create sinners in this fashion.

Bishop Méndez asked in conclusion that no positive law be imposed "under pain of mortal sin."

Liberty Is Necessary Within the Church   Bishop Huyghe made an original intervention by focusing on liberty within the Church. He said in essence:

Dialogue is possible with non-Christians only on condition that there is a prior dialogue among Christians and with the Holy Spirit. Dialogue is possible only if all members of the Church, whoever they are, are in a state of dialogue. We must learn to listen. We must see the Holy Spirit in our interlocutors.

The Church herself must become a *congregation of dialogue.* Let us insist less on administration; let us not appear jealous of our authority. What is essential is to create communion among men. Structures will follow. They are at the service of persons, not the other way around. . . .

The liberty of the children of God has not been sufficiently emphasized. As soon as anyone does anything original, the Church imposes laws on him. When a priest tries new methods, he is immediately constricted by laws. Consequently, whatever is new is suspect. . . .

The Index condemns books without giving their authors a hearing. This is contrary to the dignity of the children of God. . . .

Let us begin by initiating a dialogue within the Church that is carried on in friendship, trust, and freedom; only then will we be in a position to address the world. [Loud applause.]

We No Longer Need Fear Science   Auxiliary Bishop Wilhelm Cleven of Cologne, Germany, also spoke about the Index:

The Index does not encourage trust. Young people pay no attention to it, and see it as an instance of the Catholic ghetto. But the whole image of the Council is one of openness. . . .

The Church should no longer appear as an adversary of evolution. Christians have nothing to fear from science. Let us say clearly that the Church approves of the work of scientists, and that she does not fear great liberty in research. We must recall, of course, that salvation does not come from science, but let us try to make up for our backwardness on the scientific level.

Cardinal Frings, Archbishop of Cologne, said:

Those who criticize the schema for displaying a kind of Platonism are not wrong. Christ came to save the bodies as well as the souls of men; he came not only for individuals but for society, for nations, for the whole world. If the theology of the incarnation presented in the schema were taken literally, it would be dangerous. Bodies will be saved only by resurrection after death. Human work is not a direct preparation for the "new heaven" or the "new earth," for heaven and earth shall pass. We should therefore use the words *world*, *progress*, and *salvation* prudently. During this time of pilgrimage, the Church and the world remain distinct. The Church cannot absorb the world, nor can the world absorb the Church.

Oscar Cullmann Cited   Cardinal Silva Henríquez, Archbishop of Santiago, Chile, clarified the two meanings of the word *poverty*. In the Gospel sense it means misery. "This poverty," he said, "must be suppressed. Let us have faith in the possibility of Christians' organizing the world differently so that misery will disappear. There is no lack of natural wealth in the world."

Then the Cardinal referred to a suggestion made by Oscar Cullmann, who has long proposed that an ecumenical collection for the poor be taken up each year in the various churches, and that the money from one denomination be used, in part or in whole, to help the poor of another confession.

Avoiding Titles Archbishop Zoghby, Melkite Patriarchal Vicar in Egypt, declared, "Our witness cannot affect the world if it is not carried out in simplicity and poverty and in direct contact with the poor." And he went on:

> Since the world only recognizes authority as a function of service, let us avoid titles and insignia that are reminiscent of honors and the spirit of domination. Let us also spare the pope, the first vicar of the crucified Christ, the pain of the qualification "gloriously reigning." The popes refer to themselves as the servants of God and try to be just that. Need anything be added to "Holy Father"?

Article 58 Is Respected

There is some news concerning the declaration on religious liberty. This document, as we know, wasn't entirely satisfactory to the Pope, and he wanted improvements made before it was voted on. The measures proposed in Archbishop Felici's letter to Cardinal Bea has been abandoned as a result of the letter signed by seventeen cardinals, and another solution, this one in keeping with the Council regulations, has been suggested.

Cardinal Cigognani, Secretary of State, wrote directly to Cardinal Bea (in the Pope's name) and to Cardinal Ottaviani. He asked them to designate ten Council Fathers to form a mixed commission, half of whose members would be from the Secretariat for Promoting Christian Unity and half from the theological commission.

Archbishop Marcel Lefebvre, Superior General of the Holy Spirit Fathers, is not among the members, although the following are believed to be: Cardinal Browne of the Curia; Bishop Georges Pelletier of Three Rivers, Quebec, Canada; Archbishop Parente, and Bishop Colombo, the Pope's personal theologian.

There are two essential differences between this solution and the other: (1) the declaration on religious liberty will remain within the jurisdiction of the secretariat for unity, and (2) the commission members are to be chosen by the presidents of the theological commission and the secretariat for Unity. Thus, article 58 of the Council regulations is perfectly respected.

Several Bishops Speak Against Apartheid
and All Forms of Racial Discrimination

Archbishop Felici, in announcing yesterday that examination of chapter 4 of schema 13 would begin, asked the Fathers not to intervene orally but in writing on certain touchy points raised in the schema "because of the interpretations that might be made outside of the aula."

Patriarch Agagianian presented the report on chapter 4, which enumerates the principal problems confronting modern man. He noted that the schema was only the beginning of a dialogue with the world and that episcopal conferences should continue this dialogue by means of collective pastoral letters adapted to the particular conditions of each country. "It is necessary to know the appendixes," he added, "in order to understand the schema; they should therefore be studied."

Bishop González Martín of Astorga is renowned for having abandoned his episcopal palace in favor of a more modest house. "Let us be well aware," he said, "that the world will not respond to the Church until she first of all renews herself."

In Defense of the Nation Coptic Bishop Ghattas of Thebes, Egypt, regretted that the schema doesn't say much about the nation as such. He recalled the duty to obey governments, even if they are "bad," in the expression of Saint Paul. "I think that nationalism is dead," he added. "Let us emphasize love of country founded on the land of our ancestors. If we mention this, we can return home at peace with ourselves." (Note that Bishop Ghattas lives in Egypt.)

Cardinal Ritter, Archbishop of Saint Louis. "The human person does not take enough responsibility. The collective is sometimes substituted for the personal."

Martin Luther King Applauded Archbishop Athaide of Agra, India: "Racial segregation, apartheid, exists even in those countries that boast of being Christian. Such incredible things as slavery and the sale of human beings still exist. Such evils call for a strong remedy. Let us awaken consciences. Why not take our inspiration from Gandhi? Bhave, his disciple, sets an excellent example." This Indian travels throughout his country on foot in an effort to get landowners to share their property with those who have none. He has legal support which may soon result in abolishing private property there. "The late President John F. Kennedy," the Archbishop continued, "was in favor of racial integration; this is practical charity. Paul VI received Martin Luther King and congratulated him on his peaceful resistance." (Applause.)

Bishop Andrew G. Grutka of Gary, Indiana, denounced slums as "homes of crime." "It is a scandal," he said, "to see pastors leaving their parishes when Negroes move in. Let us cry our rejection of racial discrimination from the rooftops like the trumpet of Jericho."

Archbishop Patrick A. O'Boyle of Washington, D. C., speaking in the name of the American episcopacy, expressed a similar desire: "Racism is the most important problem of our times. Let us make a solemn declaration to this effect." (Applause.)

Bishop Barrachina Estevan of Alicante, Spain, recalled the adage of Pope Gelasius I (fifth century): "Man is God; God is man."

Promotion of Women Bishop Coderre, of St.-Jean de Québec, Canada, speaking in the name of forty bishops, intervened in favor of the promotion of women.

Bishop Bäuerlein of Srijem, Yugoslavia, thought that paragraph 21, which treats of marriage, is dangerous, and that it is wrong to center everything on conjugal love.

Bishop Pierre de la Chanonie of Clermont-Ferrand, France, insisted that the schema mention the problem of maladjusted children.

Archbishop Joseph Malula of Leopoldville, the Congo, drew applause by denouncing tribalism and requesting that the schema insist on the dignity of woman, who, he said, should be "neither an instrument of lust nor a slave."

Bishop László of Eisenstadt, Austria, made a fine distinction: "Many men today enjoy full liberty but make bad use of it. Let us protect liberty from its enemies within."

The "Subordinate" Mission of Mary

Chapter 8 of the schema *De ecclesia* was definitively approved this morning with a vote of 1,559 *placet*, 10 *non placet*, and 521 *placet juxta modum*, with 1 ballot null. It is likely that a good number of the Fathers who turned in qualified votes were not satisfied with the treatment in the new version of "Mary mediatrix." This expression has been deliberately drowned in an ocean of other epithets: advocate, auxiliatrix, adjutrix. It was the writers' way of refusing the Virgin the pre-eminence of her role as mediatrix which was specifically demanded by some Mariophiles. This view is supported by the schema itself: "Her titles are understood in such a way that they add nothing to the dignity or efficacy of Christ, the unique mediator. The Church does not hesitate to profess this subordinate role of Mary."

Thus, the chapter on the Virgin Mary finds its true place. She is not a pseudo-goddess but a creature whose nobility, if we dare so speak, was to be the mother of God, immaculately conceived and already resurrected.

Vatican II has just put away for good any temptation for the Roman Church to define new Marian dogmas. Protestants will not be the only ones to rejoice.

"The Church Has No Need of Our Pious Lies"

Archbishop Helder Câmara of Recife, vice president of the Latin American episcopal conference, spoke to the journalists on Wednesday. His talk was entitled "Schema 13, Telstar for the World." In it he praised the press, radio, and television "for their help to the Council." "We must thank you," he said, "not only for reporting what is going on in St. Peter's but especially for not watering down the truth. The Church has no need of our pious lies."

Archbishop Helder Câmara's conferences are rebellious from all points of view. They are well thought out and well delivered. The speaker's gestures, gift of mimicry, and intonations are even more eloquent than his words. Here are a few of the thoughts he expressed:

> One would have to be blind not to see the work of the Spirit during the second recess. Let us hope the third one lasts until October so the experts and the Holy Spirit will have time to improve schema 13. . . .
>
> The first encyclical that the people could understand was *Pacem in terris* because the Pope wrote in a direct, almost journalistic style. . . .
>
> We in Latin America are aware that countries behind the Iron Curtain are not the only ones where the human person is oppressed. . . .
>
> The enthusiasm with which the young want to help the "third world" makes us forget the old sin of colonialism. . . .
>
> The right to speak the truth must be won by love. . . .
>
> We must thank the former general of the Jesuits for supporting Teilhard de Chardin; may the new general see to it that his work is developed. . . .
>
> I have waited for the declaration on the Jews since my childhood. There is a man named Bea; he is a prophet and reminds us of John XXIII. . . .
>
> By what right do we say pagans are estranged from God? Perhaps they are closer to him than we are. . . .

Science demands loyalty, humility, and patience. We are too easily tempted by pride, acting as though we owned the truth, as though we were judges and censors. . . .

We have asked nuns to simplify their habits. When will bishops do as much?

OCTOBER 30

Birth Control

The Council is proceeding full speed ahead. On Tuesday the closed and pharisaical morality too long presented as that of the Church was put in the dock. Then the social advancement of woman was considered. Yesterday Vatican II began discussion on the crucial subjects of birth control and the nature of conjugal love.

One might have thought that this discussion would be veiled, timid, and circumlocutory. But it wasn't. Once more the pessimists were wrong. The Council of the twentieth century is plowing into the thick of things, and this in public view, since our regular source of information, Father Haubtmann, has been authorized to continue to give the press complete accounts of conciliar interventions.

It was a happy day for the hierarchical Church when she let herself be taught by a Maximos IV, a Suenens, a Léger. We can no longer say that the Church—that Church of "celibates," as Maximos IV put it—is afraid to admit her narrowness, her shortcomings, or even her Manicheanism. To recognized one's errors is to grow: thus, the Church grew on Thursday at Vatican II. She exorcised her own demons forcefully.

Rome finally said a clear *no* to the obsession with procreation, the unalloyed anthropology of reproduction, which is scarcely compatible with the dignity of a creature endowed with the capacity for knowledge and love. The Church said a clear *yes* to a conjugal love crowned by its interior joy without the obligation of risking what Berdyaev called "the evil infinity of children." Christianity, the religion of love, carried the day over that Catholicism which catalogued prohibitions like a counting machine.

The Church, it will perhaps be said, is breaking with her past. But in fact she is returning to her sources, which is not the same thing at all. Indeed, it is just the opposite.

Here are the principal interventions of the day as we learned of them.

Cardinal Ruffini Objects   Cardinal Ruffini spoke first. He always opens fire on the major issues. With perseverance and courage—and he needs these virtues to breast the current—he defends what has wrongly been called the traditional position. Said the Archbishop of Palermo:

> The way schema 13 talks of marriage doesn't strike me as either clear or prudent. Nothing is said about the sacramental dignity of marriage, from which all of its properties flow. It might be objected that this is because the schema is addressed to nonbelievers. But that objection has no value. Without the sacramental notion, it is clearly impossible to condemn polygamy, divorce, abortion, and other depravities of our century.
>
> To leave the choice of the number of children to the parents themselves, as the schema advocates, is dangerous. Out of respect, I will say no more. Let us imitate Saint Augustine, who did not hesitate to say that if parents do not use marriage in a Christian way, they fall into debauchery and prostitution. Let us not fear to speak the truth. We don't have to go far to find it. Catholic doctrine is very clearly defined in Pius XI's encyclical *Casti connubii* and Pius XII's address to midwives. Let us therefore redraft the schema accordingly.

So much for the Church of yesterday. Here is the voice of the Church of tomorrow.

"Human Love Is a True Goal of Marriage"   Cardinal Léger, Archbishop of Montreal, had this to say:

> The problem of the sanctity of marriage is one of our principal concerns. But many of our best faithful, struggling with daily difficulties, are in a state of doubt and anxiety. They do not find our answers satisfying. Confessors are also assailed by doubts. They no longer know what to answer. The theologians feel the need of doctrinal investigation. There is a serious malaise, and it is urgent that the Church examine it with great pastoral solicitude.

Then Cardinal Léger responded directly to Cardinal Ruffini:

> There are those who fear every renewal in theology as though it were motivated by a condemnable opportunism. But this renewal is stimulated by the anxieties of the Christian people and discoveries in the various sciences. Its aim is to encourage sanctity in marriage.
>
> Many theologians think that our present difficulties derive from an inadequate presentation of the goals of marriage. We have had a pessimistic and negative attitude toward love.
>
> This schema is intended to amend these conceptions and clarify love and its purposes: the goal of procreation and the goal of personal fulfillment. Although the schema makes a good start in this direction,

it is still incomplete. It does not present the manifestations of love as a goal of love itself.

The schema speaks well of fecundity as a goal which must be regulated with prudence and generosity. For fecundity is an obligation. But we should concentrate less on the teleology of each sexual act and more on the totality of married life.

I would like to see the dignity of mothers and fathers expressed better. We must propose human conjugal love (body and soul) as a true goal of marriage. Love is good in itself; it makes its own demands and has its own laws. The schema is too hesitant. Let us be clear; otherwise the fear of conjugal love that has so long paralyzed our theology will persist. . . .

Simple procreation is not enough. The persons ought to be loved for themselves.

We must affirm that the intimate union of the couple finds its legitimate end in itself, even when it is not directed toward procreation. For some centuries now, those who are sterile have been considered legitimately married. Even though this observation implies nothing new, it still has its importance.

Neither Laxity Nor Manicheanism   Cardinal Suenens asked:

Has an adequate study been made of all aspects of marriage? Not necessarily, for there is always progress, even in doctrine, and the Holy Spirit leads us to the truth gradually. Has an adequate balance between the different aspects of marriage been achieved? Hasn't there been too much emphasis on the passage from Genesis, "Increase and multiply," and not enough on another phrase which says, "And they shall be two in one flesh"? These two truths must be explored together. They clarify one another.

There is therefore another goal of marriage besides procreation. That is interpersonal communion. Let us develop and encourage it. By emphasizing both of these points, we can perhaps offer a partial response to the demography problem.

Let it not be said that this is laxity. No, it is simply a question of understanding our Lord's will more deeply.

The Cardinal then spoke of the progress of science:

In the time of Aristotle and in that of Saint Augustine, the same knowledge of natural laws did not prevail. Today we understand better the purpose of the conjugal union. We have a better conception of the union between the body and soul, a union that is well explained in Thomistic philosophy.

Let us have done with Manichean pessimism. In this way we will understand better what is against love and what is not against love.

The Cardinal raised his voice to insist:

I beg you, Fathers, not to repeat the trial of Galileo. One is enough in the Church.

Nor let it be objected that I am drifting into "situation ethics." No. It is our role to apply doctrine to changing situations. . . .

In conclusion, I request that an open commission be established for all experts: married men and women, doctors, theologians, [and others]. It should be both international and official in character.

The word "open" was an allusion to a study group personally called by the Pope which seems to be very private; consequently it is not possible to make direct contact with it.

Cardinal Suenens was applauded at length.

Outmoded Ideas?   Then Maximos IV, the Melkite Patriarch, intervened:

I call your attention to the problem of birth control. If we are truly pastoral, the love of Christ and men urges us to confront this issue directly.

Birth control poses an enormous and urgent problem. There is today a crisis in the Christian conscience on this point. This crisis is evidenced by a split between the official doctrine of the Church and the contrary practice of large numbers of the faithful. Some of them are forced to break with the Church; others live in a state of perpetual anguish because they cannot reconcile a normal conjugal life with the demands of their conscience. . . .

On the other hand, there is a considerable demographic increase, and in some countries there is no hope of raising the standard of living to match the population growth. Consequently, whole peoples live in misery and without hope.

Does God will such an anti-natural impasse? With confidence in the resurrected Christ and full awareness of the crisis, let us examine this problem directly, unflinchingly, and courageously. . . .

The question, then, is this: should the official positions of the Church be reviewed in the light of modern sciences and discoveries? Personal fulfillment and procreation form a whole. Neither can be neglected. We cannot distinguish between what are called the "primary" and "secondary" ends of marriage. We must consider the whole of conjugal life. . . .

Might not some of our official positions be outgrowths of outmoded ideas? Perhaps a bachelor psychosis that is ignorant of this side of life is not unrelated to these positions. There could be a kind of Manicheanism in our positions. We seem to tolerate conjugal union only for the purpose of having children. Is the external biological correctness of sexual acts the only criterion of morality in this domain, without taking into consideration the demands of prudence? Perhaps too we have relied on a biblical exegesis that is not necessarily solid. For example, the famous phrase "Increase and multiply" should be applied to mankind in general rather than to a particular individual.

As for the passage in the Bible about the crime of Onan, "It has been wrongly used as an argument against masturbation," said Maximos IV.

"Let Us Confront These Matters Courageously"   The Patriarch continued: "I agree with Cardinals Suenens and Léger that this question should be studied by specialists with the collaboration of married men and women and the other Christian churches. And why not with representatives of non-Christian religions? For this problem concerns all of humanity."

In conclusion, Maximos IV declared:

> I am not minimizing the difficulty or the delicacy of these problems nor the eventual abuses they may occasion. But it is the Church's duty to give the faithful a solid formation. This is worth more than a set of commandments blindly applied. Let us confront these matters courageously and see things as they are and not as we would like them to be. Otherwise we will be crying in the wilderness.

The moderator cut off the applause by immediately summoning the next speaker, Bishop Eugenio Beitia Aldadzabal of Santander, Spain, who declared:

> We must condemn the egoism of those couples who refuse to have children without serious reason, concerned only with their own greater comfort. . . . We must expound positive criteria that can reconcile conjugal life with the impossibility, at least temporary and in specific circumstances, of having more children. . . . It is impossible to solve all problems. Some indeed can be solved only through heroic fidelity to divine law.

Bishop Staverman of Sukarnapura, Indonesia, said:

> Let us avoid the expression "natural law" because it is equivocal. . . . Marriage is too frequently presented as an unvarying institution while in fact it is human, historical, and evolutionary. The conception of love has also evolved. Let us bring the Church's doctrine up to date

by examining it in relation to present circumstances. The whole question should be reviewed with the aid of experts and laymen, and the role of the latter should not be merely consultative.

On War and Peace

Since Cardinal Feltin will be absent when the Council discusses the problems of war and peace, the moderators permitted him to intervene on the subject during this debate. Let us recall that the Archbishop of Paris is both the international president of Pax Christi and chaplain to the armed services. He said:

> Public opinion hopes Vatican II will go as far as *Pacem in terris* and adopt this doctrine by giving it the weight and importance of a conciliar constitution. . . . This doctrine is traditional, and has been so especially since Benedict XV. Above all, public opinion expects, perhaps a little unrealistically, a very clear condemnation of modern war. We can easily understand the universal anxiety on this point. . . .

Conscientious Objection
> In our atomic age, war is becoming a less and less suitable instrument of defending violated rights. The schema says, and rightly so, that the use of ABC (atomic, biological, and chemical) weapons should be prohibited because their power of destruction can neither be tempered nor be estimated with exactness. . . .
>
> But war won't disappear simply because we speak about it frankly. The Church must bear witness to the truth. Let us be active artisans of peace. Let us not only speak about peace; let us practice it.

Cardinal Feltin made three particularly important points:

1. Disarmament: "Not just any kind of disarmament, but one that is gradual, simultaneous, and controlled. Disarmament should be principally directed at the atomic, biological, and chemical weapons."
2. Aid to underdeveloped countries: "The inequality between the advanced nations and the others is increasing, whence the tensions that lead to war, cold or otherwise. It is therefore desirable to help the underdeveloped countries. Peace and development go hand in hand. . . . We should strengthen international institutions and say more clearly that their authority is effective. Let us make explicit reference to the United Nations."
3. The teaching of peace: "Peace should be part of all our pastoral activity: Sunday sermons and catechisms for both children and adults.

Let us teach love of country and the human race. Let us get beyond nationalism. Let us be ready to forgive our enemies. We must also note with sorrow Catholics' ignorance of the encyclicals, and that has been the case for a long time."

In conclusion, Cardinal Feltin asked that some of the ideas found in the corresponding appendix be incorporated into the schema itself, especially those concerning conscientious objection and torture; and that a theological commission be formed with experts capable of making moral judgments.

OCTOBER 31

Cardinal Alfrink Asks, Is Continence the Only Solution to the Problem of Birth Control?

Debate on birth control terminated on Friday in the aula. In all, nineteen Fathers were courageous enough to discuss this abrasive and difficult question publicly. Abrasive to Catholics paralyzed by a theology which creates false problems the Protestant churches have gotten beyond, though they have sometimes avoided Scylla only to sail into Charybdis. For let us make no mistake, it is a difficult problem. For one thing, the human sciences—psychology, biology, medicine, sociology, and so on—are less developed than the natural sciences; no one yet understands very well the physiological and psychological mechanism of sexual laws of fertility and contraception. For another, neither philosophy nor theology has finished exploring human nature and its supernatural elevation.

Sexual activities are nourished by man's spiritual faculties, and inversely, sexual activities have a great influence on the intelligence, will, and sensitivity. Nothing human is foreign to sexuality. It was to Freud's credit that he made this fundamental truth evident, even though it has often been enlisted in the service of an anthropology that is outmoded in some respects. The Council deserves praise for recognizing the complexity of these problems and resisting the temptation to offer simplistic formulas as solutions. Vatican II will have to change certain attitudes, but it will not, and in fact cannot, set down precise directives.

What has been called "the Catholic pill" is an invention of the magazines, because no pill, however legitimate moralists may proclaim it, will magically resolve all the problems connected with birth control. Moreover, as more theologians are beginning to remark, every form of medication modifies nature, from the small aspirin we take to ease the pain of a headache to the anesthetics and neurological sedatives. To what extent does man have the right and sometimes even the duty to act on nature? This is the crux of the matter, and it is not easy to resolve when the sources of life are involved.

Nor do we know what treasures a genuine Christian anthropology might reveal. As early as the third century, Méthode d'Olympe said that the "Increase and multiply" of Genesis should be interpreted as an implicit recommendation for polygamy in the first age; in the second age, beginning with the coming of Christ, it should be interpreted as counseling monogamy, which would in effect reduce the number of children. Méthode d'Olympe readily believed that in the third age humanity would gather in a kind of immense monastery where men and women would no longer be asked to reproduce. In our time, Berdyaev has also expressed this idea.

Some Orientals, reacting to the galloping demography of the twentieth century, want a new prophet to rise to urge humanity in the name of God to multiply as little as possible.

In any event, we must inquire into the causes and effects of procreation, on both the religious and the scientific level, and introduce more awareness into sexual relations. Paul Valéry has written these suggestive words, in a different context, of course: "Absence of children is presence of spirit. . . ."

Eleven Fathers intervened Friday on birth control, among them three cardinals.

There Is Doubt   Cardinal Alfrink, Archbishop of Utrecht, spoke in the name of twenty-one bishops:

> All priests experience enormous difficulties with these problems. A prime example is the most generous Christian couples. Frequently they wear themselves out in tiring struggles that threaten to break down their moral values and endanger the unity of the home itself. . . .
>
> On the one hand, the Church cannot change divine law for purely circumstantial reasons. On the other, sociological analyses and personal difficulties cannot change the moral character of human acts. . . .
>
> Situation ethics is unacceptable. . . .
>
> The Church has always said and it will remain forever true that the Christian life implies sacrifices but also, let us say it clearly, joys— the joy of the resurrected Christ who conquered death. God does not rejoice in the suffering of man. The joy of the resurrection belongs to the very essence of the religious life. . . .
>
> Two essential values must be safeguarded in marriage: procreation, and the Christian and human education of children. They cannot be separated, for they form a whole. In reality, a conflict between

these two values can arise within conjugal intimacy. The human and Christian education of children is possible only when genuine conjugal love exists, a love that is normally nourished by sexual intercourse. When there is a conflict, the only solution is to make the sex act possible without procreation. Obviously, if this were done by means which are without any doubt intrinsically evil, the Church would take exception, for she can never accept the sacrifice of a particular value to save the total value of marriage. . . .

Let us distinguish well between mere biological sexuality and human sexuality. There are several theological schools on this point. It will take a good deal of time to see matters clearly. Divine law must always be protected, but this does not exclude the human aspect.

There is doubt among many couples and even among theologians. . . .

Is complete or periodic continence the only efficacious solution for the conflicts of married life from all moral and Christian standpoints? The Church must reach true veritable certainty in order to free consciences.

In conclusion, Cardinal Alfrink called for the creation of a permanent scientific and theological commission, which he deemed necessary in view of the rapid progress in the sciences.

Homage to Large Families Cardinal Ottaviani had the wisdom to keep to the safe ground of a personal testimony. His intervention had both meaning and loftiness, and will be especially appreciated by large families and even by those who have experienced the joy of only a few children. The Secretary of the Holy Office spoke calmly but with a scarcely concealed emotion that was contagious:

What the schema says about the responsibility of parents to determine the number of children does not please me. This is a new [*inauditu*] doctrine in the Church. It is contrary to the "Increase and multiply" of Holy Scripture. The "They shall be two in one flesh" does not contradict this commandment. Why should these teachings be set in opposition? . . .

Here is my personal testimony. I am the eleventh in a family of twelve children. We were poor. My father was a manual laborer. My parents never lost faith in providence, and despite our poverty, providence always came to our assistance. My parents believed what the Gospel says about the birds in the heavens and the lilies of the fields which neither toil nor spin, as well as the evangelical counsel that our first concern ought to be the kingdom of heaven, and providence will grant us all other things besides. The psalms also speak of large families and the children about the table like young olive trees. . . .

. . . The Church must at all costs avoid appearing unfaithful to her mission. The bishops gathered in the college are infallible in their teaching on faith and morals, as the schema *De Ecclesia* says. Therefore, let us be prudent. Let us not deviate one iota from sound doctrine.

Sterile Periods   Cardinal Browne of the Curia focused on doctrine:

> I asked to speak not to teach but to bear witness to traditional doctrine. I will restrict myself to what is certain, which is that the primary end of marriage is procreation and education. The second end is the mutual aid of the partners and the relief of concupiscence.
>
> But, it will be asked, what of conjugal love? We are not forgetting this. However, it is in order to distinguish between conjugal love in friendship and conjugal love in covetousness. [We might point out that these two expressions are practically equivalent to what are called *agape* and *eros*.]
>
> The love of friendship must come first; the second is not forbidden, but we must understand that if we are not careful, in the normal course of things lead it will to egoism. . . .
>
> Conjugal life will be holy if its acts are in conformity with the purpose willed by God.

The Cardinal then referred to the encyclicals *Arcanum* of Leo XIII and *Casti connubii* of Pius XI and Pius XII's speech to midwives. "There are many serious difficulties, especially with respect to determining the sterile periods. It is therefore fitting that doctors and theologians continue to study these questions. Let us wait for their conclusions before making a statement."

Not So Clear as Some Think   Auxiliary Bishop Joseph Reuss of Mainz said he personally agreed with Cardinals Léger, Suenens, and Alfrink. Then, in the name of 145 Fathers, he declared that the schema was generally good but that a number of points should be treated more deeply:

> Human sexuality should not be considered only from a biological point of view. Man's personality marks all of sexuality. . . . Let us show more deeply that marriage is founded on conjugal love, which serves the good of the home taken as a whole. . . .
>
> To increase true love, conjugal intimacy is necessary. . . .
>
> We must recall that Christian marriage is difficult to live, as is the Christian life in general. . . .

Marriage for those who are called to this vocation is a means of reaching God.

Let us recall the importance of procreation and education as well as the generosity required for this work. . . . Let us retain the idea that the parents are responsible for determining the number of children. . . .

Let us be prudent, as is the schema, because for the moment we cannot go much farther. Everything is not as clear as some think. . . . Let the Council continue to encourage study of all these questions, with the realization that there is no immediate solution.

Archbishop Urtasun of Avignon discussed the following three points, which he thought were essential: "Let us defend life against hunger and war; let us defend the human person against certain harmful experiences *in vivis;* let us condemn excesses of perverted sensuality. . . . Divorce is a great danger. It is regrettable that the schema doesn't mention it."

Eroticism Bishop Abilio del Campo y de la Barceno, of Calahorra, Spain, sounded a warning:

I would have preferred to speak in a commission meeting because I am afraid I will be misunderstood. This schema speaks too exclusively of conjugal love as if it were the source and end of marriage. But in fact it is neither the supreme norm nor the supreme term. It is merely the motor force from a psychological point of view. Conjugal love is not clearly defined. There is therefore the risk of subjective interpretation. . . .

There is a great danger because of the degraded meaning that is currently given to the word *love.* Let us be very clear, therefore, because of the contemporary context of eroticism.

Polygamy Is Increasing in Africa Bishop Joseph Nkongolo of Luebo, Leopoldville Congo, said that the schema must at all costs speak of the problems proper to Africa:

The absence of freedom of consent for the young girl is a frequent cause of divorce. We cannot speak of the indissolubility of marriage if there is no liberty. The father of the family cannot supply or force the consent required for validity. Let fathers beware of this. . . .

Nothing is said of a terrible evil: polygamy, which is gaining ground while the institution of Christian marriage is being turned more and more to derision. Let us say clearly that the return to polygamy is a regression, that it goes against the dignity of woman, and that it is a profanation of the divine order.

Bishop Nkongolo added this important remark, which will be taken up later: "In Africa, what the Church says has a great influence among the non-Christians."

Bishop Rendeiro of Faro, Portugal, said that public powers should be reminded of their role "in the protection of the sanctity of the family."

No Illegitimate Children Before God   Bishop Fiordelli of Prato, Italy, regretted that nothing was said in the schema about the education of youth, who "are not given enough to do and yet are full of resources." He also wanted to see the schema speak of the engagement period, which he thought determinative for the formation of the couple.

He requested that abortion, a veritable massacre of the innocent which is contrary to the biblical commandment "Thou shalt not kill," be mentioned. Then he added, "Let us speak of illegitimate children, for they are deprived of love and despised, and experience a certain distaste for society. They are legitimate before God. Let us not discriminate against them either on the civil plane or in the Church."

About conjugal difficulties, Bishop Fiordelli made the following remarks: "Let us not deny that there are dramatic problems, [but] it is not the Council's role to propose concrete solutions. . . . Let us not refuse the sacraments to couples in difficulty."

Bishop Hervás y Benet, Prelate Nullius of Ciudad Real, Spain, spoke in the name of 126 Fathers: "If we add nothing about the means of determining the number of children, we will give an impression of materialism. . . . Modern psychological sciences emphasize the disadvantages of a single child. . . . In large families there are many religious vocations." (Applause.)

Divorce Is a Terrible Evil   Archbishop Bernard Yago of Abidjan, Ivory Coast, agreed with what Archbishop Malula had said about the freedom of women and tribalism: "The tribe is a great problem for us, and hinders any form of international union. Moreover, it is often the foreigner who incites the tribes."

Archbishop Yago regretted that the schema did not condemn "encroaching hedonism, polygamy, or the abusive system of dowries," and said that divorce is not denounced firmly enough. "It is a terrible evil that is rampant even among Christians; sometimes there are more divorces among Christians than among pagans. Moreover, some think that the Church, and more particularly the Council, will admit divorce. This is absurd. Let us therefore be very clear on this subject."

Culture Is Not the Privilege of a Minority

The Council then went on to another important subject: culture. Six bishops spoke on this section of the schema.

Father João Ferreira, Apostolic Prefect of Portuguese Guinea, said:

> The problem of culture is not adequately treated as a function of man. Let us stress its anthropological character. . . . The Church speaks well about culture, but the world does not listen. Pious exhortations won't change anything. The Church has been cut off from the world of culture since the fifteenth century. . . .
>
> Historical Christian culture should not be identified with the culture of Christians. This culture must not resemble that of the Middle Ages because we live in a Marxist and atheistic world. We must then know the modern world in order to discern the elements of truth. . . .
>
> Let us speak at greater length of the problem of evil.

A Taste for the Truth Bishop Roger Johan of Agen, France, said that culture is not a gift, but is the fruit of labor. Therefore, Christians have a duty to defend it, develop it, and respond to it. Civilization needs this Christian influence. He continued:

> Every Christian must have a taste for the truth in itself more than a taste for authority. . . . Let us give the laity greater opportunity to study theology. . . .
>
> Let us safeguard the notion of contemplation and not only that of efficiency. There is a danger of activism today. Let us orient leisure time toward contemplation. . . .
>
> Let us recall that cultural goods are for all and not merely for a minority. We must suppress all privileges and multiply cultural centers. . . . Let us promote the science of the universal by means of international cultural relations.

Auxiliary Bishop Bohdan Bejze of Lodz, Poland, regretted that "nothing is said about 'Christian philosophy,' which the Church nonetheless recommends. [In Latin *philosophia* is used, it seems, in the sense of wisdom.] Let us state how young people should be educated from this point of view. . . . Present-day ideologies are infected with relativism, subjectivism, and existentialism." This can be counteracted by "Christian wisdom," which "gives us the true hierarchy of values. In every century there have been saints who promoted this wisdom."

In concluding, Bishop Bejze requested that John XXIII be beatified.

Respect the Culture of Others Bishop Lokuang of Tainan, Formosa, spoke of the relations between culture and mission countries: "These countries often have a very old culture, and yet missionary bulletins speak of them as 'barbarian.' Let us respect the cultural values of others in order to implant the Church."

Father Fernández, Superior General of the Dominicans, counseled, "Let us have the right hierarchy of values. What chiefly matters is the kingdom of God. The divine life of one man, as Saint Thomas said, is more important than the fate of all humanity. It is important to conserve the scale of values."

Father Fernández also said:

> Social classes of rich and poor should no longer exist; goods should be justly distributed among all men. What is true of material goods is also true of cultural goods, which should be shared among countries. . . .
>
> The schema's enumeration of the different sciences is inadequate. The philosophical and theological disciplines are overlooked. Yet these are synthesizing sciences that are especially indispensable in our specialized century.

In conclusion, Father Fernández emphasized the importance of universities, and urged dialogue among the various branches of science.

Birth Control: A Recapitulation

The least that can be said is that the last two general congregations of Vatican II have inaugurated a new era in the Roman Church. In fact, the interventions by Maximos IV and Cardinals Léger, Suenens, and Alfrink represent such a break with what is called the traditional doctrine on birth control that they mark a radical change of attitude.

They may consequently create some disarray among those faithful who are more accustomed to obeying without discussion than reflecting on their own marital problems.

The Church has until now given great encouragement to mothers and fathers of large families. Will she suddenly modify this approach? No, indeed, and Cardinal Ottaviani's intervention is proof of it.

But the Church of the twentieth century cannot stand undismayed before the demographic crises which hover over the world today and are still more likely to erupt tomorrow. Beginning in the year 2000, according to the most reliable statistics, the number of human beings will double every fifty years. The Church is therefore wise to counsel greater circumspection to parents who want large families. The number of children should be determined by salary, housing, and the capacity to provide an adequate human and Christian education.

In asking whether continence was the "only solution" to the problem of birth control, the Archbishop of Utrecht courageously raised an enormous question: whether the Church must restrict herself to recommending the Ogino method and temperature tests to remedy a high birth rate. Might at least some of the methods until now considered against nature or artificial by the Church be judged acceptable by moralists? This seems to be the case with the progesterone pills, which Father Häring and Jean Janssens are reluctant to condemn without further investigation.

The Specter of Galileo This was the meaning of Cardinal Suenens' request that the Council Fathers not repeat the trial of Galileo. For if Vatican II should, *per impossibile*, make a blanket condemnation of present or future methods of contraception, the Church could commit an "error" comparable to the Galileo affair. But as Bishop Reuss has written, there is no proof that the rules currently enforced in the Roman Church "flow from revelation."

In the final analysis, we have grounds for wondering whether the Church, thanks to Vatican II, isn't about to renounce what might be called an outmoded "semen fetish." Doesn't nature give evidence of a magnificent prodigality in this matter, and doesn't the psychology of lovers indicate that sexual relations are experienced more as a manifestation of interpersonal communion than as a means of procreation? Furthermore, hasn't the Church always recognized that couples who are sterile through no fault of their own are blameless from a Christian point of view?

The Catholic Church seems to be on the point of revising her conception of *eros* and *agape* according to the celebrated adage of Saint Augustine: "The blessed do not have what they desire but they desire what they have."

NOVEMBER, 1964

Culture

The debate on culture which began last Friday has ended. Only seven fathers requested to speak on this important chapter of schema 13. The pertinence of this subject is evident for a Church which was long the patroness of intellectual progress and the crucible of civilization, and which today not only seems to have fallen behind but also sometimes discourages research. Moreover, since the Renaissance, a secular civilization has developed.

Culture is therefore a capital question for Catholicism, and many Catholics are happy that Paul VI has made it one of his central concerns. Vatican II has merely skimmed the surface of this broad topic.

Seminary Teaching Is Inadequate   Cardinal Lercaro's intervention was widely commented upon. He said:

> This article on culture is the essence of the whole schema because it expresses the nature of the relationships between the Church and the world. Moreover, revelation can help cultural study and inversely culture can help the Church deepen her message. It is not enough to say that the Church respects culture and has confidence in scientific, artistic, and technical progress. The schema stops where it should begin. It should investigate and designate some of the essential changes that should be effected in present-day culture in relation to former cultures. . . .
>
> Evangelical culture should find its application in culture itself. How? One way would be not to remain attached to cultural forms of the past, such as the Scholastic, and to open itself to a new culture. The heritage of the past can sometimes put the light under a bushel. Evangelical poverty is not synonymous with cultural poverty. The

Church should do everything in her power to renew the horizons of culture. . . .

The Church should be present in culture like leaven. She should draw more nourishment from Scripture. Let us review the whole cycle of teaching in seminaries, which is very inadequate. Without this change it will not be possible to create a dialogue in depth with contemporary man.

Archbishop de Provenchères of Aix-en-Provence stressed the moral responsibility of scientists, especially in matters relating to genetic biology.

The Synthesis of Cultures   Archbishop Zoa of Yaounde said in sum:

> In order for the encounter of cultures to promote authentic progress, their specific values (for example, the science of the West or the religiosity of Africa) must be presented as elements of a patrimony that should be common to all peoples. The African accepts Western culture not because it is Western but because it represents a human value. The same should be true of the African's religiosity in the eyes of a Westerner. By means of this exchange of intellectual and spiritual values, we avert the causes of conflict between races and peoples of different customs, open the way to more fruitful contacts, and avoid the risk of letting the principles of atheism infiltrate a continent like Africa along with those of science. . . . The schema should state clearly that the perfect synthesis of all cultures can only be made in Christ.

Restoring Galileo to Honor   Auxiliary Bishop Elchinger of Strasbourg declared:

> Cultural values do not seem to be taken seriously enough by the Church. A fairly large sector of public opinion considers the Catholic Church, despite her former contributions to culture, very narrow-minded in this domain. It thinks she is dominated by attitudes of fear and apologetic reflexes of defense, and that she is on the outskirts of the cultural growth of modern times. . . .
>
> The memory of antimodernistic reactions in the areas of philosophy, history, and the sciences constitutes a wound that has not healed, a source of distrust. These facts oblige us to make an honest examination of conscience.

Then Bishop Elchinger asked some questions:

> Don't we have a tendency to want to circumscribe the domain of culture too narrowly, and to recognize its legitimate autonomy only reluctantly?

Don't we practice a kind of dogmatic imperialism that leads us to make quick and peremptory judgments on all research findings as though faith gave us competence in every field?

Don't we identify the theological affirmations of a given age with Christian truth as though theology consisted in lazily and unquestioningly repeating theses established once and for all?

Haven't we minimized the pastoral value of human intelligence, that is, the concern for sanctity in intellectual activity?

Don't we still have a morbid fear of rationalism and the critical spirit without recognizing what is good in them?

The case of Galileo remains a symbol of all these deficiencies in the history of modern times. Let it not be said too quickly that it is part of ancient history. The condemnation of this man has never been revoked. Many scholars today attribute to the Church the attitude of those theologians who, nearly four centuries ago, condemned this great and honest scientist. It would be an eloquent gesture if the Church, during this year which marks the fourth centenary of Galileo's birth, would humbly agree to rehabilitate him. The world today expects more from the Church than good intentions. It expects action.

In conclusion, the speaker expressed the desire that the Council encourage all major countries to create a great Christian university which, instead of duplicating similar institutions, would be a research institute and a center of influence dedicated to the tasks defined above.

Finally, in the name of seventy fathers, Bishop Proano Villalba of Riobamba, Equador, declared, "In Latin America, out of 200,000,000 men, 80,000,000 (half of them young people) are illiterate. Some 15,000,000 children cannot be accommodated in the schools. We need 20,000 new schools a year. . . . This schema is too Occidental. It says nothing about illiteracy."

The assembly then went on to the article in schema 13 relative to economic and social life.

Paul VI Emphasizes the Importance
of Papal Authority in the Church

"The presence of the pope, the visible head of the Church, reminds all that a sovereign personal power exists in the Church with authority over the whole community gathered in the name of Christ." Thus spoke Paul VI in a general audience on Wednesday, November 4.

Noting that some of the faithful manifest "distrust" or even "aversion" toward a power that is "so elevated and so indisputable," he continued:

A Protestant and Modernist attitude has spread which denies both the need and the legitimacy of an intermediary authority between the soul and God. "How many men there are between me and God" [Rousseau] is a famous expression of that attitude. Some make a distinction between a religion of authority and a religion of the spirit; they then identify the religion of authority with Catholicism and the religion of the spirit with the subjective and liberal currents of our time. And next they conclude that the first is not authentic and that the second should be exercised without any external, arbitrary, or stifling bonds.

Paul VI said that authority in the Church is not "an expression of pride or a copy of civil authority armed with the sword and clothed in glory," but a pastoral function intended to guide others and guarantee their welfare.

NOVEMBER 6

The Church Faces Economic and Social Realities

The Council is going too fast. This may not be the opinion of some, fatigued as they are by oral interventions given before an increasingly diminished audience, but the lay auditors and many observers from the outside world are concerned to see subjects as complicated as those taken up in schema 13 treated so summarily. The reasons for this haste are understandable—weariness, the desire to finish examining all the schemas during this session, and so forth—but it is nonetheless having a bad effect.

Less than two days of the Council's time has been devoted to the theme of economic and social life. This is far too little. However, it is only just to point out that some of the interventions were very much in the evangelical spirit, indeed revolutionary. Some Fathers forcefully declared that it is not stealing to take goods if one is in extreme need, and that private property is intended by God to be a means of distributing the riches of the earth equitably to all men.

Cardinal Wyszynski, intervening day before yesterday, was the first to speak on the subject: "The progressives argue that the Church has forgotten the poor. They are not aware of the harm they cause and the ammunition they furnish to the Communists. . . . The Church must speak of erroneous political systems which sacrifice man to economic objectives. . . . The essence of what is said on economic and social questions is found in the appendixes. They should form part of the schema itself."

Cardinal Richaud, Archbishop of Bordeaux, took the floor next: "Let us be more concrete. . . . Let us speak of the duty of those who hold economic power to foresee the consequences of automation. . . . Let us develop a democratic sense of responsibility that ends in a permanent education. Let us denounce excessive profit, speculations of all sorts, and usury in all of its forms."

Bishop Ángel Herrera y Oría of Málaga called the schema inadequate. "Let us be more practical. Let us denounce injustices in the distribution of goods. We desire the economic, cultural, and political advancement of workers; let us tell this to the leaders of society. . . . The workers are ignorant of our social doctrine because it isn't even applied in the life of dioceses."

Bishop Raul Zambrano Camader of Facatativa, Colombia, pointed out, "The Church does not feel bound to any economic system. . . . The classical doctrine of business' private ownership of property is not the only possible one. Today the law of supply and demand is still in play. This is unacceptable. Let us denounce arbitrary action by employers and proclaim the necessity of recourse to public powers."

Auxiliary Bishop Benítez Ávalos of Asunción, Paraguay, speaking yesterday in the name of 105 Fathers, elaborated on the consequences of the demographic explosion in Latin America, the growing disproportion between the levels of life of the rich and the poor, and the lack of political education among the illiterate. "We are talking about Catholic regions," he said. "Consequently, our responsibilities are immense. Our duty is to call urgently for far-reaching reforms."

Bishop José Alba Palacios of Tehuantepec, Mexico, speaking in the name of seventy Fathers, digressed and was called to order. But his intervention was an interesting one; he took sharp exception to the general spirit of Vatican II. "Let us restrict ourselves to what *Casti connubii* says about marriage. It is not for the faithful or parents or theologians to take decisions; this is the right of the magisterium alone. Theologians must be obedient. It would be good to recall this at a time when some are in danger of straying."

Superfluous Wealth Belongs by Right to the Poor   Archbishop Zoungrana of Ouagadougou, Upper Volta, intervened in the name of seventy African and Brazilian bishops: "Let us denounce the excessive differences between the price of imported and exported products, which depends on whether a rich or a poor country is involved. Let us say clearly that superfluous riches belong in justice to the poor."

The Council then went on to an examination of article 24 of the schema, which concerns solidarity among peoples.

Let Us Abandon Our Triumphal Clothing Cardinal Frings, Archbishop of Cologne, requested that each episcopal conference create episcopal bodies to help the poorest classes and nations. These organizations should be "more social than charitable," making no distinctions based on race or religion. "It is important," said the Cardinal, "to form technicians of all kinds. Furthermore, let the Church give tangible evidence of her democratic spirit and her spirit of service. I propose that we abandon our triumphal clothing."

This peroration was greeted with applause.

"Dialogue with Communism Could Be Profitable"

Cardinal Alfrink, Archbishop of Utrecht, made an intervention on schema 13's article 25 which will certainly rank among the most important of the Council. He spoke of the Church's attitude toward communism:

> Atheistic and Marxist ideas are everywhere. They are obviously incompatible with Christianity. But let us not forget that our obligation to charity extends to all men of good will. Many men adhere to the Communist Party not because of its philosophic doctrine but out of despair and for reasons of social justice. . . .
>
> Let us refrain from a new condemnation of communism, even though many Fathers have requested this. Why? Because it has already been done several times, and to do so again would serve no purpose. It would change nothing. There is nothing to add to what the popes have said in this respect. Furthermore, let us not forget that practical materialism, rather than theoretical materialism, is the most dangerous. . . .
>
> The experience of competent people proves that this kind of condemnation is useless and accomplishes nothing at all. On the contrary, dialogue can be profitable. Let us not prejudice such dialogue with thundering declarations. What should we do? First of all, we should insist on the real religious liberty which must be granted to all men. Everyone understands that it is normal and necessary for Christians to be able to express their faith freely. Second, it is indispensable that Christians make an effort to understand their faith better. Third, let us bring about social justice wherever there is need for it instead of limiting ourselves to principles.

"The Moment Has Come To Dialogue with Islam"

Last year Titulary Archbishop Edelby of Edessa, patriarchical counselor
of Maximos IV, a winter resident of Cairo and a summer resident of
Damas, defended married deacons and priests in the Oriental Catholic
Church. Recently he gave a talk on the Arab world at the Dutch Documentation Center. Here are some excerpts from his speech:

> Only 7,000,000 out of 100,000,000 Arabs are Christian. Fifty per-
> cent of the Christian Arabs live outside the Orient in such countries
> as America and South Africa. . . .
>
> The willful concentration of wealth in a few hands cannot con-
> tinue. One day there will be a revolt against those who have only
> one idea in their heads: to find a way of spending the income that
> comes from the outside. . . .
>
> We were constrained by the public powers to draw up a pan-
> Christian catechism in our country with the collaboration of the
> sixteen sects in our country. . . . It was a *tour de force*. It appeared
> in May, 1964, under the seal of the Arabic Cultural Union in Cairo,
> which also dictates all textbooks [used in schools]. . . .
>
> The success of Islam is not due to its loose sexual morality, as is
> sometimes said, but to its genius for responding to the deep aspira-
> tions of the Arab people—a sense of prayer, fraternity, simplicity of
> faith. . . .
>
> For you Westerners ecumenism is a luxury; for us Orientals it
> is a question of life or death. Our fragmentation into sixteen sects
> makes it impossible for any one of us to be really effective. . . .
>
> It is mandatory for the Church to share in the lives of native
> people, even under a Communist or Socialist regime. I am personally
> a member of the organization founded by Louis Massignon, in which
> we swear that we will never leave our country whatever happens. . . .
>
> The moment has come to dialogue with Islam. We have much
> to learn from it. Sometimes I think that certain Catholics with their
> many devotions appear polytheistic alongside Islam, which is a re-
> ligion of essentials. . . .
>
> Together with Cardinals Suenens, Alfrink, and Léger, and Patri-
> arch Maximos IV, I am in favor of revising the Church's positions
> on birth control.

Missionaries Should Not Appear
as Emissaries of the West

The setting as well as the subject changed at Vatican II on Friday. Paul VI presided over part of the session. He attended mass in the Ethiopian Rite celebrated by Bishop Haile Cahsay of Adigrat. It was an exceptionally long ceremony read in Geez, the classical language of Ethiopia. One of the assistants wore a tintinnabulary headgear carrying small bells. When the Gospel was enthroned, drums rolled and the celebrants, together with a number of Fathers caught up in the rhythm, clapped their hands.

Paul VI said a few words about "the grave and singular importance" of the schema on the missions. Before rendering homage "to the missioners of both sexes, to the catechists, and to all who assist the missionaries," he said: "We think, therefore, that you can easily approve the text, even after noting the necessity of final improvement."

Paul VI greeted the moderators individually, the patriarchs, and Archbishop Slipyi of Lvov, a former prisoner of the Russians.

The Pope's presence at this general congregation was variously commented upon. Most rejoiced that Paul VI, who is soon to leave for Bombay, honored the Council with his presence on the day when discussion of the missions was to begin. However, other Council Fathers wonder why discussion on schema 13 was interrupted and why the Pope did not attend the discussion on hunger in the world, as it was rumored he would. The adversaries of this schema were quick to conclude that the Pope is not too fond of the schema. But this seems a weak interpretation.

Cardinal Agagianian presented the report on the schema on the missions. He referred to the canonization of the Uganda martyrs and Paul VI's trip to Bombay. "What a highly qualified missionary," he exclaimed, and was loudly applauded. When he spoke of the bishops presently being persecuted behind the iron curtain, his voice trembled with such emotion that he was forced to pause. Then the Cardinal gave some significant statistics.

In 1870 there were only 275 ecclesiastical districts in mission countries, 68 of which were in Europe (England, Scandinavia, and the Netherlands). Today there are 770, with 270 in Africa, 79 in the two Americas, 341 in Asia, 61 in Oceania, and 19 in Europe.

At the time of Vatican I, there was not a single native bishop in these countries; today there are 41 native archbishops and 126 bishops, four of whom are cardinals. Of these 66 are in Africa and 97 in Asia. In 1870 there were hardly ten seminaries in mission countries; today there are 385 minor and 81 major seminaries.

Conquering the Weight of History   After the Pope left the aula, Bishop Lokuang of Tainan, Formosa, presented a second report. He explained particularly that the second text, which contains thirteen short propositions, was condensed from an original schema of seven chapters.

Cardinal Léger was the first to speak. He enumerated the reasons which in his opinion justified the hope that the missions would benefit greatly by Vatican II:

1. Missionaries would enjoy the necessary freedom to adapt their message to the country in which they worked. "We must conquer the weight of history in this matter," the cardinal said.
2. The restoration of the permanent diaconate would be a great help in countries where there is a shortage of priests.
3. Dialogue with non-Christian religions has begun, and Paul VI has encouraged it. "I regret that the schema has so little to say on this subject," Cardinal Léger commented.
4. Collegiality expresses the solicitude of each bishop for the whole Church. "The first task of collegiality is evangelization. Bishops are consecrated as much for the salvation of the world as for their own dioceses."

The Subordinate Role of the Curia   Then Cardinal Léger made this point, which is of great importance for the future:

> Let us clarify the paragraph in the schema concerning the creation of a central council of evangelization, because the text says that this council should be created about the Sacred Congregation for the Propagation of the Faith. What does the word *about* mean? It is ambiguous. If the council remains outside the Roman Congregation, the juxtaposition of jurisdictions could cause great difficulties. I propose therefore that the council be situated within the Roman Congregation and form its most important bureau. Thus the local churches will be better represented in Rome, and inversely, the central government will be better informed of what is going on in the various missions.

This is equivalent to asking that the curial departments become simple organisms for executing the will of the residential bishops (ratified, of course, by the pope). Until now the Curia has given orders to the bishops, supposedly in the name of the pope, who was not always fully informed, however, of the decisions taken by the various departments—

a state of affairs which prompted Maximos IV to say, "I do not fear Peter but his bureaucrats."

Welcome All Cultures Peter Cardinal Tatsuo Doi, Archbishop of Tokyo, then spoke, followed by Cardinal Rugambwa, who expressed the African point of view:

> The Church has become too Occidental in the course of the centuries, a fact that has hampered missionary expansion. The missions are the incarnation extended. The diversity of cultures has been willed by God. It is important that missionaries know the cultures as well as the philosophies and ideologies prevalent in the countries where they work. They should live as much as possible like the people in these countries, and respect their laws and customs. To be a Catholic is to be broadminded enough to welcome all forms of culture. We must make great efforts in this direction.

More than one Father in the Council was reminded of Father Lebbe's uphill struggle in the Far East. He fought all his life for missionaries to live according to local customs, and energetically and in the end successfully urged the creation of a native hierarchy.

Finally, Cardinal Bea spoke in the name of the bishops of Africa and several Asian bishops, a representation which was widely noticed owing to the ecumenical concerns of the German cardinal, who is president of the Secretariat for Promoting Christian Unity. He said:

> John XXIII . . . always thought that Vatican II would be a great stimulus to the missionary movement, which is highly essential [*maxime essentialis*] in the Church. . . .
>
> Missionaries should appear not as emissaries of the white race or of Western civilization but as true ministers of Christ. Thus, the new nations will not have an inferiority complex, for they will understand that they are full-fledged members of the Christian family. They will not be offended but honored. . . . The presence of a native clergy does not make missionary activity less necessary.

Chapter 2 of the Schema on the Bishops Is Returned to the Commission

The Fathers voted Friday on chapter 2 of the schema on the bishops. The results were 1,219 *placet*, 19 *non placet*, and 889 *placet juxta modum* votes, with 2 null ballots.

Since the majority of two-thirds was not attained, the text was returned to the commission. It will be revised in view of the amendments suggested by the 889 fathers who voted *placet juxta modi.*

The Schema on the Missions Is
Criticized by Sixteen Out of Seventeen Speakers

Saturday's general congregation was one of the most impassioned and spontaneous of the Council. Applause interrupted the interventions, which is extremely rare. Georges Bernanos would have said that joy soared, the joy of being free and courageous, the joy of communicating with the world untrammeled by fruitless worry over pleasing or displeasing anyone.

The observers were especially struck by the fact that though the Pope, during his brief appearance in the aula on Friday, said he thought the Council could "easily approve the text" of the schema on the missions, sixteen of the seventeen Fathers who intervened on Saturday demanded in no uncertain terms that the text be rejected absolutely, and declared it "unworthy" of the Council. They carried the day. This morning the Council sent the schema on the missions back to the commission.

To conformist Catholics who might be scandalized by such opposition, it is easy to answer that the Council is the freer because the Pope has and will always have the last word in the Church, and can therefore modify the conciliar texts at the last moment if he considers such modifications in the higher interests of "the people of God."

For sheer liveliness, Saturday's session was reminiscent of some of the great debates during the first session when the bishops categorically demanded the rejection of the original schemas, so infected with legalism and theological immobilism. The Fathers exhibited rare energy in discussing the schema on the missions, one that is vital for the Church. This is a sign of health, for Catholicism, unduly Westernized, has too often given the impression in the past of confusing evangelization with colonization. Not until the time of Pius XI was the need for a native clergy fully understood and the right of non-European nations to respect appreciated.

Christianity appeared in many cases to be bound to the Occident. If Pius XII's famous phrase "The Church is bound to no civilization" had such wide repercussions, it was because it seldom corresponded with the facts.

Here are some characteristic passages from the more interesting interventions.

Cardinal Frings spoke in the name of many missionary bishops and superiors general: "The question of the missions is too important to be treated in this fashion. We need a complete theological and practical schema for the fourth session. [Applause.] The office for the propagation of the faith must become a dynamic organism."

Cardinal Alfrink said, "I speak at the request of bishops and missionaries in my country. . . . The work of evangelization has scarcely begun. After twenty centuries, we are shamefaced witnesses in mission countries. . . . We need a genuine missionary treatise."

Cardinal Suenens intervened in the name of all the African bishops. "The missions pertain to the very essence of the Church," he said. "Christians are a minority, and their number decreases daily, by comparison with the world population. The task of missionaries must be provisional. The Church is not really established until there is a native laity to assume responsibility. May this day soon come!"

Archbishop Bernardin Gantin of Cotonou, Dahomey, said in the name of all the bishops of Africa and Madagascar, "The missions must overcome the prejudice that evangelization is a disguise for domination. The Church is at home in all cultures. All civilizations belong to God, who created them and loves them." The Bishop then said in French, "Exchanges between civilizations and cultures is the rendezvous of giving and receiving. The Church is supernational. She transcends all regimes." (Applause.)

Four Out of Five Men Ignorant of Christ Bishop Geise of Bogor spoke for all the bishops of Indonesia: "We are unanimous in requesting a complete schema instead of these propositions. I transmit to you the wishes of twenty-five episcopal conferences and seventy religious superiors. . . . Could anyone reading these fourteen propositions believe that the missions pertain to the very essence of the Church? The faithful will say that a mountain has brought forth a mouse."

Bishop Lamont of Umtali, Southern Rhodesia, was applauded when he called for "a schema worthy of the Council." He said that "The present text reminds one of a complete electrical system deprived of current [or] of arid and dried bones, to use Ezekiel's words. . . . Four out of five men in the world are ignorant of Christ. . . . This schema won't excite anyone or anything. We asked for bread and they gave us, I do not say a stone, but a few cold propositions from a tract on missiology."

Bishop Lamont was vigorously applauded.

Bishop Petrus Moors of Roermond, the Netherlands, urged, "Let us place ourselves in the perspective of the parousia. Let us state clearly what it is to implant the Church. For grace has preceded the coming of the Church. The encounter between missionaries and non-Christians has already been prepared by grace."

This important observation was intended to emphasize that not only have all men, Christians or not, been redeemed by Christ but also that God speaks to each through his conscience no matter what religion he belongs to.

In concluding, Bishop Moors asked this question in a skeptical tone: "Does the present structure of the Sacred Congregation for the Propagation of the Faith respond to the situation as it really exists?"

Bishop John Velasco of Amoy, expelled from China and presently living in the Philippines, declared that "The text before us today is unwittingly paternalistic. . . . Let the Council be clear on nationalism and patriotism as well as on the natural rights of emigration and labor."

Rome Is a Mission Land   Father Giocondo Grotti spoke in the name of the thirty-eight Brazilian independent prelates: "This schema is useless and irrelevant. The experts who worked on it should be sent to the missions!" He then added these words, which scored a bull's-eye: "Rome is also a mission land."

Bishop Riobé of Orléans alluded to a previous intervention in which it was said that priests who only spend a short time in the missions are "tourists." "This is an unfortunate word. . . . According to the schema *De Ecclesia*, the Council has two essential objectives: first, ecumenism, and second, the missions. Let us therefore draw up a real schema." He then added this comment: "All the members of the commission wanted a real schema. But they were not authorized to draw one up."

Bishop James Moynagh of Calabar, Nigeria, regretted that the schema said nothing about the formation of a native clergy.

Cardinal Suenens and the Ethics of Marriage

Among the remarkable interventions by Cardinals Suenens, Léger, Alfrink, and Maximos IV on conjugal love (see the reports dated October 30 and 31), the first was the most moderate. But last Saturday Cardinal Suenens undertook to answer "certain reactions of public opinion" in order to "clear up any ambiguity."

Who and what was the Cardinal thinking about? Notably, a weekly magazine (*Le Monde*) which supposedly wrote under a sketch of him, "The Church Changes Her Doctrine on Conjugal Questions."

We looked for these words in the article in question, but in vain.

It merely said, "The Council is clearly renewing traditional thinking on love and marriage."

We were surprised that this phrase could provoke Cardinal Suenens, who is known for his reformist tendencies, but were told, "When the Cardinal spoke to the Council, he had not personally read the magazine. He acted at the request of several bishops of various nationalities who were shocked by the sentence in the French weekly, which they misreported. The Cardinal was thus mistaken, and this is regrettable, because the press was made a scapegoat. The sentence in the incriminated journal is in fact irreproachable."

Here is the complete text of Cardinal Suenens' clarification:

> May I be permitted on this occasion to respond very briefly to certain reactions of public opinion interpreting my intervention on the ethics of marriage as though I had said that the doctrine and discipline of the Church had been changed.
>
> In regard to doctrine, as was clearly said, it was merely suggested that a study be done on this subject, not to revise what has been authentically and definitively proclaimed by the magisterium of the Church but rather to make a synthesis of all the principles relating to this subject.
>
> In regard to discipline, it is evident that the conclusions of the commissions involved should be submitted to the sovereign pontiff, who will pass judgment on them in the capacity of his supreme authority, as was expressly said. It is clear that the methods to be followed in carrying out such research depend solely on the same supreme authority. I say this to dissipate all misunderstanding in public opinion.

NOVEMBER 10

Will Vatican II Go as far as
Pacem in Terris on the Problem of War?

Vatican II set itself a triple task on Monday. In the course of the session it took up the subjects of the missions, aid to underdeveloped countries, and war. We shall give precedence to the last-mentioned because it is the newest and most serious topic of deliberation—new for the Council, at least; the pontifical speeches on peace and disarmament are no longer taken into account. John XXIII's encyclical *Pacem in terris*, as everyone knows, was the last and most important document from the Holy See on this question. Now everyone wants to know whether Vatican II will go as far as or even farther than John XXIII.

What does this mean? The majority of commentators on *Pacem in terris*—beginning with its principal coauthor, Monsignor Pavan—are of the opinion that the Pope did not intend to condemn all defensive war absolutely. The use of ABC (atomic, biological, and chemical) weapons and the destruction of civil targets are clearly prohibited, but though modern war has become totally ineffective for correctly regulating conflicts between peoples, it is understood that a nation nonetheless retains the right to defend its independence by the use of arms. This is in essence a recognition of the legitimacy of defense.

The major problem before the Council is, should it affirm, in the name of twentieth-century Christian morality, that all war is unjust? Or should it on the contrary proclaim that under certain conditions defensive war is legitimate?

That is the difficulty. How will the Council resolve it? It is too soon to say. At the moment we only know that schema 13 and the corresponding appendix have largely echoed *Pacem in terris*. Is that sufficient? Was it worth the trouble of gathering 2,200 bishops in Rome to repeat what the Pope had said very well in 1963? It's a good question.

Will the Church be psychologically and materially free enough vis-à-vis American strength to condemn formally the *manufacture* of ABC weapons, even though they are called "deterrent," and expressly recommend the unilateral disarmament of Christian countries? Will she make it her duty, evangelically speaking, to recommend nonviolence as a means of avoiding the dreadful holocaust of total war? Will she say that, whatever happens, it is utterly immoral and anti-Christian to use the same nuclear arms as one's enemy in self-defense? Or will she say that Christian countries have the right to use the same means?

This is what is at stake. It is a tall order. The future of the Council is in its own hands. The world will judge Vatican II and the work that goes on between sessions when schema 13 is redrafted in terms of the oral and written observations of the Fathers.

Here are some of the first opinions expressed in the aula. They reflect the uncertainty that afflicts most of the bishops.

Cardinal Alfrink, the new international president of Pax Christi, said:

> Let us go at least as far as *Pacem in terris*. It speaks more positively about disarmament than does schema 13. This must be corrected; otherwise, we will give the impression of being retrogressive. The schema says that ABC weapons have unforeseeable effects and condemns them because of that. But this seems to say that there is a "dirty" bomb which must be condemned and a "clean" bomb whose effects can be calculated. This is behind the fear that the Council is

leaving the door open for a clean bomb. Is that what it means? The text is equivocal.

Moreover, is what is said about just and unjust war appropriate? It seems to insinuate that there can be a just war with nuclear arms. But it is indispensable that we speak of such matters with the greatest prudence [*magna cautela*]. The question for public opinion is not to know whether a nuclear war can be just or not. The question is that there be no war. *Pacem in terris* goes farther because it absolutely forbids nuclear arms.

The speaker used President Kennedy's remark, "If we do not destroy nuclear arms, they will destroy us." And he concluded, "Let us make the connection between the spirit of the Gospel and the Church's duty with respect to peace."

Cardinal Alfrink noticeably interprets *Pacem in terris* more absolutely than do most exegetes.

Let Nations Absolutely Renounce the Right of War   Bishop Ancel commented:

Some see a contradiction in the text. On the one hand, war—especially atomic war—is severely condemned. On the other hand, the licitness of defense against unjust aggression is affirmed. The two statements are well founded. Without the right to defense, violence would have free reign. But this right to defense seems to imply the right to prepare atomic arms. Isn't this why, despite a general desire for peace and the work of international conferences, no progress has been made and the armaments race continues?

The Council must overcome this contradiction. Its role cannot be to find political and technical solutions; but the Church must tell the world, from the moral point of view, what the real demands of papal teaching are. The text makes an allusion to them; they are found in the progress of the community of nations and of international institutions. . . .

Two propositions can be formulated.

First, under present circumstances, the good of the human family requires that all nations definitively and absolutely renounce the right of war and consequently all that is necessary to wage war, keeping only the means serving to guarantee internal order.

Second, only international organizations should dispose of an armed force which could intervene to prevent any threat of war. It is necessary to take this step to avoid contradiction. Nations would lose nothing but their right to declare war.

Bishop Ancel was loudly applauded.

ABC Weapons and Genocide   Bishop Jacques Guilhem of Laval, France, has written a pastoral letter on nuclear arms which is by far the most courageous document on the question. In his intervention he said in part:

> The use of atomic, bacteriological, and chemical weapons, whose destructive effects can have incalculable consequences even in the future, is a crime against God and humanity. No moral principle can justify it, and the Council must condemn such genocide. . . .
>
> We must denounce the error which holds that peace is merely a matter of a balance of power and the reciprocal fear of atomic weapons. Peace is founded above all on mutual understanding and dialogue, which can overcome and resolve all divisions. . . .
>
> We must not condemn the study of atomic energy on condition that it is ordained to the good of mankind. . . . We must absolutely emphasize the fact that all men, and not just governments, can and should contribute to disarmament, and show how their manufacture absorbs fabulous amounts of money which could be used for other purposes, such as feeding, education, health. . . .

Two Years After Marx's *Das Kapital*, Vatican I Said Nothing About the Misery of Workers

The Council also ended examination of schema 13's article 24, on aid to underdeveloped countries through human solidarity. The speakers were Cardinal Rugambwa (Tanzania); Father Gerald Mahon, Superior General of the Mill Hill Fathers; Archbishop Seper of Zagreb; Bishop Floyd L. Begin of Oakland; and Cardinal Richaud of Bordeaux, in the name of seventy bishops. Father Mahon's intervention was the most interesting:

> Marx's *Das Kapital* appeared two years before Vatican I. Yet that council said nothing about social justice or the undeserved misery of workers. This was a considerable oversight. What meaning could the definition of papal infallibility have for people in hunger? . . .
>
> Vatican II has been talking about the interior problems of the Church for two years. But happily, it has not ignored crucial problems related to justice and the international order. This is great progress, for what in 1870 concerned the social classes today concerns the proletarian nations in relation to the rich nations. . . .
>
> Each year, 400,000,000 people die of hunger and more than a billion do not have enough to eat. Let us be clear before such facts. Let us imitate the Gospel and Christ, particularly the parable of the Good Samaritan. Men are not only spiritually hungry. . . .

I propose that what is said on hunger and misery be clearer and that it become one of the most important points of Vatican II. There is a duty to educate all Christians to the responsibility of social justice between nations. It is scandalous that our plea to rich nations to help poor countries is in vain.

There were still some twenty Fathers registered to speak on this subject, but the moderators did not grant them permission, because it has been decided that all schemas without exception will be discussed in the present session. Thus work during the next recess, which will be the last, can be carried on in the light of observations made in the aula.

The Schema on the Missions
Is Sent Back to the Commission

Tension Between the Pope and the Council　　After hearing six speakers on missionary problems, Monday's general assembly decided by a vote of 1,601 to 311 to send the schema back to the competent commission to be completely reworked. We cannot hide the fact that the Council's decision went contrary to the Pope's wish. His appearance last Friday in the aula was primarily to defend the schema prepared by Cardinal Agagianian.

Vatican II has given proof of a remarkable spirit of independence. Some go so far as to say that this session is ending in an atmosphere of tension between the Pope and the Council. Cardinal Suenens' clarification to the press, which we reported yesterday, is symptomatic of this state. It is inevitable that tension arise in a council convoked by the supreme authority of the Church for the specific purpose of giving greater liberty to the bishops. And the tension is healthy. In defining collegiality, which the Pope wanted done, and thereby creating two distinct subjects of supreme power, the council automatically evoked the conditions of tension. But this has not caused the slightest disorder; for the Pope, although not purely and simply above the Council because he is its head, is the final court of appeal in the Church in case of conflict. Paul VI said this in his *Ecclesiam suam* and has repeated it in his recent speeches, notably on November 4, when he recalled his "sovereign personal power," and severely criticized the outlook of Protestantism and modernism.

No "Prefabricated Christ"　　Of the six interventions on the missions, we shall report on two, the first by reason of its typically Oriental mystical character and the other because of its journalistic character, its author being a well-known American television personality.

Archbishop Zoghby, Melkite Patriarchal Vicar for Egypt, said:

The Orientals affirm with the Fathers of the Church that the mission of the redeeming Word is bound up with that of the creative Word, thus expressing the universal character of the Church's mission. The Church must begin by discovering "the divine seed" and the natural riches which are its fruit in the peoples she wishes to evangelize. Christ is at home everywhere, everywhere among his own. The Church should not impose a prefabricated Christ on people. The Church is catholic, that is, universal, insofar as she recognizes the stripped Christ of the Gospel she preaches to people in the Christ who is transfigured into the likeness of these people.

The Council and Poverty   Auxiliary Bishop Fulton J. Sheen of New York, declared:

Since the beginning of the Council, I have received thousands of letters. Each one, no matter where it came from, said, "I am in a mission country." In fact, there are no residential and missionary churches. There is only one universal Church, which is entirely missionary. Let us not separate what God has united. . . .

The Council of Trent was the council of chastity [it founded the seminaries]. Vatican I was the council of obedience. Vatican II will be the council of poverty. . . .

The crucified Christ converted the world. The crucified Church continues the mission of Christ, the Christ who said, "I have mercy on the multitudes."

NOVEMBER 11

Nuclear Disarmament

Whatever reasons prompted the moderators to accelerate the pace of the interventions as the end of the session approaches, history will record that Vatican II spoke sotto voce on the atomic bomb. The Council dealt at great length with collegiality and liturgical reform (and it cannot be blamed for this), but spent less than forty-eight hours on the most agonizing question for mankind today. Four bishops on Monday and four on Tuesday spoke for ten minutes each—altogether one hour and twenty minutes. A dozen others, it is true, submitted their interventions in writing. This was the case with Archbishop Roberts, who has authorized us to publish a résumé of his two statements, on contraception and conscientious objection.

Two Written Interventions by Archbishop Roberts   The first, on contraception, asks that a competent commission prove that contraception is forbidden by the Roman Church for reasons based on natural law or the Gospel. The way in which this question is posed implies that no such proof is possible. "Catholics," said Archbishop Roberts, "either no longer obey the Church's teaching on contraception or they suffer greatly because they find they must obey without understanding, which is an untenable position."

In his second intervention, on conscientious objection, Archbishop Roberts recalled that Great Britain allowed conscientious objection in 1916 in the middle of the First World War. The Church has not yet accepted it; thus, she is fifty years behind the times. "The Gospel," he added, "seems to be the only efficacious moral and Christian solution to the dilemma of nuclear war. Blind obedience to orders is not a Christian attitude."

Peace, Nonviolence, and the Arms Race   We must regret that the problem of conscientious objection and nonviolence were not discussed on the floor. Cardinal Feltin was the only one to make any reference to this, when he spoke a few days before the normal opening of the discussion on this subject.

It would seem that Vatican II is afraid of the burning question of war and peace. This fear is not a good augury. The Council does not seem sufficiently concerned with the disappointment the public will feel when it learns of the brief time accorded to this theme. On the other hand, Vatican II will be judged on the text of schema 13, and this won't be drafted in final form until the recess. So it is a little early to pass judgment.

Once again the Oriental Church can take credit in the person of Maximos IV for one of the clearest interventions of the Council. The Melkite Patriarch boldly declared that the Church should show the same courage as John the Baptist before Herod or Saint Ambrose before Theodosius.

We might recall that Saint Ambrose, the fourth-century bishop of Milan, refused to let Emperor Theodosius enter the Church because he had ordered a massacre of an innocent population in Thessalonica. In that age the Church knew how to confront men of power in the world, hold her own against them, and impose spiritual sanctions. How foreign this seems to Christians today who are for the most part accustomed to an attitude of complacency toward heads of states! Who in France, for example, has Bishop Guilhem's courage in protesting the arms race? The Bishop of Laval asked rhetorically, "Isn't it collective madness as well as a monstrously fraudulent diversion of funds from civilized endeavors and aid to poor countries?"

We might also note that of the eight bishops who intervened on this subject, two of them—Auxiliary Bishop Philip M. Hannan of Washington and Archbishop George Beck of Liverpool—insisted on the services the atomic bomb could render and on legitimate defense. As Archbishop Roberts told me, "Those two interventions sounded as though they were written in the Pentagon."

It wouldn't be right to take this joke literally, but it does have a symbolic meaning. The two Anglo-Saxon bishops seem to think that, should the occasion arise, Christian civilization could be defended with nuclear arms. At any rate, this is the way the two interventions will be interpreted, whatever the intentions of their authors or the obvious difficulties of the subject.

Here, in essence, is what the Fathers said about nuclear war.

Let Us Imitate Saint Ambrose, Says Maximos IV Saigh

Nuclear arms threaten us with horrible destruction. This menace is increasing steadily because of the growing numbers of those who are in possession of this infernal instrument. It is not the Council's role to make technical judgments; but it must raise its voice from the spiritual and moral standpoint. Humanity is oppressed. Let us do everything in our power to ward off this catastrophe. The intervention of 2,000 bishops could change the course of history and perhaps the fate of humanity.

Under present conditions, how can we speak of a just war? What reasons would justify such a cataclysm? If men should disappear, what purpose would our pastoral effort serve? Let us rethink our conception of a just war in terms of the current situation, and let us reject the arguments of those who would decimate humanity under the pretext of defending it. . . .

National sovereignty has limits. Humanity is looking to us with haggard eyes. We cannot remain silent. Our duty is not only to save souls but men composed of bodies and souls. We should speak as John the Baptist spoke to Herod or Saint Ambrose to Theodosius.

Pacem in terris did this; it is clear. Our schema is somewhat Platonic. . . . We must go farther and be more precise. This schema can grow as it spreads, for every truth contains a power of penetration and expansion. . . .

We can create a global climate of public opinion and reject excessive forms of nationalism. The Church might perhaps even have the right to envisage sanctions. . . .

The Council must solemnly and energetically condemn every form of atomic, bacteriological, or chemical warfare. Let us address a message to the world. The considerable sums of money poured into atomic weapons should go to relieve those who live in hunger, which is to say two men out of three. We would thus revive an ancient tradition: the bishop as defender of the city. More than ever, the world needs disinterested and courageous defenders who are not afraid to proclaim the truth. Let us not deceive the world which looks to us. The Church must remain the column of truth.

Dialogue with Professional Experts   Bishop Hengsbach of Essen spoke in the name of seventy bishops:

> This schema is excellent. It is based on principles elaborated by Pius XII and John XXIII, who developed a precise and wise theory of defensive war. Let us do the same thing, taking into account the present psychological climate, as Cardinal Alfrink requested. . . .
>
> It must be admitted that our schema does not go far enough. Can we go farther? . . . We wish to inaugurate a dialogue with the world. If this dialogue is to be real, we must treat problems that haunt the world.
>
> The difficulties of such a dialogue are real. Sometimes our inter-locutors do not have the same principles as we; sometimes we are dealing with incompetent people; sometimes we are talking to competent people such as military officials, technicians, and politicians. If we leave each of these categories to itself, they will, despite their sense of responsibility, continue to see things from their own points of view and fail to understand the Church's thinking. We must, then, bring military experts and theologians into contact with one another.

Bishop Hannan Speaks of Legitimate Defense

> [We must state] the requirements of moral theology on conducting a just war. . . . War, to be sure, is always odious; but we must clarify what cannot be done in waging a just war. [Let us not forget] that the foundation of peace is justice. . . . The schema says that everything which divides must be avoided. This is an unfortunate formula, for justice itself can divide. . . .
>
> It is said that the effects of atomic weapons are unpredictable. But in some cases, these effects can be perfectly controlled. . . .
>
> Let us not forget the Church's doctrine of legitimate defense. . . . We seem to imply that all nations have been equally negligent

in securing disarmament. This is false. There are nations which have done everything they had to do in view of the fact that their duty was to save freedom. If slavery becomes a general state, there will be no dialogue possible with militant atheists. Let us speak, then, of the duty to defend freedom."

On Unilateral Disarmament Archbishop Beck spoke in the name of "a number" of bishops of England and Wales:

> Let us speak clearly but with great care, in line with the traditional doctrine of the Church. . . . However, it is important to say unequivocally that condemnation of nuclear arms does not include all uses they may be put to. There may be objectives in a just and defensive war that would legitimize their use, even though these arms have immense power. An example would be the necessity of destroying ballistic missiles or satellites. Thus, nuclear power is not in itself evil. . . .
>
> We must remind men of their responsibilities in the use of these weapons. This use necessarily depends on the state. But let us not give the impression of blaming heads of states, because they have enormous responsibilities. Their duty is to protect not only men but also cultural and spiritual values. . . . There is no doubt that the present state of peace may be viewed as a result of "the balance of terror." . . .
>
> Let us not request unilateral disarmament or a unilateral refusal to use these weapons, because this would precipitate war. To turn the other cheek is an evangelical counsel which applies to individuals and not heads of states, who have a serious obligation to defend their citizens. . . .
>
> Let us stress at greater length the serious obligation of those in power to do everything they can to prevent war.

Among the various interventions Tuesday on schema 13, let us single out that of Bishop McGrath of Santiago de Veraguas, Panama: "Public opinion is concerned with what we are saying here in St. Peter's. It is a happy sign of the times. . . . The Church is like a doctor who has all the necessary medicines in his cabinet but cannot use them because he does not know how to diagnose the illness. Let us avoid answering before we have understood the question addressed to us. Let us also be as ardent in our temporal activities as the Communists. Otherwise, no one will believe in the Church."

A Lay Auditor Discusses
the Incontestable Efficacy of Woman

The moderator then summoned Professor Juan Vázquez of Argentina, president of the International Federation of Catholic Youth Organizations, who spoke in Spanish in the name of the lay auditors at the Council:

> Humanity expects the Council to say that it understands the positive and magnificent aspects of progress as well as the negative aspects of the terrible injustices that still afflict the world.
>
> Woman, conscious of her modern vocation, today exercises in the world—in addition to her family mission—a role that is everywhere of indisputable efficacy for the elevation and progress of humanity and the Church. She therefore deserves our infinite gratitude. However, we have not yet in practice effectively recognized her position, despite repeated declarations to this effect. . . .
>
> The preparatory work on schema 13 suffered because it did not enlist the efficacious collaboration of men and women, and of the human couple as such, who are experts in different fields. We are very much aware that the hierarchy must know the everyday world and its future. We are profoundly aware of our mission, which, in Paul VI's words, is to be a bridge, for we are the Church and we are the world.
>
> The language of the world is living. It is sometimes harsh. It demands validity of expression. This is the language we expect of the Council. Let the Council express itself in the living language of all people.

At the end of the session, Bishop Guano, the reporter for schema 13, indicated that as a result of the Fathers' observations, chapter 4 of the schema would be greatly lengthened and several of the appendixes would be integrated into the chapter itself. "Schema 13 will be the sign of the Church's passionate love for the world," Bishop Guano concluded.

Lastly, the Council took up the schema of propositions on religious.

Birth Control

We have received the following letter from Commander Joseph de Gouberville:

> For a man of my generation, the conciliar declarations on birth control are stupefying. I know that the younger generation did not

expect much. But I have seen my own mother, worn out at the end of her life after fourteen births, racked with scruples because she was terrorized by her confessor. . . . The same priest once told me I had committed a mortal sin in stealing a piece of sugar from my parents.

I must have been stupid to accept the dictatorship of spiritual directors. And I understand that clericalism provokes anticlericalism. Today we are imitating the Protestants, whom we formerly persecuted.

One ends by wondering if the Church's precepts must be believed. I remember the time when we were condemned to hell for a peccadillo and refused absolution for a mere trifle.

But happily, I have known some precursors. One was the old pastor . . . who told me, "Never talk about what goes on in the intimacy of your married life. This is no one's business, not even a priest's." . . .

NOVEMBER 12

The Fathers Demand
the *Aggiornamento* of Religious Life

Aggiornamento, like ecumenism, is moving ahead. From the moment the Church set herself the task of renewing her structures, her institutions, and her theological vision, there could be no possibility of arbitrarily stopping along the way. For this reason, efforts to limit the reforms which had to be undertaken (related to the missions, religious congregations, seminaries, and so forth) to a few elementary propositions have failed one by one. Vatican II demands further study on these matters so that no essential aspect will be overlooked.

After previous sessions on the missions, the Council is now tackling the problem of renewal in the religious life, a subject that it outlined in a special schema of propositions.

The original schema ran to a hundred pages. The present version comprises some twenty totally pedestrian propositions. The many religious among the Council Fathers (about fifty of them superiors) will find it unacceptable. They warmly desire the schema to develop the following three lines of reflection at length:

1. Religious life should be centered on "the fullness of charity" and more in touch with Christianity, the Church, and the world.
2. The text should reaffirm that celibacy is the only really constitutive

vow of the religious life, for obedience and poverty must be practiced by all priests.

3. Those entering religious life should be considered as adults instead of children under the tutelage of a superior who is more or less unconsciously inbued with authoritarianism. All masochism should be excised, as should any pointless "holocaust" of the will under the pretext of enforcing submission and humility.

It would be tedious to review Wednesday's seventeen interventions, among them addresses by seven cardinals.* Let us rather note that the majority of the Fathers complained of the inadequacy of the present schema and hoped that Vatican II would elaborate a far less skeletal text. Even Cardinal Ruffini, who is usually in the opposition, took sides with the majority on this issue. Here is the core of their statements.

Poverty as it is lived presently in religious orders and congregations has no value of witness. If individuals live poorly (which is not always the case), communities are rich or seem so. This problem must therefore be reconsidered in the light of the Gospels and present needs.

Obedience is undergoing a crisis, it is said. That is true. But it is more the fault of superiors than of subjects, for many superiors do not take the modern mentality into account, which aspires with good reason to responsibilities and participation. In women's orders in particular, authority is often confused with maternalism and obedience with infantilism (Cardinal Suenens).

The institutional aspect should not be a stranglehold. New communities must be given the necessary means to find their way in creative liberty, and older orders must retain the capacity of renewal, though without abandoning the spirit of their founders.

There are too many orders. Of course, legitimate diversity must be respected; nor should we become victims of either standardization or a leveling process, which are contrary to the genius of Christianity. But some reorganization is necessary, especially of women's congregations, whose members are leaving in disturbing numbers.

There are, we might recall, 2,000,000 religious in the world; 1,200,000 of them are women.

The contemplative and the active life should not be too sharply distinguished. They are two different forms oriented to the apostolate. Moreover, the first should benefit the second. Cloisters should dispense with some of their rigidity; they should not shackle the apostolate. The cloister is made for religious, not religious for the cloister.

* Cardinals de Barros Câmara, Ruffini, Richaud, Döpfner, Landázuri-Ricketts, Suenens, and Bea.

Some habits are ridiculously complicated. They are evidence of an aging rather than a self-renewing Church (Cardinal Suenens, who was vigorously applauded).

More prudence is necessary in fostering vocations. Nuns often use recruiting techniques that are equivalent to coercion.

The life dedicated to celibacy should not be depreciated under the guise of rediscovering the values of conjugal life, for celibacy is essentially a total consecration to God. We must also admit that the secular clergy often live in such conditions as to have greater merit than religious. There is a lack of communication between religious and the secular clergy that is regrettable.

A new schema should be drawn up with the cooperation of various experts who are more aware of the exigencies of modern psychology (Bishop Richard Guilly of Georgetown, British Guiana, who was applauded).

Many Fathers regretted that superiors general of women's congregations were not permitted to present their own problems. Now that laymen are present in the aula, there seems no good reason that nuns can't be, especially when matters directly concerning them are discussed.

Legislation on Mixed Marriages

The schema of the votum* on the sacrament of marriage was recently distributed to the Fathers. It contains, among others, some highly important propositions on the thorny question of mixed marriages, which is one of the stumbling blocks to ecumenism.

It is currently said in Protestant circles that there are two touchstones at Vatican II of the Roman Church's good will: the declaration on religious liberty and the reform of canon law with respect to mixed marriages. Here is what the new schema on marriage requests concerning the second point. The propositions are expressed in the form of a votum because they suppose an eventual reform of the canon law now in force.

> In order that canon law be more attentive, and in a more opportune manner, to the circumstances of people, in the spirit of the decrees on religious liberty and ecumenism, it is especially desirable that a clear distinction be drawn between the prescriptions on the marriage of a baptized non-Catholic partner and those concerning the marriage of a baptized partner. Consequently, the following points should be observed:

* [The term *votum*, which this schema alone carried in its title, meant an expression of the will of the Council.—Tr.]

1. For all mixed marriages, in requesting dispensation from the impediment, the Catholic partner should be gravely obligated and promise sincerely to see to the Catholic baptism and education of the children *insofar as he can* [italics added].

This last phrase constitutes a fundamental reform because for the first time the particular circumstances of each couple are taken into account, and final judgment is left to the Catholic partner on how far he can respect his commitment. It is no longer a question of a brutal order but of a pressing urgent exhortation. The text continues:

This promise is to be made by the Catholic partner alone. The non-Catholic partner should be advised of it in advance, and it should be determined that he is not opposed to it.

Likewise, the non-Catholic party should be advised of the ends and characteristics of marriage, which neither partner may reject.

2. Mixed marriages should be contracted according to canonical form [that is, before a Catholic priest], but if there are serious obstacles, in order that marriages contracted without real matrimonial consent not imply a lack of validity, it is suggested that the local ordinary be given power to dispense from the canonical form.

This last clause opens the door to mixed marriages between Catholics and Protestants that would *only be blessed* by the priest.

3. Let mixed marriages between baptized persons no longer be performed in the sacristy but during a mass. Also, let a mixed marriage between a Catholic party and a non-baptized party be performed in the church during a mass.

4. Let the excommunication directed by present canon law against those who have contracted a marriage before a non-Catholic minister be abrogated.

Although they do not resolve all the difficulties inherent in mixed marriages, these suggestions inaugurate a new spirit based on liberty of conscience and on respect for the religious convictions of non-Catholics.

Vatican II and Contraception

Mr. Edward Guitton of the University of Rennes has sent me the following communication:

Commander de Gouberville's admirably frank letter raises the important problem of our sensitivity to sin and its evolution following the junctures of history and psychology. May the new generation ask permission to reply to the older?

When my grandfather decided to send his son to the public high school, his parents were convinced that he was committing a very serious sin, and they let him know it. We no longer understand such scruples, even in Brittany.

And so with contraception: do Catholic couples still consider it a sin against the will of the Creator, or simply an infraction of a Church precept? This is the question that must be asked. When I park my car illegally, I hope that the policeman will not notice it or, if he does, will be indulgent. But I am not conscious of sinning against the supreme authority. . . .

As for the theory of "the secret domain which must never be mentioned," that too can become dated. Many Catholics, I realize, have deplored the publicity given to the Council's discussion on birth control.

But I must confess that I do not share this point of view. Happily, we have gone beyond the stage of educating by silence, which was so long the rule in both our families and the Church. The whole world is interested in this discussion. Because it took place, the risk of publicity had to be accepted. Any form of secrecy would have been taken as an insult, especially by the generation immediately concerned. Indeed, it could have been interpreted as a clerical injustice toward the laity. The Council Fathers deserve credit for having understood this so well.

I believe I can speak for my generation in saying that unless some progress, however little, is made at Vatican II in the Church's definition of the meaning and nature of marriage, young Catholics will be profoundly disappointed, and it will be difficult for them not to think that they have been deceived.

NOVEMBER 13

No Pressure Should Be Exerted
with Respect to Sacerdotal Vocations

On Thursday the Council began examination of the schema of propositions on seminaries. The renewal of seminaries is clearly one of the most urgent and most far-reaching tasks before the Church today. There will be no *aggiornamento* possible today or especially tomorrow if the very conception of seminaries is not radically revised and adapted to contemporary needs.

The present text is a summary of an original schema which was extremely long. The new document contains some twenty propositions of about twelve lines each. "It was a river and is now a walled enclosure," said Bishop Carraro, the reporter. There is general agreement that this document is one of the most open in the series of schemas of propositions. The first paragraph, a particularly important one, postulates the following rule: "In order that general rules be adapted to each people and each rite, episcopal conferences will prepare a program for the formation of their priests. This program will be continually brought up to date and submitted for the approbation of the Holy See. Thus priests can receive a formation that will enable them to respond to the spiritual needs of their country."

This proposition inaugurates a decentralization which will permit each country great freedom in adapting the style of seminaries to local requirements. It marks the end of a particularly hampering uniformity in non-European countries where seminaries did not meet local needs.

The present schema, moreover, has the essential merit of making Christ himself the standard of reference for the *aggiornamento* of seminaries. To use a word more and more fashionable in conciliar and ecclesiastical circles, the text is *Christocentric*.

The first speaker was Cardinal Bueno y Monreal, Archbishop of Seville. He first expressed his satisfaction: "The renewal of the Church depends in great part on priests. Thus the importance of seminary formation is evident." He then offered some criticisms:

> This text lacks a genuine doctrine of sacerdotal vocations. This vocation includes several elements, principally the aptitudes and desire of the candidate himself and the call of the bishop. There may be cases in which the subject has no personal inclination and has never thought of becoming a priest. When someone suggests this to him, it comes as a real revelation.

The speaker quoted concrete cases of young people who entered the seminary in this way and became outstanding priests.

Cardinal Meyer, Archbishop of Chicago, underlined the importance of the human formation of future priests. "The priest," he said, "is first of all a man, and to become a good priest he must first be a good man and a good Christian. There is no good priest if there is no basis of human qualities."

These remarks might appear banal. But they are far from that, for in many cases there is a tendency to scorn the human substratum, to believe that sanctity and spirituality make up for all deficiencies. But neither can substitute for human competence and knowledge.

Archbishop Giovanni Colombo of Milan (he is the brother of Bishop Carlo Colombo, the Pope's theologian) said:

> There remains much to do in adapting the mission and role of seminaries to present demands. There are two principal weaknesses in the formation of seminarians. The first is the lack of organic unity: spiritual, intellectual, pastoral, and disciplinary formations mutually ignore one another and remain isolated. The second is the lack of human formation: seminarians do not always acquire adequate maturity because their education is too passive, too prophylactic, that is, too exclusively concerned with protecting them from the contagion of the world and cutting them off from a society which they will one day have to evangelize.

The speaker also denounced the "improper pressures" that are sometimes exerted on young people who are not old enough to react intelligently.

Regarding the formation of seminarians, Archbishop Colombo made these fitting remarks:

> This schema is excellent in that it specifies that we must always respect the rules of healthy psychology, and treat seminarians as persons who are masters of themselves and responsible for themselves. No economic, family, or ecclesiastical pressure should be brought to bear. The fact that a candidate for the priesthood leaves the seminary should be considered as something quite normal. The seminary must be characterized by an atmosphere of total liberty, so that anyone who feels he must leave should not be embarrassed by his decision.

The Necessity of Consulting Religious

The Council has already accepted the schema on religious as a basis of discussion (by a vote of 1,155 to 882), and therefore the assembly will vote on the propositions themselves Monday. The number of negative votes was so high that practically speaking the original text will have to be completely reworked.

Eight speakers intervened on the schema Thursday, among them Bishop Huyghe of Arras, a member of the competent commission. He was particularly critical of the text, which from all appearances satisfies scarcely anyone. He said:

> This schema lacks a living spirit. It is too juridical and too Occidental. It is based on preconciliar ecclesiology. It is absolutely

necessary to draw up a new schema which shows that religious life is on the one hand a factor of unity among Christians and on the other a means of rapprochement for non-Christians. . . .

Within the Church, religious should exercise a unifying role both by example and by action. They should not separate themselves from other members of the Church; on the contrary, they should forge bonds with them, cooperate with all and fulfill an ecumenical role. . . .

In the Church's missionary activity, religious should fulfill the same role today as they have in the past. In old Christian countries, they should reflect on the form of their presence in the world, which ought to be poorer and more flexible. Everything that is not essential should be revised, especially in monasteries. In mission countries we must encourage new forms. Bishops must assume their responsibilities in the renewal of religious life.

Finally, Bishop Huyghe made this remark, which was much appreciated: "The commission should consult superiors general of women's orders, especially those who have been invited to the Council as auditors."

Pastor Marc Boegner on Ecumenism

Pastor Marc Boegner, an observer at the Council, gave a speech on Thursday evening entitled "Our Common March Toward Unity." A number of civil and religious personalities attended, including Cardinals Feltin, Gerlier, Richaud, Lefebvre, Koenig, and Bea as well as two patriarchs.

Pastor Boegner outlined the evolution of ecumenism: the formation of the World Council of Churches at the beginning of the century, the meeting in New Delhi on the eve of the Council, and the convention in Montreal. He spoke of the difficulties between Protestants and Catholics and the emotion everyone experienced when the Council was announced by John XXIII, who "created a prophetic event, provoked a deep stirring in the churches, and gave birth to a new climate."

Speaking of the Council's work, he said, "The world is waiting for schema 13." The speaker expressed the hope that the Council would not close without a declaration on religious liberty and some words about mixed marriages.

Many things still separate us, he concluded, but we must view matters in the perspective of the mystery of the Church. The march forward we have begun is irreversible. Official dialogue can now begin. We have been invited to St. Peter's, we have heard and met you, and we are moving apace with you.

Paul VI Donates His Tiara for the Poor
and Renounces the Insignia of Temporal Royalty

The Council took an intermission today, Friday. Work was suspended for an Oriental concelebration. The officiants were Archbishop Maximos IV Saigh and several other Greek Melkite bishops and archimandrites.

Two events, of unequal importance but convergent meaning, marked this long ceremony, which the Pope attended in person. The *sedia gestatoria* was prepared at the entrance of the nave. When the Pope entered the Basilica a few minutes before the ceremony began, there was the usual flutter of preparations to seat him on the ceremonial chair. But the Pope refused. He proceeded on foot to the Altar of the Confession as the deep voices of the Greek choirs resounded in the aula.

At the end of the occasion, a surprise awaited the Council Fathers and the many faithful who came to St. Peter's to attend a ceremony to which Italians are not accustomed. Archbishop Felici, secretary general of the Council, spoke. He declared in substance: "Many things have been said here during the Council about poverty. Listen, all you here present. It is as though Christ's words were echoing to us from Jerusalem: 'I have compassion on the multitude' ['*Misereor super turbam*']. The Church is truly the mother of the poor, and the Pope has decided to bear new witness to this truth by giving his tiara for the benefit of the poor."

With these words, the Pope himself carried the tiara to the altar where the concelebration has just ended.

We cannot overestimate the Pope's gesture. It was marked with the stamp of discretion which characterizes all of Paul VI's actions. Actually, the Pope has several tiaras; but the one he donated today was his coronation tiara (which is very modern and appreciably different from those of his predecessors).

Thus the Pope has begun to renounce the temporal wealth of the Vatican for the benefit of the poor. We already knew that the white Lincoln given him by the Americans is on its way to Bombay to be sold there for the poor of that country.*

The Church, in the person of her leader, is setting an example of simplification. It is bound to be followed by many others—by the Pope

* We were later to learn that the tiara was given to the Archdiocese of New York, where it was displayed while the faithful were invited to contribute to the cause of the needy, and then sold to an American museum. As for the Lincoln, when the Pope left India, he gave it to a nun who works with the poor in Bombay. The sumptuous automobile was then sold and the proceeds were given to the poor.

again and then by the bishops, who are thinking of simplifying their garb and episcopal insignia.

By giving away his tiara, Paul VI at the same time irreversibly abandoned the specific sign of his temporal royalty which made him in some sense the equal of other heads of state. We understand better now why Paul VI wanted to be received by the President of India as a simple pilgrim.

Will the Council Fathers Renounce
Their Honorific Titles and Luxurious Regalia?

Since the beginning of the first session, the Council fathers have often criticized the expensive character of their traditional regalia: the amethyst pastoral ring, the golden chain and cross with precious stones, the *cappa magna*, the ermine, the fine lace. They have also criticized the honorific ranks and titles used in ecclesiastical circles: canon, supernumerary secret chamberlain, domestic prelate, monsignor, excellency, most reverend, and so forth. These are so many vestiges of an age when clerics copied the customs and manners of the royal courts.

Cardinal Frings, Archbishop of Cologne, proposed on November 5 that his colleagues lay aside their "triumphal clothing." On October 27 a Brazilian prelate expressed the hope that the Fathers would come to the assembly in simple black soutanes (some bishops have already begun doing this). Aesthetics would lose but not the esteem of the public, who witness —sometimes with astonishment, sometimes with disdain—the spectacle of bishops and cardinals walking in the streets in their colorful attire.

Recovering Evangelical Simplicity   In an age when even military officers have abandoned the glittering uniforms of yesteryear for more modest and practical garb, ceremonial ecclesiastical vestments are a source more of irony than of respect. The gap between these clothes and the simplicity urged by the Gospel, the dichotomy between these expensive robes and the misery of so many men grows more embarrassing each day.

On the eve of the Pope's pilgrimage to India, a country of hunger, will the bishops finally resolve to translate their words into actions? Recently Cardinal Suenens complained of how "ridiculously complicated" some religious habits are, and two weeks ago Archbishop Helder Câmara of Recife wondered why the bishops didn't follow the example of the Little Sisters of the Poor.

Some bishops, it is said, were hesitant because they didn't want to seem to be teaching the Pope. But that argument no longer holds since Paul VI's decision Friday to relinquish both his *sedia gestatoria* and his tiara. The bishops now have no excuse for not following his example.

Several concrete solutions have been proposed. For example, a basket might be passed in St. Peter's in which the bishops could deposit their rings and their chains and crosses, with the proceeds of their sale going to a charitable work. Some bishops already wear simple wooden crosses and modest rings. Others have given up all their violet clothing, including buttons and socks, and dress in the black of ordinary priests. Archbishop Zoa of Yaounde always wears an ordinary clerical suit in the streets of Rome.

Several hundred bishops have recently signed a document inviting them to abandon the exterior signs of wealth and give real priority to the evangelization of the poor. There are new signers each day. Will the present session terminate without at least one practical gesture? It would be the more appropriate in that the Council has spoken explicitly of aid to underdeveloped countries and the Eucharistic Congress in Bombay will be held in a country that is singularly plagued by misery.

The Pope's Example Now that the Pope has laid aside his crown and given the sign of his terrestrial royalty to the poor, now that Christ the King appears to them in the most deprived of men as the Gospel says (Christ expressly identified himself with the hungry and naked—see Matthew 25:35–36), it would be fitting for the successors of the apostles to make similar gestures.

Such gestures would obviously be symbolic, but they would be understood by all as constituting a call to the spirit of interior poverty, which in the final analysis is what matters. It would moreover be an act of *aggiornamento* in conformity with John XXIII's wishes and still more his style of life, marked as it was by a love of poverty, particularly in his last years. There is a growing hope that John XXIII will be beatified by acclamation in the Council before the end of Vatican II.

All the great reforms in the Church have coincided in history with a return to simple customs and a renunciation of the worldly spirit, which periodically infiltrates the clergy and even religious who take a vow of poverty.

A Map of Rediscovery for the Church and the Poor Father Gauthier, a worker-priest in Nazareth who lives in a cabin and says mass each day in a grotto much like that of the Nativity, has said this with respect to schema 13:

Poverty was not included in the Council's agenda; yet John XXIII spoke these prophetic words: "The Church is for all men, and especially the poor."

The first session made this serious shortcoming clear. Subsequently, much work has been done in special meetings of a committee of twelve bishops from all countries, under the leadership of the Bishop of Tournai.

Schema 13 can be the map of rediscovery for the Church and the poor, symbolized by Paul VI's way of the cross through the crushing crowds and market places of Jerusalem.

I make mine these words of Father Häring: "The Archimedes' fulcrum of schema 13 is poverty."

A Truth To Be Shouted from the Housetops

I hope the bishops will request that the following paragraph, which appeared in the first versions of schema 13, be reinserted: "Jesus Christ willed to make his the common working condition of men during many years of his life."

This is a truth that should be shouted from the housetops. We must be careful not merely to preach poverty, which is very consoling for the rich, but especially to reveal the place of the poor in the economy of the Gospel. Christ said, "What you have done to these, the least of my brethren, you have done to me."

Let us hope that, as at the first Council of Jerusalem, apostles like Paul and Barnabas will be sent forth to evangelize the world, becoming all things to all men, even to working with their hands, in order to remove all obstacles to the Gospel.

After the Pope has given away the tiara, after the bishops renounce the exterior signs of wealth, after the Pope mingles with the immense crowds of poor Indians in Bombay, the idea of a priest working manually and personally, sharing the lives of the working class, will be stronger than in the time of Cardinal Suhard. Men like Bishop Ancel, a former worker-bishop, Father Perrin, and Father Joseph de Dorgeri, a Jesuit worker-priest who sacrificed his life so that this form of the apostolate might continue, will increasingly come to be seen as pioneers.

"The Oriental Churches Owe Almost Nothing to the West," Says Cardinal Lercaro

In a recent lecture in Rome, Cardinal Lercaro, Archbishop of Bologna and one of the Council's four moderators, said:

Apostolic and Eastern in their origins, the Oriental Churches owe almost nothing to the West. On the contrary, the West has received much from them in spirituality, liturgy, and theology itself, as the schema on ecumenism admits. . . .

Our first task is to accomplish a spiritual conversion that will be the fruit of the spirit of evangelical poverty. We must reconsider our manner of understanding the mystery of the Church and draw the resulting practical consequences. . . .

We must fully rediscover the meaning of collegiality and live it before we can say that we respect one of the most remarkable and authentic expressions of the Oriental tradition: the patriarchate and the autonomous churches. . . .

We may hope for a gradual change in the way we think about the Church and lead the Christian life. Only then can we expect to be taken seriously by our Oriental partner. Then and only then can fruitful dialogue begin.

NOVEMBER 16

The Morality Taught in Seminaries Is "Neither Principally Nor Fully Christian," Says Cardinal Léger

There are only five working days left before the closing plenary session next Saturday, which will be devoted to the promulgation of several constitutions and decrees. From now until then, it is said, one or more supplementary general congregations will be held in the afternoon.

On Saturday past, the Fathers voted on the first fourteen propositions of the schema on religious. As was expected, most of the ballots (five out of six) did not attain the required majority of two-thirds, and were sent back to the commission to be redrafted in the light of the almost 5,000 *modi* requested by the Fathers.

The substance of this general congregation was the examination of the schema of propositions on seminaries. But the Fathers were clearly divided on such questions as dialogue between seminarians and laymen within the seminary and the importance of Thomas Aquinas. The very notion of a *philosophia perennis* was questioned several times, and Cardinal Léger roundly criticized morality as it is taught in the seminaries.

A showdown on philosophy, theology, and morality was inevitable, for the intellectual and pastoral renewal of the Church, so much desired by the majority and so much feared by the minority, depends on these three fundamental disciplines. The Church, of course, is practically bound to Thomistic philosophy, which she has all but canonized.

The question is to what extent she will abandon this sure and convenient standard, which has been honored for long centuries. The Church's words of solicitude for the modern world will be empty if they are not substantiated by an effort to understand contemporary philosophies from within, instead of contemptuously passing judgment on them from without.

It is important for Vatican II to confront this problem, which poses serious difficulties. To abandon a perfectly adapted philosophy in favor of one that is still undeveloped is very hard to do. In a Church which has always taught the value of human reason against all forms of agnosticism, subjectivism, and skepticism, the renewal of philosophical teaching is at the root of all other reforms.

Among the thirteen speakers Saturday were five cardinals.

The Proper Use of Saint Thomas

I speak as one who has held positions of responsibility in seminaries for thirty years and who was for eighteen years Secretary of the Sacred Congregation of Universities and Seminaries. I grant that contacts between future priests and laymen could be beneficial, but not in seminaries. . . . This schema has a defect: it does not mention Saint Thomas in connection with philosophical formation. He is mentioned very timidly in connection with theological formation. But Saint Thomas remains the master and guide of scholarship. He is the very doctor of the Church. He is more useful than ever in fighting against modern errors.

Cardinal Léger of Montreal:

The term *philosophia perennis* is ambiguous. What does it apply to, since there are several radically different Scholastic philosophies? . . . It is the nature of philosophy to begin with an investigation into reality and not with authority.

It is evident to all that if the Council imposes the teaching of Scholastic philosophy, it will seriously inconvenience non-Western countries. Anyway, the Council has no business imposing a particular philosophy.

As applause thundered in the aula, Cardinal Léger exclaimed:

Beware of the man of one book! Beware, too, of the Church of one doctor! Rather than imposing Saint Thomas, we might propose him as a prototype of the scholar, as a master and model who knew how to turn the learning of his time to the service of the Church.

[It is well known that Saint Thomas in a way baptized Aristotle, who until then had been considered absolutely incompatible with Christianity.]

For several decades, a great number of theologians have dialogued only with the philosophies of the Middle Ages. This has its disadvantages. Let lay experts be invited into the seminaries to compare secular and religious kinds of philosophy.

Then Cardinal Léger spoke of the teaching of morality:

As Maximos IV said so well, our manuals do not correspond with the adult mind of modern man. The morality taught in seminaries suffers from several defects. It is too preoccupied with casuistry and legalism. It seems to me to be neither principally nor fully Christian.

In the future our moral theology should be intimately linked with dogmatic theology; it should be founded on Holy Scripture and centered on the love that sums up Christ's teaching. [Renewed applause.]

Cardinal de Barros Câmara of Rio de Janeiro and Cardinal Döpfner of Munich were pleased with the schema's discretion. By restricting itself to general guidelines, it protects the liberty of episcopal conferences.

"It is not enough for priests to be holy," said Cardinal Döpfner. "They must be adapted to their times. The soul of theological formation is Holy Scripture. I fully agree with what Cardinal Léger said about Saint Thomas."

Seminaries Open to the Outside World Cardinal Suenens of Malines-Brussels expressed agreement with Cardinals Léger and Döpfner, and then expounded at length on the reform of seminaries, a reform which he has personally undertaken in his diocese. He wants especially to bring them into closer contact with the outside world.

He urged a formation totally centered on the apostolate, and suggested that the order of studies be reversed: first Scripture and theology, and then (or at the same time) philosophy. The present order is two years of philosophy followed by four years of theology.

Of the other eight interventions, we shall summarize a few passages from the most interesting.

Archbishop Staffa, Secretary of the Sacred Congregation of Universities and Seminaries: "No progress is possible if we are more concerned with what is new than with the truth. The only thing that matters is the truth. The Church decides what is good in philosophy. . . . There is no valid progress without continuity with the past. Saint Thomas is not a milestone but a beacon. Let us at all costs keep the fundamental principles of Saint Thomas contained in the encyclical *Humani generis.*"

Bishop Sauvage of Annecy was in agreement with the schema, though he found it somewhat condensed. He particularly approved the predominance of the pastoral concern. He asked that seminaries correspond more with the aspirations of the seminarians themselves so that "they will feel at home in them and will not be tempted to leave."

In the spirit of the encyclical *Ecclesiam suam,* Bishop Sauvage called for dialogue between teachers and students as well as knowledge about non-Christian modern philosophies.

NOVEMBER 17

Vatican II Casts the Final Vote on Collegiality

Today, Tuesday, the Council Fathers approved chapter 3 of the schema *De ecclesia* on collegiality, amended by previous *modi.* The final vote was 2,099 for and 46 against, with 1 null ballot. The opposition was very weak at the end. Most of the bishops who had been hostile to collegiality rallied to the schema after a series of personal contacts between the Pope and members of the theological commission.

Paul VI, in fact, took a personal position. In the beginning he had come into conflict with the Theological Commission: he had wanted some corrections, and the commission members had been unanimous in wanting to conserve the text they had elaborated with such great care. Finally, matters were settled as a result of a clever compromise. The schema was not touched, but it is now preceded by a "preliminary explanatory note," which at first reading seems to give a rather restrictive interpretation to collegiality.

To approve the schema was thus to approve the note, which reflects, let us repeat, the Pope's opinion rather than the theological commission's; the latter accepted it but made specific mention of its source: "superior authority."

The intentional vagueness of this expression is suggestive. The Pope is not explicitly mentioned, a fact which scarcely attenuates the strength of this document.

It is possible that some of the forty-six opponents among today's voters were in favor of collegiality but were unfavorably impressed by the explanatory note.

The note, as everyone in Rome knows, reflects the ideas of Father Bertrams, a Jesuit who has written articles on collegiality in *Civiltà Cattolica,* and Bishop Colombo, formerly the Pope's theologian. It is difficult to analyze because it deals with theological subtleties. Essentially, it makes these points.

1. The word *college* is not taken in its strictly juridical sense, of a group of persons equal among themselves. The Pope is part of the college, but he is not an ordinary member. To avoid all confusion, the schema uses the terms *body* and *order* in addition to *college*.

2. The parallel between Peter with the other apostles and the pope with the bishops does not imply a transmission of the extraordinary powers the apostles enjoyed (for example, the personal infallibility of each apostle).

3. One becomes a member of the college in virtue of episcopal consecration and *hierarchical communion* with the head of the college and its members (the word *hierarchical* is essential here, and was added). There are thus two sources: the first, of the ontological order, is in itself the more important; the second is of the juridical order. The pope is necessary to give the function (*munus*) its *effective* power. In other words, there is no *real* exercise of episcopal responsibility without the pope's consent. Hence the necessity of a juridical, canonical determination of the exercise of the function.

The term *communion* has more than psychological value. It expresses an ontological reality. But this communion requires a juridical form, and that is why the adjective *hierarchical* was added. This precision makes it clear that implicit communion is not enough.

4. The college—which cannot exist without its head—is itself a subject of supreme and full power in the Church. Not to admit this would be tantamount to restricting the pope's power. The distinction is not between the pope and the whole body of bishops, but between the pope acting alone and the pope acting with the college or the college acting with the pope. The pope, as supreme pastor, can act whenever he judges it necessary for the good of the Church. But the college can act in a *strictly* collegial sense only with the consent of its head.

5. Finally, collegial power is not always exercised as such. But its other forms of exercise can exist only in a communion of opinion and judgment with the head of the college.

An addendum offers a comment which is important for the cause of ecumenism: "The Theological Commission did not intend to settle questions of licitness and validity of powers which exist among the separated Orientals. These points are left to the study of theologians."

The contents of this explanatory note, as it was published after several preliminary versions, create no serious difficulties. Everyone agrees that it does not affect the principle of collegiality.

On Monday, Archbishop Felici made two announcements that were intended to answer objections or questions on the part of the minority opposed to collegiality:

> Some Fathers have expressed doubts to superior authority about the·observance of the regulations during the examination of chapter 3 of the schema *De ecclesia*, as well as doubts about the doctrine contained in this chapter.
>
> In what concerns procedure, investigation shows that the regulations were strictly adhered to; in what concerns doctrine, all observations were submitted to the competent commission.

Since some Fathers asked what theological weight should be attributed to the schema *De ecclesia*, Archbishop Felici read a declaration made by the theological commission last March 6: "The Council does not define doctrine in the domain of faith and morals unless this is explicitly stated. On the other hand, what the Council proposes as the doctrine of the supreme magisterium of the Church obliges all according to the rules of theological interpretation."

The Propositions on Seminaries Continue To Find Approval

On Monday also the Fathers finished examining the schema of propositions on seminaries. This text, which was greeted with nearly unanimous approval by those who intervened, is certain to meet with the favor of the voters. Twelve more Fathers spoke on this subject, and here are some of the more salient remarks.

Cardinal Bacci Defends Saint Thomas   Cardinal Bacci of the Curia expressed his "surprise and pain" at what was said about Saint Thomas on Saturday:

> Surely no one wishes to weaken the role of the Angelic Doctor, even indirectly, since ninety pontifical documents have made the importance of this philosopher clear. If anyone opposed this teaching —which I do not believe—it would mean that the Council is not only above the popes but against them as well. This is unimaginable. . . .
>
> Some have suggested that a new commission should be created to deal competently with matters relating to seminaries. This is surprising, since such a body already exists, The Sacred Congregation of Universities and Seminaries. If another is needed, we must specify

what kind. And it should be made clear that it would depend on the Congregation of Seminaries.

Auxiliary Bishop Komba of Peramiho, Tanzania, spoke in the name of forty bishops: "Seminarians should receive state degrees so that the liberty of their vocation would be fully protected. For if they should leave the seminary, they would have less difficulty finding employment."
Bishop Schmitt of Metz said:

> This schema is good. Let us implement it without any delay. Let us emphasize the personal formation of clerics. . . .
>
> Seminary life is somewhat artificial, whence comes the necessity of contact with the outside world. The seminarian will derive great profit from this. In this way he will learn the importance of dialogue and such natural virtues as honesty and veracity. He will discover that the non-Christian man is not a spiritual nothing.

Concerning Fallen Priests Bishop Charue of Namur spoke about fallen priests:

> Often enough priests fall because their ministry is too burdensome. Frequently loneliness is alleged as the reason. But this can hardly be true, for many of these priests lived in community. Yet sometimes loneliness can be greater in community. . . . The causes of these failures are depressions, and errors stemming from a mystico-carnal syncretism. . . .
>
> Everything depends on the formation of priests. Let us avoid infantilism; let us not ordain young men who are not mature. Let us learn to wait when necessary.

Archbishop Weber of Strasbourg said, "Two excesses must be avoided, which the schema does very well: overthrowing everything and refusing to undertake a profound renewal."

Archbishop Weber noted that sometimes young people from non-Catholic schools seem more mature than those from Catholic ones. "Many difficulties in seminaries," he noted further, "are due to the disunity of the teaching body rather than the seminarians."

Coadjutor Bishop Emilio Benavent of Málaga, Spain, made several interesting remarks. Seminarians should not be ordained before engaging in two years of ministry after their studies; in this way they will learn the concrete conditions of their apostolate. Further, they should be familiar with the world of the young and the social doctrine of the Church, which is "the projection of the Gospel adapted to our times." Future priests should have the Gospel before their eyes constantly during their period of formation and their whole life; they should also be taught to base their sermons on the New Testament.

NOVEMBER 18

The Era of Collegiality
Begins in the Catholic Church

On Tuesday, November 17, the Roman Church entered the era of collegiality.

And for the most part with good grace and a spirit that the most optimistic hadn't dared hope for. Hasn't it been said often enough these past two years, and particularly the past two weeks, that this vote would be dangerous for the unity of the Church? The approach of the balloting tortured some, excited others, and depressed still others. Some experts— and they were not wrong—said that things were not mature enough, that it would take twenty years to see clearly in this matter. Some bishops wore a look which said plainly that only a last-minute miracle could save the Church from the impasse to which overly enterprising spirits had brought it. And some non-Catholic observers raised their arms to call heaven to witness that collegiality, as it has been laboriously defined by the schema, satisfied nobody: neither the Orthodox, who found it too juridical in conception and too timid in expression, nor the Protestants, to whom the suspicious strengthening of ecclesiastical authority was totally foreign.

Forty-Six Opponents Then suddenly, Tuesday morning the horizon cleared and faces relaxed. There were only forty-six opposing voices. A miracle had happened.

Who is responsible for this near-unanimity? The Pope? Haunted by the bitterness of the minority (200 or perhaps 300) and unsatisfied with the vagueness of certain passages in the schema, he untiringly multiplied contacts, personally reviewed the smallest details, and encouraged the last-minute nigglers to perfect the preliminary explanatory note (it was redrafted ten times). Paul VI played a determining role. To the end he refused to cut his losses: he would not abandon the objecting minority, who were well-intentioned, certainly terrified by this doctrinal *aggiornamento*, and yet confident of Paul VI's clearheadedness. Nor did he want to rein in the creative liberty of the Council.

Is this victory due to the theological commission, which confronted "the superior authority" face to face, jealous of its prerogatives and strong in the cohesion of its majority?

Or is it due to the subtleties of the theologians who were called upon to square the circle, supported by the Pope but harshly judged by those bishops who were skeptical of the diplomacy of intelligence?

The result is due to the convergent and divergent efforts of all these elements, to their decision to finish this matter before the end of the session so that an increasingly exhausting wait would not be prolonged.

At an exceptionally difficult moment, on a subject said to be an inevitable source of discord and one burdened with scarcely concealed passions, Vatican II proved its balance and its understanding of an age that is characterized both by its need for decentralization and freedom and by its desire for consolidation. Vatican II really completed Vatican I without breaking continuity with the past, without unnecessary or dangerous collisions, without rejecting those whose vision is riveted on the past.

Only later will we know the details of these days during which those responsible suffered hope and discouragement in turn; but what is immediately clear is the interior virtue of this success, which is a cause for optimism: the Church of tomorrow will discover the ramifications of collegiality and will deepen the concept. The pope will remain at the helm, but episcopal conferences will no longer look to Rome with the anxiety of past years.

Each bishop knows himself to be more and more involved. New bonds will be forged between the periphery and the center. It remains to define and determine these, without too much delay if we are to profit by the present thrust. For some the Council has ended; for others it has just begun.

Bishop Méndez Arceo Intervenes on the Right of Priests Returned to the Lay State to Marry

On Thursday Vatican II will vote on the declaration on religious liberty, the final draft of which has finally been distributed. Tuesday three bishops —and they were not least among the hierarchy—intervened on the schema of propositions on seminaries. It is fortunate that despite the rush of these last days, the Council found time to listen to Archbishop Garrone of Toulouse, whose high responsibilities in the Church of France lend special prestige to what he says; Bishop Méndez Arceo of Cuernavaca, whom the fathers now expect to make original interventions; and Auxiliary Bishop Reuss of Mainz, whose ideas are avant-garde. Each spoke in the name of seventy or more bishops.

Necessary Changes in the Roman Congregations   Archbishop Garrone launched a frontal attack on the problem of curial reform, speaking clearly about simple matters which some do their utmost to obscure and complicate:

> The schema gives episcopal conferences the responsibility of organizing seminaries. The consequences for the central bodies in Rome are clear. The decentralization we seek supposes a change in them. More than ever before they will become our source and confluence. . . . The Roman congregations must be revised and their structures must change. Just as episcopal conferences must have a better understanding of the needs of each nation, so the Roman Congregations must have a better understanding of the needs of the whole world.
>
> They must not limit themselves, as they have too often in the past, to negative decisions. . . .
>
> We must create very close bonds among the three congregations which deal with priests. Experts from all over the world must be called upon, and they should be physically present in Rome.
>
> Moreover, in view of the development and interdependence of the different philosophical, theological, and scientific disciplines, it is urgent to construct a synthesized viewpoint. This will require experts with a superior level of cultivation in order to avoid niggling measures.

Celibacy Should Be Neither a Trap . . .   Bishop Méndez Arceo returned to a difficult problem that is usually evaded: sacerdotal celibacy and priests in difficulty.

> Because of the taboo about this subject, we have a lame and timid statement in the schema; it lacks both dynamism and a spirit of synthesis. We must transcend the juridical spirit of the law of celibacy and clearly show its apostolic dimension as defined by Saint Paul. Celibacy is not in itself perpetual; it is an evangelical counsel which ought to be assumed freely, even though this state may be confirmed by a vow.
>
> Let us teach forcefully that virginity is a gift of God which should be desired in view of the kingdom of God. Let us once and for all put an end to the disparity between sacerdotal chastity and religious chastity. All of us priests of the Western Church are in fact monks. . . .
>
> The bishop who ordains his priests—and calls them his collaborators—does not set a trap for them [I Cor. 7:35]. He could, with the

pope's confirmation dispense them from the vow of chastity, with a total and perpetual reinstatement to the lay state. If we took this course, the doctrine of celibacy would no longer divide the Orient and the Occident. This practice would not diminish the value of celibacy but on the contrary would purify it, set hearts at peace, and increase vocations. . . .

The human and psychological problems could be confided to the congregation mentioned by Archbishop Garrone so that the following matters could be studied in depth: integration of personality, value and application of tests, suitability of methods of psychological investigation, discord between the biological and psychological evolution of sex, and the signs of maturing at puberty. . . .

Perhaps we should even use temporary vows, for example, at the time of taking minor orders.

What the speaker was asking for in sum was a psychological reversal of present attitudes. He did not ask that married men be ordained, but he clearly hoped that all who have valid psychological reasons for being dispensed will be able to obtain such dispensation normally through a return to the lay state.

The Church already does this, it might be said (although canon law does not provide for cases of psychological disturbance). But Bishop Méndez Arceo does not want this to be granted as an absolutely exceptional favor; rather, it should be a normal solution to evident difficulties. In the beginning, a young man would not promise celibacy without due reflection, which still often happens. Thus a youthful mistake, if there turned out to be one, could be adjusted in the course of formation. In this way a situation which is scarcely healthy could be made so. There are two problems here: modern psychological methods are practically speaking not used in most seminaries; and dispensations from celibacy are rarely granted to priests returned to the lay state, and then only after interminable delays.

. . . Nor an Ineluctable Renunciation It is as though the Church was afraid she would have a hemorrhage if she acted humanely toward those who think they chose the wrong vocation. Bishop Méndez Arceo said this quite plainly. In the official press communiqué we find the following: "We must not underestimate the conscience that is sometimes obsessed with the irrevocable character of sacerdotal celibacy; rather than a danger, knowledge of the possibility of a return to the lay state with a dispensation from celibacy could be a cause of peace and greater fidelity."

Bishop Reuss called for better education in the seminaries so that future priests would know what they are giving up by taking a vow of celibacy. "Celibacy," he said, "is too often considered an ineluctable renunciation in order to receive the priesthood rather than as a generous and unreserved gift to God, the Church, and the world."

Christian Education and Catholic Schools

The assembly then went on to the new schema of propositions on "Christian Education," which evolved from a previous schema on Catholic schools. The change in title shows that Vatican II refuses to consider the Catholic school as the only possible solution, and that it is aware of the large fact that many young Catholics are in secular schools.

Proposition 7 says that "Parents have the duty to send their children to Catholic schools *insofar as this is possible*" (italics added).

Five Fathers have already intervened on this schema.

Cardinal Spellman of New York said, "The question of tax support for Catholic schools is a very delicate one. Parents and not the Church should ask for such support."

Coadjutor Bishop Elchinger of Strasbourg commented:

> The schema was drawn up at a time when the authors were not aware of schema 13, or of the schemas on the lay apostolate, ecumenism, religious liberty, and non-Christians. Accordingly, it must be radically revised. . . .
> Let us emphasize that no one possesses the child—not the Church or the state or even the parents. The Gospel is against all totalitarianism. . . . If Christian education is not profoundly reformed, the Council will not be able to produce its fruits.

Archbishop Gouyon of Rennes felt that "Taking into account the necessity of a postconciliar commission, which the reporter mentioned, this schema could be approved." Cardinal Ritter shared this opinion.

Archbishop John P. Cody of New Orleans flatly contradicted Bishop Elchinger: "This schema has the advantage of taking all the others into consideration."

NOVEMBER 19

Not All Christian Education Depends on Catholic Schools, Says Bishop Henríquez Jiménez

A surprise awaited the Council fathers. It has importance in the light of what has gone on at Vatican II these past few days: the text of the preliminary explanatory note to chapter 3 of the schema *De Ecclesia* will not form part of the final schema, which was distributed to the Council Fathers on Wednesday. This schema will be promulgated by the Pope on Saturday.

The reason for this was probably that since the note has served its purpose, it has become useless. This is a good thing, because its genesis was rather extraconciliar.

This morning, Thursday, the Fathers will decide in a special ballot whether or not to vote immediately on the declaration on religious liberty. Some 200 bishops have complained to the Council presidency that they have not had the necessary time stipulated by the regulations to study the text. It was returned to them only forty-eight hours ago. Might this be considered a delaying action to put off the voting on this text until the fourth session?

Undoubtedly. But it is a valid request since the new version of this document is appreciably different from the previous one. Yet in all likelihood the majority will want to vote on it immediately.

A report follows on some of the nine interventions of the day. The reader will note the emphasis on such capital problems as freedom of inquiry, which is one of the constants of Vatican II, as well as Bishop Henríquez Jiménez's remarks on religious education and the Catholic school.

This intervention necessarily reminds one of the ideas of Canon Colomb, the creator and victim of the "progressive catechism" in France, who was ordered by the Curia to suspend his activities in 1957.

Liberty, the Sine Qua Non *of Progress*   Cardinal Léger of Montreal urged:

> Let us return this schema to the commission to be radically re-worked. My opinion is based on an analysis of concrete circumstances. We do not have enough time here for a serious study of this important schema. This text is the charter of secondary and higher education in the Church; and there is something of a crisis in higher education within the Church. . . .
>
> The problem of freedom of scientific inquiry is also involved; if freedom in the sacred sciences is not fully assured, irreparable harm could result. This is the *sine qua non* of all progress. . . .
>
> The role of the magisterium is to intervene as a last resort, but research must be encouraged and stimulated in the beginning.

Most Catholic Children Are Outside Our Schools   Auxiliary Bishop Henríquez Jiménez of Caracas also criticized the text:

This schema is too conservative and too canonical. Above all, it says nothing important about the necessary *aggiornamento* of Catholic schools. All or nearly all of Christian education is made to depend on Catholic schools. This is a serious mistake, in spite of the good intentions of the schema's authors. . . .

Let us look the facts in the face: most Catholic children are outside of Catholic schools. This is a situation we should reflect on. The Church has a duty to give a Christian education to all the baptized, without exception, and not only pupils in Catholic schools. . . .

Catholic schools are not an end in themselves but a means. If they are not fulfilling their role or fulfilling it inadequately, we have the right to reform them. Nor let us forget that the number of young Catholics in nondenominational schools will increase in the future. This is the law of our times. . . .

It is a fact that the Church is often absent from state schools, for they are looked upon as rivals. But the Church must be present and bear witness to Christ everywhere. . . .

In the name of 112 bishops, I conclude:

Let us not hesitate to engage in self-criticism.

Let us strive to promote teaching vocations for state schools.

Let us not consider everything in terms of the school, but let us think of the different means of social communication [press, radio, television, and so on].

More and more priests should be used for the work of evangelization properly speaking; laymen should be responsible for teaching in our schools.

Let us emphasize the quality and not the quantity of Catholic schools.

Let us see to it that they radiate a true testimony to the evangelical spirit.

Archbishop Nicolas Schneiders of Makassar, Indonesia, said, "The influence of the state on Catholic schools is good. Let us found schools according to the conditions laid down by the state. . . . It is a fact that students in Catholic schools are losing their faith in great numbers. Why is this? Let us face up to this lamentable situation."

Bishop Nguyen Van Hien of Dalat, Vietnam, suggested, "Let us develop Catholic schools in the missions. Let us establish normal schools. Let us have our best educators teach catechism. Too often the contrary is the case."

Coadjutor Bishop Pablo Muñoz Vega of Quito, Ecuador, said, "The Church should consider all schools and not just Catholic ones, for most of our young people are not in Catholic schools. The Church has a strict duty to these young people."

Archbishop Helder Câmara Outlines
the Governmental Structures of the Church of Tomorrow

Archbishop Helder Câmara of Recife, who has been mentioned frequently in these reports, is one of the most striking personalities at the Council. His modesty constrains him not to intervene in the aula, but his influence is immense. Everyone in Rome knows he is the bishop of the poor *par excellence*. He gave his episcopal palace to them, and they are at home in it. The Pope has a special affection for him; more, Paul VI has told the Archbishop personally how much he has been influenced by him. That is why anything this prelate says deserves the closest attention. The Dutch Documentation Center was crowded on Wednesday for a final conference before the end of the session. The secretary general of the Latin American Episcopal Conference (CELAM) spoke on a subject that is sometimes wrongly considered taboo on the pretext that it is under the Pope's jurisdiction: the reform of the Curia. He spoke as he always does, directly and boldly.

"The Holy Father," he said, "gladly listens to sincere people without ulterior motives who speak their mind to him. He himself always spoke to his superiors—and he worked with popes—objectively, respectfully, and filially, yet openly and courageously."

Here is what Archbishop Helder Câmara said. His opinions are representative of what a large number of Fathers think.

The Senate

The senate to be formed about the pope would be composed of cardinals, patriarchs, and one bishop elected by each episcopal conference for a period of ten years.

This senate would be responsible for the election of the pope, and would collaborate on programs for future councils, which might be held every ten years [the equivalent of a former century, given the acceleration of history].

An executive senate, which should be chosen for two years by the pope and whose membership should not be more than 10 percent of the plenary senate, would be convoked at least once a year to examine the problems of the Church in the world.

The Curia "The Curia would become an executive body at the service of not only the pope but the senate and postconciliar commissions as well." The Curia, the speaker continued, is composed of men who are prisoners of the past. In the future it could include new ministries and perhaps a special service, which the Archbishop defined in these words: it would be "a very sensitive antenna capable of detecting the constraints suffered throughout the world by people of whatever race, political condition, religious faith, ideological position. . . . This antenna, without prejudice to its proper function, would do everything in its power to publicize sufferings that might otherwise be anonymous and defenseless."

The postconciliar commissions:

The bishops would like to participate in the choice of these commissions, as the Pope permitted us to do for the conciliar commissions. The postconciliar commissions would no longer be under the jurisdiction of the Roman Curia. To give a specific example, we would like the Pope to invite the postconciliar commission for the reform of canon law to present its general plan to the Council Fathers, if possible during the recess.

Postconciliar commissions would prepare the application of the conciliar schemas in a legislative capacity while the senate, under the direction of the pope, would have the power of judgment and decision.

Episcopal conferences: "They would have an enormous responsibility. They should avoid apostolic atomization, which would be a sin against the collective pastorate, as well as episcopalism."

Successors of the Apostles and Successors of the Prophets   The presbyterium and the adult laity:

It is easy to speak in praise of the presbyterium and the promotion of laymen but difficult to accept in practice, truly to utilize both the presbyterium and the adult laity, masculine and feminine. It is true that the grace of the Council has worked miracles among us bishops. Real conversions have occurred, and we will perhaps be surprised to find that the priests and laity of our dioceses will want to see us as we were in the Council.

The successors of the prophets: "We bishops are too proud of being successors of the apostles. But who are the successors of the prophets and the doctors? This is a theological problem that must be investigated. The theologians in particular must be given a more explicit place in the Church.

And when we speak of theologians, we must also include laymen, both men and women."

Missionary renewal: "The Church in our day has missionary possibilities that would make men like Père Lebbe rejoice. Colonialism, let us hope, is forever dead and there will therefore no longer be any danger of confusion between the presence of colonizers and the presence of missionaries."

May the Council Canonize John XXIII   After speaking of the reform of religious orders (notably of the vow of poverty) and practical additions to schema 13, Archbishop Helder Câmara concluded:

> I would like to suggest three gestures that might be both a résumé and a symbol of the new structures of the Church of Vatican II.
>
> First, let there be a general pardon for all personal censures, and an announcement that the Index will be revised.
>
> Second, as a response to the Holy Father's gesture of donating his tiara for the benefit of the poor, let the bishops make a gesture. Let them make a *real* gesture.
>
> If it is felt that the hour for the response is not next Saturday's session, then let us bishops return to our dioceses with our memories fixed on the gesture of the Pope, who is going to India as a missionary and pilgrim. The Pope could have given money, or even a cross or a ring. By choosing to give his tiara, he intended to substantiate his speech to the Roman patriarchate and emphasize that the Church no longer is or has any desire to be a temporal power.
>
> Third, as a response to the expectation of the world, let us canonize, on the last day of the Council, Pope John, the prophet of new structures, the friend of God and of men.

NOVEMBER 20

The Pope Refuses a Request for a Vote on the Declaration on Religious Liberty During This Session

Thursday was a rough day for collegiality but perhaps in the final analysis a good one. The Council learned that the vote on religious liberty has been postponed until the next session, even though the Fathers had been told the day before that they would be consulted on this point. The bishops had the opportunity to exercise their young strength collectively in the course of by far the most dramatic session of the whole Council.

We would have to go back into history—to preceding councils—to find such a tense situation and such vigorous expressions of discontent as marked yesterday's session. A petition to the Pope immediately began circulating in their ranks. But Paul VI let it be known this morning that he had no intention of heeding the petition. Cardinal Tisserant said in Paul's name, "The Pope has received all the pressing demands for an immediate vote on the declaration on religious liberty. Nevertheless, the decision taken by the Council presidency is in conformity with the regulations. This important document will be discussed next year, during the fourth session, if possible before the others."

This declaration put an end to the hopes that had arisen.

Basically, the decision by the presidency was a wise one. It would not be fitting for the Council to vote at the last minute on a text which has been completely redrafted and which, moreover, can still be appreciably improved, in the opinion of highly qualified experts. But the method used —statement and counterstatement—was deplorable and rightly aroused the assembly's anger.

Here are the facts, in ascending order of importance.

1. First of all, as is well known, the Pope has decided he will proclaim Mary the "mother of the Church" Saturday afternoon at the Church of St. Mary Major, as he had said last year that he would do in response to the pressing desires of many bishops, notably Cardinal Wyszynski. In itself this is of no great importance, even though it evidently displeases the Protestants. But in so doing, Paul VI showed his back to the Council, which has carefully and persistently avoided this expression in the chapter on the Virgin. (The final vote, on the amendments to the chapter, was taken yesterday, with the results of 2,096 for to 23 against.) The Pope's words, therefore, whether we like it or not, will constitute a kind of disavowal of the Council on this minor point.

The Preliminary Explanatory Note 2. Archbishop Felici noted that the general vote on the schema *De Ecclesia*, as well as the vote for promulgation in the public session tomorrow, should be understood in the light of the famous explanatory note which was added, as we know, by order of "superior authority." But since this note did not appear in the booklet containing the complete schema recently distributed to the Fathers, it seemed that the note would not figure in the official acts of the Council. But that was not the case. This is a second basis for tension between the Pope and the Council. (The results of the general vote yesterday on the schema *De Ecclesia* were 2,134 for and 10 against, with 1 null ballot.)

3. After announcing that the assembly would vote today on the whole of the schema on ecumenism, Archbishop Felici read a list of changes

that "superior authority" had ordered in the text. Cardinal Bea was advised of these modifications, and in themselves they are quite minor. This one is the most regrettable: the first version stated that "Protestants find God, who speaks to them in the Bible," while the second version reads, "Protestants seek God insofar as he speaks to them in Scripture."

Of course, the Protestants reacted, especially Oscar Cullmann, who found this change in the worst possible taste. But what is more serious, the Pope practically forced Cardinal Bea to accept the changes. Thus the Council's liberty of expression was somewhat curtailed.

4. We now come to the most serious event, which provoked the anger and disarray of Thursday's session. On Wednesday, as we reported, Archbishop Felici had informed the Fathers that they would vote the next day on the suitability of an immediate vote on the schema on religious liberty. The question to settle was whether the Fathers wanted to get this text through since it had been awaited so long, or whether they thought it better to take more time to study a document that had been returned to them only the day before with appreciable differences from the previous version.

At the root of the presidency's decision (which passed by six votes against five—Cardinal Liénart, the twelfth member, is absent from Rome) was a petition that had been engineered principally by Bishop Carli of Segni, Archbishop Marcel Lefebvre of the Holy Spirit fathers, and Cardinal Larraona of the Curia. Citing article 30, paragraph 2 of the regulations, they asked that the vote on a schema so different from the first version be deferred.*

Then—and this was the incident that set off the explosion—Cardinal Tisserant said on Thursday morning:

> Several Fathers have expressed the opinion that they have not had enough time to study this new and differently structured text. . . . In these circumstances the Council presidency deemed it pointless to proceed with the preliminary vote announced yesterday. The Council presidency thinks that there is no need to ask the Fathers to vote on this decision. Consequently, the Fathers will have until January 31, 1965, to send in their observation on this declaration.

At these words, disorder broke out in the aula, and it continued intermittently all morning. The bishops could not but take this authoritarian decision badly; it took away their right, which had been recognized the day before, to make this decision themselves. The great majority of the

---

* The text of article 30, paragraph 2, reads: "The schemas must be distributed to the Fathers in such wise that they will have time to confer, to form a mature judgment, and to make a decision in regard to the voting."

Fathers were very unhappy to be so suddenly and apparently groundlessly treated like children, incapable of judging for themselves on a matter that concerned them directly. Bishops could be heard in the aula exclaiming, "We've been betrayed!" Another, an American, is credited with saying, "The bastards!"

The argument that the Fathers have not had enough time to examine the declaration on religious liberty is hardly sound. In fact, the text could have been printed and distributed much sooner than it was. These delays were very likely intended by those opposed to the schema to retard the vote.

How far was the Pope involved in this incident? Not greatly, as far as we can determine. He seems rather to have been a buffer between the four moderators, who were for an immediate vote, and the twelve presidents of the Council, who were divided. The absence of Cardinal Liénart was obviously cruelly felt.

As soon as Archbishop Felici finished speaking, there was a great commotion in the aula. Bishops rushed back and forth between the presidents and moderators. Fathers left their seats and huddled in small groups. Archbishop Felici was immediately called to the phone by the Pope, who follows the proceedings on a closed-circuit television screen. Cardinal Meyer, one of the twelve presidents, was pale with emotion, and Cardinals Ritter and Léger left to request an audience with the Pope.

A hastily drawn up petition circulated among the Fathers, and 450 signatures were gathered in less than half an hour. This was the text: "Most Holy Father, with reverence we ask Your Holiness urgently, more urgently, most urgently that the vote on the declaration on religious liberty be effected before the end of this session so that we will not lose the trust of the world, both Christian and non-Christian."

Calm was not restored until Bishop de Smedt of Bruges presented the report on the religious liberty schema. By reason of its great interest, we shall give a detailed analysis of his report. The Fathers who were standing or scattered throughout the aula spontaneously drew near the speaker to indicate their deep regard for him.

In a voice that trembled with emotion, Bishop de Smedt presented his report, interrupted now and again by applause. When he had finished, the Council broke into a fit of excitement. Applause was intense and prolonged, very like the applause for an encore in a concert hall. Two moderators joined in the applause although this is rigorously forbidden. There was never such a spectacle in St. Peter's. Bishops rose from their seats to applaud more loudly. Others shouted, "Bravo!"

We learned during the day that the Pope had declined an invitation to act directly as arbiter in the conflict. We also learned that during a

meeting of the Sacred College which was held toward the end of the
afternoon in the Pope's presence (the purpose of this meeting was to
instruct the cardinals on the reform of the Curia), one of the members
of the Sacred College, a German, arose and addressed the Pope: "In
the name of 1,500 bishops, I ask that there be a vote on religious liberty
before the end of the session!"

Bishop de Smedt's Report on the Religious Liberty Text

Here is the substance of the report presented by Bishop de Smedt, a
member of the Secretariat for Promoting Christian Unity, on the declaration on religious liberty. Clear and precise, the exposé, particularly the
last part, made a strong impression on the Fathers. This is the first time
it has been so clearly stated that truth must not be imposed by human
force and that the Church, when she is in difficulty, should avoid "seeking refuge in civil powers." This purified conception of the Church
will not fail to have repercussions in countries where Catholicism is more
or less considered as the state religion.

It is also to be noted that religious liberty is no longer based, as it
was in the first schema, on man's divine vocation but on a universally
accepted concept: the dignity of the human person.

> The present text differs greatly from the original version. We
> have carefully examined all the amendments, both written and oral,
> and in the light of these have made changes which do not affect the
> substance of the schema but modify its structure and style. The
> present text is clearer, more prudent, and better thought out.
>
> It responds to the question posed by the modern world: what
> does the Church think of the way religious liberty is most often
> respected and expressed in the social and civil life of our times?
>
> The Church is truly challenged on this point. You have observed
> how widely everything we have said here at the Council on religious
> liberty for the past two years has been studied in universities, at
> meetings of learned societies, in different Christian organizations,
> in magazines and newspapers.
>
> The whole world awaits a response. . . .
>
> I. We have paid special heed to the following observations:
>
> 1. We have taken into consideration the comments of those
> who accept the doctrine expounded in the first version but think
> that the arguments and expressions used were not clear enough,
> prudent enough, or complete enough.

2. Some Fathers also thought that they could not in conscience approve this doctrine. In such circumstances, great attention must be paid to the way the question is presented.

In our present declaration, we do not directly treat of the juridical relations between church and state, the theological problem of the right and mission of the Church to proclaim the Gospel, the moral doctrine that must be adopted with regard to non-Christians, or the arguments that make tolerance morally obligatory.

Our schema treats of the religious liberty that is due to the human person in the juridical organization of society and the city.

We affirm: no man can be the object of coercion on the part of other men. This is not the state's right or society's function. Neither has any business directing or obligating the human person in the domain of religion. Religious liberty is in fact required by human dignity itself.

Religion is above the competence of the republic. The state must recognize and defend freedom of religion for all its citizens. It must neither direct nor hinder religion.

This regulation is legitimate, and can be demanded by all men as a true right which corresponds with the principles of human reason and is altogether necessary to safeguard the personal dignity of everyone in modern society.

II. A great difficulty is the limitation imposed on religious liberty by the state. Here are the norms set down:

1. *From the moral point of view.* Man, in the external exercise of his liberty, does not have the right to violate the rights of others or to dispense with his duties toward other people.

2. *From a juridical point of view.* Man is not allowed to exercise any act of religion that would be a serious threat to public order. The civil powers must prudently supervise the exercise of religious manifestations, if this seems really necessary to safeguard public order.

III. This declaration does not at all incline toward positivism, nor can it be accused of opportunism. It simply takes into account the fact that over the centuries and with the progress of culture, human dignity has been considered more in depth and affirmed with its proper rights. . . .

Today when it is said that man must enjoy religious liberty, the Church agrees. It is a sign of progress.

The Church rejoices that she no longer has to recall the condemnations of the nineteenth century against civil powers which tried to introduce rationalism and laicism.

The Church Rejects All Coercion

IV. Does the affirmation of religious liberty contradict the rights of the Church?

The authority of the Church is willed by Christ. It is an instrument of grace. But what could be more worthy than for the Church to exercise her function independently? That is the question here, so that the Church rejects all coaction. Religious liberty properly understood does not necessarily exclude certain privileges or a certain official recognition from the state. What is excluded is the inability of a citizen freely to exercise the religion of his choice in those places where one religion is privileged. The Church asks the same thing whether she is a minority or a majority. . . .

Religious liberty is in fact the greatest of gifts. It flows from a sincere and genuine faith. Confidence in Christ's Church should never depend on secular power. [Applause.]

In her difficulties, the Church should not seek refuge in the arms of civil powers. [Applause.]

The best witness the Church can bear to the truth of the Gospel is to show herself so confident in the strength of truth that she has no need of drawing support from civil powers. [Applause.]

We must find our protection as well as the strength of the faithful in God. With good reason did a Council Father say here, "Civil leaders must abstain from all interference in religious problems." Their duty is to open the gates to the truth in which they believe so that the Church can freely teach her doctrine of salvation.

Do not fear to see error conquered by truth. Truth is a gift of God and a manifestation of his divine majesty. It can conquer every human weakness, all narrowmindedness, and even all malice.

Truth will triumph not by human force but by the arms of justice.

The Six Ages of the Church

Paul VI's gesture of giving his tiara away continues to provide theologians with food for thought. Father Gauthier, who founded a workers' cooperative in Nazareth and formerly taught at the seminary in Dijon, offers these reflections:

We can discern six stages in the history of the Church, he said:

1. The catacombs.
2. The Constantinian era, when the emperor made bishops the equivalent of senators.

3. The age of the barbarians, when the collapse of social structures forced bishops to exercise temporal power.

4. When public powers regained control, neither the bishops nor the popes were willing to give up their temporal prerogatives. Thus the quarrels between popes and princes, Canossa, and so forth.

5. Garibaldi took the Papal States by force of arms and thus relieved the Church of her temporal power. But the Church was reluctant to renounce it. The pontifical tiara was retained, and Vatican I defined the dogma of papal infallibility as a special compensation.

6. With Paul VI and Vatican II the Church is in the process of relinquishing the last vestiges of temporal power in favor of a more spiritual mission. The age of an evangelical and poor Church is beginning.

The Declaration on Hinduism, Buddhism, Islam, Judaism, and Other Non-Christian Religions

"These religions reflect a ray of truth which enlightens all men."

The new text of the declaration on Jews and non-Christians was approved this morning, Friday, by a vote of 1,651 *placet*, 99 *non placet*, and 242 *placet juxta modum*. It is entitled, "On the Relation of the Church to Non-Christian Religions." It includes five sections: (1) a preamble, (2) Hinduism, Buddhism, and other religions, (3) the Muslims, (4) the Jews, and (5) against discrimination.

The last section represents a total victory for the Secretariat for Promoting Christian Unity, directed by Cardinal Bea. The new text once again includes the word *persecution* (which is considered stronger than *vexatio*), and the persecutions are situated temporally. Also, allusion is made to "deicide" to affirm that this qualifier can in no way be applied to the Jewish people.

Here is the text in its entirety.

1. *Preamble* In our time, when day by day mankind is being drawn closer together, and the ties between different peoples are becoming stronger, the Church examines more closely her relationship to non-Christian religions. In her task of promoting unity and love among men, indeed among nations, she considers above all in this declaration what men have in common and what draws them to fellowship.

One is the community of all peoples, one their origin, for God made the whole human race to live over the face of the earth. One also is their final goal, God. His providence, his manifestations of goodness, his saving design extend to all men, until that time when the elect will be united in the Holy City, the city ablaze with the glory of God, where the nations will walk in his light.

Men expect from the various religions answers to the unsolved riddles of the human condition, which today, even as in former times, deeply stir the hearts of men: What is man? What is the meaning, the aim of our life? What is moral good, what sin? Whence suffering and what purpose does it serve? Which is the road to true happiness? What are death, judgment, and retribution after death? What, finally, is that ultimate, inexpressible mystery which encompasses our existence: whence do we come and where are we going?

2. *Hinduism and Buddhism* From ancient times down to the present, there is found among various peoples a certain perception of that hidden power which hovers over the course of things and over the events of human history; at times indeed some have come to the recognition of a Supreme Being, or even of a Father. This perception and recognition penetrates their lives with a profound religious sense.

Religions, however, that are bound up with an advanced culture have struggled to answer the same questions by means of more refined concepts and a more developed language. Thus in Hinduism, men contemplate the divine mystery and express it through an inexhaustible abundance of myths and through searching philosophical inquiry. They seek freedom from the anguish of our human condition through ascetical practices or profound meditation or a flight to God with love and trust.

Again, Buddhism, in its various forms, realizes the radical insufficiency of this changeable world; it teaches a way by which men, in a devout and confident spirit, may be able either to acquire the state of perfect liberation or attain, by their own efforts or through higher help, supreme illumination. Likewise, other religions found everywhere try to counter the restlessness of the human heart, each in its own manner, by proposing "ways," comprising teachings, rules of life, and sacred rites.

The Catholic Church rejects nothing that is true and holy in these religions. She regards with sincere reverence those ways of conduct and of life, those precepts and teachings which, though differing in many aspects from the ones she holds and sets forth, nonetheless often reflect a ray of that truth which enlightens all men. Indeed, she proclaims, and must ever proclaim Christ, "the way, the truth and the life" (John 14:6), in whom men may find the fullness of religious life, in whom God has reconciled all things to himself.

The Church, therefore, exhorts her sons, that through dialogue and collaboration with the followers of other religions, carried out with prudence and love and in witness to the Christian faith and life, they recognize, preserve, and promote the good things, spiritual and moral, as well as those sociocultural values found among these men.

3. *The Muslims*   The Church also regards with esteem the Muslims. They adore the one God, living and subsisting in himself, merciful and all powerful, the creator of heaven and earth, who has spoken to men; they take pains to submit wholeheartedly to even his inscrutable decrees, just as Abraham, with whom the faith of Islam takes pleasure in linking itself, submitted to God. Though they do not acknowledge Jesus as God, they revere him as a prophet. They also honor Mary, his virgin mother; at times they even call on her with devotion. In addition, they await the day of judgment when God will render their deserts to all those who have been raised up from the dead. Finally, they value the moral life and worship God especially through prayer, almsgiving, and fasting.

Since in the course of centuries not a few quarrels and hostilities have arisen between Christian and Muslims, this sacred Synod urges all to forget the past and to work sincerely for mutual understanding and to preserve as well as to promote together for the benefit of all mankind social justice and moral welfare, as well as peace and freedom.

4. *The Jews*   As this sacred Synod searches into the mystery of the Church, it remembers the bond that spiritually ties the people of the New Covenant to Abraham's stock.

Thus, the Church of Christ acknowledges that, according to God's saving design, the beginnings of her faith and her election are found already among the patriarchs, Moses, and the prophets. She professes that all who believe in Christ—Abraham's sons according to faith (Gal. 3:7)—are included in the same patriarch's call, and likewise that the salvation of the Church is mysteriously foreshadowed by the chosen people's exodus from the land of bondage. The Church, therefore, cannot forget that she received the revelation of the Old Testament through the people with whom God, in his inexpressible mercy, concluded the Ancient Covenant. Nor can she forget that she draws sustenance from the root of that well-cultivated olive tree onto which have been grafted the wild shoots, the Gentiles (Rom. 11:17–24). Indeed, the Church believes that by his cross Christ, Our Peace, reconciled Jews and Gentiles, making both one in himself (Eph. 2:14–16).

The Church keeps ever in mind the words of the Apostle about his kinsmen: "Theirs is the sonship and the glory and the covenants and the law and the worship and the promises; theirs are the fathers and from them is Christ according to the flesh" (Rom. 9:4–5), the Son of the Virgin Mary. She also recalls that the apostles, the Church's mainstay and pillars, as well as most of the early disciples who proclaimed Christ's Gospel to the world, sprang from the Jewish people.

As Holy Scripture testifies (Luke 19:44), Jerusalem did not recognize the time of her visitation, nor did the Jews, in large number, accept the Gospel; indeed, not a few opposed its spreading (Rom. 11:28). Nevertheless, God holds the Jews most dear because of their fathers; he does not repent of the gifts he makes or of the calls he issues—such is the witness of the Apostle (Rom. 11:28–29). In company with the prophets and the same Apostle, the Church awaits that day, known to God alone, on which all peoples will address the Lord in a single voice and "serve him shoulder to shoulder." (Soph. 3:9; Isa. 66:23; Ps. 65:4; Rom. 11:11–32).

Since the spiritual patrimony common to Christians and Jews is thus so great, this sacred synod wants to foster and recommend that mutual understanding and respect which is the fruit, above all, of biblical and theological studies as well as of fraternal dialogues.

True, the Jewish authorities and those who followed their lead pressed for the death of Christ (John 19:6), still, what happened in his passion cannot be charged against all the Jews, without distinction, then alive, nor against the Jews of today. Although the Church is the new people of God, the Jews should not be presented as rejected or accursed by God, as if this followed from the Holy Scriptures. All should see to it, then, that in catechetical work or in the preaching of the word of God they do not teach anything that does not conform with the truth of the Gospel and the spirit of Christ.

Furthermore, in her rejection of every persecution against any man, the Church, mindful of the patrimony she shares with the Jews, and moved not by political reasons but by the Gospel's spiritual love, decries hatred, persecutions, displays of anti-Semitism, directed against Jews at any time by anyone.

Besides, as the Church has always held and holds now, Christ underwent his passion and death freely, because of the sins of men and out of infinite love, in order that all may reach salvation. It is therefore the burden of the Church's preaching to proclaim the cross of Christ as the sign of God's all-embracing love and as the fountain from which every grace flows.

5. *Against Discrimination*   We cannot truly call on God, the Father of all, if we refuse to treat in a brotherly way any man, created as he is in the image of God. Man's relation to God the Father and his relation to men his brothers are so linked together that Scripture says, "He who does not love does not know God" (I John 4:8).

No foundation therefore remains for any theory or practice that leads to discrimination between man and man or people and people, so far as their human dignity and the rights flowing from it are concerned.

The Church reproves, as foreign to the mind of Christ, any discrimination against men or harassment of them because of their race, color, condition of life, or religion. On the contrary, following in the footsteps of the holy Apostles Peter and Paul, this sacred synod ardently implores the Christian faithful to "maintain good fellowship among the nations" (I Pet. 2:12), and if possible, to live for their part in peace with all men (Rom. 12:18), so that they may truly be sons of the Father who is in heaven (Matt. 5:45).

NOVEMBER 21

The Decision on the Religious Liberty Text Stands

There is calm now after the storm. But it is shadowed by a certain sadness, for Vatican II did not achieve a total victory on Friday, the last general congregation of the third session.

Supported by the Pope, the presidency did not retract its decision of the day before. This was undoubtedly correct from a procedural point of view. It also protected the freedom of the Fathers against the haste of those who would perhaps have asked for a definitive vote on the declaration on religious liberty.

But psychologically speaking, given the unhappy effects of the counterstatement, it is regrettable that some clear means was not found for the assembly to register at least an indicative vote to show that Vatican II considers religious liberty a highly precious value.

We must also bear in mind the background of this affair: the hundred or so Fathers who are hostile to this declaration and who were at the bottom of the incident on Thursday are craftier, more circumspect, and better placed that the others, who make up 95 percent of the bishops at the Council. This minority attempted—and temporarily succeeded—a final delaying maneuver which has fooled no one.

Once again the Church of yesterday plotted against the Church of today. The minority might have made themselves even more unpopular than they are. But they are too weak—and they know it—to do more than delay an inevitable result for a few months. The declaration on religious liberty, which will be adopted during the fourth session, will be better than the present schema; there is no doubt about it. At Vatican II, time has always worked against those hostile to *aggiornamento*.

But the Pope's prestige suffered. In an effort to bolster the minority, Paul VI only succeeded in displeasing the majority.

In one sense the exhibition on November 19, however painful it was, is salutary. It will help enlighten the Pope on the real psychology of the episcopal college and will prompt him to undertake a renewal of his administration without too much delay.

The Fathers Hope Paul VI Will Soon Publish a Motu Proprio Renewing Legislation on Mixed Marriages

The Council ended its work on Friday with various votes. Principally, it voted on the famous declaration on the Jews and non-Christians after a fresh effort, quickly aborted, on the part of the minority to postpone it until the fourth session. It is to be noted that 185 out of 1,969 Fathers voted against paragraph 4, concerning the Jews. The congregation also finished examination of the schema of the votum on marriage (and mixed marriages in particular), which we reported on earlier.

Cardinal Gilroy, Archbishop of Sydney, Australia, took the floor on Thursday and was the first to speak on the text. He was in general agreement with it but made the following five suggestions:

1. The impediment of "disparity of cult" in the case of a marriage between a Catholic and a non-Christian should no longer make the marriage invalid but only illicit.
2. The votum should say more clearly that the Church is firmly against mixed marriages between a Catholic and a non-Catholic Christian.
3. In mixed marriages, the promises which the schema says the Catholic partner must make should be done in the presence of the pastor and with the approval of the non-Catholic partner.
4. Canonical form should no longer be a condition of validity for mixed marriages; but in this case, the Catholic party should not be admitted

to the sacraments until he has promised the stipulated commitments before the bishop or pastor.

5. In mixed marriages, the celebration of mass should be permitted but not prescribed.

Most of the thirteen speakers on Friday were happy with the schema because it is in harmony with the double exigencies of ecumenism and religious liberty.

Cardinal Ruffini of Palermo criticized a number of passages in the text and said that the scourge of divorce and its pernicious effects should be explicitly spoken of.

Cardinal Döpfner of Munich was satisfied with the text but hoped that "The Pope will publish a motu proprio on the legislation of mixed marriages as soon as possible, taking the observations of the Fathers into consideration."

Cardinal Ritter of St. Louis was also happy with the votum. It is, he said, "wise and prudent with respect to 'canonical form,' which is neither abolished nor inflexibly retained."

Auxiliary Bishop John M. Fearns of New York, who spoke in the name of Cardinal Spellman and 100 bishops, thought that the schema had "gaps, blunders, and sometimes contradictions which would justify a total redrafting by the competent commission."

Re-emphasizing Marriage and Baptism Bishop Renard of Versailles stated:

> Just as many parents without faith ask to have their children baptized, so too many of the baptized ask for a religious marriage even though they don't believe, uniquely for reasons of convenience or because of their families. Under these conditions, marriage in the Church loses its sacred character. The result is anguish for priests and a degree of scandal for the faithful. . . .
>
> Let us re-emphasize the sacred character of marriage and baptism. Some priests demand a long preparation and sometimes refuse to perform religious marriages. Others agree to it readily without caring too much whether the couple believe or not.
>
> Both think they are acting correctly; but we must try to see clearly in this matter. The code of canon law makes no provision for this present situation. The new code should confront it directly. . . . I propose that episcopal conferences study this serious problem, and that a postconciliar commission take action in terms of the results of our investigation. Likewise for baptism.

Canon Haubtmann has told us that the French episcopacy is currently greatly preoccupied by this question.

Bishop Renard continued, "I propose obligatory preparation for marriage. The length of this could vary. Moreover, I suggest that the commission for the reform of canon law permit a priest to dispense with the presence of a witness when it is a case of marriage between Catholics who are obviously estranged from the Church."

Bishop François Charrière of Lausanne, Geneva, and Fribourg remarked, "Things have changed considerably with regard to mixed marriages."

Bishop Paul Yoshigoro Taguchi of Osaka, Japan, suggested, "Let us try to harmonize civil and religious legislation, particularly in what concerns the impediments to marriage. Mixed marriages have an apostolic value."

Marriages in the Sacristy Are like Funerals Archbishop Heenan of Westminster made a humorous intervention: "This schema deserves to be written in gold. I am particularly grateful to the experts who worked on it." The compliment was in order since Archbishop Heenan had excoriated the experts who worked on schema 13. "Mixed marriages in the sacristy are like funerals. Why shouldn't they be performed in the church? My experience proves that in England mixed marriages are not dangerous. . . . The promises demanded of the non-Catholic partner are a highly useless vexation. Let us recommend that he simply follow his conscience."

Archbishop Conway of Armagh, Ireland, spoke in the name of eighty bishops:

> I myself was born of a mixed marriage, and in my country there are many such marriages. Given the negative results of mixed marriages, it would be better to forbid them rather than encourage them. Even the separated brethren, for similar reasons, discourage mixed marriages. . . . It is not a problem which can be resolved by diplomacy or reciprocal politeness. It must be studied attentively and prudently, without falling into the kind of naïve optimism that would tempt us to legislate hastily. No assembly would act in this way when dealing with so serious a problem. It demands lengthy and mature reflection.

Love and Marriage Archbishop Djajasepoetra of Djakarta, Indonesia, criticized the text:

This schema is too juridical and too Occidental. . . . You in the West find it quite natural for those in love to marry. But you are the exceptions if humanity as a whole is considered. Our people love one another because they are married, which is not quite the same thing. We differ from Westerners in that our marriages are contracted not out of love but by the will of the parents or tribe. We marry to continue the race.

As we noted elsewhere, a large majority approved the schema of propositions on marriage and hope they will be given to the Pope, together with the observations of the Fathers, so he can personally make some decisions in this matter.

Finally, Archbishop Felici read some extracts from letters written by bishops who could not attend the Council. Then the secretary general said:

All were invited, but the sad religious conditions prevailing in some countries made it impossible for some to participate personally in our work. These bishops assure us that they are present in spirit and through their prayers and sufferings. They may rest assured that the Council has also prayed for them and for the liberty of the Church in their countries. The mass to be concelebrated by the Pope on Saturday will be offered for their intention so that God may help all those who are oppressed and so that, because of their sufferings, peace will be established in the world more quickly.

The hundred and twenty-seventh general congregation of Vatican II, the last of the third session, terminated with that invocation.

NOVEMBER 21

We Do Not Diminish Our Authority
When We Affirm Yours, Paul VI Declares

Concelebration has become a habit, and people are no longer surprised to see the Pope and the bishops saying mass about the same altar.

St. Peter's Basilica was a scene of splendor on Saturday. The bishops wore their white liturgical miters. The Pope entered the Basilica on a small-model *sedia* without his tiara, and was carried in the customary procession. He thus confirmed his renunciation of the insignia of temporal power.

After the mass, Archbishop Felici successively read the Dogmatic

Constitution on the Church, the Decree on Eastern Catholic Churches, and the Decree on Ecumenism. These were then submitted to the Fathers for an adoptive vote. The results for the three texts were, respectively, 2,110 *placet* against 39 *non placet*, 2,110 *placet* against 14 *non placet*, and 2,137 *placet* against 11 *non placet*. After these results were announced, Paul VI solemnly promulgated the three documents, using the new "collegial" formula that was inaugurated last year.

The Pope's speech was widely anticipated. We know that during the meeting of the Sacred College with the Pope last Thursday, the most important subject discussed was the reform of the Curia, a logical consequence of the new Constitution on the Church, which recognizes collegiality. Cardinal Roberti of the Curia, president of the Pontifical Commission for the Reform of the Curia and a veteran canonist who enjoys the Pope's confidence by reason of his great probity, had given a general report on the reform of the Church's governmental structures. He suggested, for example, that the Holy Office have its own prefect in the future, like the other Roman congregations. In the past the Pope fulfilled this function, an arrangement that had serious disadvantages.

The Pope waited until the last moment to write his speech. On Saturday morning the translators still did not have the text, which is normally distributed twenty-four hours in advance.

Many were struck by the beginning of the Pope's address, when he spoke of "the weak and fallible men that we are, but convinced that we are able to pronounce truths that admit neither contradiction nor termination." The Pope thus implicitly recognized his own fallibility in ordinary circumstances, and used the word *we*, to signify the episcopal body.

Paul VI alluded to "the search for the meaning of human life and history in order to give them their beauty and their unity in Christ alone." He added that "the doctrinal work of Vatican I has been accomplished, which is to say, perfected. The mystery of the Church was explored, and . . . we can henceforward enjoy a better understanding of divine thought on the mystical body."

The Pope mentioned the exacting effort made "to discover the innermost significance and substantial truth with respect to the constitutional law of the Church." He continued:

> It remains true that the most difficult and most memorable part of this spiritual effort concerned the doctrine on the episcopacy. We should like briefly to make our thoughts known to you.
>
> We shall simply say that we are satisfied that this doctrine was treated with sufficient breadth of study and discussion and with

great clarity in its conclusions. This had to be done to complete Vatican I. It was an opportune time to do it because of the modern evolution of theological studies, . . . because of the problems which the government of the Church encounters in the daily experience of its pastoral activity, and because of the expectation of many bishops to have a doctrine which directly concerns them clarified. That was also the way to handle the question.

Thus we do not hesitate, taking into account the explanations given and the terms used for the theological qualification which the Council intends to give this doctrine, we do not hesitate, with the help of God, to promulgate the present constitution *De Ecclesia.*

It would seem to us that we could make no better commentary than to say that this promulgation really changes nothing in traditional doctrine. What Christ wills, we will. What was remains. What the Church has taught for centuries we also teach. The only difference is that what has in the past only been lived is now expressly declared; what was uncertain has been clarified; what was meditated upon, discussed, and in part controverted has now reached a serene formulation.

. . . Nothing is cause for greater rejoicing than to see proclaimed the dignity of all our brothers and sons who comprise the holy people of God. . . .

How happy we are to see the constitution proclaim the dignity of our brothers in the episcopacy . . . and recognize their powers. . . . We have noted with satisfaction the manner in which the document we have just promulgated recognizes, completely and repeatedly, the first, unique, and universal charge confided by Christ to Peter and transmitted through him to his successors, the Roman pontiffs, with whose authority we, although unworthy, are today invested.

We cannot fail to be pleased by this, not for the prestige this responsibility gives to our timid and ungreedy person, but rather for the honor given to the word of Christ, for the firm cohesion with tradition and the magisterium of the Church, for the guarantee assured of the unity of the Church herself and the efficacious and sure harmony given to her government.

It was very important that such recognition of the prerogatives of the sovereign pontiff be explicitly expressed at this time when episcopal authority in the Church is being declared, so that this authority will be seen not in contrast but in just and constitutional agreement with that of the vicar of Christ, the head of the episcopal college. . . .

And it is this intimate and essential relation that makes a unified assembly of the episcopacy, that finds in the successor of Peter, not different and extraneous, but rather its center and head. This in turn makes us anxious to laud your prerogatives with ours, to rejoice in their exaltation, to vindicate their excellence, so as to integrate them with our own.

We are not afraid of diminishing our authority when we affirm and celebrate yours; on the contrary, we feel ourselves stronger through fraternal union with you, more capable of guiding the universal Church knowing that each one of you is striving for the same end."

The Pope then spoke of practical applications:

It is not easy to foresee all the practical developments that this doctrinal clarification will involve; but it is easy to foresee that they will be fruitful in deeper spiritual understanding and canonical measures. . . . The application of the decrees will necessitate many postconciliar commissions in which the collaboration of the episcopacy will be indispensable. And likewise, as questions of a general nature come up, we will have more opportunity than at present to convoke and consult certain among you, chosen according to the circumstances, to have about us the comfort of your presence, the help of your experience, the support of your advice and the assistance of your authority.

Paul VI then spoke of the reform of the Curia:

This will be all the more useful in that the reorganization of the Roman Curia, which is being actively studied, will be able to profit by the experience of diocesan bishops, thus integrating within its framework, already so efficacious in its faithful service, prelates coming from different countries and bringing the help of their wisdom and charity.

Perhaps this multiplication of studies will entail some practical difficulties, for collective action is more complicated than individual action. But if it better serves the monarchical and hierarchical character of the Church and strengthens our effort with your collaboration, we shall with prudence and charity overcome the obstacles. . . .

The Pope enumerated the repercussions that this new state of affairs will have on the faithful.

He also addressed the observers delegated by the non-Catholic churches. He greeted them respectfully and thanked them for their diligence.

"We hope," he added, "that this doctrine of the Church will be received with favor and benevolence by the Christian brethren still separated from us."

The Pope also expressed his desire for closer communion between the different churches in the future, so that one day, "if it please God," these Churches will unite.

Then Paul VI said that he believed it "opportune" to declare "the maternal function which the Virgin exercises on the Christian people," and proclaimed that the Virgin is "the most blessed mother of the Church."

The Marian theme comprised almost exactly one-half of the Pope's speech, a fact which in such a circumstance disagreeably surprised the Protestant observers and even many bishops, at least those who are ecumenically sensitive. At the last moment and for reasons that are not yet clear, Paul VI decided to deliver his speech on the Virgin, which he had prepared for the postconciliar ceremony at St. Mary Major in the afternoon, at the closing session.

Paul VI made special mention of the Fatima shrine. Rather remarkable, really.

At the end of the ceremony, the Pope pronounced cloture, and said that the fourth session would be the last of the Council.

The Contradictions of Vatican II

The third and next to last act of Vatican II ended in a curious atmosphere of mingled quiet irritation and deep satisfaction. It is as though the ancient and yet still young bark of the Church has set sail for the high seas but with a nostalgic look back from time to time at the shores she has quitted.

Much has been accomplished during this truly arduous session. All the themes on the agenda were treated. Strong words were spoken about some of them; realistic decisions were made on others. And yet so much dissatisfaction! Though generally gentle, the hand of authority was at times severe. The Pope's great and anxious desire to reconcile the irreconcilable and to bridge the chasm between a handful of immobilists and the other Fathers forced him to take initiatives that were controversial. The final revisions of the schema on ecumenism—one of the most revolutionary of all—were criticized by so well-informed an expert as Father Laurentin as "unfriendly" to non-Catholic Christians. The decree on the Oriental Churches, which was questionable to begin with, is still torn between the Catholic Uniates, to whom it was addressed, and the Orthodox it hoped to reach. It satisfied neither group and is not of a nature to improve relations with the Orient, which itself is entangled in internal contradictions, as the recent Orthodox conference in Rhodes showed.

Again, from the ecumenical point of view, Paul VI's long *fervorino* on Mary in his closing speech was disconcerting, which is the least one can say under the circumstances.

The Constitution on the Church, which history will consider the backbone of Vatican II because it is the indispensable counterbalance to Vatican I, is itself not above reproach although only five Fathers voted against it, thanks to Paul VI's efforts. On this occasion at least, his diplomatic ability was rewarded.

Finally, the bitter crisis over the vote on religious liberty disclosed both the keen sensitivities of the Council and the tenacity of a few integralists, who are adept at finding reasons for delaying decisions.

So much for the negative. But the positive is more important. One cannot but notice and even be astonished at the progress made by a Church that has until now been buried in its traditions. In three years four centuries have been bridged. The reform of the Curia, the urgency of which becomes more apparent with each passing day, will definitely be undertaken; contact has been restored with non-Catholic Christians; the real problems of the secular world have been considered.

Vatican II has clearly sided with the ideals of universal fraternity, equality, and liberty. The Jews have been unequivocally rehabilitated. Pastors have carried the day over jurists, the New Testament over the Old. A theology of evolution and human progress has been begun. Tomorrow the blunders and manipulations will be forgotten. The new impetus given will be remembered.

Vatican II has virtually ended. There is no doubt that the fourth and last session, which will be short, will ratify the schemas that are to be improved during the recess. The strength of the Council is indomitable. Its progress may be slowed slightly, but it cannot be stopped. In the final analysis, Vatican II is more a departure point than an end point. Like Jerusalem and Bombay.

Paul VI Is a True Transitional Pope

The Church has begun a double revolution, theological and pastoral. The Sacred College thought they were electing a transitional pope in Angelo Roncalli. They were wrong. John XXIII was a prophetic pope who in less than two years initiated a radical change in the Church.

John XXIII is dead. Paul VI is carrying on his work and must bring Vatican II to a good end. This council has already brought the Church much farther than was generally expected. The Holy Spirit, as the liturgy sings, is a disturber. This expression may never have found a better application than today.

The real transitional pope is Paul VI, who holds the two ends of the chain firmly in his fragile hands: the tradition of yesterday, from which nothing that is good can be abandoned, and the tradition of tomorrow, which is being born under our eyes. This is perhaps Paul VI's secret: his desire to proceed cautiously, not to break the Church in two, not to let a triumphant majority and an embattled minority rise up against one another.

A pope is primarily an arbiter. Paul VI, who like every man has his good qualities and his defects—he is not a superman—intends to play this role to the hilt, even at the risk of sometimes being misunderstood by both the majority and the minority. His loneliness is that of any man who carries heavy responsibilities. It is his lot never to be able to confide completely in anybody and to have to seek balance in the midst of daily contradictions. Hence his changes of tact, his scruples, his hesitations which are aggravated by his temperament, and his sudden symbolic gestures which open the door on the future: Jerusalem, his giving away his tiara, his pilgrimage to the poor of Bombay. These are gestures that are worthy of Paul VI's great intelligence and spirituality.

Those about him have difficulty understanding this and wonder in all good faith why he doesn't go first to Lourdes or Fatima before going to the Gentiles.

From the Abstract to the Concrete There is a double pastoral and theological lesson in the session that has just ended.

The Church is beginning to think she should stop legislating for a harem and begin speaking a language accessible to all. The first quality of an educator is to be understood. The *Ecclesia magistra* owes it to herself to revise her catechisms and her moral treatises in order to focus more on the concrete situations in which men struggle. This does not mean that she has to abandon her principles, but only that she must refuse to neglect men. She now wishes to work for the sake of flesh and blood beings, not bloodless theses. To go from the abstract to the concrete is a sign of doctrinal maturity.

On the other hand, the Church intends henceforward to ground faith in events more than in the intellect, to use "the sense of history" (this formerly suspect expression has been used by Paul VI) as a basis more than principles. In sum, she intends to renounce ideologies and systems in favor of life. A living being is organized; he has his internal unity, his proper frame of references; he believes by assimilating. He is not a scaffolding of ideas but a center of relations. This natural and supernatural center the Church finds in Christ and his Gospel before she makes a herbarium of them in Scholastic treatises. Christianity is, we have too much forgotten, a historical, existential, and personalist religion.

If the Church wishes to be the leaven in the dough as asked by her founder, then it is important that the leaven be in and not outside of the dough. Otherwise, the leaven is useless and may mold. This is precisely the cause of the divorce between the Church and the world.

As the Church draws closer to the world, without mixing in it (for then what purpose would she serve?), she will abandon the "tools of power" which have been her besetting temptation since the time of Constantine, that is, the fourth century, for the "tools of weakness" in the Gospel. She will no longer impose but propose; no longer command in an authoritarian manner but serve; no longer speak so much about the rights of the Church as of her responsibilities.

This revolution can be understood by all men of good will. For precisely, they have often seen only the hierarchical face of the Church. It deceives them because it is so much like that of the great of this world.

FOURTH SESSION

September—December, 1965

Vatican II Nears Completion

SEPTEMBER II

Achievements

Vatican II, which began three years ago, is nearing completion. Unless something unexpected happens, the fourth and last session, which opens on September 14, should end before Christmas. The 2,000 and more Council Fathers will then return to their dioceses, aware of having contributed to one of the most decisive steps in the Roman Church's long history.

The impression sometimes prevails that the work of Vatican II is finished as of now and that a series of reforms are about to get under way. This is not entirely false; an irrepressible movement of renewal has been launched. The role of the fourth session will be more to place the final seal on the conciliar documents than to innovate. Like a rotating beacon, the Council has already illuminated the horizon. Its work is now principally to work out details and perfect. Then the decisions taken must be implemented in acts. This is a delicate and long-range task; it involves problems which the Pope, with the aid of his future episcopal council, will have to resolve gradually.

Vatican II will not be fully successful until the Church of tomorrow has the courage—and she will need it—to follow in practice what has been defined in theory.

Vatican II's agenda is again very heavy. Many documents must still be revised, a work which the cumbersome conciliar machinery necessarily—and sometimes beneficially—slows down. If the session has few surprises, although the opposition is still active, it will certainly be studious, especially for the commissions. The discussions will be crowded, particularly on religious liberty and schema 13. The many votes will undoubtedly make this session appear duller than preceding ones.

It is difficult to measure the results which Vatican II has so far achieved. But one distinction can be made. There is, on the one hand, the presence of a new spirit, observable as much among the faithful, Protestants, and even unbelievers who are following the evolution in Rome as among the hierarchy. There are, on the other hand, the promulgated texts. Easy as it may be to analyze these documents, it remains difficult to form a clear idea of the mentality that is taking shape. There are contrasting reactions: joy, fear, confidence, skepticism, submission, reticence. We shall have to wait until things are more settled before we can make any definitive judgment, although the great majority of those interested in the Council are happy with the way it is going.

The Council has discussed and partially amended all the prepared documents. But it has completed work on only six out of fifteen texts. This is not much if we consider that the Council is three-quarters over, that it has held 128 general congregations and voted 277 times.

Paul VI has promulgated all the decrees and constitutions; John XXIII, who died after the first session, saw no tangible results of his initiative. Arranging these texts in increasing order of importance rather than chronologically, we might draw up the following list.

1. *The Decree on the Instruments of Social Communication* (1,960 yes, 164 no). It is a slapdash text, unworthy of a twentieth-century council, containing only a few evasive lines on the right to information. Even though it recommends the presence of the Church in the vastly important field of communications, it is full of banalities.

2. *The Decree on the Eastern Catholic Churches* (2,110 yes, 39 no). This document provoked lively criticism until the last moment. It was judged unsatisfactory by both the Orientals and the Latins; the very principle of its existence was questionable. In terms of the great progress of the ecumenical spirit in the Catholic Church, it is an outdated document. But the imbroglio of the Uniate Churches and their dissensions combined with a certain lack of understanding on the part of the Latin Fathers prevented the elaboration of a better text.

Nonetheless, this decree is an undeniable step forward. It guarantees the basis of the status of the patriarchs; to some extent it restores *communication in sacris* (reciprocal participation in the sacraments and worship) with the Orthodox (who suuffered from a recent ruling that was altogether anachronistic), and it honors certain Oriental traditions that were formerly held suspect.

3. *The Constitution on the Sacred Liturgy* (2,147 yes, 4 no). The Roman liturgy has been frozen for the past four centuries: since before the Council of Trent it has developed "artificially, in a vacuum, with a proliferation of gestures and rituals," in the words of Auxiliary Bishop Jenny of Cambrai.

Structural reforms were necessary, and likewise the liturgy needed to be freed of a kind of uniformity that was readily confused with a necessary unity. The conciliar constitution "is not a collection of little formulas for the reform of small details"; it is a kind of blueprint giving general directives and doctrinal themes which are aimed at profoundly renewing an outmoded mentality. The text embraces the reform of the mass and breviary, the sacraments, the liturgical year, and sacred music and art. Several years will be required to put all the recommended changes into practice.

Wider use of the vernacular, an issue which caused so much ink to flow, is only a secondary aspect of a much broader renewal. This innovation, we might note, satisfies 91 percent of the faithful;* the noise of those opposed is far out of proportion to their numbers.

Another capital reform: the institution of episcopal conferences and postconciliar commissions, which will be in large part the authors of renewal. The exclusive privilege of the specialized Sacred Roman congregation has ended; it will be reorganized by the Pope after the reform of the Curia.

The Central Work 4. *The Dogmatic Constitution on the Church* (2,151 yes, 5 no) is the central work of Vatican II. One of its essential aims was to complete the work of Vatican I, interrupted by the war of 1870. It deals principally with power in the Church. It strongly reaffirms the absolute sovereignty and infallibility of the pope. But the document also stresses the collegial essence of the Church, founded on Peter and the eleven other apostles. Consequently, the episcopal college—whose inseparable head is the pope—enjoys full and infallible power. This was already known in theory, but in practice it had been forgotten. The renewed accent on this doctrine will enable the bishops to be permanently associated with the central government of the Church and will give greater autonomy to national episcopal conferences.

The constitution contains many other dispositions. It defines the Church as "the people of God," as democratic a definition as possible in an essentially hierarchical society; it recognizes the "freedom of action" of laymen as well as their responsibility to make their opinions known, and it encourages them to take the initiative; it approves the diaconate as a permanent state, provided the deacons are chosen among mature men, even though they are married; it stresses the pilgrim, eschatological, and mystical Church rather than the juridical institution; finally, it comes out against a "false amplification" of the Marian cult and every form of "narrowness."

5. *The Decree on Ecumenism* (2,137 yes, 11 no) is of considerable

* See *Le Monde*, February 25, 1965.

psychological importance. It definitively lays to rest the negative, scornful, and unfriendly attitude which Rome has always had toward non-Catholic churches. This document is the most striking proof of the revolution brought about in a brief three years in the sociological mentality of the Church. It renders homage to the authentically Christian values of the "separated" communities; it recommends a study of the doctrine of these churches; it condemns any polemical spirit; it prescribes an "interior conversion" for all Christians without exception; it asks pardon for offenses committed; it exhorts the faithful "to live a purer evangelical life."

Even after Paul VI's last-minute changes, this text remains strikingly dynamic.* It is viewed as such by Protestants, who have called it, through the instrumentality of the World Council of Churches, "one of the most rich in promise" despite the many problems that still have to be resolved.

6. *The votum on mixed marriages* has been transmitted to the Pope, as stipulated in a resolution voted (1,592 yes, 427 no) November 20, 1964. On the practical level it has an importance comparable with that of the schema on religious liberty. The dispositions of the votum, without being satisfactory—for they could not be—would flatten some of the present obstacles. Separated Christians await this schema with understandable impatience. Paul VI has not yet followed up on the votum. This is surprising, but in all likelihood he will do so in the near future. The faithful will judge the value of ecumenical renewal by this text.

A Heavy Agenda

The agenda of the fourth session has an evident advantage over previous agendas: it is known beforehand, for the double reason that the list of schemas has been completed for some time and, since this session is the last, the Fathers will have to finish all the items on it.

Three clearly distinct tasks, corresponding with the various stages of development of the schemas, may be outlined.

1. In the first place, the four texts which are considered new will have to be discussed in the general congregations: religious liberty, the

* In *Civiltà Cattolica* of February 20, 1965, Father Caprile, S.J., explained how and why the Pope thought it necessary to make these changes. The commission for revising this document had rejected—as was its right—certain of the *modi* suggested by the minority. Paul VI retained some of these in the hope of obtaining a quasi-unanimous approval in the voting. *Documentation Catholique* of April 4 translated and published this "inspired" article, which also gives important details on other interventions by Paul VI during the third session.

Church in the world (schema 13), the missions, and priests. Later these schemas will have to be voted on and amended.

2. Second, the Fathers will have to vote immediately on two schemas which have already been discussed and then examine the amendments proposed by those who voted *juxta modi*. They are the schemas on revelation and on the apostolate of the laity.

3. Third, the Council will have to examine the amendments already requested and vote (singly yes or no and without discussion) on five schemas: those on bishops, non-Christian religions (the declaration on the Jews), religious, seminaries, and Christian education.

The commissions will have to work hard to revise the four schemas in the first category in so short a time (the Council is to close before Christmas). The general congregations will begin discussion on them immediately. When this is done, the essence of the conciliar work will take place in the commissions behind closed doors. Plenary sessions will then be much rarer and will be devoted principally to voting.

The Declaration on the Jews Three subjects are of prime interest: schema 13, religious liberty, and the declaration on the Jews.

There was a good deal of artificial agitation over the latter declaration during the recess, provoked by imaginative news whose origin is very difficult to determine. It was said repeatedly that the draft had been watered down owing to Arab pressure; that the term *deicide*, a word used to exonerate the Jewish people of this charge, had been deleted; that the persecutions condemned by the text were no longer mentioned. An English paper (*The Observer* of June 20, 1965) went so far as to say that the declaration had been simply taken off the agenda by order of the Coordinating Commission.

These fears seem utterly inane (Cardinal Liénart went to bat against "propagators of stupidities" in Lille on May 18) for the basic reason that last November 20 the conciliar assembly voted favorably on this schema by 1,651 to 99 against with 242 *placet juxta modi*.

It is unthinkable that the majority, who succeeded in having the expression *deicide* reinserted after it was deleted from the second version, would tolerate yet another decision. Moreover, the Council and the Pope fully intend to behave fairly by standing firm. The efforts of the Arab states to gain satisfaction hit a stone wall, whatever the customary subtle protocol and courtesy of Vatican diplomacy implied. Cardinal Bea, as is well known, is not the kind of man to accept the dismissal of a work on which he has concentrated all his authority and his fidelity to the mind of John XXIII.

The fact remains that 242 Fathers voted *placet juxta modi* and that the competent commission is the judge of how the *modi* should be taken into account without contradicting the will of the majority. According to the information given by Canon Haubtmann in his press conference of June 30, the declaration remains intact. Purely formal modifications have been introduced and an effort has been made to clarify the word *deicide* further in answer to criticisms.

The declaration on the Jews, now an integral part of the declaration on non-Christian religions, will therefore in all likelihood undergo its final vote without surprises and, let us recall, without discussion, since discussion on the text is closed. This vote will have considerable psychological repercussions throughout the world. However, anti-Semitic prejudice is so deeply rooted that miracles must not be expected from a text. Other no less catogerical statements in the past history of the Church have not been spectacularly successful.

Religious Liberty and the Opposition The fourth session will get to work immediately on the schema on religious liberty, thus putting an end —better late than never—to the mishaps that have befallen this declaration. The postponement of the vote in November, 1964, took place under circumstances which—on the surface at least—were more disputed than disputable: though the opposition had something to do with it, the Council's administration—and this was unfortunately realized only later —had found the request of the minority was upheld by the regulations. The delay was therefore perfectly regular.* Moreover, the delay permitted the Fathers to study the new schema at leisure and improve a text which, although the result of a laborious compromise, was not entirely free of faults. The subject matter, after all, is extremely complex, and the writers were also faced with the difficult task of not appearing to contradict past teachings of the magisterium.

The present schema—the seventh draft—unambiguously states man's duty to conform his life with what he believes in good faith to be the truth. God alone is the judge of this good faith, and the state has no means of understanding it. Freedom of conscience, which is vigorously asserted, implies the risk of error. The state can only prohibit certain abuses, acting according to juridical norms, for the sake of protecting public peace and morals. The schema relies heavily on New Testament references. Christ never forced anyone to follow him; *this is the real religious basis of religious liberty*.

* One of the annoying consequences of this postponement was the delay of a report on the status of Protestants in Spain which had been prepared over a long period of time.

Is this to say that this much-polished text will no longer be controversial? Nothing could be less certain.

The minority are more resolved than ever to fight, their many failures notwithstanding. Archbishop Marcel Lefebvre, Superior General of the Holy Spirit Fathers, spoke last June 6 of the "inconceivable schema" on religious liberty and compared it with a "Trojan horse" sent against the traditional magisterium of the Church.*

Another example of the opposition's activity: an organization has come into existence called Coetus Internationalis Patrum, or International Assembly of Fathers, supported by Cardinals Ruffini, Siri, and Santos with Archbishop de Proença Sigaud of Brazil as secretary. It has prepared a counterschema in conformity with article 33, paragraph 7, of the Council regulations. This article states, "If general discussion of a schema has already begun, a general statement on this schema or an organic body of amendments may be addressed to the moderator by at least fifty Fathers. The moderator will then submit it to the Coordinating Commission, which will determine what action is to be taken."

But the membership of Coetus is too weak for the action to have any chance of success. At most it can delay progress and furnish additional arguments to the enemies of the Church who think that Rome is still a hotbed of intolerance. Finally, Paul VI has shown during the recess that he favors the present schema. This should rally the support of most of the Fathers.

The Extremists The disputes among the bishops are parallel, although more seriously and with more violent expression, at the level of the Church-taught: the priests and laity.

Most of Paul VI's recent speeches indicate a persistent uneasiness because of certain disagreements in the Church that have their origin in conciliar *aggiornamento*. It is clear that some, fiercely opposed to the least reform, oppose every effort at adaptation and have only derision for those who nonetheless have an informed understanding of the changes that must be made. It is equally clear that others, although small in number, lose all sense of measure and practicability in their impatience to see the Church renewed. They tend to forget that the Church is for all and that it is important not to disturb the mass of the faithful unduly. They do not respect the continuity between the past and present, necessary for any highly hierarchized society, and indulge in formulating dangerous speculations and minimizing certain dogmas.

---

* See *Itinéraires*, July–August, 1965. It is difficult to determine whether Archbishop Lefebvre's criticisms were directed against the schema presented last November or the present text.

Both lack a sense of the obedience that the hiararchy rightly claim. The first group, more Catholic than the pope and the bishops, fancy themselves in their ignorance to be the guardians of orthodoxy. The second group think they are good Catholics if they take the letter of instructions lightly but respect the spirit.

These disturbances are aggravated by the fact that conciliar renewal has come so late. Moreover, they are inherent in all transitional periods when it is not clear where the reforms that have been launched are leading.

We must also bear in mind that ecclesiastical authorities have been too accustomed to passive obedience from priests and laymen. Today the art of persuasion and dialogue must replace authoritarianism. Each party will benefit by this, especially in a community that bases itself on a Gospel which makes a constant appeal to an inner religion.

In the present state of affairs, schema 13 will necessarily provoke divisions within the Church. It recalls that the transcendence of faith allows for diverse opinions, and that liberty is necessary in "doubtful" matters and charity in everything. It exhorts Catholics never to forget that whatever happens, what unites them is more important than what divides them. It quotes Christ's words: "By this will all men know you are my disciples, if you have love for one another."

These sensible proposals are timely. They come just after a certain French periodical, in a joust that was more spectacular than intelligent, accused a renowned theologian of being a "murderer of the faith" and the present general of the Jesuits of having "scandalous" ideas.

Schema 13: The "Crowning" of the Council

The principal feature of the fourth session will be schema 13, "On the Church in the Modern World." In his closing speech for the third session, Paul VI said it would "crown the work of the Council," and hence he gave the lie to criticisms directed againt the very principle of the schema. The Pope thus made his the hopes this schema has inspired in the Catholic laity, who would have found the labors of Vatican II markedly incomplete without schema 13.

The Church is not in fact self-sufficient. Since she defines herself as the leaven in the bread, the concerns of the world must also be hers. A Church that refused to be interested in them would have no understanding of secular realities. She would become a ghetto, and as such would be unfaithful to the Gospel, which reveals a Christ attentive to the spiritual and material needs of his contemporaries. The time has passed when a council could be exclusively concerned with the internal problems of the Church. Didn't John XXIII want Vatican II to be an essentially pastoral council? That is why the arguments of those in favor of schema 13 prevailed in the end. True, temporal questions are not directly within the Church's competency; neoclericalism must be guarded against. But if the Church is not of the world, she is in a world that was created by God and judged good, as Genesis says.

Schema 13 made a timid entrance at the third session; it was sometimes rumored that it would not be put on the agenda at all. Archbishop Felici, secretary general of the Council, provoked an incident by declaring that the schema's appendixes (on the person in society, marriage, culture, economic and social life, and peace and solidarity among men) were "altogether private" in character. He was a bit quick deciding that they would not arouse the Council's sense of responsibility, and he later had to correct himself. In the present version and by order of Cardinal Cicognani, who is both president of the Coordinating Commission and Secretary of State, the substance of the appendixes has been incorporated in the new text of the schema. This is an important change. It constitutes one more defeat for the minority—a secondary point—and, more significantly, it shows that the Church wishes to be officially concerned with the "burning questions" of the day. It marks the end of a kind of ecclesial withdrawal which prompted the Marxists to say that religion is the opium of the people because it was interested only in eternal life.

Schema 13 is defined, and this is another important point, as a "constitution." To date the Council has voted on only two constitutions, those on the liturgy and on the Church; the other pronouncements are decrees. Schema 13 will thus be the third constitution, and it will be "pastoral" rather than "doctrinal." (The fourth and last constitution will be the schema on revelation.) By making this decision, the Coordinating Commission intended to give the schema a maximum of importance. Those who wanted this text to be merely an encyclical or a message from the Council were not heeded. Vatican II will go down in history as the council of the Church *ad extra*, to use Cardinal Suenens' expression; a Council open to human problems.

The Original Text in French   It is interesting to note that the original text of schema 13 was in French. All the Fathers received this version accompanied by an official Latin translation. In addition, it was published in Italian, English, German, and Spanish. These different translations, carefully harmonized, will be distributed to the Fathers when they arrive in Rome. It is the first time that a conciliar text has been translated into several languages.

The fact that schema 13 was first composed in French contributes to the clarity and modernity of the text. The phrasing is graceful, the formulas are often happy, and the progression of thought is generally well marked. It is very easy to read, though the text could be more concise and coherent. The document comprises at least 100 pages in a large format.

Most of the theologians had hoped this text would be addressed to Christians. Their advice was not followed since the majority of Fathers, in their pastoral concern, were not of this opinion. Schema 13 will therefore be addressed to all men without exception. This is an appreciable innovation which *Pacem in terris* has made possible.

The present text is the fourth version (the first was presented to the Coordinating Commission by Cardinal Suenens in 1963). It is based on the third version, which the Fathers discussed from October 20 to November 10, 1964, in the general congregations. The new editors had to consider written interventions as well as those made orally in the aula. In all, this documentation covers 1,030 pages. This imposing bulk constitutes the best proof that Vatican II is not taking the schema lightly as some feared it would a year ago. Yet the new text will doubtless be criticized for reflecting too strongly the spirit of its authors, who are mostly Westerners, although Archbishop Zoa of Cameroun and Monsignor Satoshi from Japan have worked on it recently. The commissions were also helped by laymen and by women as well. The latter, it is said, were responsible for suppressing the expression "advancement of women." It was judged inadequate.

Schema 13 is centered on man, a perspective which by itself makes the document original. It posits the basis of a Christian anthropology, an essential part of modern theology. It expounds at length on communitarian values, on socialization and the evolutional character of society, the meaning of liberty, the respect due to man, and the necessity of abolishing all forms of discrimination based on sex, race, religion, and so forth. It denounces the damage wrought by individualistic ethics, recalls the victories of men and the autonomy of terrestrial realities, and renders glory to God. It asserts the importance of study and explicitly regrets that in past centuries the Church took positions opposed to reasonable scientific research. It notes that Christ, the alpha and omega, has sanctified all of creation, even matter, and draws the whole universe to himself. The cosmos is said to be bound up with the fate of man, and the earth is in some sense associated with the mystery of the redemption. The Church is called the sacrament of the unity of the whole human race, and Christ, according to Paul VI's beautiful expression, "is the focal point of the aspirations of history and civilization."

A second part is consecrated to particular points: marriage, culture, economic and social life, political life, and peace.

Schema 13 covers a broad range of specific consequences of the respect due the human person. Not only does it explicitly speak out against euthanasia, torture, prostitution, and the sale of children, but it censures those who neglect the rules of health and even the traffic code, and thus through indifference endanger the lives of others.

Conjugal Love Little is said about marriage, and that in a noticeably ecclesiastical style. But the accent is placed on the interpersonal love of the couple, and it is specified that marriage is not a simple means of pro-creation. There is a suggestive sentence which states that when conjugal intimacy is interrupted, fidelity may be endangered. But these points are not developed at any great length; the document says that the laws of conjugal life must be respected but does not detail their content.

The style will likely be corrected. Omissions are out of the Council's control since the Pope has reserved the right to conduct a study on birth control. The pontifical commission specially created for this purpose has worked independently of the Council, although it takes the Fathers' interventions into account. It apparently has neither concluded its work nor arrived at any clear-cut conclusions.* Every-thing is in the Pope's hands. At most we may suppose, with the *Semaine Religieuse* from Cardinal (formerly Archbishop) Duval's diocese, that the pontifical conclusions will be included in schema 13. The house organ for the Archdiocese of Algiers thinks this is "likely."

The importance of this subject is obvious. We are still in unex-plored territory, while the world, Christian or not, impatiently waits for the Church to make her position known.

Concerning political life—this chapter is completely new, which is significant—schema 13 indicates that the Church does not place her hope in privileges accorded by civil power, and even that she is ready to renounce some of her legitimately acquired rights if their exercise in any way casts doubt upon the purity of her witness. The various forms of political oppression, which are an obstacle to civil and re-ligious liberties, are vigorously denounced.

* Father de Rietmatten is the secretary of this pontifical commission on birth control, 50 percent of which are married people. The members represent three main schools of thought, which so far have not been able to reach agreement: (1) those who hold to the status quo as defined by Pius XII in 1951, (2) those in favor of using progesterone pills, and (3) those who refuse to make a distinction between artificial and natural means of birth control and think that the morality of conjugal acts should be judged in relation to the overall fertility of the couple.

The section on war was given special attention, too much perhaps, in an effort to take very divergent points of view into account. The concern for legitimate prudence and the distinctions of moralists carried the day over such prophetic interventions as that of Maximos IV Saigh last November 10 (see the report for November 11). In this sense the section is disappointing; but it may be improved during the fourth session.

Nonviolence   There are a few short lines on nonviolence, which is praised. The allusion to Martin Luther King is obvious. The case of conscientious objectors, who refuse to do military service and in time of war refuse to bear arms, is mentioned. The text expresses the desire that they be protected by law. It is clearly stated that no one has the right to give or follow orders which obviously lead to the slaughter of innocent people or prisoners.

The use of the atomic bomb is considered *in itself, objectively,* as a crime against humanity. The schema says that the conscience of mankind cannot be easily forgiven for such acts; it specifies, however, that no judgment whatsoever is passed on any person or upon the value of subjective intentions.

The "balance of terror" is condemned as monstrous; but it is also said that as long as international institutions are unable to guarantee peace, the possession of modern arms for the purpose of turning back an adversary in possession of the same arms cannot be called illegitimate in itself. It seems that the writers of the schema hesitated to state clearly that atomic *retaliation* is illegitimate.

Such as it is, schema 13 goes as far as and perhaps a little farther than *Pacem in terris* on this subject. But it is not free of the contradictions that were reflected in the conciliar interventions of 1964. Forthcoming debates on this chapter—and it contains some excellent and forceful passages—will indicate whether the Fathers will call for a more coherent and more evangelical text or whether they will be satisfied with "realistic" positions and moral exhortations. Many of the faithful, whose sense of the Church is sometimes keener than moralists want to admit, will judge the Church of Vatican II on such central issues as the atomic bomb, contraception, and religious liberty.

Lively Reactions Expected   Whatever the case, schema 13 shows a distinct liberalization of the average ecclesiastical mind. The text commits the teaching Church and sets her on a course of reflection that has been little explored: that we do not know and serve God in spite of or without the world, but through and in the world; we do not know and serve

God and hence men—it is the same commandment—except by means of events that have a providential value. God calls man to transform the world and work for its material and spiritual progress; the Church, in Paul VI's words, must "become historical." This evolutional, concrete, and optimistic vision is capable of gradually renewing the presentation of Christian doctrine and morals.

The schema will obviously provoke lively reactions from the minority. They will be tempted—and not without some reason—to complain that "Teilhardism" is invading the high places of the Church. This will be the last and in some sense the most decisive battle of Vatican II. For in fact schema 13 is the crowning effort of the marching wing of the Church, and it commands the orientation of a real apologetics for modern times. This is the first time that the hierarchical Church has addressed the Christian message to unbelievers. Many believers will benefit by this.

Coadjutor Archbishop Pailler of Rouen has written that "what is said at the Council" must not be confused with "what is said by the Council."* This appropriate remark applies to the defenders of the minority as well as the majority position. In publicizing the conciliar interventions, the Church took the risk of troubling Catholics whose religion is routine; these have difficulty understanding that bishops can be so hesitant and even contradictory about the truth. On the other hand, the Church knew that the advantages outnumbered the disadvantages. Open debate is better than the "velvet curtain" in an age when everything eventually becomes known anyway. Moreover, what is said at the Council is as interesting as what the Council says, although it remains true that only the promulgated texts are an object of faith and commit the Church.

Among the things that not only are being said at the Council but indeed the Council is preparing to say is a proposal that the pope be regularly assisted in governing the Church by an episcopal council.† This is a crucial point for implementing the Council's work at a practical level within the Church. A result of the reinforcement of collegiality, this episcopal council, in addition to episcopal conferences, should give the hierarchical Church of tomorrow an altogether new look. The proposal naturally encounters opposition from the minority. But the majority of the Fathers are confident that Paul VI will bring this innovation to pass. He has practically said as much in various of his speeches.

* *Documentation Catholique,* June 6, 1965.
† During the examination of the schema on the bishops, the Council Fathers adopted this proposal by a vote of 1,582 *placet* and 469 *placet juxta modi* against 15 *non placet.*

The Pope at the United Nations

Paul VI is progressively enlarging the Church's circle of interests. By going to the United Nations for his third journey abroad, he will prompt Christians and non-Christians alike to consider international peace the number one problem of our times.

The Pope is fond of clothing his ideas in images that the masses can understand. His first journey, to Jerusalem, had a strictly mystical and ecumenical meaning. To go to the Holy Land and meet Athenagoras was a clear indication that Rome no longer considered herself the immobile center of Christianity.

In another key, the pilgrimage to Bombay signified a desire to get out of the Christian perimeter of the West and render homage to the great Oriental religions. It was as well an expression of solicitude for the millions who suffer from chronic hunger. Paul VI has already appealed for disarmament and aid to underdeveloped countries. We are at the crossroads of the sacred and the profane.

Now a further step has been taken. Shall we say that the Pope has gone into the political arena? It would be more accurate to say that the Church is playing a greater international role. After *Pacem in terris* (John XXIII), and *Ecclesiam suam* (Paul VI), and as the Council elaborates a pastoral constitution on the modern world, the Church wants to be more present to the immediate needs of mankind.

For long centuries, the papacy—which was itself a temporal power —played a direct political role. The spiritual was contaminated by ambitions that were more or less foreign to religion. In a second phase, roughly since the eighteenth century, the temporal power of the popes weakened and then broke down completely. Then came the age of anti-clericalism and hostile laicism, and religion retreated to the inner forum.

This was a relatively short retreat. For some thirty years now, Christianity has victoriously battled against religious individualism, against an aversion to politics on the part of some of her leaders, and against the stringent separation of the temporal and the spiritual. As a result of doctrinal development and a deepening of social consciousness, religion is once again gradually penetrating the public domain.

But in a totally different way. A more discreet osmosis has replaced the clericalism of former times, which imposed authority from without. The spiritual tends to impregnate the temporal. In the West, at least, there is no longer much difference between the nations with concordats and those where church and state are separated. Furthermore, the 1948

Universal Declaration of Human Rights prohibits any religious discrimination. Brutally rejected by the profane world she formerly tried to hold in tutelage, the Roman Church is today invited to return through the front door.

The interest which the contemporary papacy is taking in international politics seems exempt from ulterior motives. Paul VI is concerned for the common good of humanity that can only develop in peace and on condition that "the third world" of the hungry and miserable be aided.

To interpret his gesture as a kind of neoclericalism would be to misinterpret it. Like the Council, the Pope wants to help an international organization in its difficult and necessary work. The United Nations needs all the help it can get.

SEPTEMBER 13

Paul VI Gives a Clear Warning
in His Encyclical on the Eucharist

The Fathers are arriving in Rome from the four corners of the earth. Some have died since last year (about seventy), but others have replaced them. New dioceses have also been created, especially in mission countries. Yet the number of bishops present at this session could be the smallest yet if the decline in attendance observed since the Council opened continues: 2,381 in 1962, 2,258 in 1963, and 2,170 in 1964.*

The bishops have taken up their Roman lodgings, most of them in religious houses, some in hotels or private homes. On Tuesday morning the tourist traffic in St. Peter's will be displaced by cars transporting the bishops. This democratic means of transportation has succeeded the sumptuous horse-drawn carriages of Vatican I. But the clothing remains the same; the same colors will sing in Tuesday morning's sun (provided, of course, the recent sullen weather improves).

This afternoon, Monday, there was a meeting of the directive bodies of the Council (the presidents, moderators, and Coordinating Commission) to determine last-minute details of the agenda. The controversial schema on religious liberty will be discussed in the first working session, to be held on Wednesday. A counterschema, as we already know, has been prepared by the minority. The Coordinating Commission will have to determine the procedure to be followed in a case of this kind. But more on that later.

* This estimate did not turn out to be correct. There were 2,264 Fathers at the first meeting of the fourth session. All of the figures correspond with the number of those enrolled at the moment each session opened.

Here is a savory detail: the opposition Fathers who have gathered in an organization called Coetus Internationalis Patrum were told to change this hyperbolic title. The Pope told them in no uncertain terms, "There is only one international assembly of Fathers, and that is the Council." Coetus was then replaced by Comitatus Episcopalis Internationalis. But though the label has changed, the mentality hasn't.

Tuesday afternoon, after the opening session in the morning (highlighted by Paul VI's speech), a procession of all the members of the Council will take place between the Basilica of the Holy Cross of Jerusalem and the neighboring Lateran Basilica.

Penance for the Faults of the Church   The Pope has said that this would be a penitential procession. He thus seems to have adopted an idea that gained currency during the first session, principally in Germany: to fight against the temptation to triumphalism, which so solemn an assembly as a council could fall into, some exterior sign should be made of collective penance for the faults committed by the Church.

The faults of the laity who have not always given an example of Christian life; the faults of theologians who have watered down, hardened, or narrowed the presentation of the faith; the faults of the clergy; the faults of the bishops; the faults of the Church as a society, some of which have become engraved in the memories of mankind and have contributed to the rupture of unity (like the Inquisition) or created a breach between science and faith (like the condemnation of Galileo); finally, the faults of the whole world—persecutions, religious or not; wars, the selfishness of affluent countries.

Many Fathers will likely be thinking of the encyclical *Mysterium fidei* during this procession. The encyclical deplores certain theological faults which constitute "a serious danger to the true faith." Commentaries on Paul VI's third encyclical abound in Rome. A document on culture was expected on the occasion of the seventh centenary of Dante's birth. *Mysterium fidei* preceded it.

And not without reason. The Pope intended to give a severe warning about a central point of Catholic doctrine as the fourth session opens. By timing it as he did, a maximum psychological effect will be attained.

We have to go back to Pius XII's *Humani generis* (1950) to find an encyclical that is essentially directed against doctrinal errors. The Dutch noticed that this was the first time an encyclical had been translated into their mother tongue, in addition to the usual languages, by the Secretariat of State. The encyclical is an undeniable warning. It will make the minority happy, and they will exploit it, should the opportunity arise, against the work of modern theologians in general.

Several further remarks might be made about *Mysterium fidei*.

The encyclical begins by mentioning the "abundant fruits" of Vatican II's liturgical renewal. The Pope noted "the sincere joy and eagerness with which the sons of the Church welcomed the conciliar constitution on the liturgy."

The Pope rejoiced that "Many worthwhile works have scrutinized and made known the doctrine of the eucharist, particularly the relationship between this mystery and that of the Church." He added that he approved "the praiseworthy desire" of those who want to investigate the mystery of the eucharist at greater length. Thus, he did not condemn all present-day doctrinal research.

The encyclical says that the faith is "immutable" and must rest "intact," but it also says that "understanding of the faith" should "progress." The Pope adopted Newman's doctrine of "development" and opposed it to evolution insofar as the latter excludes the idea of permanence.

Paul VI did not imprison faith in ancient formulas. But he did solemnly declare that the formulas already chosen by the magisterium express "concepts" that are bound to no culture and no scientific outlook. He specified that "These formulas are intelligible to men of all times and circumstances." Yet he did not say that they were the only possible formulas or the only true ones or even, theoretically speaking, the best. They are so to speak a point of departure and an obligatory norm for any ulterior reflection. This is very important: the encyclical does not condemn research and closes no door on future presentations of the faith which might be developed within the framework of other philosophies— whether present or future, whether Occidental, African, or Oriental. This is the price of the Roman church's catholicity.

Of immediate interest is the fact that Paul VI did not explicitly condemn such expressions as *transsignification* or *transfinalization*. He merely declared that they are not satisfactory.

SEPTEMBER, 1965

In Opening the Last Session of the Council,
Paul VI Announces the Creation of an Episcopal Synod

Here in Rome especially, one understands that the liturgy is primarily a spectacle. A ceremony like the opening of a conciliar session is an incomparably majestic display of color and ritual. Everything is for the eye, and we must admit that such pomp can distract from what is essential in a religious gathering—the collective and individual prayer of the faithful.

The mass was concelebrated by twenty-six bishops and the Pope, the first bishop of the Church. When it was over the conciliar session was officially opened. It began with the solemn enthronement of the Gospel, the ceremony of obedience, the *"Veni creator"* (intoned by Paul VI), and the profession of faith. Then Archbishop Felici, secretary general of the Council, announced that the hundred and twenty-eighth general congregation of Vatican II would begin on Wednesday at 9 o'clock.

The Pope then read his speech in his usual level and deliberate voice that transmitted the concentration of his thought and the strength of his conviction. Once again the Fathers were struck by the lyricism of his remarks and the classic beauty of his rich and harmonious phraseology.

The big news of the day was the Pope's announcement, at the end of his speech, of the creation of an episcopal synod. Such a body has been requested many times by the Fathers. The Pope did not wait until the end of the Council and promulgation of the decree on bishops to take a position. He respected the assembly's wishes and gave the Fathers total satisfaction.

It is important that the majority of members of this synod will be elected by episcopal conferences and not named by the Pope. The Roman Church has finally adopted a system of greater representation. If we dare use the word, she is becoming as democratic as her essentially hierarchical structure permits.

Here in its entirety is the passage relating to the creation of this senate:

> . . . we are happy to make [the announcement] to you of the establishment, in accordance with the wishes of the Council, of an episcopal synod composed of bishops to be chosen for the greater part by the episcopal conferences and approved by us, which will be convened, according to the needs of the Church, by the Roman pontiff for consultation and collaboration when this will seem opportune to us for the general good of the Church. We consider it superfluous to add that this collaboration of the episcopacy is meant to turn out to be of the greatest help to the Holy See and to the whole Church. And in a special way it can be of use in the day-to-day work of the Roman Curia, to which we owe so much gratitude for its effective help. Just as the bishops in their dioceses, so we too always need the Curia for carrying out our apostolic responsibilities. Further details will be brought to the notice of this assembly as soon as possible. We did not wish to deprive ourselves of the honor and pleasure of making this brief announcement to you, in order to give you a further proof of our confidence and brotherly esteem. We are placing this new proposal, which is full of such splendid possibilities, under the protection of Mary Most Holy.

Paul VI also spoke of his trip to the United Nations; he hoped that his voice would speak for all the bishops. "We shall absent ourselves for a short time," the Pope said, "in order to carry to the representatives of the United Nations a message of honor and peace. We would like to believe that our message will have your unanimous support."

A Vocation of Charity Speaking of the totality of the Council's work, the Pope declared:

> The fourth session now begins in the basilica, which is dedicated to the memory of the Apostle Peter, the visible foundation of the Church of Christ. The Catholic hierarchy has expressed, strengthened, and illustrated the bonds which unite it in a loyal and unambiguous communion. Such a communion might seem impossible in view of the diversity of our human origins and the implacable divisions which separate men from one another.

After recalling Saint Paul's words, "For we are God's helpers," the Pope called for "the development in charity" of the Council. The Council, he went on, "has stirred hidden powers within us. It has fired in our souls the spirit of prophecy which is proper to the Church of God. . . It seems that [in this Council] we express to God the world's burden of sorrow, of toil, of miseries, and of spreading errors."

Paul VI then affirmed the communitarian character of the Church in these words:

> . . . we are a people, the people of God, the Catholic Church, a unique society which is at once visible and spiritual. The Council makes us realize more clearly that our Church is a society founded on the unity of faith and on the universality of love.
>
> The search for a perfect and higher form of social living constitutes the fundamental and seemingly insoluble problems of history, even if we think of the endless vicissitudes of Babylon which are being so tragically repeated in our age. But at least in its basic principles, this search has ended for us, although it has in fact been completed only virtually.

The Pope then spoke of "the repeated experience of disillusionment" owing to "strife among men" and of "the irresistible march of nations towards unification." The Church needed "to verify experimentally the unity that makes us all the family and temple of God, the mystical body of Christ." He continued:

> The mandate that flows from the love of Christ, to feed his flock, still continues to exist and is the basis for the existence of this [Apostolic] See, just as it . . . is the basis for the existence of each of your episcopal sees. And today this mandate is affirmed with full awareness and new power. This is what the Council says: the Church is a society founded on love and governed by love. . . . [The Council] has emphasized the universality of apostolic zeal, stressing that it must embrace all men, all races, all nations, and all classes.

The Unity of All Christians and Love for the World   Then Paul VI greeted the non-Catholic Christians: "The Church of the Second Vatican Council is affectionately open to all the Christian brethren who are still outside the perfect communion with our Church, one, holy, Catholic, and apostolic." He pointed out, "If there has been one recurring and moving note in the deliberations of this Council, it has been the theme . . . of reintegrating all Christians in the unity willed by Christ with its difficulties and its hopes. Is this not, venerable brothers and reverend and very dear observers, a mark of charity?"

The Pope then spoke about schema 13: "Can the Church, can we ourselves, do anything but look upon [the world] and love it? This contemplation of the world will be one of the principal activities of the Council session just beginning. Again, and above all, love; love for all men of today, whoever they are or wherever they are. . . . The Council is a solemn act of love for mankind."

Paul VI then mentioned the countries behind the iron curtain:

> At the present time this pacific Council must bear with grievous wrongs. Several who should be sitting here have not been able to respond to our invitation because they have been unjustly prevented from coming. This is an indication of the grave and sorrowful oppression of the Church that still exists in several countries, where with cold calculation, men attempt to stifle and suppress her. This thought fills us with sadness.

Nonetheless, the Pope insisted on the fact that the Council wishes "to testify our humble love," and recalled the evanglical teaching: "Love your enemies and pray for those who persecute you." He added:

> This Council will indeed remain clear and firm in what concerns fidelity to doctrine. Yet toward those who, as a result of blind antireligious prejudices or unjustified opposition, still inflict so much suffering on her, the Church, instead of pronouncing condemnations, will entertain feelings only of love. For them she will pray; yes, we will all pray, with love, that our enemies will receive God's mercy which we beg for ourselves. May the love for all prevail!

Vatican II: The Council of the Episcopacy

On the eve of the fourth session, the encyclical on the eucharist had created some uneasiness here and there. To censure before the entire world a few intellectuals who erred struck some as severe and gave rise to fears that the opening speech of this session would be full of warnings.

Yet Paul VI's allocution impressed the great majority of Fathers as a liberating document. "It is like John XXIII's best," observers commented spontaneously. They were won over by the spirituality and generosity of a text in which no trace of anxiety appeared. The observers from the Patriarchate of Moscow were not the last to note Paul VI's invitation to the Council to condemn no one and to practice love for the Church's enemies.

When the Pope announced the creation of an episcopal synod, applause broke out in St. Peter's. One of the principal—if not the principal—hopes of the Council on the level of the inner reorganization of the Church has been largely satisfied. It is a direct consequence of collegiality, which Vatican II defined last year. The establishment of this council in practice and not merely in theory tolls the passing bell for absolute monarchy in the Church. It is an innovation, to be sure, but it is also a return to the sources, for the Church had similar structures from the fourth to the sixteenth centuries.

Some bishops dared not hope that this senate (which was hinted at in the Pope's opening speech to the second session on September 29, 1963) would be composed mostly of bishops elected by episcopal conferences rather than named by the Pope.

Does this mean that Paul VI followed all of the suggestions made in previous conciliar interventions? No, because he did not announce that this senate would be convoked on a statutory or regular basis. Paul VI seems to want some freedom in this matter. The synod will be called to sit when the good of the Church seems to him to require this. But there will be a permanent secretariat in Rome,

Moreover, this reform is not enough in itself; what is needed is a radical reform of the Curia, promised by the Pope just before the second session (September 21, 1963). This supposes that the sacred Roman congregations will in the future be essentially administrative bodies and will no longer hold bishops under their yoke, forming thus a kind of screen between the residential bishops and the Pope.

The progressive status of episcopal conferences, enjoying a certain autonomy and real powers, will also contribute to the effective decentralizion of the Church's government.

It is today more evident than ever that Vatican II will go down in history as the council of the episcopacy, as Vatican I was the council of the papacy. Will a future council, which many think will be held outside of Italy, be that of the laity?

SEPTEMBER 15

The Schema on Religious Liberty Declares
That Public Powers Must Respect Freedom of Religious Choice

The first general congregation of the fourth session began discussion on the schema on religious liberty. The new text was inspired by Bishop Carlo Colombo, former theologian to Cardinal Montini. It seems of a nature to satisfy most of the Fathers; moreover, the long and eventful history of this document has prepared the bishops to welcome it favorably. The honor of Vatican II vis-à-vis non-Catholic Christians is at stake on this crucial issue.

In order to enable our readers to follow this debate more closely, we shall present large extracts from the schema. Of course, the Fathers are free to amend and polish it further. Every schema is a point of departure, and experience proves that the Fathers have never failed to improve on the texts prepared by the competent commissions. Nor will they fail in the present case.

The schema comprises four parts: (1) a preliminary declaration, (2) the doctrine of religious liberty as drawn from reason, (3) the doctrine of religious liberty in the light of revelation, and (4) a conclusion.

The schema is essentially a juridical one and claims the same liberty for all religions.

1. Preliminary Declaration

Religious liberty means that all men are to be immune from coercion on the part of individuals or of social groups and of any human power, in such wise that in matters religious no one is to be forced to act in a manner contrary to his conscience, whether privately or publicly, whether alone or in association with others, within due limits.

This right . . . is to be recognized in the constitutional law whereby society is governed. Thus it is to become a civil right to which all men and religious communities can legitimately lay claim. Responsibility for this right belongs both to the citizens and to the public powers, each in their specific way.

It does not follow from this affirmation of religious liberty that man has no obligation in religious matters, or that he is emancipated from the authority of God. Indeed, religious liberty does not imply that man may put truth and falsehood on the same level or be dispensed from the obligation of forming a true opinion, or that he may arbitrarily decide whether he wishes or not to serve God, in this religion or in that manner. For the principle of religious liberty leaves intact Catholic doctrine that the Church of Christ represents the one true religion.

2. The Doctrine of Religious Liberty as Drawn from Reason

Man perceives and acknowledges the imperatives of the divine law by means of his conscience: this pertains to the very dignity of the human person. That is why each person is bound to follow his conscience faithfully in all his activity in order that he may come to God, who is his goal.

Man has the power and the right to seek truth in matters religious in order that, utilizing appropriate means, he may prudently form sure judgments of conscience. Truth should be sought in a human fashion, that is, through free investigation; and once he has found it, man can adhere to it firmly through free assent. Moreover, since man has a social nature, truth is sought and found through the teaching authority or the institution and by communication and dialogue, by means of which the truth . . . can be exchanged. . . .

There is therefore a solemn moral principle which prohibits anyone from being forced to act against his conscience. . . .

An injustice is committed if, while man's right to religious liberty is recognized, he is at the same time refused free exercise of his religion in society within the limits required by public order.

Moreover, religious acts by which men order their lives to God in private and in public, by a spiritual decision and by their very nature, transcend the terrestrial and temporal order of things. But the competence of civil power . . . is restricted to the temporal and terrestrial order. . . . The civil power exceeds its limits when it interferes in man's relationship with God. It cannot therefore be said that the natural dignity of civil power suffers in any way when it . . . limits itself to temporal things. . . . The dignity of the human person requires that no one be prevented, even by public authority, from acting according to his conscience in matters religious, whether publicly or privately. . . .

Regarding the limits to religious liberty, the declaration sets these norms:

1. *Moral norm.* Men taken as individuals and social groups must bear in mind the rights of others and their duties toward others, for we must act toward others in accordance with justice and humanity.

2. *Juridical norm.* Civil society has the right to protect itself against abuses. It pertains principally to civil power to furnish this protection, not arbitrarily but according to the juridical norms which are required for public order.

. . . The exercise of religion in a society cannot be prohibited legitimately by the coercive intervention of the civil power unless the public peace is disturbed, public morals are compromised, or the rights of others are infringed upon. Moreover, the rule of law must be observed according to which the greatest possible freedom must be given to man, and it should be limited only insofar as this is necessary.

3. *Care of religious liberty.* To protect and promote the inviolable rights of man constitutes the principal responsibility of any civil

power. That is why this civil power must by just laws effectively assume the protection and care of the religious liberty of all its citizens. It must see to it that the juridical equality of its citizens is never harmed for religious reasons.

Public powers are not therefore permitted to impose by force or fear, or other unjust means, the profession or rejection of any religion or hinder men from joining or leaving a religious community. All the more is it a violation of the will of God and of the sacred rights of the person and the family of nations when force is brought to bear in any way in order to destroy or repress religion, in the whole of mankind or in a particular country or in a definite community.

It is the will of this Council that the right of the human person to religious liberty be recognized in all the cities of the world, that it be fortified by effective legal protection, and that it be provided with the means appropriate to encouraging citizens truly to exercise their religious rights and fulfill their religious duties. . . .

If in view of the particular historical circumstances obtaining among peoples, special civil recognition is given to one religious community in the constitutional order of society, it is at the same time imperative that the right of all citizens and religious communities to religious freedom should be recognized and made effective in practice.

4. *Liberty for Religious communities.* The religious liberty which individuals rightly claim must be recognized for religious communities as well: the right not to be impeded by legal means or an administrative action of the civil power from choosing and educating their own ministers, from communicating with the authorities and religious communities located in other countries, and from acquiring and disposing of the means necessary to their subsistence.

Religious communities have the right not to be prevented from teaching and bearing public witness to their faith, either orally or in writing, as long as the legitimate requirements of public order are not violated. . . . All coercion and all dishonest persuasion must be abstained from, especially in the case of simple and poor people.

5. *Religious liberty for families.* The right to determine the kind of religious formation to give their children accrues to families. Moreover, the civil power must recognize the parents' right to choose in all liberty schools or other means of education. Unjust burdens must not be imposed on them because of this freedom of choice. Civil power violates the rights of parents when it imposes a single form of education that excludes all religious formation.

3. Religious Liberty in the Light of Revelation

. . . God created man in his image and willed that man freely adhere to him in a sacred society. . . .

God sent his Son, who gave the commandment of **love** to his disciples who freely approached him. . . .

Jesus also distinguished between what is Caesar's and what is God's, so that Christians must obey Caesar in those things which are Caesar's and God in those things which are inviolably God's. . . .

Although some of God's people have followed ways that were scarcely in conformity with the Gospel, the doctrine of the Church has always remained steadfast, teaching that no one must be forced to adhere to the faith. . . .

God calls men to serve him, but he never coerces them. For he considers the dignity of the human person whom he himself created. . . .

Christ patiently attracted and invited his disciples. He always refused to work miracles that would seem violently to extort the assent of faith from men. Those around him asked for such signs, but Christ refused. He reprimanded the apostles when they asked him to ring down fire from heaven to devour the wicked.

. . . The apostles followed the example of Christ.

. . . The Church, faithful to the truth of the Gospels, follows the way of Christ and the apostles when she recognizes and favors the principle of religious liberty. . . .

One of the most important principles of Catholic doctrine is that man must respond to God in a free act of faith; consequently, no one must be forced to embrace the faith against his will. . . .

It is everywhere and always very important for the Church to enjoy the necessary freedom to carry out her ministry of salvation. . . . This liberty is holy, and is so proper to the Church that those who attack it act against the will of God. . . .

The Church must claim freedom for herself before any public power. . . .

By the will of God, the Catholic Church is the teacher of truth, and her function is to announce and teach this authentic truth. The charity of Christ urges the Christian to act with love, prudence, and patience toward men who are in error or ignorant of the faith.

4. Conclusion

Religious liberty is already affirmed in many constitutions as a civil right and is recognized by international organizations. But there are regimes which, although their constitutions recognize man's right to worship God, nonetheless endeavor to prevent their citizens from professing their religion and make life very difficult and dangerous for religious communities. . . .

The Vatican Council exhorts all, and especially those charged with educating others, to try to form men who are obedient to legitimate authority and deeply attached to genuine liberty.

SEPTEMBER 16

Eight Cardinals Have Already Intervened on Religious Liberty

Examination of the declaration on religious liberty began yesterday. So far, eight cardinals have already intervened. The minority has protested much less than one would have expected. There is one important exception, however: Cardinal de Arriba y Castro, Archbishop of Tarragona, made what most of the audience considered "frightening" remarks.

That a bishop, even though a Spaniard, could defend such a sectarian position in 1965 is reason to ponder the effects of a kind of theology that was formerly held in honor. It is also a measure of the progress we have made since. Such an intervention is useful in the sense that it helps the Church recognize her past errors, which history explains without excusing.

The interventions carried contradictory opinions on the question of church-state relations. Some seem inclined toward separation of church and state; others, who are more explicit, favor the system of concordats which grant special privileges to the Catholic Church. The most pertinent objection to state recognition of the Church was made by Cardinal Alfrink, who showed that such a system is a two-edged sword, for it follows logically that the state could also grant privileges to a nonreligious ideology.

Bishop de Smedt of Bruges, a member of the Secretariat for Promoting Christian Unity, explained the general outline of the schema in his introductory report. He clearly pointed out its limits; the declaration is essentially a juridical one, and affirms that public powers have no right to constrain persons or groups in religious matters, a domain in which they have no competence.

The reporter noted that it is very difficult to say that religious liberty as modern man understands it is a juridical consequence of the Gospel. "There are arguments of convenience," he said, "but no more; this question is of another order."

The kind of religious liberty treated in the schema, he added, is not tolerance, because the text adopts a juridical perspective and speaks of the respect due the human person.

In 1947, Bishop de Smedt noted, religious liberty was recognized by some fifty states; today it is mentioned in the constitutions of more than 100 states.

Cardinal Spellman was the first to intervene; his Latin was so badly pronounced that he was extremely difficult to follow. He praised "the clarity and the excellence" of the declaration but wanted a "better developed and more systematic" text. "The Church," he said, "wants the state to be impartial, and not concern itself with the religious question. If this were the case, both would benefit." Then the Cardinal stressed the capital importance of the schema from the ecumenical point of view.

Cardinal Frings, Archbishop of Cologne, said he was satisfied because "We feel the spirit of the Gospel, which is respect for the human person, in this text." He quoted the parable of the wheat and the tares, noting that we cannot remove one without danger of destroying the other.

He proposed a different structure for the declaration, and thought that the section on the doctrine of religious liberty as drawn from reason ought to be suppressed since it falls within the competence of philosophers and not the Council.

He also thought some other paragraphs of the schema ought to be deleted because they tend to be confusing.

The Danger of Indifferentism   Cardinal Ruffini, Archbishop of Palermo, declared that the schema contained some excellent considerations of a technical and juridical order on the dignity of the human person, his right and duty to follow his conscience, the liberty of the act of faith, and consequently the necessity to avoid all coercion in religious matters. Then he said:

> However, in order to avoid serious difficulties, we must distinguish between psychological freedom and moral freedom. Only the latter has reference to the truth. The truth is one; one also is the true religion, which in itself alone has a right to liberty. It is the duty of those responsible for the common good to guarantee liberty of worship to those who profess the true religion.
>
> The Council cannot limit itself to asking the state to observe articles 18, 19, and 20 of the Universal Declaration of Human Rights. We must praise the intention of the United Nations to promote peace among men of different faiths, but this intention is tainted with religious indifference. . . .
>
> The passage in the schema which says that the competence of

public powers is restricted to the temporal domain is ambiguous. Public authorities in effect have the obligation to render God the worship that is his due, and they have the responsibility of promoting the total wellbeing of each individual. No one can deny that religion contributes greatly to moral development. It is not enough to say that in certain historical circumstances the state can confer a special juridical privilege upon a religious confession. Such an affirmation does not explain the agreement which the Holy See has signed with different states. . . .

I fear that we seem to be saying, that we give the impression that the separation of church and state is a good thing. But the *Syllabus* says exactly the opposite, as does Pius X. Who would dare assert that they were wrong?

"In Italy, for example, the concordat says that the Catholic religion is the state religion, and the state gives special privileges to the Church. It would be dangerous and false to go against the concordat policy of the popes.

Passing to another subject, Cardinal Ruffini remarked that Christ occasionally used violence, as when he chased the money changers from the Temple.

Cardinal Siri, Archbishop of Genoa, also criticized the schema:

Let us speak not against liberty but against the abuses of liberty. Liberty involves the possibility of sinning, but it in no way implies God's approval or even tolerance of sin. In several places the schema claims liberty for all religious communities, even those that are estranged from the natural law and are contrary to good human morals. We cannot legitimize what God merely tolerates; we can only tolerate it, and that within the limits of the common good. We cannot therefore accept the proposed schema insofar as it recommends liberty for all without discrimination. . . .

We should consider more carefully the contribution of theological sources to this problem of religious liberty and determine whether or not the contents of this schema can be reconciled with the teachings of Leo XIII, Pius XI, and Pius XII. Otherwise, we weaken our own authority and compromise our apostolic effort.

Only the Catholic Church Has the Right To Preach the Gospel   Cardinal de Arriba y Castro recognized that:

This is probably the most delicate problem of the whole Council with respect to the faith. We must clearly affirm this basic principle:

only the Catholic Church has the duty and the right to preach the Gospel. That is why proselytism on the part of non-Catholics among Catholics is illicit and should be prevented by the civil authorities as well as by the Church, as the common good requires. . . .

The Council must be careful not to decree the ruin of Catholicism in those countries where it is in fact the only religion. The problem should be referred to episcopal conferences, which, with the approval of the Holy See, are in a better position to apply the principles of the declaration to local situations. . . .

It cannot be disputed that non-Catholics have the right to practice their faith, provided they do so in private. Nor can it be disputed that no one can be forced to practice a given religion.

Cardinal Urbani, Patriarch of Venice, spoke in the name of thirty-two Italian bishops. (We might note that he is one of the three provisory presidents of the Italian episcopal conference.)

Substantially, this text pleases me. The Council is dealing here with a very complicated and in a sense new subject. Let us therefore take into account the ancient documents of the magisterium, though of other factors as well. Let us distinguish carefully between the juridical and moral aspects of religious liberty. The argument from reason in defense of the civil right to religious liberty does not seem clear enough; it calls for more visible proofs. There should also be a fuller explanation of the duties of civil authority and the moral aspects of religious liberty. . . .

Finally, it would be good to study more attentively how the natural right to religious liberty demands a precise definition which, however, can vary according to circumstances.

The Gospel of Liberty   Said Cardinal Cushing, Archbishop of Boston:

This schema responds to the expectations of the Church and the world. Everything in it is solidly based on the doctrine of the Church. . . . The right to religious liberty is founded on the truth which constitutes the foundation of all human and social rights: the dignity of the person. Thus the basis of this right is not something subjective, but is based on the most exact moral theology. Liberty comes from grace and the natural law; the right to religious liberty is one with the human vocation to liberty in the Gospel.

Let us not fear to preach the Gospel of liberty. There are dangers everywhere, to be sure, but one of the greatest is to deny liberty. Once again, we should preach the whole Gospel, and the first witness to this preaching is the approval of the text now under study. The influence of this declaration will be exceptional.

Cardinal Alfrink, Archbishop of Utrecht, made the last intervention of the day:

> On the whole, this text deserves the approval of the majority. . . . The description of religious liberty given in the first lines of the declaration, however, seems too negative. Liberty is not only the absence of constraint; it is primarily the faculty of adhering to values which contribute to the perfection of the person. . . .
>
> On the other hand, the passage concerning special recognition by the state for a given religion is too affirmative. In fact, all such recognition is always bound up with political circumstances or concrete conditions.

The Cardinal thought it dangerous to admit that the state should normally confer privileges upon the Catholic religion. To admit this, he said, is by the same token to be obliged to admit that in other circumstances the state could privilege a non-Christian ideology. That is why Cardinal Alfrink requested that the corresponding passage in the schema be expressed in a concessive rather than an affirmative way.

The Episcopal Synod Will Have Deliberative Powers Under Certain Circumstances

Here are the principal provisions of Paul VI's motu proprio containing the rules for the future episcopal synod, read to the Council on Wednesday in the Pope's presence:

1. The synod, which will depend directly upon the pope and not the Curia, will be constituted of representatives of the episcopacy from all over the world. Its work and the time of the meetings will be determined by circumstances.
2. It will have an informative and consultative role and, should the pope think it in the interests of the Church, a deliberative one as well. Its function will be to tighten the bonds between the pope and the bishops, to collect precise information on the interior life of the Church and her action in the world, and to permit the expression of a common opinion on questions touching doctrine or pastoral action.
3. The pope will convoke and determine the place of meetings. He will ratify the election of its members and determine the agenda at least six months in advance, insofar as this is possible. He will send the partici-

pants the materials necessary for preparing discussion. He will preside over the meeting personally or through a delegate.

4. The synod may meet in a general, extraordinary, or special assembly.

   The following will participate in the general assembly:

   a. The heads of the Oriental Catholic Churches (patriarchs, major archbishops, and those metropolitans who do not depend on a patriarchate).
   b. Bishops elected by continental episcopal conferences.
   c. Ten religious elected by the Roman Union of Superiors General.
   d. Cardinals who are in charge of the Roman congregations.

   The following will participate in the extraordinary assembly:

   a. The heads of the Oriental Churches.
   b. The presidents of episcopal conferences.
   c. Three religious.
   d. The cardinals who are heads of congregations.

   The special assembly will have an analogous composition but will be regional in character.

5. Episcopal conferences will be represented in proportion to their membership: one delegate for a conference of at least twenty-five members, two for a conference of fifty members, three for a conference of 100 members, and four for a conference of more than 100 members.

6. The pope can add to the synod members of his own choice to the amount of 15 percent of the elected membership.

7. The rights and duties of the members of an assembly will cease upon cloture of the assembly.

8. The synod will have a permanent secretary and secretariat. Each assembly of the synod will have its own secretary, whose function will last as long as the meeting. The secretaries will be named by the pope.

These regulations provide for representation from the whole Oriental Church as well as the Western Church. With the exception of cardinals who head congregations, the heads of the Oriental Churches, and experts chosen by the pope, this synod will be composed of elected members. It will therefore be representative of the thinking of residential bishops throughout the world. It will be a kind of miniature ecumenical council convoked periodically. It will assure a continuous liaison between Rome and the rest of the Church; it thus marks the end of the Holy See's isolation and, let us hope, of the psychological obstacles caused by unilateral decisions on the part of Rome.

Cardinal Alfrink Talks About the Problems
of Ecclesiastical Celibacy

The backwash produced in a large sector of Italian opinion by the abusive interpretation of Paul VI's recent encyclical found an epilogue in a lecture given Wednesday afternoon at the Dutch Documentation Center by Cardinal Alfrink, Archbishop of Utrecht.

The Primate of the Netherlands, considering his Church calumniated, took up the gauntlet. He did so with a total frankness quite different from the circumscribed tones in which bishops normally speak. In this regard, Cardinal Alfrink's talk was exemplary, and was reminiscent of one given last year by Father Hans Küng, on honesty in the Church (see the report for October 8, 1964).

Vatican II is creating a new kind of bishop, one who is no longer afraid of words and is unconcerned about courting the powerful. The many Council Fathers present at this lecture were in agreement with the Cardinal's remarks. The collegial spirit is thus borne out in practice. The age of a timid and more or less servile episcopacy is beginning to fade. Deserving of special mention is the way Cardinal Alfrink spoke of the tensions in the Council, the celibacy of priests, and the anti-Roman spirit.

Here are the most striking passages of the lecture, one of whose principal objectives was to indicate the vitality of the Christian community in the Lowlands, which had been unjustly attacked.

> It has been clear during these years of the Council how important Vatican II has been in propagating the theological development of recent decades to the Church as a whole. After the Council, there will be no more reactionary regions, so to speak. The whole body of bishops has been raised to an equal theological level. After each session, the 2,000 bishops of the Church have returned home enriched. The Dutch Documentation Center has rendered eminent service to the bishops of the Church.

Calumny

> ... Let me say a word in protest against the unilateral, negative, twisted, and almost calumnious fashion in which the Catholic community of the Netherlands has been spoken of for some months. If you do not immediately grasp what I am talking about, permit me to refer you to some recent publications of the Italian press.
>
> I am sure you believe that I am perfectly aware of what is de-

fective in our Catholic community in the Netherlands, where sometimes opinions are expressed that are not altogether acceptable even
by those who are in favor of free and public discussion.

Press stories which express half-truths that are onesidedly tendentious and indict the whole community of the Netherlands announce
the danger, indeed more or less the certitude, of an imminent schism.

A Schism?

A Council is always a period of struggle for the Church, when
the battle lines become more sharply drawn and contrary opinions
clash. For these reasons, Christian charity can be endangered. We
could even say that these reasons augment the possibilities of a schism.
But if in fact a schism broke out, it would be because of many other
factors.

A French writer has said that it is a sign of the Church's lack of
vitality that a schism has not already taken place. Couldn't we say
just the opposite, that it is a sign of the Church's vitality that, despite
the present tensions, no schism has arisen? Can we not see in this the
proof that love for the Church and fidelity to the Church are so well
rooted that we wish, despite tensions and complaints, to remain in
the Church? . . .

The evolution of the Church begun at Vatican I in 1870 has, I
think, too clearly shown that he who abandons Peter at the same
time breaks a bond with Christ for a real schism to have any chance
of success.

. . . I am optimistic enough to think that the Catholic community
of the Netherlands is so profoundly attached to the Holy See that
the idea of a schism could only have originated outside of the Netherlands. But mightn't it still be true—as is often suggested by articles
in the aforementioned press—that the Dutch Catholic community is
infected with an anti-Roman spirit?

The Anti-Roman Spirit is Encountered Everywhere

If the term *anti-Roman* means "anti-papal," then I can in all good
conscience deny the charge categorically. Quite the contrary. But if
we mean that some members of the Catholic community of the
Netherlands object, and sometimes vehemently, to certain methods
of the Roman government apparatus and to the way certain persons
use these methods, then I could not and would not deny it.

Perhaps I should say in all honesty, not that certain persons *use*
these methods, but rather that they *used* them. For the whole world

knows that under the influence of the Council as well as the initiative of Popes John and Paul, many things have already changed for the better. But it would be a heartbreaking error to think that this anti-Roman spirit is found only in the Netherlands. It is found just about everywhere, even in Rome. . . .

The Council has stirred up minds, and there is scarcely a subject that is not discussed in the Church. What in other countries is thought and discussed privately is published in my country. But it would be an error to think that problems would disappear if certain ideas and opinions were suppressed. It would be a very serious error which could do considerable damage to the Church. Isn't open discussion, even if it sometimes goes too far, preferable to a smoldering fire? In the latter case, a destructive conflagration would not be impossible.

The Catholic community of the Netherlands is criticized, for example, for publicly discussing the value of priestly celibacy. In this discussion, the positive and negative sides were debated. But wouldn't we be wrong to think that in the absence of such discussion the problems and needs would no longer exist?

Elsewhere, other methods are used. I know a country where people write anonymous letters to foreign cardinals, hoping they will be understanding and sympathetic toward this problem. I do not want to say this method is more or less preferable than the other. But once again, we must stop thinking that there is no problem just because no one has the courage to say what he thinks in public.

SEPTEMBER 17

The Declaration on Religious Liberty Under Fire

The discussion on religious liberty will occupy the Council for two or three more days. It is not known whether the International Episcopal Committee has transmitted its counterschema to the moderators. Perhaps the members have become aware of the futility of their effort and have decided at the last moment to concentrate their criticism on the official text. We will soon know.

Beginning next week, the Council will start to vote on the schema on revelation, which was discussed last year, and will then go on to an examination of schema 13. On Thursday, five cardinals spoke on religious liberty. Five of the seventeen speakers were largely negative, sometimes in violent terms; nine had some important reservations; and three declared themselves satisfied.

The balance of praise and criticism makes it impossible to draw any clear conclusion about the general thinking of the Fathers. It is psycholog-ically normal that most of the bishops who intervene are counted among the dissatisfied. It is likely that the majority of the Fathers are ready to vote on the text as it presently stands. The amendments are proposed by a relatively small number of Fathers; furthermore, their proposals are often contradictory. The competent commissions will determine what course of action is to be followed.

Let us begin with the negative interventions.

Archbishop Morcillo González of Madrid:

> We must defend religious liberty with all our strength; but the schema is not acceptable. It is a declaration and not a conciliar con-stitution. Now, a declaration implies a judgment made on a particular situation about a specific problem and includes practical directives. The contemporary world is characterized by religious pluralism, by the development of international relations, by ecumenism, by reci-procity between different religious in the exercise of liberties and rights, and also by a moral impossibility for many to find religious truth. These considerations seem sufficient to justify a declaration on religious liberty. But the scriptural and philosophical arguments ad-vanced in the schema are not valid. Man has the right to act accord-ing to the dictates of his conscience, but first of all he has the duty to seek religious and moral truth and the right to be aided in this quest. . . .
>
> It is true that the state is not competent in matters religious, but it can always listen to and accept what the Church teaches. The biblical arguments in the schema prove nothing. Christ also chased the money changers from the Temple. The teaching of the popes since Leo XIII is practically ignored. We must correct these serious shortcomings. Let us avoid basing this declaration on arguments which pretend to be absolute. Otherwise we would do violence to tradition, to the magisterium, and to Scripture.

Bishop Lokuang of Tainan, Formosa:

> The new version of the schema does not dissipate the ambiguity of a number of points. In treating religious liberty for all, the text seems uniquely concerned with negative considerations, and there seems to be a certain reticence in expressing the Church's right to declare herself unique and true. One would therefore like to see a more positive tone impregnate the whole declaration. . . .
>
> We must not be silent on the opinion we all hold in common that a Catholic state is preferable to one that is indifferent or neutral. This would also involve a change in some obscure and dangerous

expressions. The world in fact counts on this declaration, and it is good that it should correspond with the expectations of our times.

Bishop Velasco of Amoy, China:

The schema is totally unacceptable because it has the same faults as the previous version. It is infected with juridical legalism and contradicts the traditional doctrine of the Church. It could breed pragmatism, indifferentism, and neutralism. It seems to admit of a kind of subjectivism in matters religious and does not distinguish between truth and error. It could cause innumerable doubts and anxieties among the faithful. . . .

The text was revised with partiality. Account was taken only of those amendments that were partisan to the previous text. All the other amendments were systematically ignored. Yet the minority must be heard. . . .

What have they done with history? It is impossible to reconcile this text with the magisterium of the nineteenth or even the twentieth century. Perhaps I have misunderstood this document. . . . But if that is the case, what about the faithful?

Bishop Carli of Segni, Italy:

The commission's report recognizes that there is a great distance between scriptural doctrine and the modern conception of religious liberty. In order to bring them closer together, the commission had a choice of either bending the modern conception or bending the teaching of Scripture. It chose the second alternative. . . .

The subjective is canonized. . . . The schema is founded on the affirmation that man has a real natural and objective right to spread his religious and moral ideas without restraint, provided he observes the limits fixed by civil authority. We are trying to find a positive and absolute basis for a basically negative right. The scriptural argument for such a basis used in the schema is invalid. . . . The texts from the Old Testament concern psychological liberty alone. The choice of these texts is onesided; it would be easy to find others that would be extremenly hard on those who propagate error or refuse to listen to the Church. . . .

We cannot say that in the time of Christ all who were in error were of bad faith while today they are in good faith. There can be no positive right to spread error among Catholics. In this matter we can only prevent or tolerate.

Bishop Emilio Tagle Covarrubias of Valparaiso, Chile, in the name of forty-five Latin American Bishops:

I am very much against this schema. It merely rearranges the previous version, and it contains a number of contradictions. . . . Many passages are too complacent toward false religions and run the risk of indifferentism and liberalism. It does not seem possible to grant the same rights to all religions indiscriminately. Only the one true Church has the right to religious liberty, strictly speaking. Other religions can only be tolerated, depending upon the circumstances and persons.

Many Reservations Here, now, are the more moderate interventions.

Cardinal Meouchi, Maronite Patriarch of Antioch, asked for a change in terminology and method:

> The terminology is very important. Christians and non-Christians use the same words without meaning the same thing by them. The problems themselves issued from concrete circumstances and carry a certain impulse; but we are accustomed to going from principles to the concrete. To dialogue with the world today we must take into account the mentality of the present as well as the future which we should be preparing.
>
> Moreover, the method used to expound the doctrine of this schema should not be theological or philosophical but should be based on experience. Then all will understand better what religious liberty, the basis for a dialogue in friendship and truth, means in the light of faith.

Cardinal Slipyi of Lvov:

> The activity of a Council should always correspond with the needs of an age. Now, today, the violation of the Church's liberty is a very painful wound. This should be said more clearly. . . . Too, religious liberty is a benefit not only for the Church but also for the state. The limits of religious liberty should be clarified further to prevent abuses on the part of civil authority. . . .
>
> The text reproaches those states which are opposed to religious education for children; but we should also speak of those states that impose an atheistic education. . . . The scriptural passages are not always convincing. . . .
>
> In the final analysis, man can abuse any form of liberty; the schema should emphasize this, and instead of appealing to human dignity, it should refer to the virtue of nobility which impels man to dominate and transcend his egoism.

"Noblesse oblige," he said several times.

Archbishop Nicodemo of Bari thought the text as a whole was acceptable. But, he said, the subject is so serious that several points should be clarified:

> Thus, the right to religious liberty calls for a better definition. We should also add a few words to make it quite clear that the Council accepts as its own the Church's doctrine on this subject. The formulation of the declaration should be concise. What is said about the relationship between the Church and the state does not seem to coincide with the teaching of the magisterium. . . .
>
> We should not speak of public order but of the common good considered in its fullest sense and in its historical context. Let us not appear to grant concessions where we should be firm. The relationship which must exist between the faithful and ecclesiastical authority should be made clear. And above all, let us avoid using obscure expressions that favor individualism and even contempt for religion.

Archbishop Gregorio Modrego y Cosáus of Barcelona:

> This schema is a considerable improvement over the previous version. Nonetheless, its doctrine is substantially the same. It should be radically revised. The text does not explain clearly what the common good is. The affirmations are neither demonstrated nor confirmed by the passages from Scripture that are quoted; quite the contrary, they are in patent conflict with papal teaching. . . .
>
> Religious truth is one of the elements of man's common good. Now, the common good falls within the competence of the state. The state, therefore, cannot be indifferent to the truth or the falsity of religious confessions.

Coadjutor Archbishop Duraisami Lourdusami of Bangalore, India:

> This schema will help maintain and improve relations between Catholics and non-Catholics. But some passages should be modified. To communicate the truth, for example, is something which is not only useful but necessary. The law should protect the faith on the basis of its obligation to communicate the truth. . . .
>
> It would be desirable if we deleted everything in the text relating to the recognition of a particular religion; for this is difficult to understand today, and in non-Catholic regions this passage could constitute an obstacle to the diffusion of Catholicism.

Archbishop Juan Carlos Aramburu of Tucumán, Argentina:

> We should modify the passage which affirms that civil authority can prohibit the right to religious liberty for reasons of the practical

order or of public peace. For in fact this opens the door to every kind of abuse. Christians have always troubled public peace. Christ himself was an agitator. We should specify that public peace is founded on the universal rights of man; otherwise public powers will be able to judge what constitutes a breach of public peace as they please. It would be easy for them to condemn preaching in pagan or Communist countries. Likewise, the abolition of racial discrimination or in general any missionary activity could be considered unjust.

Bishop Mason, Apostolic Vicar to the Sudan:

Let us suppress the passage about the state's recognition of the Church. . . . Let us issue pedagogical directives, because it is necessary to form our youth so that they will respect the convictions of others. . . . Let us stress the responsibility of governments not only to proclaim the right to religious liberty but to see to it that it is respected. Religious liberty is inseparable from the other rights of man. In many countries of Asia and Africa, where religious problems are frequently connected with racial questions, violations of religious liberty can have unfortunate consequences for the Church.

Bishop Giuseppe Marafini of Veroli, Italy: "It would be good to add that religious liberty does not dispense the state from following the moral and religious principles of the natural order. The state cannot be confessional, but it ought not be antireligious, indifferent, or amoral."

Mixed Marriages   Maronite Archbishop Ziadé of Beirut spoke of religious rights in mixed marriages:

I hope this expression will be banned from canon law, for those who have received the same baptism participate in the sacrament. . . . We cannot force the non-Catholic party to act against his conscience, in what concerns the education of children, for example. Everything depends on the non-Catholic's or non-Christian's convictions. If he professes a religious conviction, we should only ask him to let the Catholic party act according to his faith. In all cases, collaboration between the pastors of the two spouses is necessary.

Charity, Justice, and Logic Demand the Schema's Adoption   Here, now, are the three most favorable interventions.
Cardinal Jaeger, Archbishop of Paderborn, Germany:

This schema in no way favors indifferentism. It clearly affirms that the Catholic Church is the only true religion. Moreover, it strongly emphasizes the obligation of each individual to seek the truth and form his conscience according to God's law. The affirmation of this obligation could be further strengthened. Furthermore, we must avoid confusing religious liberty in its juridical and moral senses. This distinction enables us to resolve difficulties raised by cases of those who are responsible for their error. . . . But this problem does not concern the state, which cannot judge the conscience of its citizens.

Cardinal Silva Henríquez, Archbishop of Santiago, Chile:

This schema deserves to be approved by reason of both its formulation and its contents. From the pastoral point of view, the declaration represents a splendid victory which will give new meaning to the apostolate. It brings out the spirit and the importance of the Gospel's message, and rather than favoring relativism, it exhorts responsibility. According to Saint Ireneus, the Gospel is "the unknown terrain of liberty." The apostles preached the liberty of the Gospel and left to their successors the mission of promoting it. . . .

The schema refers to the deep meaning of evangelical liberty and thus presents Christianity in perfect harmony with the dignity of the human person. The whole apostolate should be impregnated with this spirit. A serious examination of conscience is necessary. Let us abstain from all constraint that originates in a desire for money, propaganda, and authoritarianism vis-à-vis pagans, non-Catholics, or the faithful.

Cardinal Ritter, Archbishop of St. Louis:

Those who elaborated this schema merit our deepest gratitude. Their work leaves nothing to be desired. Charity, justice, and logic permit no further delays and no further objection to approval of this schema, which is awaited by the whole world.

Charity demands it because this declaration is the only means of offering help to all those who suffer persecution because of their religion and fidelity to their consciences. Justice demands it because sometimes the official behavior of authorities in certain Catholic countries imposes mortifying restrictions upon non-Catholics whose Christian conscience is nonetheless sincere. Logic demands it, finally, because without this declaration, many affirmations in the Constitution on the Church and the Decree on Ecumenism would make no sense. If the declaration were not approved, the Council Fathers could be accused of infidelity to the Gospel.

Religious Liberty and Atheism

Liberty is indivisible. It cannot be proclaimed for some and denied to others. Religious liberty is a special instance of liberty of conscience, of the freedom to express one's convictions in words, writing, or actions. If the Catholic Church believes in freedom for all religions, she must begin by giving the example herself.

The schema on religious liberty not only asserts liberty of action for Protestants but also implicitly urges the Catholic Church to be more respectful and understanding toward her own faithful. Thus she must become more liberal toward scholars—exegetes and theologians—for truth is reached only gradually. The Church must not hamper their work or remove them from their natural milieu, although this does not mean that the hierarchy does not have the right and responsibility to pass judgment on the orthodoxy of such scholars.

Nor can the Church refuse unbelievers or atheists the rights she acknowledges for believers. In 1961 at New Delhi, the World Council of Churches asserted man's right to unbelief without incurring external sanctions. At Odessa in 1964, Dr. Nolde, in the name of the executive committee of that organization, declared that atheists had as much right to proselytize as believers.

Bishop de Smedt of Bruges gave a lecture on Thursday, attended by a number of bishops, in which he expressed similar ideas. "An atheist, a Hindu, a Protestant, Orthodox, or Catholic," he said, "has the same rights as anyone else. That is, the state, groups, or individuals cannot intervene to prevent him from expressing his convictions."

SEPTEMBER 18

The Debate on Religious Liberty
Reveals Two Irreconcilable Viewpoints

Vatican II has discussed religious liberty for only two days and already the debate has declined considerably in interest. In fact, the interventions repeat the same arguments, either for or against. Still, it is intriguing to see that various Fathers contradict each other so categorically. Thus on Friday morning, Archbishop Baldassari of Ravenna declared, "Religious liberty must be based on Scripture and not the natural law." Then Coadjutor Bishop Elchinger of Strasbourg asserted, "There is no point in invoking the Gospel; rational arguments suffice."

A few minutes later, Archbishop Paul J. Hallinan of Atlanta affirmed,

"This schema is exempt from any taint of agnosticism or indifferentism." He was followed by Bishop Gasbarri, Apostolic Administrator of Grosseto, who accused the same text of "agnosticism, indifferentism, positivism, liberalism, laicism, legalism, existentialism, pragmatism, and Kantianism."

No less.

The debate makes it clear that there are two apparently irreconcilable viewpoints among the Fathers, which might be characterized in this fashion.

The first camp comprises "notional" types; they are attached to abstract truths and "theses"; they are more or less indifferent to the subjective values of conscience and sincerity. If they sometimes consent, under the most favorable conditions, to recognize religious liberty for non-Catholics, they do so with regret and only because of the unfortunate circumstances of our pluralistic age. At most, they will grant a niggardly modicum of tolerance. This same attitude looks on the confessional state as ideal: since the Catholic Church alone has the truth, she has absolute rights in every respect. These Fathers rely heavily on the past teaching of the magisterium, like Pius IX's *Syllabus* or Pius X's celebrated passage, which they would gladly repeat if they dared:

> Freedom of worship is a monstrous error, an insanity, a freedom of perdition, an error most fatal to the Catholic Church and the salvation of souls. A disastrous heresy forever to be deplored, a dreadful system. Freedom of worship corrupts morals and the spirit; it protects the pestilence of indifference; it constitutes a veritable social crime.

The second attitude is more "existentialist." It believes in the truth of Catholicism but is more concerned with granting religious liberty to all without exception; respect for conscience (even erroneous) seems to it to have a primordial value which flows from the teaching of Christ. Those who have this viewpoint speak not of tolerance but of liberty. They hold the human person to be more important than the objective value of his convictions. Man comes before ideas.

They do not consider themselves unfaithful to the Church's tradition, for they distinguish what is decadent, outmoded, and defective in past teaching from what is permanent. We might also recall that, contrary to a widespread prejudice in religiously ignorant circles, pontifical infallibility is not involved in a document like the *Syllabus*. In any event, the dogma was not defined in 1864; and even had it been, what we say would still be true.

Since that time, Catholicism has come to a deeper understanding of certain truths. It has mastered the idea that freedom necessarily inheres in an ideology incompatible with the faith. Not all of the Fathers have ex-

perienced this evolution. The challenge facing any assembly, including a
religious one, is to unite persons of unequal intellectual maturity and divergent ideas. There are bishops who act and think as if they were living
in the nineteenth century; they have no sense of the development of
human thought. Others live in their own age; they may even be avant-
garde. Thus they welcome intellectual *aggiornamento*. Happily, these
outnumber the former.

There is perhaps only one point on which all the Fathers agree: the
act of faith must be free, in accordance with what canon law teaches. Too,
most of the bishops agree on this fundamental conclusion: religious liberty
is a good or at least a necessary lesser evil. But there is considerable disagreement as to the doctrinal justification of such religious liberty. That is why
the writers of the schema were wise to restrict it to a juridical point of
view until a greater common understanding can be reached. We will have
to wait many years yet before the Church can put forth a truly coherent
philosophical doctrine harmonizing these two equally absolute values:
truth and liberty.

Let us return to Friday's general congregation. Six cardinals and
twelve bishops (three of them French) intervened. For reasons of space
we cannot cover all of the speeches, and so will limit our report to the
following, which by definition must represent a somewhat arbitrary
choice.

Cardinal Heenan, Archbishop of Westminster:

> We must put an end to the accusation that the Church claims
> liberty when she is a minority and suppresses it when she is in the
> majority. We must recall the not too distant *historical* circumstances
> when Protestants and Catholics persecuted each other and accepted
> the principle *cuius regio eius religio*. This intolerance has disap-
> peared. . . .
>
> Yet some still hold that error has no rights. But persons have
> rights, whether they are right or wrong, and the schema affirms this.
>
> The principle that each must obey his conscience is indisputable.
> Cardinal Newman said he obeyed his conscience first and then the
> pope.

Cardinal Conway, Archbishop of Armagh, Ireland: "Let us not give
the impression that the state has nothing to do with religion, because religion forms part of the common good. This is also true of non-Christian
religions. A state that was indifferent to the religious fact would be inhuman, for man has a religious dimension."

Cardinal Ottaviani, Secretary of the Holy Office: "The schema goes against traditional doctrine. In one passage the true and false are put on the same level. . . . The dignity of man cannot be the basis of religious liberty. . . . Let us not forget that hell is mentioned frequently in the New Testament. Like the apostles, the Church must say, *non possumus non loqui* [we cannot not speak]. Let us revise the whole schema."

Bishop Sauvage of Annecy: "In general this schema pleases me; after a final revision it should command unanimity."

Archbishop Cantero Cuadrado of Saragossa: "In the perspective of this schema, the real foundation of religious liberty is, even before the dignity of man, the fact that the state is incompetent in the inner domain of religion."

Bishop Rupp of Monaco:

> The schema smacks of a liberal nineteenth-century conception of freedom. This is a serious error because the young have gone beyond this mentality. It risks drawing the comment that once again the Church is behind the times with respect to ideas, reform, and revolution. . . .
>
> Let us be content to adopt the seven-point declaration recently proclaimed by the World Council of Churches. . . .
>
> Article 44 of the *Syllabus* turned out to be prophetic because it condemned totalitarian states.

Auxiliary Bishop Charles G. Maloney of Louisville: "The auditors at the Council approve this schema. This is an important fact we must take into consideration."

Archbishop García de Sierra of Burgos: "The schema contains a number of unacceptable points. Sound doctrine should guide us and not the will of the majority. . . . Let us revise the text from top to bottom [*ab ovo*]."

SEPTEMBER 20

Vatican II Understands Its Own Freedom Better in Reflecting on Religious Liberty

Religious liberty: There has been no more perplexing problem for the Fathers of Vatican II. More than "the expectation of the world," a hyperbolic expression that tends to be abused in Catholic circles, this perplexity has constituted the interest of the present debates. In fact, it is profoundly indicative of the crisis of conscience the bishops are experiencing.

We might say that each bishop is testing religious liberty in the inti-

macy of his own liberty of conscience. The line of division is in this case
less between the majority and minority than within each bishop's conscience.

As we have already stressed, Catholic thinking in its present stage is
somewhat unequipped before the question of religious liberty. The Council Fathers' pastoral instinct inclines them toward religious liberty. They
sense that here is an existential truth they must proclaim.

Paradoxically, the bishop least disposed to accept religious liberty is
usually the most doctrinally sound. This anguish has been lived day after
day for two years by members of the Secretariat for Promoting Christian
Unity, who are responsible for elaborating this schema. There is, in fact,
a double anguish: (1) to find a theological basis for the necessity of religious liberty on theology, and above all, (2) to reconcile this doctrine
with the past teaching of the magisterium.

The second point has practically no solution. It is all very well to
argue from the historical and philosophical situation of the nineteenth century; there is only one intellectually honest way to get off the horns of this
dilemma—admit that the popes erred on this particular point. But the
Church will likely never admit this officially. She is still too enamored of
herself, still too much a prisoner of her past, still too imbued with her
authority considered as a service. This is psychologically explicable, and
there would be no point in deploring it without qualifications. If we
think of the average mentality of a great number of faithful who are accustomed to idolizing everything that comes from the hierarchy, then the
Church has good reason to be hesitant about such an admission. The masses
would have difficulty weathering the trauma.

As for the theological difficulty mentioned above, there is one way of
solving it, which the schema tries to make use of in the third part: to
show that the religious basis is found in the Gospel. Several Fathers have
pointed out that the scriptural passages are not convincing. This is true
in the sense that, strictly speaking, the civil right to religious liberty cannot be proven from the Gospel. There is undeniably a difference in levels.
On the other hand, it also cannot be denied that the overall movement of
the Gospel is toward religious liberty. What purpose is served by quibbling
over the strength of a given scriptural text? The twenty centuries of our
era prove beyond any shadow of a doubt that the Gospel is a school of
liberty. Every time the West has forged an ideology that was directly anti-
Christian (we say anti-Christian and not anti-Catholic), man's freedom has
decreased. We have only to think of Fascism, Nazism, or even Marxism.

The Gospel is essentially a ferment of liberty that has inspired all the
Christian mystiques of the East and the West. Politics, and not truly religious men, corrupted the vitality of this seminal idea. When the French

launched their Revolution with the motto "Liberty, equality, and fraternity" in 1789, it was evident to any reflective spirit that this trilogy expressed a Christian ideal cut off from its roots. Scarcely anyone today, even in the Church, disputes this.

The "Divine Right of Tares"   As Jean Vogel wrote after one of the conciliar interventions, there is a "divine right of tares" in the Gospel. Christ said that the tares should not be weeded out for fear of destroying the good grain. Only when Christ comes in judgment at the end of time will the tares be separated from the wheat. Meanwhile, the Church of Christ must respect the tares. She also received the command not to judge, that is, *not to condemn*. At bottom, this command is pure wisdom. For experience teaches that we find truth through error. Freedom to err is a condition of freedom of thought. He who wants never to make a mistake will never think!

In reflecting on religious liberty, the Council is humbly learning to understand its own liberty better. That is undobutedly why there is so much interest in and sometimes sympathy for this issue from the outside world. For the rest, the schema on religious liberty would have no reason for existence if the Church had kept the evangelical spirit throughout her history.

The Cause of Ecumenism Is Making Progress, Declares Cardinal Bea

Late Saturday afternoon Cardinal Bea, president of the Secretariat for Promoting Christian Unity, hosted a reception for the observer delegates and the guests of the secretariat. A few Catholic observers were also invited.

When he greeted the observers, the Cardinal expressed pleasure that the number of churches, federations, and communities represented at the fourth session had increased. Then, speaking of the spirit in which "We wish to realize our common task with absolute fidelity to the truth," the Cardinal continued:

> I would like to add a thought about the inevitable difficulties we encounter in our work. This thought is prompted by what happened at the end of the third session. I want to speak about the last-minute difficulties with the text on ecumenism, the disappointments they caused for many people, and the fears they raised about the future of ecumenical dialogue. I do not wish to minimize the facts; I know it

required much effort from various quarters gradually to restore calm; and I would not say that it has yet been restored everywhere.

I mainly want to emphasize the fact that in spite of all this, considerable progress has been made in the ecumenical field. We have only to think of such important events as the exchange of official visits between the Ecumenical Patriarchate of Constantinople and the Roman Catholic Church, and the creation of a mixed committee between the World Council of Churches and the Roman Catholic Church as well as between the latter and the World Lutheran Federation. . . .

We are sure to encounter further difficulties in the course of this session. It is enough to think of the number and importance of the schemas that remain to be finished, several of which have a great bearing on the ecumenical movement. That is why . . . I would ask you to join us in considering all things calmly, supernatural charity, and trust. We aslo ask your daily prayers that "He who has begun this work will bring it to its completion" [Phil. 1:6].

In the name of the observers, Reverend Dr. Douglas Horton, a Congregationalist, thanked Cardinal Bea for all the facilities and marks of friendship given to the observers, and declared that they will give a new impetus to the ecumenical movement. He continued:

To be sure, there are a few differences of theology and polity which have developed between the Roman Church and the rest of us during the centuries in which we have been studying how to keep separate. We shall have to trust the generations . . . to come to give us the chance to resolve them. But it is evident that the friendship you have shown us has cleared the ground in which a reconciliation can take root. . . . Because you have made us your friends, nothing that is important to you can be unimportant for us. We will never be indifferent, whatever our disagreements, to what concerns your theology and your liturgy.

SEPTEMBER 21

The Church Today Is Expiating Her Own Violations of Religious Liberty, Says Cardinal Beran

Since Paul VI insisted that the discussion on religious liberty not be cut off abruptly, interventions on the subject continued Monday morning. The Fathers agreed to close the debate by the end of Tuesday morning.

Let us return to the contents of the schema. In a conference given in Rome, Cardinal Jaeger, a member of the secretariat for unity, said this text was comparable to a Copernican revolution. It is the first conciliar schema to begin not with God but with man (schema 13 is also centered on man). This is an intellectual advance which is still rather rare among the hierarchy and which horrifies the ultraconservatives.

Rousseauistic Error   Consider, for example, the following intervention by Archbishop Lefebvre of the Congregation of the Holy Spirit:

> The schema recognizes equal rights for all religions and recommends the neutrality of the state, which would intervene only for reasons of the common good. The reporter said that this conception was arrived at after a long evolution. But it only goes back to the eighteenth century; it cannot therefore be considered traditional. The real sources of this schema are the philosophers of the eighteenth century—Hobbes, Hume, Locke, Rousseau, and the liberal Catholicism of Félicité de Lamennais, which was condemned by Leo XIII. Should the conservation of public order be the norm for intervention on the part of the state? Communists do not hesitate to persecute Catholics in the name of this principle. Should human dignity be the basis of religious liberty? But the Communists attack our religion, which they consider an alienation, in the name of this principle.
>
> Non-Catholic approval of this schema is indicative. A Freemason has written that he puts all his hope in a positive vote. Protestants also want this. In reality, this schema is based neither on tradition nor on Scripture, but on a false Rousseauistic conception. . . .
>
> The Catholic Church alone has a strict right to liberty. With regard to other communities and religions, each particular case must be examined.

The Testimony of the Persecuted   Aside from this piece of bravura, the like of which no longer impresses the Fathers, Monday's general congregation experienced a marked renewal of interest, essentially because of three particularly stirring interventions.

The first was by Cardinal Wyszynski, Archbishop of Warsaw, who has long stressed the radically different meanings attached to such expressions as *states' rights, society,* and *liberty* by dialectical materialism and Christianity. "It is well to remember this," he said, "in order to understand the situation of the Church in countries dominated by regimes which adopt the principles of dialectical materialism. In such cases, Catholics must remember that they have only one alternative: to suffer and bear their cross. Let our text be elaborated in terms of these two radically different universes."

The Fathers then heard Josef Cardinal Beran, Archbishop of Prague. This was his first appearance at the Council after many years of imprison-

ment. He was greeted with a long ovation as he approached the microphone to speak.

> Here is my humble personal testimony. This schema applies to all
> true liberties of conscience, and its theological scope is considerable.
> From the moment liberty of conscience was radically restricted in my
> country, experience proved that constraint forced men to sin against
> God. One could observe among the faithful and priests not only
> serious dangers to the faith but serious temptations to living, hypoc-
> risy, and other vices. These deplorable effects are the same when con-
> straint is exercised in the name of religion. . . .
>
> One can say that in Bohemia the Church today is expiating such
> violations of religious liberty as the death of John Huss in the fifteenth
> century and the forced conversion of a large part of the population in
> the eighteenth century. Present experience and history demand, there-
> fore, that the Council proclaim the principle of religious liberty,
> clearly and without restriction, in a spirit of penance for past faults.
>
> It would then be possible to intervene in favor of our persecuted
> brethren. . . . The conclusion of the declaration should be addressed
> to governments; they should be requested to stop interfering with
> religious liberty, to release imprisoned priests and laymen, to permit
> bishops and priests to resume their functions, to leave the Church free
> to govern herself, to let religious congregations revive, and to give real
> freedom to Christian families.

*Urgent Necessity of the Declaration for the Peaceful Unification of the
World*   Finally, Joseph Cardinal Cardijn, the founder of the Young Christian Workers, spoke. He was the first cardinal of the workers to be heard.
This miner's son is more accustomed to improvisations and meetings than
to the formality of conciliar declarations. "This will be the first time I have
ever spoken from a written text," he confided to a friend.

> My experience of sixty years in the apostolate of young workers
> all over the world shows that a clear and solemn declaration on jurid-
> ical freedom in matters religious is an urgent necessity for the peace-
> ful unification of today's pluralistic world. Trust between men is a
> requisite condition for the construction of a more human world. Trust
> is not possible without religious liberty. Likewise, religious liberty is
> a condition for effective ecumenical and missionary activity. . . . In
> countries where Christians are a small minority, their action can only
> be based on the strength of God's word, on the poverty and witness of
> the layman's life. . . . Nor should we forget the educative and pedagog-
> ical value of liberty.

Most of Monday's interventions (in all, nine cardinals and four bishops) were favorable to the schema. Joseph Cardinal Lefebvre, Archbishop of Bourges, firmly refuted the six most common objections to the schema. Cardinal Shehan, Archbishop of Baltimore, and Auxiliary Bishop Thomas W. Muldoon of Sydney both proposed that the declaration be preceded by a sort of explanatory preface. Angelo Cardinal Rossi, Archbishop of São Paulo, said in the name of eighty-three Brazilian bishops that he wanted a special paragraph added to the schema explaining the historical errors of the Church in matters of religious liberty. Bishop John Gran of Oslo declared himself very satisfied, and recalled that Christ asked his disciples not to do to others what they would not have done unto them.

Cardinal Browne of the Curia expressed a typical minority opinion, though let us note that he is not a member of the Comitatus Episcopalis Internationalis as he was thought to be because of his sympathies with members of that organization. "We can grant equal rights to all religions," he said, "but the propagation of other religions in Catholic countries is a violation of public morality. It should be prohibited."

The Schema on Revelation: 354 Juxta Modi *Votes on Chapter 2*   The Council Fathers have voted on chapter 2 of the schema on revelation, taken as a whole. The results: 1,874 *placet*, 9 *non placet*, and 354 *placet juxta modi*. We might also note that the Comitatus Episcopalis Internationalis, the official organ of the minority, has distributed its suggestions for amendments to the Fathers.

SEPTEMBER 22

Ninety Percent of the Fathers Accept the Schema on Religious Liberty as a Basis for the Final Declaration

The machinery of the Council is functioning smoothly, as it should after four years of use. The majority has become aware of its formerly unsuspected strength. They have learned to avoid conflicts with the minority and have discovered less onerous methods of gaining ground.

The minority, for their part, have become aware of their actual limits. Confronted with hard realities, they have learned from their failures. They are less inclined to see themselves as guardians of orthodoxy since perceiving that the last two popes, while remaining above the fray, have not only not automatically supported them but have urged them unceasingly to undertake their own *aggiornamento*.

This throws some light on the events of the last thirty-six hours, which could have provoked a crisis. It is said that 127 Fathers, doubtless including several cardinals, asked Paul VI to take the schema on religious liberty out of the hands of the unity secretariat and give it to a commission of theologians composed of members not belonging to this body. Unless I am mistaken, this request has been rejected.*

Early Monday evening, the directive bodies of the Council met to decide on the suitability of an indicative vote on the schema to clarify the position of the majority or at least an orientation vote to determine whether the Fathers will accept the present schema as a basis of discussion. The "caliphate" of the Council, as it is familiarly referred to in Rome, did not reach an agreement, it seems, which is not the first time such a situation has occurred. The Council was in a delicate position, for the discussion of the schema on religious liberty had revealed serious internal contradictions which made it difficult for the unity secretariat to determine the specific orientations it should follow in redrafting the schema.

The Pope's Intervention   At this point the Pope intervened—a last-minute decision, judging by the tardiness of Cardinal Tisserant (president), Cardinal Agagianian (moderator), and Archbishop Felici (secretary general) at Tuesday morning's general congregation. Paul VI proposed the solution of having the Council vote on the following question: "Does the text on religious liberty please the Fathers as the basis for the definitive declaration which will be perfected later, in accordance with Catholic doctrine on the true religion and with the amendments proposed by the Fathers in the course of the discussion, which are to be approved in conformity with the Council rules?" The following results were obtained: of 2,222 votes, 1,997 were *placet* and 224 *non placet*, with 1 null ballot.

The systematic opposition to the schema can now be seen proportionally: it is very weak, about 10 percent of the assembly. In one fell swoop the Council broke out of its impasse. The cleverness of the question is remarkable. To mention conformity with Catholic doctrine is not so bad as it sounds. The allusion had the purpose of reassuring the minority, who have repeated *ad nauseam* that the schema is unorthodox.

Moreover, Bishop de Smedt indicated in his terminal report that the secretariat for unity would be happy to profit "by the cooperation of all the Fathers, whatever their opinions, in order to draw up the best possible formulation." We may assume that no special commission will be named to revise the schema, although the secretariat for unity may be helped in its work by particular theologians.

Cardinal Journet and Maritain   Cardinal Journet will certainly be in the first rank of these theologians. His intervention on Tuesday morning made

---

* Also, it is now known that the Comitatus Episcopalis Internationalis has decided not to present a counterschema, as we foresaw.

a profound impression. The Swiss theologian was recently elevated to the purple by Paul VI because of the soundness of his doctrine. His thought and writings have always been linked with those of Jacques Maritain. Mr. Salleron wrote in *Le Monde* of September 21 that Maritain was the philosopher most qualified to clarify the situation. Cardinal Journet declared:

The differences of opinion in the aula could be reduced if several points already made in the schema were set in relief.

First, the human person is a member of two societies, the temporal and the spiritual.

Second, we should not forget that the human person, although a member of the political society, transcends it, and that this society must respect his convictions. But the person is not free with respect to God's truth.

Third, in the case of an erroneous conscience, we should not forget that even in error the person remains a person and should be considered as such. He cannot be constrained unless he is a real threat to public order. But he is no less responsible before God, who alone is the judge of his culpability.

Fourth, it is the state's duty to respect God. How? By not being ignorant of the different religions and by acting in such a way that all can freely honor God.

Fifth, in addition to the natural law, the Church has the supernatural law to preach the Gospel to all.

And finally, the leaders of the Church since the time of Constantine have had recourse to the secular arm. This was the Christian system. But under the influence of the Gospel itself, a clear distinction gradually emerged between civil society and the society of the Church. Today the distinction between the two orders is accepted by all. . . .

Does it follow that temporal matters are not subject to revelation? Certainly not. But this subordination is done in a different and better way than formerly. To propagate the faith we now have recourse to "the weapons of light" and not military weapons [*arma castronum*]. . . .

The declaration on religious liberty should be approved in its entirety; everything I have said is in the present text. We have only to clarify it.

The Cohesion of the Council　　We shall now briefly note three other interventions, the last at Vatican II on this subject.

Cardinal Dante of the Curia said the schema was in the spirit of Lamennais and the principles of the French Revolution which are still condemned. Archbishop Kozlowiecki of Lusaka, Zambia, said he liked the schema very much. Coadjutor Bishop Muñoz Vega of Quito affirmed in the name of the bishops of Ecuador that the schema was acceptable, but he said that it did not seem theological enough.

And so the most difficult debate of the Council ended in serenity. There is reasonable hope that the final vote on the schema will be almost unanimous. In solving this problem without serious setbacks, the Council has once again proven that it is capable of transcending its contradictions. Everyone agrees that this is due primarily to the Pope's skill and tact.

We cannot overemphasize the importance of the fact that the Secretariat for Promoting Christian Unity remains in charge of the schema on religious liberty. This body, which has become the moving spirit of ecumenism in the Roman Church thanks to John XXIII and Paul VI, will have played a decisive role at one of the Council's most critical moments.

Lifting Excommunications

Dr. W. Michaelis of Hamburg, a Protestant and a judge, has suggested that the excommunications of Photius (867), Michael Cerularius, Ecumenical Patriarch of Constantinople at the time of the schism with the East (1064), and Martin Luther (1520) be lifted.

Dr. Michaelis thinks this measure is possible, he said, because it would not involve taking a position on the truth or falsehood of the dogmatic opinions held by these persons. "The canonization of Joan of Arc in 1920 [condemned to death in 1431 and rehabilitated in 1456 by an annulment of the condemnation] is an eternal sign of the Roman Catholic Church's reparation for the crimes of the Inquisition. It can also be interpreted as a precedent for the gesture I am suggesting, one which I am convinced would be of great moral value."

Five Cardinals Have Already Spoken on Schema 13

On Tuesday the Church also began examination of the new schema "On the Church in the Modern World." Archbishop Garrone of Toulouse, vice president of the executive committee of the French episcopacy, replaced Bishop Guano, who is ill, as reporter. The Archbishop traced the history of the schema, which let us recall is addressed to all men without exception, Christian or not. The new version contains an outline of Christion anthropology, and the appendixes have been incorporated into the main body of the text.

"This schema," Archbishop Garrone said, "is in the spirit of Paul VI's

Ecclesiam suam, which recommends dialogue between the Church and the world." We have already analyzed this schema in some detail.*

Five cardinals intervened.

Military Service Cardinal Spellman, Archbishop of New York, praised the tone and style of the schema, and said it should be acceptable to all. But he thought it ought to give much more emphasis on the values of obedience and authority in the Church.

Cardinal Spellman made a number of listeners smile when he spoke about the chapter on war:

> I do object to one section. From the wording of section 101, the notion could arise that military service can never be obligatory. . . . But if the leaders of a nation decide in good faith and after mature deliberation that military service by their citizens is absolutely necessary for the defense of peace and justice, how can the individual citizen justly refuse military service? As it is said in the same section of the schema, the legitimate authority is presumed to be acting within its competence. . . . I strongly urge that section 101 be entirely revised.

Cardinal Landázuri-Ricketts, Archbishop of Lima, Peru, asked that the schema be a proclamation rather than a constitution. He also thought the text is too long (some 100 pages) and contains too many repetitions. Some terms, like *church* and *world*, are used in different senses. This might cause confusion.

Cardinal Silva Henríquez, Archbishop of Santiago, Chile, also thought the schema was too long, and asked that the adjective *pastoral* which qualifies the title *constitution* be removed. Otherwise, it might be thought that this text is being distinguished from the dogmatic constitutions.

Cardinal Jaeger, Archbishop of Paderborn, found the schema satisfactory and balanced but too optimistic. It does not take sufficiently into account the permanent conflict between God and Satan in this world, he said. In its opening lines the document should stress the necessity of cooperation with the separated brethren. In addition, a permanent body should be created after the Council to be specially concerned with the relationship between the Church and the world.

Finally, Cardinal Bea sharply criticized the Latin translation (the original version was in French). "An attempt was made to use classical Latin," he said. "For new concepts, we need new words. Let us create them. No one can understand this. I have been familiar with Latin for forty years but I couldn't read this without referring to the French text, which has no official status."

* See pp. 570 ff.

Four More Speakers on Religious Liberty

Wednesday's general congregation treated two themes: religious liberty and schema 13. Although the debate on religious liberty is over, four more Fathers spoke on the subject. The regulations permit this, provided each speaker represents at least seventy bishops. Those who intervened were Archbishop Wojtyla of Cracow; Maronite Bishop Michael Doumith of Sarba, Lebanon; Bishop Grotti of Tunigaba, Brazil; and Auxiliary Bishop Ancel of Lyon. Bishop Ancel remarked:

> The schema does not show the connection between the obligation to seek truth and religious liberty. Yet it is precisely this obligation which constitutes the ontological foundation of religious liberty. Every man has the duty to seek objective truth. This obligation flows from human nature, and can be admitted even by nonbelievers.
>
> If man is to fulfill this obligation, he must dispose of more than psychological liberty; he must also be free from all external constraint. . . . These ideas should be more clearly expressed in the preliminary declaration, which will be the best-known part of the document.

Taking up a theme previously expressed by Cardinal Alfrink in a similar way, Bishop Doumith said the schema should not speak of a confessional state. When the confessional state is not Christian (the speaker was evidently thinking of the Muslim state) and makes civil law depend on religious law, then those who do not profess the state religion are discriminated against.

Two Observations   Here are two further observations on Tuesday's indicative vote.

1. It is likely that the Pope's forthcoming trip to the United Nations in company with eight cardinals helped bring about a satisfactory solution quickly. Now Paul VI will be able to go before the United Nations with this positive result on the books.

2. In addition to the conservatives, who are more or less hostile to the schema, the 224 Fathers who voted against the schema include a certain number of bishops who favor the document but think it is altogether too weak. They demand that the text be completely redrafted on a much broader basis than the purely juridical. Two French bishops are said to be of this opinion.

It would therefore be a mistake to think that 224 Fathers are "negative" opponents. In fact, these are few in number.

Five Out of Twelve Interventions Hostile to Schema 13

Schema 13 was subjected to severe criticisms by five of the twelve speakers on Wednesday morning.

Cardinal Ruffini of Palermo was first to the attack. He found the schema too long, sometimes obscure, and not precise enough.

> The text does not refer to the great number of sins, the corruption of morals, or all the abominable evils of the modern world. . . . It says nothing about the problem of suffering. . . . It is too prone to show the Church on her knees asking pardon for her faults. I don't like this at all. We are forgetting everything that civilization and culture owes to the Church. Let us speak of doctrine rather than describing the world.

Cardinal Siri, Archbishop of Genoa complained that there is "not a word on relativism, indifferentism, or laicism. The Church cannot neglect her own problems in favor of those of the world. This scandalizes Christions. Let us talk about the Gospel."

Archbishop Giuseppe Amici of Modena said, "This schema does not respond to the hopes it raised in the press. It will disappoint unbelievers as well as the faithful because of its weak exposition of doctrine. Let us refer everything to the norms of the Gospel without considering the present situation. This is not the Church's mission."

A Dubious Compromise Bishop Russell J. McVinney of Providence, Rhode Island, said the text is "a dubious compromise with those who are at the root of the evils that afflict humanity, like the decay of morals." The speaker then launched into a long diatribe against the modern world.

"Speak about the schema," the moderator interrupted.

"That is precisely what I am doing," retorted the Bishop. "Many young people and even priests no longer obey the Church."

The intervention most hostile to the schema was made by Archbishop de Proença Sigaud of Diamantina, Brazil, secretary of the Comitatus Episcopalis Internationalis.

His personal secretary is a layman, Mr. Enrique Barbosa Chavés, who calls himself the director of the Brazilian Society for the Defense of Family Tradition and Property (Rio de Janeiro branch). This is not surprising when one knows the ultraconservative social positions of the Archbishop of Diamantina. But many other bishops in his country are working in the opposite direction, for a redistribution of land and reforms that are urgently needed.

Teilhard and Babel   Archbishop de Proença Sigaud personally explained to us the reason for his intervention. He said that the schema is inspired by the principles of modern phenomenology and not the philosophy of Thomas Aquinas, recommended by the Pope. There is a great danger in this.

We already have a schema on the world in the twenty volumes of Pius XII's speeches, which contain clear and profound doctrines on all problems. Let us make a compilation from this encyclopedia, and let the schema take inspiration from this supernatural light. The Archbishop complained that "The present schema forgets original sin and ascesis. . . . Teilhard de Chardin's ideas about the formation of the world are dangerous, and threaten to plunge us into catastrophe. The tower of Babel was also intended to be a new construction of the world."

Seven Favorable Interventions   The seven other speakers were quite favorable to the schema, but expressed different wishes.

Cardinal Koenig, Archbishop of Vienna, thanked the commission for its work, and directly opposed Cardinal Siri and Archbishop Amici in saying: "The Church must be concerned with the world because of her supernatural mission. Otherwise, she would fail to carry out her responsibility. . . . A new and altogether satisfying conciliar style has been found here. Let us clarify the contents of the schema and approve it."

Cardinal Döpfner, Archbishop of Munich, spoke in the name of ninety-one German and Scandinavian bishops: "The schema is much better than its predecessor, but it suffers from several important weaknesses: an inadequate distinction between the natural and supernatural orders. . . . Sin is not emphasized enough. . . . But even though it is imperfect, we must adopt it."

Archbishop Anthony Jordan of Edmonton, Alberta, Canada, said, "The Church is well presented as the humble servant of the human race. The schema is capable of reaching all men. But let us emphasize the bond between man's work and the liturgy."

Archbishop Aramburu of Tucumán, Argentina, suggested, "Let us imitate the method of Saint Thomas who always began with the natural basis."

Italian Archbishop Giuseppe D'Avack of the Curia said, "The schema seems too naturalistic. Its conclusion should make the secret of Christianity clear: charity lived in grace which was earned for us by the cross of Christ."

Bishop Rusch of Innsbruck-Feldkirch, Austria, felt that the text is overly philosophical. "It should have a dynamic and practical theological dimension. The tone is too moralistic and not biblical or historical enough."

Ukrainian Rite Archbishop Hermaniuk of Winnipeg said, "*Placet juxta modum.* I am happy because of the concern shown for non-Christian religions and because of the humble way in which the Church is presented. The style is simple and pastoral." The schema has defects—it is too complicated in structure and too Scholastic in form—but these can easily be corrected.

Schema 13 Elaborates "a Theology of the World," Says Father Chenu

In a conference at the Dutch Documentation Center Wednesday, Father Chenu said that history was "consubstantial" with Christianity. Man, he went on, "is God's partner." And he quoted Karl Barth: "Since God became man, man has been the measure of all things."

Criticizing the Cartesian kind of dualism, the speaker said that Vatican II is helping erase traces of angelism from the Christian conception of man, who lives in the world and in history.

"The construction of the world," he said, "has been reintegrated into the economy of salvation. Grace works through and in man to influence the world, which is an extension of man's body." Father Chenu noted, however, that profane history is not salvific. "Evangelization is of another order than civilization. But profane values are stepping stones. Socialization, for example, has opened up new ways to express fraternal love."

By elaborating a theology of the world, the Council is renewing the theology of creation. The construction of the world and the fulfillment of temporal tasks constitute a continuing creation which will be recapitulated in Christ. Christian hope is an absolute; but terrestrial hope calls for Christian hope. "The two hopes influence one another, the second nourishing the first."

Father Chenu proposed that schema 13 be more closely related to the Constitution *De ecclesia* and that explicit mention of the Messiah be made. Purged of the error of millenarianism, the messianic theme, he concluded, is one of the most striking signs of our time.

SEPTEMBER 24

Schema 13 Supposes a Still Inchoate Theology of Terrestrial Realities

For a militant layman trained in Catholic Action, especially if he is a transalpinist, schema 13 seems like a collection of commonplaces, and on some subjects, like marriage, culture, and war, it is singularly deficient in both courage and depth. On the other hand, many bishops find it extremely new, indeed revolutionary. This is the first time, we might recall, that a council has been concerned with man and the world as such. One should therefore not be surprised by the weaknesses of the schema; it contains, if in a minor key, lines of reflection that suppose a still inchoate theology of terrestrial realities.

The laymen who worked on the preparatory commissions are unanimous in saying that for the most part the ecclesiastics they were associated with live in a totally different world, a world of abstractions and theological logomachy. The laymen were naturally inclined to begin with facts and develop principles in terms of those facts, while their interlocutors were accustomed to the opposite procedure.

Nonetheless, a great deal of work went into schema 13; it has been revised twenty times and isn't finished yet. The chapter on culture, for example, is still very unsatisfactory and will be revised before the criticisms of the Council are made. The Germans deserve credit for accepting the schema even though it lacks the *Weltanschauung* they are so fond of —an epic in which the powers of good and evil are locked in a permanent historic battle.

At the moment the conciliar debates are with few exceptions on the dismal side. They are still concerned with an examination of the schema as a whole and the preliminary exposition. Here are the subjects of the sections corresponding with the first two parts, which deal largely with generalities:

A. Introduction: (1) solidarity of the Church with the whole human family, (2) those to whom the Council is speaking, (3) the service of man.

B. *Preliminary exposition* on the human condition in the world today: (4) hopes and anxieties, (5) a profound transformation, (6) changes in the social order, (7) psychological, moral, and religious changes, (8) the imbalance of the modern world, (9) the increasing universality of deep aspirations.

By way of example, here is a passage from the last section:

Many scientific, human and religious factors have contributed to the transformation of the world, whence its both global and complex character.

Thus the modern world appears to be both powerful and weak, capable of better and worse things, poised between freedom and slavery, between progress and regression, between brotherhood and hatred. Man can only make his choices to his advantage by transcending himself. . . . What is the meaning of suffering, evil, death, which persist despite all progress? What awaits us after life? What is the meaning of existence and human efforts? What purpose does it all have?

The Latin into which it was translated from the original French version has been widely criticized. It is cast in a Ciceronian mold and the effects are considered deplorable, so much so that many Fathers have requested, to the great chagrin of the purists, that stylistic considerations be cast to the winds. They suggest that instead of using ridiculous circumlocutions, the schema should rely on such straightforward terms as *cultura, responsabilitas, valores, civilisatio, structura,* and *socialisatio.* The word *sport* is presently translated *ludicra certamina.* This expression is so obviously vague that its meaning was put between parentheses in French, in the manner of children who spell out what they are trying to draw.

The Odor of Capitalism It would be pointless, in the present state of discussion, to give a detailed report of each intervention. There were eleven on Thursday, including three cardinals. Here are some of the more salient points made.

Most of the bishops called for a more concise text. Two Indians—Coadjutor Archbishop Lourdusamy of Bangalore, who spoke in the name of sixty-two bishops from his country, and Bishop Abasolo of Vijayapuram—regretted the absence of a religious message or a natural spirituality. They also remarked, as did Cardinal Rugambwa of Bukoba, Tanzania, that the text seemed to be addressed to developed countries, and hence it is difficult to see how the document could make a universal impact.

Archbishop Morcillo González of Madrid and Archbishop Boleslaw Kominek of Wroclaw, who spoke in the name of sixty-two Polish bishops, agreed that schema 13 smacked of capitalism. This prompted Monsignor Haubtmann, one of the editors of the schema, to say *ex aula,* "Some employers don't think so!"

Archibishop Baudoux of St. Boniface, Manitoba, Canada, was happy with the "holy optimism" and the clarity of the text. He urged that it be as modern as possible. "Our style is still too apologetic. Let us be more forthright and bolder."

Péguy's Ducks Bishop Renard of Versailles was sorry that the schema played down original sin and did not bring out "the existential ambiguity of human values." In the concrete, these do not always lead to Christ. "The self-sufficiency of these values is a danger," he said. "They are seen too much as stepping stones to grace and not enough as possible obstacles."

The Bishop cited Charles Péguy, speaking of the evil effects of a desiccating moralism: "They do not get wet in grace any more than a duck gets wet in water."

Let Us Speak to Youth Virilely and Not Paternally, Says Cardinal Cardijn

The intervention of Cardinal Cardijn of Belgium was warmly applauded:

> This schema is excellent. Let us consider men in the concrete as well as in the abstract. . . . I will speak of workers later. Today I would like to speak of youth and the deprived.
>
> Let us put more emphasis on youth [schema 13 scarcely mentions them]. They represent half of humanity. Let us speak to them in terms of the future. The world depends on youth and not on us. Let us realize that their life is very different from what their elders knew. Their work or pleasure frequently takes them away from their family or even their country. We must make them understand that the Church has confidence in them. Let us invite them virilely and not paternally to assume their responsibilities. Let us appeal to their sense of freedom. They have a magnificent vocation to fulfill in the domain of international relations and peace. . . .
>
> As for the one-third of the world that lives in misery, let us talk to them about the necessity of attaining a standard of living equal to that of other countries. The scandal of international injustice must cease in a world where the only rich nations are the Christian nations. Christians can play a considerable educative role. The underdeveloped countries have a right to respect for their own genius.

Religious Liberty Again

Religious liberty is one of those subjects that are not easily disposed of. Although the schema has left the limelight for the laborious silence of the commissions, it is still widely discussed in the corridors of Vatican II.

The history of religious liberty in the Church, as traced by Father Gerest, a Dominican, makes it clear, according to many Fathers, that great progress has been made.

In the first period, liberty was considered a temptation. Erasmus was condemned in 1557, and the Inquisition reigned balefully. It is only fair to note that the suppression of religious liberty was the responsibility of all the churches of that time.

In a second stage, (the eighteenth and nineteenth centuries), liberty was considered, in reaction against liberalism, as an insanity, in the celebrated term of Pius VI which was repeated by Gregory XVI and Pius IX. Lamennais was condemned by the encyclical *Mirari vos* in 1832. The papacy could not see then how freedom of religion could be disassociated from a philosophy of subjectivism and indifferentism. This was the cause of the intransigence which we consider unacceptable today.

In a third period, religious liberty was looked upon as a concession. After the *Syllabus* (1864), Bishop Dupanloup spread the thesis-antithesis theory which led to a more or less parsimonious tolerance. Leo XIII was the pope of this tolerance.

In a fourth period, particularly with Pius XI and Pius XII, religious liberty came to be seen more and more as a good. In the encyclicals *Mit brennender Sorge* (1938), which condemned Nazism, and *Summi pontifici* (1939), the Papacy protested against the oppression of consciences.

John XXIII, in *Pacem in terris*, became the champion of liberty. It remains for Vatican II only to follow his directives and affirm that "the dignity of the human person demands that man enjoy freedom of action."

We are on the threshold of a fifth period, in which universal awareness will have long preceded all doctrinal substantiation. An eternal sign of the times.

Two Fathers Think That Christians and Even the Church Are Often a Cause of Atheism

The relatively high number of interventions hostile to schema 13 proved to be misleading. Consulted on the suitability of this document as a basis of discussion, 2,111 Fathers answered in the affirmative and only 44 in the negative. Thus examination of schema 13 proceeded full speed ahead on Friday morning, with twelve interventions. Many added something new and constructive.

We can pass over such oft-repeated criticisms as: the schema is too long; it doesn't speak enough about sin, the cross, redemption; it is too optimistic; it uses the word *world* in different senses, which could cause confusion; it does not distinguish clearly enough between human progress and supernatural salvation (Cardinal Frings).

These were the most interesting interventions.

Coadjutor Bishop Elchinger of Strasbourg said:

> The schema has a good deal to say about what the world should do but too little about what the Church proposes to do to meet the

world and truly understand it. Christ asked us to be witnesses, that is, not only to spread his message but to adopt a new way of loving men and aiding them concretely. . . .

Men today ask of the Church a healthy freedom, a profound sincerity, brotherhood in work, and the exchange of ideas. . . .

One means of encouraging respect for human dignity and effectively developing the sense of personal liberty would undoubtedly be a concerted effort to increase the decentralization of economic, social, and even ecclesiastical life at every level of the hierarchy. This decentralization would in fact enable different persons to express themselves frankly and assume the kind of responsibility that is compatible with adult dignity, without, of course, denying the necessity and value of superior authority. . . .

It is not enough for the schema to expound beautiful thoughts about unbelief and atheism. The Church has the obligation to suppress within her own structure anything that might nourish unbelief. She must have the missionary boldness to send forth real witnesses to Christ who will adopt new forms of the apostolate, especially in places where the message of God and Christ has never been heard.

Cardinal Seper, Archbishop of Zagreb, told the Fathers:

It is obligatory that the schema treat atheism. But let us speak about it in terms of the atheistic mind. Many look upon atheism as progress. Let us try to understand this psychology. Many of our contemporaries were born atheists. It is therefore not their fault. . . .

Christians are much too frequently partisan to a past order and are themselves often the cause of atheism. Many Christians are opposed to the progress of the world; yet it is God's explicit will that there be more justice in the world.

Bishop Himmer of Tournai said:

Workers are not given adequate treatment in the schema; yet they constitute the greatest part of the human race. Even when they are under the influence of Marxist ideology, we must dialogue with them.

The advancement of workers is real progress for mankind. Let us say this clearly. The working world is coming to respect more and more professional ability rather than money. Money is seen now more as the fruit of labor than as the product of capital.

Man Divinized The Oriental interventions were once again a precious enrichment for the Latin Church. If it is true that the Church of the Orient is not concerned enough with the world, it is no less true that the Church of the Occident has to some extent lost the eschatological perspective and "the new earth" spoke of by Saint Paul.

Cardinal Meouchi of Antioch made these points:

> The importance of Christ's resurrection is not emphasized enough. Yet it is a cosmic event that bears upon the future of the world, all of nature, and matter itself. In the West too much stress is laid on the passion and not enough on the resurrection of Christ, who definitively conquered death. . . .
>
> Nor is the Holy Spirit adequately treated. . . . The anthropology that is outlined is not sufficiently based on Scripture or patristics. It is still too rational. . . .
>
> The image of God is not only man as the lord of creation; it is above all man divinized. Only an eschatological perspective can reconcile the Orient, which insists on the vanity of things terrestrial, and the Occident, which is more sensitive to their value.

Maronite Archbishop Ziadé of Beirut also spoke about the resurrection. "It is necessary," he said, "for the seed to die in the earth in order to rise again. Man's activity is such a grain; it must die to receive the illumination of the Spirit. The experience of Christ is ontological, 'mysterious,' not merely moral."

Neoclericalism   Finally, Archibshop Cantero Cuadrado of Saragossa said he was worried about the schema because it attached too much importance to the things of this world. "Isn't this clericalism?" he asked. "The things of the world are not those of the Church. . . . The schema is ingenuously optimistic; it is also Occidental. . . . Its method must be reversed: begin with theology and then come to the facts, not vice versa."

Other speakers of the day were Cardinal Richaud of Bordeaux, Cardinal Santos of Manila; Bishop Volk of Mainz, and Bishop Marafini of Veroli, Italy.

What Schema 13 Says About Atheism

On Friday Vatican II began examination of the first part of schema 13. It is entitled, "The Church and the Human Condition." The first chapter of this part is consecrated to "The Vocation of the Human Person," and comprises ten sections: "Man in the Image of God," "The Dignity of the Human Body," "The Dignity of the Soul and Particularly of the Intelligence," "The Dignity of Conscience," "The Grandeur of Liberty," "The

Social Character of Man," "Victory over Death," "The Knowledge of God," "The Problem of Atheism," and "Christ, the Perfect Man."

Section 19, on atheism, was criticized by Cardinal Seper and Bishop Elchinger, and strikes many as being unsatisfactory. Here is the text. One cannot avoid noticing its churchy style:

> Many systematically deny God; this is one of the most serious facts of our time. Indeed, there are very diverse forms of atheism; they cannot be simply reduced to a common pattern. In many regions atheism is deliberately propagated and may even enjoy the support of the public powers, and it is spread with the help of various means of social pressure, especially in the education of youth, in contempt of the liberty of citizens.
>
> According to one of these ideologies, in determined social conditions man, enslaved by all sorts of adversities, sees the perfection of liberty and happiness as a divine, superterrestrial being. He then subjects himself to the product of his own imagination, expecting salvation from it, and thus turns away from his worldly responsibilities. In this way he becomes a kind of stranger to himself. Man must be liberated from this alienation, this slavery, at all costs in order that he may consecrate all his energies to economic and social progress and establish his happiness on this earth.
>
> This atheism uses psuedo-scientific arguments and methods that are often gravely injurious to the dignity of the person in order to stamp out the faith in the hearts of the masses. Yet many martyrs have borne and still bear splendid witness to the living God before the world. The Church, faithful to God and faithful to man, will continue to repudiate, sorrowfully but firmly, those poisonous doctrines and actions which contradict reason and the common experience of humanity, and dethrone man from his native excellence.
>
> We invite those who defend such systems to ask themselves sincerely whether or not their opposition to God can be based on solid and irreproachable arguments. We ask, moreover, by what right civil authorities make a distinction between believers and unbelievers, and why they do not recognize the fundamental rights of the human person. In rejecting atheism, the Church sincerely admits that all men, whether believers or not, must live together in the same world and that all must work to build it up. But at the same time she demands the liberty and the possibility for believers to build also the temple of God in this world, notably the community of Christians gathered in the Church.
>
> The Church knows perfectly that she is in harmony with the

most secret desires of the human heart when she champions the dignity of the human vocation, restoring hope to those who have already despaired of anything higher than their present lot. Far from diminishing man, her message brings to his development light, life, and freedom. Apart from this message, nothing will avail to fill up the heart of man: "Thou hast made us for thyself, O Lord, and our hearts are restless until they rest in thee."

The Isms of the Council

The sociology of the Council remains to be done. But this is hard work. It is easier to catalogue the vocabulary used by the bishops. Depending on whether they belong to the minority or the majority, they repeat a certain number of words periodically with characteristic insistence. Tell me how you speak and I will tell you what you are. This adage is verified every day at Vatican II.

Here is a preliminary list of a few key words ending in *ism*. As is natural, the minority, who are obsessed by heresies, are more articulate than the majority. But both groups are conditioned by their language.

MAJORITY	MINORITY
Triumphalism	Subjectivism
Formalism	Relativism
Legalism	Liberalism
Clericalism	Indifferentism
Occidentalism	Positivism
Paternalism	Pragmatism
Individualism	Naturalism
Dogmatism	Existentialism
Conceptualism	Laicism
	Modernism
	Rationalism
	Kantianism
	Collectivism
	Marxism
	Teilhardism

Conferences on Schema 13
by Pastor Vischer and Father Congar

In a conference on schema 13, Pastor Lukas Vischer, an observer delegated by the World Council of Churches, emphasized the high ecumenical value of this document. The world that is discussed in this schema, he said, is the meeting point for all churches. Thus the world plays a privileged role as mediator.

The schema should not give the impression that the Church is intact. "That would not be the truth. We are divided. Let us not hide this." The speaker also regretted that the orders of nature and grace were not more sharply distinguished.

Father Yves Congar showed how the Church has long lived with a monastic type of spirituality that was based on contempt for the world and women (derived from Saint Augustine, Saint Jerome, and others). Schema 13 is proof that this period has passed.

"I think," said Father Congar, "that the number-one problem in theology, catechesis, and preaching is to reunite anthropology and theology. The Bible, a Jewish writer has said, is not a theology for man but an anthropology for God. The contents of revelation is less the mystery of God than the God-man relationship."

In conclusion, Father Congar declared that just as the Council of Trent created a new kind of bishop who was a pastor and not a lord, so would Vatican II create an original kind of bishop who will be "the evangelical conscience of the world."

SEPTEMBER 28

On Atheism, Worker-Priests, and the Arms Race

Schema 13's treatment of atheism is "impoverished." The word is on everyone's lips today. How can one explain this meagerness on a subject that is at the heart of the contemporary religious problem? Catholic publications have diagnosed the case at length. In France alone such figures as Jacques Maritain, Jean Lacroix, Étienne Borne, and Father Liégé have written about it—not to mention a certain pastoral letter by Cardinal Montini as Archbishop of Milan and recently his encyclical *Ecclesiam suam*.

The explanation is simple though disturbing. The writers of schema 13 once again had to take contradictory recommendations into account. Some think that the condemnation of atheism is the be-all and end-all of Christian theology and pastoral concern. Such bishops still exist. Others want to talk about atheism in an understanding spirit, realizing that contemporary atheists are the product of a superstitious and distorted Christianity. Generations of Christians have believed and still believe in God as though he were an idol. Some think they possess truth, which is to say God ("I am the truth," Christ said), as one would possess a bank account; others use Him as an excuse for not assuming social responsibility.

Caught between these two contradictory attitudes, the writers of schema 13 were paralyzed. The Council Fathers seem determined to overcome these obstacles. Some brilliant interventions on Monday proved this, among which must be included those of Maximos IV Saigh and Archbishop D'Souza of Bhopal, India. Father Pedro Arrupe, General of the Jesuits, stressed effectiveness in his intervention, good disciple of Saint Ignatius that he is. This Spaniard spoke like an army man who would sacrifice anything for results. He also took the occasion to underline the virtue of total and unconditional obedience to the sovereign pontiff. This was variously commented upon, and disturbed the Protestant observers.

Three speakers referred more or less directly to the need for worker-priests, thus proving that Vatican II cannot, despite the efforts of some, avoid the real problems of the modern apostolate.

And, for the first time as far as we know, the name of Freud was mentioned in the Council with reference to the Church's backwardness in assimilating the thinking of the great geniuses of humanity.

Condemning Atheism Is Pointless Cardinal Koenig made these remarks on the schema's treatment of atheism:

> Section 19 is inadequate. The different forms of atheism must be distinguished. . . . Atheism is propagated throughout the world, and yet the human soul is naturally Christian. . . . It seems that the roots of atheism are found only in the Western world. Historically, atheism was encouraged by the failings of Christians themselves, many of whom had and have no precise idea of God or exact image of man. The possible remedies against atheism are intense cooperation to foster Christian unity, the Church's efforts to promote social justice without discrimination, and the struggle against religious ignorance. . . .
>
> Priests and Christians must share in the life of atheists. These are the real Christian weapons. . . . A new condemnation of atheism would be absolutely pointless.

Real Socialism Is Christianity Maximos IV Saigh said:

> Section 19 is too negative. It is obvious that we are not going to save mankind from atheism by condemning Marxism. We must also

denounce the causes of Communistic atheism, especially by proposing a dynamic mysticism and a vigorous social morality.

This section could profitably be replaced by the following passage from Paul VI's *Ecclesiam suam:* "Sometimes, too, the atheist is spurred on by noble sentiments and by impatience with the mediocrity and self-seeking of so many contemporary social settings. He knows well how to borrow from our Gospel modes and expressions of solidarity and human compassion. Shall we not be able to lead him back one day to the Christian source of such manifestations of moral worth?"

Paul VI takes up the thread of John XXIII's *Pacem in terris* when he says, "The doctrines of such movements, once elaborated and defined, remain always the same, whereas the movements themselves cannot help but evolve and undergo changes, even of a profound nature, but we do not despair that they may some day be able to enter into a more positive dialogue with the Church than the present one, which we now of necessity deplore and lament."

These two texts seem preferable to the present schema, which itself merely deplores and laments. We all know from experience that many atheists are not against the Church. Some are very close to her. What they really seek is a truer presentation of God, a religion in accord with the historical evolution of humanity, and above all a Church that sustains not only the poor but also the efforts toward solidarity among the poor. They are often scandalized by a mediocre and selfish Christianity, hobbled by money and base riches, even taking up arms to defend, not its faith which can never be defended by force, but its short-range interests and security. . . .

Some have asked that the schema denounce the sins of the world. But that is precisely the enormous sin of the world, continually denounced by Christ in the Gospel: namely, selfishness and the exploitation of man by man. Some would like the text to speak more about the necessity of carrying the cross and accepting one's lot with resignation. But who in fact carries a greater cross than the oppressed masses, who are trying to shake off their misery by means of work, solidarity, and even socialization? It is only unfortunate that they do this within atheistic systems. But hasn't the selfishness of certain Christians provoked much of the atheism of the masses?

Christ cautions us against scandalizing the little ones, that is, the humble. Many atheists, like Lazarus in the Gospel, are scandalized by the rich who call themselves Christian.

Let us therefore be courageous enough to redirect the moral values that are solidarity, fraternity, and socialization to their true sources, which are Christian. Let us show that true socialism is Christianity fully lived with a just distribution of goods and fundamental equality.

Modern forms of economy and sociology need not condemnation but the leaven of the Gospel to break away from atheism and accomplish their objectives in a harmonious fashion.

Rather than a banal condemnation, which we already have, let us send the working world an ever greater number of priests and laymen who are prepared to share the life of workers and the social effort of contemporary man, and thus reveal to them the God they reject but secretly seek.

Archbishop D'Souza observed:

In reading this schema one gets the impression that it is a "digest." The work of the Council is not to sum up everything that has been written these past few years on the problems of the world; rather, it is to give a new impetus to the Church, which must respond without further delay to the appeals which God addresses to her through events. The Church is often behind the times. Today, a hundred and fifty years after religious liberty became part of the social life of many countries, we are just getting around to defining it. We had to wait forty years after Marx's *Manifesto* before *Rerum novarum* was published. We are all familiar with the condemnation of Galileo. But he wasn't the only one. Think of Lamennais, Freud, Teilhard de Chardin. . . . Let us speak of them here, and let us henceworth avoid condemnations and the Index. . . .

Are we ourselves altogether men of our times? We monologue and no one understands us any longer. Happily, there are coffee bars at the Council where we can exchange ideas.

Thereupon the assembly broke into laughter.

Less Talk and More Action Father Arrupe's talk was followed attentively. It was his first speech in the aula, and everyone knows that the Pope has given the Jesuits the task of fighting atheism. There is a curious mixture in Father Arrupe of a modern, practical, scientific mind and an attitude of a bygone age that considers the Church as an army poised for attack. Basque in origin, Father Arrupe is a fierce defender of Christian institutions. He dreams of a neo-Christianity. Let us listen:

The intention of section 19 is good, but as usual with us it is too intellectual. We must go further. The spirit of the world is steeped in materialism; it infiltrates everywhere. It is the great evil of the century, and it is becoming more organized. Confronted with it, our efforts seem dispersed. Let's get organized. In 1961, 18 percent of the world was Catholic; in 1965, it is only 16 percent. Our pastoral methods are inadequate. Our intellectual positions are like a refuge and a subterfuge. Let us act more and talk less.

Atheism is not primarily theoretical and philosophical. It is not enough to fight it with arguments. We must counter it with the reality of a Christian community. Let us rebuild a Christian society, not enclosed in a ghetto but in the midst of the world. We must create circumstances favorable to the Christian development of all men. I propose (1) that specialists make a thorough investigation from which a general plan of action might be deduced; (2) that the Pope assign responsibility in this matter—we owe the Pope absolute and unconditional obedience [Father Arrupe repeated this twice], for he must direct the whole Church; and (3) that all believers be invited to collaborate in our plan.

The Infernal Cycle of Armaments Archbishop Guerry of Cambrai referred to arming for deterrence and the infernal cycle of armaments:

> The Council should explicitly and solemnly repeat Pope Paul's appeal in Bombay. The Holy Father asked nations to consecrate a part of the resources used to defray military expenses to the struggle against hunger and the development of backward nations. The appeal in Bombay did not merely diagnose the cause of the evil but proposed positive solutions. This appeal is more necessary than ever, because we are confronted with the frightening, almost tragic impotence of heads of state to put an end to the infernal cycle that is forcing one nation after another, against its will, to invent and manufacture greater quantities of more expensive and more devastating weapons.
>
> Each invokes the right to legitimate defense and thinks it is creating a deterrent force. But everyone wants to be in possession of what has become a symbol of power. The armaments race aggravates the disparity between rich and poor nations in a truly scandalous manner. It imposes very heavy sacrifices.

Bishop Pildáin y Zapiáin of the Canary Islands said, "Let us vigorously denounce liberal capitalism. It is a cause of atheism which we should solemnly condemn, as Cardinal Suhard did in his day. The goods of the earth are destined for all, and we cannot tolerate the existence of enormous, unexploited wealth side by side with great poverty."

A Pestilence Cardinal Florit of Florence said, "Section 19 does not stress the fact that atheism by its very nature is wicked. No conciliation with it is possible; any form of collaboration would be dangerous. The philosophical theories of our time have led to atheism and scientism. The problem of evil is the chief obstacle to accepting God."

Byzantine Rite Bishop Nicholas Elko of Pittsburgh had this criticism:

> The schema seems to excuse atheistic materialism. Now, atheism brings about the ruin of the social order. It is a terrible sign of our times; it is a pestilence. It must be condemned; otherwise future centuries will accuse us of cowardice. Let us not oppose one pope to another, for they have all said the same thing. As a remedy, I propose that we correct our possible errors, that we promote social justice, that we inform ourselves on atheism. . . .

Bishop Ruotolo of Ugento urged, "Let us not give the impression of discrediting the Church by evoking historical faults. Let us leave the past to historians. Let us draw up a special declaration, or at least a special chapter, on atheism."

Other speakers included Father Fernández, Master General of the Dominicans, whose intervention was abstract and very theoretical ("Principles are more important than applications," he said, thus contradicting, no doubt unwittingly, what the general of the Jesuits had said); Bishop Corboy of Monze, Zambia; Bishop Klepacz of Lodz, Poland; and Cardinal Rossi, Archbishop of São Paulo, Brazil. The last mentioned stressed the fact that Latin America has undergone a political revolution but has yet to experience the necessary social revolution.

By Monday, September 27, there had been twenty-two votes on the schema on the lay apostolate. There were 287 *placet juxta modum* votes for chapter 4 and 230 for chapter 5, which proposes a permanent secretariat for the laity in Rome. Thus, all the chapters have been approved with the required two-thirds majority. The commission will now examine the proposed amendments before returning the schema to the assembly for the last time.

Why the Directive Bodies of the Council Suffer from Chronic Impotence

The recent failure of the meeting of the directors of Vatican II (that is, the four moderators, the twelve presidents, and the six members of the

Coordinating Commission, along with the secretary general) calls for some comment. We recall that the meeting convened September 20 was to determine whether or not—and if so, in what form—to interrogate the Fathers on the religious liberty schema. The results of this meeting, as we reported, were negative. The majority (either 13 to 7 or 15 to 9; it is difficult to verify the figures) were against a vote. The majority seemed to fear the test of an indicative vote. They thought that the opposition would either be very strong or on the contrary very weak. In the first case, it would be a partial defeat for the conciliar majority; in the second case, it would be a total defeat for the minority.

Whatever the case, we are told that a personal intervention on the part of the Pope was necessary to set matters right. It is a constant fact (demonstrated in October, 1963, in November, 1963, and again in November, 1964, apropos of schema 13) that the directive bodies of the Council have never been able to resolve the difficulties of Vatican II by themselves. It is also a fact that "These bodies are more sluggish than the will of the immense majority of the assembly,"* more sluggish indeed than the will of the moderators delegated by the Pope to preside over the operation of the Council.

Why?

Because though three out of the four moderators are dynamic and open men, the same is not true of most of the Council presidency. In fact, the moderators have not been able to fulfill their role as of spurring the Council. The tricephalic nature of the conciliar leadership paralyzes its activity. The three heads neutralize one another. As a consequence, the conciliar commissions have exhorbitant power, for it falls to them to interpret the desires of the Council.

It is worthwhile noting that none of the presidents or moderators was elected by the assembly. They were named by John XXIII and Paul VI. This is the root of the difficulty. The Council presidency is not reflecting the image of the Council.

It is obviously unhealthy that the Pope has to intervene in order for the Council to be itself. This is one of the major defects in the conciliar structure. For this reason, collegiality has not yet been entirely borne out in practice. It will take some time to throw off the dead weight of a certain tradition and teach the episcopal body to assume its new responsibilities.

* Father René Laurentin, *Bilan de la troisième session*, Paris, Éditions du Seuil, 1965.

Dialogue with Modern Man Requires
a Knowledge of Psychoanalysis

All believers owe a debt of gratitude to unbelievers. As Paul Valéry wrote, "It is unfortunate that the Church, which has understood and assimilated so many things, has not been able to absorb the unbelievers, those great promoters and confessors of the spirit."

Unbelief has over the centuries forced religion to purify itself. The first Christians who refused to worship pagan gods were treated as atheists. Who forced Christianity to draw up a doctrine of religious liberty if not the descendants of those unbelievers who launched the French Revolution? *Oportet haereses esse.* What helped the faith rid itself of superstitions if not science, whose progress is closely connected with a methodological ignorance of God and the supernatural? Scientists taught their believing brothers that God would never take the place of second causes. Theology and metaphysics owe a great deal to science.

With Freud, the great unbeliever of the modern world, humanity made a revolutionary breakthrough. The "Know thyself" of antiquity found unsuspected fulfillment in depth psychology. Psychoanalysis is more capable than any previous discipline of determining the real place of religious feeling and detecting its deviations. It is difficult to see how Christianity can do without a method of investigation that has turned the traditional conception of man upside down. We are becoming more aware today of the affinities that exist between psychoanalysis and spirituality.

Despite the Church's contempt for psychoanalysis, it is very interesting to note the prudence of the Holy Office in a monitum of July 15, 1961. It said essentially this: (1) it is false to assert that psychoanalytic training is an *absolutely* necessary condition for priestly ordination; (2) priests and religious cannot consult psychoanalysis without the permission of their bishops and a serious reason.

The door is not completely closed, as is sometimes said. In any case, it is a credit to Vatican II that Bishop Méndez Arceo of Cuernavaca devoted most of his intervention on Tuesday morning to the benefits of psychoanalysis.* Here is the substance of what he said:

> I cannot understand why schema 13 is silent about psychoanalysis. It is a real science with its own object, method, and theories. It is not an entirely mature science and it is not without dangers,

* Bishop Méndez Arceo directs the diocese in which a Benedictine monastery is making systematic use of the techniques of psychoanalysis.

which must be taken into account; but we cannot for all of that ignore the psychoanalytic revolution. It is at least as important as the technological revolution.

Analysis forms part of human culture, has proposed a renewed concept of man, and raises problems we didn't even suspect the existence of before. The Church, because of the anti-Christian dogmatism of certain analysts, has taken a position that is reminiscent of the case of Galileo. But nothing is more relevant to pastoral activity than psychoanalysis.

The Church's statements, which have been too infected with mistrust, have never had any influence on those who practice this profession. Some Catholics harbor the illusion of a Christian or Catholic psychoanalysis; but true science is neither Christian nor non-Christian.

If, therefore, the Church wishes to initiate sincere and honest dialogue with contemporary man, she cannot ignore genuine analysts. She must address them directly and not through the intermediary of morality or theology. This would have very beneficial results, for psychoanalysis as a science has a power of purification that could be of great help to men whose faith is commingled with psychological deviations that pervert or inhibit it.

This courageous intervention was the most notable of the fifteen speeches at Tuesday's general congregation. Here is a sketch of the others.

Armenian Rite Patriarch Ignace Pierre XIV Batanian of Cilicia thought it inappropriate for the schema to include the following quotation from the Hindu sage Rabindranath Tagore in section 40: "I turned my face from you and spelled by means of your letters, whose meaning I no longer understood." The speaker also requested a special paragraph on "situation ethics," which he called one of the greatest deviations of our times.

Bishop Paul Hnilica, a Jesuit and Titular Bishop of Rusado, Czechoslovakia, made a moving plea for the bishops who were imprisoned behind the iron curtain and asked pardon for their enemies.

Encountering Atheism   Archbishop Marty of Riems declared:

Whether they are positivist, Marxist, existentialist, or formed in the school of psychoanalysis, atheists do not deny God systematically. They refuse to believe in God because, in their eyes, belief is an illusion that diminishes man.

Those priests and laymen who have tried know that dialogue between Christians and atheists is difficult and demanding for both parties. When a Christian encounters an atheist in the flesh, he must always strive for greater honesty. To be real, such an encounter demands a purification of one's own faith and a deeper understanding of its contents. The natural and the supernatural must be better distinguished in order to be better united. The same is true of sacred history and profane history, theological hope and terrestrial hope.

Archbishop Marty said that section 19 of the schema, which he thought unsatisfactory, should be completely redrafted by the Secretariat for Relations with Non-Christian Religions, created last year by Paul VI. We might add that this new office is still feeling its way. Most Catholics, including bishops, have not yet grasped its importance; this will only gradually emerge as believers become more and more imbued with a true missionary spirit.

Archbishop Garrone of Toulouse intervened next:

Today when religion itself, not only Christianity, is questioned, the greatest service we can render men is to show that God is the author of the world. But even Christians have an inadequate understanding of this truth of the faith. Many reduce creation to the origin of the world; they do not understand that it implies the permanent and essential dependence of all things on God. The believer thus sees the creative presence of God in all terrestrial realities. This dependence on God is the profound reason for the spirit of poverty which we have spoken of so often. . . . Concerning the relationship between the earthly city and the heavenly city, we must show that charity animates the world of today, and its presence in all things will be manifested when Christ returns.

The Dogma of Universal Fraternity Auxiliary Bishop Michel Rusnack of Toronto, a Ukrainian Rite prelate, said: "It would be scandalous if a twentieth-century council did not deal with communism. We must publicly denounce its errors and lies." This bishop also spoke of the Ukrainian bishops who were imprisoned and priests who were forced to do manual labor.

Bishop Soares de Resende of Beira, Mozambique, asked, "Let us say something about the regime of secrecy by means of which the Soviets violate consciences and brainwash the youth. It is a destructive pestilence. . . . Let us confront the revolution of hatred with the revolution of fraternity. Let the Council make a solemn declaration proclaiming the dogmatic definition of the universal fraternity of men."

Archbishop António Mosquera Corral of Guayaquil, Ecuador, said,

"Let us stress the proper role of the Christian layman. He must become the salt and the light and the evangelical leaven for all other men."

Bishop Romero Menjíbar of Jaén, Spain, declared, "Nothing is better suited to the modern world than the paschal message of the resurrection."

Today, Wednesday, the Council began examination of the second part of schema 13, which deals with such burning questions as marriage, war, the misery of underdeveloped countries, and political and social life.

SEPTEMBER 30

In Certain Cases of Adultery, Let the Injured Partner Remarry?

With the second part of schema 13, Vatican II leaves the domain of theological and philosophical generalities to deal with the concrete problems confronting men today. In so doing, the Council is fulfilling the pastoral vocation John XXIII assigned to it. The subjects of the chapters in the second part, let us recall, are marriage, culture, socioeconomic life, political life, the community of nations, and peace.

We have already noted the weakness of the chapter on marriage. It is also unbalanced as a result of conflicting opinions among the commission Fathers. Let us point out once again that one of the essential factors of marriage has been removed from the chapter: birth control. This was at the Pope's wish; he will supervise a special study of this thorny problem. If Paul VI did not have the confidence of the whole Council, which recognizes his great intelligence and cultivation and is aware of the scrupulous care with which he informs himself before making a move, Vatican II could feel more frustrated.* For the problem of marital relations is far and away the most important which the schema treats, and last year the Fathers proved that they had some specific things to say about it.

Nonetheless, schema 13 does say that the parents themselves determine the number of children they think they can have "in response to the gift of God and the requirements of true love." Moreover, the schema defines marriage as "not a simple instrument of procreation, although it is ordained to this," and as "an institution ordained to the procreation and education of children."

The Fathers commented on these definitions in their interventions.

* We are in a position to say that the Pontifical Commission on Birth Control is composed of sixty-one members, among them Archbishop Leo Binz of St. Paul, Auxiliary Bishop Reuss of Mainz, and experts, priests, religious, and laymen from various countries; they are theologians, philosophers, demographers, psychiatrists, gynecologists, moralists, sociologists, and physicians, among other specialists.

The most interesting were those of Cardinals Léger and Suenens (who made headlines last year with his pronouncements on marriage) and Bishop Volk.

But the day was dominated by the revolutionary intervention of Archbishop Zoghby, Greek Melkite Patriarchal Vicar for Egypt. For the first time in the contemporary Church, someone has officially asked the Church to give the broadest possible interpretation to Matthew 5:32 and 19:9 by granting that in the case of adultery the injured partner may remarry. This intervention will have great repercussions among the many faithful who find the present canonical legislation very painful.

It would be unrealistic to think that Archbishop Zoghby will be listened to; but the fact that he could make such a suggestion is of considerable importance. It will give Catholics caught in irresolvable situations if not hope at least the consolation of knowing that some pastors share their distress.

Presently the Church never annuls a marriage that is valid, sacramental, and consummated. She may declare a marriage null because it was not validly contracted. She grants separations but not the right to remarry, except in very rare cases. On the other hand, Protestantism permits divorce and remarriage in cases of adultery, as does the Greek Orthodox Church. However, this privilege is not granted to the guilty party.

A divorced person may continue to receive the sacraments. But if he remarries while his partner is still living, he cannot receive absolution, go to communion, or have a religious burial except in very rare cases.

The Pauline and Petrine Privileges We should also mention the Pauline and Petrine privileges. The first concerns unbaptized persons: if one of the partners converts to the Catholic Church and the other does not follow or refuses to live in peace with him, then this nonsacramental marriage can be dissolved (canons 1120–1127).

The Petrine privilege, whose invocation is reserved, as its name indicates, to the sovereign pontiff, is not mentioned under this designation either in canon law or in the manuals of moral theology. It goes beyond the Pauline privilege. It says that the pope, by reason of this privilege, can dissolve sacramental marriages which are apparently valid and consummated, for example, between two Protestants if one of the partners converts to Catholicism and the other is opposed to it.

We might also mention the following case: in Germany after the Second World War, the Church and the state agreed jointly that if the husband had disappeared for a period of six years, he was to be presumed dead. The wife, who was then presumed to be a widow, might remarry both civilly and religiously.

Frankness and Humanity   Outside of these cases, the intransigence of the Roman Church is absolute. And she is the cause of many agonies of conscience. What is striking about Archbishop Zoghby's intervention is its humane character. It was also frank, for who dares to speak of the scandal provoked among the faithful as well as unbelievers by the "casuistic gymnastics" that permits the indissolubility of marriage to be gotten around?

Archbishop Zoghy's proposal is capable of putting an end to many hypocrisies and giving peace to many minds.

Here is the entire text of this intervention, one of the most revolutionary of the whole Council:

> There is a problem that is still more agonizing than birth control: that is the problem of an innocent partner who, still young and in no way guilty, is left alone by reason of adultery. A short time after the marriage (which seemed happy), one of the partners, because of human weakness or with premeditation, abandons the home and contracts a new union. The innocent partner goes to see the pastor or the bishop. There is only one answer: "I cannot help you. Pray and resign yourself to living alone and in continence for the rest of your life!" This solution supposes heroic virtue, a rare faith, and an unusual temperament. It cannot, therefore, be for everybody.
>
> The young man and woman, who have each married because they do not feel called to perpetual continence, thus find themselves forced, in order to keep from becoming neurotic, to contract an illegitimate union outside of the Church. Once courageous people and normal Catholics, they now find themselves living with a tormented conscience. They have only one alternative: either become exceptional people overnight, or perish!
>
> We know from experience that the solution of perpetual continence is not for the normal run of Christians. In other words, we know that we leave these young victims with no court of appeal. We ask them to rely on the kind of faith that moves mountains; but such faith is not given to everyone. Even many of us bishops don't have it.

"Shift for Yourself"

The question which these tortured souls are asking the Council is this: does the Church have the right to answer an innocent person, whatever the nature of the problem torturing him, "Shift for yourself [in French in the text: *débrouillez-vous*], I have no solution to your case"? Or, at best, can the Church provide such cases with only an exceptional solution which is only for exceptional persons? The Church has certainly received sufficient authority from Christ to offer her children the means of salvation proportionate to their strength and aided by divine grace. Heroism, the state of perfection, was never imposed by Christ under pain of perdition: "If you would be perfect . . . ," Christ said.

Therefore, the Church does not lack the authority to protect such persons. It does not seem normal that perpetual continence, which pertains to the state of perfection, can be imposed as a punishment upon an innocent and betrayed partner. The Oriental Churches separated from Rome have always been aware of this authority and have always exercised it in favor of the innocent person. The matrimonial bond was certainly made indissoluble by Christ, except as the Gospel according to Matthew (5:32 and 19:9) indicates: *in cases of adultery*. The Church must judge the meaning of this interpolation. While the Roman Church has always interpreted it in a restrictive sense; the Oriental Church has always interpreted it in favor of a possible remarriage for the innocent partner.

It is true that the Council of Trent, session 24, sanctioned the restrictive Roman interpretation (canon 7 *de matrimonio*). But it is well known that the formula adopted by that council was deliberately recast so as not to exclude the Oriental tradition which followed a practice contrary to that of Rome. The theologians of Venice deserve credit for this; they were familiar with the Greek tradition based on the interpretation of the Greek fathers and even certain Western fathers like Saint Ambrose of Milan.

We know how the fathers of the Oriental Church tried to discourage widows and widowers from second marriages, following in this the Apostle's counsel; but they never intended to deprive an innocent partner, unjustly abandoned, of the right to remarry. This tradition, conserved in the East and never retracted during the ten centuries of union, could today be adopted by Catholics. The progress in patristic studies has made the doctrine of the Oriental fathers clearer; and they were just as good exegetes and just as good moralists as the Western fathers.

Pastoral concern for difficult marriages has been expressed differently by the Western canonists. They endeavor, by means of subtle casuistry which sometimes resembles gymnastics, to unearth any impediment that might invalidate the contract. They certainly do so out of pastoral concern, but sometimes it redounds to the detriment of souls. For example, sometimes after ten or twenty years

of marriage, hitherto unsuspected impediments of affinity are discovered that make it possible to resolve everything as though by
magic. Jurists find this natural and normal; but as pastors we must
admit that the faithful are often shocked and scandalized.

Isn't the Oriental tradition more suitable than impediments for
showing divine mercy to Christian spouses? Of course, we must
be careful. Abuses are always possible.

In this time of ecumenism and dialogue, the Catholic Church
must recognize the tradition and morality of the Orthodox Church.
I hope that theologians will study this problem, and be in a position
to offer some remedy for the anguish of innocent spouses who have
been abandoned by their partners, and deliver them from the serious
predicament which endangers their souls.

The Other Interventions   Here is a brief analysis of some of the other
interesting interventions.

Cardinal Ruffini said:

Clearer reference should be made to the teachings in the encyclical *Casti connubii*. The description of the ends of marriage is all the
more obscure because the Church's traditional distinction between
the primary and secondary ends is neglected. . . .

The text condemns abortion but says nothing about divorce
and the various forms of onanism. . . . The criteria and principles
used to urge responsibility threaten to provoke doubts and anxieties,
even among honest and religious couples. This attitude is all the more
surprising in that it is difficult to find a moral problem in marriage
that has not been solved by the ordinary magisterium of the Church.
. . . The schema speaks of the licitness of periodic continence but
doesn't emphasize that any artificial means used to turn conjugal
union from its natural end is improper and against nature.

Marriage Is a Community of Life and Love   Cardinal Léger said something quite different:

I fear that the doctrine propounded here will deceive the legitimate expectations of the faithful. The chapter will seem inadequate
to the most fervent Christians. The formula which defines marriage
as an institution ordained to the procreation and education of children is incomplete and ambiguous.

This formula perhaps explains the meaning of marriage for
the human race, but for persons marriage is more than an institution

ordained to the procreation of children. It is also and primarily a community of life and love. I therefore propose (1) that we say clearly and openly that marriage is an intimate community of life and love; (2) that we explain in detail the deep meaning the child has for conjugal life, in such wise that parents will understand that fecundity is the summit of love; and (3) that we say, finally, it is the will of God for parents to have children and thus become his cooperators.

Cardinal Léger also noted that this chapter is not very cohesive; ideas are juxtaposed without logic. Sometimes the text speaks in an exhortatory tone, and other times it moralizes. He concluded: "Despite the great doctrinal difficulties the Council has encountered in treating these questions, I believe it cannot promulgate a text that will be difficult for pastors to understand."

Cardinal Suenens made these suggestions:

The Council should appeal to scholars so that studies of sexual life might be broadened and coordinated. It is necessary to know more about the laws of human fertility, the psychological laws of self-control, especially the conditioning of reflexes, and the laws of conjugal life taken as a whole. Such an invitation should serve as a guideline for Catholic universities.

Furthermore, the Church honors the practice of renewing baptismal vows, the vows of religion, and so forth. Why not have an annual renewal of the sacred vows of marriage? This could be done collectively or in private. It would be a powerful stimulus to conjugal fidelity. . . . Finally, it is regrettable that the Council has said nothing about the alarming increase of early marriages, which are contracted lightly, and hasn't reminded public authorities of their duty to react against the immorality that is invading our streets, the cinema screen, and our literature. It is a disgrace to a so-called Christian civilization.

Cardinal Colombo, Archbishop of Milan, spoke in the name of thirty-two Italian bishops. His words were very positive, an indication of the present point of evolution the Italian episcopacy has reached:

We can accept the schema's fully human and personalist perspective without any reservation. However, we cannot accept anything that vitiates conjugal relations. The schema should eliminate any equivocation about this. . . . We need not seek the justification of this moral law in the fact that the physical integrity of the conjugal act constitutes a moral value in and for itself but rather in the fact that the physical perfection of the relations is an intrinsic and inseparable element of the will to love one another and procreate.

Archbishop Muñoyerro, Military Vicar of the Spanish armed forces, complained, "The text talks too much about conjugal love. We must re-affirm with the Holy Office that the first end of marriage is the procreation and education of children."

Auxiliary Bishop Kazimierz Majdanski of Wloclawek spoke in the name of the Polish episcopacy: "Even Catholics are almost indifferent to abortion. This scourge is as serious as the problem of the atomic bomb. Specialists say there are more abortions than births. Let us say more about this scourge than the handful of words in the schema."

Archbishop Nicodemo of Bari protested, "What the schema says about large families seems almost insincere."

Bishop Volk of Mainz said, "Today no one any longer understands how man can freely commit himself to a permanent state. Yet nothing favors true liberty more than such a commitment. This is what constitutes the greatness of man. It is the culminating point of liberty. Moreover, it corresponds with the deepest aspirations of love. Marriage is great because of this. For nothing is great without sacrifice."

OCTOBER, 1965

Cardinal Journet Critizes
the Orthodox Tradition of Remarriage

Vatican II is a Council of pastors rather than theologians or doctors. Sometimes the latter regret their subordinate role, more subordinate than in some previous councils. If this were not the case, it is sometimes said, Vatican II would accomplish more. But that isn't necessarily true; for the real efficacy of a council is a function of its educative influence and the large number of people who are personally affected by its work. It is therefore good that the principal actors of the Council are bishops, despite the hesitations, delays, and temporary impasses this might involve.

Schema 13 furnishes a case in point. "In its present state," a lay professor attending the Council said, "I wouldn't sign it." This opinion is fairly widespread. But it is easy to criticize. What is important is the slow decantation of ideas, the gradual maturation of the bishops' thinking as they labor over a deficient and perfectible text.

There is no doubt that the observations made these past few days, despite their disagreement, will contribute to an appreciable improvement of the schema on the modern world. The voice of the laity, who are directly interested, was heard in the aula Thursday morning through the intermediary of Bishop de Roo of Victoria, British Columbia. He said:

> The faithful also have something to say about morality. They want us to lay more stress on the values of marriage than on the difficulties of marriage. They will feel frustrated if dualism persists in the teaching on the ends of marriage. The laity intuitively live these ends as though they were one. They think we do not present the home as a center of love clearly enough and that we ought to say more about the affection owed to children.

Auxiliary Bishop Reuss of Mainz is superior of the major seminary of that city, one of the most modern in Europe. It is well known that this bishop is a member of the Pontifical Commission on Birth Control. His intervention thus commanded special attention: "An excellent pastoral spirit animates the chapter on marriage, but the style is too rhetorical and should be improved. . . . With good reason does it say that love can be considered an end of marriage, but this should be understood in its ontological sense. In a pyschological sense, love is only a motor force. It is love which intrinsically requires the indissolubility of marriage."

Bishop Reuss also commented, "What Cardinal Ruffini said on Wednesday is not altogether clear. Otherwise, why would the Pope have formed a special commission to study the problem of birth control?" (Cardinal Ruffini had referred to the "horrible so-called Catholic pill.") "On the other hand, I am in entire agreement with Cardinal Suenens' intervention."

Bishop Franz von Streng of Basel and Lugano stressed the scourge of abortion and deplored the indifference of public opinion to what theologians call direct murder (*occisio directa*).

Cardinals Heenan (Westminster), Rossi (São Paulo), Conway (Armagh), and Browne (of the Curia) all thought what the schema said about the double end of marriage and contraception was inadequate.

The intervention of Archbishop Djajasepoetra of Djakarta was very similar to the one he made during the third session. "You in the West," he said, "always say one marries because he is in love. With us, the opposite is the case. One marries first and then loves." The speaker obviously thought the second method superior to the first.

Archbishop Francisco da Silva of Braga, Portugal, was satisfied on the whole. But he thought what the schema said about conscientious objection was dangerous. He suggested such qualifications as "insofar as possible" or "if the common good is protected."

Cardinal Journet's intervention was a direct response to Archbishop Zoghby's proposal about remarriage the day before.

This intervention was the event of the day, and drew much protest from Oriental circles and those favorable to the Churches of the Orient.

The historical sources of the Swiss cardinal's talk were widely contested. In any event, his remarks about the Western Church confirm what we wrote Thursday: that there is practically no chance the Roman Church will adopt the Orthodox tradition on remarriage at this time. Cardinal Journet said:

The doctrine of the Catholic Church on the indissolubility of marriage is the doctrine of Christ himself. Saint Mark, chapter 10, reports Christ's answer to the Pharisees: "What God has joined together, let no man put asunder." Christ said that any man who puts away his wife and marries another commits adultery. Saint Paul teaches the same doctrine, not in his own name but in the name of the Lord, in his first Epistle to the Corinthians. [Archbishop Zoghby quoted the same source yesterday.] Saint Matthew's teaching must be interpreted in light of these texts: it proves the licitness of separation in cases of adultery but not the legitimacy of remarriage.

Certain Oriental Churches admit divorce in case of adultery and permit the innocent party to remarry. But this practice was introduced by reason of the relations which existed between church and state and under the influence of civil law, which permits divorce in similar cases. Justinian introduced a new law into the canon which acknowledged various causes for divorce. To justify this innovation, the Oriental Churches then had recourse to the text in Saint Matthew about separation in case of adultery. But the fact that these Churches admit other reasons for divorce besides adultery shows that they acted more in human terms than according to the Gospel.

At any rate, the evangelical doctrine of the indissolubility of sacramental marriage has always been in effect in the Catholic Church, and it is of divine right. The Church looks with great compassion upon unhappy situations that call for a heroic life; they remain insoluble in the eyes of men but not before God.

And yet there have been and are theological opinions that show a contrary view. Let us look at a few.

Saint Epiphanius, Bishop of Constantia of Cyprus (fourth century): "Divine law does not condemn a man who has been abandoned by his wife nor a woman who has been abandoned by her husband for remarrying."

Saint Basil, Bishop of Caesarea of Cappodocia (fourth century): "I am not sure a woman who lives with a man who has been abandoned by his wife could be called adulterous."

Saint Theodoret, Bishop of Cyrrhus (fifth century): "The Creator has prohibited the dissolution of marriage except for one reason."

Archbishop Guerrero of Grenada (sixteenth century): "Canon 7 of the Council of Trent forbidding remarriage in case of adultery does not please me because it contradicts the holy doctors."

And Father Bartmann, a contemporary professor of theology, writes:

> The Greeks in general and some Latins see a reason for divorce in adultery, and permit remarriage. This was the viewpoint of Tertullian and Lactantius. Saint Basil personally considered the new

marriage illicit; but he tolerated it, as was the custom then, for the innocent party. Saint Cyril of Alexandria thought that marriage is dissolved by adultery. Saint John Chrysostom reserved judgment, although he leaned toward the Greek opinion. This is also true of Theodoret of Cyrrhus, Victor of Antioch, and the later Greeks of the eleventh and twelfth centuries.

Archbishop Zoghby Denies That the Orthodox Tradition of Remarriage Is the Result of Civil Influence　After Cardinal Journet's intervention Thursday, we solicited two interviews. The first was with Archbishop Zoghby himself, whose position was directly attacked by Cardinal Journet. The second was with an Orthodox observer who is particularly well informed but prefers to remain anonymous.

It will be noticed that the second interview is much more subtle than the first. But it affirms no less solidly that the Orthodox tradition of remarriage is in no way imputable to the influence of civil legislation, and this is what the controversy is all about.

The problem of two different interpretations for the same text from Saint Matthew will never be resolved until the Churches of the East and West are reconciled. This is a distant but nonetheless inevitable perspective.

Archbishop Zoghby told us:

It goes without saying that the Oriental communities in communion with Rome all follow Roman discipline and practices with regard to marriage. . . .

The fathers and doctors of the Oriental Church who developed the basis of Christian doctrine, and who constituted the overwhelming majority of the fathers at the great ecumenical councils, could not have been influenced by politics in interpreting Christ's words as reported by Saint Matthew, chapters 5 and 19, as they did. To pretend this would be to forget what the universal Church owes to their knowledge and holiness.

The Justinian Code which was promulgated toward the end of the sixth century adopted the Oriental discipline on marriage. But it could scarcely have influenced Origen, Saint Basil, Saint John Chrysostom, and others who lived 350 years before this code, which merely reflected the previous doctrine and practices of the Oriental Churches.

The Oriental Churches adopted this interpretation and this practice in favor of the innocent party long before the schism with Rome. Yet they were never condemned during the centuries of union, nor were they disapproved by the ecumenical councils presided over by representatives of the Bishop of Rome and attended by the Churches of both the East and West. This is proof that the Roman Church never contested the legitimacy of the Oriental discipline in this matter.

Our other interviewee declared:

We are scarcely in favor of a prolonged discussion on the conception and practice of marriage in the Orient and the Occident. It is a delicate problem. The two traditions accept the same basic doctrine regarding this sacrament. Further development of theological reflection, a calmer approach, and proven pastoral concern—these are the necessary conditions for discussion. It is clear that the question is too big, too serious, to be handled in a polemical spirit or treated simply by a series of statements. The ecumenical spirit abroad today precludes this.

The Orthodox Church—and this is often forgotten—has always clearly affirmed the sanctity and indissolubility of the sacrament of marriage. And surely her theology and liturgical tradition are at least as developed as are those of the Western Church. The Orthodox Church views marriage essentially as a mystery, a sign of the new eschatological reconciliation in the Incarnate Word of all of creation. This reconciliation is founded on the indissoluble bond between Christ and the Church, his spouse, but personally—we must stress the personal dimension—manifested and actualized by the husband and wife before the altar.

Those who have attended Orthodox weddings will have noticed the special ceremony of crowning the couple. This is an unequivocal sign of the "royal" dignity of the whole person—man and woman—which was lost in original sin and restored in and by Christ. In the Orthodox Church the marriage ceremony emphasizes the partners' reception of Christ's grace, while in the Occidental Church, more influenced as it is by Roman law and the Germanic customs of the Middle Ages, the emphasis is on the consent of the partners, the formal element of marriage.

Nonetheless, in practice the Orthodox Church allows the remarriage of the innocent party. This in no way contradicts what we have said, nor is it in any way the effect of civil legislation, as was alleged in the aula on Thursday morning.

The Orthodox Church acts out of pastoral concern and in the name of evangelical realism. In clear-cut cases the Church permits a second and sometimes a third marriage to protect the innocent party. In the Orient this practice falls within an economy that is best translated into Western terms by "dispensation." This economy in no way contradicts the indissolubility of marriage; it merely, I repeat, represents a pastoral concern in well-defined cases. Let us note, too, that the celebration of the second and third marriage is considerably simplified. A third marriage is in fact little more than a blessing. For those familiar with the liturgical tradition of the Orient, this is significant.

I have somewhat simplified the presentation of the problem, particularly as regards the spirituality of marriage in contemporary Catholicism, which is experiencing a remarkable renewal. I should also add that many abuses have disfigured the Orthodox practice. But this is a matter of abuses and not the truth of the Church.

The small tempest caused by the conciliar interventions should not in my opinion abet the polemical spirit. This would scarcely be conducive to solving the problem.

The Amended Text of the Jews
Distributed to the Fathers

The amended text of the declaration "On the Relation of the Church to Non-Christian Religions" (since November, 1964, the title has no longer said, "Particularly Toward the Jews") has been distributed to the Fathers. They will be called to cast a final vote on it next Wednesday, October 6.

The intense curiosity raised by this text has now subsided. Here are some of the more important passages concerning the Jews, but we should not forget that the rarely mentioned sections on other religions, Islam in particular, are also of great interest.

> True, the Jewish authorities and those who followed their lead pressed for the death of Christ, still, what happened in his passion cannot be charged against all the Jews, without distinction, then alive, nor against the Jews of today. Although the Church is the new people of God, the Jews should not be presented as rejected or accursed by God, as if this followed from the Holy Scriptures. All should see to it, then, that in catechetical work or in the preaching of the word of God they do not teach anything that does not conform to the truth of the Gospel and the spirit of Christ.
>
> Furthermore, in her rejection of every persecution against any man, the Church, mindful of the patrimony she shares with the Jews and moved not by political reasons but by the Gospel's spiritual love, decries hatred, persecutions, displays of anti-Semitism, directed against Jews at any time by anyone.

Exegetes will be inclined to draw sometimes more, sometimes less from the text than it contains. We shall restrict ourselves to a few observations. Although insistent, Arab pressure to have the text suppressed failed; so too did the efforts to have it watered down. Although the word *deicide* has disappeared, at least for the time being, it remains no less true that the Jews (and not the "Jewish people," as previously), whether in the time of Christ or living today, cannot as a whole be accused of having caused the death of Christ. This death is historically imputed only to the Jewish authorities and those who followed them; this is something new in the text.

All persecutions are decried (the word *condemned*, which was formerly coupled with the word *decried*, has disappeared), and furthermore, "displays of anti-Semitism" has been added.

The expression "by anyone" indicates unequivocally that the Church herself and Christians are aware of having participated in such persecutions and displays of anti-Semitism.

It remains for the Fathers to say by means of their vote in the near future whether they are satisfied or whether they want to see the text strengthened still more. There is no danger of its being weakened. The overwhelming majority of the Fathers, let us recall once again, adopted the text last year as a basis of discussion. Only 99 were opposed and only 242 voted *placet juxta modi*. Since debate on the subject closed in November, 1964, there will be no new discussion in the aula this year.

OCTOBER 2

The Modern World Has Helped Improve the Church

On Friday Vatican II began discussion on chapter 2, on culture, of the second part of schema 13. Most of the interventions were interesting. It is clear that the theme of culture is taken seriously by the Fathers. They have had a year to reflect on this complex subject. The chapter is expected to be radically revised.

The Council heard Bishop Schmitt of Metz speak in the name of seventy bishops on the introduction to the second part. His intervention deserves credit for getting the discussion out of the rut it had fallen into. So much has been said in the Council about the modern world and its evils! Bishop Schmitt took a different tack and spoke of the virtues of the modern world, praising it for having contributed to the betterment of the Church. He enumerated the following facts:

> The Church is indebted to the world for her greater awareness of religious liberty; thanks to socialization, her greater emphasis on

her communitarian and collegial dimension; her greater appreciation of justice and even charity; her living her Catholicity better, thanks to the new wave of independence among peoples and civilizations, the renewal of her traditional doctrine on war, *Pacem in terris* being a promising step in this evolution; her ability to show forth her true transcendence better, by helping her solve her problems vis-à-vis politics; her better understanding of the living character of tradition, thanks to the spirit of research and invention in the secular world; and her deepening and purifying of the meaning of man's relation to God as a result of the world's attempts to give a better definition of man's total meaning.

The Church should be grateful for everything in the world that represents an effort toward greater humanity, and should endeavor to assimilate the positive values of the contemporary world, especially the sense of liberty and human dignity and the concern for scientific and historical truth, even though she will have to revise some of her structures in order to achieve greater evangelical humanity.

The Church must recognize that her future is necessarily bound up with man and the world, to which she must be present. Only on this condition will she be able to free the aspirations of modern man from their ambiguity.

Encouragement for the Creative Mind Coadjutor Bishop Elchinger of Strasbourg said:

> Even in countries with a Christian tradition, many men retain a mistrust of the Church because of her narrowmindedness, her spirit of domination, and her lack of respect and love for man's cultural efforts, an accusation which has been cast against her for the last five centuries. Moreover, for the past few centuries, the Church has been imprisoned in a kind of culture that is tied to a determined philosophy, which has made her unable to understand the thought and language of men accustomed to other intellectual categories.
>
> For a long time the Church has not paid sufficient heed to the world, and for that reason she has failed to some degree in her apostolic mission. . . .
>
> Let the Church establish contact with the cultures of the whole world by means of dialogue and collaboration, guided solely by a spirit of service and not domination.
>
> Let the Church take care to have theologians who know how to integrate everything that is positive in modern philosophies into

their own studies. This is not a simple question of pastoral methods; it is an intellectual problem. It is a question of reorienting theological thinking itself. To do this, it would be desirable for the Church to encourage theologians who have a creative mind.

Bishop Julien le Couedic of Troyes, France, declared, "Assembly-line work is dehumanizing, as are the amoral laws of anonymous production which separate workers from the results of their endeavors. . . . Man should use things and not be at their service. True culture puts man at the center of all creation and raises him to God."

Long Live Sports! Bishop Lucien Lebrun of Autun sang the praises of sports. They are of considerable importance to modern man, he said. "The athletic spirit is an important element in the contemporary mind. Sports are a source of the mind's control over the body, of endurance, and fairness. They contribute to the ability to make decisions and to cooperate; they help people get to know one another better."

Archbishop Blanchet, Rector of the Catholic Institute of Paris:

> This chapter lacks vigor; it does not correspond with the virile and dramatic character of intellectual research. It says nothing about history, to which modern men are very sensitive because it enables them to understand themselves better and gives them a healthy notion of the relative.
>
> Let us insist on a philosophy which is open to synthesizing, which is at the basis of all true humanism, and which provides an antidote to false humanisms. Let scholars in the universities put an end to the factious conflict between science and faith. We must not think only about scandalizing the weak; we can also scandalize the strong.

Sincerity for All Archbishop Michele Pellegrino, named to Turin, is the youngest of the Italian bishops. This was his first intervention at the Council, and it was quite different from those of most of his Italian colleagues. The reader can judge for himself:

> The history of men and the history of salvation are closely connected. Theology must become more historical, as the Pope said to Professor Skydsgaard, a Lutheran observer at the Council.
>
> The magisterium renders great service in detecting errors, but it should do so with respect for persons. This was not always the case, particularly during the period of modernism. There is even a lack of respect for certain cardinals. . . . Formerly theologians were

exiled; today they are experts at the Council, which is proof that the magisterium should have great regard for persons. . . . We must make it possible for everyone to be sincere."

Auxiliary Bishop Padin, Secretary General of Catholic Action in Brazil, felt that "A universal culture is neither possible nor desirable. All cultures should dialogue and recognize each other as complementary. Let us avoid leveling. . . . We still too often give a privileged place to classical culture."

Other speakers were Father Fernández, Master General of the Dominicans; Cardinals Gracias of Bombay and Slipyi, Ukrainian Archbishop of Lvov; Bishop Ddungu, of Masaka, Uganda; and Auxiliary Bishop Hacault of St. Boniface, Manitoba.

In the course of Friday's general congregation, Archbishop Felici read a message which the Pope will send to the United Nations in his name and in the name of all the Fathers before arriving in New York. In it the Pope expresses his respect for liberty and the dignity of men, and says that the United Nations cannot be destroyed (*deleri non potest*).

The Text of the Declaration on the Jews

Here is the whole text of the new version of the declaration on the Jews. All words in italic have been added since the last version.

As the sacred synod searches into the mystery of the Church, it remembers the bond that *spiritually* ties the people of the New Covenant to Abraham's stock.

Thus, the Church of Christ acknowledges [the expression "with a grateful heart" is omitted here] that, according to God's saving design, the beginnings of her faith and her election are found already among the patriarchs, Moses, and the prophets. She professes that all who believe in Christ, Abraham's sons according to the faith, are included in the same Patriarch's call, and likewise that the salvation of the Church is mysteriously *foreshadowed* by the chosen people's exodus from the land of bondage. The Church, therefore, cannot forget that she received the revelation of the Old Testament through the people with whom God in his inexpressible mercy concluded the Ancient Covenant. Nor can she forget that she draws sustenance from the root of that well-cultivated olive tree onto which have been grafted the wild shoots, the Gentiles. Indeed the Church believes that by his cross Christ our peace reconciled Jews and Gentiles, making both one *in himself*.

The Church keeps ever in mind the words of the apostle about his kinsmen: "Theirs is the sonship and the glory and the covenants and the law and the worship and the promises; theirs are the fathers and from them is Christ according to the flesh" (Rom. 9:4–5), the Son of the Virgin Mary. She also recalls that the apostles, the Church's mainstay and pillars, as well as most of the early disciples who proclaimed Christ's Gospel to the world, sprang from the Jewish people.

As Holy Scripture testifies, Jerusalem did not recognize the time of her visitation, nor did the Jews, in large number, accept the Gospel; *indeed not a few opposed its spreading.* Nevertheless, God holds the Jews most dear for the sake of their fathers; he does not repent of the gifts he makes or of the calls he issues. In company with the prophets and the same apostles, the Jews await the day on which all peoples will address the Lord in a single voice and "serve him shoulder to shoulder" (Soph. 3:9).

Since the spiritual patrimony common to Christians and Jews is thus so great, this sacred synod wants to foster and recommend that mutual understanding and respect which is the fruit, above all, of biblical and theological studies as well as of fraternal dialogues.

True, the Jewish authorities and those who followed their lead pressed for the death of Christ, still, what happened in his passion cannot be charged against all the Jews, without distinction, then alive, nor against the Jews of today. Although the Church is the new people of God, the Jews should not be presented as rejected *or accursed by God, as if this followed from the Holy Scriptures.* All should see to it, then, that in catechetical work or in the preaching of the word of God they do not teach *anything that does not conform to the truth of the Gospel and the spirit of Christ.*

Furthermore, in her rejection of every persecution against any man, the Church, mindful of the patrimony she shares with the Jews and moved not by political reasons but by the Gospel's spiritual love, decries [the expression "and condemns" is omitted] hatred, persecutions, *displays of anti-Semitism, directed* against Jews at any time by anyone.

Besides, as the Church has always held and holds now, Christ underwent his passion and death freely, because of the sins of men and out of infinite love, *in order that all may reach salvation.* It is, therefore, the burden of the Church's preaching to proclaim the cross of Christ as the sign of God's all-embracing love and as the fountain from which every grace flows.

Paul VI Reveals His Perplexity
About the Birth Control Problem

Problems confronting the Church today—relations with the world, reform of the Curia, ecumenism, birth control—were discussed by the Pope in an interview with a correspondent from the *Corriere della Sera*.

Speaking of the evolution within the Church, the Pope said:

> The Council is in the process of proving that alongside the crisis of faith in the world, there is happily no crisis within the Church. The most serious themes, like religious liberty, have been debated with love by the Church. . . . The formation of two schools— progressive and nonprogressive—never involves the problem of fidelity. All are interested in the good of the Church. There has been no defection; nor are there any signs of interior disunity. If there were, the Pope would be very concerned and would say so. That is what he is there for.

Paul VI had this to say about the birth control problem:

> The world is wondering what we think and we must give an answer. But what? The Church has never in her history confronted such a problem. This is a strange subject for men of the Church to be discussing, even humanly embarrassing. The commissions are in session and mountains of reports are piling up. There is a good deal of study going on; but we have to make the decision. This is our responsibility alone. Deciding is not as easy as studying. But we must say something. What? . . . God must truly enlighten us.

On the Curia: "You know all the accusations about centralization, about Romanization. We can now see the problem clearly. One has only to come to Rome to see that the Church is in very good shape and that certain faults are not critical." The Church is no longer dominated by kings and emperors, the Pope said; there is no nepotism or simony. "Technical reforms are necessary to facilitate our work," he continued. "There will be personality conflicts. But there will be no serious problems. Should they arise, we would make every effort to solve them."

On ecumenism: "We must be under no illusion; but meanwhile the atmosphere has changed." The Pope recalled an anecdote. One day a Walthusian observer greeted him with these words: "How do you do. We haven't seen one another for five hundred years."

On the United Nations: "We have agreed to go. The Pope can't say, 'Thanks very much but I haven't the time.' Personally we would rather save the time and money. But this is the first time the heads of states from all over the world have expressed a desire to hear the representative of Christ, and we must go."

Archbishop Zoghby Clarifies His Intervention on Remarriage

Thesis, antithesis, synthesis: this dialectic applies to what has been referred to in Rome these past four days as the Zoghby affair. The Patriarchal Vicar of Maximos IV suggested on his own responsibility that the Catholic Church might permit the remarriage of an innocent partner in certain cases of adultery.

This intervention, which every impartial observer considered of the highest importance, was the thesis. It is good to underline its importance because some Catholic papers contested it. The antithesis was defended next day by Cardinal Journet, who somewhat imprudently (this is the least we can say) attacked the Oriental tradition. Matters then quieted down. The interview with the Orthodox observer in *Le Monde* October 2 very definitely contributed to this appeasement.

On Monday Archbishop Zoghby clarified his intervention in the aula. This third intervention has the triple merit of being clear, averting all controversy, and presenting the initial proposal as a simple extension of the Petrine privilege.

Both the Orient and the Occident affirm the immutable principle of the indissolubility of marriage; but the Orthodox tradition admits an exception which, at least for the time being, the Roman Church rejects.

A Simple Extension of the Petrine Privilege We quoted earlier some patristic passages upon which the Oriental tradition is based. These passages are not widely known in the West—and for good reason—but they are important. It is only honest to admit that there are two traditions. To opt for one should not lead us to depreciate the other.

Archbishop Zoghby said:

> 1. My intervention had a strictly pastoral aim: to suggest a solution for the agonizing problem of so many young husbands and wives who are condemned to live in a state of forced continence through no fault of their own.
> 2. I clearly affirmed the immutable principle of the indissolubility

of marriage, and I deliberately avoided using the word *divorce* because, in Catholic usage, this word signifies an infraction of the principle. . . .

3. This indissolubility is so rooted in the traditions of both Churches that it could not conceivably be questioned in a conciliar intervention. Indeed, that same Orthodox tradition has always held marriage to be as indissoluble as the union of Christ and the Church, his spouse, a union which remains the exemplary model of the sacramental monogamy of Christians. In theology, divorce is only a dispensation accorded to the innocent party in well-defined cases in virtue of what the Orthodox call "the principle of economy," which means "dispensation" or "condescension." This dispensation does not exclude the principle of the indissolubility of marriage. Indeed, it protects this principle, as do the dispensations granted to valid marriages by the Roman Church in virtue of the Petrine privilege. . . .

4. . . . I was envisaging the possibility of eventually adding to the grounds for dispensation already admitted by the Catholic Church, the ground of fornication and desertion of one partner by the other. Whether or not these further reasons for dispensation, which are analagous to those admitted by the Petrine privilege, can be accepted remains for the Church to judge.

5. This is no empty proposal because it is based on the indisputable authority of the holy fathers and doctors of the Oriental Church, who cannot lightly be accused of accommodating political and human motives.

Contrasting Interventions on Economic and Social Life

Monday morning Vatican II ended examination of the chapter on culture with five interventions, including one by Coadjutor Archbishop Veuillot of Paris, and began discussion on economic and social life. Three cardinals and seven bishops spoke. We shall report later on this interesting debate. It revealed extraordinarily deep conflicts: some found the chapter too traditional, too indulgent toward private property, and too little concerned with the social advancement of the workingman, while others regretted its audacity, its recklessness, its harsh judgment of private property, and its sympathy for agrarian reform, for the right to strike and to form unions.

The intervention by Bishop Hengsbach of Essen was particularly noted. He spoke in the name of eighty of his German colleagues and was strongly on the side of the conservatives. This was the surprise of the day.

A number of Fathers, including Bishop Franič of Split, Archbishop Fernandes of Delhi, Archbishop Thangalathil of Trivandrum, India, Auxiliary Bishop Edward E. Swanstrom of New York, and Cardinal de Arriba y Castro of Tarragona, agreed that a permanent postconciliar bureau should be set up in Rome to implement the Church's social doctrine and encourage the reforms that are pressingly needed in one or another country.

Bishop Ancel on Celibacy

It's a fact. It is no longer taboo to contest the law of ecclesiastical celibacy. This is a switch from the solemn declarations of yesteryear. Four months ago Bishop Boillon of Verdun said that, for all he knew, the present situation could change. Now Auxiliary Bishop Ancel of Lyon has given a talk in Rome on this critical issue, which no one can any longer avoid.

The Superior General of the Prado, a former working bishop, is a man to tackle difficult issues. With classical reserve and yet an open mind, Bishop Ancel is undoubtedly the man who can most contribute to an evolution of thinking in the episcopacy on this question.

The prelate outlined the objections to a married clergy before a room jammed with priests and Council Fathers, notably Brazilians. He could not forget that he was speaking in a country where the number of priests living in concubinage is fairly relatively high (particularly in Sicily) and where the Holy Office is now almost never asked to grant priests reduced to the lay state permission to marry. Nor did he forget that the Council is soon to vote on a text giving the reasons for clerical celibacy.

Actually, no one denies that a celibate clergy is a good thing. The evangelical, spiritual, and practical reasons for it are obvious. But the difficulty arises when what is merely highly suitable is made into an obligatory law. The example of the Orthodox Church is there to prove that a man can be married and a good priest, just as a Protestant can be both a pastor and a married man.

Another problem: is it reasonable to continue to deprive the Church of men who might have a vocation to the priesthood but not to celibacy?

Bishop Ancel enumerated the following arguments in favor of married priests:

1. There are not enough priests.
2. A married clergy would not diminish the value of a celibate clergy as is seen from the example of the East, where chastity is held in high esteem.

3. It is better to have a married clergy than the scandal of unfaithful priests.

These were some of the arguments against:

1. It would be more difficult for the bishop to transfer a married priest.
2. If a married priest had only one child, he would be accused of practicing birth control. If he had twelve children, he would have no time for his parishioners.
3. It would be difficult to pay him a living wage.
4. The married priest would have an inferiority complex in the presence of celibates.

Bishop Ancel said the following arguments "impressed him":

1. Priests are becoming more and more associated with the bishop; it is fitting, therefore, that they be associated with his celibacy.
2. Priests require a longer and broader formation today.
3. It doesn't make much sense to administer the sacraments without evangelizing.

"I am not taking sides," Bishop Ancel concluded. "The Church has spoken, and I can go no farther."

He did say, however, that a married diaconate side by side with a celibate clergy struck him as a good solution. Moreover, priests in the future will be required to live in greater evangelical poverty.

Bishop Ancel also noted that formerly the priest was warned, "Beware of women." Today it is more a question of teaching him how to conduct himself with women. "We should not receive affection that belongs to Christ," he said. "In the past there was one major preoccupation in seminaries: avoid particular friendships. Today we should have recourse to the psychological sciences and teach the young aspirant how he should behave with women. The priest can renounce women but he cannot be heartless. Repression is not a good way to educate the emotions."

The speaker thought the best solution was priests working in teams.

He also stressed the importance of helping priests who are in trouble with women. Finally, he made this important suggestion: that the future code of canon law permit priests to be dispensed from perpetual vows.

Text of Pope Paul's Speech to the United Nations

Here is the text of the speech Pope Paul VI delivered yesterday afternoon, Monday, at the United Nations:

As we begin our address to this audience, unique in the world, we wish first to express our profound gratitude to Mr. Thant, your Secretary General, for the invitation which he extended to us to visit the United Nations on the occasion of the twentieth anniversary of this world institution for peace and cooperation among the peoples of all the earth.

Thanks also to the President of the General Assembly, Mr. Amintore Fanfani, who has had such kind words for us from the very day he took office.

Thanks to all of you here present for your warm welcome. . . .

Simplicity and Grandeur

You are all well aware that this meeting between us is of a two-fold nature: it bears the stamp both of simplicity and of grandeur. Simplicity, because he who speaks to you is a man like you; he is your brother, and even one of the least among you, representing as you do sovereign states, for he is vested—if it please you so to think of us—with only a minute and quasi-symbolic temporal sovereignty, only so much as is needed to leave him free to exercise his spiritual mission and to assure all those who treat with him that he is independent of every worldly sovereignty. He has no temporal power, no ambition to compete with you. In point of fact, we have nothing to ask for, no question to raise; at most a wish to express and a permission to request: to serve you, within our competence, disinterestedly, humbly, and in love.

This is the first statement we have to make. As you see, it is so simple that it may seem insignificant to this assembly, accustomed as it is to dealing with extremely important and difficult matters.

The End of a Laborious Pilgrimage

And yet we said to you—and you all feel it—that this moment bears the stamp of a special grandeur. Grandeur for us, grandeur for you.

First, for us. Oh! You well know who we are. Whatever your opinion of the Roman Pontiff, you know our mission: we are the bearer of a message for all mankind. This we are, not only in our own name and in the name of the great Catholic family, but also in the name of those Christian brethren who share the feelings we express here, and particularly of those who charged us explicitly to be their spokesman here. And like the messenger who, at the end of a long journey, delivers the letter entrusted to him, we are conscious of living a privileged moment—short as it may be—which fulfills a wish we have been carrying in our heart for nearly twenty centuries. Yes, you do remember. We have been on the way for a long time and we bear with us a long history; here we celebrate the end of a laborious pilgrimage in search of a colloquy with the whole world, a pilgrimage which began when we were given the command, "Go and bring the good news to all nations." And it is you who represent all nations.

A Moral and Solemn Ratification

Allow us to tell you that we have a message for you all. Yes! A happy message to deliver to each of you.

We wish our message first of all to be a moral and solemn ratification of this high institution. The message comes of our experience of history. It is as an "expert in humanity" that we bring to this organization the voices of our latest predecessors, those of the whole Catholic episcopacy, and our own, convinced as we are that this organization represents the obligatory road of modern civilization and of world peace.

In saying this, we are aware that we are making our own the voices both of the dead and of the living: of the dead who fell in the terrible wars of the past while dreaming of harmony and world peace; of the living who survived war and already in their hearts condemn those who would try to bring it again; and of still others of the living, the young generations of today going forward confidently in rightful expectation of a better humanity. We also make our own the voice of the poor, the disinherited, the unfortunate; of those who yearn for justice, for dignity of life, for freedom, for well-being, and for progress. The peoples turn to the United Nations as to the ultimate hope for harmony and peace. We venture to bring here their tribute of honor and hope, together with our own. And that is why this moment is great for you too.

We know that you are fully aware of this. Listen now to the rest of our message. It looks wholly to the future. The building you have made must never again fall in ruins; it must be perfected and conformed to the demands world history will make. You mark a stage in the development of mankind: henceforth no turning back; you must go forward.

To the majority of states, no longer able to ignore each other, you offer an extremely simple and fruitful form of coexistence. It is this: first of all, you recognize and distinguish *one another*. You do not, of course, confer existence upon states, but you qualify each nation as worthy to sit in the ordered assembly of the peoples; you grant to each national sovereign community a recognition of high moral and juridical value, and you guarantee it an honorable international citizenship. This in itself is a great service to the cause of mankind: clearly to define and to honor the national entities of the world community, and to establish them in a juridical status which entitles them to be recognized and respected by all and from which there may derive an ordered and stable system of international life. You give sanction to the great principle that relations between the peoples should be regulated by reason, by justice, by law, by negotiation; not by force or by violence or by war, neither by fear nor by fraud.

So it should be. And allow us to congratulate you on having had the wisdom to leave the door to this assembly open to the young peoples, to the states which have but lately attained national independence and freedom; their presence here is proof of the universality and magnanimity which inform the principles of this institution.

So it should be. This is what we praise and what we wish for you, and, as you see, these virtues we ascribe to you do not come from without. We draw them from within, from the very genius of your institution.

Strive To Bring Back Any Who Have Left

Your Charter goes even further; and our message goes forward with it. You exist and work to unite the nations, to associate the states together. Let us use the formula: to bring together *one and another*. You are an association. You are a bridge between the peoples. You are a network of relations among the states. We are tempted to say that your character in some sort reflects in the temporal order what our Catholic Church seeks to be in the spiritual order—unique and universal. Nothing higher can be imagined on the natural level, in the ideological structure of mankind. Your vocation is to bring not only some of the peoples but all of the peoples to fraternize. A difficult undertaking? No doubt. But such is the undertaking, your most noble undertaking. Who does not see the need thus progressively to set up a world authority, able to act effectively on the juridical and political plane?

Once more we repeat our wish for you: go forward. We shall say more: strive to bring back among you any who may have left you; consider means of calling into your pact of brotherhood, in honor and loyalty, those who do not yet share in it. Act so that those still outside will desire and deserve the confidence of all; and then be generous in granting it. And you, who have the good fortune and the honor to sit in this assembly of the peaceful community, hear us: so act that there may never be an attempt on the mutual confidence which unites you and enables you to do good and great things, that it may never be betrayed.

Let No One Be Superior

The reason for this wish, which might be said to pertain to the structure of your organization, leads us to complete it with other formulas. They are these. Let no one, as a member of your association, be superior to the others—*not one above another*. This is the formula of equality. We well know that there are other factors to be considered besides that of mere membership of this body. But equality, too, is a part of its constitution; not that you are equal, but that here you make yourselves equal. And it may be that for several among you this is an act of high virtue; allow us to say this to you, we who represent a religion which works salvation through the humility of its divine founder. It is impossible to be a brother if one is not humble. For it is pride, however inevitable it may seem, which provokes tensions, struggles for prestige, predominance, colonialism, selfishness; it is pride that shatters brotherhood.

And here our message reaches its highest point, negatively at first. It is the word you are expecting from us, and we cannot utter it without being conscious of its gravity and solemnity: *never again one against another*, never, never again! Is it not to this end above all that the United Nations was born: against war and for peace? Listen to the lucid words of a great man now departed, John Kennedy, who declared four years ago, "Mankind must put an end to war, or war will put an end to mankind." There is no need of long speeches to proclaim the supreme finality of this institution. Suffice it to recall that the blood of millions of men, that countless and unheard-of sufferings, that useless massacres and fearful ruins have sealed the pact uniting you, with a vow which must change the future history of the world: never again war, war never again! Peace, it is peace which must guard the destiny of the peoples and of all mankind!

Thanks to you, glory to you, who for twenty years have labored for peace and have even given illustrious victims to this holy cause. Thanks to you and glory to you for the conflicts you have prevented and for those you have settled. The results of your efforts for peace, up to these last days, even if not yet decisive, deserve that we venture to interpret the feelings of the whole world and in its name express to you both congratulations and gratitude.

You, gentlemen, have done and are doing a great work: you are teaching men peace. The United Nations is the great school where that education is acquired, and we are here in the *aula magna* of that school. Whoever takes a place here becomes both pupil and teacher in the art of building peace. And when you leave this hall, the world looks to you as to the architects, the builders of peace.

Peace, as you know, is built not only by means of politics and the balance of forces and interests. It is built with the spirit, with ideas, with works of peace. You are laboring at this great work. But you are as yet only at the beginning of your labors. Will the world ever succeed in changing the exclusive and bellicose state of mind which up to now has woven so much of its history? This is hard to foresee; but it is easy to affirm that we must resolutely take the road toward a new history, a peaceful history, one that will be truly and fully human, the very history God promised to men of good will. The roads to it are mapped for you: the first is that of disarmament.

If you wish to be brothers, let the weapons fall from your hands. You cannot love with offensive weapons in your hands. Even before they cause victims and ruins, weapons, especially the terrible weapons modern science has given you, beget bad dreams, nourish bad feelings, create nightmares, mistrust, and somber resolves; they exact enormous expenditures; they bring to a halt projects of useful work undertaken in solidarity; they warp the psychology of peoples. So long as man remains the weak, changeable, and even wicked being that he often shows himself to be, defensive arms will alas be necessary. But you, your courage and valor spur you to study ways of guaranteeing the security of international life without recourse to arms: this is an aim worthy of your efforts, this is what the peoples expect of you. This is what must be attained. And for this, unanimous trust in this institution must grow; its authority must grow; and the goal, it is to be hoped, will then be reached. Then you will win the gratitude of all peoples, relieved of the crushing expense of armaments and delivered from the nightmare of ever imminent war.

We know—and how could we not rejoice in the knowledge?— that many among you looked with favor upon the invitation in the cause of peace that we addressed to all states from Bombay last December: to devote to the benefit of the developing countries at least part of the savings which can be realized by reducing armaments. We here renew that invitation, with the confidence your sentiments of humanity and generosity inspire in us.

Working One for Another

To speak of humanity and generosity is to echo another constituent principle of the United Nations, the very highest: you are laboring here not only to exorcise conflicts between states, but to make states capable of working *one for another*. You are not satisfied with making coexistence between nations easier; you are taking a much greater step forward, a step deserving of our praise and our support; you are organizing brotherly cooperation among the peoples. Here a system of solidarity is being set up, so that the high aims of civilized order may win the unanimous and ordered support of the whole family of peoples, to the good of all and everyone. This is what is most beautiful in the United Nations; this is its most truly human face; this is the ideal which mankind dreams of on its pilgrimage through time; this is the world's greatest hope. We presume to say that this is the reflection of God's design—a transcendent design and full of love—for the progress of the human society on earth, a reflection in which we see the message of the Gospel, which is heavenly, become earthly. Indeed, it seems to us that here we catch an echo of the voice of our predecessors, particularly of Pope John XXIII, whose message of *Pacem in terris* evoked among you so honorable and significant a response.

Control of Births

What you proclaim here are the fundamental rights and duties of man, his dignity, his freedom, and above all his religious freedom. We feel that you are the interpreters of what is highest in human wisdom, we would almost say of its sacred character. For it is above all the life of man that is in question, and the life of man is sacred; no one may dare offend it. It is in your assembly that respect for life, even insofar as the great problem of the birth rate is concerned, must find its highest affirmation and its most reasoned defense. Your task is to ensure that there is enough bread on the table of mankind, and not to favor an artificial control of births, which would be irrational, in order to lessen the number of guests at the banquet of life.

But it is not enough to feed the starving; each man must also be assured of a life consistent with his dignity. And this is what you are striving to achieve. Is this not the realization, before our eyes and thanks to you, of the prophetic utterance so well suited to your institution: "They shall beat their swords into ploughshares and their

spears into pruning hooks"? [Is. 2:4] Are you not using the prodigious energies of the earth and the magnificent inventions of science,
no longer as instruments of death, but as tools of life for the new era
of mankind?

We know with what growing intensity and effectiveness the
United Nations and its related world agencies render help to governments which need it to speed their economic and social progress.

We know how ardently you work to conquer illiteracy and to
spread culture throughout the world; to give men proper and modern
medical assistance; to put at man's service the marvelous resources of
science and of the technique of organization. All this is magnificent
and deserving of everyone's praise and support, including our own.

We ourself would also like to set an example, even though the
smallness of our means is inadequate to the practical and quantitative
needs. We wish to intensify the efforts of our charitable institutions
against the world's hunger and to meet its chief needs. It is thus, and
in no other way, that peace is built.

The Moment of "Conversion" Has Come

One word more, gentlemen, one last word: this edifice you are
building does not rest upon purely material and earthly foundations,
for it would then be a house built on sand; above all, it rests on our
consciences. Yes! The moment of "conversion" has come, of personal
transformation, of inner renewal. We must accustom ourselves to
think of man in a new way; and in a new way also of men's life in
common; finally, in a new way of the paths of history and the destiny
of the world, in accordance with the words of Saint Paul, to "put on
the new man which, after God, is created in righteousness and the
holiness of truth" [Eph. 4:24].

Now the hour for a halt is upon us, a moment of meditation, of
reflection, almost of prayer; a moment to think anew of our common
origin, our history, our common destiny. Never before has there
been such a need for an appeal to the moral conscience of man as there
is today, in an era marked by such human progress. For the peril comes
neither from progress nor from science; on the contrary, properly
used, they could resolve many of the grave problems which beset
mankind. The real peril is in man, who has at hand ever more powerful
instruments, suited as much to destruction as to the highest conquests.

In a word, the edifice of modern civilization must be built on
spiritual principles, which alone can not only support it but also
illuminate and animate it. And it is our conviction, as you know, that
these indispensable principles of higher wisdom can rest only on faith

in God—the unknown God of whom Saint Paul spoke to the Athenians on the Areopagus?—unknown to those who, without realizing it, yet sought him and had him near them, as happens to so many men of our century. . . . To us, in any case, and to all those who receive the ineffable revelation which Christ has given us of him, he is the living God, the Father of all men.

Paul VI "Defends Imperialism" at the United Nations, Says an Albanian Newspaper

"Pope Paul VI went to the United Nations to defend publicly the lost cause of American imperialism. He enlisted the aid of his spiritual sons, in accordance with the secular traditions of the Vatican, to bless the politics of aggression, the war initiated by imperialists, and their collaboration with Khrushchevian revisionists," declared the Albanian paper *Zeri i Popullit*. The article continued:

Paul VI spoke as a representative and spiritual leader of the Vatican, the most retrograde and obscurantist power of our age. Those who know anything about Vatican ideology know that these words are addressed to the weak and not the powerful, the oppressed and not the oppressors.

Thus, from the point of view of Vatican politics and morality, this means: "Vietnamese soldier, do not fight against the American Marines."

In his speech the Pope praised the United Nations, an organization that so far has betrayed the hope of peoples by becoming an instrument of the politics of aggression and American imperialism. He sang the glories of the United States and met with President Johnson, who has launched a war of extermination in Vietnam.

Pope Paul did not condemn the war of extermination that American imperialists are waging in Vietnam, not a word in condemnation of genocide. Nor did he have any word to the Indian reactionaries who are unjustly fighting Pakistan.

It is not surprising that the Pope was enthusiastically received at the United Nations by the American imperialists and all the reactionaries as well as the revisionists who see in him an ally. No wonder Andrei Gromyko, the representative of modern revisionism, listened to the Pope's words "with rapt attention."

What Schema 13 Says About Political Life

The chapter of schema 13 concerning the life of the political community is four and a half pages long. The titles of the first three sections are "Public Life Today," "The Nature and End of Political Society," and "The Collaboration of All in Political Life." Here are some excerpts from the chapter:

> All Christians must be aware of their own specific vocation within the political community. It is for them to give an example by their sense of responsibility and their service of the common good. In this way they are to demonstrate concretely how authority can be compatible with freedom, personal initiative with the solidarity of the whole social organism, and the advantages of unity with fruitful diversity. They must recognize the legitimacy of different opinions with regard to temporal solutions, and respect citizens who, even as a group, defend their points by honest methods. . . .
>
> Political parties, for their part, must promote those things which in their judgment are required for the common good. Great care must be taken about civic and political formation, which is of the utmost necessity today for the population as a whole, and especially for youth, so that all citizens can play their part in the life of the political community. Those who are suited or can become suited should prepare themselves for the difficult but at the same time the very noble art of politics, and should seek to practice this art without regard for their own interests or for material advantages. With integrity and wisdom, they must take action against any form of injustice and tyranny, against arbitrary domination by an individual or a political party and any intolerance. They should dedicate themselves to the service of all with sincerity and fairness, indeed, with the charity and fortitude demanded by the political life.

The fourth section is entitled "The Church and Public Society." In it we read:

> The Church does not place her trust in the privileges offered by civil society. She will even give up the exercise of certain rights which have been legitimately acquired, if it becomes clear that their use will cast doubt upon the sincerity of her witness or that new ways of life demand new methods. She does not at all reject genuine collaboration with public powers; indeed, she ardently desires this. But it is only right that at all times and in all places, the Church should have true freedom to preach the faith, to teach her social

doctrine, to exercise her role freely among men, and also to pass moral judgment in those matters which regard public order when the fundamental rights of a person or the salvation of souls requires it. In this, she should make use of all the means—but only those— which accord with the Gospel, and which correspond with the general good according to the diversity of times and circumstances.

The Debate on Political Life Was Brief

The unexpected always happens. As Paul VI was making the most political gesture of any contemporary pope, altogether by happenstance Vatican II was beginning discussion of the section of schema 13 concerning the political community. Examination of this chapter was practically nonexistent. Only three Fathers spoke on the question, which is so essential that it was thought proper to add a long passage to it during the recess. A few moments later, Paul VI arrived in St. Peter's from his visit to the United Nations.

There is only one explanation, though no excuse, for this anomaly: the bishops are not yet fully aware of the importance of the political domain and are hesitant to speak on the subject, despite its importance. They have inherited a reticence from the past toward certain involvements as damaging for the temporal power as for the spiritual. "Don't dirty your hands," Péguy would have said; flee the compromises of power, remain above the melee, contemplate the world rather than change it. This is still the temptation of many churchmen and faithful. They would be well advised to meditate further on the striking example Paul VI has just given.

As a consequence of these dangerous prejudices, the so-called Christian nations have often had heads who were anything but Christian: Mussolini, Hitler, Salazar, Franco. And yet the Gospel implies a political creed. To let a dichotomy develop between religious and political life under the pretext that a theocracy is wrong is not a Christian attitude, because it contradicts the economy of the incarnation.

These were some of the remarks heard in the corridors of the Council after the almost nonexistent debate. It was one of the low-water marks of Vatican II.

The first of the bishops who intervened was Bishop del Campo of Calahorra, Spain, who limited himself mainly to the notion that just tax laws are binding in conscience.

Next the Council heard retired Bishop Beitia of Santander:

It is good, as the schema points out, for the Church to abandon some of her privileges on occasion. But let us not forget the rights of the Church. Separation of church and state has been condemned several times by the magisterium. We seem to have forgotten this. . . . The thesis-antithesis theory ought not be forgotten, for it is the expression of the truth itself. Because of it, pluralism can be respected.

Archbishop Baraniak of Poznan, Poland, told the Fathers: "The real problem today is the attitude of Christians in countries with atheistic regimes. They have the right to cooperate, of that there can be no doubt; still, they wonder if they can participate in activities that are good in themselves but are used to promote atheism. The schema should throw some light on this problem."

Archbishop Hurley of Durban, South Africa, spoke in the name of seventy Fathers:

The schema is right not to speak of two perfect societies, the Church and the state. For this is inexact. There is the presence of the Church in the world. It is the sign and guarantee of man's transcendence. . . . Conflicts are undoubtedly inevitable, and the Church must demand her liberty to defend the rights of man. But when there is conflict with political authority, she should conduct herself as a witness to Christ's love. The schema should say this.

A Dangerous Schema?   In the course of the same congregation on Tuesday, the Council completed the examination begun the day before of the section on social and economic life. There were in all twenty-one interventions on this subject. Two conflicting conceptions of the Church clashed. Some think that the Church ought to be as little concerned as possible with such questions, and hence that the schema should be restricted to general principles lest it become quickly dated. Thus, Cardinal Siri of Genoa asked that nothing be said about agrarian reforms, and Archbishop García de Sierra of Burgos found the remarks about labor unions out of place. The Spanish prelate referred to Christ in the desert resisting Satan's temptation to temporal power. "This schema is too messianic," he then said. "It is dangerous. It risks upsetting the established order."

Those in the other camp thought the Council should give specific directives. Archbishop Thangalathil of Trivandrum felt the schema should say more about the misery of the poor (which is an occasion of sin) and the equitable distribution of goods. Coadjutor Bishop Fernandes of Delhi was of the opinion that this chapter furnishes a unique opportunity to speak about the problems of underdeveloped countries. Several Fathers thought with Bishop Franič of Split that this section could be reworked by the episcopal synod and perhaps issued as an encyclical.

Bishop Hengsbach of Essen found that the schema does not put enough emphasis on private property, which is, he said, "something fundamental." He asked that the schema avoid forecasting. Bishop Coderre of St.-Jean de Québec was of the opposite opinion; he called for a more prophetic tone and asked consequently that the schema speak more of future prospects.

Cardinal Wyszynski, Primate of Poland, said, "Let the Council condemn both liberal capitalism and atheistic communism; let it trace out a new way in which everything will be subordinated to respect for the human person. Let us study further the phenomenon of emigration."

The Responsibility of Employers   Cardinal Cardijn, founder of the Young Christian Workers, said:

> Let us talk more concretely about the workers. Most of them, throughout the world, live in undeserved abominable misery. They cannot gain professional training or social security. They are sometimes prohibited from forming unions. They have neither homes nor schools. This is the modern world's enormous sin against man and against God. . . .
>
> Let the Church support the appeals from workers in underdeveloped countries. Let her remind employers of their responsibilities before God. . . . May something concrete in favor of the poor come out of Paul VI's pilgrimage.

Bishop Himmer of Tournai wanted the schema to "stress the theological basis. Man is a creator much like God himself. He is made in the image of God, and he should create not for riches but out of love."

The Right to Progress   Bishop Larraín Errázuriz of Talca, Chile, president of the Latin American Episcopal Conference, has just written an incisive pastoral letter to the faithful of his diocese about the tragic consequences of underdevelopment. He once again reminded the Council of the seriousness of the socioeconomic situation in Latin America. It is "a constant menace to peace," he said. The Chilean bishop quoted Cardinal Feltin: "Progress is the new name for peace." Then he continued, "Progress is not only a duty but a right. The end of the economy is not gain but man, as the schema fittingly reminds us."

Importance of Agriculture   Bishop Bernardino Echeverría Ruiz of Ambato, Ecuador, argued: "The world today needs not declarations but action. Let us create a permanent secretariat for social justice in Rome." This desire has been expressed by a number of Fathers, and it seems likely that the Pope will take some kind of action on it.

Bishop Carlos Parteli of Tacuarembo, Uruguay, spoke about agriculture: "The reduction of misery depends upon the progress of agriculture. . . . We must praise the impartial work of the United Nations Food and Agriculture Organization."

Bishop de Vito of Lucknow, India, commented upon the erroneous impression many have that Christ said, "The poor you will have with you always." Actually, it is a bad translation: the evangelist used the present and not the future tense. The speaker recalled the beatitude of poverty and mentioned the crimes of abortion and prostitution, which are, he said, consequences of misery.

Schema 13 in the Eyes of Two Non-Catholic Observers: Pastor Hébert Roux and Professor Paul Evdokimov

We asked a Protestant and an Orthodox their reactions to schema 13. Pastor Hébert Roux of the Reformed Church of France said:

> Everyone agrees that with schema 13 the Council faces its most difficult challenge. This difficulty ought to remind all Christians to be sober and moderate when they treat issues that are so closely bound up with men's hopes and anxieties.
>
> What bothers me most about the schema is what I would call its false modesty. This appears first of all in the simple fact that, after having defined her proper essence as a mysterious relationship with Christ in the original vocation of a messianic people of God ordained to a universal mission, the Catholic Church feels obliged to hedge her concern for men with all sorts of precautions and justifications. We are told that this is a method, a humble attitude that will give the schema a better chance for success, that the Church is taking a new stance toward the world. Perhaps. . . . But in that case why the long dissertation about man in general before coming to grips with the concrete problems confronting contemporary man? Why ask the question, "What is man?" and answer it with a synthesis of elements borrowed from Christian metaphysics and humanist anthropology?
>
> In the constitution *De Ecclesia,* the Church defines herself in the light of the Gospel. Why then, when she considers the world *ad extra,* does the Church think that this light which enlightens

all men really only enlightens those within the fold, and that those outside can be affected only by a kind of indirect lighting through the instrumentality not of the clear mirror of the Gospel but rather of the protective and reassuring screen of philosophy? I am not saying that this philosophy is not true; it is even helpful. But I think it is out of place. It is as though the Church were making a detour in an effort to establish a sort of collusion between human thought and Christian thought. She thinks Christianly for the purpose of those inside the Church and humanly for those outside, when perhaps the opposite should be done, precisely because there is not and should not be an inside and an outside in the Church's relationship to the world.

We forget, meanwhile, that millions of men are thinking of nothing except survival. It would be a serious failing if this gigantic effort, however generous it may be, to break down the wall of separation, misunderstanding, and hostility that has arisen over the centuries between the Church and the world were compromised by a false modesty that made the Church look as though she were in some sense holding back or not clearly articulating the only answer she can give: the Man Jesus Christ.

The real answer to the question "What is man?" is to be found in the Gospel. For there the justice of God is revealed, that is, the way God acts to create a new humanity. In addressing the world, the Church should not be afraid of using her own language, provided of course that it is the language of the Gospel. It would surely be more human today, rather than beginning with the first Adam and his metaphysical adventures in order to lay out a disguised apologetics and justify the participation of Christians in the construction of a world that is already dead, to begin with Christ, the second Adam, whose obedience made satisfaction for the original disobedience by inscribing in his very flesh the decisive act which is the basis of our hopes and in the final analysis justifies an optimism that is not unconditional but very concretely conditioned.

We read this admirable expression in the schema: "The Gospel judges the Church." If this is true, and it is, then the Gospel should be the criterion and foundation of everything the Church says and does for the world and mankind.

But the Gospel is not a manual of formulas or a code of laws saying what is permitted and not permitted to natural man. The Gospel is the proclamation of God's judgment and grace in the person of Jesus Christ. This is the foundation upon which the Church is built; without this there is no Church. And on this foundation also, the Gospel becomes the divine law of regenerated mankind. This means that all men are called to be reborn and to discover in the Gospel not formulas for salvation but the way to live the new life with a new vision of the world in Jesus Christ.

Whether it is a question of dialogue with atheists, religious liberty, marriage, or social justice, the Church is first of all called to convert herself. Otherwise the Church will seem qualified only to speak like everybody else, following what the apostle calls "Conformity with the present time." Or she will settle for moralizing and enunciating principles of natural law, leaving aside their concrete fulfillment out of prudence. And this is altogether too modest, falsely modest.

True modesty should consist for the Church in effacing herself and letting the truth of what she affirms, the reality and activity of the Spirit, of Christ and his Gospel, shine through her. This supposes a considerable reversal in our way of thinking, acting, and living; the renunciation of habits and categories that are in no sense essential but are nonetheless deep-seated; and finally, the elaboration of a theology of the world that is more biblical than philosophical and a theology of man that is more human because more evangelical. If the Church does this, she will always be a disappointment to those in search of pills, palliatives, and panaceas; but she will be doing what she is intended to do—treating human problems in their real depth and thus giving men a hope that is worthy of their dignity.

Professor Paul Evdokimov, who teaches moral theology at the Institut St.-Serge in Paris, made this statement:

Schema 13 is admirable for its thoroughness, its style, and its openness. That is its strength and its weakness. It is addressed to both believers and nonbelievers, but it will not likely satisfy either because it lacks depth. The document in fact lacks nerve. It is too calm; its optimism is not "crucified." Even a difficult text is immediately understood if it answers to the real problems of men, which are the same everywhere. . . . It is a pity that the text mentions only devils and not angels, which is a very real dimension of human existence.

The first part offers an anthropology based on the image of God. But for the average man the notion of image is an abstraction that won't be very clear. In any case, to mention the image is not enough. The schema should speak of the redeemed image, of the "new creature" in Christ. And it should speak in a manner capable of touching all men.

As well, where the schema speaks of Atheism, it would be good to see the analysis pushed much further. And I would like to see it treat the frighteningly frequent phenomenon of the state of an atheistic soul that is emptied of all spiritual substance. Sartre's famous *Nausea* is that retching of human nature when it is ranging along the moving frontier between the human and the demonic. The spiritual person speaks of mysticism, ascesis, *acedia*. In human terms this means that the human spirit is completely broken, in despair, with madness or suicide as its outcome. It postulates a whole theology of the real scourge of our times, which is boredom. Man is bored; he yawns his life away. As Dostoevsky said, a man will perish not from wars but from boredom. From a great gaping yawn big as the world of boredom will emerge the Devil.

Men expect from the Church a new and powerful word of consolation in which they can feel the irresistible breath of the Spirit, advocate and comforter. The dialectic of Father and Son has replaced the old dialectic of master and slave. At this level, human life is a passionate adventure; it is marked with the violence of the Gospel. John Chrysostom said men who had partaken of the eucharistic banquet were like lions. . . .

To respond to God's calls, we must place ourselves on his level and decipher the divine plan in the world, define the ultimate end of human activity, the grandiose meaning of culture, and its intimate link with the values of the kingdom. We might reverse the terms of "the Church in the world" and ask what we want to do with the world, how theology concretely sees the world in the Church.

This brings me to the question of marriage. The Roman and Orthodox Churches as institutions are based on monasticism and celibacy. The classical conception of monasticism relates it to "the angelic state." But angels are in the service of men. The eschatological maximalism of monks is no solution for the world. If everyone were a monk, there could be no human vocation in this world. That is why the Church serves the world, and the world is centered on the conjugal state. Biblical and patristic teachings confer ecclesial dignity upon marriage and see in it the "little Church," the organic cell of the mystical body. The meaning of the prophetic and royal priesthood of the laity with their triple office is found here.

In the East the matter of the sacrament of marriage is not a promise but love rendered charismatically. Unfortunately, history shows that we profaned and disfigured love even before we came to understand it. But we have only to read the end of the Canticle of Canticles, where love between a man and a woman is fired with an eternal flame. It is divine by nature. The Christian couple realizes the *plerum*, the fulfilled man, the redeemed Adam and Eve. Within this recreated plenitude, man is called to build the city of men and at its summit etch the icon of the kingdom, anticipate it, and introduce it into this world. To seek the kingdom means to change this world into the kingdom. Clement of Alexandria speaks of "the paradisial grace" given to marriage which makes it totally charismatic. Formerly married people wore the monastic tonsure which made marriage "interiorized monasticism," a conjugal priesthood in the service of the Lord.

This leads us to touch upon the painful question of mixed marriages. We all suffer from Christian disunity; but mixed marriages suffer from it in the flesh. They are privileged occasions for ecumenism which the Church should understand. Visibly, the Church understands today that married people are not children upon whom decisions are imposed. They are adults, members of the conjugal priesthood, and no one, not even God and much less ecclesiastical authorities, can take decisions relating to their destiny and their role. The beautiful words in the texts on ecumenism and religious liberty should find their application in mixed marriages. Any demand of a promise is somewhat degrading for the conscience. But for those who are free, adult, and priestly in their very substance, there is no question of a promise. Nor, indeed, can there be. The desires of the Council are tending in this direction. The world expects a solution that might in some sense be miraculous, for all councils are related to the apostolic Council of Jerusalem and its great cry of jubilation, "It was good for the Holy Spirit and for us.'

OCTOBER 7

All the Interventions Call for a More Energetic and More Cohesive Text on War

Vatican II, as is well known, wishes to address schema 13 to all men of good will, even those who are unbelievers. The laymen we have interviewed think this is rather pretentious, at least when it comes to chapter 5, on war. We have already mentioned this section's weakness, but we must say more about it now since the Council is discussing it.

Let us note first of all that, unlike the rest of schema 13, this chapter was written directly in Latin and not first in French, which does not make translation easy. But it is far weaker in substance than form. Here are some criticisms:

1. A meandering line of thought tries to reconcile conflicting opinions: on the one hand, that of bishops who find it normal and fitting that Christian countries manufacture and stockpile nuclear arms which are capable of annihilating whole continents; on the other hand, the viewpoint of prelates who think this attitude is difficult to justify in the light of the morality of the Gospels.
2. No reference whatsoever is made to the Gospel (the chapter, which is entitled "The Community of Nations and the Building of Peace," runs to some 400 lines).
3. In section 100 we read that the possession of nuclear arms for purposes of deterrence is not "illegitimate in itself." This clause, although qualified by other passages, strikes a good number of Christians as perfectly ridiculous.
4. Unable to choose between a casuistic perspective that tends to legitimize the possession of nuclear arms and a prophetic perspective that would condemn the manufacture of such arms as insane, schema 13 satisfies nobody—not even its writer, if our information is correct.

These four criticisms notwithstanding, schema 13 contains some excellent passages condemning the "balance of terror" and the use of atomic bombs, and proclaiming the necessity of viable international institutions and the legitimacy of conscientious objection and nonviolence. Still, the text as a whole lacks a firm backbone and is hardly worthy of a council. One would hope for a version that is more cohesive, more rigorous, centered on the future, and less complacent about the transitional period we are now going through when the world has not been able to establish an international power. One thinks of a remark by Charles Maurras apropos of the French Republic: "A plague cannot be ameliorated." This could be applied to the present situation with respect to nuclear arms. Of course, it would be puerile to imagine that the solution of the problem is easy. We are, in fact, confronted with conflicting demands, as is characteristic of every absurd situation.

A member of Pax Christi who is very dissatisfied with the weakness of this chapter told us, "In our present circumstances, the manufacture of nuclear arms for purposes of deterrence could be proof of a greater love." Our interlocutor is far from being a warmonger, but he considers himself a "realist"; he believes in the virtues of deterrence.

An expert at Vatican II expressed this opinion to us: "This chapter is like a Spanish inn. We find in it what we bring to it. So many concessions have been made to atomic powers that the Council will have to react."

It is interesting to note that nowhere does schema 13 address itself directly to heads of Christian states; they are nowhere asked to set the example of atomic disarmament.

Realism or Prophecy? In a public conference Tuesday, Father Dubarle, a Dominican who is known for his balanced thinking, said:

> The Church has not yet thrown off the theology of the just war. This was perhaps valid for the fourteenth century, but it does not respond to the twentieth-century situation. The text of schema 13 is too weak, muddled, and shifty [*sic*]. It is scandalous to tolerate what the schema calls "minor" (in Latin, *minores*) wars which are odiously cruel and hypocritical. These conflicts are experimental wars, moreover, and remind one of the Spanish Civil War. . . .
>
> We must take sides. War is a crime in itself. The armaments race is a vicious circle. The Council is losing a unique occasion to come to the defense of the innocent, who are always victimized by war. . . . The Church must be more decisive. In this schema, she should both defend the small people and give specific directives to scientists because they do not know how to resolve their own conflicts of conscience.

Father Dubarle chose to speak in Rome as a prophet. But when addressed as a moralist, he replied, "The present situation prevents my theologian's conscience from saying that it is immoral to manufacture atomic bombs as long as there are no effective international institutions."

How does Father Dubarle the prophet accommodate Father Dubarle the theologian? This difficulty set off a lively discussion between the speaker and his audience. In the final analysis, Father Dubarle said, he would be very happy if the Council ignored his theologian's scruples.

The Theory of a Just War Is Obsolete These various considerations enable us to define better the climate in which the Fathers made their interventions Tuesday and Wednesday. There has been a marked intellectual evolution in the episcopacy over the past year. Everyone has been struck by the forthrightness of the interventions. Still, it is symptomatic that the Council Fathers do not give the impression of having studied the doctrinal basis of nonviolence, or of applying the commandment "Thou shall not kill" broadly enough, or of adequately evoking the pacific teachings of Christ. Not all the texts in the Gospel go in the same direction, but it cannot be denied that the spirit of the Gospel as a whole supports the theory of nonviolence.

The most pertinent criticism of the chapter seems to be this: that it stops at the limits of a natural morality and does not rise to the level of the pacific spirituality of Christ. Or, as Pastor Hébert Roux has just told *Le Monde*, "The Gospel judges the Church."

An account of the first interventions follows. Most of the bishops want to go beyond the theory of a just war, and some of them are sympathetic to nonviolence. It is a sign of the times. A good part of Cardinal Léger's speech brought De Gaulle's politics inescapably to mind, which naturally didn't go unnoticed. It was the first time in Vatican II that so clear an allusion had been made to a head of state.

On Tuesday, Cardinal Alfrink of Utrecht opened the debate on chapter 5:

> This chapter treats a difficult and controversial subject in a satisfactory way; but the connection between the ideas should be more firmly established so that the readers can grasp the fundamental points at the outset. . . .
>
> It is necessary to make a distinction between the possession of arms and their use, given the unfortunate fact that peace today depends to a great extent upon the balance of terror. However, we must avoid the ambiguities that could arise from the statement, just in itself, that positive results could be born of this unhappy and precarious state. We must proclaim openly that the only remedy for the balance of terror is the reduction and then the abolition of nuclear weapons, as both Pius XII and John XXIII said. Their words could usefully be incorporated in this schema.
>
> There is some confusion in the text about so-called minor wars and the activity connected with war. The problem posed by obedience to orders ought to be more clearly expounded. The passage concerning conscientious objection could be retained, provided we mention that it falls to civil authorities to prevent possible abuses.

Cardinal Liénart was the first speaker yesterday. He said:

> The world today presents a painful contrast between the desire for peace of most men and the reality of war. The Church, faithful to the Gospel, has always been against war; she ranks it among the worst scourges, along with plague and famine. Attentive to the signs of the times, she understands that she has a greater role to play today. Weapons exist which can annihilate not only entire cities but the entire world. War has become a crime against God and against man. The classical distinction between a just war and an unjust war is no longer adequate. Recourse to arms can be permitted

only for the sake of establishing justice. But how can this end be achieved with inhuman means? Today men should no longer think of defending their rights with arms but rather of suppressing the injustices which provoke wars by putting justice and fraternity into practice.

Cardinal Léger of Montreal took the floor next to say:

Many expect the Council to place its whole authority in the service of peace; some would like a solemn condemnation of military activity and particularly destructive weapons. The schema wants to respond to this desire. But the text must be corrected, for it is ambiguous and even contradictory. It both contains an absolute condemnation and at the same time says there can be exceptions under certain circumstances. . . .

The problem presents itself in a new way today. The classical theory of a just war has become practically inapplicable because of the nature of modern warfare. We must cast this theory aside. The text should show the horrors of modern war and say, in a few brief but strong words, that war cannot be a suitable means of restoring violated rights.

Concerning the necessity of an international authority, the schema should affirm more energetically the responsibilities of governments, and sound a warning against inertia, the anachronistic cult of the sovereignty of the state, nationalism, selfishness, contempt for international society—whether expressed in words or in deeds— and a lack of education in the international perspective. . . .

What is said about conscientious objection pleases me. But this should be motivated less by "meekness" than by charity and an evangelical spirit. . . . Finally, we should explicitly call for cooperation between Christians and non-Christian believers, especially Buddhists.

The Backwardness of States Cardinal Duval, Archbishop of Algiers, spoke in the name of the episcopal conference of North Africa:

This text should be stronger. It should indicate more clearly why a reform of international commerce is necessary; in its present form, it increases the differentiation between rich and poor nations. . . . Racism is only mildly reproved. . . . The horror of war is not sufficiently emphasized, and the condemnation of total war is not clear. . . . The chapter should be more synthesized in form in order to show how the problems of hunger, ignorance, and peace are interrelated. . . .

The passage which states that the intentions of those who declare war are not being judged should be deleted and replaced with one that says just the opposite. [Bishop Pal Brezanoczy, Apostolic Administrator of Eger, called for a similar correction in the name of the bishops of Hungary.] We must state that war is intrinsically evil. Furthermore, the problem of peace should be treated in a more positive fashion. . . . We must establish new ways of thinking and a new political morality. The cooperation of all is necessary for this. The Council should address itself to political and economic leaders, emphasizing the necessity of a world authority as well as the backwardness of states that do not want to give any consideration to international institutions. Moreover, Vatican II should address itself to scientists and underline the moral rules of scientific research; finally, it should appeal to all men, showing them that evil is first of all in our hearts, and urge each to work for the establishment of peace.

Archbishop Garrone of Toulouse declared:

The text is balanced, but it could be more unified and effective. . . . We must take into account the serious ambiguities which exist in the minds of many men; for them peace is merely the absence of war, and they confuse fear of war with love of peace. But the possibility of war will never disappear until every effort is made to establish justice and men are taught to master their passions. We must do everything we can to outlaw war. . . .

The truths expounded in the first part of the schema are only implicit in the second part; they should be explicit there, too. . . . The text would be more effective if it were more positive; it should be especially clear on the serious obligations incumbent upon the consciences of heads of state today. [Here Archbishop Garrone used the expression *sub gravi*, which in moral theology designates mortal sin.]

Several Allusions to Conscientious Objection Father Butler, Superior General of the English Benedictines, stated:

The paragraph which says that the possession of nuclear weapons for purposes of deterrence cannot be considered illegitimate puzzles me, for how could such an intention be discerned? If one truly intends not to use such arms, then there is no point in having them. Let us therefore delete this paragraph.

Nor do I think we should insist on the duty to obey legitimate authority, for in wartime such authority is often abused. It would be better to call attention to the responsibility of those who too readily obey immoral orders and then invoke the duty of obedience to justify crimes committed in wartime. . . .

Conscientious objection is not limited to military service. Moreover, objectors can play a prophetic role. Only spiritual arms are Christian.

Coadjutor Bishop Gordon Wheeler of Middlesbrough, England, thought conscientious objection constituted a positive value. "It is not enough not to condemn it," he said.

The same bishop and Auxiliary Bishop Charles Grant of Northampton, England, asked that the "equivocal" passage which says the possession of modern weapons is not illegitimate in itself be deleted.

Bishop Castan Lacoma of Siguenza, Spain, took a different tack: "Let us leave judgment about conscientious objection to civil authorities. . . . In case of atomic aggression, it is legitimate to retaliate with similar weapons. The real solution lies in suppressing these arms altogether." The speaker was the only one to say that atomic defensive war is legitimate.

Bishop Rusch of Innsbruck, Austria, said, "Not only should classical wars be condemned but also the so-called subversive or ideological wars as well as all narrowminded nationalism. We must proclaim that Christ's words 'Blessed are the peacemakers' apply to nations as well as to individuals." The Bishop also suggested that a secretariat be created in Rome to deal with military matters.

A Doubtful Law Does Not Oblige

The intervention by Bishop Simons of Indore, India, rather unexpected in a debate on war, was one of the most revolutionary of the whole Council. The Indian prelate spoke on birth control, and expressed the desire that the Church authorize contraceptives on the basis of the principle of moral theology that a doubtful law does not oblige (*lex dubia non obligat*):

> The demographic explosion is a striking phenomenon of our times. It is predicted that the population of the globe will have doubled in a few dozen years. To resolve this problem, we must do more than rely on the natural riches of the earth; they are not inexhaustible. The decreased mortality rate as a result of progress in the medical sciences contributes to a constant increase of the world population. We must investigate possible ways of arresting this demographic expansion, bearing in mind that laws are made

for man and not vice versa. Why couldn't theologians study the application of principles that constitute an obstacle to the solution of this problem? Let us distinguish between natural laws and moral laws. Theologians and moralists have stopped short with conceptions which do not correspond with reality. From the point of view of the common good, contraceptives could change our whole approach to this problem. A doubtful law does not oblige.

Schema on Bishops Ready for Promulgation

The whole schema on bishops was voted on by the Fathers on Wednesday. The results: of 2,181 votes, 2,167 were affirmative and 14 negative. We might note that none of the fourteen *modi* transmitted to the competent commission by the Pope at the request of Bishop Carli of Segni (the leader of the minority on the commission) were incorporated. The schema is now ready for promulgation.

OCTOBER 8

The Debate on Schema 13 Continues

Why, a humorist has asked, hasn't a bishop had the courage to praise the atomic bomb? Isn't it the most daring weapon ever created by man? Isn't it because of nuclear arms that we have avoided the horror of a third world war? Doesn't it furnish irrefutable proof that war has become absurd? Doesn't it thereby represent decisive progress for humanity?

Like all paradoxes, this position has its interest and, all things considered, is no more scandalous than the following, which is much more popular: it is good for nations to possess atomic bombs as long as there is no effective international organization. The Council is becoming more and more reluctant to use this kind of language, although it is inclined to adopt a realistic position. The whole question here is whether or not the Council is competent to make such a judgment; it may be logical, but with good reason it can disturb public opinion, and it has nothing to do with the Gospel.

Doesn't the world expect 2,000 bishops, whose profession is to preach the Gospel, formally to condemn the armaments race and all its consequences? A give-and-take policy isn't valid. Yet this is what the present schema does, torn as it is between two contradictory positions. That is why it is so weak.

If Vatican II followed through on its still diffuse thinking, it should absolutely condemn all forms of war, "minor" or not, atomic or classical, local or worldwide. It is more important to condemn war than to condemn the manufacture of the atomic bomb, although one would imply the other.

If the Church were as adept at drawing consequences from the fifth commandment as she is from the sixth, the world would certainly be changed. Maximos IV Saigh said this in an admirable way during the third session, as did Archbishop Roberts, formerly of Bombay.

Here is a summary of the last eight interventions on Thursday concerning war.

Bishop Carli of Segni took to the attack:

> The present text on conscientious objection is illogical, incomplete, and obscure. The Council should be silent about this question. The theologians do not agree. Let us leave the subject to them. The manner in which the document speaks is too imprecise; more distinctions are in order. There can be just wars, in which case military service is not only legitimate but necessary. Such service is even useful in peacetime, for we must prepare for defensive wars. To affirm outright that conscientious objection is good is to infringe on the prerogatives of the state, which alone is competent in this matter. The authors of the schema are biased in favor of conscientious objection. They thus go against the traditional doctrine of the Church and against morality.

Archbishop Cantero Cuadrado of Saragossa was of a similar opinion. He termed conscientious objection "inadmissable."

The Balance of Terror Bishop Mariano Gaviola of Cabanatuan, the Philippines, said:

> The balance of terror cannot be considered the best and unique instrument for avoiding war, from either the moral or the legal point of view. Today, however, it is unfortunately the only way to achieve minimal security. Nations fear war, and they have the right and responsibility to take the most suitable means of preventing it. We should encourage the participation of Catholics in organizations of international and national peace, particularly Pax Christi.

The tone of the five other interventions was quite different.

Archbishop George Beck of Liverpool was very partial to conscientious objection, which seemed to him to be a direct consequence of religious liberty. He also asked this question:

How can we make a practical judgment about a government's intention to deter the enemy? . . . The fragmentation of the world into 170 sovereign states is beyond a shadow of a doubt an obstacle to international cooperation. . . . Too often we teach history to the young as an illustration of national glory, and every country automatically justifies the wars it has initiated.

We should, on the contrary, strive to establish an international authority that is capable of preventing wars."

Cardinal Martin, Archbishop of Rouen, complained, "This text is too cold. . . . The distinctions between defensive and offensive wars, as well as between just and unjust wars, is obsolete today. It has become necessary to condemn all forms of war as a means of resolving international problems. Christians should be the first to organize a universal peace movement, in the name of humanity and the Gospel. 'Never again war,' Paul VI said at the United Nations."

The Right To Revolt   Cardinal Ottaviani, Secretary of the Holy Office, made an energetic and widely discussed declaration. Of particular interest was what he said about a nation's right to revolution:

Several Fathers have said that war should be condemned altogether. I am in entire agreement. I would like to see the schema treat at greater length the means of promoting and maintaining peace and resolving international conflicts in a peaceful way. We must manifest the value of the weapons of justice and charity. The civil and religious education of nations should help eliminate all conflict between classes and races as well as every form of political or economical imperialism. . . .

We must spread the spirit of fraternity among nations according to the principles of the Gospel in order that they will be disposed to accept the sacrifices necessary to the common good of humanity. Totalitarianism, the principal cause of wars, should be eliminated. We should strengthen such international institutions as the International Court of Justice at the Hague and the United Nations. . . .

The schema should explain clearly the different forms of violence; the word *war* is too vague. Armed revolution, guerrilla warfare, terrorism, and sabotage should also be condemned. We must remember that communism stirs up wars and aggression, although they call it the liberation of the masses. . . .

According to Saint Thomas, the representatives of a people or the people themselves can revolt against a government preparing for a war that would be the ruination of the country. . . .

The Council should express the desire that all nations join together in a single worldwide republic.

Bishop Klepacz of Lodz, Poland, spoke of the causes of war:

We all live with the nightmare of an unprecedented world conflict. Therefore, it is not enough to speak of peace and condemn war, we must try to reform institutions and man himself. Selfishness, cupidity, utilitarianism—these are the real causes of war, and our theories about justice, truth, and solidarity are so much empty wind. Let the Council take objective account of the truth and show the possibility of improvement.

Archbishop Gouyon of Rennes spoke of the necessity of avoiding violence:

The Gospel urges us to do everything we can to avoid violence, which it condemns. But we cannot refuse a nation the right to defend itself against an unjust aggressor. Nonetheless, every war, even a limited one, is an exceptionally serious evil, aggravated by the fact that we never know where it will lead us. Any nation that declares war should be condemned by the conscience of mankind. Only an international authority should have the right to protect violated rights by means of arms. Let nations desist in favor of this solution."

Toward the end of the session on Thursday, the Fathers decided by a show of hands to close discussion on schema 13. They then began examination of the schema on the missions. We will report on this later.

OCTOBER 9

Despite the Cloture Vote,
the Council Resumes the Debate on War

On Friday, five more Fathers intervened on chapter 5, each in the name of seventy or more bishops as the regulations require.

Auxiliary Bishop Ancel of Lyon spoke first:

It is true that the writers of the schema have been unable to give adequate expression to the Church's efforts for peace. The Council should bear witness to the truth in the name of Christ. What is required, therefore, are clear statements and not a casuistic exposition. We must above all solemnly affirm the necessity of instituting an international authority. The time has come for all nations to submit to an effective supranational authority. Let the Council make a solemn declaration to this effect.

Bishop Rupp of Monaco said, "This schema goes farther than *Pacem in terris*. . . . It is absolutely essential that we mention the right to emigrate. Those who live in overpopulated areas have a strict right to new land."

Bishop Luigi Faveri of Tivoli urged the Fathers, "Let us emphasize charity. The exercise of love remains the only center and the surest basis of the Council, as Paul VI said in his opening speech to the fourth session."

Bishop Philbin of Down and Connor, Ireland, felt that "The conclusions of the draft seem to underestimate the meaning and bearing of the Gospel, which is ignored in most of the document. The text has a didactic and philosophical tone. We must stress the fact that without Christ man can do nothing."

Bishop Boillon of Verdun declared:

> The text makes distinctions that are out of date. We cannot distinguish between conventional and nonconventional weapons. As early as 1917, conventional arms killed over a million people at Verdun. Nor can we distinguish between combatants and noncombatants. Nor should we speak of limited wars, for an inexorable law risks transforming it into a total war. It is no longer possible to predict the effects of modern weapons. We should add that wars between so-called Christian nations have been a scandal to non-Christians and an obstacle to evangelization. We must rally public opinion in favor of justice and against violence.

Archbishop Garrone, the reporter for schema 13, thanked the Fathers for their constructive criticism. He said that the schema would be shortened, in keeping with a general desire, and that the writers would try to give it "the prophetic fire it lacks."

The Council then went on to the chapter on the missions, on which there were eleven interventions.

Paul VI Is Considering an Intercontinental Trip

Named a citizen of the world—a title that would have pleased John XXIII—by the International Registry of World Citizens, Paul VI returned to his modern apartments in the Vatican to ponder his next trip. The Pope of Jerusalem, Bombay, and the United Nations has clearly started a new trend. Some say his next voyage will be to Poland, behind the iron curtain, and in the same stride Africa, Latin America, and perhaps a Marian shrine like Lourdes.

All this puzzles the Curia. Never has a pope been so disconcerting as Paul VI. Never has a pope said such brutal things about them or about Roman nobility as has Paul VI. Never has a pope so disturbed the thousand-year tradition of protocol: tiaras given away, the *sedia* and *flabella* cast aside, his title as a temporal power relinquished; and even in his visits abroad as head of the Church he has preferred to be known as a pilgrim, a brother, an "expert in humanity."

The Curia and other prelates throughout the world are exhausted trying to follow Paul VI, both literally and figuratively. Nothing is more characteristic of the Pope than the speed of these official disruptions. For example, when he proceeds through the nave of St. Peter's, his retinue have all they can do to keep up. The reforms already accomplished are nothing in comparison with those to come.

UNESCO at the Vatican? It is no longer a secret that Paul VI is seeking a sophisticated and practical means of dissociating himself further from Vatican City (with its various palaces and museums) in order to show the modern world that the Church is free from all compromise with temporal wealth. It is sometimes said that the Pope would like to turn over part of the Vatican to UNESCO. Psychologically speaking, it is of the greatest importance that the vicar of Christ resemble his master, who persistently rejected the honors and pomp of power and lived a simple life close to the people whom he wished to serve. When Paul VI makes this determining gesture, he will break with the Constantinian era to rejoin the early traditions of the primitive Church.

A week after Paul VI's visit to the United Nations, we can report with fair accuracy on what is being said or rumored.

A List of Questions The opinion of some is clear: let the Pope not forget that the majority of men today are no longer Christian and are little concerned with the praiseworthy intentions of the sovereign pontiff. Why did the Pope want to give his support to the United Nations, which is well known for its intrigues and narrowmindedness? Why did he flatter the members of this international organization? Why does he refuse to come into contact with the nonreligious masses who know nothing of Catholicism? It certainly doesn't please God that Paul VI scurries from continent to continent in search of a superficial and transitory popularity, and so forth and so on.

Many other questions are asked by those who sense confusedly that religion goes beyond their conception of it, and that the most prestigious of contemporary courts is gradually but surely breaking with a long tradition of isolation and pomp.

The Pope's immediate company—one or two persons at the most— and some members of the Curia are happy that the Pope's trip to the U.N. was so perfectly understood by the masses but roundly criticized in certain Roman chambers.

We read such surprising things as these in the papers: "The Pope's trip to the United Nations is not to be taken seriously. The conciliar declaration on the Jews is much more important"; "The Pope has become a diplomat, a man of politics"; "The Pope went to the United Nations because he is haunted by war" or "because he is aware of personal failure in his own circles."

Are these things true? We should rather say that not for a moment did the Pope step down from the spiritual and moral plane which is his while mingling with politicians and diplomats. This is quite different from the reasons cited above, not only on the level of the Pope's personal intentions but also on the level of facts. The Pope didn't go to the United Nations primarily because he was afraid of war—who isn't?—but because he believes that under the present circumstances, the United Nations is the body most capable of advancing humanity toward its destiny of unity. We are thus at the opposite pole of machinations. Paul VI feels—as Teilhard de Chardin described so admirably—that man is gradually being forced to renounce war and outmoded national sovereignties, and that it is his duty to support this tendency, however disproportionate his gesture might be. For anything that helps human progress rightly interests Christianity. The United Nations is in some sense the secular and embryonic replica of the international Church.

Recognition of an Adult Humanity Paul VI is aware that mankind is no longer seeking its balance around the altar or the Vatican but in secular structures. In visiting the United Nations, he showed he recognized that the temporal powers, having attained their maturity, have also acquired independence vis-à-vis the Church, and that mankind is adult enough to build a natural morality which is not explicitly based on religion. Men today are no longer religious and in fact do not consider themselves as such, but they have faith in themselves. Paul VI has in some sense baptized this purely secular faith, somewhat as Aquinas baptized the philosophy of Aristotle in the Middle Ages and revealed its unsuspected affinity with Christianity. You will be gods, the New Testament affirms. Twentieth-century man, however heretical he may be, has taken the Gospel literally. He is following out the logic of the incarnation. Humanity is the body of God.

The Leaven　Paul VI's visit to the United Nations also signaled the end of Christian Manicheanism, the end of the divorce between terrestial or political values and the values of the Spirit. It represents Catholicism rediscovering the true meaning of laicism. After centuries of Jansenism, idealism, and contempt for the world, it means the rehabilitation of the political order, an invitation to specific political commitment. It is in some sense the dawn of the New Middle Ages Berdyaev spoke about, of a neo-Christianity at the antipodes of the old Christianity: not authoritarian or vindictive, not narrowly institutional or closed in upon itself, but open, considerate, charitable, an invisible leaven in society and more effective because it is invisible.

People are sometimes surprised to hear Paul VI speak of himself as a brother rather than a father, a friend rather than a prince. But in our view it would have been more surprising had Paul VI gone to the United Nations in a regal capacity. Soon, as Catholics either hope or fear, the Pope will become a globetrotter. He will express his concern for all men: black African, white American, European Socialist, whatever. He will demonstrate that if men need God, then necessarily so does God's vicar. Thus the public at large will understand better that the Pope's aims are not political or diplomatic or even specifically religious (Christ came to abolish religions), but simply human and spiritual. The "expert in humanity" has just begun his course among his brothers, all men. When he became Bishop of Rome, Paul VI swore that he would re-establish a bridge between the Church and the world. He is well on the way to keeping his promise.

OCTOBER 11

Bishop Koop of Brazil
Urges a Married Clergy in Latin America

The question of a married clergy is progressively gaining attention. The influence of the Oriental Church has something to do with this. But there are other influences as well. The Latin American episcopacy, with their strongly pastoral bent, are becoming more and more concerned about the catastrophic situation of the Church on that continent. We can say without any exaggeration that if there isn't a large increase in the Latin American clergy and soon, the presence of the Church will be finished within a few years. That presence is already seriously compromised; it is very late in the day.

Religious history proves that the Church has no taste for suicide. She is often tardy in undertaking necessary reforms, it is true, but in the end she makes them. This is likely what will happen with a married clergy. The door was partly opened when Vatican II approved a married diaconate.

The intervention reported below was to be pronounced in the aula when the discussion on priests comes up by Bishop Pedro Koop, of Lins, Brazil. Bishop Koop, sixty-one, is of Dutch origin, and belongs to the Missionaries of the Sacred Heart. Two other Brazilian bishops intended to intervene in a similar vein. The speech in question was submitted to the secretariat of the Council, as is usual. But the moderators told Bishop Koop that they thought it unwise for him to give it orally in the aula. For this reason, it is said, he is preparing a more moderate speech than the one published here.

The document will remain one of Vatican II's boldest efforts. Even though it will have no immediate practical effects, it will be an important factor in the eventual solution of this problem.

Here is the substance of Bishop Koop's intervention:*

Venerable Fathers, I want to come right to the point: if we are to save the Church in Latin America, we must introduce a married clergy, chosen from men of outstanding character, as soon as possible. However, the law of eccesiastical celibacy would remain in effect.

Statistics prove that the Catholic Church is gradually losing ground in the world in general and particularly in Latin America because of the population increase, attacks by the atheists and the non-Catholic sects, and other factors.

The principal reason for this is the lack of priests. The shortage is increasing daily in relation to the population growth.

Latin America represents 33 percent of the universal Church. Yet it has only 6 percent of all priests. In the year 2000 Latin America will have 600,000,000 souls. That would be 50 percent of the universal Church. Consequently, we would need 120,000 priests in order to provide a pastor for every 5,000 souls, ignoring for the moment the abnormal distances that each would have to cover.

The new ruling concerning the diaconate will help the situation somewhat, but it will never remedy it. Primarily for pastoral reasons—

---

* To prevent any misunderstanding, let me note that Bishop Koop did not personally give me or have me given the text of his intervention. Mimeographed copies have been in the hands of nearly all the Council Fathers and experts for several days. One of these authorized me to publish it.

to save the faith of many souls, to administer the sacraments of penance and the eucharist, to give extreme unction, to preach, and especially to offer mass—we have an urgent need of priests.

It is urgent that priests be multiplied a hundredfold, and in our own day, so that the Church may be brought to men and so that she may seek them where they live, because owing to the inadequate number of church buildings men cannot find their way to her.

There is a population of 80,000,000 in Brazil; 60,000,000 of the faithful are ordinarily not reached by the Church because there are not enough priests living near the people, either socially or in a community sense.

Venerable and very zealous Fathers and pastors! By virtue of the divine command to conserve and propagate the faith, I propose that the Council make it possible to confer the priesthood on worthy laymen who have been married for at least five years. After suitable formation they would exercise the priestly ministry as substitutes and assistants. They could administer to small communities in their free time.

This solution has always been in effect in the Oriental Church, which has married priests who are exceptionally worthy and truly apostolic.

Married priests could enlist their conjugal, familiar, and socioeconomic experience in the service of the ministry. This would indubitably make it more effective. They would be fully dependent upon the bishop, and would exercise their ministry in determined places, particularly in smaller communities. Thus, nothing would be changed. But a new pastoral instrument would be created, one capable of alleviating our distressing religious situation now and for the future.

Let the bishops be under no illusion: the fate of the Church in Latin America is in great danger. The choice is urgent: either we multiply the number of priests, or we can expect the fall of the Church in Latin America.

I propose that we add the following sentences to paragraph 14 of the schema on priests, beginning with line 16:

Since the number of celibate priests in great regions of the Church is totally inadequate and tends to diminish because of the disproportionate population increase, the Council, considering the good of the many souls to save and by virtue of the divine commandment, has decided that it pertains to the competent territorial episcopal conferences, with the approbation of the sovereign pontiff, to decide whether or not, for the good of souls, the priesthood can be conferred with the consent of the Roman pontiff on mature men who have been married for at least five years, according to the norms established by the Apostle Paul in his epistles to Titus and Timothy.

OCTOBER 12

Paul VI Discourages Discussion
of a Married Clergy in the Council

One could feel the storm coming. Once again, the fear of those whom the Pope himself has called "nonprogressives" seem to have set the wheels in motion.

Paul VI recently received in audience a number of cardinals (including Cardinal de Barros Câmara, Archbishop of San Sebastian, Rio de Janeiro) who had come to urge him to dam the flood of interventions in favor of a married clergy. An increasing number of Council Fathers are recommending this solution in the name of pastoral demands. They have no intention of tampering with the law of celibacy presently in force; rather, they would like to create an auxiliary clergy chosen from among married men to assist the traditional clergy. They see this as a possible remedy for the catastrophic religious situation in Latin America.

Then the Pope intervened, although not quite in the way the "nonprogressives" had expected him to. Here is the substance of what Paul VI wrote in a letter addressed to Cardinal Tisserant and read to the assembly by Archbishop Felici on Monday. This version is the official communiqué from the French press bureau.

> We know that some Fathers intend to discuss in the Council the law of ecclesiastical celibacy as it is established in the Latin Church. Thus, while respecting the assembly's freedom of expression, we would like to offer our personal opinion: this is not the time to debate publicly a subject which requires the greatest prudence and is of such importance.
>
> It is our purpose not only to do everything we can to conserve this ancient, holy, and providential law but to enforce its greater observance,* reminding the priests of the Latin Church of the causes and reasons which, especially today, should make us consider this same law as highly fitting, because it enables priests to consecrate their love uniquely to Christ and give themselves totally and generously to the service of the Church and souls. [Applause.] If any Father wants to talk about this question, let him do so in writing,

* This is a reference to the laxity of clerical morality in many Latin American countries.

and let him remit his exposition to the Council presidency, which will in turn transmit it to us.

A few moments before this letter was officially communicated to the Fathers, they voted on the amended paragraph 10 of the schema on seminaries. This paragraph stresses the value of consecrated celibacy as a precious gift from God and not merely a law, and urges those responsible to see to it that seminarians are mature enough to accept celibacy as a benefit and not as a mere profession.

This paragraph, which noted the Oriental tradition of a married clergy, was recently strengthened (the word *chastity* was replaced by *celibacy*). Here are the results of the vote: of 1,989 ballots, 1,971 were *placet*, 16 *non placet*, and 2 invalid.

Total Confusion Thus the situation seems clear. Almost all the Fathers declared themselves in favor of ecclesiastical celibacy.

Things began to get a little muddled with the interpretation which certain commentators want to make of these two events on Monday, the Pope's letter and the vote on paragraph 10.

What do these commentators say? That the vote proves that only sixteen out of 1,989 bishops are in favor of a married clergy in addition to a celibate clergy, that it shows the bishops' thinking, and that the vote is all the more convincing because it took place before the Pope's letter was read.

But isn't this a somewhat hasty interpretation? There is only one method which would furnish convincing proof, and that would be to put a direct question to the Council: are you for or against an auxiliary married clergy? When such a question was asked on September 29, 1964, with respect to a married diaconate, 1,598 Fathers voted affirmatively, against 629.

This method wasn't used in the present case, and with reason: it is probable that a good number of positive votes would have been registered, thus making it clear to everyone that the bishops are divided in their judgments on the question.

Not only was such a vote not taken, but the Pope used his authority to prohibit oral and public discussion of the question (we might note that this applies to both proponents and opponents of a married clergy). This is the second time that the Pope has discouraged the Council, in each case on a matter involving chastity; the first instance was the birth control problem. This limitation of the Council's liberty indicates that Paul VI doesn't want Vatican II to go too far or too fast.

Does this mean that the Pope is personally opposed to a married clergy? Not really, because supporters of the idea like Bishop Koop have made it quite clear that they are talking about a second, auxiliary clergy. There is no question of supplanting the celibate clergy. In fact, most of the Fathers would be against this. Thus, there is a double equivocation in certain minds: they both refuse to consider the pastoral problem as Bishop Koop, for example, outlined it, and want to believe that the majority of the bishops are against an auxiliary married clergy.

We would not have stressed this equivocation were it not for the fact that those who have an official reponsibility to disseminate information are contaminated by it. From the evidence, they have become spokesmen, sometimes without great conviction, for those bishops who are partisan to the status quo.

Strict honesty demands that we make it clear that the Pope has not closed the door. He has simply asked the Council not to talk about the subject and to inform him of their ideas directly and discreetly.

The problem of celibacy, which is of intimate concern to all priests, is the touchstone of the rapid evolution in the thinking of some Fathers as well as the Pope's attitude. Paul VI intends to remain in control of the situation, no matter what trends develop in the Council. He does not think the hour has come. And there is no doubt that he has every right to act as he did, in spite of the definition of collegiality contained in the conciliar Constitution on the Church, *Lumen gentium*, promulgated last year.

Monday morning eleven Fathers spoke on the schema on the missions.

Archbishop Roberts on Conscientious Objection

A speech by Archbishop Roberts is always a paraconciliar event. Monday night was no exception. This bishop has never spoken on the Council floor, or more exactly, if we understand him correctly, he has never been given the opportunity.

"Tonight I will give you the intervention I had prepared for the Council," he said, "but was not able to give, although I sent it to the secretariat in August. Some, like Cardinal Ruffini, have intervened several dozen times. They always seem to have a green light; but I never do."

He gave his opinion on conscientious objection in these terms:

> The Catholic Church is behind English legislation by fifty years. She greatly underestimates the role of conscientious objection. I am not accusing any one bishop; the Church as a whole is to blame. Most of the opposition comes from Italians. All the Protestant states have explicitly accepted conscientious objection, but I don't know of one

Catholic state that has. I ask that the Council support a man's right not to obey blindly. I disagree with what the schema says about *presomptio juris.*

The Schema on the Missions

This morning Wednesday, Vatican II began examination of the schema on priests, which in principle will be the last one discussed in public. It was introduced by Archbishop Marty of Reims, Superior of the Mission de France. We will have more to say about this text. It has been awaited with legitimate impatience and curiosity by the priests of the whole world, the men in the first lines of the apostolate, who don't want to be forgotten by Vatican II.

The tone of Archbishop Marty's report made a forceful impact. It is both simple and strong. A good deal is at stake in this schema. The revival of the priest-worker movement, for example, depends upon it in some degree. This movement has been under study for the past two years by a mysterious pontifical commission. Nobody seems to know who its members are or what they are doing. It is said that seventeen cardinals are registered to speak on the schema on priests.

For the moment, let us go back to the thirty-nine interventions (twelve of them by cardinals) which have been made on the missions these last few days. Here are some of the key ideas presented.

1. Membership in the visible Church is the normal way of salvation, but one can be saved without being baptized. One has only to follow the imperatives of his conscience. For the Holy Spirit is effectively present in every creature of good faith and in all of creation. All religions contain truth. Grace acts everywhere, even in non-Christian religions, for there is no salvation outside of Christ.

2. The aim of the missions is not so much to save souls as to implant the Church. This satisfies a double requirement: obedience to Christ, who sent his apostles forth to evangelize the whole world; and obedience to the Church, which is obligated by her very nature to spread throughout the world.

3. We cannot argue from the fact that men can be saved without apparent assistance from the Church to the notion that the missions are useless or optional. They are of divine right and pertain to the very essence of the Church. All men have a right to the total truth of Christ, and the Church has a strict responsibility to Christianize all human communities without exception.

4. The divisions between the Christian churches is a scandal and constitutes a serious obstacle to the progress of the missions.

5. Dialogue with non-Christians is a pastoral necessity. But the schema ignores atheism, which infects a third of the world. It would be desirable for the future Congregation for the Propagation of the Faith to work in close collaboration with the recently created Secretariat for Relations with Non-Christian Religions.

6. Missionaries must be given a special formation, giving them an intimate knowledge of the peoples they are to evangelize.

7. The apostolate of lay missionaries is very important. There should be close cooperation between lay and clerical missionaries.

8. Dioceses with an abundance of vocations should be obligated to send priests to mission countries where there is an urgent need for them.

9. The schema is too Occidental. It seems to take no account of the churches in Africa and Asia. It is as though mission countries were of no real interest to the Church of the West. This is a totally anachronistic perspective. Today the Church has been implanted everywhere, and the young churches have an equal role in propagating the faith. There must be a reciprocity of services between the old and young churches.

10. The schema does not defend missionary institutes sufficiently. These suffer from a serious shortage of vocations, largely because they are not adapted to the needs of the twentieth century. Let them undertake their *aggiornamento*.

Infantilism and Sentimentalism   The intervention on Tuesday by Father Pedro Arrupe, General of the Jesuits, was of exceptional interest. Here is a summary.

We must completely overhaul our concept of missionary work. Several false ideas, which discourage vocations, must be rectified:

1. The center of the world's gravity is rapidly becoming Asia, given the population growth on that continent. The Church ought to be present there right now. It is high time. In Japan eighty years ago, there were few cultural institutions; today there are ninety universities in Tokyo alone.

2. Some think that misionary work is easy, but it is extremely complex. Missionary work is often presented in the West in an infantile and sentimental manner.

3. The West's superiority complex is not justified. Simple good will is not enough for a missionary vocation. Men of strong personality are needed.

4. The missionaries are presented as beggars. But this way of doing things

should be changed. Such a change supposes a radical reorganization of methods.

Father Arrupe concluded by calling for information offices run by the Congregation for the Propagation of the Faith and episcopal conferences. He concluded with these words from Saint Augustine: "*Si aliquando cur non modo; si non modo cur aliquando?*" which might be translated: "If something has to be done eventually, why not now; if it is not done now, why should it be done eventually?"

A Maneuver We might note that the schema on the missions contains a paragraph on the reform of the Roman Congregation for the Propagation of the Faith. But the Fathers familiar with the work of the commissions have observed that the passage in question does not correspond with what the Commission for the Missions originally proposed. As a result of an action by Cardinal Roberti, president of the extraconciliar Commission on the Reform of the Roman Curia, the text of the paragraph was watered down. This turn of events caused much surprise and dissatisfaction. It seems that the more influential members of the Congregation for the Propagation of the Faith took it upon themselves to modify the passage in an effort to retain all of their authority over the missions, a highly anticollegial maneuver. Will their effort be thwarted? This is what everyone is wondering at the moment. It is of one cloth with the whole question of curial reform.

The Price of Law

The agitation created in conciliar circles by the Pope's refusal to let the Council debate the celibacy issue publicly and the publication of Bishop Koop's projected intervention in *Le Monde* has not died down. And for several reasons.

The Holy Office and residential bishops are swamped by the innumerable problems relating to the law of ecclesiastical celibacy together with the many infractions of this discipline, particularly in the Latin countries but also, it is said, in Germany. This situaton is a wound in the Church's flank which greatly disturbs the bishops.

For an appreciable number of priests, celibacy is patently more a burden than a liberation. Even when it is borne heroically, there is no evidence that it is an aid to the apostolate.

It is reasonable to think that the Church will be stricter in the future in selecting men for the priesthood so as not to perpetuate the painful situations that presently exist. This seems to be what the Pope meant when he said that the observance of the law must be strengthened. But then the number of vocations, already tragically inadequate, would be still further diminished.

A stringent division of the clergy between rich and poor dioceses will become mandatory. This supposes a complete reformation of present practices and will only gradually be effected.

The Fathers are not very happy about the fact that their written interventions—the only kind permitted—will not contribute to the construction of the conciliar schema since they will be directly transmitted to the pope.

Many of the Fathers are highly uneasy. Almost all conversation is centered about the events of the past two days.

On the other hand, a very large number of Fathers are not ready for the idea of a second, married clergy. In France, for example, where there is no need for such a solution, and the bishops who would accept this plan for South America could be counted on the fingers of one hand. What makes this so tragic is that they have no alternate plan to propose. Canon law affirms the strict right of the baptized to the sacraments, and this law cannot be respected on many continents because of the shortage of priests.

OCTOBER 14

Archbishop Marty Underlines the Pastoral Demands of the Priest's Missionary Vocation

On Wednesday, Vatican II finished voting on the schema on seminaries: 2,196 Fathers voted *placet* and only 15 *non placet*. The text was transmitted to the Pope. It is now ready for promulgation, as are the schemas on bishops and religious life. The three texts could be promulgated at the public session which the Pope has decided the Council will hold on October 28, and which Archbishop Felici announced in the aula on Tuesday.

Most of Wednesday's general congregation was devoted to discussion on the missions by speakers who invoked the seventy-signature rule. Ten fathers intervened, as did Mr. Eusèbe Adjakpley, a Negro lay auditor from Togo who is the African regional secretary for the International Federation of Catholic Youth. There were few new ideas expressed; however, the following are worthy of note.

Father Omer Degrijse, Superior General of the missions of Scheut, Belgium, stated: "The schema does not adequately bring out the connection between missionary activity and ecumenical activity. The ecumenical movement makes more progress in concrete acts, such as those of John

XXIII and Paul VI, than in theological discussion. Let us implement ecumenism with deeds, not words. Let us undertake a catechesis and evangelization in common with the separated brethren."

Bishop Nagae of Urawa, Japan, declared, "There should be a mutual exchange of ideas, persons, and means between the old and the young in the Church."

Expelled Bishop Velasco of Amoy, China, was so critical of the schema that he was hardly convincing. He thought it insisted too much on communitarian salvation and not enough on individual salvation. It speaks of human values, he said, but not of evangelical values. It admits theological pluralism, which is altogether regrettable. "This schema is based on a false irenism, a false theology, and a false ecumenism."

Mr. Adjakpley spoke about the process of edification that heightens the desire of all peoples not only to receive but also to assert themselves and to give.

> I am sure that I can speak for all laymen—men and women, young and old, married and unmarried—who want, each according to his vocation, to put their witness and their skills at the service of the evangelizing mission of the Church. We hope that the present discussion will help increasing numbers of laymen to hear the call of the missions and understand the role they have to play, especially in bearing witness to a living Christianity among their own people and striving to make the Church present in all domains like a leaven.
>
> We would like to appeal in a special way to the young, whether in mission or in Christian countries. They are enthusiastic about secular challenges. They must also feel equally committed to the essential work of Christians: bringing Christ to the world and the world to Christ. . . .
>
> All Christians must try to express spiritual values to the secular world. We are all called in Christ to make the evangelical leaven permeate society.

Many Fathers have signed a petition expressing their stupefaction (*maxime obstupefacti*) at the extraconciliar modification of the passage in the schema relevant to the reform of the congregation for the Propagation of the Faith. The change bears on the nature of missionary bishops' participation in the work of the congregation. The signers urge the adoption of the text originally proposed.

Here are some of the more telling passages from Archbishop Marty's report on the schema on priests. Simply presented, they are nonetheless original ideas. They are indicative of the progress made in the last two years in awareness of the essentially missionary role of the priest, whose spirituality should be rooted in his pastoral activity and not in an abstract relationship with God. The priest is at the service of men, all men.

In Archbishop Marty the spirituality of the Mission de France, founded by Cardinal Suhard, makes its entrance in the aula. It still encounters opposition but is gaining ground each day.

> The priest exercises his mission among men by taking part in their lives. The pastoral mission of the priest is intrinsically universal. It concerns non-Christians as much as the faithful. . . .
>
> The priest is never isolated. His pastoral mission integrates him into the network of ecclesial communion. He shares in the episcopal mission, and together with other priests he forms the bishop's presbyterium. He works in constant contact with the laity. . . . The pastoral mission of the priest, exercised in the name of Christ and the Church, must be the basis of his holiness and nourish his spiritual life. It is in relation to this mission, and the universal love it supposes, that we must measure the importance of the evangelical counsels in the priestly life. . . .
>
> We all know very well that we cannot accomplish the mission confided to us without the daily cooperation of our priests. Working in the vineyard of the Lord at a turning point in the history of the Church, priests expect substantial nourishment from us. Let us not fail them. Their mission is difficult and requires great fidelity from all. May they discover a little better through our words that the yoke of Christ is easy to carry and his burden light!

The Council also began voting on the schema on Christian education. This schema has been exhaustively reworked on the basis of observations made by the Fathers in 1964. Even so, it has been judged so inadequate by some Fathers that they have petitioned the Council's administrators to let the schema be discussed again in the aula or at least be the object of *placet juxta modi* votes, which would enable them to propose further amendments, instead of simply the yes-no balloting the regulations call for. This appeal was rejected.

The schema mentions the obligation of parents to choose the Christian school, but adds the qualification, "with the necessary discretion." This version is the result of contradictory amendments indicating the different situations in different countries.

In his report, Bishop Daem of Antwerp said that the schema deals particularly with Catholic schools but includes the whole enterprise of Christian education in its scope, as the title indicates. The family is chiefly responsible for the education of the child. The schema warns against a state monopoly of education, although it admits that the state has an important role to play, depending on the economic, social, and cultural evolution of the country in question.

Given the extreme diversity of circumstances in the world, the text had to be very general. Episcopal conferences are charged with adapting the principles to the concrete conditions of each country.

Thirteen votes took place on the schema Wednesday. The number of *non placet* votes was relatively high, ranging from 16 to 132, with the average at 84.

"Good Will and Moral Exhortations" Cannot Resolve the Crisis of the Preisthood, Says Father Pin

On Wednesday the Dutch Documentation Center invited Father Jean Pin, the Jesuit sociologist from France who teaches at the Gregorian, to give a lecture entitled "The Crisis of the Priesthood."

"There is such a crisis," Father Pin said. "The vocation shortage is critical. A good number of apparently excellent candidates leave the seminary; many priests are uneasy because of criticism from the laity, and are aware that they have scarcely any influence. Celibacy, we must admit, is increasingly the subject of conversation in those very circles where it was formerly accepted."

Father Pin said that we aren't too clear about what a priest is, that the stable norms are crumbling, and that theologians are divided on the definition of the priesthood. He then analyzed the causes of "the collapse of structures" we observe today:

> Not only is the priest not of this world but he isn't in the world as he once was, in the time of a sacral society. Formerly, he was something like a superior officer at the summit of a hierarchical pyramid.
>
> Now that the sacral society has dissolved and given way to a technological and secular society, a crisis has emerged that cannot be remedied by either good will or moral exhortations.

Father Pin declined to propose any solutions, he said, because he didn't want to be regarded "as a visionary." However, he thought it desirable that there be more small units in the Church with their own leaders, who should exercise a profession in the world and lead a normal family life. Father Pin didn't say whether they should be composed of priests, deacons, or laymen. The present clergy should be more differentiated and specialized. Furthermore, they should exercise their apostolate in complementary teams.

"Public opinion is not yet mature," the speaker said to excuse his noncommittal stand. But this seems rather intentionally evasive. It appears to us that public opinion is perfectly well aware of the changes that must be effected in this domain and is awaiting them impatiently.

The Vote on the Declaration on the Jews

The vote on the declaration on non-Christian religions, including the statement on the Jews, began today, Thursday. The first passage of the section on the Jews was approved 1,937 to 153.

In his report, Cardinal Bea explained the conditions under which the text on the Jews had been revised, and added, "I beg you to consider this change in the light of pastoral prudence and evangelical charity." We know that the most important modification was the deletion of the expression "guilty of deicide." Here are the two reasons officially given for the change. They are not convincing.

1. "The word *deicide*, whatever the context, has an odious connotation. For that reason, it should be banned from the Christian vocabulary."
2. "Moreover, the word *deicide* might lead to false theological interpretations. . . . This has happened in the past and has given rise to arguments of a pastoral and ecumenical nature in dialogue with certain churches."

Three Fathers Ask That the Declaration Be Rejected   We have learned that Archbishop Lefebvre of the Holy Spirit Congregation, Archbishop de Proença Sigaud of Diamantina, Brazil, and Bishop Carli of Segni—all three are members of the International Episcopal Committee—have sent a letter to the Fathers asking them to reject the declaration on the Jews so the Pope will not promulgate it.

They are of the opinion that (1) this text does not respect what the Gospel says about the responsibility incurred by the Jews in the death of Christ, (2) it does not refer to the eventual conversion of the Jews, and (3) Holy Scripture and tradition use such words as *reprobation* and *cursed* with respect to the Jews, while the declaration avoids them.

Why Not Women Priests?

Women are a frequent subject of conversation at the Council, if not in the aula, then at least in the corridors at Vatican II, where the council of tomorrow is assuredly in preparation.

When a married diaconate was approved, a giant step forward was taken. It will implicitly keep the question of married priests alive, despite all the precautionary disclaimers to the contrary. And the married diaconate brings women into the antechamber of the sanctuary.

But why should the Church stop there? In the name of what principles or theological prejudices? The International Alliance of Joan of Arc has put the question to ecclesiastical authorities: why not women priests? Protestants accept women pastors.

Jesuit Father Daniélou, who is hardly a rabid liberal, recently stated his mind on the subject: "I am partisan to the idea that the Council authorize the ordination of deaconesses without delay, indeed before the end of the Council. As for an eventual female priesthood, there is no basic theological objection to it."

This expert's opinion is not likely to meet with universal approval among the theologians, and certainly not among the bishops. But at least the question remains open, and we must not judge a future possibility with old-fashioned ideas.

The Archbishop of Atlanta on Women And indeed, Archbishop Paul J. Hallinan of Atlanta, Georgia, has submitted a document to the secretariat of the Council in which he requests a more important role for women in modern life and in the Church.

The prelate suggests that women be allowed to serve mass, read the Gospel, become professors of theology, and be ordained deaconesses. He also asks that they be given a place on the postconciliar commission for implementing the schema on the laity, and that they be represented in the Vatican Congregation of religious as well as on the Commission for the Revision of the Code of Canon Law.

OCTOBER 15

Vatican II To Pronounce on the Declaration on the Jews

During the general congregation today, Friday, the Council should vote on the rest of the statement on the Jews, included as section 4 in the declaration on the Church and non-Christian religions.

On Thursday, Cardinal Bea's report on this text was one of the three subjects of interest, along with the voting on the education schema and the final discussion of the schema on priests.

Cardinal Bea's report was listened to with exceptional attentiveness. Because the text of his report was distributed to the journalists in French, we are in a position to quote from it at some length:

> The Secretariat for Promoting Christian Unity used the follow-
> ing method to deal with the contents of this chapter: in addition to

close examination of the proposed *modi* and lengthy discussion on them, we thought it advisable to make several trips to contact the Catholic and non-Catholic hierarchies of those countries where this schema has created the most difficulty during the past year. All efforts have aimed first, as far as possible, to prevent inaccurate interpretations of the theological doctrine propounded in the schema, and second, to make its exclusively religious nature clear so that political motives could not be read into it.

Concerning the latter point, the secretariat thought that the reasons for rejecting persecutions against the Jews should be made clearer by inserting these words: "The Church, . . . moved not by political reasons but by the Gospel's spiritual love, decries . . . ," and adds the rejection of "any kind" of persecution, whomever it might be directed against. . . . Thus we may hope that all political interpretation of this document will be impossible, or at least that the falsity of such interpretation can be demonstrated.

Concerning theological clarity, may I make explicit mention of the very difficult point in the schema regarding the responsibility of the Jews in the death of Christ.

Cardinal Bea read the new version of this passage in the schema, and then went on:

It is clear from this text that (1) the schema completely safeguards and expounds evangelical truth; (2) at the same time, it excludes unjust affirmations and accusations directed indiscriminately against all Jews living in the time of Christ or Jews living today, namely, that they are all guilty of Christ's condemnation and because of that rejected and cursed; and (3) the Council exhorts all to see to it that catechetical work and preaching conform to the truth of the Gospel and the spirit of Christ.

Suppression of the Word Deicide

By a comparison of this text with the one you approved last year, it can be seen that the secretariat has deleted the expression "guilty of deicide." Why? We know that the difficulties and controversies, as though the schema contradicted the Gospel, arose mostly from a *de facto* use of this expression. Moreover, anyone who reads the text we have just read and explained will see clearly that the doctrine we wanted to express in the previous version is exactly and completely expressed in substance in the present text.

I know that many attach great psychological importance to

this expression. Nevertheless, I say: if the word is misunderstood in several regions, and if the same concept can be expressed in other more apt words, don't pastoral prudence and Christian charity prohibit its use, indeed make it imperative that we express the concept in other words? And I say this is required by the same "evangelical religious love" which impelled John XXIII to order the preparation of this declaration and which inspired you to approve it last year. Our secretariat thinks that this modification is of great importance for an exact understanding of the declaration and, despite difficulties of all kinds, for its universal reception. For these reasons, I beg you to consider this change in the light of pastoral prudence and evangelical charity.

On Christian Education and the Priesthood

The schema on Christian education was adopted by 1,912 votes against 183. The number of negative votes is higher than usual. This is because the schema was severely criticized by several Fathers. In the partial voting that preceded the final vote on the whole text, the *non placet* ballots ranged from 16 to 132, as we said; they numbered 102 on the ninth question, regarding the duty of parents to support Catholic schools and send their children to them whenever possible.

The discussion on priests continues to be interesting. There have been twelve interventions in all, including seven by cardinals. They dealt with such themes as manual labor, the necessity of holiness, the priest and the unbeliever, and the cosmic dimensions of the priesthood. Here is the substance of what was said.

Cardinal Meouchi, Marionite Patriarch of Antioch: "This schema is still too juridical. It doesn't sufficiently highlight the mystery of the unity between the Church and the transforming activity of the Holy Spirit. . . . Let us talk about the virtue of obedience, but we should not forget that the priest must also obey the will of God as it is manifested in events and in history."

Cardinal Ruffini of Palermo: "This schema is altogether praiseworthy; it is a fine ecclesiastical document." Then he touched on a taboo subject: "Ecclesiastical celibacy is honored not only in the West but in a good part of the Orient as well. Let us thank all who have understood this."

Cardinal Léger of Montreal: "Priests should be given neither a lay nor a religious spirituality but rather one adapted to their state."

This is what the schema says on the subject, a passage highly praised by the Cardinal: "Let priests seek the way of perfection that is proper to their state, and at the same time seek the principle of unity for their life and work, in pastoral charity itself."

"Unfortunately," Cardinal Léger said, "the conclusions that flow from these correct principles have not yet been developed. . . ."

Cardinal Richaud of Bordeaux: "We must not forget the theocentric point of view. The priest's mission does not contain the whole essence of the priesthood."

Cardinal Colombo, Archbishop of Milan: "It would be good to emphasize that the pastoral ministry has its primary origin in an intimate bond with the fullness of the priesthood in bishops; we should also make it clearer that the relationship between Christ and bishops and priests is best seen in the diocesan clergy. This would be a measure of consolation to the latter in their loneliness and labor. . . ."

Manual Labor for Priests Bishop Argaya of Mondonedo, Spain, who is sixty-two, spoke of the critical issue of manual labor for priests. It is interesting to note that a Spanish bishop was the first to treat this subject in the aula. He said:

> Manual labor for priests is a pressing question. Why not speak of it? This form of work is as praiseworthy as any other—even better [*valde decet*], since Christ and Saint Paul worked with their hands. . . . However, priests must be cautioned against what might be called the heresy of action. . . . Let Vatican II, following the example of the Council of Trent, give us the kind of priest who is adapted to the modern world.

Bishop Guyot of Coutances:

> Many are pondering the nature and condition of the priest's life. They would be disappointed if this schema did not respond to these questions, which priests have always asked themselves. To this end, the text should show more clearly how the Holy Spirit works through the priest's life and ministry, as well as the priest's responsibility to the nonbeliever in the world today. These two considerations are connected. . . . The schema would then have a prophetic, ecumenical, and missionary dimension which it now lacks. . . . Paul VI has said that Christians today have to confront the same problems as the first Christians living in a pagan society. The evangelization of those who do not know Christ, or do not recognize him as the Savior, is one of the great concerns of priests. The schema should take this into account, at least in a general way. . . . We should say explicitly that

episcopal conferences have the responsibility of determining the concrete implementation of what is contained in the schema.

Bishop Guyot didn't say so explicitly, but it was quite clear to anyone who knows the man at all that in speaking of the powers of episcopal conferences, he was thinking of the question of worker-priests, at least for France. The plenary assembly of the French episcopacy is going to have to discuss this question sooner or later. Vatican II will have contributed to the bishops' thinking on the problem.

The Cosmic Dimensions of the Priesthood Auxiliary Bishop Henríquez Jiménez of Caracas, Venezuela, alluded to Saint Paul and Teilhard de Chardin:

> The schema should put more emphasis on the value of the priesthood for the salvation and progress of the human race and for the consummation of all things in Christ. . . . The priesthood has cosmic dimensions. Let us tell priests so. It would inspire them with zeal and optimism. . . . The crisis of obedience and authority will not be solved by means of a theological vision of the priesthood.

OCTOBER 16

Definitively Adopted by the Council,
The Declaration on the Jews Draws a Mixed Reaction

Yesterday the Council adopted the declaration of non-Christians 1,763 to 250, with 10 null ballots. The vote puts an end to the incredible number of pressures, diplomatic maneuvers, visits, letters, and pamphlets and tracts that have assailed the Secretariat for Promoting Christian Unity for more than three years. When the details of the various attempts to abort or water down the conciliar declaration are known, we will be stunned by such passion, aberration, hatred, and, to put it bluntly, ignorance and stupidity.

Many regret, and with good reason, that the last version of the text presented by the secretariat for unity was somewhat weaker. It is above all a pity that the real reasons for the changes were screened behind pious clichés. Roman diplomacy carried the day over total frankness. Many Fathers are saying this quietly to each other.

But it must be admitted that the declaration, in the form voted on, has retained the essential. Those who spread the most alarming rumors during the recess were grossly mistaken. In clearly rejecting anti-Semitism, Vatican II has fullfilled John XXIII's hopes in a general way. The Church has implicitly acknowledged her past faults in this connection; they are serious, enduring, and numerous. The new ecumenical mentality has over-come the prejudices of yesteryear. In this respect Friday's vote turns a new page in the history of relations between Rome and the Jews.

Until the last, anti-Semitic Catholics combined in an effort to muzzle the Council. We called attention last year (see the report for September 29, 1964), to a pamphlet contending that a "Judeo-Masonic" plot had trapped the Council. Another, by a Frenchman, Léon de Poncins, accused the bishops of "unconsciousness" for having approved last year's text.

A Declaration "Only an Antipope or a Secret Conspiracy Could Approve"
But we must make special mention of a four-page document the bishops have recently received. It is prefaced by this long and puzzling title: "No Council and No Pope Can Condemn Jesus, the Apostolic and Roman Catholic Church, Her Sovereign Pontiffs,* and Her Most Illustrious Councils. The Declaration on the Jews Implies Such a Condemnation. For This Reason It Must Be Rejected."

The text includes such wild remárks as these:

> The Fathers who have been so interested, during Vatican II, in freeing the Jews from their part in the death of Christ actually want to force the Church implicitly to condemn and contradict herself before the whole world. It is obvious that only an antipope or a secret conspiracy could approve a declaration of this kind. An increasing number of Catholics throughout the world share this opinion, and they are determined to act in any way that is necessary to save the Church from such an outrage.

Twenty-eight Catholic movements signed this pamphlet: three each from the United States, Italy, and Mexico; two each from Spain, Argentina, Portugal, and Chile; one each from Germany, Austria, Brazil, Ecuador, Venezuela, and from Jordan; and, giving her the sad privilege of leading the list, five from France.

Let us add that it is very difficult to interpret the negative votes we have just reported—10 abstentions and 250 *non placet* ballots. The most we can say is that they represent a mixture in unknown proportions of bishops from Arab countries, bishops of the extreme right, and bishops who are dissatisfied because the new version is weaker than the 1964 text.

---

* The brochure names fifteen popes whom "Jews attack . . . and accuse . . . of anti-Semitism because, having realized the excesses and crimes committed by Jews against Christians as well as Jewish plots against the Church and Christian states, they had the courage to adopt strong anti-Jewish measures."

Reactions to the Declaration on the Jews

The World Council of Churches: Satisfaction   In the name of the World Council of Churches, which represents 214 Christian Churches, Mr. Visser t'Hooft, Secretary General, released the following communiqué in Geneva:

> We are happy that the Council has adopted the declaration, for it clearly expresses the biblical truth, which has been hidden in all the churches, that it is through the Jewish people that divine revelation first came to men and that the profound bond which exists between Christians and Jews should be not merely a memory but a reality. . . .
>
> Anti-Semitism is therefore a denial of the Christian faith itself. The World Council of Churches attempted to express this at the New Delhi conference in 1961.

The Orthodox Patriarch of Antioch: Some Criticisms   A statement by Theodosios VI, Orthodox Patriarch of Antioch and the Orient, was published in Damascus on Friday in which he criticized the text adopted by the Council saying that the Jews cannot be held collectively responsible for the death of Christ.

According to the Orthodox Patriarch, only those Jews who followed Christ and believed in his teaching merit salvation and are exempt from the eternal Christian curse that weighs upon them.

Jacques Madaule: A New Era in Jewish Christian relationships   Mr. Jacques Madaule, president of Amitié Judéo-Chrétienne, notified us of the following statement:

> [Despite its weaknesses,] the declaration on the Jews adopted by the Council is a cause for rejoicing. Great pressure was exerted against this document. . . . We cannot find praise enough for the courage and tenacity of men like Cardinals Bea and Liénart and a great number of other bishops. Owing to their efforts the Catholic Church has finally made a solemn declaration on this serious problem.
>
> I see the document as a beginning, a point of departure. After so many bloody centuries, the Church has finally renewed authentic dialogue with Judaism. We must now see to it that the dialogue is as fruitful as possible. I am convinced that it opens a new era not only in Jewish-Christian relationships but in the relationship between Christians and all non-Christian religions, especially Islam.

Rabbi Kaplan: The Jews Have Not Been cleared of the Accusation of Deicide   Chief Rabbi Jacob Kaplan, in a recent interview, declared:

> It must be admitted that in 1965 the word *deicide* no longer makes any sense and furthermore has an odious ring. But precisely because of all the harm this false accusation has caused the Jews for seventeen centuries, the schema should have said that it is groundless. . . . But it doesn't. It seems clear that those responsible for modifying last year's text have no intention of clearing the Jews of the charge of deicide, and this is an extremely serious matter.

The American Jewish Committee: An Act of Justice   Mr. Zachariah Shuster, European director of the American Jewish Committee, made the following statement:

> The declaration on the Jews adopted by Vatican II is a significant event in the history of Judeo-Christian relations and cannot fail to have wide repercussions in various parts of the world.
>
> It is nonetheless regrettable that the declaration contains certain passages—notably those referring to ancient times and the origin of Christianity—that can cause misunderstandings and confusions.
>
> But we must recognize that the declaration rejects the myth of the collective responsibility of the Jews for the crucifixion, a myth that has caused so much harm in the past.
>
> The declaration also protests against persecutions and anti-Semitism. This should have been said a long time ago; it constitutes an elementary act of justice. Let us hope that the Council's plea for mutual respect and fraternal dialogue will contribute to a better understanding between religious groups, and that the positive principles proclaimed in the declaration will improve Judeo-Christian relations.

Mr. Morris B. Abram, President of the American Jewish Committee, also said the declaration was "an act of justice" that has "long been awaited."

Israel: A Point of Departure   The declaration on the Jews is on the whole being well received in Israel, though many find it unfortunate that the original version was "weakened" and that the Council merely "regrets" anti-Semitism and no longer condemns it.

It is thought, however, that this document constitutes a point of departure for abolishing the religious justifications for anti-Semitism. Everything will depend, it is said, on the steps taken in the future to conform religious teaching in Catholic countries with the declaration.

The Priest and the Modern World

Sixteen Fathers, including seven cardinals, intervened Friday on the schema concerning priests. It is a good sign that Vatican II is taking some time with this document; its importance to the Church is considerable. Here is a report on what was said:

Cardinal Döpfner of Munich, in the name of seventy-five bishops: "This text is too much like spiritual reading. The text should be more sober and accurate. It does not sufficiently bring out the difficulties of priests living in de-Christianized surroundings: great loneliness, and anxiety especially among older priests which can go to the point of endangering the faith."

Cardinal Alfrink of Utrecht: "Let us speak more on the priest's responsibility to dialogue with marginal Christians and atheists. Let us deepen the theology of the priesthood, for everything depends on it."

Cardinal Suenens of Malines-Brussels: "The schema is still too conceptual and untimely. When the priest tries to establish contact with the modern world, he finds that an abyss separates him from it. Even in the Church he feels squeezed between the laymen, who are taking more and more initiatives, and the bishops. . . . The priest's activity should be centered on the eucharistic sacrifice."

Cardinal Jaeger of Paderborn: "The schema is substantial, but it doesn't go far enough. The Council of Trent gave us a kind of priest adapted to the needs of the age. Vatican II must do as much for the twentieth century."

Cardinal Herrera y Oría of Málaga: "There is no relationship between what is taught in the seminary and what takes place in life. Deacons should have a year of pastoral experience before being ordained. Seminarians should be taught more about social realities."

Archbishop Miranda y Gómez of Mexico City: "In Mexico the number one problem is a shortage of priests. The remedies are a unification and cooperation among all the movements of the apostolate, and scientifically conducted sociological studies from which relevant consequences can be drawn."

Bishop Franič of Split: "We should praise rather than exhort priests. Some have given their lives for Christ. . . . Bishops should live in community with their priests."

Melkite Archbishop Nabaa of Beirut: "The material conditions of some priests' lives is distressing. . . . Scandalous inequalities among priests must cease. The whole people of God as well as bishops are responsible for their priests."

Auxiliary Bishop Stanislaus Brazana of Buffalo: "Let us be charitable toward priests in trouble. Human weakness and not ill will is the cause. Their confrères should do everything to facilitate reconciliation. The whole Church has a responsibility in this matter; a less rigorous way of dealing with it would not scandalize good priests, who know the parable of the good Samaritan."

Bishop Renard of Versailles: "Obedience and love should never be separated. . . . Let us be clear about the means bishops must use to sanctify their priests." Auxiliary Bishop Tito Mancini of Porto and Santa Rufino, Italy: "Priests should be encouraged to take initiatives. Let us trust them. We must not require a passive obedience; otherwise we kill zeal in priests and disgust them."

OCTOBER 1 8

Cardinal Bea Intervenes
in Favor of the Oriental Clergy

With the schema on priests, the Council has taken up the essential question for the Church's efficacy. The definition of collegiality in the Constitution on the Church and schema 13 itself would remain inoperative if the Council did not give priests practical directives for acting in the modern world.

Bishop Soares of Beira, Mozambique, said Saturday that the Church would have to wait for the next Council to obtain a good schema on priests. Is this too pessimistic? Actually, the essential merit of the present schema is that it recognizes episcopal conferences as empowered to make concrete applications in their respective countries. Bishop Guyot, among others, said this, last Thursday.

The Council is very aware that it must at all costs avoid legislating in detail for each local church. Vatican II is the council of open doors. Even on the burning issue of eventually instituting an auxiliary married clergy, at least for Latin America, the Pope did not close the door. Even the integralists admit this. What the Pope said was: "This is not the time to debate publicly a subject which requires the greatest prudence and is of such importance."

However important this question is (and if it is "important," it must exist), it remains secondary. It is not at the heart of the problems of modern priests. A good number of them find fulfillment in celibacy. It is clear to everyone that the best priests will be those who remain celibate, provided they have a real vocation to celibacy.

The nub of the sacerdotal problem is elsewhere. It has been said a hundred times that the priest must be a missionary, and that mission and Church are coextensive terms. But this will be a mere play on words until priests are given the real possibility to be truly missionary. In the present "technological and secular society," as Father Pin put it, the priest cannot be what he was in the former "sacral" world. The Jesuit sociologist deserves credit for stating this clearly.

If priests of the second half of the twentieth century wish to be leaven in the dough, in the evangelical image, they must live in the midst of the world and know its difficulties, hopes, and anguish from within. We can only evangelize those we understand. The good pastor, as Christ said, knows his sheep. How can he know them if he remains a man of one isolated specialty, a solitary and distant witness to the sacred? Cardinal Suhard knew this when he launched the worker-priest movement. Vatican II is vaguely aware that it must follow this trend and strengthen it, that it must make it possible to form priests rooted in the world, in all parts of the world, not only in the working world but all others. The war (soldier-priests), captivity (prisoner-priests), and the Mission de Paris (worker-priests) have done more for the Church than dozens of volumes on the spirituality of the priest. Cardinal Heenan expressed it well on Saturday: "It is better to administer the sacraments than to write books on the Church as the people of God."

The Church of tomorrow will be a missionary Church only on condition that, somewhat as the Jesuits have succeeded in doing, she sends priests into all sectors of society and especially to the working world, where our future civilization is being forged.

It is significant that Archbishop Marty of the Mission de France was chosen by Vatican II to rewrite the schema on priests. It was a vote of confidence in this specialist in evangelization among the most paganized workers and peasants.

To date, forty-four Fathers have spoken on the schema on priests, and discussion will not end until October 25. Here are some new ideas expressed in Saturday's interventions.

Cardinal Florit, Archbishop of Florence: "Let us stress the close connection between the priesthood and poverty. Priests must be concrete proof of what the Church of the poor is. They should make a special vow of poverty at the time of their ordination. If there had to be only one poor man in a rich parish, it should be the priest." Some bishops thought he should have added, "And if there had to be only one poor man in the diocese, it should be the bishop."

Cardinal Heenan of Westminster: "Let us give more attention in the schema to priests in serious difficulty. This is essential." The speaker was referring to difficulties with celibacy. "All priests are responsible for one another. No priest should ever ask Cain's question, 'Am I my brother's keeper?' Exhortations to charity are not enough; we must speak of the responsibility of fraternal correction. Priests should strengthen the bonds of friendship among themselves. The lonely priest is exposed to grave peril."

Cardinal Bea, president of the Secretariat for Promoting Christian Unity, made an important intervention, one expected from Maximos IV Saigh. The Oriental Father had a speech already prepared, it is said, but has not been able to give it owing to the Pope's directive of October 11. Or perhaps Maximos IV voluntarily declined to speak. In any event, the two versions are in circulation. Furthermore, the fact that a Latin cardinal spoke on this subject lent it more weight:

> The schema speaks well of celibacy, but it does not demonstrate that celibacy is necessarily bound up with the priesthood. Because so much emphasis has been laid on the appropriateness of celibacy for the priesthood, one might be led to believe that there is some kind of inner contradiction between marriage and the priestly state. What about married Oriental priests, then? Are they not priests in the full sense of the word? Married Oriental priests do not represent a concession. To say this would be antitraditional. . . .
>
> Vatican II is an ecumenical council, and it should consider the whole Catholic priesthood in its double tradition. We must distinguish clearly between the condition of the priesthood in the Latin Church and in the Oriental Church, where there are married priests. This is important. The married priests of the Orient must not be looked upon as poor relatives.

In Defense of Assistants   Auxiliary Bishop Leven of San Antonio presented some original ideas, as he did last year. He spoke of assistant pastors, and his intervention is likely to have great repercussions outside of Rome. Vatican II, he said, should speak of assistants. More than 50 percent of priests fall into this category. Assistants are neither irresponsible nor adolescent; they are adult and free. But only the pastor takes decisions, and sometimes pastors are enfeebled by age when they are named. This gives rise to serious crises, which should be no surprise. Bishop Leven asked, "Would modern . . . industry spend so much time and money to train men and use them so poorly? Successful modern managers have learned that treating grown men as individuals worthy of reverence and trust and confidence increases effectiveness and does not lessen authority . . . This schema should assist in teaching [that lesson.]" Bishop Leven's speech received loud applause.

Bishop Albert Ndongmo of Nkongsamba, Cameroun, quoted Cardinal

Suhard's words, "The priest is Christ," and then said, "The Holy Spirit breathes on priests. Let us say this."

The debate having been declared closed, Archbishop Marty, reporter for the schema, explicitly indicated that episcopal conferences would eventually legislate on the work of priests.

The Church's Encounters with Various Cultures Are Sometimes Painful, Says Father Arrupe

In a conference given at the Council's press bureau on "Culture and Missions," Father Arrupe, Superior General of the Jesuits, envisaged

. . . the possibility of reconstructing with new materials the old medieval *universitas* which has been supplanted since the Renaissance and which was a synthesis of culture in and by the faith. Man must be initiated once again to the art of harmonious self-fulfillment which was symbolized by the *universitas*. . . .

The Church loves with a same love the different cultures in which men live in the expectation of God. We must say emphatically that the Church can only save men in and with the living context which forms their culture. . . .

At the same time the Church contributes to the development of cultures, she also receives much from them. The Church learns from man and the world how to be more herself. She is led to reflect more deeply on the contents of the evangelical message, and thus she contributes to the development of man's self-awareness in history. Each culture confronts her with a challenge that is an occasion to discover her own riches. Examples abound: the Greco-Roman culture (the encounter between Hellenic currents of thought and the theology of the Trinity), the humanism of the twelfth and thirteenth centuries (the theological thinking of Thomas Aquinas in confrontation with the currents of his time, particularly the Aristotelian), the notion of tolerance and religious liberty (the evolution of these made possible only by the evolution of human consciousness). . . .

Furthermore, cultures furnish the Church with an opportunity to rid herself of forms and expressions which she tends to think are definitive and necessary. Today, the encounter, or one might say the collision, with cultures leads the Church to penetrate to new depths, sometimes painfully. How can the apostle of the Gospel become

"Greeks with the Greeks" or "Chinese with the Chinese" without distorting himself or making an artificial adaptation? How can the Church, with the necessary weight of her institutions, respect the needs of so many diverse cultures without disturbance? How can she present the Gospel without reference to past cultures which enabled her to know and express herself?

These questions are often painful; but they are salutary for the Church, because they bring her back to the essential, which is the message of Christ. . . .

The Church cannot be uninterested for supposedly spiritual reasons in the cultural changes that are taking place before her eyes, because the very authenticity of her preaching is involved.

OCTOBER 22

Father Loew: "Let Us Clear the Clogged Pipes of Our Faith"

Among those who went to the conference by Father Loew at St.-Louis-le-Grand Thursday evening were Cardinal Tisserant, Dean of the Sacred College; Cardinals Richaud of Bordeaux, Martin of Rouen, and Roy of Quebec; some thirty other Council Fathers; and Mr. Brouillet, French Ambassador to the Vatican, together with a large number of clerics and laymen. Father Loew, a Dominican, is a former dockworker in Marseilles and one of the first worker-priests.

The speaker made no explicit mention of manual labor for priests, but he stressed the fact that the Church must find an effective way of reaching the masses.

In the direct and colorful speech he learned from his erstwhile coworkers, Father Loew spoke about the absence of God in the contemporary world. "This absence, according to Léon Bloy, has become one of the attributes of God," he said. The major portion of his lecture explained why and how the Church must purge herself of everything that could prevent the word of God from reaching contemporary man. He said:

> Let us clear the clogged pipes of our faith. Too many things block us. The mystery of the faith has been flattened out by casuistry. The people are deluged. Problems have replaced certitude; we must rediscover the great axes of the faith. . . . *Aggiornamento* is not enough in itself. The primordial truths must glow. This is the indispensable condition for conversion. . . .

May the Council encourage this cleansing so that ordinary people can understand us. Let us become poor so that we can offer the one thing necessary. Let us form small cells in every quarter of the city that are faithful to the breaking of the bread and prayer. Let us share the suffering of the poor.

In Turin Commenting on the declaration on the Jews in *La Stampa* of Turin, A. C. Jemolo writes:

Two facts are universally known: Arabic threats, and the existence in all American and European countries of Nazi and Fascist currents. They don't have many adherents but these are active, and in Catholic countries they like to appear very attached to the Church. Some are even inclined to put themselves forward as depositories of the faith against the pope and the bishops. . . .

Wouldn't it be wise for the Church to state clearly, particularly to the young, that fascism and the cross can have nothing in common? Wouldn't it also be well for the Church to see to it that no solemn declaration on her part could in any way be interpreted in favor of anti-Semitism?

Intense Activity in the Conciliar Commissions

The conciliar aula is momentarily deserted, but the commissions of Vatican II are hard at work. The subcommission in charge of revising the schema on priests, presided over conjointly by Archbishop Marty (France) and Bishop Nagae (Japan), has been meeting in Rome for the past three days.

At Nemi, in the enchanting setting of the Alban Hills, the subcommission in charge of revising the schema on the missions is at work.

The Theological Commission is preparing to examine certain pontifical *modi* which it is said that the Pope will ask to have added to the schema on revelation. As is well known, this schema treats the very delicate question of the relationship between Scripture and tradition. Paul VI's projected request makes the Protestant observers uneasy; they fear, rightly or wrongly, that ecumenical dialogue will suffer if this schema becomes too specific.

Finally, the commission for schema 13 has been in session every day since the thirteen subcommissions finished revising the different parts of that document. This commission will be at work until about October 30. Thus the schema could be printed around November 8, after having been edited by the coordinating Commission. At least fifty votes are expected on this long document.

Unless something unexpected happens, the fourth and last conciliar session will probably close on December 8.

Cardinal Alfrink on War

A large audience was attracted by the press conference by Cardinal Alfrink, Archbishop of Utrecht, Military Vicar of the Netherlands, International President of Pax Christi, and one of the twelve presidents of Vatican II. The Cardinal spoke on war and peace, one of the most bitterly debated themes of the Council, the two principal camps comprising those who defend the traditional teaching of the Church on the one hand and on the other those who want a more prophetic answer to the challenge of our times.

It was interesting to note that almost all the questions addressed to the speaker touched on the same key points: is it still reasonable, in 1965, to think a defensive atomic war is just; and is the manufacture of atomic weapons compatible with evangelical morality?

Vatican II seems to have come to a crossroads. It can no longer approve both nuclear arms and the nonviolence of a Gandhi or a Martin Luther King. It must choose.

Cardinal Alfrink noted that the draft of schema 13 written during the recess was wrong not to have referred to the Gospel and to have overlooked the revolutionary force of spiritual weapons (fasting, prayer, and so forth). He assured the audience that the new version would be better, and went so far as to say, "The only platform common to all men of good will, whether of the East or of the West, is the defense of peace."

Here is the substance of his speech:

> This is the crux of the moral problem we now face: it is no longer a question of war or peace; it is a question of life or death.
>
> Different pacifist movements think that all war is a flagrant contradiction of the Gospel; they conclude that a Christian cannot in good conscience participate in acts of war. We can accept this position up to a point, for it is certain that the Gospel preaches love, and that all war is monstrous. On the other hand, this principle cannot be the exclusive basis of peace. Because of human imperfection, very complicated situations arise in which the defense of peace does not depend on only one of the parties involved, and the human conscience must resolve other very serious problems.

Today, for example, peace can only be guaranteed by abstracting from the question of defense.

It is difficult to see how a defensive war can be justified if it results in total destruction. In this sense, war has become an absurdity and not a remedy for injustices. But perhaps a distinction is in order. If we admit that it is legitimate to defend ourselves against injustices, it follows that a defensive war is legitimate even in this frightening atomic age. However, the defense of violated rights does not justify the use of means that can wreak total destruction. This is objectively a crime, whatever the intentions of those who use such means. Although the schema does lend itself to casuistic discussions, it affirms this principle clearly. It is evident that the unlimited use of modern arms is morally unacceptable and that we must strive to abolish them altogether.

The schema also makes a distinction (I regret that it appears in the text, but it is nonetheless valid in moral theology) between the use and the possession of such arms. The danger now, in the present balance of terror, is that each nation will think it has a right to manufacture these weapons for the purpose of maintaining peace. But far from lessening the risk of war, this can only increase it.

Cardinal Alfrink was asked this question: "Will the Council explicitly condemn communism as requested in a recent petition signed by 450 Fathers?" His answer was: "Communism has already been condemned many times by the Church. Why do it again?"

OCTOBER 25

The French Episcopacy Authorizes Priests
To Work Full Time in Factories

The decision on Saturday by the French episcopacy to let priests work full time in factories and elsewhere will not surprise readers of *Le Monde*. In the past year we have indicated several times that this was possible, given the new spirit created by Vatican II both within the Curia and among the bishops.

This decision, six years after the Roman prohibition of the practice, will have an immediate influence on the schema on priests presently being redrafted under the direction of Archbishop Marty. It has already created a great stir among the Council Fathers and is being widely discussed.

Between the third and fourth sessions, a survey was conducted through the intermediary of the apostolic nuncio in France. The results were clear: the great majority of French bishops who have had worker-priests in their dioceses wanted the experiment to be resumed, either because of personal inclination or, more frequently, out of pastoral concern.

We must emphasize the extraordinary reversal which the new Roman position represents. The Pope excepted, almost exactly the same Curia cardinals who were opposed in principle to worker-priests have today changed their minds.

Remarkable Progress in the Curia There are several reasons for this evolution.

1. *The change in circumstances.* The circumstances which gave rise to the worker-priest movement after the Second World War were such that Rome felt obliged to stop it. The real reasons for this decision were the danger of contamination of the priesthood by political involvement, a so-called traditional conception of the priesthood, the attraction of Marxism, and fear of the independence and even the rebellion of a certain number of worker-priests at that time.

As always in such cases, the hierarchy offered a theoretical justification for its refusal. Some went so far as to say that there was an incompatibility between the priestly function and the worker state and to deny that the workers were so de-Christianized that priestly presence among them was indispensable.

2. *The Change of popes.* John XXIII, much more traditional than Paul VI, thought that the worker-priest movement was a rash solution. The present Pope, as he wrote many times when he was Archbishop of Milan, understood very well that workers would never return to the Church if priests did not first live among them. Paul VI, the missionary pope *par excellence* as his recent voyages have proven, feels and knows that the zeal of apostles of the Gospel must not balk at any bold innovation. That is why, after some hesitation in the beginning and a closer examination of the situation, the Pope came to accept the solution of priests working full time in big industries.

We are in a position to say that it was at the Pope's personal request that the Holy Office authorized the French episcopacy to take this decision before the end of the Council and thus in Rome itself, a circumstance that confers additional weight on this initiative.

3. *Collegiality is becoming a fact.* Under the influence of Vatican II and the conciliar Constitution on the Church, the Curia is beginning to recognize that it cannot legislate everything for everybody and that

it cannot replace the episcopal conferences. Bishops know local problems better than the Curia and are responsible for their own communities. It is obvious today that the episcopacy alone is capable of making an adequate judgment of local pastoral problems and proposing suitable remedies. For what could an Italian cardinal who has never been in France know of the conditions of the worker in a Renault factory? He would likely be inclined to think a factory chaplain (a solution long recommended in Italy) would meet the needs of the apostolate.

We know, for example, that Cardinal Ottaviani has changed his mind; he is now disposed to trust the local episcopacy. It is being repeated just about all over Rome that the Secretary of the Holy Office has said in substance, "Consider what it means for a dozen cardinals of the Curia to have changed their minds so quickly and on such a capital issue." It is only fair to say that the Curia, in the few years since Vatican II began, has made a sincere effort toward *aggiornamento*. This is all the more remarkable in that most of the cardinals are advanced in age. It took no small degree of courage, and supposes a laudable flexibility as well as a sensitvity to events.

Features of the New Experiment   What are the principal characteristics of the new experiment?

1. First of all, the expression worker-priest has given place to *working priest*. People will probably not notice this subtlety and will continue to speak of worker-priests. They will be correct, although there are appreciable differences between the present and the former experiment.

2. Working priests will no longer be considered freelancers working in isolation and more or less cut off from their ecclesiastical attachments. They will be in regular contact with such Christian institutions as the parish, other working priests, religious congregations, missionary organizations, and Catholic Action groups. They will no longer go it alone. This not only is very important psychologically but is in keeping with the objective requirements of evangelization.

3. The working priest will have to be constantly mindful that he is first of all a priest and that his essential mission is evangelization. Whatever interest he may take in improving the material conditions of workers, the working priest is above all a man of the Church, charged by his bishop with preaching Christ. In other words, Father Montuclart's formula, "Let us humanize first and then evangelize," is no longer valid. This position was rightly condemned by the Church. In reality evangelization and humanization are inseparable. The error lay in seeing them as two successive steps of the Church's mission.

4. Working priests will be chosen more carefully than before. Their intellectual, spiritual, and social formation will be very thorough. Only those who have markedly balanced personalities and proven faith will be selected. This seems to indicate that working priests will be taken from among men who have already had some experience with the world of labor.

5. The working priest will not be allowed to take union or political responsibilites, at least for the three-year period currently envisaged. He can of course join a union, but—and this is a major difference from the former system—he is not to become an activist, except behind the scenes, so that his colleagues will not be misled concerning the profound meaning of a priest's presence among them.

5. Working priests will be directly responsible to Archbishop Veuillot of Paris, president of the Episcopal Committee for the Apostolate of Workers. Cardinal Lefebvre, who was named to the Holy Office last year by Paul VI, will be the liaison with Rome. Also on the committee are Bishop Ancel, Bishop Pierre Puech of Carcassonne, Auxiliary Bishop de Cambourg of Bourges, and Bishop Huyghe of Arras. The last named is the committee's representative from the Mission de France, which will undoubtedly play an important role in getting the experiment off the ground.

Because of the work already done by the worker apostolate, under the control of the episcopal committee, the working priests will form part of a total missionary effort.

A Modest Resumption   The working priests, at least in the beginning, will be few in number—perhaps a few dozen. Thus we must not entertain unrealistic expectations about the immediate effect of the French episcopacy's decision. Indeed, there is still an obvious imbalance between the need for evangilzation among workers and the response that is being made to it today. There are no grounds for thinking that the missionary problem, which is the number one problem of our age, has been or is even about to be resolved. At the moment there is only a modest seeding. But the seeding is rich in promise.

We cannot overemphasize that this experiment must not be allowed to fail as its predecessor did; for if it does, "That would be the end of this kind of apostolate for a long time to come," said Bishop Haubtmann, spokesman for the French episcopacy.

There is no doubt that the first worker-priest experiment was poorly thought out, and it eventually took a dubious turn. But at this memorable time when the French episcopacy has been given liberty to resume Cardinal Suhard's great work, it is fitting to render homage to those pioneers, whatever their errors or faults might have been. They were victims of a lack of maturity on the part of the local parishes, hesitation on the part of the episcopacy, and total misunderstanding on the part of Rome. Without the pioneers, without the lessons learned from their apostolate, without their sacrifice—some literally died of broken hearts when Rome stopped the experiment—without their courage and their creative imagination and without the efforts of those who never gave up hope in an apparently insoluble situation, what has taken place today would have been impossible.

A Seminar on the Diaconate

For the first time, an international seminar on the diaconate has been held in Rome. It has just ended at the Domus Mariae. Some three to four hundred persons participated, including Council Fathers, clerics, and laymen from various countries. The French and German groups were the largest. The sessions were alternately presided over by Cardinals Döpfner, Seper, and Silva Henríquez. Here are some of the principal ideas advanced during the seminar.

1. The diaconate has already been exhaustively studied in theory. Only practice can now bring further clarifications.
2. The deacon can perform three functions: liturgical, catechetic, and charitable (Japan, for example, only needs catechists).
3. The deacon should belong fully to his milieu; ideally his formation should not separate him from it either materially or culturally.
4. Most of the reports were in favor of married deacons who exercise a civil profession. Celibate deacons could live in diocesan communities. The age limit for candidates remains very flexible. The deacon's witness as a married man fulfilling a role in society will help give the Church a more accurate image than the one provided by the celibate clergy alone.
5. Some regretted that the conciliar Constitution *Lumen gentium* does not mention the case of permanent deacons.
6. Non-Catholic churches already have deacons. Those of the Orthodox Church may marry or not. The Russian Church leads with 15,000 deacons and 50,000 priests (these statistics date from 1914). The Anglican Church has for some time had married deacons who exercise a profession. Protestants also have deaconesses.

The New Draft of the Schema on Religious Liberty

The new version of the schema on religious liberty has been distributed to the Fathers, and it seems to be meeting with general approval. Voting —some dozen ballots will be necessary—began today, Tuesday.

During the hundred and fifty-second general congregation on Monday, Bishop de Smedt, in the name of the Secretariat for Promoting Christian Unity, took the floor for the sixth time to report on the text.

This document was revised in conformity with the vote of September 21, when by a majority of 1,997 to 224 the Fathers accepted the text then under discussion as a basis of the final version to be drawn up "according to Catholic doctrine on the true religion" and the observations made.

Bishop de Smedt's report was divided into seven points. Here they are as they were distributed by the official communiqué of the press bureau for Vatican II.

1. *Duties toward the truth and toward the Church.* The introduction to the schema makes two points: first, religious liberty consists in the absence of constraint from either men or laws; second, no one can be dispensed from his moral obligations toward the truth and the true Church. Different passages through the text show how this principle is to be applied in concrete cases.

2. *Clarification of the notion of religious liberty.* The new subtitle of the declaration specifies that it is a question of "the right of the person and communities to social and civil liberty in matters of religion." Thus it is a question not of the relationship between man and God or between the faithful and ecclesiastical authority, but of the relationship between man and civil authority. The text is concerned with guaranteeing man's right to seek and follow truth in the religious domain in a free and responsible way. This juridical guarantee obviously does not dispense men from the moral duty of using their freedom in conformity with the objective moral law and, if they are Catholics, in conformity with the laws of the Church, which speaks in the name of Christ.

3. *The basis of the right to religious liberty.* This basis is presented in the form of a teaching, as befits a Council. It is found in the Catholic doctrine of the dignity of the human person, a doctrine that has been evolved by the popes during the past several decades. The dignity of the person requires man to seek truth, to adhere to and conform his

life with it in a free and responsible way. The doctrine is first of all stated in a way that can be understood and admitted by all, believers or not; then it is treated more in depth in the perspective of man's duties toward God.

4. *Synthesis of pontifical documents.* Papal teaching on religious life in society has developed along two lines. The older documents were principally objective: they stressed the truth which must be recognized and the rights of the Church. Then there is a subjective perspective which has formed over the centuries, concerning the rights of nature and free choice.

These two tendencies are harmoniously synthesized in the present doctrine of religious liberty. Theologians will perfect the synthesis still more in the future. The declaration restricts itself to fundamental and well-established points: (a) God makes the truth and his will known to man through the objective and unchanging eternal law and through revelation; (b) it is God's will that man adhere to this truth as an intelligent, free, and therefore responsible person; (c) the free and responsible response of man is impossible if external constraint exercised by other men, social groups, or public authority prevents him from seeking, choosing, and deciding in matters religious; (d) man must therefore be legally protected so that he is not forced to act against his conscience or prevented from acting according to his conscience; and (e) man has the right to enjoy the liberty thus guaranteed in conformity with the moral law.

5. *Limits of religious liberty.* The commission paid special attention to the observations of the Fathers requesting that the passages concerning the limits of religious liberty be clarified in such wise that the declaration could not be unjustly used by public authorities to restrict religious liberty. The passage to the effect that civil society might sometimes recognize a specific religion was retained, for this is a fact in many countries and it seemed necessary to say just how such a system could accord with religious liberty.

6. *The basis in revelation.* The section which studies religious liberty in the light of revelation was reviewed by specialists in the social sciences. This part is intended to show that revelation affirms the general principles which the doctrine of religious liberty is based on. Religious liberty is thus anchored in Scripture and in the spirit of Christ and the apostles.

7. *The freedom of the Church.* The text clarifies the rights of the Church: on the one hand, she has a right which comes to her from the mission received from God; on the other hand, she has a natural right—

her members have the same rights as other men in society. The two rights are not in conflict; both are respected when religious liberty, social and civil, is guaranteed by society.

In conclusion, Bishop de Smedt thanked the Fathers for their help in the revision of the schema, in which questions that are not ripe have been left aside, the doctrine of religious liberty has been clearly distinguished from related questions, and the text has been based on solid principles. If the declaration is proclaimed by the Council, he said, it will open new paths for the exercise of religious liberty in the world, and the Catholic Church will be, both in fact and by right, in a better position to accomplish the mission she has received from God. Respect for and confidence in the Church will be strengthened, and the real meaning of the Church's mission as Paul VI defined it in his encyclical *Ecclesiam suam* will be easier for men to understand.

Further Discussion on Priests

Seven more Fathers spoke on the schema on priests. Each spoke, as the regulations require, in the name of seventy bishops. Obviously tired by the length of these discussions, the Fathers listened to the interventions with something less than attentiveness. At times the chattering was so loud in the aula that the speakers could scarcely be heard.

Bishop Román Arrieta Villalobos of Tilaran, Costa Rica, spoke of equalizing the distribution of priests between rich dioceses and countries and poor ones. "Priests who have nothing to do could be sent where there is work," he said.

Bishop de Roo of Victoria, British Columbia, said, "It is necessary to show very clearly how the pastoral mission of the priest illumines and unifies his life and ministry. If the schema is not corrected to this effect, it will appear anachronistic beside the ecumenical events of the present time and will be of no help to priests who have to face up to the exceptional demands of the modern world."

Bishop Charbonneau of Hull, Quebec, reflected:

> The bishop cannot be content with giving orders; he must communicate a spirit to his priests that will make them true pastors of their faithful. . . . The priest shares in the function of pastor with all the responsibilities that implies: personal judgment, initiative, study. . . . The schema should therefore be revised in view of replacing a negative conception of obedience with a more theological

vision of its true dimensions. The bishop should be more a father than a boss, and should be concerned with the spirituality of his priests.

Bishop Jaime Flores Martín of Barbastro, Spain, suggested, "If theological and public considerations of the unique priesthood of Christ were substituted for the treatment of the priesthood in the Old Testament, the schema would be improved. Only Christ's priesthood can sanctify because it is eternal and perfect."

Archbishop Thomas A. Connolly of Seattle stated, "Obedience is more necessary than ever today. The priest's promise of obedience on the day of his ordination is not merely a legal act. In reality, obedience is essential to his mission. Priests may and frequently do have their ideas on the problems and needs of a diocese, but the unity of the Church and the good of souls always require obedience."

Bishop José García Lahiguera of Huelva, Spain, spoke in the name of 184 bishops from various countries: "We must emphasize the responsibilities of bishops in what concerns the spiritual life of priests. The schema seems to underrate the importance of spiritual direction."

OCTOBER 27

Archbishop Pellegrino, the Newest Italian Bishop, Praises Intelligence

The hundred and fifty-third general congregation, on Tuesday, terminated on a mixed note of weariness, satisfaction, and the nostalgia that accompanies the completion of a difficult labor. It was the last time the Fathers would intervene orally in the aula at Vatican II.

The following spoke during that session: Bishop Foley of Lancaster, England; Archbishop Fares of Catanzaro, Italy; Bishop Enrique Pechuan Marín of Cruz del Eje, Argentina; Bishop Compagnone of Anagni, Italy; and Archbishop Pellegrino of Turin.

Archbishop Pellegrino was consecrated very recently and represents a totally new kind of bishop. It was no accident that this brilliant prelate of a large industrial diocese was chosen to close the debates of Vatican II. We may consider this symbolic of a Church in the process of renewing herself and putting trust in her most dynamic elements.

It is also significant that the last intervention of Vatican II was in praise of intelligence. Vatican II is in certain respects the continuation of Vatican I. And Vatican I, in a more or less fideistic age when reason was depreciated, vigorously affirmed that man's intelligence was *capax*

Dei, according to Saint Augustine's attractive definition. The twentieth century has not yet completely shaken off the troublesome heritage of the nineteenth. Intelligence does not always get a good press, even from clergymen. Archbishop Pellegrino's defense of intelligence had something of the prophetic about it.

Here is a résumé of his intervention, as it was reported to the journalists by Assumptionist Father Bernard, who is in charge of the French-speaking section of Vatican II's press bureau:

> The schema should put more stress on the importance of intellectual activity in the life and ministry of the priest. Profane and sacred sciences are both relevant. The Constitution on the Church said that it was possible for a priest to undertake profane activity provided his life remained primarily ordained to his ministry. It was noted that a priest may engage in manual labor; we should say as much for intellectual work. Given the present shortage of priests, none of them should be permitted, except in special cases, to be exclusively concerned with purely literary or scientific work, although this does not apply to those who are engaged in the study and teaching of such profane disciplines as philosophy, history, biology, and physics. These are related to theology because they contribute to the formation of a new *Weltanschauung.* This is not the case with all disciplines, however. . . . The schema should be more firm in what it says about sacred sciences. . . .
>
> We must react against a still widespread pragmatic mentality which emphasizes outward results and neglects study and the interior life. Sometimes pastors and administrators consider those engaged in studies as second-rate priests. Often professors in seminaries are underpaid, and libraries are endangered because of lack of funds. . . . No doubt the Church is often poor, but many expensive buildings are still being constructed. There are intellectually underdeveloped regions as a result of lack of respect for the work of intelligence. [Many thought of Italy and the United States at this point.]
>
> There will be two temptations after the Council: some will still cling to the old, others will want to emphasize what is new. It will be necessary to have a clear vision of the problems and the historical conditions in which these will have to be resolved. The Church will need the laity for this work but she will be especially in need of priests who are endowed with both a solid intellectual formation and an authentic pastoral sense, priests who will know how to go forward with safety along new trails.

The First Votes on the Religious Liberty Text

The results of the first seven ballots on the schema on religious liberty were reported late this morning, Wednesday. The first six were cast yesterday, and the seventh today.

First ballot: 2,232 voters; 2,031 affirmative, 193 negative, 8 null.
Second ballot: 2,234 voters; 2,000 affirmative, 228 negative, 6 null.
Third ballot: 2,236 voters; 2,026 affirmative, 206 negative, 4 null.
Fourth ballot: 2,223 voters; 2,034 affirmative, 186 negative, 3 null.
Fifth ballot, on the first five paragraphs of the schema: 2,161 voters; 1,539 affirmative, 65 negative, 543 with reservations, 14 null.
Sixth ballot, on the sixth through eighth paragraph: 2,161 voters; 1,715 affirmative, 68 negative, 373 with reservations, 5 null.
Seventh ballot: 2,238 voters; 2,087 affirmative, 146 negative, 5 null.

Cardinal Koenig on Communism

"There is a growing Christian ferment in the Soviet Union today," said Cardinal Koenig, Archbishop of Vienna and head of the new Vatican Secretariat for Relations with Nonbelievers, in an interview with *Corriere della Sera.*

"Perhaps the Communists themselves are beginning to understand that religion is not a superstructure but a spiritual need of man in every society."

The prelate said that the role of his secretariat is only to study the nature of modern atheism, nothing more; it does not have the task of seeking out possibilities of agreement between Catholicism and atheism. Then he said, "Study and knowledge mean understanding and respect and hence not attacks against individuals. But we must avoid confusion and define the limits of the dialogue. For example, there will be no contact with governments, no participation in the political manifestations of atheism, and no individual initiative. The role of the secretariat is thus to instruct and inform the bishops on atheism."

The Cardinal gave this report on the initial efforts of the secretariat:

> Marxist atheism is the most dangerous form of atheism ever known in history. Marxism is a pseudo-religion, and its official doctrine seems to be crystallized. . . . [However,] Marxist atheism in France, Italy, and Yugoslavia has somewhat changed its attitude

toward religion, in contradiction with the Soviet position and the coercive measures leveled against believers in Communist countries.

Some Marxists today are in favor of collaboration with Catholics and try to demonstrate that even Marxist orthodoxy admits of peaceful coexistence between ideologies. These changes are real enough, but at the moment it is difficult to say whether they are designed to attract believers or whether they represent an effective evolution with respect to religion.

The Problem of a Double Clergy

A petition signed by laymen from twelves countries has been forwarded to the Council Fathers asking them to establish a postconciliar commission to study the connection between celibacy and the priesthood.

After noting that the change in man's conception of himself in modern society could lead to a change in our conception of the priest, the document goes on to say:

> There is a certain disproportion between the image of the Church which the bishops are forging and the image which priests, who represent her, are obliged to give of the same Church. In many regions the indissoluble bond between celibacy and the priesthood particularly must often prevent the face of the Church from continuing to look the same way. We unavoidably recall here the many married bishops and priests who were excellent representatives of Christ in the Church for centuries; and even today, in one or another part of the Church, there are still married priests who are real signs of Christ.
>
> We are not at all arguing that all priests should be married; we would like only to maintain that the Church should investigate whether she should not allow priests to live their priesthood either as celibates or as married men.
>
> We are in a critical situation now: either priests feel that celibacy is an obstacle to the fulfillment of their ministry, or they feel they can no longer live chastely and consequently renounce their ministry or in practice stop observing their vow of chastity. . . .
>
> We would like to emphasize that we do not want to question in any way the great value the law of celibacy has had for the edification of the Church and the sanctification of priests. Nor do we in any way want to question that virginity, chosen for the kingdom of heaven, is an eminent and desirable ideal.

Last-Ditch Attacks Against
the Religious Liberty Schema Fail

Wednesday's event (October 27) was the last five of the eleven ballots on the schema on religious liberty. We have already reported some of the results of this voting.

The number of *placet juxta modum* votes for the first eight paragraphs (543 for paragraphs 1–5 and 373 for paragraphs 6–8) reveals once again the weakness of the opposition, especially in view of the fact that at least 100 of the votes were cast by Fathers who thought the schema was not strong enough.

Eleventh-Hour Efforts by the Opposition   The opposition was hard at it until the last moment. Comitatus Episcopalis Internationalis or equivalent organizations distributed three kinds of documents.

The first is a mimeographed text which attempts to prove that the schema on religious liberty is in contradiction with papal teaching (several pontifical texts such as the *Syllabus* are quoted). The pamphlet speaks of "fraud." It criticizes the passage in the schema which mentions the historical errors of Christians with respect to religious liberty (such "self-accusation" is termed "intolerable"), and concludes: "We can then with good reason fear that if the schema is approved, it will be said, 'The ordinary magisterium of the sovereign pontiffs and the bishops is finished in the Church.' "

The second publication lists many texts from the Old and New Testaments to show that the Bible does not support the theory of religious liberty.

The third document offers a list of amendments that would substantially transform the present version.

The password for the Comitatus was: vote *non placet*. And, as a secondary ploy: vote *placet juxta modum*. But this organization succeeded in convincing very few Fathers. More than four-fifths of the bishops ignored them, as the voting attested.

It is now obvious that the Roman Church has gotten over her yearning for the past. To the many Protestants and freethinkers who doubted that the Church has really changed her position on the crucial question of religious liberty Vatican II offers an unequivocal answer. What yesterday seemed improbable to certain outside observers, despite the optimistic prognosis of insiders, is now an undeniable fact.

It is also significant that on the very day when Vatican II cast a favorable vote on religious liberty, Cardinal Ottaviani, Secretary of the Holy Office, expressed the depth of the Church's *aggiornamento* in an interview for an Italian publication.

A Pastor Speaks in the Aula

Wednesday's general congregation also heard an address by Monsignor Thomas Falls of Philadelphia, one of the priest-auditors at the Council. His intervention focused on the schema on priests. He stressed the need of a truly adapted spirituality for priests, and saw the model for such a spirituality in the parable of the good shepherd.

"I Am Like an Old Policeman Serving the Church Blindly," Says Cardinal Ottaviani

An interview Cardinal Ottaviani granted *Corriere della Sera* of Milan is of considerable interest. More than anyone else, the Secretary of the Holy Office, who will celebrate his seventy-fifth birthday October 29, illustrates how much John XXIII, Paul VI, and Vatican II have transformed the Church. The Cardinal admitted that a change had taken place, and with touching simplicity spoke of his resistance to the change and his fidelity to the Church as she now is.

In the most moving passage of the interview, the Cardinal compared himself with a policeman, alluding to his nearly total sightlessness and expressing his desire to serve the Church of today and tomorrow blindly. Such admirable abnegation and faith are a lesson for all who are tempted to resist the new direction which the Church has taken under the influence of Vatican II.

Corriere della serra also announced that the name of the Holy Office is going to be changed to "the Congregation for the Protection of Faith and Morals." Paul VI thinks the new name is psychologically desirable since the Holy Office is undergoing a reform; the new name is much less likely to recall unhappy memories.

Answering questions from the journalists, Cardinal Ottaviani said:

> I am the policeman who guards the gold reserve. Do you think I would be doing my duty if I abandoned my post? Dear sons, seventy-five years is seventy-five years. I have spent them defending certain principles and laws. If you tell an old policeman that the laws are going to change, it is clear that as an old policeman he will do what he can to see that they don't change.

But if they change anyway, God will certainly give him the strength to defend a new treasure in which he believes. Once the new laws have become part of the Church's treasure, an enrichment of the gold reserve, there is only one principle to go by: serve the Church. And this service signifies: to be faithful to its laws. Like a blind man. Like the blind man I am.

Paul VI Promulgates the Declaration on Non-Christian Religions

The public session on Thursday, October 28, marked a new step forward for Vatican II. Five new conciliar decrees were promulgated by the Pope in union with the Fathers.

The new texts are the declarations on non-Christian religions (incorporating the statement on the Jews) and Christian education and the decrees on bishops, religious, and seminaries.

With the five documents adopted during the second and third sessions, these pronouncements bring the total to ten. Six schemas remain, including the Pastoral Constitution on the Church in the Modern World (schema 13), which will be promulgated at the end of the session since it is not quite ready yet.

Here are the results of the final voting on the texts just promulgated by the Pope:

The Decree on the Pastoral Office of Bishops in the Church: 2,322 voters; 2,319 affirmative, 2 negative, 1 null.

The Decree on the Appropriate Renewal of the Religious Life: 2,325 voters; 2,321 affirmative, 4 negative.

The Decree on Priestly Formation: 2,321 voters; 2,318 affirmative, 3 negative.

The Declaration on Christian Education: 2,325 voters; 2,290 affirmative, 35 negative.

The Declaration on the Relationship of the Church to Non-Christian Religions (and especially the Jews): 2,312 voters; 2,221 affirmative, 88 negative, 2 with reservations, 1 null.*

This was the program of Thursday's session: enthronement of the Gospel, singing of the *"Veni creator,"* reading of the five decrees, the

* This is the first time votes with reservations have been registered on the day of promulgation. Moreover, there were nine to thirteen fewer voters on this text than on the others. It seems that the declaration still created problems of conscience for some bishops.

voting, mass for peace concelebrated with the Pope, report on the results of the voting, and last the Pope's allocution.

The Pope concelebrated mass with twenty-four Council Fathers, among them six cardinals and several bishops from Communist countries.

The Pope's speech was brief and not too original. He did, however, stress the "solemn [declaration] on the relationships between the Catholic Church and those who profess other religions." He returned to this question at the end of his speech:

> May our Christian brethren still separated from full communion with the Catholic Church wish to contemplate this new manifestation of her renovated face. May such contemplation come also from the followers of other religions, and among them those whom one same relationship to Abraham unites, especially the Jews, who are objects certainly not of reprobation or distrust but of respect, love, and hope.

Paul VI also noted that the day's ceremonies coincided with the seventh anniversary of John XXIII's election, and he alluded to the suffering of bishops "who represent countries where liberty . . . is restricted, if not refused," as well as of those whose countries are presently at war.

OCTOBER 29

The Catholic Church's Sexual Morality Is Not so Rigorous as It Seems

The present silence in Rome about the birth control question is deceptive. Paul VI is continually examining this difficult problem, as he said in an interview in the *Corriere della Sera* earlier this month.*

We may be sure that the Pope will not dodge this question and that he will make a statement when he feels he is in a position to do so.

The Pope's indecision—and many are grateful to him for having admitted it publicly—is understandable. The special commission he called has not yet reached any clear conclusions; moreover, it has undergone a marked evolution in favor of relaxing present ecclesiastical discipline. The Church's current position rejects the so-called "artificial" methods of birth control and approves only such "natural" means as the Ogino method and temperature tests. Paul VI is very hesitant because, although it seems inevitable that the present limits of sexual morality will have to be broadened, there is a danger of falling into a form of laxity. Actually, Catholic rigorism in sexual matters is largely theoretical since

* See pages 658–659.

many confessors and spiritual directors have taken upon themselves the responsibility of advising a more liberal course for the faithful. The problem is to accept this officially for certain cases, and thus put an end to a hyprocrisy that is harmful to the reputation of Catholic morality.

The Pope is said to have asked the Holy Office to make a study of this question, which would add another document to the paperwork. It is unlikely that Cardinal Ottaviani's congregation has very progressive ideas on this question or most any other, for that matter; the negative influence which the conclusions reached by this organism could exert is already causing concern.

It is important to understand this problem of Catholic sexual morality clearly. There is a peculiarity here: while the general public is aware of the casuistry used regarding a just war for instance—a casuistry, moreover, that scandalizes many Catholics—it is largely unaware of the casuistry in the sexual domain. Even priests are poorly informed since seminary instruction on this question is usually rather rudimentary.

But this is not the case in Rome. For example, at the pontifical university, the Gregorian, which is conducted by the Jesuits, Father Joseph Fuchs gives seminarians a course on sexual morality that would surprise the uninitiated. Here are some excerpts from his course notes, which can be procured at the Gregorian.* The technical explanations which follow are indispensable for an understanding of the subject. They make it abundantly clear that the Church's morality today is much more open than is commonly thought; the principles may be rigorous, but their application is far less so.

A woman who has been subjected to physical or moral violence, making it impossible for her to resist sexual intercourse, may use a douche, although some moralists dispute this.

Likewise, a woman in danger of being violated may licitly prevent fertilization by using a pessary or taking pills that make her temporarily sterile.

Some moralists think that a douche is probably licit after fornication if the woman repents of her sin or at least if there would be serious difficulty in educating a possible child (Aloro, 1960; R. D. Alberti, 1915). But she could not use this means to sin more freely (P. Vermersch, 1919).

Some authors apply the arguments apropos of the rights of a violated woman to a wife who is subjected to real violence on the

* Rev. Joseph Fuchs, S.J., *"De casitate et ordine sexuali (ad usum auditorum),"* 3rd ed., Rome, Gregorian University, 1963, pp. 93–96.

part of her husband (except in circumstances where she is not considered to satisfy her husband).

Father Fuchs cites the case of drunkenness. H. Noldin and A. Schmitt (1940), G. Mausbach and G. Ermecke (1956) allow the use of preventive measures even in this case.

> The temporary sterilization of a woman who is in danger of violation, as is often true in wartime, is not illicit.

> The use of pills which prevent ovulation is licit during the period of lactation when nature fails to cause sterility.

> It would be reasonable to delay ovulation for a few days to avoid a seriously inconvenient [*molestam*] menstruation, as for example if one had to take a trip or participate in a ceremony and no other means were available.

Morality and Biology   What can we conclude from all this? Father Schillebeeckx, the Dominican theologian of the Dutch episcopacy, put it well in a recent conference. Referring to the licitness of using contraceptives in instances of violation, he said, "In this particular case, the principle of human dignity must take precedence over the law of biological finality. But then it seems a matter of situation ethics; therefore, the law is neither absolute nor moral. It is the negation of the principle according to which biological structures as such are the basis of a moral obligation."

Put more simply, the use of contraceptives is not an *intrinsic* evil. Otherwise moralists could not admit that they are licit under certain circumstances. Thus we are justified in thinking that the Church can evolve without denying the fundamental and unchanging principles of morality which she cannot interfere with. It is an adaptation of the law that is desirable, and not a change strictly speaking.

OCTOBER 30

The Schema on Revelation Is Considered
the Most Important Theological Text of Vatican II

On Friday, after the reports by Cardinal Florit and Bishop Charne (substituting for Bishop van Dodewaard) explaining the amendments to the schema on revelation, the Fathers voted on these modifications. There was a vote for each chapter of the schema, six in all. The *non placet* ballots ranged between 8 and 55. The vote on the whole text, the last before promulgation, yielded these results: 2,115 voters; 2081 affirmative, 27 negative, and 7 null.

In its present form, the schema on revelation seems to be the most important theological text of the whole Council. With the schema *De ecumenismo*, it is of the greatest importance for ecumenical dialogue. It was very carefully elaborated with the help of such experts as Father Congar, Monsignor Philips, and Father Benoît, director of the Biblical School of Jerusalem. Some last-minute *modi* suggested by the Pope were incorporated; they make the text more precise.

This is particularly true with respect to the relationship between Scripture and tradition. The first version of the schema spoke of "two sources" of revelation. This was a much-contested expression and has been excised, although the new formula leaves no doubt of the importance of tradition in Catholicism. The present text says in substance that the Church does not draw from Scripture alone her *certitude* (note the word) of all that has been revealed. This manner of speaking brings out the irreplaceable role of tradition without either over- or underemphasizing its importance. It is clear, for example, that the dogma of the assumption is based primarily on Tradition although from the Catholic point of view it is not only not in contradiction with Scripture but is in some sense implicitly contained in it.

No Conflict Between Scripture and Tradition   The schema—and this is very important—distinguishes between but never opposes Scripture and tradition. Scripture is always read within tradition. Thus Scripture and tradition mutually reinforce one another. Tradition transmits the word of God integrally. Scripture and tradition must be the object of the same devotion and the same respect. Tradition must not be presented as a mere quantitative supplement to Scripture, and inversely Scripture must not be presented as a complete codification of revelation.

What do the Protestant observers think of this final version of the schema? Some of them are disappointed because the Pope's *modi* accentuate the role of tradition, but they admit that this is within Catholic logic. Others, although bothered by the added emphasis, think that the schema constitutes "an effective basis for ecumenical dialogue with all open-minded Protestants." They recall that the Montreal meeting of the Faith and Constitution committee (the theological department of the World Council of Churches) recognized the great importance of tradition, to the extent that at one point the expression *sola traditio* was almost adopted. This was rejected in the end because it seemed to contradict the formula used in the churches of the Reformation, *sola scriptura.*

Beyond the Counter-Reformation and Antimodernism   The schema contains passages, which many Catholic theologians judge to be excellent, on how the inerrancy of the Bible should be understood, on the historicity of the Gospels, "literary genres," the Old Testament (which is happily defined as "a preparation for the Gospel"), the role of the magisterium (which has received the "charism of truth," according to the expression of Saint Ireneus), and Scripture (which is called "the soul of theology").

As a whole the schema on revelation is being highly praised. Jesuit Father Martelet, a student of Father de Lubac's, told us, "This is a great document. The schema is essential for relations with the Orthodoxy and is capable of reconciling us with them. I think that this document is the milestone which indicates that we have gone beyond the Counter-Reformation and antimodernism."

Friday's general congregation terminated with the report of Wednesday's voting on the declaration on religious liberty. The results of the last two ballots, the tenth and eleventh, showed only 417 and 307 *placet juxta modi* votes and 60 and 70 *non placet* respectively.

The different parts of the text have all been adopted with the required majority of two-thirds, so that the commission is not obliged to take the amendments into account. It will do so anyway, as it always has at Vatican II.

The general congregations will break for the week of All Saints' and reconvene on November 9. The Fathers are expected to have the revised text of schema 13 by November 11.

Beginning November 9, the presidents of the episcopal conferences will report in the aula on the conclusions their conferences have drawn about various subjects assigned to them by the Pope, starting with indulgences. We are all aware of the deplorable role played by indulgences at the time of the Reformation. But there is wide agreement that the doctrine of indulgences is very badly presented in the Church even today. Some priests are bitterly critical of it. Father Jean Steinmann, a renowned biblical scholar and author of a *Life of Jesus,* said in one of his classes, "The Church has not even stopped at the foolishness of taxing the blood of Christ."

An Ecumenical Act by the Council:
The Vote on the Schema on Revelation

Pastor Max Thurian made the following analysis of the Council's pronouncement on revelation:

On October 29 the Council adopted the definitive text on revelation by an overwhelming majority—2,081 against 27. To those who have followed the evolution of this text from the first through the fourth sessions, it is altogether marvelous to see how the Council Fathers have brought the Catholic Church to a more authentically traditional understanding of the problem of God's revelation to his people. The ecumenical influence played a considerable role in this. It is one more proof that in the future the Catholic Church cannot live and progress unless she maintains dialogue with all Christians.

The schema ends the simplistic polemic about the sources of revelation. Of course, it does not solve all the problems of ecumenical dialogue on this critical point in Christian theology; the problem of the Church's authority in matters of faith, the problem of the magisterium, as it is called, remains. Nonetheless, the text marks a decisive step toward Christian unity.

In simplified and general terms we might say that Catholic-Protestant disagreement on revelation comes to this. For Catholics, revealed truth is found *partly* in the Bible and *partly* in the tradition of the Church. When a dogmatic truth cannot be found in Scripture, it must be found in tradition. There are thus two sources of revelation. For protestants, the Bible *alone* contains all of revealed truth. Tradition is merely the witness to this unique biblical truth.

For the churches which belong to the World Council of Churches, a decisive step was taken at the world conference in Montreal in 1963. In a report that was "discussed in depth by the committee, which approved it unanimously" (article 41), the conference stated: "It is now necessary to review these positions [on the relationship between scripture and tradition]. . . . We are also aware that the concept of tradition is being subjected to a radical examination in Roman Catholic theology. . . . Under the present circumstances, we wish to take up the question of Scripture and tradition again. . . . Therefore, we can say that we exist as Christians through the tradition of the Gospel, attested to in Scripture and transmitted in and by the Church under the guidance of the Spirit. Understood in this sense, tradition is actualized in the preaching of the word, in the administration of the sacraments, in worship, in

Christian teaching, in theology, and in the mission and witness to Christ by the lives of members of the Church. . . . We can speak of Christian tradition, the contents of which is the revelation of God and the gift which he makes of himself in Christ, his presence in the life of the Church" (articles 44–46).

Thus, for Protestants who can accept the consensus of the theologians at Montreal, who represented all the member congregations of the World Council of Churches, the tradition of the Church preceded Scripture and transmits Scripture by interpreting it: "As documents, the Scriptures are only 'the letter.' It is the Spirit who is the Lord and who gives us life. That is why we can say that the correct interpretation (taking this word in its broadest sense) is the interpretation that is guided by the Holy Spirit" (article 52).

There is a striking parallel between chapter 2 of the schema on revelation ("The Transmission of Divine Revelation") and the Montreal report in what concerns the relationship between Scripture and tradition. The Council has resolutely rejected the idea that revealed truths are to be found partly in the Bible and partly in tradition, as though the truths of tradition were *quantitatively added* to those of Scripture. Cardinal Florit of Florence made this clear in his intervention before the last vote: "Tradition is not presented as a quantitative addition to Scripture, and Scripture is not presented as a codification of all of revelation."

The Bible is not a code of laws which completely exhausts the meaning of revealed truth. The Church's correct interpretation, tradition, is necessary to determine the full meaning of "the letter" of Scripture. Obviously there is a problem here of knowing what the Church which interprets is and what the correct tradition is. If one step has already been taken in our common understanding of the relationship between Scripture and tradition, others must be taken before we reach unity; they concern the concept of the Church and authority in the Church.

But the terms of the Council have the same ring to our ears as the Montreal conference report quoted above. The Council affirms: "This tradition which comes from the apostles develops in the Church with the help of the Holy Spirit. For there is a growth in the understanding of the realities and the words which have been handed down. This happens through the contemplation and study made by believers, who treasure these things in their hearts (see Luke 2:19, 51), through a penetrating understanding of the spiritual realities which they experience, and through the preaching of those who have received through episcopal succession the sure gift of truth. For as the centuries succeed one another, the Church constantly moves forward toward the fullness of divine truth until the words of God reach their complete fulfillment in her" (chapter 2, section 8).

This living tradition is closely connected with the revelation contained in Holy Scripture: "For Sacred Scripture is the word of God inasmuch as it is consigned to writing under the inspiration of the divine Spirit, while sacred tradition takes the word of God entrusted by Christ the Lord and the Holy Spirit to the apostles, and hands it on to their successors in its full purity, so that led by the light of the Spirit of truth, they may in proclaiming it preserve this word of God faithfully, explain it, and make it more widely known. Consequently it is not from Sacred Scripture alone that the Church draws her certainty about everything which has been revealed" (chapter 2, section 9).

The last phrase was suggested by the Pope and accepted by the commission as a clarification that did not change the substance of the text. Cardinal Florit pointed this out. Like the Montreal conference, Vatican II wanted to remove an ambiguity that has caused controversy between Protestants and Catholics since the Council of Trent. To say that Scripture is the inspired word of God does not mean that it must be *isolated* (*sola scriptura*) from the life of the Church, from the tradition which interprets it in the Church. The Bible is not a code from heaven whose truths are self-evident; it needs the Church to discern the word of God in it and transmit it integrally in a faithful tradition. The Council affirms that *tradition adds nothing quantitative to Scripture;* objectively, tradition does not contain truths which are not in Scripture. It strengthens the Church's *certitude* concerning the truths which are revealed in Scripture but which are not totally explicit in Scripture alone. On such truths "Tradition can make a decisive contribution" (Cardinal Florit). But we must remember that it is a contribution confirming the Church's certitude about the objective existence of those truths which are revealed in Scripture.

This clarification in the ecumenical dialogue should lead all Christians to have greater fidelity to Holy Scripture, the word of God, understood according to a correct interpretation which is clarified by tradition. Difficulties concerning the criteria of this correct interpretation and the authority which guarantees the fidelity of tradition remain. These are problems that have yet to be solved. The Council has at least removed certain obstacles and taken a first step. This is ground for real hope.

NOVEMBER, 1965

The Declaration on Non-Christian Religions Speaks with Great Respect of Hinduism, Buddhism, and Islam

Will Rome become a center for the comparative study of religions and even of unbelief? Paul VI envisaged this possibility in his encyclical *Ecclesiam suam.* He hopes to broaden the dialogue with not only non-Catholic Christian religions but other religious confessions as well and even atheism, which he analyzed in some detail. He recently created a Secretariat for Relations with Non-Christian Religions as well as a Secretariat for Relations with Nonbelievers.

Following this same path, the Council consecrated a special document to non-Christian religions, which was promulgated October 28, as we know. And schema 13 did not ignore atheism, which is one of the basic positions of the twentieth century.

The section on the Jews has been the most frequently discussed part of the schema on non-Christian religions. Granting the importance of that statement, the radical novelty of the sections dealing with Hinduism, Buddhism, Islam, and "other religions" should not be overlooked.

Whether we recognize it or not, this sudden extension of Rome's religious horizon marks a rupture with a certain tradition. It would not have been possible without the combined efforts of John XXIII and Cardinal Bea as well as the sustained collaboration of Vatican II. This new mentality is in keeping with the will of Christ, who established the principle of the fulfillment of all religions in a unique revelation that is universally valid in space and time. Missionary activity is not merely an important aspect of Christianity; it constitutes its very essence. Moreover, Christianity is not merely one religion among others. It defines an original type of interpersonal relations between man and God (sonship and love) which considers all confessional beliefs in relation to "the one thing necessary."

Here are some key passages from the text of the Declaration on the Relation of the Church to Non-Christian Religions. (We have already quoted section 4, on the Jews.)

After affirming the increasing unification of mankind and recalling the common origin of the human race as well as its unique end, God, the declaration reviews various religions:

> 2. . . . . Thus in Hinduism, men contemplate the divine mystery and express it through an inexhaustible abundance of myths and through searching philosophical inquiry. They seek freedom from the anguish of our human condition through ascetical practices or profound meditation or a flight to God with love and trust.
>
> Again, Buddhism, in its various forms, realizes the radical insufficiency of this changeable world; it teaches a way by which men, in a devout and confident spirit, may be able either to acquire the state of perfect liberation or to attain, by their own efforts or through higher help, supreme illumination.

A Ray of Truth

Likewise, other religions found everywhere try to counter the restlessness of the human heart, each in its own manner, by proposing "ways," comprising teachings, rules of life, and sacred rites.

The Catholic Church rejects nothing that is true and holy in these religions. She regards with sincere reverence those ways of conduct and life, those precepts and teachings which, though differing in many aspects from the ones she holds and sets forth, nonetheless often reflect a ray of that Truth which enlightens all men. Indeed, she proclaims and ever must proclaim Christ, "the way, the truth, and the life" (Jn. 14:6), in whom men may find the fullness of religious life, in whom God has reconciled all things to himself.

The Church therefore exhorts her sons that through dialogue and collaboration with the followers of other religions, carried out with prudence and love and in witness to the Christian faith and life, they recognize, preserve, and promote the good things, spiritual and moral, as well as the sociocultural values found among these men.

Respect for Muslims

3. The Church regards with esteem also the Muslims. They adore the one God, living and subsisting in himself, merciful and all-powerful, the creator of heaven and earth, who has spoken to men; they take pains to submit wholeheartedly to even his inscrutable decrees, just as Abraham, with whom the faith of Islam takes pleasure

in linking itself, submitted to God. Though they do not acknowledge Jesus as God, they revere him as a prophet. They also honor Mary, his virgin mother; at times they even call on her with devotion. In addition, they await the day of judgment when God will render their deserts to all those who have been raised up from the dead. Finally, they value the moral life, and worship God especially through prayer, almsgiving, and fasting.

Since in the course of centuries not a few quarrels and hostilities have arisen between Christians and Muslims, this sacred synod urges all to forget the past and to work sincerely for mutual understanding and to preserve as well as to promote together for the benefit of all mankind social justice and moral welfare, as well as peace and freedom. . . .

Rejection of All Discrimination

5. We cannot truly call on God, the Father of all, if we refuse to treat in a brotherly way any man, created as he is in the image of God. Man's relation to God the Father and his relation to men his brothers are so linked together that Scripture says, "He who does not love does not know God" (I John 4:8).

No foundation therefore remains for any theory or practice that leads to discrimination between man and man or people and people, so far as their human dignity and the rights flowing from it are concerned.

The Church reproves, as foreign to the mind of Christ, any discrimination against men or harassment of them because of their race, color, condition of life, or religion. On the contrary, following in the footsteps of the holy Apostles Peter and Paul, this sacred synod ardently implores the Christian faithful to "maintain good fellowship among the nations" (I Pet. 2:12), and if possible to live for their part in peace with all men, so that they may truly be sons of the Father who is in heaven.

NOVEMBER 5

The Divorce Proceedings Between the Church and the World Seem Today To Have Been Halted

Vatican II has entered upon its final phase. Only six texts remain to be dealt with (in some cases by a vote on the amendments, in others by a vote on the schema itself, in all cases by the vote of promulgation). These are the documents on religious liberty, revelation, the laity, the Church in the world (schema 13), the missions, and priests. The first three will be promulgated on November 18 and the last three on December 7, the eve of final cloture.

Since there will be no more discussion but only balloting, we can make a preliminary assessment of this session. The commissions are putting the finishing touches on schema 13; history will relate the details of the bitter conflicts, which continue even at this moment, occasioned by the revision of such chapters as the one on war.

These inevitable and theoretically secret altercations aside, it is correct to say that the fourth session has generally pursued its objectives with freedom, serenity, and efficiency.

The violent upheavals of the first session, a period of demolition, are no more; even the tensions between the Pope and the Council that emerged at the end of the third session over religious liberty, ecumenism, and collegiality have passed. Paul VI has not had to impose his authority in an extraconciliar fashion at all during the present session. It has often been rumored during the past weeks that the Pope would request a "prefatory note" or impose *modi* of his own. But he hasn't. The superior authority intervened once or twice at most, and then through the intermediary of the Council machinery and always with great discretion. Only once did the Pope appeal directly to the Council Fathers, when he asked them not to debate the celibacy issue publicly and to make their thoughts known to him personally.

Old Wine and New Bottles In general the Pope and the Council, of which he is the head, got on marvelously well. The announcement of the creation of an episcopal synod, the consultation of episcopal conferences in Rome itself, the imminent reform of the Curia, and the votes on such important documents as those on religious liberty, the Jews, and revelation all contributed to creating a new conciliar climate.

The Fathers' habit of working together, their satisfaction at having set the Church on new or renewed paths, the certainty that Vatican II has introduced an extraordinary evolution in ecumenical relationships and in the presentation of the faith, an evolution whose consequences can be drawn only in the future—all these helped give the fourth session an originality of its own.

The time of harvest has come. It is obvious that the new wine in preparation cannot, in the Gospel's image, be put in old bottles. The *aggiornamento* dear to John XXIII, which Vatican II, with Paul VI's support, is in the process of achieving, already seems too cautious a word. We have begun a second stage.

Aggiornamento or Change? Father Heckenroth, university chaplain in Paris, said this in a highly intelligent booklet which he wrote in cooperation with qualified experts:

> There is good reason to ask whether or not the first achievements of Vatican II have not laid the groundwork—by a process of chain reactions and are awakening of the critical spirit reinforced by the relativization of ecclesial discipline in a secular perspective—for a general questioning of the Church herself, a re-evaluation of more and more aspects of ecclesiology which is so radical that it seems destined to go beyond mere *aggiornamento* and end with a real change in traditional Catholicism.

This change, needless to point out, would not affect the essence of the Church or the necessary continuity of the ecclesial body. It would rather be the result of a deeper understanding of the nature of Catholicism and its evangelizing mission. Never have we understood better than today that if the Church wishes to remain faithful to her founder, she must reform herself and be open to all the changes that are or will be requisite.

The fourth session proved the impotence of a minority opposition that did everything in its power to prevent or at least slow down the inevitable evolution. It really only succeeded in bringing out the best in the majority. Still attached to a dying past, contemptuous of the modern world even though the last two popes have tried to make them see its greatness and the advantages it offered, the opposition Fathers, numbering between fifty and three hundred perhaps, finally rallied to the support of schemas that ruffled their sensibilities and troubled their normal patterns of thought. They must be given credit for this.

Remarkable Unity The fourth session also proved that the episcopal body is in robust health and has remarkable unity despite its differences, which are important certainly but are nonetheless secondary in the order of faith.

This great harmony of thinking which in no way damps the desire for renewal, sets a good example for non-Catholic churches. They are beginning to look at Rome in another light and find support for their own desire for renewal.

As the Council ends in Rome, a greater convergence of the dynamic elements in Christianity is discernible. We may with reason look upon this phenomenon as a first step toward the eventual convergence of the dynamic elements of all the great religions.

It is high time. For humanly speaking, the Catholic Church seemed condemned to become a sect unless she undertook a simultaneously intellectual, spiritual, and pastoral renewal. The astute observer can see that the divorce proceedings between the Church and world seem today to have been halted. For Vatican II can in no way be considered a parenthesis, undoubtedly prestigious but only transitory, in the history of Catholicism.

"Growth or decline of the Church?" Cardinal Suhard asked on the eve of World War II. The postconciliar period will soon make the answer clear.

NOVEMBER 9

Will Vatican II Take Action
Against Exterior Signs of Wealth in the Church?

"We are dressed like marchionesses. All we need is earrings." Everyone in Rome is familiar with this crack by an American prelate whose pastoral zeal and humility disarms all criticism. It is reminiscent of Saint Bernard's campaign in the twelfth century against the pomp in which bishops, "covered with ermine," ensconced themselves; "One would think they were newlyweds on the day of their marriage," he wrote. Father Congar points out that the title *eminence* is of Byzantine origin, and that *excellency* gained currency in the time of Mussolini so that bishops would not be less honored than the Italian officials who had the same title.

A good many of the ceremonial rituals presently in use at the Vatican were directly copied from Renaissance customs. The episcopal cross appeared in Rome during the eleventh century and the ring during the eighth century in Spain and Gaul. Several Council Fathers have called for a simplification of these exterior signs of wealth and power. Archbishop Gouyon of Rennes urged the suppression of the expensive *cappa magna*. By comparison with the past, the Church has made some progress. At the third Lateran Council (1179), prelates came equipped with twenty or thirty horses; at the Council of Constance, the Archbishop of Mainz had a retinue of 452 persons and the Bishop of Salzburg 260; at the Council of Trent, Ercole Cardinal Gonzaga came with an entourage of 160 and Alessandro Cardinal Farnese (the future Paul III) had 360 servants.

Since that time, some bishops have dispensed with wearing the ring except on rare occasions. Others have replaced the gold pectoral cross with one made of ordinary metal or wood and have stopped wearing colorful frills on the street.

A State of Mind   In giving away his personal tiara, Paul VI set an example which the whole world understood. When he visited the United Nations, he offered U Thant one of Pius XII's pectoral crosses, said to be valued at 150,000,000 lira. Similar gestures are expected from the Vatican in the near future. Will the Council take a collective decision before it ends to show the bishops' concern for evangelical poverty? It is possible, although many are opposed to such an action. They argue, "Let us not ease our consciences so cheaply. Poverty is a state of mind."

The bishops of this opinion are the same who said two years ago, "Let us not presume to set an example for the Pope." But Paul VI has made that argument invalid. The bishops in favor of a collective gesture answer, "It is not to ease our consciences that we should make such a decision. Rather it is for the sake of those familiar with our way of life, who expect a visible sign of our spirit of detachment. There are more effective signs than high-minded speeches and learned schemas. We are judged most often on appearances. Let us make an effort to imitate the first successors of the apostles, who lived poorly and refused all honors."

In any case, judging by the letters published in the press and the conversations of the laity, the old-fashioned ceremonial of bishops has become the object of increasingly bitter criticism. Jean Sullivan, a priest and essayist, recently wrote, "Doctors abandoned uniforms when medicine became serious." Experience proves that bishops are more respected and loved when their way of life is as simple as possible. Bishops know that their best laymen want these changes. Father René Laurentin, an expert at the Council, said the other day that "Archbishop Felici's description of the different clothing to be worn by the various ranks of prelates on October 28 makes one think of an ecclesiastical fashion show." These remarks are perhaps shocking to a certain traditional kind of Catholic, but they reflect the thinking of Catholic actionists as a whole, which is to say precisely those upon whom the hierarchy is relying to build the Church of tomorrow.

The Example of the Synod of the Melkite Bishops   It is worth noting that the Catholic Melkite bishops, gathered in synod under the leadership of Maximos IV Saigh, have already taken action. An official document enumerates the following practical suggestions:

1. Let us avoid using any gold in our personal effects when simpler material is available.
2. The gesture of giving up our rings would bring us closer to our Orthodox brethren; would reconfirm the real meaning of the bishop's

hands, which alone are sacred and deserve to be kissed by the faithful; and would win over our hesitant Latin brothers.

3. Let us suppress every sign of ostentation from our clothing that is not required by the liturgy.

4. Let us strive to modify our style of life [with less expensive automobiles and so forth].

5. Let us support legitimate strikes even if this means losing a rich benefactor. Let us call for just salaries, and let us begin by applying this advice to those who serve the diocese or the Church.

6. Let us set an example by turning our large holdings into cooperatives.

7. Perhaps we could dispense with the honorific titles which the Occident awards: *excellency, monsignor,* [and so forth].

8. Let us be inspired by the Spirit, who will urge us to give up our episcopal palaces, divide our real estate, and sell the sacred vessels.

This document is not very well known in the West. Many Latin Fathers hope Vatican II will act on such an attitude before terminating a few weeks hence. In countries like the Latin American, where there is extreme poverty and where the Church is associated with the ruling class, she sins most frequently by omission when asked to side with the poor. It is urgent that the Church do just the opposite. The Council would rightly be considered a failure in those areas if it does not inspire such practical resolutions.

How can Vatican II not make its own the words Bishop Guyot of Coutances penned in 1963?

> Poverty is the sign of the incarnation; it should also be the sign of the Church. Throughout history usages have been introduced, both in ecclesiastical morals and in the divine cult itself, that were inspired more by worldly vanity than by the simplicity and fraternity of the Gospel. We can surely hope that the Council will respond to the aspirations of many pastors and faithful in this domain.

NOVEMBER 10

The Reform of Indulgences Recommended by the Curia
Is Judged Inadequate by the Fathers

Although it was extraconciliar, the part of the hundred and fifty-sixth general congregation on Tuesday consecrated to indulgences was one of the most colorful and provocative moments of the fourth session. Paul VI deliberately had this discussion take place in the aula before the Protestant and Orthodox observers at the Council. Cardinal Cento, the Grand Penitentiary, and Monsignor Giovanno Sessolo, his regent, read the report on the draft of a decree requested by the Pope which proposes a reform in the practice of indulgences.

What is a grand penitentiary? A figure right out of the Middle Ages. He directs the Sacred Apostolic Penitentiary, one of the four tribunals of the Roman Curia founded in the thirteenth century. His insignia is a long wooden rod with which he touches the head of those who kneel before him. This used to be worth an indulgence of 100 days, and still is in some cases. Even today the confessionals in St. Peter's that are used by the grand penitentiary's "delegates" are furnished with this rod, angled like a flagpole.

So much for the colorful.

The subject of the report is much more serious than it seems. *Aggiornamento* could not honestly avoid the question of indulgences, which poisoned the air at the time of the Reformation.

Indulgences, a major factor in Luther's revolution, were sold to raise money for the completion of St. Peter's Basilica. In reopening the case of indulgences, Paul VI intends to purge the Church of an unsavory element in her past. As usual he has proceeded by stages. Today a cardinal from the Curia spoke and proposed a slight reform. Tomorrow the presidents of episcopal conferences will take the floor.

A Relic of the Past   Canon law devotes no less than a whole chapter, divided into twenty-six articles, to indulgences (canons 911–936). The doctrine of indulgences holds that the Church has the power to remit the "temporal penalty" incurred by sins which have already been forgiven in the sacrament of penance. The earliest plenary indulgence (total remission of the penalty) dates from the First Crusade. Indulgences applicable to the souls in purgatory only appeared in the fifteenth century. In the time of Luther, indulgences were the object of shameless commercial traffic, and the Church waited until the Council of Trent to decree that they were gratuitous. The last official catalogue of indulgences dates from 1938. It abrogated certain formulas like "seven years and seven quarantines."

It would not be just to say that the whole question of indulgences is ridiculous and scandalous. The principle is to be found in the beautiful dogma of the communion of saints, so much admired by men like Léon Bloy and Paul Claudel. By virtue of the reversibility of merits, the Church uses her "power of the keys" spoken of in the Gospel to dispose of her spiritual treasure for the benefit of sinners. The problem began when the Church undertook to evaluate merit mathematically and to speak of days,

months, and years of indulgences, a result of transposing ancient penitential disciplines which today no longer correspond with anything, not even
a memory since most of the faithful are ignorant of the Church's distant
history.

The reform proposed by Cardinal Cento, Grand Penitentiary, in the
name of the special extraconciliar commission created by Paul VI, is not
concerned with theology. It merely gives practical norms for the present
canonical prescriptions, such as eliminating the numerical calculation of
indulgences. The value of an indulgence, according to the new proposal,
would be equal to the meritorious value of the act of piety to which a
partial indulgence is attached. In the case of a medal or scapulary, the indulgence would be proportionate to the value of the act of piety denoted
by wearing such an object. In other words, as Father François Bernard
of the Council's press service explained, the Church would "double" the
merit by her intervention. Thus, although the old arithmetical method
is abandoned, the idea of measure is retained. This is the root of the difficulty. The proposals seem more a simplification than a profound reform.

In fact, the report was disappointing; this is the general consensus
of the Council Fathers and experts we interviewed. One of them said,
"We must go much farther and give a pious burial to the whole practice
of indulgences; it is outdated." A humorist remarked, "We can't be too
hard on indulgences." The Oriental Catholic Fathers are among the
harshest critics, for the practice of indulgences is totally foreign to their
tradition.

African, Indian, German, Dutch, and English-speaking bishops among
others also have serious reservations about Cardinal Cento's report. One
expert told us it is "theologically poor and canonically debatable." Beginning this morning, Wednesday, the presidents of episcopal conferences
will give their opinions. We may expect severe indictments of the practice if not the very principle of indulgences.

Unimportant though it may seem, the matter of indulgences is far
from negligible. It is another cumbersome relic from the past. New thinking on the subject is essential for ecumenical dialogue.

NOVEMBER 11

Lively Intervention by Maximos IV on Indulgences

During the hundred and fifty-seventh general congregation, the Fathers
heard the first interventions by presidents of episcopal conferences on indulgences. The proposals presented in the aula by the Curia yesterday
were judged timid and awkward, and the speakers today voiced their

displeasure with them. Cardinal Sidarouss, speaking in the name of the Coptic Patriarchical Synod of Alexandria, was the only one who approved the report. The most remarkable intervention of the morning was by Maximos IV. As usual it was characterized by independent thinking and frankness.

An incident created an extra stir about this intervention by the Greek Melkite Patriarch, who was elevated to the purple by Paul VI last January. At the last minute, the secretary general of the Council asked him to delete certain passages from his oral presentation. Here are the two passages in question:

> When the use of public canonical sanctions was eliminated from the Church's discipline, indulgences should also have been eliminated since their purpose was to temper or take away altogether these canonical sanctions. In maintaining them the Church drew an unjustifiable and overly specific analogy between the human and canonical system of accounting and the divine. . . .
>
> [The practice of indulgences too often encourages] fetishes, superstition, and a kind of religious capitalism.

The official communiqué from the press bureau of Vatican II made no mention of the interventions made by the presidents of episcopal conferences on indulgences. The reason given officially was that they are extraconciliar. But curiously enough the bulletin said that Cardinals Maximos IV Saigh, Sidarouss, Manuel Gonçalves Cerejeira of Lisbon, Gilroy of Sydney, and Shehan of Baltimore "gave general approval to the proposals already submitted, although they requested various changes."

Yet what Maximos IV said could scarcely be interpreted as approval of the proposals. It is to be noted that the Patriarch said the "equation" between the Church's intercession and the remission of sins by God has no theological basis whatsoever. This is the heart of the matter. Here, in substance, is Maximos IV's text:

No Theological Basis

There is no doubt that the Church can add a supplementary propitiatory value to the pious acts of Christians by virtue of the communion of saints and the infinite merits of Christ. Nor is there any doubt that the Church's power of intercession can obtain the remission of temporal penalties, partial or total.

But it is impossible to establish an equation between the intercession of the Church and God's forgiveness. Not only is there no theological basis for this, but it has been the source of numerous and serious abuses which have done irreparable harm to the Church.

Nothing in the early and universal tradition of the Church proves that indulgences were known and practiced as they have been in the West since the Middle Ages. There was no trace of indulgences for at least eleven centuries. Even today this practice is foreign to the Orthodox. In this they are faithful to early tradition.

The theological reasoning which tries to justify the late introduction of indulgences in the West is, in our opinion, a series of deductions in which each conclusion claims a little more than is warranted by the premises. . . .

In imposing sanctions or in mitigating or removing them, the early Church in no way intended to interfere with God's judgment in order to lead him to suppress all penalties or reduce them in a determined fashion. [The first deleted passage came here.]

In the Middle Ages, indulgences were treated to innumerable abuses which occasioned serious scandals for Christianity. Even today it seems to us that the practice of indulgences too often encourages [the second deleted passage came here] a kind of pious accounting with no concern for what is essential, namely, the sacred and a personal gesture of penance.

In conclusion, we suggest the following:

1. The suppression of all enumeration of days, years, and centuries, as the schema does.
2. The suppression of any mathematical equation between merit of penitent and satisfactory contribution by the Church; for the Church does not multiply the merit of the faithful by a determined coefficient.
3. Suppression, even in plenary indulgences, of all automatic assurance of total remissions.
4. Development of a theology in which the accent is placed upon personal satisfaction by the faithful, validated and elevated by the merits of Christ.

. . . By so doing, the Catholic Church would avoid doctrinal difficulties with Protestants, at least disciplinary difficulties with the Orthodox, and pastoral difficulties with Catholics themselves.

On Wednesday the Council Fathers also voted on the whole schema on the laity. Here are the results: 2,108 voters; 2,101 affirmative, 2 negative, and 5 null ballots.

This document is now ready for promulgation.

Several Protestant Observers Applaud
Cardinal Döpfner's Intervention on Indulgences

Faithful to directives received from the Curia, the official press bureau
of Vatican II continues to be silent about the interventions by the presidents of episcopal conferences, expressing their opinions on the Sacred
Apostolic Penitentiary's proposals for the reform of indulgences. There
were only twenty lines in the bulletin for November 10 and seven in that
of November 11.

Apparently the Curia finds it very hard to stomach open criticism
by the presidents of organizations which in the future (and beginning
even now) will dispose of powers that until the present have been in its
hands.

This effort to keep the press in the dark is a mistake because the newsmen know what is being said in the aula despite the lack of official information. Once again Father Bernard, one of the editors of the French bulletin,
has kindly consented to tell us something about what went on Thursday.

After Cardinal Wyszynski, president of the Polish episcopal conference, suggested some changes in details, Cardinal Alfrink, in the name of
the Dutch episcopal conference, pointed out "a fundamental imbalance
between the practice of indulgences and contemporary theology. The
commission's proposals are inadequate. The penalty attached to sin is
not a punishment but a purification. It is a question of quality, not quantity."

Speaking for Spain, Cardinal de Arriba y Castro preceded Cardinal
Urbani, president of the Italian episcopal conference. Then Cardinal
Koenig of Austria spoke. He also thought the proposals were out of touch
with contemporary theology, and that they were too "juridical" and not
"biblical" enough. "The concept of an inner conversion is not brought
out," he said.

Finally, Cardinal Döpfner, president of the episcopal conference of
Germany and one of the four Council moderators, recalled (as had Maximos IV the day before) that in the Middle Ages the Church had made an
unjustifiable transference from temporal penalties to the divine order.
"The fundamental question is charity," he said. "Reparation for sin is a
function of an increase in charity. When we speak of the Church's 'treasure,' we are speaking analogically. What we are really talking about is
God's gift of divine life to man."

He also noted that the proposals are doctrinally weak. They cannot
be published as such, he said. A new commission should be formed with

theologians from different schools. "With the Italian episcopal conference, I think that the new schema should include a complete doctrinal exposition," Cardinal Döpfner concluded.

He was loudly applauded by the assembly. But what is most noteworthy is that the English-speaking Protestant observers (who have simultaneous translation thanks to a system that was installed last year and paid for by the Americans) also applauded.

Paul VI, who as we know follows the Council's work on a closed-circuit television set, must have been pleased with these developments. For it was his will that the problem of indulgences, however painful for the feelings of the Curia and however delicate for Protestants, be dealt with in the aula.

As Father Daniel O'Hanlon said in a press conference:

> Almost all the jurists on the commission that prepared these proposals are members of the Sacred Apostolic Penitentiary. . . . It seems that they wanted them promulgated without consulting the bishops. The matter was brought to the attention of the episcopal conferences as a result of the Pope's intervention. . . .

> The present document is an angry reminder of the way certain schemas were prepared before the Council and rejected by the Fathers during the first session.

NOVEMBER 13

The New Schema on Priests Mentions Worker-Priests

The Fathers continued to vote on the schema on the missions yesterday, Friday, and began voting on the schema on priests. Here are two symptomatic facts.

1. The first concerns a maneuver on the part of the Sacred Congregation for the Propagation of the Faith which succeeded in weakening the passage in the missions schema that recommends participation of residential missionary bishops in the work of this congregation. The words "with a deliberative voice" mysteriously disappeared from the schema and a more general expression was substituted. The Fathers took note of this, because 712 of them voted *placet juxta modi* on this section. (Of the 2,153 votes cast, 1,428 approved and only 9 voted no). Consequently, the commission will have to amend this passage.

2. Second, these words have been added to the schema on priests: "All priests are sent forth as coworkers in the same undertaking, whether they are engaged in a parochial or extraparochial ministry, whether they

devote their efforts to scientific research or teaching, whether by manual labor they share in the lot of workers themselves, with the approval of competent authority."

Even the most optimistic hadn't expected this. The addendum is the direct result of the revival of the worker-priest experiment in France, which has made a deep impression on many Council Fathers, and the efforts of Archbishop Marty, Superior of the Mission de France, who played an important part in the writing of this draft.

The new passage is proof positive that Vatican II is a revolutionary council. Who would have thought a year ago that worker-priests would be officially mentioned in the schema? The outside hope then was that episcopal conferences might wangle Rome's consent to revive this form of the apostolate six months or a year after Vatican II.

Archbishop Felici made this announcement to the assembly on Friday: "Some Fathers have asked whether or not the lectures organized at Domus Mariae had an official character or were authorized in any way by the general secretariat. The answer to both questions is negative."

NOVEMBER 15

The New Version of Schema 13
Speaks Far More Forcefully Against the Arms Race

The new version of schema 13 was distributed to the Fathers in two stages: on Friday they received the second part of the schema, which incorporates the former appendixes; then on Saturday they were given the first part, on anthropology. This important schema has undergone a number of modifications. We might note immediately the happy fact that it has been shortened as the Fathers requested. The present text comprises some ten or twelve fewer pages than the previous version. The chapter on war has been appreciably improved; it is much less casuistical.

Voting on schema 13—there will be forty separate ballots—began this morning, Monday. Many *modi* are expected, especially for the second part of the document, which treats marriage, culture, economic and social questions, political life, and peace, among other subjects.

How will the Council handle the chapter on war? Will the American bishops, for example, accept the new text, which is much more severe with respect to the arms race and deterrent weapons?

Here are the principal stipulations of this new chapter, which shows a clear victory of the "prophet" over the "legalist."

1. The most striking change is the suppression of the passage which

affirmed that in present circumstances the possession of deterrent weapons is not "illegitimate in itself." Also to be noted is the appeal for a renewal of the traditional theology of war.

2. The new text firmly proclaims "the permanent binding force of universal natural law and its all-embracing principles." It condemns genocide and commends those who are courageous enough to refuse openly to follow immoral orders.

3. The passage on nonviolence is retained, as is the passage urging legal protection for conscientious objectors.

4. Governments have a right to legitimate defense provided they have exhausted every effort to find a peaceful solution.

5. Not everything is permitted to combatants, and international agreements modifying the atrocity of war must be respected.

6. Total war in this century of the atomic bomb is condemned without reservation (*nulla ratione licitum est*). It is senseless to believe that war is the best way to restore violated rights. "All of these considerations compel us to undertake an evaluation of war with an entirely new attitude." (This phrase is new.)

7. The paragraph on the subjective intentions of those who declare war is suppressed. The schema says that any act of war aimed indiscriminately at the total destruction of cities or nations "is a crime against God and man himself. It merits unequivocal and unhesitating condemnation." This is followed by a solemn appeal addressed to heads of state and military leaders urging them "to give unremitting thought to their gigantic responsibility before God and the entire human race."

8. The balance of terror and the arms race are severely condemned. The arms race, far from eliminating the causes of war, aggravates them. It "is an utterly treacherous trap for humanity, and one which ensnares the poor to an intolerable degree." And the schema adds, "It is much to be feared that if this race persists, it will eventually spawn all the lethal ruin whose path it is now making ready. Divine providence urgently demands of us that we free ourselves from the age-old slavery of war. If we refuse to make this effort, we do not know where we will be led by the evil road we have set upon."

9. The schema says that "It is our clear duty, therefore, to strain every muscle in working for the time when all war can be completely outlawed by international consent." The document then stresses at some length the necessity of effective international organizations and the usefuless of meetings to foster peace and disarmament.

More than 2,000 Fathers
Approve Manual Labor for Priests

L'Osservatore della Dominica (the Sunday edition of *L'Osservatore Romano*) of November 14 published a letter the Pope sent to Cardinal Alfrink this past July 19. The letter, which had never been published before in Italy, thanked the Cardinal for his vigilance in preserving the traditional doctrine on the eucharist "free of all error."

The fact that the letter was published in Italy is significant. The encyclical *Mysterium fidei* of September 11, 1965, might have given some malevolent spirits the impression that Paul VI was trying to stop theological study of the eucharist or even that he was implicitly casting aspersions on certain bishops who were too indulgent toward the promoters of doctrinal renewal. But that was not the case at all. Although the Curia periodically shows its mistrust of *aggiornamento* in theology—as of research on the eucharist, for example—the Pope is in favor of it. Just recently Paul VI authorized the bishops to criticize publicly the Sacred Penitentiary's conception of the practice of indulgences. The interventions on the part of the presidents of episcopal conferences prompted Archbishop Felici, secretary general of the Council, to issue this warning in St. Peter's on Saturday: "Some of the theological points of view expressed in the aula have elicited reservations."

Whom was he thinking of? And what authority has expressed reservations? Archbishop Felici did not say, but it is certain that he was voicing more than a personal opinion.

We are sure of one thing: the Curia has tried to muzzle the presidents of episcopal conferences with respect to indulgences. The press service showed little sense in not reporting on this issue under the pretext that it was extraconciliar while at the same time the official bulletin gave considerable space to a competitive exhibition of photographic art which the press bureau organized. An obvious double standard.

It is also worth noting that public discussion of indulgences has ended. The episcopal conferences whose presidents have not spoken have been invited to submit their remarks in writing.

On Saturday the Council continued voting on the schema on priests; 2,016 Fathers against 84 (with 20 null ballots) approved the supplementary passage concerning worker-priests.

We might also note that another paragraph has been added to the schema exhorting the married priests of the Orient to set an example of fidelity and chastity and to give a good education to their children. The

Pope asked for this addendum at Cardinal Bea's request. The passage is inserted where the text speaks of the many advantages of a celibate clergy.

The two passages were overwhelmingly approved (2,005 against 65). This indicates that the bishops are open to the various forms the priesthood can take.

No Condemnation of Communism in Schema 13

Once again, and for the next to last time, schema 13 is the center of attention. Monday morning, after a general report by Archbishop Garrone of Toulouse and the detailed report by Bishop McGrath of Santiago de Varaguas, Panama, the Fathers began voting, first on the preface and introduction and then on the beginning of the first part. Here are the results of the first vote: 2,187 voters; 2,009 affirmative, 41 negative, 134 with reservations, and 3 null ballots. The second vote: 2,113 voters; 2,074 affirmative, 27 negative, and 12 null ballots.

The bishops were told that all amendments must be submitted by Wednesday, November 17. Many fathers very much regret that the time given is so short; they think, with good reason, that they need a longer period to reflect on this particularly difficult document. The revision of schema 13 will surely suffer as a result, and many feel that it would be more reasonable (some do not hesitate to say "more conscientious") to determine the closing date of the Council in terms of the time needed to amend this schema, rather than the other way around.

Here are the highlights of Monday morning's reports.

Schema 13 responds to an inner need of the Council. The schema is the indispensable counterpart of the Constitution on the Church.

The present designation of the schema as a "pastoral constitution" will be the object of a special vote.

Atheism, marriage, and war are the three most difficult and urgent questions. The passage on atheism was revised with the collaboration of the secretariat for nonbelievers.

The competent commission has for the third time rejectd a plea that communism be explicitly mentioned. Why? Because this corresponds with the clearly defined positions of John XXIII and Paul VI.

The Divinization of Man The schema has been accused of being too optimistic about the modern world. This optimism has been tempered at the request of many Fathers. The present text places more emphasis on sin.

Man's specific contribution to society has received greater stress.

The schema is less exclusively Occidental than in former versions.

The bishops of Asia, Latin America, Africa, and Central Europe have collaborated on the present draft.

The schema notes that the first reason for man's "imbalance" is that he is called to a divine vocation. A second reason is sin. The authors of the schema attach great importance to the first of these reasons. For in fact Christian anthropology is based on the affirmation that man can only find true fulfillment by responding to supernatural grace, which raises him above himself. An awareness that humanity has been called to become divinized as a result of the incarnation is essential to the Christian conception of man. The fundamental optimism of Christianity is found at this level and nowhere else.

The fifteen votes on the schema on priests were completed on Saturday, and the last five were reported yesterday. All the chapters of this schema obtained the required majority of two-thirds. Still, the number of *placet juxta modi* votes was relatively high (they climbed to 630), and the commission will have to take them into account.

NOVEMBER 17

Schema 13 Reproaches Christians Who "Conceal Rather than Reveal the Authentic Face of God"

Although schema 13 says nothing about communism, it says a great deal about atheism. Actually, a condemnation of atheistic communism could be interpreted, rightly or wrongly, as ambiguous, for communism is primarily an economic and political system, and all its applications cannot be declared evil. But in examining and judging atheism, the Church is on surer ground, which no one can contest as being her own.

Schema 13 does not condemn atheism *ex professo;* this would serve no purpose. It does much more and much better. It tries to circumscribe the massive fact of contemporary atheism within some 100 lines, and seeks to describe, explain, and appreciate it from a theological and philosophical point of view.

The subcommission which reviewed this text (it is much better than the previous version) was composed of Cardinals Koenig and Seper, Fathers de Lubac and Daniélou, and five members from the secretariat for nonbelievers.

Here are substantial extracts from the schema's discussion of atheism.

On the Forces and Roots of Atheism

The word *atheism* is applied to phenomena which are quite distinct from one another. For while God is expressly denied by some, others believe that man can assert absolutely nothing about him. Still others use such a method to scrutinize the question of God as to make it seem devoid of meaning. Many, unduly transgressing the limits of the positive sciences, contend that everything can be explained by this kind of scientific reasoning alone, or by contrast, they altogether disallow that there is any absolute truth. Some laud man so extravagantly that their faith in God lapses into a kind of anemia, though they seem more inclined to affirm man than to deny God. Again, some form for themselves such a fallacious idea of God that when they repudiate this figment they are by no means rejecting the God of the Gospel. Some never get to the point of raising questions about God, since they seem to experience no religious stirrings, nor do they see why they should trouble themselves about religion. Moreover, atheism results not rarely from a violent protest against the evil in this world, or from the absolute character with which certain human values are unduly invested, and which thereby already accords them the stature of God. Modern civilization itself often complicates the approach to God not for any essential reason but because it is so heavily engrossed in earthly affairs.

Undeniably, those who willfully shut out God from their hearts and try to dodge religious questions are not following the dictates of their conscience, and hence are not free from blame; yet believers themselves frequently bear some responsibility for this situation. For taken as a whole, atheism is not a spontaneous development but stems from a variety of causes, including a critical reaction against religious beliefs, and in some places against the Christian religion in particular. Hence believers can have more than a little to do with the birth of atheism. To the extent that they neglect their own training in the faith, or teach erroneous doctrine, or are deficient in their religious, moral, and social life, they must be said to conceal rather than reveal the authentic face of God and religion.

On Modern Atheism

Modern atheism often takes on a systematic expression which, in addition to other causes, stretches the desire for human independence to such a point that it poses difficulties against any kind of dependence on God. Those who profess atheism of this sort maintain that it gives man freedom to be an end unto himself, the sole artisan and creator of his own history. They claim that this freedom cannot be reconciled with the affirmation of a Lord who is author and purpose of all things, or at least that this freedom makes such an affirmation altogether superfluous. Favoring this doctrine can be the sense of power which modern technical progress generates in man.

Not to be overlooked among the forms of modern atheism is that which anticipates the liberation of man especially through his economic and social emancipation. This form argues that by its nature religion thwarts this liberation by arousing man's hope for a deceptive future life, thereby diverting him from the constructing of the earthly city. Consequently, when the proponents of this doctrine gain governmental power, they vigorously fight against religion and promote atheism by using, especially in the education of youth, those means of pressure which public power has at its disposal.

The Church's Attitude Toward Atheism

In her loyal devotion to God and men, the Church has already repudiated, and cannot cease repudiating, sorrowfully but as firmly as possible, those poisonous doctrines and actions which contradict reason and the common experience of humanity, and dethrone man from his native excellence.

Still, she strives to detect in the atheistic mind the hidden causes for the denial of God; conscious of how weighty are the questions which atheism raises and motivated by love for all men, she believes these questions ought to be examined seriously and more profoundly.

The Church holds that the recognition of God is in no way hostile to man's dignity, since this dignity is rooted and perfected in God. For man was made an intelligent and free member of society by the God who created him; but even more important, he is called as a son to commune with God and share in his happiness. She further teaches that a hope related to the end of time does not diminish the importance of intervening duties but rather undergirds the acquittal of them with fresh incentives. By contrast, when a divine substructure and the hope of eternal life are wanting, man's dignity is most grievously lacerated, as current events aften attest; the riddles of life and death, of guilt and grief go unsolved, with the frequent result that men succumb to despair.

Meanwhile every man remains to himself an unsolved puzzle, however obscurely he may perceive it. For on certain occasions no one can entirely escape the kind of self-questioning mentioned earlier, especially when life's major events take place. To this questioning only God fully and most certainly provides an answer as he summons man to higher knowledge and humbler probing.

The remedy which must be applied to atheism, however, is to be sought in a proper presentation of the Church's teaching as well as in the integral life of the Church and her members. For it is the function of the Church, led by the Holy Spirit who renews and purifies her ceaselessly, to make God the Father and his incarnate Son present and in a sense visible. This result is achieved chiefly by the witness of a living and mature faith, namely, one trained to see difficulties clearly and master them.

Cooperation and Dialogue Necessary Between Believers and Nonbelievers

Many martyrs have given luminous witness to this faith and con-continue to do so. This faith needs to prove its fruitfulness by penetrating the believer's entire life, including its worldly dimensions, and by activating him toward justice and love, especially regarding the needy. What does the most to reveal God's presence, however, is the brotherly charity of the faithful who are united in spirit as they work together for the faith of the Gospel and who prove themselves a sign of unity.

While rejecting atheism root and branch, the Church sincerely professes that all men, believers and unbelievers alike, ought to work for the rightful betterment of this world, in which all alike live; such an ideal cannot be realized, however, apart from sincere and prudent dialogue. Hence the Church protests against the distinction which some state authorities make between believers and unbelievers, with prejudice to the fundamental rights of the human person. The Church calls for the active liberty of believers to build up in this world God's temple too. She courteously invites atheists to examine the Gospel of Christ with an open mind.

Above all, the Church knows that her message is in harmony with the most secret desires of the human heart when she champions the dignity of the human vocation, restoring hope to those who have already despaired of anything higher than their present lot. Far from diminishing man, her message brings to his development light, life, and freedom. Apart from this message nothing will avail to fill up the heart of man: "Thou hast made us for thyself," O Lord, "and our hearts are restless until they rest in thee" [Saint Augustine, *Confessions*, I, 1].

In the course of Tuesday's general congregation, the fathers completed no fewer than fifteen votes on schema 13. The first seven, along with Monday's ballots, covered the introduction and chapters 1, 2, 3, and 4 of the first part. The number of *placet juxta modi* votes for each chapter as a whole was respectively 453, 388, 467, and 284. The reservations on chapter 1 were thus the highest; this chapter, on "The Dignity of the Human Person," contains the passages on atheism. Since the two-thirds majority of affirmative votes was obtained, the competent commission will consider only those *modi* that are in agreement with the general tone of the text.

Vatican II Requests the Creation of a Postconciliar Secretariat To Promote the Underdeveloped Countries

Vatican II finished voting on the different sections of schema 13 on Wednesday. The chapter on marriage and the family was approved by a vote of 1,524 affirmative, 72 negative, and 484 *placet juxta modi*. A new passage has been added to this chapter calling upon scholars, biologists, sociologists, and psychologists to elucidate the various conditions of human procreation. In other words, the Council deems it desirable for study on the laws of how life is transmitted to progress, so that the married couple will be able to procreate more and more intelligently and freely.

Vatican II said no more on this subject because Paul VI has reserved the right to speak personally on birth control. But in urging scientists to shed new light on the problem, the Council leaves the door open to an evolution in the application of the present principles of sexual morality.

The chapter on culture drew 44 negative votes and 185 *placet juxta modi* (there were 1,909 affirmative votes). One paragraph in this chapter speaks of the responsibility of the faithful to keep in close contact with the cultural world of their age. The chapter also states that theology courses, whether in seminaries or in universities, should be accessible to laymen. The latter have a right to freedom of study, thought, and expression.

We shall say more later about the section on social and economic life. Voting on the chapter as a whole resulted in 1,740 affirmative votes, 41 negative, and 469 *placet juxta modi*.

Results of the voting on the chapter on the political community will be published Friday.

Finally, the Fathers voted on the chapter relating to peace and the community of nations. There is a new paragraph in this section which reads:

> The Council, considering the immensity of the hardships which still afflict the greater part of mankind today, regards it as most opportune that an organism of the universal Church be set up in order that both the justice and love of Christ toward the poor might be developed everywhere. The role of such an organism would be to

stimulate the Catholic community to promote progress in needy regions and international social justice.

Thus we may expect the creation of an office in the service of the
underdeveloped countries. This request by Vatican II leads us to believe
that the postconciliar Church will do everything it can to reduce progressively the distinction between rich and poor countries.

This secretariat would also establish contacts with other organizations
interested in underdeveloped countries, notably the United Nations. It
would have the further task, together with the already existing secretariats,
of maintaining liaison with the World Council of Churches and other
religious groups to insure as broad collaboration as possible.

Finally, the new body would watch over the theological and spiritual
welfare of Christians engaged in the work of international organizations,
technical assistance missions, and all other enterprises dedicated to peace,
development, and international justice. All too often isolation and lack
of information hamper effective action on the part of Christians.

The Pope Announces the Imminent Publication of a New Statute for the Holy Office, the Progressive Reform of the Curia, and the Opening of Beatification Proceedings for Pius XII and John XXIII

The public congregation this morning, Thursday, was distinguished by
Paul VI's speech, undoubtedly one of the most important the present
pope has given. Several points impressed the audience:

1. Paul VI's promptness in taking the reform action requested by the
Council. He emphasized several times that he is anxious to proceed
with this.
2. The announcement that the episcopal senate will meet for the first
time in 1967 since 1966 will be entirely devoted to "other postconciliar
concerns."
3. The establishment of postconciliar commissions "to complete the
norms" laid down in the decrees of Vatican II.
4. The Pope's emphasis on episcopal conferences.
5. His recognition that the Curia must be improved. The Pope said he
didn't think structural changes were called for, but he mentioned the
need to replace personnel as well as "for not a few reforms, for some
simplifications and other improvements" in that body.

6. The announcement of the imminent publication of a new statute for the Holy Office.

7. The opening of the canonical procedure of beatification for Pius XII and John XXIII according to the usual norms. (Thus the Pope did not accept a suggestion made by several Fathers for canonization by acclamation.)

8. The announcement of a special jubilee to open on December 8 and close on Pentecost, 1966.

The mass of the day was concelebrated by the Pope with twelve superiors of religious congregations, eleven experts, and one pastor. Father Henri de Lubac, who played an active role in elaborating the conciliar documents, was one of the concelebrants. The Pope quoted this Jesuit theologian in one of his recent speeches.

Two new conciliar texts were promulgated by the Pope "in union with the Fathers": the Dogmatic Constitution on Divine Revelation and the Decree on the Apostolate of the Laity. The formal vote on the revelation document was 2,344 affirmative and 6 negative, and the lay apostolate decree was adopted 2,305 to 2.

Following are the principal passages of the Pope's allocution:

Let it suffice now to direct our thoughts to a few consequences that we said were related to the ending of the ecumenical council. This ending is rather a beginning for many projects, the establishment of organizations to collaborate with us in laying down the norms desired by the decrees of the council. It is our intention to proceed as soon as possible to establish them, since we are resolved to put into speedy execution the holy deliberations of this ecumenical synod.

We have already set up three postconciliar commissions: one for the sacred liturgy, a second for the revision of the code of canon law, and a third which is already endeavoring to implement the provisions of the decree on communications.

We have not waited for the approval of the schema on the pastoral duty of bishops in the Church in order to grant in full the request contained in it. Instead, we have already announced the institution of the episcopal synod which, God willing, we hope to convoke for the first time, if not next year, which will be entirely taken up by other postconciliar concerns, at least in 1967, when we shall have to commemorate in a suitable manner the centenary of the martyrdom of the Apostle Peter, an observance which was already instituted in the last century by our predecessor of revered memory, Pius IX.

In the same way also we shall be eager to institute, as early as possible, the commissions which the council has voted to set up in order to complete the norms of the conciliar decrees or to carry out the special projects connected with their application. New offices will be opened for those new services which may be rendered necessary by the statutes of the council and by the demands of the renewal of the Church.

On our part we shall not be wanting in the will to bring to a happy conclusion the unfinished business resulting from the celebration of the ecumenical synod and to carry out the activities initiated by it, like those of the three secretariats now doing excellent work, namely, the one which is fostering the unification of all Christians in the same Church, the second which is promoting relations with non-Christian religions, and the third entrusted with the study and care of nonbelievers. May the Lord sustain our will and grant us the strength and means to fulfill these new obligations.

This, however, venerable brothers, will take some time. In any case please do not interpret this as a lack of fidelity to the proposals which we are going to announce, if these and other developments of the central offices of Church government take place with reasonable gradualness and if they are so studied and carried out as to avoid the encumbrances of bureaucracy and useless financial burdens. . . .

The newly recognized power of episcopal conferences is an important fact in the organic growth of canon law, and as we have readily welcomed and promoted it, so too we hope it will confer a salutary and respected blessing on Holy Church in the various nations and regions. . . . This we will promote; and the central offices of ecclesiastical government, and foremost among these the Roman Curia, will be of effective assistance to us and at the same time of valuable service to the whole structure of the Church.

The Roman Curia

With regard to the Roman Curia, permit us, at the conclusion of this great proof of the spiritual and organizational resources of the Catholic Church, to commend this body to your generous recognition. If the Catholic Church finds herself today in that state of well-being in which, by God's grace, we can see her to be, she owes it in good measure to the services of this industrious and faithful instrument of the apostolic office.

It would be wrong to consider it antiquated or inefficient, selfish or corrupt; we are bound to bear testimony to its efficient service. By the constant mercy of God the defects imputed in other times to this human organization which surrounds and serves the Roman pontiffs no longer exist today. On the contrary, a religious spirit and a true love for Jesus Christ, fidelity and obedience, zeal for the Church and readiness to favor progress are happily the guiding principles of the Roman Curia, rendering it well fitted for its important function and entitling it to the confidence of the whole Church.

We do not hereby intend to exclude the possibility that the Roman Curia may need improving. Everything human, everything that is temporal can easily be weak and imperfect. Moreover, the higher a man's office and the greater the demands his task imposes on his moral integrity and Christian holiness, the more manifest and lamentable his shortcomings appear. We ourselves are the first to recognize this fact, and we have taken measures to ensure that the Roman Curia will be appropriately reorganized, in accordance with paragraph 9 of the recent Decree on the Pastoral Office of Bishops in the Church. We will likewise be the first to see to it that the genuine spirit of Jesus Christ penetrates and animates to an ever higher degree all those who have the honor of belonging to this body.

We can assure you, venerable brothers, that we have not been idle in this matter in recent times, although overburdened with so many other cares. The studies undertaken with a view to the reform of the Roman Curia have been advanced and have made good progress. We can say at once that apart from the replacement of personnel, there is no great necessity for structural changes. On the other hand, there is need for not a few reforms, for some simplifications and other improvements. The criteria that should animate this body will be determined and formulated with greater clarity. The desired transformation will seem slow and partial. It cannot be otherwise if due respect is to be had for persons and traditions. But this transformation will surely come.

However, in order to give some tangible proof of our words, we can announce that within a short time a new statute will be published to legislate for the principal sacred congregation, that of the Holy Office.

Pre-eminence of Moral and Spiritual Renewal   Then the Pope focused on the pre-eminence which must be given to "moral and spiritual renewal." He expressed his gratitude to the experts for their effectiveness and competence.

Finally, let us quote this widely noted passage, which illustrates the way Paul VI thinks and acts:

The Church is settling down with new norms she has received from the Council. Fidelity is their characteristic. In these norms there is a new element, that of increased awareness of the ecclesial communion, of her marvelous structure, of the greater charity which should unify, vivify, and sanctify the hierarchical communion of the Church.

This is the period of the true *aggiornamento* proclaimed by our predecessor of venerable memory, John XXIII. This word, which described his goal, certainly did not have the meaning for him which some try to give it, as if it allowed for the "relativization," according to the spirit of the world, of everything in the Church—dogmas, laws, structures, traditions. His sense of the doctrinal and structural stability of the Church was so vital and strong that it was the basis and foundation of his thought and of his work. From now on *aggiornamento* will signify for us a wisely undertaken quest for a deeper understanding of the spirit of the past Council and the faithful application of the norms it has happily and prayerfully provided.

NOVEMBER 19

The Schema on Religious Liberty
Is Subjected to Final Votes Before Promulgation

This morning, Friday, the Council voted on the Declaration on Religious Liberty, in the last step before promulgation. This is the time for the *expansio modorum*, the expression of *placet* or *non placet* only—the amendments stage is over—toward the final text, which incorporates the *modi* sumbitted previously.

Bishop de Smedt presented the last report on a schema whose history, we know, has been long, very complicated, and punctuated by a number of sabotage efforts. The Pope himself asked that the voting begin on Friday morning, only forty-eight hours after the Fathers received the final draft of the schema, to cut short any last-minute attempts by the unhappy minority to scuttle it. We haven't heard much about recent intrigues in this matter, but tongues will no doubt wag when the final vote has been cast.

One change has caused difficulty in the eyes of the majority: "Religious liberty . . . leaves untouched traditional Catholic doctrine on the moral duty of men and societies toward the true religion and toward the one Church of Christ."

The new words here are "traditional" and "societies."

The first might indicate that the Church is not renouncing the thesis-hypothesis theory which the majority of Fathers criticized in the debates. The second might be read, in a strict interpretation, as an allusion to a Catholic state. We say in a strict interpretation because the text says simply "societies" and not "civil societies."

There is no doubt that the two words were added to placate the minority; nor is there any doubt that the latter will exploit the addenda in the directions just indicated. However, such a strict interpretation would be artificial since the spirit of the schema as a whole is far different; a later paragraph, for example, evokes the necessity of developing the doctrine of recent pontiffs on the inviolable rights of the human person. This is a discreet but clear way of saying that certain aspects of previous doctrine must continue to evolve.

Votes on Schema 13

The results of the last votes on schema 13 were made public today. The chapter on political life was adopted by a vote of 1,970 to 54, with 210 *placet juxta modi* and 7 null ballots.

The last chapter, on peace and war, and the conclusion of the whole schema were adopted 1,656 to 45, with 523 *placet juxta modi* and 3 null ballots.

The competent subcommissions are hard at work on the *modi*. The number of reservations on the last chapter is noteworthy.

NOVEMBER 20

The Vote on Religious Liberty Marks a Historic Date

The definitive votes on the Declaration on Religious Liberty cast Friday, November 19, less than a month after the vote on the statement on the Jews (in the schema on non-Christian religions), constitute another historic event to add to the annals of Vatican II. Here are the results of the five votes on the Declaration on Religious Liberty:

First vote: 2,242 voters; 1,989 affirmative, 246 negative, 7 null ballots.
Second vote: 2,200 voters; 1,957 affirmative, 237 negative, 6 null ballots.
Third vote: 2,210 voters; 1,989 affirmative, 217 negative, 4 null ballots.
Fourth vote: 2,228 voters; 2,033 affirmative, 190 negative, 5 null ballots.
Fifth vote, on the whole of the schema: 2,216 voters; 1,954 affirmative, 249 negative, and 13 null ballots.

No other schema has suffered such vicissitudes. The Protestants rightly look upon it as a test of the good will—indeed, of the good faith—of the Roman Church. The schema removes one of the principal obstacles to ecumenism. What was impossible yesterday will be possible tomorrow.

In creating the Secretariat for Promoting Christian Unity and then giving it full powers to write and present conciliar schemas, John XXIII was aware that this body (which he confided to the direction of his friend Cardinal Bea) would encounter great difficulties. The Curia could only look with mistrust on an office designed to take away some of the Holy Office's traditional powers. Today we can say that Cardinal Bea and his team have won an almost total victory.

The fury of the enemies of this text was extraordinary. In one sense, it surpassed their bitterness toward the Jewish statement, for the reasons invoked in this case were more convincing than those advanced against the schema on the Jews.

Doctrinal dogmatism made a bold stand. The minority argued from previous pontifical documents and even brandished the dangers of laicism and indifferentism. But the Church of pastors carried the day over certain doctors who are armed with quotations but do not see that all doctrine, including Catholic doctrine, is subject to organic evolution. The weight of the past was very heavy; it took the combined efforts of the most open theologians, the pastoral instincts of the bishops, and the resolute will of the Pope to overcome the resistance.

Once again the majority at Vatican II has shown itself understanding toward the minority. They have not been repaid in kind, at least thus far, since in the final vote there was still a total of 262 Fathers out of 2,116 who refused to accept the schema. That is a high figure when we consider the efforts made by both the commission and the Pope to win over the opposition.

Two pamphlets circulated in the aula Friday morning, both dated November 18. They were sponsored by the famous Comitatus Episcopalis Internationalis and urged a *non placet* vote.

"Our episcopal conscience cannot compromise," we read in one of the pamphlets. "There is now no hope of having the schema corrected by the commission. Our only hope lies in the Pope's intervention. But it would be difficult for him to intervene if the Fathers are almost unanimously in favor of it."

The text rather smoothly leaves this escape hatch open: "On the day of promulgation, each can vote according to the judgment of the Sovereign Pontiff, if he thinks he can do so in conscience."

It seems likely, then, that at the public session on December 7 the minority will weaken appreciably; thus the concessions made to them in the present text will have proven helpful.

The schema has been voted on; it now must be put into practice. This will not be automatic, especially in countries where religious liberty is seriously threatened. A Latin American ambassador told us recently, "The Council should not use the expression *religious liberty; tolerance* would be enough."

Because we provided most of the previous text on religious liberty [see the report of September 15, 1965], we will not publish the present version. But it is in order to make some clarifications. Bishop de Smedt's report, as it was given in the official press bulletin, will be helpful in this respect.

Bishop de Smedt's Report The reporter noted three items in particular that emerged from the previous voting and the amendments:

1. Some Fathers thought that the text did not show well enough how the schema avoided contradicting the doctrine of popes before Leo XIII. As the previous report had mentioned, pontifical documents before Leo XIII principally stressed the moral duties of public powers toward religion; since Leo XIII, the same teaching has been retained but the emphasis has been on another obligation incumbent upon public powers, namely, that of respecting the rights of the human person in matters religious. The text has been amended to express more clearly the duties of public powers toward the true religion although the main purpose of the declaration is to clarify the second obligation.

2. The Fathers now admitted that we need a declaration on what we mean technically by "religious liberty."

3. They unanimously accepted the doctrine expounded by Pius XII: in present-day society, the common good requires that religious liberty be recognized and established everywhere legally.

Bishop de Smedt then explained why the secretariat did not consider some of the suggestions made. He said that those Fathers who disagreed with the development given this doctrine of recent popes did not want the schema to mention the *right of the person* to religious liberty. They admitted only to a *civil positive right*, to be established within the present framework of society. The secretariat would make three observations to these Fathers. First, this would change the meaning of the text, which was adopted with the required two-thirds majority. Again, it would endanger the Catholic Church's liberty and independence, which would then depend on the will of legislators. We must think of the good of the whole Church. But finally, this does not mean that the Council is concerned only with the Catholic Church's liberty. The declaration bases religious liberty on the dignity of the human person, who in the image of God is endowed with free will and personal responsibility.

Then Bishop de Smedt gave an account of the amendments accepted, which have the purpose of preventing errors of interpretation. He presented them in four groups:

1. Some Fathers feared that the paragraph on "the duty of men and societies toward the true religion" might make the text less acceptable to

non-Catholics or non-Christians. But the Council must clearly and sincerely show how recognition of religious liberty leaves intact for Christians the duties toward the true religion. Two amendments have a particular importance in this respect. First, at the end of the preceding paragraph, concerning the Catholic faith in the one Church of Christ, the text simply affirms that all men are bound to seek truth, especially in what concerns God and his Church, and that the truth they come to know must be adhered to and observed. Then the next paragraph states more clearly that religious liberty leaves untouched traditional Catholic doctrine on the moral duty of men and societies toward the true religion and the one Church of Christ.

2. Some Fathers were afraid that certain passages could be interpreted as though the Council recognized the right to spread error and accepted religious indifferentism. The present text more clearly states that each person must form "correct and true" judgments of conscience; that dishonest proselytism must be considered as an abuse of and infringement on the rights of others; that religious communities must not be impeded from showing the value of their doctrine for the organization and inspiration of society; and finally, that parents have the right to choose schools for their children in keeping with their religious convictions.

3. A good number of Fathers feared that the text laid itself open to the charge of laicism, as though the practice of religion were not part of the common good. Thus the text now specifies that public powers who are responsible for the common good must recognize and encourage the religious life of citizens. But they do not have the right to impose or prevent religious acts. It also specifies that individuals, social groups, public powers, the Church, and other religious communities have a responsibility toward religious liberty, each in its own manner, "in virtue of the duty of all toward the common good"; the text further specifies that the legal equality of all citizens, whatever their beliefs, is an element of the common good.

4. With respect to the limits of religious liberty, some Fathers asked that the text not speak of "public order" or at least do so more prudently; "the common good" was suggested as a substitute. Bishop de Smedt noted the gravity of this matter. He stressed that when it is a question of protecting or promoting religious liberty, "the common good" is envisaged in its widest scope; when it is a question of limiting religious liberty, "the common good" is considered to mean its fundamental part. This segment is precisely designated today by the term *public order* in civil law and various constitutions, and the text must adopt the technical term currently used in society. The Council can help clarify this question by carefully pointing out the contents of the notion of public order. The commission

therefore adopted the text while retaining its substance. This text shows that the limits of religious liberty are founded on the necessity of guaranteeing the rights of all and their pacific coexistence—public peace—and of protecting public morality. In this section, the term *public order* is not used but an immediate qualification is added to the effect that religious liberty is an essential part of the common good and therefore pertains to public order.

Reactions to the Pope's Last Speech

Now that extraconciliar conversation is not dominated by the vote on the religious liberty declaration, the Council Fathers and experts have more time to discuss the Pope's speech of November 18. It was not universally praised as was, for example, his homily on the opening of the fourth session. Commentators can be classed in two groups.

The first group is composed of those who are especially interested in the important announcements made by the Pope: heading the list, the news of a new statute for the Holy Office; then the promise of a meeting of the episcopal synod in 1967; and finally the announcement that postconciliar offices will be created as soon as possible to put the general directives of Vatican II into practice.

The bishops are also happy that Paul VI stressed the importance of the episcopal conferences presently being reorganized; their status will be determined by future canonical legislation.

Too, everyone is happy that the process for the beatification of John XXIII has been begun, even though many hoped he would be made a saint by acclamation.

It is noted that the process for Pius XII should normally take much longer to finish—if indeed it is ever finished, as Paul VI was prudent enough to say. The reason for this is the great number of speeches Pius XII delivered over nineteen years, each of which will have to be minutely sifted by competent clerics from the Congregation of Rites.

It is also noted that Paul VI intentionally associated the two last popes, both of whom, he said, are very dear to him. This is one more act of diplomacy to the present pope's credit, for the two pontiffs he has brought together were very different in both temperament and destiny. Admirers of Pius XII are not always those of John XXIII, although it is rather pointless to contrast the two popes, "to whom the Church herself and the world owe so much," in Paul VI's words. Nonetheless, the two were loved in different ways.

In the second group of commentators are those who are unhappy with the Pope's long eulogy of the Curia and deplore the effect this will have outside of Italy. But those familiar with the Italian mentality see the Pope's psychology as correct. He obviously wanted to recognize the zeal of devoted old servants, and especially appease their discomfiture over the reforms to come.

Critics in this group also noted the moderation with which the Pope spoke about reform; this will be less radical than some had expected and will be done very gradually.

Paul VI Justifies the Existence of Canon Law

"Obedience does not stifle liberty but perfects it by stimulating activity and exalting the human person. Disobedience, on the other hand, disperses energies and makes man the slave of his passions," said the Pope in a speech given in Latin on the occasion of an audience granted to the sixty cardinals and seventy advisers of the pontifical commission for the reform of canon law.

Responding to critics who question the Church's power of jurisdiction by saying that the law oppresses liberty, Paul VI declared:

> We must not listen to those who have contempt for canon law and affirm that the letter kills while the spirit quickens. Even though we can say that the letter must not be contrary to the spirit, the law nonetheless needs the letter insofar as it needs a clear exposition in writing. This is abundantly proven by the code of canon law. . . .
>
> Moreover, some make a distinction between the juridical or organizational Church and the Church of charity by saying that the latter is in keeping with the first commandment and that all the evils which afflict the Church stem from her "legalism." Nonetheless, just as the soul cannot be separated from the body without causing death, so too the Church of charity cannot exist without the "legal" Church. We cannot ignore that the Church is by divine will a visible society, endowed with institutions intended to assure her external government. Christ conferred upon his apostles and their successors the power of jurisdiction. This is clear from a reading of the Gospels, and Saint Paul discusses it at length in his first letter to the Corinthians.

After saying one could not subscribe to the opinion of those who maintain that the Church should not be a hierarchy by a "ministry" of the word (since nothing should come between Christ and the faithful), the Pope added:

Nor should we believe those who affirm that the nature of the Church is contrary to the nature of law and who admit only a sacramental law, the hierarchy being necessary only for the administration of the sacraments. . . .

All of these errors deny the positive law itself and are in contradiction with the Gospel, according to which Christ instituted the hierarchy and endowed it with special powers in order that it might feed the flock authoritatively.

NOVEMBER 21

Underdeveloped Countries

Father Gauthier, founder of the Society of Companions of Jesus the Carpenter, held a round-table discussion at his Roman residence this morning, Sunday. Attending were a number of bishops who are specialists in Indian and Chinese questions, and French and Italian laymen and journalists. The subject: aid to underdeveloped countries.

Father Gauthier, a worker-priest in Nazareth and a prime mover behind the conciliar group promoting the "Church of the poor," is the gray eminence of the Council. History will record with what singlemindedness he has tried to make the Western bishops understand that Vatican II will be a failure if it does not lead to practical efforts to evangelize the poor and strip the Church of her wealth.

The following opinions are recorded anonymously at the request of those attending the meeting.

Marxists are more faithful to the evangelical command to feed the hungry, said a bishop. It is a mystery to me why non-Christians have been more evangelical than Christians. Communism is a testimony of our failure.

India has a Christian constitution that makes provisions for the poor, another bishop informed the group. In 1947 and 1948 Nehru broke up the 630 feudal principalities of his country. The English failed to do this, and to protect the production of their own country, they failed to equip India industrially.

The Council would have been more effective, said several laymen, if it had asked sociologists to provide data on the problem of hunger when schema 13 was being discussed. Many bishops will return home without having really understood the complexity of this problem. Moreover, the public has been disappointed in Vatican II because the Council has attached such importance to problems within the Church and has given so little time to the question of world poverty. There was time to discuss indulgences in the aula but no time to inform bishops about the problems of underdeveloped countries.

Generally speaking, said a bishop, Westerners do not understand the dramatic and explosive character of world hunger. There are bishops at the Council who are aware of this. But they dared not speak because they felt they belonged to another world, and they were not encouraged to instruct their peers.

Father Gauthier had the final word. He put this anguished question to the group: "Will the postconciliar Church be able to go among the nations, as did the early Church?"

NOVEMBER 23

Schema 13 Was the Only One Formally Desired by John XXIII, Says Archbishop Garrone

Archbishop Garrone of Toulouse, vice president of the standing committee of the French episcopacy, delivered a lecture at the Vatican's official press bureau on Monday. It was remarkable for its vigor and clarity. The reporter for schema 13, Archbishop Garrone was particularly well qualified to talk about the meaning of this text, its necessity, and its value, which he did without minimizing its imperfections.

The speaker began with the latter. There are several reasons for these imperfections. Schema 13 is in a sense a catchall for themes that couldn't be fitted in elsewhere; it was drawn up late and amended hastily at the end of the Council; the subject is a totally new one, and consequently has no conciliar tradition behind it to profit by; finally, it deals with burning questions for which the Church has no ready-made or definitive answers. "We must not think that the Church has easy solutions for all problems," Archbishop Garrone said.

The audience was particularly attentive when the speaker said:

> Schema 13 is the very heart of the Council. We might almost say it was the only schema formally desired by John XXIII. It is the continuation of the Constitution *Lumen gentium* on the Church, which was an effort to ready the Church for authentic and timely dialogue with the world. In *Lumen gentium*, the Church got herself bathed and dressed to speak to the world. As time goes by, we understand better that the relationship between the Constitution on the Church and schema 13 is the relationship between a preparation and an action. . . .
>
> The idea of service impregnates schema 13. It is a question of

the Church's fraternal presence to the world. The Church's attitude toward the world is one of open cooperation. The schema is centered on man, the pivot of creation. Allow me to express the hope that commentators on this text will emphasize the first part [on anthropology], for this determines the applications in the second part.

Nor did the speaker dodge the thorny question of birth control. We gather from what Archbishop Garrone said that the Pope will present his conclusions "in the near future."

Bishop Ancel, who accompanied Archbishop Garrone, made the following remarks about the chapter on war, which he personally helped write.

At the request of many bishops, this chapter now refrains from entering into casuistical details. We never have the right to resort to war to obtain justice, and yet every country has the right to legitimate defense. Total war, whether atomic or not, can never be justified. Finally, the arms race not only exposes the world to grave dangers but constitutes a genuine injustice toward poor countries, which have a strict right to be helped by rich countries.

The remarks of these two bishops make us see more clearly that schema 13 has begun the desired dialogue between the Church and the world, awkwardly perhaps but with obvious good will.

We might add that in our personal opinion an ambiguity remains in schema 13. It could give the impression that the Church and the world are two absolutely distinct realities, that the two have in some sense to confront one another. Many think this is not correct, holding on the contrary that the world and the Church are two complementary and inseparable aspects of a single reality: creation. The Church is the privileged part of the world which has received the mission to announce the Gospel to those who do not yet know it explicity but who are *de facto* under the influence of grace and the Spirit, who, as the liturgy sings, "fills the whole earth."

NOVEMBER 24

The Excommunications of 1054

The question of removing the reciprocal excommunications of 1054 between Rome and Constantinople has been studied very quietly by a mixed commission which met from Sunday through Tuesday at Fener, the seat of the Patriarchate of Constantinople.

The delegation from the Vatican was under the leadership of Bishop Jan Willebrands, secretary of the Secretariat for Promoting Christian

Unity, and that of the Ecumenical Patriarchate of Constantinople under Metropolitan Meliton of Heliopolis and Thyra.

The meeting, according to a Catholic spokesman, took place 'in an atmosphere of calm and charity." He added, "A reciprocal gesture was made."

However, as an Orthodox spokesman said, it is the responsibility of Pope Paul VI and Patriarch Athenagoras I, to whom the commission's report will be submittted, to define the future aspects of dialogue between the two churches.

NOVEMBER 25

The Chapter on War Criticized

Archbishop Philip Hannan of New Orleans, who intervened on the Council floor last year in favor of authorizing the use of atomic weapons within certain limits, was quoted recently by the Divine Word news service as saying that if schema 13 were approved in its present form, "It would be considered ridiculous in political and military circles throughout the world."

Archbishop Hannan was referring especially to the passage in the chapter on war concerning the possession of nuclear arms and the principle which excludes recourse to force even to restore violated rights.

The prelate said it would be wrong to condemn the use of atomic arms indiscriminately because "Many of them have very precise and limited destructive power."

Archbishop Hannan said he was against the idea that Catholics should be taught all wars are morally unjustifiable and unjust. "This would be an error that would have a harmful effect on the efforts realized by free countries to protect their liberties against aggression."

"Political Colonialism Has Ended
but Economic Colonialism Remains, Heavy and Suffocating,"
Says Archbishop Helder Câmara

Archbishop Helder Câmara of Recife, Brazil, has never spoken on the Council floor, but he has had a great deal of influence at Vatican II. His reputation extends beyond the borders of Latin America, where he has inspired various social undertakings and is known for his extraordinary cordiality toward the poor. Now and again we hear talk about the spirit of prophecy in the Church. If there is one bishop who merits the title of prophet, it is Archbishop Helder Câmara, whose spirit of faith and poverty, spontaneity, and humor have made him one of the most colorful and effective bishops at the Council.

He gave a lecture Wednesday evening at the Dutch Documentation Center entitled "What the Council Couldn't Say." His words need no commentary. He speaks with the voice of a bold and free man who is not concerned about displeasing the powerful. For instance: "Almost two thousand years after the death of Christ, at a time when the Declaration on Religious Liberty is to be promulgated, nearly two-thirds of humanity live in a subhuman condition which makes it impossible for them to understand the real meaning of liberty."

Speaking of the Church's responsibility in Latin America, the Archbishop said, "Underdevelopment has plunged Latin America and the whole 'third world' into a situation that is unworthy of the human person; it constitutes a real insult to creation. A revolt against the Church on the part of Latin American Christians is inevitable if the Church sins by omission today, at an hour of oppression and slavery."

Then the speaker alluded to North America's responsibility: "I am a bishop of the Church before I am the Bishop of Recife. The day when North America takes the decision to incite all nations to re-examine in depth the international politics of business—the only way to go to the heart of the problem of harmonious and overall development—the world will be nearer to peace than if all the nuclear stockpiles were destroyed."

The prelate suggested:

[Let the Latin American hierarchy] take an open position in favor of the underdeveloped masses; let them try to dispose of their real estate holdings, especially if they are unproductive; let them give moral support to any nonviolent movement against landowners who are still in the Middle Ages and have a colonial mentality. This colonialism is the worst that I know; we still have medieval barons in our country.

Is it asking too much of the Latin American hierarchy to inspire, stimulate, and follow a new Bolivarism, directed in this case not toward political independence but toward socioeconomic independence? When Latin America confronts the incursions of international trusts that are stronger than the strongest states [the speaker repeated this twice], when regional and continental blocs multiply and organize in defense of their interests, a common Latin American market will become mandatory.

Political colonialism has ended but economic colonialism remains, heavy and suffocating. The antitrust laws which exist in the United States should be applied to commerce with the third world.

After paying homage to the remarkable work of Martin Luther King, Archbishop Helder Câmara concluded, "The Communist masses will be convinced when they understand that they do not have to deny God and eternal life to love men and fight for justice on earth. The Communist masses will look upon religion with interest and sympathy when they discover that it is determined not to cover for injustices committed in the name of private property and enterprise."

NOVEMBER 26

Last-Minute Difficulties with the Chapter on Marriage

There have been some last-minute difficulties with the chapter on marriage in schema 13. The Secretariat of State sent a letter to the competent commission asking that four *modi* be inserted in the text. The practical effect of these would be to prohibit all forms of contraception, in line with Pius XI's *Casti connubii* and Pius XII's famous speech to midwives.

Almost all the members of the commission took exception to both the substance and the form of this request, since the text of the schema is almost ready for the printer.

The question is, does the Pope personally approve these *modi* or has he simply consented to transmit them to the commission in order to please the minority? The latter is more likely. Similar instances have not been unknown in the past. As we write these lines, the matter is still up in the air. The commission held an extraordinary meeting on Friday to discuss this affair. When news of the goings-on leaked out, there was a good deal of consternation.

Schema 13 and Communism

Despite all the minority's efforts, Vatican II refused to condemn communism. However, in the latest—and definitive—version of schema 13, a clarification has been added so that no one will have reason to think the magisterium has broken with its former official position.

The passage comes in the section on atheism. Where it is said that the Church "cannot cease repudiating [atheistic doctrines], sorrowfully but as firmly as possible," these supplementary words were inserted, as we have seen: "the Church has already repudiated." A footnote refers the reader to various texts in which the last four popes more or less directly condemned atheistic communism.

DECEMBER, 1965

Birth Control: Paul VI Agrees To Let the Competent
Commission Attenuate the Amendments He Suggested

The competent commission for schema 13 received the Pope's permission
to alter appreciably the amendments he himself has proposed. It is another
proof of Paul VI's flexibility.

The expression "illicit contraceptive methods" suggested by the pope
has been replaced by "illicit methods against life," which is much more
general. Elsewhere, since Paul VI has said that either the present or the
future tense may be used, two formulas are possible: "the methods which
have been denied by the magisterium *or will be* denied," or "the methods
which have been denied . . . *and are* denied." The commission naturally
chose the second formula because it leaves the future open.

The schema now refers explicitly, at Paul VI's request, to Pius XI's
Casti connubii and Pius XII's address to midwives in 1951, which reject
nonnatural means of birth control. The prescent text doesn't deny that
there could be an eventual evolution of current doctrine; it doesn't mention this at all. As it stands, the schema represents no progress over previous
doctrine. Many Fathers are surprised that Paul VI, having removed the
question of birth control from their hands last year, is now forcing them
to take a reactionary position without their consent. It would seem the
Pope is afraid that the Council might draw up a doctrine that would be in
conflict with what Pius XI and Pius XII said on this subject.

The problem in brief is this: if the Church permits couples to have
conjugal relations that are *intentionally unfruitful* through the use of the
Ogino method or temperature measurement, is it licit to bring about temporary sterilization in one of the partners by medical means, that is, to
supplant nature?

It seems clear that the Pope is reluctant to give a direct answer to this
question, even for the case of those who are disposed to have as many

children as their situation permits. While Protestants are liberal in this matter, Catholic theology is very strict for anthropological reasons (a certain concept of "human nature") and perhaps also for fear of indirectly encouraging extramarital relations or, more directly, conjugal selfishness.

"Situation Ethics" and "Ethics of a Situation"   Most confessors and spiritual directors have in recent years been rather permissive in this domain. In practice, they frequently let married couples take responsibility for their acts, though cautioning them that each time they fail to "respect nature," they are objectively guilty in the light of the traditional sexual morality of the Catholic Church. Actually, this traditional morality is less and less respected in our aphrodisiacal and from that viewpoint decadent civilization. Certainly this is not reason enough to change moral principles if they are solidly established. But to the nondeterminative argument of expediency (does a law that is universally violated remain a good law?) can be added arguments based on a clearer conception of sexual functioning in the light of science, which has already definitively laid a certain number of myths to rest.

Certain theologians want a change of perspective. The Church should not, they say, draw up a detailed list of licit and illicit methods; experience proves that such a list is constantly subject to revision. The magisterium should limit itself to recalling that anything which is intended to deprive human love of one of its essential aspects, that is, "procreation," does not correspond with the ideal toward which the married couple should be striving, although on the other hand the couple must learn to assess their particular circumstances correctly. The Church condemns *situation ethics,* but she has the highest regard for the *ethics of a situation.*

It is clear that the Church favors periodic continence as the most adequate solution whenever it is justified by the spiritual and emotional maturity of the couple and the concrete circumstances of the particular home authorize it. But this solution is impracticable and ineffective in a great number of homes. Moreover, it is not always advisable for the harmony of the marriage. Nonetheless, training in greater control of the senses is desirable in all cases, and seems the most human measure since it brings the will to bear.

Whatever the value of these different approaches to the problem, which are more complementary than contradictory, Catholics will soon learn what decisions Paul VI will take in the wake of schema 13.

Vote on the Amendments
to the Schema on the Missions

The hundred and sixty-fifth general congregation was held yesterday, Tuesday morning, and during the meeting the Fathers voted on the amendments to the schema on the missions. The Pope surprised the assembly by attending the mass, which was concelebrated by Cardinal Meouchi, Patriarch of Antioch, and eight other Maronite Rite bishops.

The results of the first three votes, on chapters 1 and 2 of the schema, have already been published. The number of *non placet* ballots varied between 18 and 26.

One of the most important amendments accepted concerns the reorganization of the Congregation for the Propagation of the Faith. It specifies, in accordance with the request of 461 Fathers, that the representatives of all those who are engaged in missionary activities (bishops, religious superiors, directors of pontifical works) and participate in the administration of this body have "a deliberative voice."

On the other hand, the commission refused to accept a suggestion made by the same 461 Fathers that these bishops be chosen by episcopal conferences. The Pope will select them after consulting the episcopal conferences.

Archbishop Felici, secretary general of the Council, corrected a material error caused by a failure in the computer when the votes for promulgation of the schema on the laity were being tallied. Thirty-five *placet* votes had been mutilated by the machine and had not been counted. The correct figures are 2,342 voters, with 2,340 affirmative and 2 negative.

Schema 13 Firmly Against Artificial Birth Control

The difficulties which arose last week over the chapter on marriage have been resolved.

Last Thursday, after Cardinal Cicognani, Secretary of State, had requested the commission to insert four *modi* making specific reference to the encyclical *Casti connubii* and Pius XII's 1951 speech to Italian midwives, Cardinal Léger intervened to ask—as he had last year—that the Council not prejudice scientific and doctrinal study presently under way. Moreover, the lay auditors at the Council asked Paul VI not to include anything in schema 13 that would appear to be a final judgment on birth control since this problem is now being examined by a special pontifical commission.

Thereupon Cardinal Cicognani addressed a new letter to the conciliar commission. He said that the four amendments contained in his first letter were suggested by the Pope but that he would leave the commission free to propose a better formulation. According to some observers, the Pope wants schema 13 to furnish a firm and doctrinally sound statement on this question. Later he can assess the situation in the light of the findings of the special commission and propose relatively liberal concrete applications.

This was also what the conciliar subcommission understood. According to *L'Avvenire d'Italia,* which is usually well informed, this subcommission "will express a firm condemnation of contraceptive 'abuses' but will not stress the purpose of procreation any more than the other ends or aspects of marriage."

The same paper reported Father Häring, one of the chief experts on the commission, as saying that this does not absolutely exclude all human intervention in the natural processes which regulate birth.

DECEMBER 2

Archbishop Helder Câmara Calls for the Reform of Diocesan Curias

Archbishop Helder Câmara has given another repercussive conference. Speaking of simplifying the life of bishops, he said:

> We have had enough of bishop-princes who remain aloof from their people. We have had enough of a Church that wants to be served, that always wants to be first, that does not have the humility or the realism to accept the fact of religious pluralism. When will we bishops have the humility and the intelligence to learn like the laity, and particularly journalists, how to talk and be interesting, how to talk and be understood?

Speaking of the urgency of structural reform in the local churches, the bishop called for a change in diocesan curias analogous to the proposed changes in the Roman Curia. For, he said, "Our priests and laity are as critical of the diocesan curia as we are of the Roman congregations."

Regarding priests, the Archbishop said:

> The world of today needs priests who do not have to look upon women as almost synonymous with sin in order to be pure, who do not have to hate the world to love heaven, who can discover in the love of men the best way of loving God. . . .

The world does not listen to priests who are always moralizing, always scolding, always begging. . . .

Our priests are not seminarians. Let us establish real dialogue with them. They expect us bishops to be the first to put into practice the documents we have adopted.

On religious: "Immense houses, opulent chapels, enormous estates—these are a frequent cause of scandal in the 'third world.' "

On the laity: "Sometimes laymen are more clerical than priests. Sometimes they force priests to be clerical."

On the jubilee announced by the Pope: "We hope that this jubilee will bring pardon for all the censures that the Holy Office has issued and that it will make things easier for our brothers, the priests who have left us. . . ."

DECEMBER 3

Vote on the Schema on Priests

The Council Fathers voted on the schema on priests yesterday, Thursday. It was overwhelmingly approved. This is the last vote before promulgation on December 7. Archbishop Marty of Reims presented the report on the examination of the *modi*, which numbered over 10,000 for a text of only fifteen pages. The explanatory brochure on the amendments comprises more than 100 pages. This is the best answer to those who feared Vatican II would neglect priests.

It is most interesting to see how the competent commission revised this schema. Some of the amendments touched on points of capital importance: the nature of the priesthood, worker-priests, celibacy, and married priests.

Some Fathers wanted the Council to adopt the "traditional" definition of the priesthood as the power to celebrate the eucharist. But the commission did not follow their recommendation. For in fact the Council's perspective is different, and focuses on a theological innovation. It views the priesthood of the priest as in the line of and depending upon the priesthood of the bishop, as a participation in the power of teaching, sanctifying, and governing the faithful. The schema cites Saint Paul's words to the Romans, "that I should be a minister of Christ Jesus to the Gentiles; sanctifying the Gospel of God, that the offering up of the Gentiles may become acceptable, being sanctified by the Holy Spirit" (Rom. 15:16). Hence the schema directly associates the priesthood with evangelization. The priest offers the cult only because he evangelizes. Moreover, the priest is not isolated; he is defined in constant reference to the people—Christian and non-Christian; the unbeliever cannot be neglected. Finally, the priest is considered as a member of the sacerdotal body. His specific spirituality is essentially bound up with the exercise of his ministry. The priest is above all a missionary.

As we know, following the official decision by the French episcopacy to revive the worker-priest movement—an action the Pope willed expressly—the schema was enriched with the expressions "manual labor" and "share in the lot of the workers themselves."

Three hundred and sixty-eight Fathers asked for the suppression of these additions to chapter 2, agreeing in this with the Comitatus Episcopalis Internationalis. The commission paid them no heed, as was to be expected. It explained that since this form of the apostolate has already been established "in some nations in the Latin Church as well as in some Oriental Churches," the Council could not ignore it. However, the commission did replace the formula "with the approval of competent authority" with a more precise expression: "if there seems to be need for this and competent authority approves."

Only thirty-eight Fathers voted against the changes in this chapter.

Celibate and Married Clergy   The sections on celibacy, contained in chapter 3, have been improved. There were eleven pages of amendments on this subject. A total of 234 Fathers wanted the paragraph which makes mention of the Oriental married clergy, introduced at Cardinal Bea's request, suppressed; the commission ignored them. Again, 332 wanted the schema to say that celibate priests have a *more* intimate relationship with Christ; the commission ignored them too. This is indicative of a concern not to devaluate the Oriental married clergy. Moreover, a quotation was added from Pius XI's encyclical on the priesthood in 1935: "This holy synod in no way intends to alter that different discipline which legitimately flourishes in the Eastern Churches."

The previous text urged the married priests of the Oriental Church to set a perfect example of conjugal love and give their children a sound education. These recommendations were deleted from the new version. They do not apply specifically to Latin priests and might be considered discourteous.

Only twenty-seven Fathers voted against this chapter.

Rejection of the Pope's Suggestion   Finally, we might note that the commission rejected an amendment thought to have originated with the Pope since it was transmitted by the Cardinal Secretary of State. The Pope's *modus* suggested that the deacon pronounce "a temporary tacit vow of celibacy" on the day of his ordination and the priest a "perpetual tacit vow." The commission did not accept the *modus* because it represented "a substantial change" in a schema that had already been adopted by more than two-thirds of the conciliar assembly. By such signs we recognize the appearance of a new collegial mentality in the Church.

At the end of the general congregation, Archbishop Garrone of Toulouse presented the report on the amendments to schema 13 that will be voted on Saturday. We will report further on the changes in the sections on conscientious objectors (it was improved) as well as in the chapter on war and peace.

Voting on the schema on the missions ended Tuesday. The schema as a whole was accepted by 2,162 affirmative votes to 18 negative, with 2 null ballots.

DECEMBER 4

The Final Version of Schema 13 Insists on the Right to Legitimate Defense but Remains Steadfastly Against Total War

With a feverish haste that bordered on a dead run, the Fathers and experts worked day and night to finish examining the 30,000 *modi* that were submitted on schema 13. The results of their labor are published in two books totaling 411 pages. They contain reports, presentations of amendments, and the reasons some were accepted and others rejected, either partially or totally. The Council Fathers have but a few hours to study the complex contents of these pages.

Twelve votes will be necessary to complete work on this schema, nine today, Saturday, and three on Monday.

Attention is centered on the chapter on war. It has been vigorously contested by the American Cardinals Spellman and Shehan along with eight other bishops. This late maneuver has set off a lively controversy, but it is evident that nothing important in the schema will be changed.

This chapter has undergone some changes. The new text strengthens the passage concerning the right to legitimate defense but says clearly that total war goes "far beyond the limits" of such legitimate defense. This unequivocal passage was also retained: "Any act of war aimed indiscriminately at the destruction of entire cities or of extensive areas along with their population is a crime against God and man himself. It merits unequivocal and unhesitating condemnation."

The paragraph on armaments was amended in such a way that it cannot be said that the Council had any specific nation in mind. The passage on the danger of modern weapons was retained—they "can catapult men into the most atrocious decisions"—as well as the solemn appeal to heads of state and military leaders.

The changes relative to conscientious objection are more serious. Archbishop Garrone's report on this section was badly interpreted. He was trying to answer some bishops (notably Italians) whose objections were not considered substantial. His explanation concerned both the old and the new version, but some thought he was commenting on a newly inserted amendment. That was not the case at all.

"We must note," Archbishop Garrone said, "that the text [the former as well as the present version] makes no judgment about the objective morality of conscientious objection, nor does it establish a right to refuse to bear arms. It merely affirms that humane provisions should be made in such cases."

Here is the text of the previous schema: "Moreover, it seems right that laws make humane provisions for the case of those who, out of personal and mature conviction and frequently prompted by religious reasons, refuse in conscience to bear arms, provided, however, that they agree to serve the human community in some other way."

The new text reads: "Moreover, it seems right that laws make humane provisions for the case of those who for reasons of conscience refuse to bear arms, provided, however, that they agree to serve the human community in some other way."

Over Two Hundred Modi *on Communism* Archbishop Garrone made three important remarks about the passage on atheism. First, 209 *modi* requested a formal and explicit condemnation of communism. Second, the written petition which was remitted previously on the same subject was signed by 332 Fathers. (Those who were responsible for this petition reported the figure at 450.) And owing to an "involuntary mishap," this petition, which was submitted within the time limit, was not examined by members of the commission.

A Note on Birth Control In the new version of schema 13, the passage referring to the Church's present teaching on birth control is accompanied by this explanatory note from the commission:

> Certain questions which need further and more careful investigation have been handed over, at the command of the Supreme Pontiff, to a commission for the study of population, family, and births, in order that, after it fulfills its function, the Supreme Pontiff may pass judgment. Since the doctrine of the magisterium is such, this holy Snyod does not intend to propose immediately concrete solutions.

The best Vatican II can do under the circumstances is suggest that the norms presently in force may be modified by the Pope in the future.

DECEMBER 5

Meaningful Ecumenical Celebration
at St. Paul's Outside the Walls

The liturgical ecumenical celebration held Saturday afternoon at St. Paul's Outside the Walls had high symbolic value. The preparations for this ceremony were very discreet to avoid upsetting those who are not yet cognizant of the ecumenical progress made during the Council. Journalists were not admitted; nor were priests. The assembly was exclusively composed of non-Catholic observers, Council Fathers, and Paul VI. Strictly speaking the Pope did not preside over this ceremony, although he was the most important person present.

Representatives of different churches took turns praying, and the Pope pronounced a homily. After the ceremony the non-Catholic observers met privately with the Pope. Interestingly enough, they met in the Benedictine monastery where John XXIII first announced his intention to convoke a Council to a group of astonished cardinals.

This was a meaningful and intentional coincidence.

DECEMBER 6

On Atheism, 131 *Non Placet* Votes

The results of the first five votes on schema 13 (the introduction and the first section) were published at the end of the hundred and sixty-seventh general congregation on Saturday.

The second ballot, on atheism, drew 131 *non placet* votes. One reason for this high number might be the fact that the Council refused to condemn communism *ex professo*.

The other *non placet* votes ranged between 62 and 75, the latter drawn in the fifth ballot, on the chapter which recognizes the positive contribution of all Christian churches to the concept of human dignity. The same chapter states that the Catholic Church can be helped in many ways by men and society in preaching the Gospel.

The results of the vote on the whole schema on priests—the last before the promulgation vote of December 7—have been released: of 2,257 votes, 2,243 were affirmative and 11 negative, with 3 invalid ballots.

On the Eve of Cloture: Paul VI Changes the Name
and Methods of the Holy Office

Paul VI did not want the Council to end without keeping his promise, made November 18, to publish a statute on the Holy Office. *L'Osservatore Romano*'s issues of December 6 and 7 contain the motu proprio *Integrae servandae*, in which the Pope outlines changes in both the name and the methods of the Holy Office. By so doing he has responded to one of the fondest hopes of Vatican II, expressed innumerable times under different forms in the general congregations as well as in the "vota" which were submitted during the preparatory period of the Council. We recall in particular Cardinal Frings's intervention of November 8, 1963, in which he spoke of the "scandal" that the procedures used by the Holy Office caused in the world. He requested that the Holy Office follow the rules of legal process as they are laid down in canon 1555. He urged further that in the future no one be condemned without first having been heard, advised of the charges against him, and given a chance to defend himself. Applause then filled the aula. It was a cruel blow to Cardinal Ottaviani, who declared with tears in his eyes, "To attack the Holy Office is to offend the Pope, who is its head."

Now, two years later, Paul VI, who was pope then and seems not to have taken offense, is requiting the brave cardinal who dared pit himself against the "supreme" congregation.

Without the reform of the Holy Office, no other reform could go far in the Church. The blame here falls less on men than on an institution that is radically corrupted by secrecy, by a unilateral procedure, and by its occult omnipotence. If it were not poor sportsmanship to hit a man when he is down, we might recount in some detail how men of the Church have suffered at the hands of the Holy Office, have had their reputations tarnished, their lives broken, their consciences torn; and how many Christians have lost their faith because of this office. The "inquisition of the Inquisition," as Archbishop Roberts, formerly of Bombay, put it, had to be undertaken one day. Paul VI is truly performing an operation for religious health, an operation that was undeniably urgent. Who would take the schema on religious liberty seriously if the Church didn't practice it within her own structures?

Banishing Fear Today the abscess has been lanced, one further reason for joy as the Fathers prepare to disband. December 7, 1965, will go down in the history of the Roman Church as a great day for ecclesiastical freedom.

The contents and especially the tone of the preface to the motu proprio are noteworthy. The Pope affirms that the reform of the Curia "must begin with the Congregation of the Holy Office, since it has been given charge of the weightiest of all the matters entrusted to the Roman Curia, those in fact which deal with the doctrine of faith and morals. . . ."

Paul VI quotes I John 4:18, "Perfect love banishes fear." He then continues:

> . . . it seems more appropriate now to preserve the faith by means of an office for promoting doctrine. Although it will still correct errors and gently recall those in error to moral excellence, a new emphasis is to be given to the preaching of the Gospel. Besides, the progress of human civilization, whose influence on religion cannot be overlooked, is affecting the faithful in such a way that they will follow the Church's lead more fully and more lovingly if they are provided with full explanations for the Church's definitions and laws, insofar as matters of faith and morals by their nature allow.

It would be difficult to define the spirit of reform more clearly. And it is directly opposed to the spirit that has reigned in the Holy Office, which never gave reasons for its condemnations and never permitted the accused to defend himself. Usually the latter wasn't aware of what was going on; frequently even his bishop didn't know.

Here are the twelve points of reform. We see particularly that trials will no longer be secret, the accused writer will be given a hearing and the right to defend himself, and his bishop will always be informed. Moreover, the consultors to the Holy Office will be chosen from all over the world and can be assisted by experts, especially university professors. Thus Paul VI has put an end to such revolting abuses as great theologians' being judged by men of little education and no openmindedness whatsoever.

The Twelve Points

1. The Congregation for the Doctrine of the Faith, the new name of the Holy Office, will have the task of protecting doctrine relating to faith and morals throughout the whole Catholic world.
2. The congregation will be presided over by the pope and directed by a cardinal secretary with the aid of an assessor, a deputy, and a promoter of justice. There is no longer a commissary. Thus another vestige of the Inquisition has been eliminated.
3. The congregation, which is no longer called "supreme," will be com-

petent in all questions touching the doctrine of faith and morals or bearing any relationship to this doctrine.

4. The congregation will examine new doctrine and opinions, however these might be diffused. It will organize studies and encourage meetings of scholars. This is an innovation. The congregation will also condemn doctrine that is contrary to faith, after consulting the bishops concerned.

5. The congregation will "diligently" examine books referred to it and, if necessary, will reprove them, after having heard the author's point of view. The latter will have the opportunity to defend himself, even in writing, and his bishop will be advised, as called for in the Constitution *Sollicita ac provida* of Benedict XIV.

6. The congregation is competent, in theory and in practice, in all questions relating notably to marriage between baptized and nonbaptized persons or annulment of such unions.

7. The congregation will pass judgment on errors according to the norms of legal process. This puts an end to the special privileges the Holy Office enjoyed in this respect.

8. The congregation will watch over the dignity of the sacrament of penance according to norms that the bishops are to be informed of. Another innovation: those concerned will have the right to defend themselves and choose their counsel among qualified experts who are approved by the congregation.

9. The congregation will maintain liaison with the Pontifical Biblical Commission. This is also new.

10. In addition to consultors chosen by the Pope for "their learning, prudence, and specialization," others may be chosen from among university professors when their services are required by the case in question.

11. The congregation will exercise its mandate in the administrative and judiciary domains.

12. The regulations governing the congregation will be made public. Until now they have been secret.

DECEMBER 7

The Last General Congregation:
Only 251 Council Fathers Voted Against Schema 13

The hundred and sixty-eighth and last general congregation of Vatican II, on Monday, December 6, was devoted to voting on schema 13. After the mass, celebrated in the Slavic Byzantine rite by Bishop Elko of Pittsburgh for the Ruthenians of North America, the Gospel was enthroned by Archbishop Martin Johnson of Vancouver, British Columbia. Cardinal Suenens was moderator.

Everyone wondered how many Fathers would follow the advice given by Cardinals Spellman and Shehan and eight other bishops to vote against schema 13 as a whole because of chapter 5, on war, in its second part. A letter by these Fathers set off a train of events. First of all, the Pope let it be known that he was in entire agreement with the contents of chapter 5. Then Bishop Schröffer of Eichstätt, West Germany, president of the subcommission for chapter 5, and Archbishop Garrone of Toulouse, reporter for schema 13, counterattacked with a letter that was distributed to the Council Fathers Monday morning in the aula.

The signatories of this letter rebutted the argument of the Spellman coterie point by point:

> One has only to read the schema carefully and the explanation of the amendments to see that criticism of them is unfounded. In fact, the schema does not say that possession of nuclear arms is immoral. It merely speaks of "danger," "menace," and so forth. Nor does it say that possession of these arms can only be a temporary stopgap; it merely denies that the arms race is a sure means of maintaining peace. Nor is it said that nuclear arms are a cause of war, but merely that they threaten to aggravate the causes of war. Finally, the text does not deny in anyway the right to legitimate defense. . . .

It was learned in the course of the session that Cardinal Spellman had changed his mind and was asking the Fathers in his camp to vote *placet* on the whole schema. Chapter 5 nonetheless had drawn a large number of negative votes when it was voted on Saturday; of 2,201 voters, 1,710 were affirmative and 483 were negative, with 8 null ballots.

But the negative votes were reduced by half in Monday's vote on the schema as a whole. Of 2,373 voters (an exceptionally high number), 2,111 were affirmative and 251 negative, with 11 null ballots.

The general congregation concluded with a series of thank-you speeches. Archbishop Felici, secretary general of the Council, expressed his gratitude in verse. This amused the Fathers. Cardinal Suenens rendered thanks to the Blessed Trinity, invoked each day since the beginning of Vatican II, and expressed his gratitude to Archbishop Felici, whose "patience," "humor," and perfect Latin elocution were much appreciated during the whole course of the Council.

Toward a Life of Strict Poverty

"This is schema 14."

There is much more than humor in this remark about a document in several languages which was sent to the Council Fathers and the Pope by a group of anonymous bishops.

A hard core of some fifty bishops (with several hundred sympathizers) from different countries constitutes this group. Since the first session, the group—Cardinal Gerlier, now dead, was one of the most assiduous members—has been meeting to examine the theme of "the Church of the poor." From time to time they prayed in the catacombs, although always discreetly to avoid giving a holier-than-thou impression and also to protect their anonymity. They have now taken an important initiative in alerting their peers to their "project," a project which represents a solemn commitment for them.

Here is the substance of their document, which many observers consider one of the most precious fruits of Vatican II:

> We bishops, having come to see that we are not living a life of evangelical poverty, and encouraged by each other in a common effort in which each of us wants to avoid pretention and presumption; . . . in humility and an awareness of our weakness, yet with the determination and strength given us by God's grace, we have committed ourselves to the following:
>
> We will try to live like the ordinary people in our dioceses in all that concerns housing, food, [and so forth].
>
> We renounce forever both the appearance and the reality of wealth, particularly in regard to clothing . . . and insignia. . . .
>
> We will have no property, furniture, bank accounts . . . in our own name; what we are obliged to possess we will put in the name of the diocese or social or charitable organizations.
>
> We will, insofar as possible, confide the financial and material administration of our diocese to a committee of competent laymen who are aware of their apostolate, so that we may be more pastors and apostles and less administrators.
>
> We renounce . . . all titles signifying grandeur and power (for example, eminence, excellence, monsignor). We prefer the evangelical "father."
>
> We will avoid in our behavior and social relations everything that can constitute privileges, priorities, and any preference whatever for the rich and powerful (such as giving or accepting banquets . . .).
>
> We will likewise avoid encouraging or flattering the vanity of

anyone in view of obtaining gifts or for any other reason. We will invite our faithful to consider their contributions as a normal participation in worship, the apostolate, and social action.

We will give as much of our time as possible to . . . workers, the economically deprived, and the underdeveloped, without prejudice to other groups in our diocese. We will support laymen, religious, deacons, or priests whom the Lord calls to evangelize the poor by sharing in their lives.

Aware of the demands of justice and charity and of their interrelationship, we will strive to convert all charitable works into social organizations based on justice and charity, which will . . . [serve] as a humble service of the competent public organisms.

We will bend every effort to urge the officials of our government and our public powers to adopt and apply the social laws, structures, and institutions required for justice, equality, and the full and harmonious development of the whole man with the whole of mankind, thus preparing the advent of a new social order worthy of the sons of man and the sons of God.

We commit ourselves to sharing . . . our lives with our brothers in Christ—priests, religious, and laymen—in order that our ministry be a true service. Thus, we will strive to reform "our life" together with them. We will encourage collaborators in order to be moving forces in the world's terms. We will try to be more humanly present and receptive; we will be open to all, whatever their religion.

When we return to our respective dioceses, we will make our intentions known to the faithful, asking them to help us with their understanding, their collaboration, and their prayers.

Each point in this document was accompanied by quotes from the New Testament. There are thirty-six in all.

A Speech by the Pope   In an allocution to the Italian hierarchy, the Pope also spoke of poverty. After expressing the need for "an organic doctrinal description of the bishop as the Council has defined him," the Pope referred to the age "when pastoral authority was bound up with temporal authority." He said:

Who doesn't remember the crosier and the sword? Episcopal insignias were then symbols of superiority, of external pomp, of honor, and sometimes of privilege, pleasure, and wealth. In that era this was not scandalous. . . . But today that is not the case, nor can it be the case. The faithful, far from admiring, are shocked and scandalized if the bishop appears clothed in anachronistic signs of dignity, and remind him of the Gospel. . . .

Happily, we no longer have the power symbolized by the insignia. . .

Let us thank God for everything worldly and exterior that we have abandoned. Love must always be evident; the bishop must be a father, a master, an educator, a consoler, a friend, a counselor.

Elsewhere in his speech, Paul VI dwelt at some length on the necessity for the bishop to have human contact with his community and especially with priests.

"A Wave of Affection and Admiration Flowed from the Council over the Modern World," the Pope Declares

The last plenary session of Vatican II opened this morning at 9 o'clock. St. Peter's was aglow with light, the sunshine from outside and the clusters of brighter electric lights studding the interior arches of the Basilica like constellations of stars.

The time had come for the Fathers to cast the last votes of the Second Vatican Council, expressing their collective will on the remaining conciliar documents. They adopted schema 13, the Pastoral Constitution on the Church in the Modern World, by 2,309 to 75, with 7 null ballots. The Declaration on Religious Liberty won 2,308 to 70 votes, with 8 null ballots. The Decree on the Ministry and Life of Priests was adopted 2,390 to 4, and the Decree on the Mission Activity of the Church 2,394 to 5.

The Pope had entered St. Peter's on foot—without the *sedia gestatoria* —wearing a miter on his head and carrying his pastoral staff in his hand. After the traditional ceremony of obedience, a declaration drawn up by the Patriarchate of Constantinople and the Catholic Church concerning "the events of 1054" was read. This expression, intentionally vague and reserved, evokes the reciprocal anathemas of the Oriental schism which have now been lifted. The Pope concelebrated mass with twenty-four presidents of episcopal conferences according to the Ambrosian Rite. The Gospel, from Matthew 5, repeated Christ's words "You are the salt of the earth."

Following the promulgation of the Declaration on Religious Liberty, the Pastoral Constitution on the Church in the Modern World, and the two decrees on the missions and priests, Cardinal Bea read the papal brief on the events of 1054. Athenagoras I, Ecumenical Patriarch of Constantinople, had sent Metropolitan Meliton of Heliopolis to represent him in Rome. It was to him the Pope gave the papal brief after it was read. When Meliton approached to kiss his ring, Paul VI raised him and embraced him twice as tumultuous applause broke out among the bishops and faithful attending the ceremony.

After a penitential ceremony, during which the bishops asked pardon of God for any sins against charity they might have committed during the conciliar discussions, the Pope added a special prayer in the name of all: "Since our conscience fears that ignorance has led us into error and a precipitate will has made us stray from the path of justice, we pray and beg you, O Lord, to forgive us if we have committed any offense during this Council."

The accents of the "*Te Deum*," chanted by the whole assembly, terminated this ceremony on a note of profound spiritual joy.

"A feeling of boundless sympathy" for man "has permeated the whole" of the Council, said the Pope. He defended the Council against those who accused it of doctrinal laxity and of having missed the essential by stressing man: ". . . the Catholic religion and human life," he said, "reaffirm their alliance with one another, the fact that they converge on one single human reality: the Catholic religion is for mankind."

Here are the principal passages of this fine speech. By defining a modern Christian humanism, it indicates the work of the Church in the future.

> We should like to devote this precious moment to one single thought which bends down our spirits in humility and at the same time raises them up to the summit of our aspirations. And that thought is this: what is the religious value of this Council? . . .
>
> [Ours is] a time which everyone admits is oriented toward the conquest of the kingdom of earth rather than of that of heaven; a time in which forgetfulness of God has become habitual, and seems, quite wrongly, to be prompted by the progress of science; . . . a time in which secularism seems the legitimate consequence of modern thought and the highest wisdom in the temporal ordering of society; . . . a time, finally, which is characterized by upheavals and a hitherto unknown decline even in the great world religions. . . .
>
> God is—and more, he is real, he lives, a personal, provident God, . . . our creator, our truth, our happiness. . . .
>
> The Church has gathered herself together in deep spiritual awareness, not to produce a learned analysis of religious psychology, or an

account of her own experiences, not even to devote herself to re-affirming her rights and explaining her laws. Rather, it was to find in herself, active and alive, the Holy Spirit, the word of Christ. . . .

The Council documents . . . leave wide open to view this pri-mary and focal religious intention, and show how clear and fresh and rich is the spiritual stream which contact with the living God causes to well up in the heart of the Church. . . .

No Deviation from the Religious Orientation

But we cannot pass over one important consideration in our analysis of the religious meaning of the council: it has been deeply committed to the study of the modern world. Never before perhaps, so much as on this occasion, has the Church felt the need to know, to draw near to, to understand, to penetrate, serve, and evangelize the society in which she lives, and to get to grips with it, almost to run after it, in its rapid and continuous change. This attitude, a response to the distances and divisions we have witnessed over recent centuries, in the last century and in our own especially, between the Church and secular society—this attitude has been strongly and un-ceasingly at work in the Council, so much so that some have been inclined to suspect that an easy-going and excessive responsiveness to the outside world, to passing events, cultural fashions, temporary needs, an alien way of thinking . . . may have swayed persons and acts of the ecumenical synod, at the expense of the fidelity which is due to tradition, and this to the detriment of the religious orientation of the Council itself. We do not believe that this shortcoming should be imputed to it, to its real and deep intentions, to its authentic manifestations.

We prefer to point out how charity has been the principal re-ligious feature of this council. Now, no one can reprove as want of religion or infidelity to the Gospel such a basic orientation, when we recall that it is Christ himself who taught us that love for our brothers is the distinctive mark of his disciples [see John 13:35] . . . ?

Yes, the Church of the Council has been concerned, not just with herself and with her relationship of union with God, but with man—man as he really is today: living man, man all wrapped up in himself, man who makes himself not only the center of his every interest but dares to claim that he is the principle and explanation of all reality. . . .

Secular humanism, revealing itself in its horrible anticlerical reality, has in a certain sense defied the Council. The religion of the

God who became man has met the religion (for such it is) of man who makes himself God. And what happened? Was there a clash, a battle, a condemnation?

We More Than Anyone Honor Mankind

There could have been, but there was none. The old story of the Samaritan has been the model of the spirituality of the Council. A feeling of boundless sympathy has permeated the whole of it. The attention of our Council has been absorbed by the discovery of human needs (and these needs grow in proportion to the greatness which the son of the earth claims for himself). But we call upon those who term themselves modern humanists, and who have renounced the transcendent value of the highest realities, to give the Council credit at least for one quality and to recognize our own new type of humanism: we too, in fact we more than any others, honor mankind.

And what aspect of humanity has this august senate studied? . . . Its attitude was very much and deliberately optimistic. A wave of affection and admiration flowed from the Council over the modern world of humanity. Errors were condemned, indeed, because charity demanded this no less than did truth, but for the persons themselves there was only warning, respect, and love. Instead of depressing diagnoses, encouraging remedies; instead of direful prognostics, messages of trust issued from the Council to the present-day world. The modern world's values were not only respected but honored, its efforts approved, its aspirations purified and blessed.

But one thing must be noted here, namely, that the teaching authority of the Church, even though not wishing to issue extraordinary dogmatic pronouncements, has made thoroughly known its authoritative teaching on a number of questions which today weigh upon man's conscience and activity, descending, so to speak, into a dialogue with him, but ever preserving its own authority and force. . . .

Another point we must stress is this: all this rich teaching is channeled in one direction, the service of mankind. . . .

It might be said that all this and everything else we might say about the human values of the Council have diverted the attention of the Church in council to the trend of modern culture, centered on humanity. We would say not diverted but rather directed. . . .

The modern mind, accustomed to assess everything in terms of usefulness, will readily admit that the Council's value is great if only because everything has been referred to human usefulness. Hence no one should ever say that a religion like the Catholic religion is without use, seeing that when it has its greatest self-awareness and effectiveness, as it has in council, it declares itself entirely on the side of man and in his service. In this way the Catholic religion and human life reaffirm their alliance with one another, the fact that they converge on one single human reality: the Catholic religion is for mankind. In a certain sense it is the life of mankind. . . .

Consequently, if we remember, venerable brothers and all of you, our children, gathered here, how in everyone we can and must recognize the countenance of Christ, . . . and if we can and must recognize in Christ's countenance the countenance of our heavenly Father, . . . our humanism becomes Christianity, our Christianity becomes centered on God; in such sort that we may say, to put it differently: a knowledge of man is a prerequisite for a knowledge of God. . . .

And so this council can be summed up in its ultimate religious meaning, which is none other than a pressing and friendly invitation to mankind of today to rediscover God. . . .

DECEMBER 8

The Solemn Ceremony of Cloture in St. Peter's Square: Paul VI Speaks to All Mankind

Vatican II ended Wednesday with a grandiose ceremony in the great circular court outside St. Peter's that is ringed by Bernini's columns.

The fact that it was held in the open air is symbolic of the Council's desire to set no limits to the Church's concern. As the Pope said explicitly during the mass of cloture, the Church loves the whole world, excluding no one, especially her enemies, and every loved one, he added, is present.

He then said:

The hour for departure and dispersion has come. In a few moments you will leave the conciliar assembly to go forth to meet mankind, taking with you the good news of Christ's Gospel and the renewal of his Church for which we have been working together these past four years.

This is a unique moment, a moment of incomparable meaning and richness. The past, present, and future converge in this universal gathering, in this privileged point of time and space: the past, for here the Church of Christ is united with her tradition, her history, her councils, her doctors, and her saints; the present, for we are taking leave of one another to go into the world of today with its miseries, its suffering, its sins, but also its prodigious accomplishments, its values, its virtues; and finally, the future is here in the urgent appeal from the peoples of the world for greater justice, in their desire for peace, in their conscious or unconscious thirst for a higher life, that life precisely which the Church of Christ can and wishes to give them.

We seem to hear from every corner of the world an immense and confused voice, the questions of all those who look toward the council and ask us anxiously: "Have you not a word for us?" For us rulers? For us intellectuals, workers, artists? And for us women? For us of the younger generation, for us, the sick and the poor?

These pleading voices will not remain unheeded. It is for all these categories of men that the Council has been working for four years. It is for them that the Constitution on the Church in the Modern World, which we promulgated yesterday amidst the enthusiastic applause of your assembly, has been prepared.

From our long meditation on Christ and his Church there should spring forth at this moment a first announcement of peace and salvation for the waiting multitudes. Before separating, the Council wishes to fulfill this prophetic function and translate the "good news" which it has for the world into brief messages in a language accessible to all men. Some of its most respected spokesmen will now pronounce these messages for all mankind in your name.

Various Council Fathers then read seven messages from the Pope to the following categories of recipients: government leaders, intellectuals and scientists, artists, women, the sick, workers, and youth. Each text was then given to a representative person or group of addressees. Here are some extracts.

To Intellectuals and Scientists
. . . our paths could not fail to cross. Your road is ours. Your paths are never foreign to ours. We are friends of your vocation as seekers, companions in your weariness, admirers of your successes, and, if necessary, consolers in your discouragement and your failures.

To Women
Women of the entire universe, whether Christian or nonbelieving, you to whom life is entrusted at this grave moment in history, it is for you to save the peace of the world.

To Workers
We wish also to be witnesses before you of the Church's great love for you workingmen, and we declare to you with all the con-

viction of our souls: the Church is your friend. Have confidence in her. Unfortunate misunderstandings in the past have too long maintained a spirit of mistrust and lack of understanding between us, and both the Church and the working class have suffered from this. Today the hour for reconciliation has sounded, and the Church of the Council invites you to celebrate this hour without suspicion.

To Youth

Rich with a long past ever living in her, and marching on toward human perfection in time and the ultimate destinies of history and of life, the Church is the real youth of the world. She possesses what constitutes the strength and the charm of youth, that is, the faculty of taking joy in what is beginning, of giving herself without reservation, of renewing herself and setting out again for new conquests. Look upon the Church and you will discover in her the face of Christ, the genuine hero, humble and wise, the prophet of truth and love, the companion and friend of youth.

The Pope personally gave the message to intellectuals to Jacques Maritain.

Paul VI also donated checks for $30,000 to a hospital in Bethlehem, $20,000 to the Little Brothers of Jesus in Argentina, and $15,000 for a charitable organization in Pakistan and $10,000 for one in Cambodia.

After mass, Paul VI blessed the cornerstone of a parochial church to be erected in the suburbs of Rome in honor of the Council.

Archbishop Felici, secretary general of the Council, read the decree of cloture for Vatican II. Finally, five bishops, representing the five parts of the world, went before the enthroned Gospel to chant a hymn of praise. with the whole assembly responding. These are traditional invocations which have been sung for the closing of councils since Chalcedon in 451.

The assembly then sang these words:

"May the peace of Christ be granted to all who have been redeemed by his blood.
Feliciter! Feliciter! Feliciter!
May the kingdom of Christ come.
Let us give thanks to God! Amen."

And the Pope then gave his solemn blessing.

As Paul VI went back to his quarters and the bishops left St. Peter's square for the last time, the bells of the churches of Rome rang at full peal.

An Opening to the World

John XXIII said one day that the idea of convoking a council came to him while he was reflecting on the problems of the modern world. He thought the purpose of such a council should be to begin a dialogue in the language of contemporary man. The Pope found himself confirmed in his intention when he asked himself how unity between divided Christians could be re-established: the *aggiornamento* of the Roman Church, brought about by a council, seemed to him the indispensable condition for any serious ecumenical dialogue.

Throughout the long forty-five months of preparation, as during the four sessions and the fruitful recesses, Vatican II pursued this double objective.

Today, as the Council closed with deliberately restricted pomp, it is easy to find shadows: silence on questions which are daily obsessions for some of the faithful; projects which were halted at the level of good intentions; the fears, hesitations, or opposition of certain minorities. But this is to underestimate the fact that many were very much surprised at the events of the Council's early days, the encyclical *Pacem in terris*, the questioning of so much of the status quo, and the evolution of so many minds. Those who ignored this evidence took their hopes for reality.

Even independently of the far-reaching reforms in the government of the Church and the role of the clergy and the laity, who could have believed in 1959 that the Council would have fulfilled John XXIII's double objective as well as it did?

On Tuesday, December 7, Rome and Constantinople solemnly lifted the mutual excommunications of 1054 and publicly admitted the faults committed on both sides at that time. True, Athenagoras I's authority extends to but a small part of Orthodoxy. Nonetheless, the first concrete step has been taken toward abolishing the schism which has divided the Christians of the East and West for nearly a thousand years.

The farewell ceremony for the observers, held the previous Saturday at St. Paul's Outside the Walls, was the real ecumenical summit of the

Council, a prelude, while a still unforeseeable reunion is awaited, to the development of closer relations between Rome and the other Christian churches. There is no doubt, as John XXIII foresaw, that the inner reform of the Catholic Church has disarmed the other confessions of many accusations.

The same reform has also enabled Catholicism to open dialogue not only with the other great religions but also with a whole segment of the world which, whether Marxist or not, saw in it primarily a relic of the past, a symbol of conservatism and obscurantism. As Paul VI said on Tuesday, Vatican II, despite great pressure, condemned no one; its outlook was "very much and deliberately optimistic." And the Pope exclaimed, "We too, in fact we more than any others, honor man."

In this opening to the world, the Council has intentionally, although no doubt inadequately, given priority to the poor. That is why the Pope invited the episcopacy to adopt a style of life more in conformity with the spirit of the Gospel.

It remains to be seen whether or not the will of the Pope and the episcopal college will change the behavior of the 400,000,000 Catholics in the world. If the contents of the evangelical message, whose relevance schema 13, despite its imperfections, has demonstrated, were lived by even a portion of the mass of Catholics, wouldn't the future of humanity be radically changed?

A First Assessment of Vatican II: Closed Doors?

Vatican II has now closed. John XXIII, who convoked it, has passed on. But both are so present in our minds that there is little place for nostalgia at this year's end of 1965, which will go down in history as the transitional date between two very distinct eras of Christianity. The more time passes, the better we will see this paradoxical truth the Council lived: a discontinuity in the continuity of the Church. With Vatican II Rome finally entered the twentieth century, which is indicative of both the Church's backwardness and her efforts toward *aggiornamento*. The Council abolished the notion that the Catholic Church, however widespread throughout the world, is a sect—a Western religion, bound in practice to Greco-Latin civilization, a religion of wealthy countries, a stranger to the great currents of history and contemporary thought as well as to the major preoccupations of modern man.

The Council, so to speak, broke down the walls of the citadel and let some "fresh air" in, to use John XXIII's image. At the same time the outside world saw something of the spiritual treasure of a Church that is not only an institution and a hierarchy but a center of faith, hope, and charity.

The Church of Vatican II was undeniably more concerned with seeking new truths and new ways of serving men than with jealously protecting her rights and privileges. In a word, the Roman Church is now more imbued with the spirit of the Gospels, much to the surprise of anticlerics. All of a sudden Rome became both critical toward herself and more indulgent toward others. This change was possible because the majority of Council Fathers overcame their fear. Rather than showing herself aggressive and negative and brandishing anathemas and condemnations as the minority had hoped, the Church acted like an adult. Vatican II put out into the deep. It understood that it must be a leaven in the dough, that is, be present at the heart of humanity. The Roman Church really abandoned the legalistic spirit, inherited from the Old Testament, for the Gospel's spirit of freedom.

Is this to say that the Council was a total success, that it achieved the much-needed pastoral and doctrinal renewal in every domain? Far from it. To be honest, an assessment must take the negative into account as well as the positive.

Temporary Failures Where did Vatican II fail, at least temporarily and in appearance? Here are some indications.

The Council came up short against a number of issues, which relate to marriage and at least two of which directly concern interpersonal relations between man and woman. Should this surprise us in a Church that is run by celibates who have long regarded woman as a suspect and dangerous creature?

1. The first of these issues is birth control. Would Vatican II have solved it had the Pope given the Fathers a free hand? We cannot be sure, although such great interventions as those by Maximos IV Saigh, Cardinal Suenens, Cardinal Léger, and Cardinal Alfrink during the third session made a deep impression on public opinion. Paul VI is troubled by this question. He confided it to a special extraconciliar commission which has so far come to no clear-cut conclusions. Thus the Pope has not made any definitive pronouncement. Unquestionably, this delay strikes those who do not understand the complexity of the problem as unduly long and disappointing. Still, we should not forget that schema 13, although silent on this subject as was ordered, nonetheless emphasized the love of the spouses, thus leaving the door ajar for the future.

2. Vatican II succeeded in instituting a married diaconate (by a final vote of 2,099 to 46). This is a partial solution to the serious vocation shortage in the Church. But the Council was forbidden by the Pope to

discuss the appropriateness of a married clergy in addition to the traditional celibate priesthood. It would seem that the time is not ripe for such a discussion. The majority withdrew within the framework of the status quo, and sought to mix the notion of the suitability of celibacy in the priesthood—which is unquestionable and unquestioned—with the notion of its innate necessity. The future will show whether and to what degree this psychologically understandable withdrawal is conditional. Perhaps the catastrophic situation in Latin America will impose exceptional solutions *ad experimentum*.

3. Vatican II did not confront the problem, which is so serious and painful for many of the faithful, of the possibility that an innocent partner who has been deserted might remarry, as is the tradition in the Orthodox Church. Only one Father, a Melkite bishop, took the risk of raising this question, apparently unsuccessfully. However, Father René Laurentin, an expert at the Council, courageously defended Maximos IV's position.

4. The Council's desires concerning mixed marriages have remained without issue. Millions of future couples await a liberating text that has not materialized. Many fear that the motu proprio which Paul VI is now preparing will be far less liberal than Vatican II had hoped.

5. Despite the Pope's example in solemnly relinquishing his tiara, the symbol of his temporal power, and several other unequivocal acts of deprivation, the Council Fathers did not heed those who suggested that they make a *collective* gesture renouncing the external signs of wealth (precious jewels, estates, palaces, and so forth) and the titles from another age which are a stumbling block to an increasing number of the faithful today. A small group of bishops did make a private gesture to this effect in the catacombs. It is perhaps a harbinger of things to come, but little more.

6. On the institutional plane, Vatican II refused to fix a retirement age for residential bishops. In this respect the Pope has gone farther than the Council, since it is confirmed that a mandatory retirement age will be part of the reform of the Curia, which will follow very shortly on the reform of the Holy Office which the Pope has just announced.

7. Nor did the Council do anything about the way bishops are nominated. To say the least, the present system scarcely corresponds with the legitimate aspirations of the "people of God"—to use the definition of the Church in the conciliar Constitution *Lumen gentium*, which was adopted by a vote of 2,151 to 5.

Youth and Optimism These seem to us to be the principal shortcomings of Vatican II. They are inevitable in a society that is as top-heavy and complex as the Roman Church, heavily dependent on her past and sometimes obsessed by fidelity to her traditions. It is difficult to draw the line between what can and should be changed and what can and should be conserved. An admirable point about Vatican II is that 2,200 bishops of a generally advanced age, frequently cut off from the daily realities of life, could show such flexibility and youthful spirit. The only objective explanation for this is the evangelical message of which the Church is the guardian. This message is formed above all of a rejection of immobilism, a great trust in redeemed man, the certitude that the Spirit is constantly at work everywhere in the world and that final victory over the forces of evil rests with him. Christianity is an optimistic religion. It teaches, as Henri Bergson said so well, that "The world is a machine for making gods." Vatican II has helped highlight this central truth by de-mummifying the Church.

Open Doors

We now turn to an assessment of Vatican II's achievements, which are considerable.

The Council, officially baptized "ecumenical," was more ecumenical by its object than by its nature. What does this mean? It could not, despite its very strong desire to do so, reunite all Christians in a constitutive manner. Vatican II could not be a council of union but only, more modestly, a council to prepare union. On the other hand, it was sufficiently pastoral to accomplish a number of desirable reforms. It is only fair to recognize that the old Roman Church made a considerable effort to rejuvenate herself, an effort that was to a large extent crowned with success: not only the word but the idea of *aggiornamento* developed beyond all expectations.

Most of the majority's aims were satisfied. Thanks to the support of two popes, on the one hand, and the hopes of the faithful, on the other, the Church teaching—the episcopacy—did not balk at the reasonable demands of the Church taught—the priests and laity. The "people of God" played an important role at the Council. Vatican II, an open house almost from the outset, welcomed the more or less prophetic aspirations of the unranked. This could only shock the small number who thought of the Church as static and purely authoritarian, forgetting the communitarian aspect of a society which owes the best of itself to inspirations coming from its base. Thanks to the mass media, information was easily passed from the bottom to the top. This is a just redress of the balance after centuries of authoritarianism. Vatican II, without any doubt, precipitated this evolution.

The Workers and the "Third World" The best example of this is the worker-priest. Against all hope, this form of the apostolate was explicitly approved by the Council. The credit must go to the dedicated work of a few unknown priests who gradually succeeded in persuading the Pope, the Curia, and the bishops of the virtues of this practice. Six years after the movement was condemned, the Council legalized the right of priests to work in factories. This spectacular turnabout is pregnant with possibilities, for it is no exaggeration to say that the keystone of evangelizing the working class is to be found here and nowhere else. The Church now has the urgent task of finding a way to be present among the deprived masses in the countries of the "third world." There the decisive battle for the Church in our century will be won or lost.

It is impossible to list once again the reforms achieved or begun by Vatican II. But we shall mention some salient points.

Without denying what is best in her tradition, the Church has stopped considering herself as having a monopoly on truth. She has liberally honored the truths contained in any other religion, beginning with her sister churches, the non-Catholic Christian confessions. In less than four years Rome entered the front ranks of the ecumenical movement, from which she had been tragically absent. The other churches can no longer accuse Catholicism of arrogance and pharisaism. The conservative elements in the Roman Church, like the non-Catholic integralists, have lost considerable ground; their anger is some measure of their disarray.

Psychological and Doctrinal Liberalism The Jews, who have suffered so much at the hands of Christians, obtained justice, at least on the books. Vatican II, eschewing profitless anathemas, began to dialogue even with atheists; this dialogue will expand with time. And finally the council declared peace to the whole world, secular and religious, including the Communists, of whom John XXIII said, "They claim they are enemies of the Church, but the Church has no enemies."

This is not merely psychological liberalism. It is at bottom doctrinal. Let there be no mistake about it. This does not mean that the Church no longer considers herself the spiritual beacon of mankind, or that the successor of Peter is hesitating to recognize his mission as the great shepherd of the Christianity to be; it only means that both have recognized the element of relativism and imperfection inherent in any human work, and no longer look to secular powers for support that is at best suspect. This is the profound meaning of the Declaration on Religious Liberty. At the same time, the Roman Church has established the bases of respect for the human person within her own organism. By throwing off the totalitarian spirit of the Holy Office and the Inquisition, she has finally rejected her besetting temptation to persecute minds and consciences. Liturgical, biblical, theological, pastoral, and philosophical study will be stimulated by this.

It will take time, of course, for this new attitude to be translated into action, but the course is irreversibly set.

The Structures of Dialogue   The layman too, until now considered subject to the Church's beck and call, has been recognized—oh, timidly, to be sure—as a full-fledged citizen whose specific competence must be respected and solicited. An age of dialogue and trust has succeeded the age of passive obedience.

As a consequence, the Church of Vatican II has provided means of encouraging pluralism and dialogue. Episcopal conferences have stripped the Curia of a number of special privileges. The episcopal synod will be a permanent body of cogovernment, as Pope Paul said in his speech opening the fourth session on September 14. The Roman congregations will be gradually reorganized, reformed, and internationalized.

At the diocesan level, the new status of the presbyterium should eventually overcome episcopal paternalism. We may reasonably hope that bishops will soon cease to be distant, omnipotent, and arbitrary commanders. The present pope seems disposed to trust the regional episcopacies so that the hierarchy's actions will be more pertinent and their control more sensitive to local problems. But this attractive program can only be achieved in the measure that all responsible parties keep on the alert. For the weight of the past is still heavy.

God or Mammon   On the social plane, Vatican II clearly affirmed the primacy of an equitable distribution of wealth over private property. This is a giant step forward. The episcopacies of underdeveloped countries must draw the practical consequences of this emphasis and vigorously denounce the scandalous injustice of societies that are pagan both in their structures and in their customs. Will the postconciliar Church take up the challenge of those who say, not without reason, that Christian governments serve Mammon more than God?

Intellectual Updating   If the Council succeeded in reforming institutions and inspiring some shifts of opinion, it was because of a theological renewal, and hence an intellectual updating.

Vatican II rang the death knell for a conceptualistic, notional, Scholastic type of theology and ushered in a personalist and so to speak "existentialist" theology. It got out of the thesis-hypothesis rut which has hampered Catholic thought for over a century. The new orientation has these aspects, among others:

1. Truth is no longer considered as something inanimate which we possess; rather it is the mystery of a living person, of whom the God-Man is the model. Likewise, dogmas and institutions are no longer considered as ends but as means.

2. Individualism has given place to a communitarian vision of human reality. The perspectives of theology and morality have been profoundly modified as a result.

3. A new anthropology is being elaborated. We are now aware that we take nothing away from God when we give to man; quite the contrary. Love of God is a function of love for men, and the construction of the heavenly city is a function of the construction of our earthly city. As a consequence a "mystique of the world" is emerging which restores to the universe its fundamental religious meaning. Teilhard de Chardin was one of the great inspirers of the Council.

4. The concept of evolution has been exorcised. The idea of organic growth has carried the day over an unrealistic notion of the immutability of principles based on an infantile fear of change. The frames of reference necessary to all thinking are now seen as motor axes rather than inert breakwaters.

5. The notion of tradition has been purified. Movement is no longer considered an evil but a requisite for progress. A desire for more perfect forms has been substituted for a fetishism of the past.

6. Theology is being penetrated by history and is turning its attention to the future. Eschatological thought has been restored to a place of honor. Saint Paul and Teilhard de Chardin have gained the march over the Scholastic and Descartes.

Liberty, Equality, and Fraternity This liberation of Catholic thought, too long imprisoned in the negative tide of the Counter-Reformation, in a way enables the Church to take up the standard of the French Revolution, which made the rounds of the secular world before coming to rest in Catholicism, whence it originated. Liberty, equality, fraternity: this glorious motto was the quintessence of Vatican II, as Hans Küng recently suggested.

The postconciliar Church must now assimilate the astonishingly rich contribution of Vatican II and project it onto all levels. This is an enormous task which will require as much wisdom as boldness. It will be furthered by the new collective awareness in the episcopacy which was forged by the Council. Also, the Pope's moral authority has been increased by the test of the Council. The great Catholic body is more attached than ever to its head; this is a good thing, because a strong supreme authority is all the more necessary now that the Church is becoming more diversified and decentralized as a result of Vatican II.

Young people, who are again becoming interested in religion, will be in a better position than their elders to discern to what extent the Council has inaugurated a new era of Christianity. To be sure, the Church cannot cut any of the vital moorings that anchor her to the evangelical message; but with time, these moorings will become fewer in number and less restrictive.

Young Catholics, both clerical and lay, who are responsible for the fate of the future Church, will undoubtedly accelerate the pace of the reforms proposed by the Council. It will be up to them to see that Vatican II becomes a point of departure rather than a parenthesis in the life of the Church.

INDEX

Renard, Bishop: Church and modern world, 623–24; laity, 415; mixed marriages, 549–50; priests, 716
Rendeiro, Bishop: marriage, 480
Reuss, Bishop Joseph: birth control, 478–479, 648; marriage, 648
Revelation, *see* Sources of revelation, schema on
Richard-Molard, Pastor Georges: Church renewal, 367–69
Richaud, Paul Cardinal: 12, 141; bishops, 207; diaconate, 154; economic and social life, 488; episcopal powers, 316–17; priests, 710
Riobé, Bishop Guy: 228; missions, 496
Ritter, Joseph Cardinal: 70–71; ecumenism, 254; episcopal conferences, 225; mixed marriages, 549; nation vs. individual, 466; religious liberty, 239, 340, 603
Roberti, Francesco Cardinal: 701; religious liberty, 348
Roberts, Archbishop Thomas D.: 3, 39; conscientious objectors, 698–99; on the press, 191–92
Rodríguez Ballon, Archbishop Leonardo: priests, 419
Roman Curia, *see* Curia
Romeo, Mgr.: 416
Romero Menjibar, Bishop Felix: Church and modern world, 453, 459
Roo, Bishop Remi de: laity, 392; morality, 647; priests, 730
Rosales, Archbishop Julio: priests, 418
Rossi, Angelo Cardinal: 329; marriage, 648; religious liberty, 613
Roux, Pastor Hébert: 682; on Church and modern world, 675–77
Roy, Archbishop Maurice: Church and modern world, 445
Rubio, Fr. Luciano: revelation, 382
Ruffini, Ernesto Cardinal: 22, 210, 223; birth control, 469–70; Church and modern world, 438, 619; Church's infallibility, 272; collegiality, 146; Curia, 217; declaration on Jews, 359; *De ecclesia*, 93; diaconate, 142; ecumenism, 238–39; eschatology, 307; laity, 170; liturgy, 34; marriage, 549, 644; press conference, 205–6; priests, 709; religious liberty, 336–37, 590–91; revelation, 75, 380, 383; Virgin Mary, 310
Rugambwa, Laurean Cardinal: 46; Church and modern world, 623; laity, 177;

missions, 493
Ruotolo, Bishop Giuseppe: atheism, 635; laity, 185, 401
Rupp, Bishop Jean: 208; episcopal powers, 317; religious liberty, 607; war, 690
Rusch, Bishop: Church and modern world, 620; war, 685
Rusnack, Bishop Michel: communism, 639

Saboia Bandeira de Mello, Bishop Carlos: on Bishops, 145
Sacred Liturgy, schema on: 19, 25, 71; amendments to, 92; breviary, 62, 63–64; communion under two species, 47–48; in Communist lands, 47; Divine Office, 60; ecumenical implications, 32; episcopal powers, 34–35; extreme unction, 61; funerals, 61–62; liturgical reform, 31–33, 42, 56–57; liturgical year, 60; marriage, 59–60; music, 60; preparation of, 32; priesthood of the faithful, 47; sacraments, 57, 59–60, 61–62; sacred art, 60; syncretism, 46–47, 48; variant texts, 34; vernacular vs. Latin, 8–9, 19, 32–33, 38, 40–42, 47, 61, 62; vestments, 60, 68; votes on, 69, 83, 151, 154–55, 163, 251–52, 278; *see also* Commission on the Sacred Liturgy; Constitution on the Sacred Liturgy
Sansierra, Bishop Ildefonso: 204
Santin, Archbishop Antonio: 231
Santo Quadri, Bishop: theology of work, 459
Sapelak, Bishop Andrea: ecumenism, 246
Sauvage, Bishop Jean: collegiality, 165; religious liberty, 607; seminaries, 523
Scandar, Bishop Alexander: 235, 267; laity, 188
Schema 13, Schema 17: *see* Church and the modern world
Schemas: "counterschema," 129; preparation of, 18–21; questioned by Council, 25; redrafting of, 93–95, 114–15; regrouping of, 92, 105–6; scope of, 10–11; *see also* Proposition schemas; under subject matter of schema
Schick, Bishop Eduard: 157; revelation, 387
Schillebeeckx, Fr. Edward: birth control, 740; Church and modern world, 308, 309; revelation, 384–85
Schlink, Dr. Edmund: 269–70

Suenens, Leo Cardinal (*continued*)
for bishops, 226; seminaries, 308, 522;
Virgin Mary, 313
Syllabus of Errors: 13, 67, 241, 605, 735

Tagle Covarrubias, Bishop Emilio: religious liberty, 599–600
Taguchi, Bishop Paul Yoshigoro: mixed marriages, 550
Taizé, Community of: 54–55, 266
Talamás Camandari, Bishop Manuel: diaconate, 159
Tappouni, Ignace Cardinal: 22, 150; declaration on Jews, 358–59
Tardini, Domenico Cardinal: 6
Tatsuo Doi, Peter Cardinal: missions, 493
Tawil, Archbishop Joseph: ecumenism, 255
Tchidimbo, Archbishop Raymond: Church and modern world, 451; laity, 182
Teilhard de Chardin, Fr. Pierre: 19, 79, 114, 116, 309, 444, 445, 451, 458, 460, 468, 620, 711
Thangalathil, Archbishop Gregorios: 58; economic and social life, 673
Theodosios VI, Patriarch: 713
Theological Commission, *see* Commission for Faith and Morals, Doctrinal
Thiandoum, Archbishop Hyacinthe: 46; Islam, 264; press conference, 222–23
Thunemann, Bishop: 39
Thurian, Pastor Max: revelation, 743–45
Tisserant, Eugène Cardinal: 22, 59, 77, 118, 253; liturgy, 71; religious liberty, 538; vernacular vs. Latin, 38
Tracy, Bishop Robert E.: racism, 189
Tromp, Fr. Sebastian: 60
Tyrrel, George: 114

Underdeveloped countries: 780–81; secretariat for proposed, 768–69
Uniates, *see* Oriental Churches
Unity, Christian, *see* Ecumenism; Secretariat for Promoting Christian Unity; Unity of the Church, schema on
Unity of the Church, schema on: 20, 83, 119–20, 124–25
Urbani, Cardinal: eschatology, 307; indulgences, 758; religious liberty, 592
Uriarte Bengoa, Bishop León de: ecumenism, 247

Uribe Jaramillo, Bishop Alfonso: laity, 186
Urtasun, Archbishop: 235, 479

Vairo, Bishop Giuseppe: Church and modern world, 442
Varillon, Fr.: 39
Vatican Council II: addressed by Paul VI, 299–301; agenda, 106–7, 290–95, 566–567; auditors, 134, 334–35; ceremonies, 37, 96–98, 118–28; "concentrated council," 83–84; "directors," 635–36; evaluation, 99–100, 112–13, 282–83, 287–90, 556–59, 563–66, 750–51, 808–16; French Protestant attitude toward, 301–2; homage to John XXIII, 195–96; "isms" and, 629; Italian representation at, 48–49; lay participation, 129; message to Catholic priests of the world, 266; "Message to the world," 28, 29–31, 72; "moderators" for, 115, 203–4, 220–21; openmindedness of, 160–62; Oriental Churches, 190–91; Popes and, 110–11, 749; preparation for, 90–91; press coverage of, 36–37, 143, 446–48, 456; recesses, 103–17; regulations, 129; secrecy rules, 131, 143, 171, 305–6; translation services, 53, 205, 295; undersecretaries, 26; women and, 184, 296–97, 334
Vazquez, Juan: women, 507
Veiga Coutinho, Bishop Fortunato da: 252; laity, 194; papal primacy, 164
Velasco, Bishop John: missions, 496, 703; religious liberty, 599
Vet, Bishop Gerhardt de: Church and modern world, 453; laity, 397
Veuillot, Archbishop Pierre: 146, 211; episcopal powers, 316; laity, 397–98
Villalba, Bishop Proano: culture, 486
Villot, Coadjutor Archbishop Jean: 26
Virgin Mary, schema on: 86, 132, 135, 196–197, 310–12, 313–15; inclusion in *De ecclesia* schema, 190, 199; *see also De ecclesia* schema
Vischer, Pastor Lukas: Church and modern world, 630
Visser 'tHooft, W.A.: 8, 12; declaration on Jews, 713
Vito, Bishop Albert de: 159; economic and social life, 675; laity, 397
Vito Chang, Bishop: 252
Volk, Bishop Hermann: 53, 140, 251; marriage, 646; revelation, 390

About the Author
Henri Fesquet

covered the Ecumenical Council throughout all four sessions from June 1962 to December 1965 for the prestigious French daily Le Monde, *for which he has reported religious news since 1950. Mr. Fesquet was a student of Jean Guitton, first Catholic lay observer at the Council, and of Father Yves Congar, O.P. Henri Fesquet is also the author of* Catholicism: Religion of Tomorrow?

About the Translator
Bernard Murchland

teaches philosophy at the State University of New York at Buffalo. He is the editor of Two Views of Man *and* The Meaning of the DEATH OF GOD, *which is published by Random House. Mr. Murchland has translated Lepp's* The Anthentic Morality *and other books.*